The Arab World Today

The
Arab World
Today

William R. Polk

Harvard University Press

Cambridge, Massachusetts

London, England   1991

This is the fifth edition of *The United States and the Arab World*

This book is printed on acid-free paper, and its binding materials
have been chosen for strength and durability.

Library of Congress Cataloging-in-Publication Data

Polk, William Roe, 1929–
    The Arab world today / William R. Polk.—5th ed.
        p.   cm.
    Rev. ed. of: The Arab world. 4th ed. 1980.
    Includes bibliographical references and index.
    ISBN 0–674–04319–7 (cloth). —ISBN 0–674–04320–0 (paper)
    1. Arab countries—History. 2. United States—Foreign relations—
Arab countries. 3. Arab countries—Foreign relations—United
States. I. Polk, William Roe, 1929–   Arab world. II. Title.
DS39.P64   1991
327.73017'4927—dc20   91–8768
                                                            CIP

For Elisabeth

Contents

Contents

Maps and Figures

Preface to the 1991 Edition

The quarter-century since *The United States and the Arab World* was first published has been one of the most turbulent periods in Middle Eastern history. The external features of this turbulence are easy to identify: rivalry between the Soviet Union and the United States, which have been skillfully played upon by regional powers as often as they themselves have manipulated these powers; major international wars between Israel and the Arabs and between Iraq and Iran, interspersed with aggressive and ruinously expensive arms races; and tragic, brutal, degrading civil wars in Yemen, Lebanon, and the Sudan. Most recently, of course, Iraq has invaded Kuwait, an action that moved the United States, joined by a disparate band of allies now including the Soviet Union and acting partially under United Nations auspices, to send an armada unmatched since the Vietnam conflict to try to restore the status quo ante. As this book goes to press, the spectacular, indeed stunning, shooting war in Iraq has ended and the much more perplexing but less dramatic problem of peace seeking has begun.

These are happenings that impinge almost daily upon our thoughts, for rarely has the Middle East been long absent from the front pages of American newspapers or from our television screens.

Since I first visited the Arab world at the end of World War II, I have seen American involvement go from almost total detachment, through the years in which the Middle East was seen as a sort of annex to the Cold War, then through a period in which we recognized our great dependence upon its oil, and finally to large-scale and possibly more or less permanent armed intervention in 1990. For Americans, naturally, these happenings are compelling and form the focus of our current interest.

But the last quarter-century has also witnessed trends and changes that, viewed over the longer sweep of time, may prove more lasting and significant than the more dramatic and more accessible "news." So, without closing our eyes to the latest events, we need to understand the background and the longer-term trends.

To do this, we cannot look only at the Arab world. We must also try to understand what has happened to us, the Europeans, and the Russians in this past quarter-century. In other words, we must try to understand also what lies in the eyes of the beholders. Historical observation is always, and particularly in this instance, an interplay between what *they* are and what *we* can see. Effective understanding, on which our future may in no small part depend, derives not only from "objective" influences (in terms of measurable units of population, wealth, power, and production) but also from subjective influences. The Arab world we see today is very different from the one we saw twenty-five years ago, and most of us view it differently as well.

To attempt to encompass the elements of this interpretation requires thus not only an account of current events but an appreciation of what the Arabs have become and how we Americans interact with them. With the prejudice of a historian, I do not think we can develop a "checklist" to be sure we comprehend the present, without doing so in reference to the past. Further, I see these various trends and elements not as a state but as a still-evolving process.

These are somewhat ephemeral and certainly shifting qualities; so to take what was originally a 1960's book and make it into a 1990's book is a matter not merely of altering a few numbers but of recasting perceptions. For a better understanding of the chapters that follow, a general discussion of the issues will be helpful. Let me begin with the (more or less) "objective" changes.

The first and most spectacular change is external to the Middle East. It is the sudden end to the Cold War. For nearly half a century, the preeminent American interest in the Arab world, an interest first articulated in the time of President Truman and made the centerpiece of—one might almost say the sole justification for—American policy in the administration of President Eisenhower, was to "deny" hegemony over the Arab world to the Soviet Union. That remained the top priority of American policy in the Kennedy and Johnson years. To secretaries of state Acheson, Dulles, and Rusk, any prophet who foretold the events of the fall of 1990 would have appeared completely wrongheaded. Yet, in recent months, we have seen the United States welcome the Soviet Union into our armed coalition and the Soviet Union use events in the Persian Gulf to symbolize and prove the end of the Cold War.

Does this mean (the reader should ask at this point) that everything written about the Middle East before is now out of date and of little value in understanding today's events or tomorrow's trends? The answer, I think, is no. History is full of examples that are hardly less dramatic. Even in our own times, we have seen a comparable shift as Germany, Italy, and Japan suddenly ceased to be our enemies and became our friends and allies. But, more subtly put, the question of relevance suggests that many of our perceptions about the Arabs and of theirs about us—and themselves— need to be critically reexamined.

As I shall argue in the relevant parts of this book, external events, like the Cold War itself, were (in Middle Eastern terms) always significant primarily because they impinged upon, augmented, or justified local trends and events. The Cold War, viewed by such Arab leaders as presidents Nasser and Sadat, was a source for new and greater means (namely generous American and Soviet aid and military supply) to accomplish what were seen as regional objectives. Rare was the Arab statesman who viewed the Cold War or the Soviet threat in anything like the terms of Messrs. Acheson, Dulles, Rusk, or Kissinger. Those who did had short tenures in office. Our failure to understand this was a root cause of the frequent disappointments and frustrations of American policy.

So, as I originally said, I believe that we must approach an understanding of this and similar issues through an exploration of perceptions as well as "facts." How the Arabs perceived what we and the Russians did became as crucial as what we and the Russians actually did. Even more crucial is the achievement of an understanding of what we and the Arabs thought we and they were doing, why, and how.

I have analyzed the Arab side of this complex and subtle problem in the historical and cultural sections of this work, Parts Two through Five. They are essentially unchanged from the form they took in *The United States and the Arab World*. I argued in 1965 and I still remain convinced that a thorough understanding of the material discussed there is essential for an appreciation of contemporary events. Were I primarily concerned here with history *qua* history, I should wish to recast some of this material to take advantage of recent scholarship, but the changes I would make would be marginal. I stand by both the need for this kind of analysis and the analysis I have offered.

Let me now highlight what I see as the most significant of the regional changes I will discuss.

The first and most striking change is in the numbers of people. In all the Arab countries, populations have risen dramatically. The Egyptian population, the largest, has doubled in the last quarter-century to at least 55 million. This compares to the estimated population of pharaonic Egypt of about 4 million. In short, all of ancient Egypt had less than a fourth of the population of today's Cairo. One of the smaller societies, Saudi Arabia, probably quadrupled in size (if we can trust the population guesses) to about 16 million.

Of course, while populations have exploded, usable land has increased only marginally. Malthus and other classical economists were largely right in supposing that agricultural expansion usually brings poorer lands into production. Large-scale irrigation projects, deriving from the construction of great dams and reservoirs, have allowed the reclaiming of some desert tracts and double or triple cropping of some existing lands, but the results have nearly all been disappointing. As economists put it, such reclamation is rarely "cost effective." Productivity is often very low, much reclaimed land is already in the process of being lost, and the side effects are environmentally damaging. The Egyptian High Dam is the prime example, an example which, unfortunately, is being widely copied. But however they are evaluated, such projects have certainly resulted in only slightly more living space for the children and grandchildren of the people I first met in 1946. Egypt was then already a country of crowds; today, it is by far the most densely populated area on earth. Some additional lands have been reclaimed from deserts, particularly in Syria, Iraq, and Saudi Arabia, but these will not fundamentally change the way of life of the people, since the whole Middle East is and will remain chronically short of water.

So the population increase has forced a move into cities. Egypt again provides the most dramatic example: when I first visited

Cairo in 1946, the population was about 2 million. Today, although no one knows the true figure, it appears to be just short of 20 million. Baghdad, Jiddah, Riyadh, Kuwait, and Amman were then scarcely more than villages. When I first visited them, Jiddah, Sanaa, Muscat, and Kuwait were still little "islands" in the desert, surrounded by defensive walls. Few had hotels, sewage systems, or piped residential water. Today, their populations are reckoned in the millions. They now join us in the struggle with traffic jams and pollution.

Few urban areas—and no rural areas—had more than token medical facilities. Such industry as existed was hardly more than cottage in scale. And education was restricted in both access and quality; even the best was little better than elementary. Today, schools, universities, and even advanced scientific institutions are widespread and often free.

Standards of living have improved dramatically. Studies done at the end of World War II usually began with the stark fact of pervasive hunger. Large portions of the Arab population lived on the brink of starvation. Debilitating and crippling diseases were evident in practically every family. Infant mortality claimed as many as one child in two. Life expectancy was short.

From a detached viewpoint, there can be no doubt that what has been accomplished is nearly miraculous. But politics allows few detached viewpoints. What a participant would have thought an impossible dream in 1946 has become today's nightmare. The accomplishment is real, but the scale according to which it is judged has been recalibrated.

This is so not only because all of us quickly forget the "bad old days," remembering only selected parts as the "good old days," but also because development in the Arab countries has been grossly uneven. The unevenness has two aspects. Within any given country, some people live in opulence next-door to people whose level of poverty has been unknown in the West for centuries. And between the oil-rich and the farm-poor countries is a comparable divide. Put another way, not even the "super-rich" of the developed Western world live on a scale comparable to that of the rich of the Third World. And the difference between a Kuwait, with a per capita average income of $10,500, and a Sudan, with $340, means, among other things, that Sudan is the "factory" that produces the menial servants for the rich countries. We must view these kinds of difference not only in statistical but also in political terms.

Add to these terms another dimension—time. Access to the modern world varies greatly among the sectors of any given population. Health care is an obvious category: the rural poor do not have it; the urban rich do. Yet some of the new, oil-rich societies maintain the most modern hospitals available anywhere. Similar categories and similar disparities can be discerned throughout the Arab societies. Even where bus lines hardly function, countries maintain commercial airlines with the most modern jet airplanes. Peasants drafted into the military may have never ridden in an automobile but are quickly placed behind the wheel of giant tank transports. Huge petrochemical and even atomic power complexes take shape near farmers who labor to lift water with an Archimedean screw. In Saudi Arabia, Yemen, and the Gulf states, sons of men who weighed Maria Teresa silver dollars in their bazaar stalls now watch their computer screens to track money markets in Zurich, London, Tokyo, and New York. In the early 1950's, Iraq had a total of five mechanical engineers; today, count has been lost in the thousands. All of the Arab countries together at the end of World War II could hardly have filled a conference hall with their technicians; today, whole cities are devoted to them.

The strides made in these years have, in fact, been enormous. Yet, also in fact, they add up to failure when weighed in the scales of today's expectations. There is increasing evidence that significant parts of the population in most of the Arab countries no longer believe in development. This is a sentiment shared more widely than we would imagine throughout the so-called Third World. The great dreams of the 1960's have given way to a tired and often troubled wakefulness in the 1980's.

To understand this, we must expand our view beyond economics to include other aspects of the Arabs' self-image and aspiration.

When I first began to study the Arab world, many of its younger men and women were still grappling with the problem of identity. "Who are the Arabs?" was a question not just dreamed up by Western scholars but avidly debated in Middle Eastern coffeehouses and offices. No simple answers were found. One that had satisfied many in the prewar days was "anti-imperialists." Young people in Egypt, Syria, Palestine, and Iraq in the 1920's and 1930's found a common enemy in the foreign powers, mainly Britain and France, that ruled their lives. To a degree, the definition was satisfying. But, as first Britain and ultimately France learned to work through native elites, nationalism lost both its "purity" and its coherence. Activists in Egypt found that they did not share enemies with their counterparts in Syria, and both found that the older leaders, many of whom had reached accommodations with the imperial powers, had become their principal enemies.

Nasser's coup d'état in Egypt in 1952, in which he ousted the monarchy and the older nationalists, and his stand against Britain, France, and Israel (and in part America) in the Suez crisis, made him the hero of his generation. But even his supporters saw early on that his regime was deeply flawed. In retrospect, we can see that he was held aloft more by his opponents than by his friends. By the time he died, in 1970, his image was severely tarnished.

No one man has been able to take Nasser's place, although Arabs, like Americans, crave a hero or "star." One after another, the candidates have proved to have feet of clay. Sadat was never a serious contender, and his regime was tainted with corruption from its early days. He was far more popular in the West than in the Arab world. The Egyptians were glad to ease away from Nasser's stern brand of Arabism, but they never admired Sadat for catering to their desires. Qaddafi has used Libya's wealth to foster his candidacy, but to most Arabs he always appeared unstable, reckless, and immature. Arafat, of course, appealed only to a single constituency, the more moderate of the Palestinian refugees. His more radical rivals are comparatively unknown. Husain of Jordan was respected for his ability to survive but was fatally compromised by his title as king, and lacked, in Jordan, a significant political base. Assad of Syria never inspired love or affection, even within his own country. And Saddam Husain of Iraq, a thoroughly unlovable man in the best of times, has acquired some pretense of heroism only from the fact that foreign powers and the richer Arab leaders have opposed his expansion. The quest for a hero has thus proved not only unhealthy but also, at least so far, vain.

In part, of course, this quest was for the unity that a single hero would symbolize. If nationalism in the older sense did not provide it, recent generations thought that Arabism, *Arabiyah*, might. But the symbolism of the hero and the dream of unity, both already flawed, interacted to fatally weaken each other. As the would-be heroes clashed, the lack of real unity became painfully manifest.

Ironically, development hastened this process. Countries that once lived more or less isolated from one another now view their neighbors with envy and fear. As Saddam Husain has illustrated, modernization confers mobility and military might, even if it does not satisfy the desires for a better life. And with the old external enemies now gone or less evident, hostility to the foreigner no longer unifies. Thus, nationalism is swinging away from Arabism toward something else. Precisely what that is or will be confuses the Arabs today, just as it did our ancestors in Europe when the medieval synthesis of Christianity broke down.

As they sought to galvanize their domestic power, each of the leaders came to emphasize local nationalism at the expense of Arab unity. The most recent hero, Saddam Husain, has wavered: should he cast himself, his movement, the Baath Party, and Iraq as Arab or as Mesopotamian? Some believe that his attack on neighboring Kuwait, surely a "brother" Arab land, is the last nail in the coffin of Arabism.

For many, this outcome would be satisfying. But it appears almost too tidy to be likely. Let us look briefly at it.

Is not Kuwait a "brother" Arab land? Yes, of course. But Kuwait is also part of the heritage of imperialism. It was, after all, established by the British as a protectorate to block the northern end of the Persian Gulf just before World War I. It is also an immensely rich land, with deposits of about 100 billion barrels of oil. In one generation its people have gone from backward poverty to financial power, and in making this transition they have flaunted their wealth indiscreetly. Not only the Iraqis but many others have envied and disliked them. True, they have given generously to Iraq during its war with Iran and to other Arab countries in their quest for development, but as we Americans have painfully learned, such contributions do not create popularity or affection. Even among the Saudis, with their comparable wealth, Kuwait has been viewed as a parasite.

Saddam Husain was not the first Iraqi leader to seek to "reclaim" Kuwait. The historical basis for that claim is weak, but the weakness did not stop his predecessors from trying. For generations, Iraqis have claimed that Kuwait was (and should be again) an integral part of Iraq.

I believe that a public opinion poll among Arabs today (were such really possible) would reveal that few know or care about the historical validity of the claim. Most would, however, assert that Kuwait is a rich, selfish legacy of a hated past, an enclave which the Western powers and Japan are anxious to keep as it is because they want cheap gasoline. Most would scoff at the idea that we have been driven by international standards of justice to defend it or to make aggression unprofitable. They would find much in our governmental policy papers to sustain their accusation.

Were they more subtle, they might further argue that (like most of Africa and Asia) they have no legal and peaceful means to reorder the world they have inherited from imperialism. Pakistan and India have not found better ways; neither have Vietnam and dozens of other countries. However we Americans may feel about it, and our actions show that we often agree, force is still the most common means of rewriting the past.

The attempt by Iraq to take over Kuwait is thus, I think and fear, not a discrete episode but a chapter in a current and future series. It certainly exacerbates Arab disunity, but this is hardly new. The Arabs have endured much from one another: coups in Iraq, Syria, Libya, the Sudan, Yemen; civil war in Lebanon, Jordan, Yemen, the Sudan; inter-Arab wars in Yemen, Oman, Syria, Lebanon, Libya, and Egypt. And Saddam Husain is scarcely the first Arab hero to be opportunistic. He cannot be credited with destroying the belief in Arab unity, any more than he can be claimed as its hero. But recent events in which he has been deeply involved tend to confirm the pervasive sense that Arab unity is as elusive as ever and that Arab nationalism is a weak reed.

What remains? The answer of the richer countries, particularly those of the Arabian peninsula, is "the good life." For Kuwait and some other countries, the definition may have been cast too narrowly and crassly. But in the broad sense, the pattern was set when President Nasser decided to build the High Dam in Egypt. The Arabs could achieve the identity and dignity they sought, he and many other Arabs believed, only if they became "modern." To be modern, a country had to have industry. And to acquire industry, it had to develop its resources.

Since no Arab country had a tradition of private enterprise, everything depended upon the state. As in ancient Egypt and Mesopotamia, the state alone was believed to have the capacity to organize resources. Even in conservative Saudi Arabia, it is the state that sets the goals, provides the capital, mobilizes the manpower, and often buys the product of the nascent industry. The state has a monopoly on education, health care, social welfare, law, and internal security—most of which were traditionally not thought of as parts of its role.

With this scheme of state intervention in the lives of citizens, the Arabs are finding two kinds of failure. First, like the Russians, many see waste, corruption, inefficiency, lack of incentive. An example: I recall visiting a model farm in Egypt a few years ago. Proudly the director showed me the modern, expensive, imported irrigation system. It was not working, and when, to demonstrate, he ordered it put into operation, spouts of water erupted everywhere: all the pipes were broken or wrongly connected. Potemkin, at least, had had the sense not to try to cook a meal in one of his villages. Even where the investment has been well managed, as (to be fair) it often has, the stark fact is that, other than in derivatives of the petroleum industry, there is little in the Arab world that favors industry. Everyone is still trying, and some are trying ruinously hard, but much of the hope and spirit has gone out of the struggle.

The second kind of disillusionment is of a different sort. It is the growing belief that the road to the "good life," whatever that may be, does not run through materialism. Some of those who never heard a radio as children, and who now have every sort of electronic tool and toy, are wondering if they are happier. As inflation has bitten into savings, many of those who have toiled for years in distant lands find that they have gained little. Families have begun to disintegrate as they did long ago among Western societies, but in the Middle East the change has been more rapid, recent, and dramatic.

A part of the disenchantment with leaders, ideas, and things is today becoming manifest in the resurgence of Islam. Now, surprisingly to many (and I must admit I was not one of the prophets of this change), Islam is recapturing the minds of many Arabs as it has of many Iranians. I believe it likely that this trend will be accelerated by the recent events in the Gulf and particularly by the intervention of the United States.

For reasons we can illustrate but not completely explain, the Arabs have ever been a fractious people. It is in the nature of tribal society to split, and even after tribalism (or at least nomadism) ceased to be the dominant social and economic pattern, the Arabs have had trouble uniting except in the face of an external enemy, and then only briefly. Their problem, as the greatest of the Arab students of the Arabs, Ibn Khaldun, put it, was to get everyone's "face turning in the same direction." We shall see example after example of this challenge, and solution after attempted solution. Of all these, Islam was the most spectacularly successful, and Arabs today, like other Muslims in Iran and elsewhere, look back with pride and envy to the clarity, unity, and purpose of early Islam. Even Arab Christians—and in previous times Arab Jews—found Islamic civilization a haven from discord and conflict. As we shall see, in the nineteenth century, Islam had fallen into a kind of comfortable disrepair—although we now realize that it was decrepit more in comparison to the extraordinary changes of the West than in terms of its own societies' needs and demands. But in the eyes first of foreigners and then of its own people, Islam was backward, narrow, unacceptable. And, superficially at least, it was simply swept aside. Associated with it, if not caused by it, were all the ills or evils of the past. A few clung to it but they were either the pitiful poor, the threadbare divines, or the eccentric. By the end of World War II, most observers would have said that Islam was simply irrelevant to political life. And then it was probably true.

But all the other ways to "turn faces in the same direction" failed. Indeed, the very suggestion of new or better ways of achieving unity caused further splits in existing unities. Nowhere was this more evident than among the Palestinians, who, in the face of the Israeli threat and the often even more destructive support of the Arab states, found a Palestinian community insufficient as a means to achieve internal cohesion. The Palestinians have not yet turned to Islam because so many of the more militant and able are Christian, but if they are faced with further failure they may do so in the future. Other groups have done this, and it seems likely that the example of the Persian revolution will affect the thought and actions of Arabs despite significant differences in temperament, experience, and political and religious organization. This is so because of yet another cause of disappointment widely felt in the poorer nations—a disappointment with materialism.

Materialism is a complex issue in recent historical experience. The poor desperately want the *things* of the West, yet blame the West for what they feel to be its excessive emphasis on things; the rich, themselves having too many things, often are shocked by the crude materialism of the poor. But often the "developed" and the "less developed" fail to perceive what one another is saying. When Westerners say to the poor that they should avoid the excesses of materialism so that they can control pollution, for example, or use "appropriate technology," the poor often interpret this to mean "stay poor." When the poor say the West is materialistic and should be more concerned with man's fate, Westerners often remember Aesop's fable of sour grapes or think that they are merely talking unrealistically and ignorantly. The quest for more and better goods has generally been a disappointing one for most of the world's poor. It has proven either unattainable (like the grapes to the fox), or, in much of the Middle East, sour (like the fox imagined the grapes to be). And it is not only the recent experience of such national shopping centers as Kuwait, where it has been found that there is a limit to the number of radios and watches and pens one can enjoy. More generally, it has been found that a five percent rate of growth in gross national product does not necessarily, or even often, equate to stability or happiness. Curiously, the lesson could have been learned from earlier experience. It is not often realized that, relatively speaking, parts of the Middle East were materially quite advanced not only in ancient times, to which modern polemicists like to refer, but even in this century. As Charles Issawi has pointed out, "By 1913 Egypt had a higher railway mileage per unit of *inhabited* area than almost any country in the world, and per unit of population than most countries . . . Egypt had its first railway before Sweden or Japan, and it was not until the 1870's that the *total* railway mileage of Argentina and Brazil surpassed that of Egypt, while Japan did not catch up until the 1890's and China until after 1900."* Yet, as we shall see, these were years of national humiliation for Egypt. Materialism per se did not produce power, whether or not the reverse was true. And the lesson has been painfully relearned in the several Arab-Israeli wars. *Things* do not constitute or cause development (although we persist in thinking that they do), or power (although we and the weak hope that they will), or unity or stability. But if they do not, what will? This question underlies much of the history of the recent Middle East, and it is not surprising that, having tried nationalism and what was understood to be socialism and forced-draft development (of which Iran was, after all, the world's showcase), many would think of going back to their roots in religion. We are, I now believe, at the beginning of a movement that in various forms may occupy our attention for the rest of this century.

More concrete and more demanding in certain ways is the transformation of the refugees of the 1948–1949 and 1967 Arab-Israeli wars into a community, if not yet into a state. In 1965, in their diaspora, the Palestinians were the objects of pity and scorn; by 1980 they had become the key to the puzzle of Middle Eastern peace. Even those who hate and fear them—hate and fear themselves being new emotions—now realize that no lasting peace can be made that disregards them. One might, indeed, go so far as to say that in some ways they are the most complete nation in the

* See Charles Issawi, "Asymmetrical Development and Transport in Egypt, 1800–1914," in William R. Polk and Richard L. Chambers (eds.), *Beginnings of Modernization in the Middle East* (Chicago, 1968).

Arab world—even without a territory or a statehood or a tactical consensus. Their story is a difficult one but central to the Middle East in our times.

Since 1965 much has changed about the United States as well. The euphoria of the early 1960's and the deep pessimism of the late 1960's dwindled in the 1970's into a gray, self-questioning, somber view of ourselves and the world. The sudden realization of our dependence upon others, most obvious today in terms of the energy shortage, has been provoked by our recognition that the world is indeed imperiled by the explosion of population, by maldistribution of wealth, and by growing environmental hazards.

Sadly, we have done little about any of these dangers. One that is again upon us is illustrated by the oil crisis. We were stunned by the oil crisis of 1979. We determined to find alternate sources of energy, and even the Saudi Arabians, recognizing as they did at that early date that it was unhealthy for us to depend so much upon their oil, tried to help us in this quest. But our resolve quickly petered out. Budgets to support the insulation of buildings, the development of solar and wind power, and the construction of efficient mass transit systems were cut away; we went back to the wasteful use of gasoline; and we rallied against nuclear energy. In the Iraqi invasion of Kuwait, we suddenly found ourselves confronted by a new oil crisis. Essentially, we lost, at least temporarily, access to about a quarter of the world's oil. At least in part, we intervened in the Kuwait crisis because of this fact.

Will we learn from the crisis? Our record is not good. It appears that we will get through these hard times of oil shortage and high prices relatively easily, but somewhere down the road, the Middle East (and other areas) will run out of oil. We have been drawing down the reserves, and, of course, no new deposits are or will be made. So, probably within the coming twenty-five years, the ultimate oil crisis will be upon us. With this in mind, let us look briefly at what has happened in this aspect of our relations with the Arabs.

Not until the first oil crisis did we realize how crucial cheap energy has been to the development of Western industry and how formative to our living patterns. Discounted for inflation, oil *fell* from $1.71 a barrel in 1950 to $0.98 a barrel in 1970. After the major price rise in the aftermath of the 1973 Arab-Israeli war, it reached only $3.68 (in terms of the value of 1950 dollars) in 1976. Today, with inflation the norm, the rise in the price of oil, although dramatic and disquieting, is more than matched by the rise in the price of many other commodities, especially metals. There seems no end or even slowing down in sight.

Beyond the statistics, one can see that an enormous change has occurred in the world economy, and much of it is a function of the price of energy. This change has three basic aspects.

First, in the oil-producing countries, there has been a move literally from rags to riches. In Saudi Arabia, for example, total government revenues for 1946 were $10 million. By the time the first edition of this book was published, they had reached $7 billion. In 1980 they reached $85 billion. Then came a sort of "phony peace" in the energy "war." The price of oil again fell, and in 1985 traders talked, shortsightedly but in their terms realistically, of an "oil glut." Today prices have risen again to figures comparable to those, not discounted for inflation, reached in 1983. Before the crisis, Saudi Arabia was exporting about 1.4 billion barrels a year at roughly $15 a barrel, for a total income of about $21 billion. In the midst of the crisis, the price of oil rose briefly to over $40 a barrel and Saudi production increased by about one fourth.

Second, if the current trends continue, Saudi Arabia should again become the major player it was in the 1970's in international financial markets and the major customer it was for many of the world's industries. And it is not only an important player in the West's financial future: Saudi Arabia has been and doubtless will again become a source of significant aid to developing countries. Its foreign aid program in the late 1970's lent or gave about $10 billion yearly. One hopes it will again shoulder that burden. More directly, it has contracted for the services of millions of workers from Africa, southern Arabia, Egypt, Pakistan, the Philippines, and Korea who live in Arabia and send their salaries home.

The third aspect is the impact upon the United States. In the 1930's much of the Middle East was as unknown to Americans as Tibet. Biblical scholars and oil men were almost the only visitors. The United States at that time *exported* oil, and the dollar was accepted as the lynchpin of world finance. This remained true until 1965. Major changes have since taken place, and more appear likely.

Partly as a result of and partly coincident with the rise in world petroleum prices, America's *relative* wealth and power in the world community have declined. Few Americans would have understood the phrase "balance of payments" in 1965 except as a problem faced by the benighted countries of Africa and Asia. Today we are no longer able to export enough to pay for all we import: to simplify, the food and industrial production of our people and land does not match our industrial and energy demands from foreign sources. We are making up the difference by a transfer of capital to the oil producers and to industrial nations such as Germany and Japan. This has caused a fall in the value of the dollar. Today many readers who never before thought of these matters scan the newspapers for quotations on the dollar and on gold in the Zurich, Tokyo, and London markets.

This is not merely a financial or foreign-policy issue: we built suburban America to fit the automobile and the automobile depended upon cheap energy. Now that gasoline has gone from about $0.15 a gallon to over $1—still cheap compared to prices in Europe of about $4—the use of the automobile will not be so easy or so free. Before the end of the 1980's our balance-of-payments problem, partly as a result of energy imports, grew seriously worse.

The strain of this transformation has, in turn, affected another aspect of international relations. Now, for the first time in history, massive wealth is being transferred from the strong to the weak. So far this has not been too painful a process, but the future bodes ill for the energy users. Consider the issue before the United States. Few political leaders will choose to tell their constituents that they can no longer freely cruise the supermarkets, highways, and suburbias of America because we cannot afford it. Some may delight in focusing discontent on the oil producers. Ugly, racial cartoons have already appeared, showing fat "oil sheikhs" choking the gas pumps. This happened in 1979 and has recurred in 1990, although this time the perceived enemy was not an "oil sheikh"—he is now our ally—but Saddam Husain.

Military deployment has certainly been popular in the United States. Forgotten are the terrible costs of the Vietnam conflict. No one doubted America's ability to win a shooting war, but the long-term costs of such a war are yet to be reckoned. It does seem clear, however, that the perception of events will differ in the United States and in the Arab world: doubtless in the latter, whatever the justification, whatever the provocation, America's actions will be weighed in different scales.

The question of the high cost of energy will arise if we do not find our way toward a more conservative policy on the use of energy. Domestic oil production has declined about 12 percent and consumption has risen about 12 percent over the past decade. Consequently the United States is now importing close to 7 million barrels of oil a day. A large part of this is used to fuel our nearly

200 million automobiles. What does this cost? Begin with oil that sells for $30–40 a barrel and add to that the "security costs" necessary to assure our access to it, deployment of military forces, aid to key nations, and the pressure on our national debt. The real figure is thus probably double the list price. Given the downward trend in the American economy and the likelihood of a continued adverse balance of payments, this kind of outflow will come to seem a nearly intolerable burden. It is a burden we can choose to lighten either at home or abroad.

Another issue on which perceptions in America and in the Arab world differ and with which I shall have to deal is terrorism. "Terrorist" is a word associated in the American mind today with Arabs and Persians—whom many Americans see as blended into one people. The association has done much to color the climate of public opinion in which our political process works.

Terrorism is not an easy subject to address, for several reasons. First, anyone who seeks to analyze it finds himself constantly saying, "Of course, I don't condone it, but to understand how . . ." The subject is even more distasteful than espionage. Worse, it is murkier. Dozens of books and hundreds of articles have been written on the subject, but when they are subjected to careful reading, few are illuminating. Most are set in a "James Bond" atmosphere more suitable to a movie than to the real world. I will have a certain amount to say about the subject when I discuss the problem of Palestine. Some of those involved in terrorism, of course, are psychopaths. If all of them were, terrorist movements would quickly die out, as some already have. But most are politically motivated. We see this in part because when the political conditions that gave rise to their movements continue, they are able to tap a steady stream of new recruits. This explains, I think, why any serious attempt to deal with terrorism must begin with politics.

Part 1 of this book sets the stage and introduces the actors. For my purposes, I have defined the Arab world to include the Sudan and Libya but not Tunisia, Algeria, and Morocco. To have included them would have greatly widened the scope and blurred the focus of the book.

In Part 2, I examine four aspects of history that I believe crucial to an understanding of present mentality. To a degree remarkable to secure, wealthy, industrialized Americans, the Arabs are bound by a code of honor that they have inherited from ancient times and that is relearned by each generation through the study of its literary heritage. Islam, the religion of the overwhelming majority of Arabs, permeates every aspect of society. Islam must be thought of as at once a religion and a social order. Like Americans, many Arabs today do not practice or even profess their religion. For those who do, the formal religion of the Koran is only a part of their religious heritage. Woven into that heritage are residues of older religions and folk beliefs, and out of the austere, relatively simple religion of the ancestors has emerged a veritable thicket of belief and custom. Never fixed or dead, this has been transmuted by history, geography, and climate. Today, as other ideologies and creeds have been found wanting, it has acquired a new relevance.

Particularly in an age of painful weakness that is the immediate background of contemporary Arabs, the memory of glorious yesterdays has been almost hypnotic. Preoccupation with the past has both sustained the Arabs in the face of contemporary adversity and prevented them from making some of the adaptations that might have mitigated their adversity. Thus, the definition of the past has been an issue in contemporary politics. What was so painful was precisely the fact that it was over. From roughly the European Middle Ages onward, very few Arabs lived under Arab rule. So habituated were the Arabs to the rule of alien empires, particularly of the Turks, that when Napoleon invaded Egypt at the end of the eighteenth century he found its people unwilling to take even the limited degree of self-rule that he offered. These, in my view, constitute the main legacies of the more distant past.

In Part 3, I discuss the "impact of the West," beginning with the "opening" of the Middle East by Napoleon. In some ways, this period may be likened to Commodore Perry's "opening" of Japan; the initial responses of Arabs and Japanese were in significant ways comparable. However, the Middle East was too near Europe, lacked essential intellectual and social prerequisites for rapid modernization, and was too attractive a target to be left to find its own way into the modern era. Modernization was bought at a high price. Intellectually, the thinkers of the Arab world were undecided as to what they could change and what they must save. Although attempts were made to redefine religion in acceptably modern terms and to find a basis in linguistic or cultural nationalism, it was not until the First World War that the Arabs found—indeed virtually had thrust upon them—a cause that was capable of sustaining an independence movement.

In Part 4, I deal with the "school" of national independence that was created by Great Britain and France in the areas that subsequently became Iraq, Syria, Lebanon, and Trans-Jordan. "Graduation" from the school of the Mandates constituted entry into the international state system. Arabia stood apart from this process, whereas Egypt was subject less to education than to detention. In both countries, the costs were being paid in the 1970's. Another contrast is offered by Libya and the Sudan, both once subject to imperial control—the latter under the rule of modern equivalents of platonic philosopher-kings and the former under a brutal, inefficient fascist regime. Finally, Palestine, the tragic issue that permeates modern Middle Eastern history, is analyzed in its pre-1948 form.

Part 5 recounts the years during which all the Arab states gained independence and began to face the intricate and critical challenges of statehood. Chapter 13 deals with the initial frustrations and missed chances, Chapter 14 with the frenetic attempts to find new political forms, more efficient means of coping with the legacies of the past, and some passable definition of legitimacy. Chapters 15, 16, and 17 return to the theme of Palestine, emphasizing the two wars of 1967 and 1973 and the tragic Palestine Arab diaspora.

Part 6 analyzes economic, social, and intellectual change.

Part 7, "War, Fragmentation, and Uprising," looks at the war between Iraq and Iran in the 1980's but sets that war in the context of older historical memories, particularly the interplay of Islam and traditional Iranian nationalism and religion, and the complex problems of geography, including the separate identity and aspirations of the Kurdish people. Chapter 22 describes and analyzes what I have called the maelstrom of the Levant. In Lebanon this took the form of a civil and international war of tragic complexity that has virtually destroyed that little country and brutalized its society. Events in Lebanon stimulate, interact with, and offset happenings in the occupied territories. There the thwarted nationalism of the Palestinians, the quest for Greater Israel, the shifting alliances of the Arab states, religious competition, problems of "security," and the overarching diplomatic relations of the powers are issues that must be heard above the relentless drumbeat of violence.

Part 8 discusses the involvement of the United States in the Arab world up to and including the deployment of American troops in Saudi Arabia in 1990. In Chapter 27, I discuss terrorism and analyze the nature of political violence in its various forms.

In a work such as this, of course, far more must be left out than can be included. Consequently, I have provided an extensive, annotated section on complementary readings in European languages.

Here I would like to add a few words on the growth of my own perspective on the nature of international politics. When the first edition of this book was being prepared, I was a member of the Policy Planning Council of the State Department. In 1965 I resigned from the State Department to become professor of history and director of the Center for Middle Eastern Studies at the University of Chicago. During the 1967 Arab-Israel war, I was briefly called back to government service in the White House. Twice after that time, I have been asked to undertake confidential diplomatic missions, once by the American government and once by the Israeli government. Otherwise, I have maintained no formal connection with government. Thus, within the frame of scholarship, I can speak openly and, in a special sense, "irresponsibly" about government policies.

In 1967 I became president of the Adlai Stevenson Institute of International Affairs. My work in the Institute exposed me to a wide range of contemporary public-policy problems, particularly in the fields of development, population growth, the environment, and peace seeking. These experiences broadened and deepened, as well as called into question, some of the conceptions with which I originally undertook my study of the Middle East. The rewriting of a book cast years earlier about a volatile part of the world in a volatile era of history is a sobering experience. I find that I have moved far from some of the complacency that now seems to me to be evident in the first edition of the book. My view of the developmental process has certainly broadened and my perception of the international process has dramatically changed. That new perspective will be reflected in this edition.

In the 1960's, I held the standard view of international affairs. This view, taught throughout the American and European academic community and echoed in the Soviet Union as well as in the Middle East, is that international affairs consists of interchange among *states*. The issues at stake are matters of national interest. The action takes place in terms of strategy. In the late 1950's the computer revolution, the impact of mathematicians like John von Neumann, and the emphasis, primarily by the military, on programming, planning, and gaming seemed to point toward a science of international affairs in which all issues could be "objectified" and many could be quantified. The great issues of the time were assumed to be relatively little disturbed by those human interactions that are generally called politics. It ought to be possible, argued the strategists, to identify interests clearly by means of criteria that were themselves so evident and "neutral," and to define rules of conduct that were so universal, that nations need no longer be subject to the irrationality of politics. Hans Morgenthau has offered an analysis based on power. Like almost everyone else in the early 1960's, I was fascinated by this vision of a rational world. If men could truly determine, by a self-evident logic, what they *had* to do, then conflict would be either avoidable or meaningless. The trick was to make national interest evident, and within acceptable limits to demonstrate the capacity and the will to protect it. The Cuban missile crisis seemed to many of us the quintessential war game. We and the Russians had, apparently, both added up the column of figures the same way and the outcome appeared to have been predictable.

I began to have serious misgivings about this system, however, even before the Cuban missile crisis; by the time I left the government in 1965, my belief in the possibility of objectifying international affairs had been profoundly shaken. My return to government briefly in June 1967 confirmed my doubts. I had been in charge of writing the basic national policy paper, then considered operative, on the Middle East. That paper had been approved by every significant office of the executive branch of our government. Yet it not only did not guide the conduct of our foreign policy but was not even considered.

Over the last few years, as I have thought about the nature of the international political system, I have reached some tentative conclusions. Briefly put, there are two. First, international politics occurs among *governments,* not states, and it is the *perception* of national interest—rather than some abstract codification—which governs. Governments cannot operate, abstractly, on grand designs but must move within the perceptions of bureaucracies, political parties, interest groups, and ideologies. Their actions and inactions often neglect or thwart the more abstract interests of the state. There is no more hope for a science in international affairs than in domestic affairs. Politics will reign supreme. The question is how enlightened and informed the politics is.

And although it is useful, indeed even necessary, to discuss in broad and crisp terms grand conceptions of international politics, these are merely the starting points of discussion and will be shaped, modified, and rendered effective or ineffective by other forces. The concept of national interest may be a road map, but the choice of the vehicle, the speed of the movement, the safety or danger of the drive will be dependent upon forces that cannot be predicted or generated or controlled.

In American policies of the 1950's and 1960's we can see the results of these theoretical misperceptions. Time after time we tried to bring about peace in the Middle East in ways we knew would not work—because they made no *political* sense—in our own society. We redrew frontiers, offered means to divide river waters, suggested arms control measures, imposed token police forces, tried to "defuse" the issue of Palestine, and helped feed people. It was not that these were bad moves, or that they were made with ill intent, but merely that people, leaders, politicians, bureaucrats, officers, governments could not deal with them apart from a political context.

Second, the agenda of the world's great issues is changing. Some of the most crucial problems are now to be seen as multinational but not international, domestic but domestic in a number of nations. This is another way of saying that ours is an age characterized by a high degree of politicization. International relations today cannot be carried on without regard to the prejudices, desires, fears, and impulses of national populations. Thus, while the "interests" of nations are undoubtedly real and compelling in general, in the specific they may prove to be impossible bases for governments to act upon, or possible only if clothed in different apparel.

Immediately before us is a period in which issues of poverty, population, the environment, and cultural identity will, I believe, increasingly predominate. These will be much more important factors—even in resolving the troubled relationships of the Arab states—than arms balances, frontiers, and other issues of "the old diplomacy." Since this book is weighted with these factors in mind, I think it is fair to the reader to expose them at the outset.

A reviewer criticized the first edition of this book on the ground that it dwelled too long on the cultural context in which Arab political affairs unfold. I remain unmoved by this line of criticism. On the contrary, experiences of the last ten years have strengthened my initial conviction that unless the cultural context for politics is understood, nothing significant can be said about Arab political affairs or about the relations between the United States and the Arab world. I assert with added conviction that if we are to understand how and why people act as they do, we must first pose and answer *intra*-cultural and *intra*-system questions and only then proceed to pose and answer *inter*-cultural and *inter*-system questions. The sequence, as stated, is the one followed in this book.

Another matter falls into place at this point. To what degree does an outsider's deep and prolonged saturation in the culture of another people become an equivalent for sympathy or identification with it? In the Department of State, one of the most telling criticisms of an ambassador was that he had "localitis"—meaning that he had identified himself too closely with the people to whom he had been sent as an ambassador.

In their encounter with an alien culture, most students pass through several stages of emotional commitment. In the first stage it is perhaps necessary, if not inevitable, that they should identify themselves with the people whom they are trying to understand. Students who fail to make this identification are likely to attain little more than a superficial appreciation of the motive forces that run deep in the culture being studied. In fact, a psychic identification with the culture is required, if only to sustain the extraordinary effort required to master its language thoroughly. Then comes a second stage in which students are repelled by the manifest shortcomings in the practices of the people under study, or even by the very essence of the culture. The simple fact of physical weariness from the demands of careful study may heighten the repulsion and the inclination toward rejection.

When the first and second stages are passed through, however, the individual student achieves a personal, artistic interpretation of the other culture—an interpretation whose quality depends on the student's personal aptitudes. At that third stage, he or she is in a position to say: "This I approve of, and that I dislike, but both I understand."

The student who reaches this stage must be reconciled to the likelihood that he will satisfy neither the opponents nor the proponents of the political system under study. I realized this fact after the appearance of the first edition of this book. In Israel the book was severely criticized. In Egypt it was banned outright. By some it was regarded as an exercise in pro-Arab sentimentalism, by others it was regarded as clever Zionist propaganda. In my own view, the only sensible criterion for evaluating a book on politics is to be found in the extent to which the book helps in the task of predicting the future and guiding people toward rational goals. That was my purpose in the first edition. It remains my purpose today.

If a reader is interested in the forces at work in world history instead of in current propaganda, he will be rewarded if he makes the effort to understand the Arabs for themselves instead of viewing them narrowly through the lens of the tragic Arab-Israeli competition for a corner of the Middle East, or merely as the suppliers of our petroleum. This kind of understanding has an essential and direct bearing both on the long view of trends in world history and on the more immediate attempt to achieve peace in the Middle East. To fail to see that the Arabs in themselves are a people worthy of sympathy and understanding is not only to betray a certain poverty of human spirit, but also to declare one's indifference to the needs of world peace. It is my own object in this book to portray a major component of the world population and to perceive in all of its dimensions a culture that must be understood for its own sake, and also for its bearing on the quest for world peace.

Many people have assisted in the growth of my knowledge, interests, and prejudices. It is impossible to name them all, but I would be remiss in not thanking a few to whom I am particularly indebted.

My own work on the Arab world goes back to 1946. Over the years, I have learned much from teachers, colleagues, students, friends, and others. Alas, a number of them are no longer alive, but I want to record their contribution to my study. Without sharing responsibility for my words with them, I want to mention Jamal Mohammed Ahmad, Edmund Asfour, John Badeau, Gabriel Baer, Leonard Binder, Lord Caradon, John Cooley, Charles Cremeans, Salah Dessouki, Nabih Faris, Hassan Fathy, Saul Friedlander, Mordechai Gazit, Sir Hamilton Gibb, Manfred Halpern, Hume Horan, Albert Hourani, J. C. Hurewitz, Fuad Jabber, Adib al-Jader, Peter Jennings, Hassan Sabry al-Kholy, Mounah Khoury, Bona Malwal, John Marshall, Emrys Peters, my brother George Polk, Yevgeni Maximovich Primakov, Chaim Rabin, Walt Rostow, Eric Rouleau, Herbert Salzman, James Spain, Jaroslav Stetkevych, U Thant, Speros Vryonis, and Zaki Yamani. I also wish to thank the John Simon Guggenheim Foundation, the Rockefeller Foundation, the Ford Foundation, and the Adlai Stevenson Institute, all of which, at critical stages, supported my research.

William R. Polk
Vence, France
January 1991

The Arab World at a Glance

Bahrain has 520,186 people (July 1990), of whom 40 percent are literate; a total area of 620 square kilometers, of which 10 percent is cultivated; and a GDP (Gross Domestic Product) of $3.5 billion, or $7,550 (1987) per capita.

Egypt has 54,705,746 people (July 1990), of whom 45 percent are literate; a total area of 1,001,450 square kilometers, of which 5 percent is cultivated; and a GDP of $38.3 billion, or $700 per capita.

Iraq has 18,781,770 people (July 1990), of whom 55–65 percent are literate (1989 estimate); a total area of 434,920 square kilometers, of which 13 percent is cultivated (plus 12 percent pastures and woodland); and a GNP (Gross National Product) of $35 billion, or $1,940 per capita.

Jordan has 3,064,508 people (July 1990), of whom an estimated 71 percent are literate; a total area of 91,880 square kilometers, of which 4.5 percent is cultivated (plus 1.5 percent pastures and woodland); and a GNP of $6.2 billion, or $1,760 per capita.

Kuwait has 2,123,711 people (July 1990); a total area of 17,820 square kilometers, of which none is cultivated and 8 percent is meadows and pastures; and a GDP of $20.5 billion, or $10,500 per capita.

Lebanon has 3,339,333 people (July 1990), of whom 75 percent are literate; a total area of 10,400 square kilometers, of which 30 percent is cultivated (plus 9 percent meadows and woodlands); and a GDP of $2.3 billion, or $700 per capita.

Libya has 4,221,141 people (July 1990), of whom 50–60 percent are literate; a total area of 1,759,540 square kilometers, of which 1 percent is cultivated and 8 percent is meadows and pastures; and a GNP of $20 billion, or $5,410 per capita.

Oman has 1,457,000 people (July 1990), of whom 20 percent are literate; a total area of 212,460 square kilometers, of which 5 percent is meadows and pastures; and a GDP of $7.8 billion, or $6,000 per capita.

Qatar has 490,897 people, of whom 40 percent are literate; a total area of 11,000 square kilometers, of which 5 percent is meadows and pastures; and a GDP of $5.4 billion, or $17,070 per capita.

Saudi Arabia has 17,115,728 people (July 1990), of whom 52 percent are literate; a total area of 2,149,690 square kilometers, of which 1 percent is cultivated and 40 percent is meadows and woodlands; and a GDP of $73 billion, or $4,720 per capita.

Sudan has 24,971,806 people (July 1990), of whom 33 percent are literate (1986); an area of 2,505,810 square kilometers, of which 5 percent is cultivated and 4 percent is meadows and woodlands; and a GDP of $8.5 billion, or $340 per capita (Fiscal Year 1987).

Syria has 12,483,440 people (July 1990), of whom 49 percent are literate; a total area of 185,180 square kilometers, of which 31 percent is cultivated and 49 percent is meadows and woodlands; and a GDP of $18.5 billion, or $1,540 per capita.

United Arab Emirates has 2,253,624 people (July 1990), of whom 68 percent are literate; a total area of 83,600 square kilometers, of which 2 percent is meadows and pastures; and a GNP of $25.3 billion, or $11,680 per capita.

Yemen Arab Republic has 7,160,981 people (July 1990), of whom an estimated 15 percent are literate; a total area of 195,000 square kilometers, of which 14 percent is cultivated, plus 44 percent meadows and woodlands; and a GDP of $5.5 billion, or $820 per capita.

Yemen (People's Democratic Republic of) has 2,585,484 people (July 1990), of whom 25 percent are literate; a total area of 332,970 square kilometers, of which 1 percent is cultivated, plus 34 percent pastures and woodlands; and a GNP of $1.2 billion, or $495 per capita.

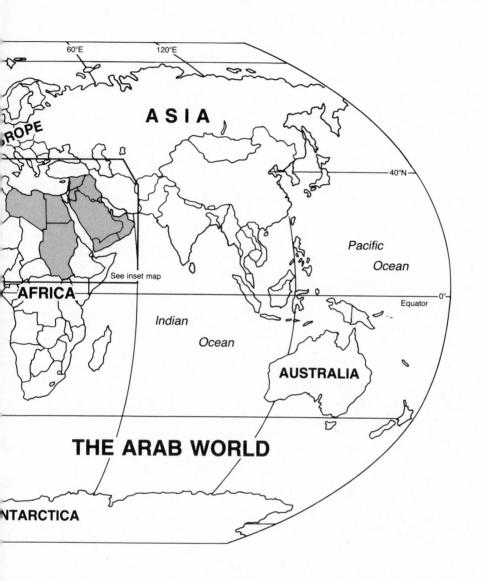

60°E 120°E

EUROPE

ASIA

40°N

ROPE

See inset map

AFRICA

Pacific

Ocean

Equator 0°

Indian

Ocean

AUSTRALIA

THE ARAB WORLD

NTARCTICA

PART 1
Introduction

1

The People on the Land

THE Middle Eastern Arab World—encompassing Egypt, Libya, the Sudan, the Arabian peninsula, Jordan, Lebanon, Syria, and Iraq—is a vast stretch of mostly barren land joining northeastern Africa to western Asia. Slightly larger than the United States, the Arab World has a climate similar to that of the Great Plains. The summers are intensely hot and dry; the winters are often bitterly cold. From the point of view of the inhabitants, perhaps the most significant physical feature is the lack of sufficient rainfall to support agriculture in most of the area. This fact has had and today continues to have a profound impact on every aspect of life. From the perspective of outsiders even more significant is the fact that the Arab World is the junction between Africa and Asia and Europe. The linchpin is Egypt, through whose land, sea, and air routes pass much of the world's commerce. Taken together the area constitutes a great highway—or a roadblock.

These two factors, the internal poverty and the strategic importance of the area, have from the dawn of history brought invading armies to the Middle Eastern shores and today make the Arab World a cockpit of international conflict. These same factors have also driven the people to occasional bursts of energy and inventive genius to which the world's civilization owes a vast debt. Indeed, civilization began in the valleys of the Nile and the Tigris and Euphrates. Occasionally, too, the people of the area, frustrated by their harsh environment, have lunged outward to conquer vast empires or create far-flung commercial links.

Every American school child is familiar with the Phoenicians, the Babylonians, and the ancient Egyptians, but the Arabs came upon the stage of history at a time when our historical focus had shifted westward. It is difficult, therefore, for Americans to speak with precision of the Arabs, their history, and their culture. But it is also difficult for the Arabs themselves to formulate a commonly accepted definition of Arab, Arabism, and Arabdom.

The Arabs, wrote one of their early poets, are "parasites of the camel." The true Arab was a nomad. Only in his veins coursed the pure Arab blood and only on his tongue the pure Arabic language. Corruption and weakness are the vices of settled life. When the plow crosses the threshold, said an Arab proverb, manhood departs. Thus, "nobility" could be measured by the distance of penetration into the great sand seas of western Asia.

Actually, however, the great majority of the people who speak Arabic are peasants and city dwellers. The bedouin nomads are today, as they probably always have been, a minority of the population. About as few Arabs today can trace their origins to the Arabian Peninsula as Americans can to England. Arabs, like Americans, are a mixed lot. The overwhelming proportion of those who are today called Arab are descendants of the native populations, once called Babylonians, Phoenicians, or Egyptians, who have adopted the Arabic language during the last fourteen centuries since the coming of Islam. Yet so deeply have the Arabs impressed their image upon those with whom they came in contact that the drawing of distinctions on ethnic or linguistic grounds is pointless. The Iraqi is, in a political and cultural sense, no less an Arab than is the Saudi Arabian. To understand the modern Arab world an appreciation of the impact of what has come to be called Arabism is essential.

It was not the desert which was the matrix of Islamic civilization. Islam was always an urban culture. To call a Muslim of the Islamic middle ages an Arab would have been an insult. His was a different order of culture, a different mode of life, and he held the nomad in a contempt tempered by fear. Some of his values he derived from the nomad, whose marvelous poetry, that thread on which Arabic civilization has been strung and in which are embodied the values of Arabic society, he relished. But the city man found in the Islamic order of society, in brotherhoods and guilds, and in fixity of dwelling new norms of life alien to those of the nomad.

Between these two, as wheat between grindstones, was the peasant.

Taxed and exploited by the one, he was bled or evicted by the other. Lacking the organization and resources of the one, he was weaker and less warlike than the other. Never was he able fully to participate in the culture of either. Both despised him. Yet he literally furnished the wheat of Middle Eastern life. Upon his labor was built urban civilization and upon his resources the bedouin drew in the frequent lean years of drought.

These three, the bedouin, the peasant, and the city man, are the Arabs. Between them are wide and deep cultural, economic, and political schisms. Yet between them are also important bridges of mutual dependence. And across these bridges, throughout history, a steady stream of men have moved.

Impelled as they were by the harsh and unpredictable conditions of their environment and aided by the fierce qualities they possessed as warriors, the bedouin constantly encroached upon their settled cousins. The clash of the desert and the sown, the parable of Abel and Cain, is a persistent theme in Arabic history. Usually the bedouin were content to levy a tribute and retire when the coming of the rains and the absence of more powerful foes made the desert again safe, but periodically groups spilled into the settled lands and remained. Throughout recorded history there has been a tendency toward what has been called sedentarization. In the last century sedentarization has increased, but only the scale, not the fact of sedentarization is new.

Indeed, the gradations from a purely nomadic to a purely settled way of life are imprecise. Practically all bedouin plow some land. Even in the midst of the vast deserts, one encounters plots where water seepage, flash floods, or occasional rainfall periodically make agriculture possible. These men sow seed, move on with their herds, and return to harvest a crop. In the belt of steppe lands between the desert and the true agricultural lands the villages are semi-nomadic. Their populations fluctuate with the seasons. During the winter rains part of the village will move off to pasture the flocks, returning in the late spring to work the land and harvest the crops. Even in the "black lands," the irrigated plains, the villagers are in part herdsmen.

Yet in general terms the "frontier" between the desert and the sown land can be drawn with considerable precision on a map. In order to stay in one place to cultivate the land, a farmer must have the equivalent of at least eight inches of rainfall yearly. Where this much water is available from rain, oases, or rivers, men have settled. Where the water amounts to less than eight inches or is unreliable, men have had to move. In the Arab World the frontier between these two ways of life has been called the "Fertile Crescent" as it is a great arc running from Jerusalem northward to Aleppo, eastward to

Mosul, and south to Basra. Inside the arc only by irrigation can men settle to farm.

Let us examine the area to see how the physical facts have shaped society and culture.

The vast majority of the Arab World is today, and has been throughout history, desert. In Egypt, for example, the total land area is the size of Texas and New Mexico but 97 percent of this is waterless sand and rock. More richly endowed are Iraq, about two-thirds the size of Texas, which is 70 percent steppe and desert, and Syria which is about half desert. Jordan is about 80 percent desert while Saudi Arabia and Kuwait, comprising about 630,000 square miles or an

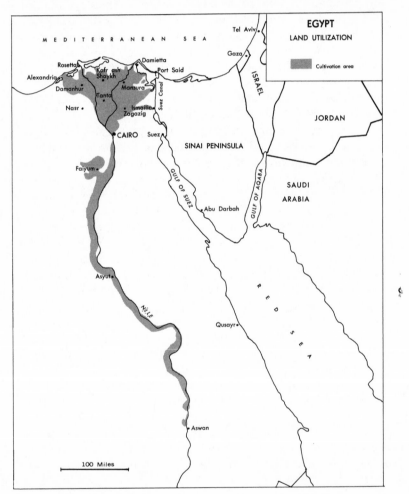

area one fifth the size of the United States, have an agricultural area only about twice the size of Long Island or one tenth of one percent of the total.

Scattered in the vast empty areas are "islands." Some are large oases where an outpouring of spring water makes settled agricultural life possible; others are merely cisterns where rain water is collected and stored for men and animals. Normally these cisterns and some of the oases are meeting places for nomads when the intense heat of the summer desiccates the desert's plant life. Then, as the winter rains come, the nomads and their flocks move out into the suddenly, and briefly, lush pasture.

The rainy season is short, normally about two months, and the summer is long, about six months, but the bedouin manage to stay in the desert or the fringes of the desert upwards of eight months. Only

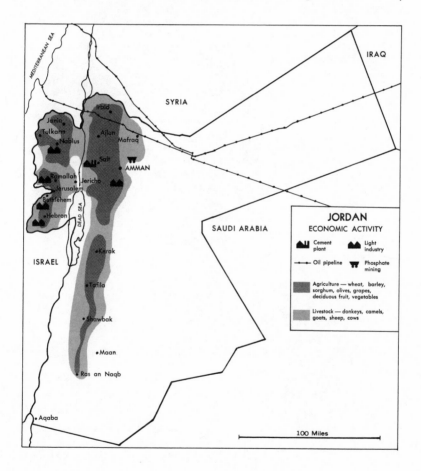

by living in small groups and by moving about can men and animals live there.

In the last decade, dramatic changes have taken place in the structure of bedouin life, the size of populations, and the relationship with settled peoples. In many areas, the advent of the truck and the lure of the city lights have all but wiped out nomadism. These changes will be discussed more fully subsequently, but here the bedouin is considered as he has lived for over 2,000 years and has left his imprint on Arabic culture.

Many, including settled Arabs, have thought of the bedouin as aimlessly wandering gypsies who, to avoid the hard physical labor of

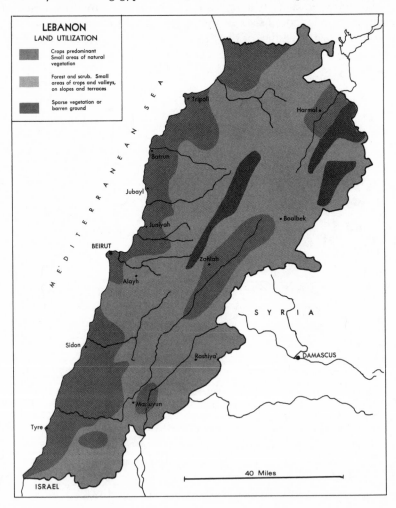

settled life, follow their animals around the deserts, stealing a bit now and then from their hard-working cousins, the peasants, and contributing nothing to the well-being of their fellow men.

The reality is quite different. The bedouin way of life, like that of the Eskimo, is a highly sophisticated adaptation to an extraordinarily difficult environment. It takes great skill, daring, and perseverance to live in the desert. And unless one is constantly supplied from outside, as armies and explorers are, he must move to live. The resources of the desert can be exploited only by the bedouin through his animals. The animals which can stand desert life are the camel, the sheep, and the goat. Others, even the horse, are, like man, ill-fitted for desert life. But, though the desert is harsh and poor in any particular area during most of the year, the resources of the desert taken in the large are immense. Winter rains create vast and lush pastures for short periods and fill water tanks and cisterns. Chance thunderstorms, with their telltale flickers of lightning, are watched as eagerly by the water-hungry bedouin as guides to green valleys as are thunderheads by the Polynesian sailors of the western Pacific as guides to unseen islands. When rain falls, the patches of desert which receive it burst into meadow lands to which the bedouin and their herds must hurry before sun and wind destroy the grass and flowers. The Arabs, whose whole artistic powers have been channeled through their language,

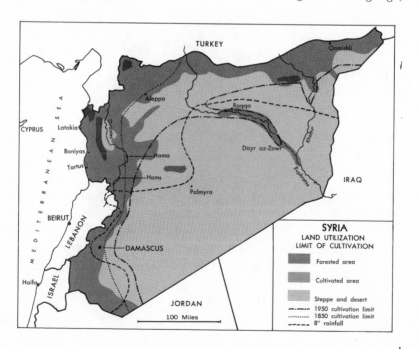

SYRIA
LAND UTILIZATION
LIMIT OF CULTIVATION

Forested area

Cultivated area

Steppe and desert
—·—·— 1950 cultivation limit
··········· 1850 cultivation limit
— — — — 8" rainfall

100 Miles

even have a particular verb, *shāma,* which means "to watch for flashes of lightning to see where the rain will fall." Few scenes in Arabic literature are treated with more care, sensitivity, and delight than the coming of a rain storm.

Apart from movement to take advantage of a chance rainfall, the bedouin must move for two other reasons. The animals quickly exhaust the pasture and both men and animals quickly drink up the water in wells and cisterns. If the season is cool and the vegetation wet, the animals drink little water and men live on their milk. But even camels need some water. The change of seasons provides another reason for migration. In the summer the desert is the literal hell described in the Koran. Scorching heat, suffocating sand storms, and raging winds bring unquenched and maddening thirst and are murderous to plants, animals, and men. The plants that grow in the desert survive underground but men and animals must move to the cooler areas of the hill country where they can find water holes and some grazing. Even there the water may be so brackish and undrinkable that men must live on camel milk. It is not without reason that the bedouin has been called the parasite of the camel. Indeed, until

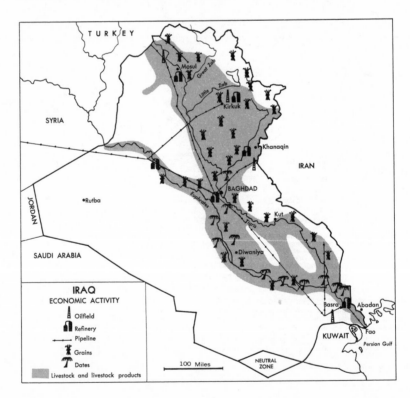

the camel was domesticated, sometime around 800 B.C., there were no true desert nomads. Men could move into the desert only short distances, for brief periods, but could not cross the great deserts or remain within them. Historically speaking, the bedouin way of life did not develop until several thousand years after the agricultural revolution. With the coming of cold and rainy weather biting, icy winds drive the nomads back to the lowlands, for the camel needs warm areas to breed. With rain the desert once again becomes the "Garden of Allah."

A true tribal map of the Arab nomadic areas would be unlike any other land map. What it would show is the route of march with an area of approximate winter pasture at one end and summer pasture at the other. Perhaps the best analogy would be a map of the sea showing fishing areas: one could trace the route of the boats and their general location but could not predict exactly where they would be, for this would depend on where the men found fish. So, for the Arabs, little or nothing is fixed and their civilization traditionally has lacked the concepts, so strong in our civilization, of home, homeland, and

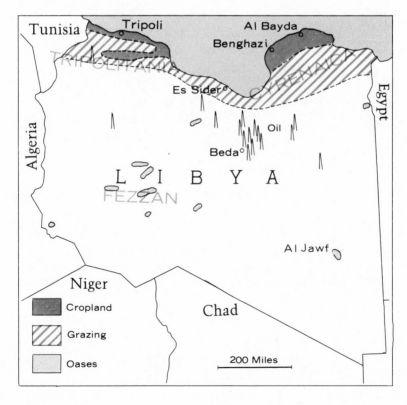

patriotism. The sentiment which we find in place of birth, home, and death exists for the nomad, of course, but it attaches to people, not to land. It is the family, the clan, and the tribe which capture loyalty and devotion. In the classical literature, the pre-Islamic poetry, the nomad is usually pictured as he happens upon an abandoned campsite, but for him the place means nothing—on it he lavishes no brilliant description—it only serves to remind him of a loved one. It is to

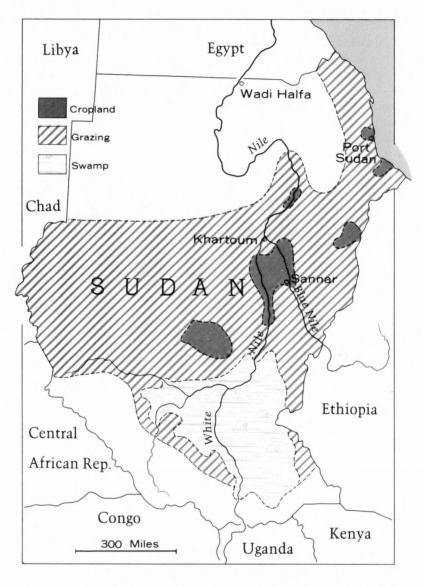

scenes of desert life as a prelude to the glorification of his folk that the poet addresses himself. Land per se has little meaning for him, and the Arabic word which comes closest to meaning "homeland" has none of the emotional overtones of *patria*.

In other ways, as well, the material conditions of bedouin life are reflected in his social organization and thought. In the desert no man can live alone. The bedouin is required by his harsh environment to be a social animal. Resources are too scattered for large numbers of people to live together, but efficient utilization of those resources requires team effort. Under normal conditions the "team" appropriate to the task is what the Arabs call the *qawm* or the clan. The "tribe," of hundreds or thousands of men, based on genealogy and on grazing areas and water rights, can have effective existence only when enough water and fodder is available—and that can only be sporadically. It is the clan that lives, herds animals, and fights as a corporate group. It normally is composed of several generations of children of a single man but often absorbs clients whom it agrees to protect and others who, in the Arabic expression, "put on its skin."

To the qawm the individual owes total loyalty and from his membership in it he derives social identity and legal standing. Since the primary function of the qawm is to enable the individual to live in a hostile environment, every cultural and social pressure is brought to bear on the individual to do his part in making the qawm cohesive, strong, and effective. Within the qawm property distinctions are minimal.

In a society without external institutions or means of coercion, a man's safety depends upon the ability and willingness of the clan to protect him. But, since the mode of life of the bedouin demands that he spend much of his time alone and far from his fellows, the notion of vengeance came to be substituted for protection. Failure to take vengeance, of course, would reduce the credibility of the threat and so undermine the safety of everyone. However, unlimited warfare and the taking of vengeance would destroy that minimum element of security which makes life in the desert possible. So, as we shall see in the next chapter, various other sorts of safeguards were created to give men a degree of tranquility.

Bedouin society has always been a pulsating organism, subject to rapid coagulation and to equally rapid disintegration. As one clan grows rich and numerous, other clans will ally themselves to it and it will absorb numbers of clients. When it outruns its resources or becomes politically unwieldy, the clan subdivides.

There never have been large numbers of bedouin and today their numbers are decreasing. Reliable statistics do not exist, but there are probably not more than a million bedouin in all of the Arab countries.

In many areas, even those bedouin who remain have radically altered their ways of life. In the summer months, they crowd into the fringes of the cities and towns where water is available and part-time work can be found. In the winter and spring, they often establish *fixed* encampments or outposts on the edge of the sandy deserts. There, supplied by truck with water, they pasture their herds on the rain-fed grazing. Technology has allowed them to develop an anomaly: a settled life in the desert. However, these are but extensions and amplifications of an old pattern.

Always, the lure of city comforts attracted and the unpredictability of the desert climate expelled some nomads. Now, with the tractor reaching out to plow the steppe lands and the pump bringing more areas under regular cultivation, with property rights of the settled peoples enforced by governments whose weapons are carried on airplanes, tanks, and trucks and who are guided by radios, the bedouin are held in check. As the market for camels has declined, with the coming of the airplane, railroad, and truck for transport and beef cattle for meat, the bedouin have ceased to command markets and perform services which once gave them an assured place in the economy. Moreover in the last century it has been the policy of governments to force the bedouin to settle so that they can be controlled, conscripted, and taxed. As a result the frontier of settlement has moved out into the desert areas further each generation, and by the 1930's a French sociologist could accurately say, "the contemporary Arab East is a vast peasant farm." About two thirds of the Egyptians, Syrians, Iraqis, and Jordanians today derive their living from agriculture.

Agriculture is historically much older than camel-borne nomadism. Beginning about 20,000 years ago, two major changes slowly occurred in the Middle East. First, Middle Eastern hunters grew more skilled and more numerous and, second, the climate of the Middle East grew more harsh. Gradually, the wild animals were exterminated. The larger animals and those which depended upon an abundance of water went first. This presented a dilemma comparable to one which, in modern times, afflicted the Eskimos. The new technology, rifles in the case of the Eskimos, and the bow and arrow in the case of the ancient Middle Easterner, enabled men to destroy their ecosystem. Famine was probably averted in part by migration, but those who did not migrate had to find an alternate source of food. Either by genius or by accident, they began to experiment with agriculture. Wherever they may have first tried, they first succeeded in the relatively wet areas of southern Anatolia.

It was in southern Anatolia, roughly 10,000 years ago, that men began to experiment with agriculture. For several thousand years investment in agriculture was probably relatively casual, as it remains today among the bedouin of Central Arabia, but gradually, as men became more proficient, they began to remain with their fields and to build permanent dwellings. As grasses were planted, techniques and seed were slowly refined. Little by little groups must have wandered back into the ancestral hunting grounds, particularly along the Tigris-Euphrates Valley, bringing with them the new agricultural technology. There they experimented with alternate sources of water, particularly with digging ditches to bring the water from the rivers to their fields. The results, of course, were spectacularly better than in the cold, thin soil of the rain-fed mountains. The sun, the thick black soil, and the abundant river water enabled them to produce agricultural surpluses beyond the dreams of their forebears. By roughly 4,000 B.C., villages were being transformed into towns. In these, the accumulation of an agricultural surplus allowed for increasing differentiation of labor and the beginning of civilization as we know it. The progeny of this "urban revolution," in varying degrees of complexity, at various levels of scale, not only accounts for the vast bulk of the population of the Middle East, but is the base upon which all of its religions and cultures have been built.

There is no "typical" village in the Middle East, but certain characteristics are sufficiently widespread to give an idea of peasant life. Most villages define themselves in terms of kinship, locality, livelihood, and religion. Like the nomadic encampment the village is predicated upon the proximity of water; but unlike it the village is relatively fixed. There has been distinct and constant change in the location of villages. The frontier of settlement of Syria and Iraq as well as, but more dramatically than, Egypt has varied a great deal in the last century, and old tax registers of even such relatively stable areas as Lebanon show great changes over the centuries. Yet village life presents perhaps the most stable element in the area.

Villages are small worlds unto themselves. Today, with the advance of the motor car and the radio, this is less the case than formerly, but it is still pronounced. Villagers tend to marry within their villages. Of the nearly 400 marriages contracted over the last century in one Lebanese village, for example, only 40 were with "foreigners" from neighboring towns. The vast majority were with cousins inside the large extended families or clans. Thus, the village and its component families achieve a high degree of homogeneity and control over people and resources which might otherwise have been alienated. Real or ascribed kinship becomes a conceptual scheme by which all contemporary relationships are explained and codified.

Subdivisions within a large kindred among villagers, as among the nomads, re-enforce their kinship with neighborhood. In many mountain and hill villages in the Levant the neighborhood of a clan is a miniature fort whose houses present a windowless wall to the outside and front on a courtyard in which a well or cistern is shared by all. Within the court the women go about their daily chores unveiled and the children play as members of one family. Often the rules of inheritance will result in a graphic portrayal of the family tree on the ground. For example, one can observe in a Lebanese village the sort of "geography of kinship" illustrated in the accompanying diagram.

Other parts of the village may be held in common. In Jordan and parts of Syria and Iraq a sort of village commune has existed. In this system land is reapportioned among inhabitants from time to time. In other villages, where the custom of individual holdings is stronger, the village might hold grazing lands and a market place in common. Resources, such as access to a spring or cistern, would be carefully

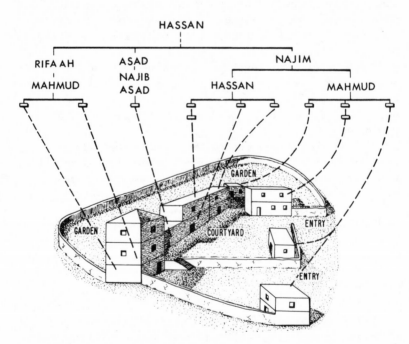

The geography of kinship in a Lebanese village

regulated by custom or even by a written "treaty" between the major clans of the village.

The fact of life most central to all is the community of the village: any threat to the stability or economic well-being of a part of the village is necessarily a threat to all. As in the nomadic life the rights of the individual are severely subordinated to those of the group; above all, the system is conservative. Major dislocations by migration, death, or impoverishment have to be righted by social means, so the village brings in or excludes outsiders as it sees fit, protects village rights to water or land, and endows shrines and religious organizations.

Whereas the bedouin can protect himself, his fellows, and his animals by moving, the villager, tied to his plot of land, his house, and his access to water, can not leave except in dire emergency and at high price. In times of unrest or anarchy villagers did become partly or wholly nomadic. The perceptive Swiss traveler John Lewis Burckhardt noted in 1810—a time of anarchy—that few Syrian peasants died in the same village in which they were born, so oppressed were they by the government tax collectors and the rapacious bedouin raiders. Even today and even on irrigated lands, the Iraqi peasant is at least semi-nomadic, partly out of the habits of insecurity and partly because for nearly a thousand years the central government has failed to regulate irrigation and drainage. But for most of the peasants in the Middle East, kinship has been replaced by geography and the central function of all organization is to protect one's little world from outside encroachment.

Among settled people, as among the nomads, those are most safe who are least easy to reach. And so the inhabitants of the remote mountain villages of Yemen, Hadhramaut, Oman, Iraq, Syria, and Lebanon have been able to preserve, through the changing times of many centuries, their culture and their independence, while the peasants of the open plains of Syria and the river deltas of Egypt and Iraq could not. It is not surprising, therefore, that the minority communities and religious sects are often to be found in the mountains while there is more homogeneity in the plains.

The large-scale, irrigated agriculture of the Middle East has, historically, given the area its wealth. Indeed, it is probable that the "birth" of civilization as we know it, in the sense of human organization on a large scale, is intimately associated with the need to control the mighty rivers of the Middle East. This problem, it has been suggested, is at the base of oriental despotism. It is certainly clear that the settled agricultural areas have always lived under highly centralized, autocratic governments which have closely regulated not only the

17

commerce but also the details of agricultural production. In fact, so intimately have the governments, from ancient Egyptian and Babylonian times, intervened in the lives of the people that they represented the whole spectrum of organized life from economic, military, bureaucratic, and legal power to matters of personal status and religion. But the people fear and resent this interference and usually resist by withdrawal, having as little to do with government as possible while submitting to its outward power. As Father Ayrout observed in *The Peasant,* "They have changed their masters, their religion, their language and their crops, but not their way of life. From the beginnings of the Old Kingdom to the climax of the Ptolemaic period the Egyptian people preserved and maintained themselves. Possessed in turn by Persians, Greeks, Romans, Byzantines, Arabs, Turks, French and English, they remained unchanged . . . A receptive people, yet unyielding; patient, yet resistant." So accustomed are they to living apart from government and yet so pliant are they before government that they make both the development programs of today and the attempts at representative government of recent years extremely difficult.

The peasant is deeply suspicious of any move the government may make—even if, on the surface, it appears to be to his benefit. When the governments tried to get him to register his lands, he often did so in someone else's name, fearing taxes and conscription. When modern governments have sought to get him to use better methods and seed, he has been reluctant, since the old ways, though perhaps not the best, were known, trusted, and reliable. The peasant can ill afford to gamble and is little disposed, in any case, to trust any government. And indeed governments of the last century, even when occasionally proclaimed in his name, nearly always were or became centers of power for the landlords to oppose all measures designed to help the peasant. It was, after all, the elected Iraqi parliament which in 1932, upon achieving independence, passed a law to convert free tribesmen into serfs, bound to the land and policed by machinery of the state. It was the elected Egyptian parliament which stoutly resisted to the bitter end any moves to enforce equitable taxation, introduce better and cheaper fertilizers, or to give the peasant a share in the land.

The city, as personified by the government, always has lived leechlike on the countryside and often gave little in return. Between the way of life in the cities and that in the countryside there has been always a vast gulf, unbridged even by a common culture, for the peasant actively partook little of the Islamic culture of the urban areas or the Arabic culture of the bedouin, although he was the passive recipient of both.

Like the bedouin, who was attracted to settled life, the peasant was constantly lured by the city. In times of rural anarchy and chaos men huddled in walled towns for protection. As economic opportunity or political considerations led them, they moved to cities or garrisons or palaces and, by encamping around them, created new urban areas. At several times in the Islamic period such movements have been particularly pronounced. During the Islamic conquests the early caliphate, to keep the hastily assembled tribal armies from fading into the countryside, encouraged them to settle around the garrison-administrative centers which gradually grew into such cities as Basra, Kufa, and old Cairo. When Baghdad was laid out in 762, its founder, the Abbasid Caliph Mansur, planned only a palace and an administrative center but founded, in fact, the core of a city. And, finally, in the period of rapidly expanding commerce that has extended over the last century the cities have grown considerably in size and, like magnets drawing together iron filings, have clustered around themselves concentric rings of shanty towns.

But, of course, rings of shanty towns are not cities. And the Middle East has had an unbroken urban tradition from the earliest historic times. This is particularly evident in Egypt and Mesopotamia but Damascus, Palmyra, Petra, Tripoli, Sidon, Tyre, Jerusalem, Medina, and Mecca have their roots deep in the past. Jerusalem and Damascus were well enough known, but Mecca, even before the birth of Muhammad in A.D. 570, was a significant international entrepôt, controlling through diplomatic and military ties with the "nations" of Arabia, the bedouin tribes, and a caravan trade covering thousands of miles. This center had a sophisticated oligarchy dealing with intricate problems of commercial law, money, and banking, and an urban pride and sense of identity celebrated in the pantheon, the Kaaba, which long before Islam was a focal point of Arabian religion and commerce.

The coming of Islam provided a powerful stimulus to urban life. Muhammad was a city man who thought in urban terms. His "Constitution of Medina" was, among other things, an attempt to transcend the limits of kinship and neighborhood of the tribe and village by creating a sense of community which would embrace rival groups of kindred, men of different hamlets, and even men separated by the frontiers of religion. Inherent in the structure Muhammad created in Medina is the intricate social pattern of the medieval Islamic city, interlaced as it became with religious and craft guilds and neighborhoods centering on mosque schools, with its markets patrolled and organized by inspectors of weights and measures, police, and law courts. The civic pride of the medieval cities was often further expressed in great popular religious festivals while wealth, learning, and power were institutionalized in foundations, libraries, and schools.

To a tragic degree this aspect of the Arab cultural heritage was destroyed by the invasions of the Mongols and the Turks, in which such great urban centers as Baghdad, Aleppo, and Damascus were virtually obliterated and by the centuries of waste and neglect which brought foods, famine, and pestilence in their wake. Baghdad, which in the twelfth century had a population of nearly a million—or five times that which Paris was to achieve two centuries later—was sacked and massacred in 1258. When this happened, culture, which in Iraq in Islamic times was always an urban phenomenon, withered like a plant in the scorching blast of a desert summer. Unlike the plant, the culture was not deeply rooted in the soil and little survived for the refreshing nourishment of subsequent, peaceful centuries. Moreover, when centralized control over the vast and complex irrigation system was ended, great tracts of land were ruined. Irrigation and drainage ditches were allowed to fill with silt, the desert broke in to the black lands, and much of the best land turned into a swamp. With its rural base sapped, the urban structure of Iraq did not again reach the scale of its medieval days until this century.

Yet, by the end of the eighteenth century urban life was beginning to recover, and some cities, such as Aleppo and Damascus, though small by modern terms, had again developed relatively high standards of cultural and commercial life. Damascus was described by a French visitor in 1833 as "a vast factory town comparable to Lyon." And the merchants of even such small seaports as Jiddah were able to buy and sell shiploads of merchandise from Zanzibar, India, and the Red Sea ports. Little towns like Gaza derived their importance in part from the fact that the caravan routes passed through them and they were trading centers for the bedouin.

The point is that a real urban society existed. It offered both an urban government and a satisfying community life, based upon villagelike neighborhoods and laced together by religious foundations, brotherhoods, and guilds. Life was sufficiently organized to encourage cultural and educational development, and so to keep alive the forms of Islamic culture.

The three levels of Arab society, the nomadic, the village, and the city, though separated in important ways culturally, politically, and geographically, historically have been in other ways dependent upon one another. The bedouin furnished meat, wool, and transportation to the villagers who raised the grain that sustained the bedouin in bad years and the urban people always as well as the cotton and silk which were fashioned in the cities and sent out again on the backs of bedouin camels. These patterns of life interacted and for all their differences were accepted. As we shall see, it was in part the dislocation of this pattern which has been a prominent feature of society in our times. For today, in the Arab countries as in most society, the urban areas are growing rapidly in numbers and in power at the expense of both the steppe and the sown cultures. Cairo today has a larger population than all of Egypt had in 1800 and Beirut has grown from about 10,000 in 1830 to a million in 1973. As industry develops relative to agriculture this trend will continue.

The "frontier" between desert and sown land, as we have seen, is a highly determining factor in the structure of the Arab world. Another of the "frontiers" of Middle Eastern Arab society is religion. Before the advent of Islam some Arabs had become Christians and Jews, but most of the nomads were pagans with rudimentary cults of gods and goddesses often symbolized by stones. As we shall see, Islam became a great codifier of society, giving not only law but also highly specific rules and mores, and a unifier of society in that it set forth principles that transcended the boundaries of clan, tribal, village, and regional strife. Islam also tried to transcend religious differences by marking out the rights and duties not only of its own citizens, the Muslims, but also of the members of other religions. More than other great religions, notably medieval Christianity, Islam was highly successful in extending the perimeters of tolerance. One measure of this fact is that for many centuries after the conquest the peoples of the new empire of Islam retained their separate languages and religions. Conversion to Islam is still far from complete in the Arab lands and as late as the last century many whose descendants now regard themselves as Arabs spoke other languages.

In the Arabic community are many who are not today Muslim while among the Muslim community are several sects and many non-Arabs. Historically these differences were abetted by the Muslim rulers who allowed each community, as distinguished by religion, to rule itself in matters of personal status, taxation, and internal security. Western powers have often been associated with these minority groups. The Italians and Greeks had their own nationals in several of the Arab countries; the French protected the Catholic community; and tsarist Russia aided the Orthodox community. Great Britain traditionally aided the Druze and the Jews, and private American groups helped to create and then foster Protestants. So the existence of minority communities has import both in domestic and international terms.

21

Egypt has about five million Copts. The word Copt is a corruption of the Greek word for Egyptian; the Copts are the remnant of Hellenized ancient Egypt. Today, they share with other Egyptians the Arabic language but remain monophysite Christians under an unbroken line of 118 patriarchs since the Council of Chalcedon in A.D. 451. Like minorities elsewhere, the sect was often used by, and lent themselves to use by, alien rulers who knew that the Copts, while having detailed knowledge of the country, could never threaten their rule. Thus, the Copts tended to become identified as a clerical class, although many are peasants, and to be tarred with the brush of governmental tyranny and alien privilege. As late as the end of World War I almost half of the Egyptian civil service was Coptic.

Egypt also has had large communities of Jews, Greeks, and Italians, although all three have declined greatly in recent years. They benefited to such an extent from alien patronage that hardly any members of these communities could be brought to an Egyptian court for any offense and virtually all were able to escape taxes and other obligations. Quite naturally they were resented, often bitterly, by the less fortunate natives. As an English satirical writer once said, in every wave of nationalist violence it was the Greek grocers who laid down their lives for Britain. The Greek grocer was the usurer of the typical Egyptian village. Alexandria became again in the nineteenth century and remained until quite recently a predominantly Greek city. The Italians aroused less ire but have suffered in the generally anti-foreign feelings which followed the coming of independence.

The Jews have suffered proportionally as violence and hatred between Egypt and Israel have increased. As early as the 1930's, when Zionism became strong in the Palestine Mandate, there were anti-Jewish demonstrations, and when Israel defeated Egypt in 1948–49, public feeling increased in violence. The Egyptian government took various steps to control the animosity but when, in 1956, Israel attacked Egypt, it openly encouraged Jewish emigration.

Lebanon, on the contrary, as a vast natural fortress of steep valley sides and rocky crags, has been historically a refuge of minorities. Indeed, Lebanon has no true majority. In a population of some 2.9 million about 6 percent are Armenian, and 0.5 percent are Jews. Of the rest, the Arabs, the latest estimates give this breakdown: 7 percent Druze, members of a heretical offshoot of Islam, 18 percent Shii or non-Orthodox Muslim, 20 percent Sunni or Orthodox Muslim, 38 percent Uniate Christian, 16 percent Orthodox Christian and 1 percent Protestant. These subdivisions are so woven into the "confessional" system of Lebanese political and administrative life as to enable each community effectively to defend itself today as, behind the

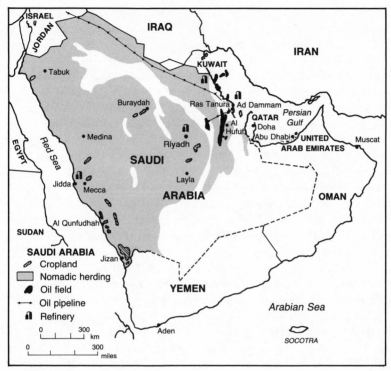

SAUDI ARABIA
- 🐟 Cropland
- ▧ Nomadic herding
- 🔴 Oil field
- ⟶ Oil pipeline
- ▥ Refinery

walls of villages and the rocks of steep mountain sides, it did traditionally.

In Jordan (including the West Bank of the Jordan under Israeli occupation) about 2 percent of the population of three million are Circassians whose ancestors in the last century migrated from the Caucasus to escape the Russians, and 1 percent are Armenians who came
for similar reasons. Nine percent of the people are Christian, mostly
living in what used to be the mandate of Palestine on the west bank of
the Jordan River, and all the rest are Orthodox Muslims.

Of the roughly 18.7 million Iraqis over 75 percent are Arabic-
speaking and about 20 percent Kurdish and Turkoman. The Arabs
are divided into the Sunnis and the somewhat more numerous Shiis
while the Kurds and Turkomans are mostly Sunnis. Iraq, like Lebanon, has no true majority: religiously, the Sunnis are preponderant
but are divided ethnically and linguistically between Arabs and
Kurds while ethnically and linguistically the Arabs form the majority
but are divided religiously and culturally between Sunnis and Shiis.
Other minorities include the Chaldeans, Armenians, Jews, Yezidis
(popularly called "Devil Worshipers"), and Assyrians, each in small
numbers.

23

Syria, with a population of 12.5 million, is basically Sunni Muslim but contains 13 percent Christian, 11 percent Alawi, 3 percent Druze, and 1 percent Ismaili minorities.

Alone among the Arab areas, the Arabian Peninsula is comparatively devoid of minorities. North and south Arabic dialects are written in the same script, and almost everyone today is Muslim. Shii minorities inhabit eastern Saudi Arabia and comprise most of the populations of Yemen and Oman; otherwise the Muslims are Sunni. Racially, of course, not all Muslims are "Arab." Along the seacoasts, the Red Sea, the Indian Ocean, and the Persian Gulf, significant numbers of blacks, South Asians, and Persians are to be found. Over 1,000 years of annual pilgrimages to the Islamic holy cities have left behind little pockets of Muslims from Central Asia, China, East and West Africa, Turkey, and the Balkans. Statistically and politically, however, these groups are not significant.

Yemen did have a large Jewish minority and was once ruled by Jewish kings; but in recent centuries it has been ruled by an imam who represented the Zaidi branch of Shii Islam, which they share with the population of Oman to the east.

The total population of the Arab Middle East has exploded in the last century. The birth rate, apparently, has always been high but it was canceled in large part by a very high rate of infant mortality and by famine and plague. Centuries ago the Arabs of the desert, aware that the settled areas were sources of disease, strove to remain in the cleaner air of the desert, but drought and famine drove them in tidal pulsations toward the urban centers. Hunger is the compelling image in some of the most graphic and tragic pieces of Arabic literature. The peasants usually managed to eat, but their economy hovered barely above mere subsistence. It was partly for this reason that they resisted growing nonfood crops like cotton. For the food they grew they paid a heavy toll in their exposure to malaria, bilharzia—the snail-borne disease associated with irrigation—and dysentery.

There are no accurate population statistics even now for most of the Arab countries—figures for Saudi Arabia over the last decade have varied from 2 to 20 million—but reasonable estimates in the third decade of the nineteenth century give the basis for an informed guess that there were then about six million Arabs in the Middle East, of whom half lived in Egypt. Today, Egypt's population is more than 55 million and, increasing at 2.5 percent yearly, will double in a quarter of a century. It is clear that this extremely rapid rate of growth places the most serious pressure on the economies of the Arab countries, which will require enormous investment of capital and skill to enable them to feed their people. But not only are the actual numbers of people increasing; the minimum scale of living for which they are prepared to settle is also rising. Thus, in political and economic terms the difference between 1830 and 1990 is not just 6 million compared to roughly 153 million, but 6 million at a certain living standard and 153 million at a living standard several times as high. Today, economies must not only feed and clothe but furnish medical care, education, consumer goods, industrial plants, roads, dams, and, unfortunately, highly sophisticated and highly expensive weapons for large armies.

In most natural resources other than oil, the Middle East is poor. Even where minerals exist, they either are difficult of access or are not present in usable combinations. For example, Egypt has iron deposits but no coal; Jordan has phosphate rock but no power with which to process it. The whole area is deficient in timber. Therefore, most industry is still primarily engaged in processing agricultural products.

Oil is the great exception to generalizations about the Middle East. Here, Middle Eastern Arab resources are tremendous. Kuwait, the golden land of the Middle East, with an area of 17,820 square kilometers (roughly the size of Connecticut) and a population of 2.1 million, has estimated oil deposits of 100 billion barrels, which give it an income of $20 billion. Saudi Arabia has reserves of 250 billion barrels; Iraq, 100; Libya, 22; and the UAE, 100.

As Europe recovered from World War II and the whole world took to wheels and wings, the oil industry and the oil-producing countries prospered. The Arabs now draw over $50 billion yearly from royalties on their oil. But, tragically for the economic impact of this flow of capital, oil is primarily to be found in those areas of the Middle East least suited for human habitation and where nature has provided little else in which people could invest. It is only recently that the Arabs have found ways in which the income from petroleum could be put to work effectively in the Arab area rather than causing a boom in the real estate markets of Cairo, Beirut, and Lausanne.

From the point of view of outsiders, the Arab Middle East contains assets of great world importance. The Suez Canal, which yields about $250 million yearly to Egypt, is of enormous value to international commerce and industry. In 1979, 235 million tons of cargo in some 20,289 ships passed through the canal. But even before the canal was dug, Egypt was a transit point in international commerce and communication. In the Middle Ages, Egypt waxed rich on this trade. Its later poverty was in part a consequence of one of the great blockades of all time, the seizure of control over the mouth of the Red Sea, to close off Venetian-Egyptian commerce, which was the consequence of the Portuguese sailor Vasco da Gama's great feat in rounding the Cape of Good Hope in 1498. For both Napoleon and the British, Egypt seemed a key to Europe's control over India. Finally, the existence of the canal was a major causative factor in the Anglo-French invasion of Egypt in November 1956.

And, in this age of air travel, the airspace over and the landing and transit facilities in the several Arab countries, but most importantly in Lebanon and Egypt, are of the greatest importance in international relations.

In their own terms, the Arabs face the problems of poverty, backwardness, and ambition shared by the "developing" nations of Africa and Asia. But, as Arabs, as Middle Easterners, and as heirs to a particular historical experience, they face the common problems in a highly individual way. To discern the particular in the communality and the communality in the particular is, perhaps, the supreme challenge in international understanding. Thus, for themselves, for their assets, and for their very weaknesses, the Arabs will command the attention of the world in our time.

PART 2

Four Legacies from the Arab Past

2

The Ancient Arabs: The Code of Honor

Like most peoples, the Arabs cherish a memory of times of glory, halcyon days when the world paused to allow men to aspire to the fullness of their bravery, strength, and refinement, and which, ever after, set a banner on the pinnacle of their achievement and a seal on their aspirations. Ancient song and story, in its content and form of expression, forms the core of a classical tradition, the quarry of artistic endeavor, and the repository of national ethic. The Arabs call these *Aiyamu'l-Arab* or "the Days of the Arabs." For all those who speak and relish the richness of the Arabic language and who call themselves Arab, the Days of the Arabs are an ideal past.

Such a period in Western civilization was the Age of Pericles, or, in a slightly different form, the England of the Arthurian Legends. Americans, even with our short history and variegated backgrounds, have already begun to make of the early years of the Republic—or of the Wild West—an idealized past in which men stood straighter, strove more nobly, and reached more surely for glory.

An idealized past, even one with which a person can identify only by great stretch of imagination, is a mirror for the present. However dimly it may be related to a real past, it provides a clear and bright picture of the aspirations and values of the present. What then has come down to modern Arabs from this dim, distant, and wild past?

The traditions and values of the ancient Arabs are not simply of antiquarian interest. Ancient Arabic poetry is today the syllabus of linguistic and literary study in every Arab school. Poetry to the Arabs is what folk stories, drama, legend, and epic are to the West. Few indeed are the Arabs, even those who are illiterate, who have not memorized hundreds of lines of poetry, and few are the political discussions, social gatherings, or entertainments in which poetry does not figure prominently. On its poetry Arabic civilization has lavished all of the inventive genius which in other cultures has been spread over the whole range of the arts. Study, memorization, and repetition of ancient Arabic poetry tie the modern age to previous ages and on this string is hung that sense of continuity which makes those who live in the modern Middle Eastern Arab states think of themselves as Arab. It is not only a living tradition, it is the essence of tradition.

By their British and French rulers and by many Western visitors, the modern bedouin nomads, and so by extension ancient Arabs, were regarded as the "good Arabs," a wild, childlike people, indolent perhaps and unproductive of social well-being, but whose courage and simplicity one could admire in contrast to the superficially Westernized, devious, difficult "town Arabs." Others, including their Turkish governors under the Ottoman Empire, have thought of the bedouin as gypsies, a people wandering aimlessly through the deserts, or pirates who, living in the vast inner sand sea of the Middle East, raided and plundered the coast and then retired, out of reach, to their distant "islands" and "fishing grounds." Arab philosophers have thought of the bedouin in terms similar to the eighteenth century European philosophers' "Natural Man"—the bedouin were the simple, pristine, children of God, uncorrupted and untamed by civilization, a bloodbank of new vigor for jaded urban society.

These attitudes have led, of course, to different policies. The British attempted to police the bedouin while protecting them from the city Arabs. Transjordan was to be their state, and in Iraq they were to have a strong voice in parliament. The French were less protective but, if anything, more appreciative of *la civilisation du désert*. The Turks generally sought to destroy the bedouin as others have sought to destroy pirates. Punitive expeditions were tried repeatedly but succeeded only against the settled or semi-nomadic tribes, who, having invested in lands and houses, could be caught. The true nomads vanished before the slow Turkish infantry only to reappear before isolated garrisons. Few were those governors wise enough to lure the bedouin to settle so that they might be controlled.

The attitude of the urban Arabs themselves was and still is ambivalent. The Arabs glory in the traditions and art of the bedouin as ancient Arabs, and nobility is claimed by descent from the bedouin.

Historically to say of a student of Arabic that he studied with the bedouin was to accord him the best of credentials. Classical Arabic was the language of the bedouin of the Arabian highlands. Yet, the bedouin are feared and even hated, for if they have infused new vigor into society they have also drained off the old life and have overthrown existing orders of society. Today in the Arab World there is no government which can be said to be sympathetic with the bedouin. All seek to convert him into a settled peasant and all have upset the administrative arrangements which set him apart from other citizens.

Actually, nomadism has been in decline for at least a half a century. Settled peoples have not needed the meat and wool of the bedouin camels, for they could get them elsewhere cheaper. They have found cheaper and faster means of transport. And, with the use of the airplane and the truck with a machine gun mounted on top, they could prevent the nomads from raiding one another and the settled lands as never before. As the high commissioner of Iraq wrote in 1924 in his report to the League of Nations, "now, almost before the would-be rebel has formulated his plans, the droning of the aeroplanes is heard overhead." Always bedouin life has been fragile; now the delicate balance of conditions which sustained it has been upset. The bedouin, like the knight and the cowboy, is rapidly passing from the scene, but like all heroic figures he leaves behind a legend which dwarfs reality.

As we have seen, the harsh realities of desert life shaped bedouin society and thought. The bedouin never lived under government, and even their own tribes were loose federations in which every man was an equal. The shaikh was little more than a respected arbiter and generous host, never a ruler to his people. Burckhardt, one of the great observers of bedouin life, wrote in *Notes on Bedouins and Wahabys,* "the shaikh has no actual authority over the individuals of his tribe; he may, however, by his personal qualities obtain considerable influence. His commands would be treated with contempt; but deference is paid to his advice . . . thus the Bedouin truly says that he acknowledges no master . . . and in fact, the most powerful chief dares not inflict a trifling punishment on the poorest man of his tribe."

But, if the desert gives scope for such democracy, it also puts a heavy premium on social cohesion. Life in the desert is and must be a team effort. The clan or qawm is the group of kindred which lives, herds animals, fights, and makes peace together. The qawm was the effective social unit—it was, in reality, the nation-state of the bedouin. No larger or more elaborate social gathering had more than transitory existence and none had real authority over the clan. Since there was no "international" law and no supraclan institutions, the identity and protection of the individual were derived from membership in a clan. It was the certainty that a man's clan would protect him where possible and exact retaliation when he was harmed that gave him security of property and person.

Pride in folk and boasting of their qualities is one of the common features of the Arabic poem. The poet, the propagandist of his day, finds many ways to enhance the reputation of his folk, detailing their bravery, their wisdom, their generosity. As an-Nabighah sang,

> . . . . a people are they whose might in battle shall never fail
> When goes forth their host to war, above them in circles wheel battalions of eagles, pointing the path to battalions more:
> Their friendship is old and tried—fast comrades in foray, bred to look unafraid on blood, as hounds to the chase well trained . . .
>
> Of steeds in the spear-play skilled, with lips for the fight drawn back, their bodies with wounds all scarred, some bleeding and some half-healed.
> And down leap the riders where the battle is strait and stern and spring in the face of Death like stallions amid the herd;
>
> Between them they give and take deep draughts of the wine of Doom as their hands ply the white swords, thin and keen in the smiting-edge.
>
> In them no defect is found, save only that in their swords are notches a many, gained from smiting of host on host.
>
> (translated by Lyall)

Behind the boast of his folk is the poet's implied and, at the end of the poem, explicit boast of his own virtues.

Most of the poet's virtues could be shown in performance of the duties of the tribe but the ultimate in personal bravery was to pit oneself against all mankind and all nature. If a man were expelled by his qawm he was literally an outlaw against whom the hand of every man was turned, living as Hobbes said in "continuall feare and danger of violent death." Since the ideal of rugged individualism always clashed with that of corporate subordination, some Arabs, including some of the greatest of the poets, were expelled from their clans and tried to "go it alone" by feats of almost superhuman endurance. As the greatest of these outlaw poets, Shanfara, sang,

> By your life, the earth is not so narrow that a man cannot find elbow room,
>
> As long as he uses his wits and by desire or fear travels in night's black gloom.

In supreme irony, the poet expels his own folk, choosing wolves for his qawm, since wolves do not break confidence and live by a sterner code than fickle men. He fears nothing as, accompanied by his three companions—a stout heart, a glistening sword, and a long singing bow—he moves through deserts so awesome that before them even riding camels panic and in weather so hellish in the "dog days" of summer that the very mirages melt and vipers writhe on the stones, "prolonging my hunger so long that it is the *hunger* I kill and I become unmindful of it." But the outlaw-poet wants his audience to know that he does not punish himself for masochistic reasons. "Were it not to avoid a shameful action, no drinking bout or feast would be found without my being there."

> But a proud and bitter soul will not uphold me in the face of wrong, except as I plot my vengeance.
>
> I am the master of patience draping its gown over the heart of a wolf and tenacity I wear for sandals.

Such stark and unbending glorification of egotism, violence, and hatred led to lives that were often, as Hobbes put it of *his* man in nature, "solitary, poore, nasty, brutish and short."

The centrifugal forces of individualism limited the centripetal forces of clan cohesion. In the last resort, at terrifying personal sacrifice, the individual could save his own honor even at the expense of loss of his folk. In this direction lay heroism and poetic ennoblement. In more normal circumstances a family quarrel could be ended by a split of the qawm into two parts, each of which could live normally, or by grafting the weaker group onto another clan in the same tribe much as one might migrate and become naturalized in another nation. In this direction lay salvation.

Westerners—and most Arabs—may find the content of this poetry of bravery, as the Arabs called it, objectionable, but its grand gesture, its eloquence, the flow of its language, cannot but sway men's emotions. No one who has watched an Arabic audience can fail to have noted the extent to which linguistic virtuosity hypnotizes the people. It is this which has given to the radio station in our own time such extraordinary influence throughout the Arab World and which allows even vitriolic and vile propaganda, if well said, to be accepted.

Ironically, even in the poems which express hatred of one man for others or one folk for another, and which are, therefore, divisive propaganda at its most effective, there is a force for cultural unity. Over the years, as names and events were forgotten, the poems lost their political sting and came to be a common heritage of all Arabs. It was, indeed, the sharing of the classical literature which provided the common cultural experience of the ancient Arabs.

The contrary sentiment to a rugged individualism bordering on suicide is the intense emotional attachment to one's clansmen, right or wrong, and the personal acceptance of responsibility for any and all of their acts. The Arabic word for the sentiment which bound together the clan is the same as the modern word for nationalism, *qawmiyah*. In one of the most widely quoted poems in Arabic, this sentiment is summed up by a bedouin poet of the clan of Ghaziyah. The clansmen have been on a raid and foolishly stop their retreat before they are out of reach of their enemies. The poet Duraid bin Simma, having warned them and realizing their folly will probably cost him his life, stays to fight for, as he said,

> When they spurned me, I was still with them, having seen their folly and my own imprudence
>
> For what am I apart from Ghaziyah—if the clan goes astray, so I,
>
> And if Ghaziyah is rightly guided, I too am rightly guided.

Then he fought the

> Fight of a man who nurses his brother with his own person, knowing that man is not immortal.

Failure to protect one's kinsmen or, if they are killed or wronged, to retaliate against those who inflicted a wrong would destroy the meager protection the individual could find in desert tribal life. It was the categorical imperative of bedouin life and honor. To fail or shirk was a cowardly action which stained the individual and his kindred with the "stain of shame." Only the blood of the enemy could wash away this stain. And virtually every Arabic poem has some reference to the fear of blame for not acting as a man should.

This duty was incumbent upon a clan not only for its own members but also for those they undertook to protect. Annoyance at the "protected stranger" often showed through the lines of the poems. As Urwa bin Ward sang:

> God curse the starving thief who concealed by the blackness of night steals behind the tents to suck the marrow bones in the refuse heap.
>
> Who counts as the riches of his lot to be every night where he can demand hospitality from a luckier friend.

But each poet boasts of his folk's generosity and protectiveness toward the guests or dependents. And no more bitter reproach could be made of a qawm than that it had failed in this duty. In the earliest of all known Arabic poems, the Basus Cycle, the poetess taunts her protectors by warning a friend that she is in "the encampment of such a folk that even when a wolf attacks he always seizes *my* lamb." Her protector, insulted beyond all compare, prepared to take vengeance on those who have harmed her after begging mankind not to blame him for "My protected one, know you one and all, is of the closest of kin." And so, like the Trojan War, began, poetically at least, a war of honor. For the Arab, said one of the greatest of Arab poets, must be a "spring pasture to the protected strangers." This is one of the deepest of obligations which has been rooted in Arabic civilization and nurtured by the tradition embodied in Arabic poetry.

The wise man is not foolhardy. Patience, cunning, and reserve are so much the attributes of the perfect man that they even spill into Islamic thought. Indeed, in the Koran God is described as the "best of the Plotters" (iii.54). But the final and greatest quality of the perfect man is generosity. The arbitrator is "one above the fray, possessed of such a generosity as leads him to aid others to show their generosity."

Generosity is not a virtue among the weak. For them the proper road is retaliation which should lead to the status quo ante. Other ways, however, could create a new balance of power. If the wrongdoer offered to pay recompense, the wronged could, after a decent interval, accept, and peace could be made. The strong, on the other hand, could be generous and could make peace without loss of face. One of the seven "Golden Odes" of ancient Arabia celebrates the peacemaker, who by his personal generosity and wisdom manages to stop war between two clans.

> . . . If we set our hands to Peace, base it broad and firm by the giving of gifts and fair words of friendship, all will be well.

> "Yea, glory ye gained . . . the highest—God guide you right! who gains without blame a treasure of glory, how great is he!"

> (Translated by Lyall)

Otherwise war to the knife was not only sanctioned but demanded by the social ethic. Even if it meant death, no man could with honor or pride shirk his duty of retaliating, goaded as he was by his womenfolk and the very ghost of the slain and wracked by a "burning fever"—"Hearts are cured of rancour-sickness, whether men against us war, or we carry death among them: dying, slaying, healing comes."

To Western tastes some of the value system embodied in classical Arabic poetry is not appealing. The boasts of the poets, the thirst for vengeance, the hunger for fame, and the fascination for the wounding of the foe, though not unfamiliar to readers of classical Greek literature, are not attractive. But to understand their impact on modern Arabic thought is vital to an understanding of politics in the Arab Middle East. For the imperative of preserving or achieving dignity, the fear of reproach as being unworthy or impotent people, and finally, the importance of the form of action and the word of communication as equal to or surpassing that of the content, greatly influences Arab political behavior. To outsiders who would understand, whether condoning or opposing, this is the beginning of knowledge.

3

Islam: The Regulation of Society

ISLAM never made peace with bedouin society. In the Koran the bedouin Arab is scorned as one who, failing to believe in the religion, merely submits to the outward power of the religious state. However, Islam was born in an Arabia deeply colored by the values, the presence, and the literature of the bedouin Arabs. And Islam defined itself in the framework of a corporate, tribal society. The wonder is not that Islam was so influenced by Arabian experience but rather that Muslims were able so to elaborate the structure they inherited as to form one of the great religious civilizations of human history.

The historical role of Muhammad, the society of early Islam, and the Islamic creed are here set forth in bare outline. But this bears to the civilization of Islam the relationship of a skeleton to a man: omitted are the nerves, brain, heart, and flesh, an account of which would fill more than this volume. In short compass, this chapter will attempt to show the structure of the skeleton and to suggest the richness of the whole body.

Muhammad, the Messenger, who delivered the Word of God to the Arabs in Arabic, as the Koran explains, was born in the commercial city of Mecca about A.D. 570. Around his life has grown an immense literature of fact and fiction, devotion and scorn, conjecture and artifice. But from the Koran and the Traditions related by his early followers we know that he was born into a poor branch of Mecca's ruling oligarchy and was an orphan from his early youth. When about twenty-five, he married a wealthy widow whose business agent he had become. With her capital he acquired some status in the community while engaging in the caravan trade with Yemen and the Levant.

Then, apparently quite suddenly, when he was about forty, Muhammad had a vision of the Angel Gabriel who ordered him to "Recite in the Name of the Lord." The stunned and frightened Muhammad is said to have stammered, "But what shall I recite?" After an interval in which he received no further visions, he transmitted to his people, in an unending stream until his death in 632, what has been collected by his followers as the Koran.

For his contemporaries as for later, non-Muslim writers, Muhammad has proved to be a difficult and complex figure. To some Western medieval writers he appeared as a satanic adventurer who sought to undermine Christendom or, to the more fanciful, a "fallen" cardinal who, having been passed over for the Papacy, set out to create his own religion. Modern writers have portrayed him as an epileptic, a sufferer from hysteria, a self-deceiving spiritualist, a madman, or a dupe of the Devil. The pagan oligarchs of his own city were unconcerned with precise labels. To them, he was a troublemaker who was upsetting the pagan religion on which was based the prosperity of Mecca.

For himself, Muhammad claimed no superhuman attributes except one: he was the messenger through whom God's Word—the same Word as that delivered by previous prophets, both Christian and Jewish, to their peoples in their languages in former times—was to be taken in Arabic to the Arabs. He admitted that he could perform no miracles although Jesus, with God's permission had; though Islam specifically denies the divinity of Jesus, it does ascribe to him an exalted place in Creation. But God intended, the Muslims hold, that Muhammad, in his time and in his language and among his people, should be the leader of men to the Highroad of the Virtuous.

After some initial success in converting members of the community of Mecca, although few among the citizens of the oligarchy, Muhammad reached what appeared to be a dead end in his mission: with the popular support he had he was at once too weak to defend himself and win more converts to his faith and too strong to be tolerated by the defenders of the pagan cults which intertwined Meccan commercial practice and political structure. Meccan prosperity was conditional upon pan-Arab recognition of the city's special status as a sanctuary in which no fighting could take place and of the "Forbidden" months when men could trade freely throughout Arabia without fear of raid or vendetta. The fact that the new religion would upset this balance was apparent both to the rulers and the ruled—the one viewed it as sedition and the other as a rallying point for opposition to their oppressers. Probably it was not lost upon the oligarchs of Mecca either that to accept Islam meant accepting the primacy of its prophet.

The fact that Muhammad was tolerated at all was due to the requirement of Arab society that his clansmen protect him. Then in 619 the clan found a way to expel him as one who behaved disreputably toward his fellows. In that year in quick succession died Muhammad's first (then his only) wife and an uncle who though a pagan had been his main support. When Muhammad was asked if his uncle was in the Islamic Heaven as a virtuous man or in its Hell as a pagan, he replied "in Hell." He was immediately repudiated by his clan and became an outlaw, exposed to the fury of the Meccans. In desperation he fled from Mecca to find a safer haven.

First, Muhammad took his message to the nearby town of Taif which, like Mecca, was prosperous, well-organized, and conservative. Like Mecca it had a pagan pantheon intimately associated with its trade. Poor soil it was for the seed of Islam. As a Meccan, Muhammad was able to command an audience of Taif's chief men but, as the Victorian scholar Sir William Muir imagined, "the disproportion to the outward eye between the magnitude of the prophet's claims and his present solitary condition turned fear into contempt." The men of Taif set their slaves and street urchins against Muhammad, stoned him, and literally ran him out of town. Bloody, exhausted, and shaken, Muhammad returned to a hostile Mecca where he lived in seclusion for over a year, until, feeling that "his thorn had been cut," another Meccan gave him protection· and succor.

But others had heard of his mission. To Mecca came men of many of the Arabian towns and tribes to trade, to experience the delights of a market town, to exchange information, and to listen to the soothsayers, poets, and storytellers. Mecca was the intellectual and cultural, as well as the commercial, market of Arabia. Under the "peace" of the Meccan gods men who would have fought—would have *had* to have fought on sight—elsewhere were able to mingle freely. In such a situation Muhammad met some of the men of the northern Arabian town then called Yathrib and later (and now) called Medina.

Medina, unlike Taif and Mecca, was agricultural. Moreover it had no pantheon, and, inhabited by a Jewish or Judaized Arab community, it was familiar with monotheism. More important, Medina had no organized corporate life, being less a town than a collection of hamlets, midway between a bedouin encampment and a city. Like the former it lacked a government to settle differences and enforce security but like the town it so constricted its members that they could not escape from one another as could nomads. Hostility could be settled neither by official pressure as in Mecca nor by movement as in the desert. In Medina a perpetual civil war threatened the very life of the community. The situation, in fact, had so far degenerated a few years before Muhammad's mission that in an orgy of destruction the rival clans had hacked down one another's trees and almost ruined the economy.

In this circumstance it was natural that the town should seek a neutral arbitrator to settle their differences. This, it seems, was what they sought in Muhammad. The fact that Muhammad was a Meccan lent prestige to his name and that he was a man of religion gave him a moral stance above the partisan politics of Medina. Whereas both Mecca and Taif felt endangered by a new creed, Medina welcomed any solution to its war and agreed to obey Muhammad "in all that is right."

Muhammad, with the painful memory of his Taif adventure fresh in mind, carefully negotiated for over a year on what his status would be and sent ahead, by small parties, about 150 of his followers to form, as it were, his qawm in Medina. It was as a prophet armed that he was to enter the city. Glad to be rid of him, the people of Mecca did nothing to halt this migration until the very end when they decided to take no chances on the future by assassinating him. At the last minute Muhammad slipped away and rode northward to his new home. This was the Hijra, the "Flight," from which the Islamic calendar is dated.

Upon entering Medina, Muhammad faced the initial problem of winning an immediate peace; then he had to settle his followers; and finally he had to secure his own power. All of these tasks he approached within the political traditions of Arabia. The pattern which emerged is expressed in a document called the "Constitution of Medina," dating from the second year after the Hijra.

With a flash of brilliance, Muhammad established his people as a part of the economy of Medina by arranging for each immigrant to be adopted as a "brother" by some member of the community. Like most things Muhammad did, this was to linger through Islamic history as a social ideal—all Muslims are supposed to be brothers and to assist one another in personal as well as institutional ways.

The central problem, however, was to get the warring clans of Medina to sink their differences in some larger social organization. The theoretical unit larger than the clan in Arabic society was the tribe, but among the nomads, due to the nature of the desert economy, the tribe rarely had actual existence. Its "chief" had no real power and was merely the most respected clan shaikh. But within the tribe it was possible to negotiate an end to hostilities, through the payment of "bloodmoney," whereas against foreigners the settling of hostilities was far more difficult. Therefore, it was both natural and reasonable that Muhammad should think of the city in terms analogous to a tribe. And, indeed, the community he set out to create in Medina was to have the same essential qualities.

Like the Arab tribe, the new community of Islam laid upon its members obligations for the defense of the whole. The "believers and adherents" were to struggle together and jointly to pay blood money or ransom. If an outsider harmed a member of the community, in a way parallel again to tribal society, the entire force of the community was brought to bear against him—"the Believers to a man will be against him." The community of believers was enjoined never to abandon one crushed by debts, and jointly to oppose those sowing sedition. Believers, the "clansmen of Islam," were ordered never to kill believers or to help others against believers. Like the tribe, the Islamic community could grant protection, for "the protection of God is one," and the weakest Muslim could impose this obligation upon all his brothers. As in the tribe, so in the Islamic community, foreigners could seek protection and succor. And as befit the new basis of society, religion, in a way parallel to the old basis, kinship, not only men of different kindred but also those of different religions could be so protected. The Jewish clans of Medina were confirmed in their customary rights, property, and practices, but, since they did not fight in the militia of the community, they were obliged to contribute to the defense of the whole through taxation. Lastly, the community was bound to act together; the clans were prevented from making a separate peace and had to accept responsibility for the acts of all.

Muhammad had profited from his one major failure by learning that in order to establish the religion of God in a moral society he needed political power. In a corporate society this could only be "tribal," and the tribe is the essence of the early Islamic community. The boundaries of Muhammad's tribe, however, were religious rather than genealogical.

It was the Koran which was to set the moral tone and the way, or sunna, of the community. This again was not an alien thought in Arabia. As the pre-Islamic poet Labid, in one of the *Golden Odes*, sang, "And we are of a clan whose forefathers laid down for them a sunna since each qawm has its sunna and its imams."

Whereas the tribe had no fixed abode, Islam, being based on a town, did. Muhammad, borrowing from his native city, institution-alized Medina as a sanctuary in which no fighting could take place. Theoretically, throughout Islamic history the *Daru'l-Islam* or the abode of Islam has been a place of peace in distinction to other areas which were the abode of war. In this abode of peace lived Muslims and men of other religions and men of many clans.

When Muhammad died eleven years after the Hijra, in A.D. 632, he had barely had time to draft the outlines of his conception of the com-munity. As we shall see, he appointed no successor—indeed, there could be no successor as the Messenger of God—to govern the com-munity. Few of his followers understood his concept. To the "adher-ents," those who formed the bulk of the new "religious tribe," Mu-hammad had been a sort of paramount chief to whom, as a person, they submitted, and whose death freed them from all obligation. The true believers were few and, without Muhammad, without a guide. Consequently, it appeared that like other empires based on a tribal structure, Islam would not survive the founder's death.

Islam started as a community and only much later became a sys-tem of thought. This sequence, markedly different from the history of Christianity, has deeply colored the system itself. Muslim theologians and jurists have worked from precedent—the Traditions of the Prophet (*Hadith*)—as much as from the Book. From the beginning they were as much concerned with the regulation of man in earthly society as with the preparation of man for Divine Judgment.

The sunna, or "way," of Islam is based upon the society which Muhammad created in Medina. In this code, men are separated from one another by their religions. Each is entitled, within certain bounds, to practice his own faith, but Islam is recognized as the proper religion for Arabs. And though all three of the then-known monotheistic religions are theoretically the same, as the religion of Abraham, both the Jews and the Christians are said to have cor-rupted what they received from God. Muslims hold that the Jews have distorted their texts and altered various practices (Islam is closer to the less Orthodox Jewish sects) and that the Christians have com-mitted the sin of associating Jesus with God, who is Alone, One, and Unapproachable. To correct these mistakes and to guide a new peo-ple, the Arabs, God revealed again, in Arabic, His one and unchang-ing message to Muhammad.

Concerned as Islam was with precise definitions and with the prac-tical administration and moral tone of the Medina community, we should expect to find, and do find, explicit and full treatment in the Koran of such affairs as property rights, inheritance, marriage, di-

vorce, punishment of theft and adultery, treatment of slaves and or-
phans, commercial practices, food, drink, games, and bribery.

Islam envisaged no division of Church and State. To be precise, it
foresaw no Church at all. Society, if not a State per se, encompassed
all aspects of man's proper life. Indeed, in early Islam those functions
we call "religious" play a utilitarian part—in a new society fighting
for its life against external enemies and beset by internal divisions,
even the ceremonial of public prayer had a disciplinary quality not
different from the drill of new recruits in an army. But Islam went beyond simply laying down the rules of society by addressing itself to
the method of living the correct life in all of its detail.

Formally, the religion of Islam was extremely simple. To be a
Muslim, a man must affirm the Unity of God and the Prophecy of
Muhammad, saying, "there is no god but God and Muhammad is
His messenger." Beyond that, the latitude of action or inaction is
wide. Muslims are supposed to pray in a prescribed manner, give
alms in a certain amount, fast during the daylight hours of the Holy
Month, perform the pilgrimage at least once, and "strive in the way
of God."

These are the "pillars" of the faith. To convert these into the elaborate, formal civilization of Islam, as the subsequent centuries were to
know it, was the work of generations of scholars, theologians, and
jurists who, mining the lodes of the Koran and the Traditions, fabri-
cated from this simple ore an elaborate structure. Their task, difficult
enough in a changing and growing society, was complicated by the
gaps, alterations, and conflicts within the materials they worked.
Since Islam, like Christianity, is divided into many sects, it is well to
understand something of this early source of difference.

The 6000 verses which have come to us as the Koran were not
written down in the lifetime of Muhammad. It was the fact that
many of those who had memorized the verses were being killed in
warfare that led Muhammad's successors to collect his messages. Naturally, there were different renditions. Several of the more famous
were collected into "rival" Korans, which began to spread throughout the Islamic world. Individual versions tended to become associated with regional or tribal groupings. Ultimately this situation became so dangerous that a single authorized codex was prepared and
all other copies were ordered destroyed.

However, Arabic writing at that period, like early notations in
Western music, allowed considerable interpretation; the letters were,
in fact, prompters for those who knew the text. Not only were vowels
not written (so that, for example, the first part of this sentence would
read "nt nl wr vwls nt wrttn") but no distinction was made between a

number of consonants (for example between n, t, th, y, and b). Therefore, a single line could have more than one meaning. Thus, within the official text a number of different interpretations were equally orthodox. In fact, in a typical commentary on the Koran one finds after most verses, "but so-and-so reads it thus and another reads it thus."

Later, the issue was further complicated when various religious thinkers and, indeed, whole sects within the family of Islam suggested that the text of the Koran itself was subject to an inner meaning and required allegorical interpretation.

So complex was this problem to become, even early in Islam, that the religion developed not a priesthood but a legal profession who specialized in the application of Koranic law to social problems. This body of jurists and scholars of the Law has remained the cardinal organizational cadre of Islam to the present day.

The absence of a priesthood, holy men, and saints in Islam was felt early in its history. The religion, in the limited sense of man's relationship to the godhead, was in primitive, Orthodox Islam—as it is today in such puritanical sects as the Wahhabis of Arabia—an austere, stark, and cold system. Between man and the all-powerful, unrelenting God-Judge was a vast gulf, across which no man could help another, since not even Muhammad was an intercessor. Nor was the religion satisfyingly visible. It began by destroying the visible signs of pagan cults and was even hostile to the sensual representation of religious subjects. A patch of desert was as "holy" or acceptable to God as a place of prayer as the most beautiful and elaborate mosque.

It is not surprising, therefore, that early in Islam men sought softer, warmer, and shorter ways to reach God. As Islam spread to areas which had known other religions, elements of sensualism, sainthood, and ecstasy were injected into it. The early followers of Muhammad were accorded a position not unlike that of the Apostles. Locally revered good men achieved locally recognized sainthood and their graves became places of pilgrimage—often, indeed, these places were associated with the gods of former religions. The intercession of such figures was devoutly sought despite the formal anathema of Islam. Ultimately, a religious art grew, although this never flourished among the Arabs, and great care in the design of religious buildings brought about an architecture comparable to Gothic Europe. Finally, the faith received a symbol in some ways akin to the Crucifixion when the grandson of Muhammad was killed on the battlefield against a government which many regarded as oppressive and secular. Those who opposed that government, who came to be called the Shiis or Partisans, seized upon the death of Husain, Muhammad's grandson, as the emotional nucleus of their political rebellion against the Orthodox State.

But the Shiis, even more than the Orthodox or Sunni Muslims, became deeply divided amongst themselves over points of dogma and interpretation. Some of the Shiis actually merged their imams with the godhead, ascribing to them, in inherited succession, the "spirit" of God. Others expressed in a religious medium their political, social, or economic differences from the rulers in a theocracy. Thus it is that many of the conquered people, who were treated as second-class citizens in the new Islamic empire, expressed their resentment against the Establishment by espousing unorthodox religious beliefs. Even Orthodox Islam, coping with the multifarious problems of a vastly expanded society and drawing on various sources, developed four distinct schools of law.

The greatest of the merits of Islam is that it has been able to retain the simplicity of its beginnings, so that to be or become a Muslim is easy, while being flexible enough to embrace a wide variety of practice, to accommodate dissent, and even to submit to total reinterpretation. For this flexibility a price has been paid. The religion has never made possible the weaving of the strands of society into a social fabric capable of clothing in one garment the whole Islamic world.

In Islam, as in tribal life, geographical division and separate historical experience gave additional scope for diversity. It is for this reason that the Arabs hark to language—the language of the Koran and of the poets—as the immutable base of their dream of nationhood.

4

Conquests and the Caliphate: Glorious Yesterdays

HEN in A.D. 622 Muhammad moved his Meccan followers and fled himself from the hostility of the Meccans to Medina, he set the stage for the growth of the Islamic community. What distinguished the move to Medina from the abortive venture in Taif was that Muhammad went as a Prophet armed with the nucleus of a state. The fact that he had his own partisans raised him above the position of a neutral arbitrator and gave him the balance of power in the community. With his Book—and his sword—Muhammad was able to fuse the natives of Medina, who were composed of two Arab and several Jewish tribes, with his own followers to make a new and much larger tribe whose membership was defined not by kinship but by religion. Within the group no fighting was allowed and the hand of every man was turned against the common external enemy, but the enemy always had the option of joining the group, as believers in Islam or as adherents who accepted its suzerainty.

In this arrangement was a powerful stimulus to growth since the energies of the groups of members, formerly balanced one against another, were now turned outward. The community of Islam was spurred to action and given certainty of victory by the messianic force of God's favor to their leader. But the proof of divine grace was the conquest of Mecca. Muhammad realized that he must prevail over Mecca, the chief city of western Arabia, or fail in his mission.

To humble Mecca was not easy since the Meccans were rich, numerous, and experienced; but they were divided internally and lacked the fervor—and the lean hunger—of the new rival. Moreover, Mecca, depending as it did on the caravan trade, was vulnerable to blockade. As a former merchant himself, Muhammad began his "campaigns" with a thrust at Mecca's lifeline by attempting to intercept a caravan. The raid failed, however, when bedouin tribes allied to Mecca gave warning. It thus became evident that though the strategy was correct, its first tactical step must be to subdue and bring within the Islamic community the tribes who controlled the desert.

A normal tribal group, the clan, was small. When the groups it encountered were also small it could survive. Muhammad, however, had found a way to combine a number of clans into a large unit. Since no fighting was allowed within this unit, all its warlike energies were turned outward. Thus, it brought overwhelming force to bear on each clan it battled. The old balance of power had been upset. The tribe attacked was unable to combine with other tribes, since its only means of achieving a limited degree of political cohesion was based on real or imagined kinship, and alone it could not stand against the larger Islamic community while facing other, traditional tribal enemies. Only by submitting could it save itself, and, having submitted, it had to renounce the use of its force against other members of the Islamic Community and so its power was added to that directed outward against other tribes. In this way a large if ephemeral tribal "empire" was rapidly created. And, finally after several encounters, Mecca itself submitted to Muhammad in A.D. 630. The prestige thus gained and the addition of the most sophisticated and able men in Arabia in turn brought in to at least nominal submission tribes from all over the peninsula.

The tribes, however necessary as a force against external enemies, were always regarded with great suspicion by Muhammad and the early Muslims, who were, after all, urban Arabs. Tribesmen at best were lukewarm adherents rather than true believers (Koran xlix.14) and had to be taught civilized manners toward the Messenger (Koran xlix. 1–5) and treated severely if they got out of line. More economical than trying constantly to suppress the tribes was to give them a target for their warlike energies. Only in this way could they be made loyal members of the Islamic Community. Thus, shortly before his death in A.D. 632, Muhammad had planned a foray into Palestine.

Muhammad's death presented the community with what might have been a mortal crisis. So completely had his mission captured the imagination of his inner group of followers, the true believers, that some could not accept the fact of his death. Muhammad himself had made no provision for his succession. He had established no formal organization of statehood or of religion; only in his person was the state manifest to believers and adherents alike. The only "office" held by anyone in the community was leadership of public prayer in the absence or sickness of Muhammad. It was this office which was seized upon by Muhammad's inner circle and imposed upon the rest of the community. And it is from this humble beginning that the caliphate (caliph meaning successor) derives.

To the tribes, however, this innovation was unacceptable; in their eyes Muhammad's death dissolved all bonds of allegiance. Throughout Arabia the empire, like a mirage, vanished, as the tribes, in the religious terminology of later Muslims, "apostatized." The caliph appeared to have inherited a memory. So strong was the hold of Muhammad over his inner circle that the caliph nevertheless honored Muhammad's last command by dispatching the small remnant of the Muslim army into Palestine on a raid. It was with great difficulty that Medina withstood attacking bedouin until the army returned with booty and boasts of successes yet to come. The nearer bedouin once again leaped aboard the bandwagon of success, wealth, and glory and as before were turned against the other tribes in what became the bloodiest and most repressive war in Arabian history. So successful were the flying columns of cavalry scouring Arabia that they fused, almost imperceptibly, into an army of conquest. Their leader, Khalid ibn al-Walid, nicknamed the "Sword of God," was one of the great generals of all time.

To understand what happened next, it is important to realize that the two great Middle Eastern empires of that era, Byzantium or Eastern Rome and Sassanian Iran, had fought one another to an exhausted standstill. In A.D. 611 the Persians had invaded Syria and Palestine and in 614 had captured Jerusalem. Returning to the attack, the Byzantine forces slowly won back their lost ground, took repressive measures against the pro-Sassanian Jewish community, and tried, vainly, to enforce the Orthodox faith among the monophysite Christians who prevailed in Syria and Palestine. Both empires were exhausted, faced financial crises, and were rent by internal schisms. To economize, the Byzantines stopped paying subsidies to the Christian Arab tribes who had guarded the steppe lands of Syria and Jordan. This may have been the crucial factor in the Muslim Arab success.

In 633 the caliph launched probes of tribal forces northward into Byzantine territory; in the following year his great general marched northward in Iraq and, turning westward, rode straight across the Great Syrian Desert for 500 miles, appearing suddenly outside the walls of Damascus. After looting Damascus this army and the other

Arab tribal groups fought several brief battles with Byzantine forces, until in July of 636 on the Yarmuk River in what is now Jordan they met and destroyed the assembled Byzantine forces led by the emperor.

What had started as a punitive expedition became a raid, and the raid became a war of conquest. Spurred on by the very shock of their success and by the tales of glory and booty, a torrent of tribes poured out of Arabia. In the words of Sir William Muir, "It was the scent of war that now turned the sullen temper of the Arab tribes into eager loyalty: for thus the brigand spirit of the Bedawi was brought into unison with the newborn fire of Islam. The call to battle reverberated throughout the land, and was answered eagerly . . . warrior after warrior, column after column, whole tribes in endless succession with their women and children, issued forth to fight. And ever, at the marvellous tale of cities conquered; of rapine rich beyond compute; of maidens parted on the very field of battle 'to every man a damsel or two'; and at the sight of the royal fifth [the caliph's share] fresh tribes arose and went. Onward and still onward, like swarms from the hive, or flights of locusts darkening the land, tribe after tribe issued forth and hastening northward, spread in great masses to the East and to the West."[*]

The defeated Byzantine forces fell back upon the seacoast, abandoning the hinterland to the Arabs. The caliph himself came to Jerusalem in 637 to make peace and organize the new province. In the chronicles he is described as riding a white camel, dressed in worn and torn robes, as he came to pray at the place where Muhammad dreamed he had ascended to Heaven and to which the early Muslims had directed their prayers, as modern Arabs do to Mecca. As in Arabia, so in the new empire, the "People of the Book," the Christians and Jews, were given the status of protected clients and allowed to continue to practice their religions, to manage their internal community affairs, and to avoid military service by payment of a tax.

The Muslims, who regarded Islam as the religion of the Arabs and who wanted revenue more than soldiers, put little effort in an attempt to convert anyone to their religion. Meanwhile, a world was waiting to be won. In the same year as the caliph's visit to Jerusalem an Arab army defeated the forces of the Sassanian emperor and captured his capital of Ctesiphon near modern Baghdad. Now all Persia was open before them. Shortly thereafter, another Arab general convinced the caliph to let him conquer Egypt. He is related as saying "its people are playthings, its soil is gold and it belongs to those strong enough to

---

[*] *The Caliphate, Its Rise, Decline and Fall* (Edinburgh, 1915), p. 43.

take it." With a force of Yemenite cavalry the general defeated the first Byzantine garrison he met. Reinforced and aided by the local Coptic Christian community he then captured Babylon, near modern Cairo, and laid siege to Alexandria, which surrendered in 642. By 669 the Arabs had created a navy and had attacked Cyprus; six years later this force was able to destroy the bulk of the Byzantine fleet of 500 ships. Meanwhile, Arab armies were plunging deep into Anatolia to the north and eastward into Afghanistan.

The Caliph Omar, the second caliph, was assassinated by a Persian slave in 644. Once again the young Islamic state was left without a designated successor. This time the powerful Meccan oligarchy, which had chafed under the puritanical rule of the first two caliphs as it watched others reap the spoils of the conquests, managed to get one of its own number, Uthman of the Umayyad clan, elected caliph. Quick to profit from their new position, the old oligarchy reached out to gather the fruits of power and majesty from the vast new empire.

The empire itself was the jerry-built creation of expedience. The tribal armies, interested in loot rather than in rule, would have melted away had they not been gathered into cantonments or garrisons and paid a share of the booty. The garrisons, Kufa, Basra, Qum (in Iran), Old Cairo, and Qairawan (in Tunisia), rapidly grew into towns and cities as the local people flocked to them and settled to sell goods and services to the soldiers in exchange for their newly won riches. But the gathering, conversion, and transportation of the caliph's fifth of the booty, the payment of the army, and the administration of taxes and governmental expenditures were vast new undertakings. The inner core of Muhammad's followers were not fitted by experience for these tasks; alone among the Arabs, the oligarchy of Mecca was. Eagerly they sought to reap this worldwide harvest. For their private gain, they were immensely aided by the fact that there were no universal laws or customary practices and little thought of ethics. In most parts of the new empire the old practice and often the old civil servants were maintained, with only such changes as were necessary to accommodate a different ruling group in the place of the Byzantine or Sassanian overlords. For men of wit, and the Meccans were certainly that, the interstices in the several conflicting tax systems opened onto enormous fortunes.

Resentment grew against the old Meccan oligarchy, the latecomers to Islam, the men who had driven the Prophet from their city and who only submitted when they were beaten, and yet who now reaped the Muslim harvest. The resentment came to rest upon the third caliph who, though personally a good and pious man, was an "agent" of the Meccans. Not only Arabs grew resentful but also the conquered, who found in the rich and pompous Meccans a target for this hostility against the victors. So, while Islam rolled from one brilliant victory to another, internally it was wracked by dissension and corruption. Finally, in 656, after a campaign of extensive public criticism of his rule, the caliph was murdered by a group of Arabs from the mutinous army in Egypt.

Never again were the Arabs to be united. As universal as the discontent had been, it had no internal cohesion. Ali, son-in-law and cousin of Muhammad, was proclaimed caliph by those who had murdered Uthman, but he had to fight for his title, first against the other members of the "old guard" of Islam, including a widow of the Prophet, and next against the entrenched relatives of the slain caliph. Even his own followers were split into mutually hostile groups so that he could never direct his force against his major rivals. Finally after a sequence of pitched battles, truces, and conferences, Ali himself was murdered by a fellow Muslim in 661 in his new capital of Kufa. His reign was brief, but his name and memory linger on as the spiritual leader of the movement of dissent in Islam, the Shiis.

The provincial governor of Syria who defeated Ali and became caliph was the nephew of the Umayyad Caliph Uthman. With the forces of discontent against the Umayyads scattered and defeated, he set about unabashedly to found a dynasty which was little concerned with Islam. Under his successors this Arab kingdom held sway until 750 from Syria; after a brief hiatus it managed to re-establish itself in Spain where it lasted until 1030. The Umayyads were great patrons of the Arab poets and laid heavy emphasis on the bedouin virtues of hardihood, chivalry, and enjoyment of life within a code of honor. Little did they care for the spiritual life in Islam. Yet, their armies won for Islam its vast empire. They attacked Constantinople itself in 669, and blockaded it from 673 to 678. Their armies thrust eastward into Afghanistan, taking Kabul in 664, and northward across the Oxus to take Bukhara in 674 and Samarkand in 676. To the west they took Carthage, in modern Tunisia, in 698. From 708 to 715, Arab armies plunged deep into India and in 711 began the invasion of Spain. In 717 they tried again to seize Constantinople and invaded France. By 733 they had conquered Georgia in the Caucasus and in 738 reached their highwater mark at the battle of Tours or Poitiers in France. At that time their empire was probably the largest yet known in history.

But the Umayyads were never able to find an acceptable foundation for their empire. The real bases of their power were the Arab tribes of Syria, but these were so scattered over the vast empire that the government ultimately had to hire mercenary armies of Arme-

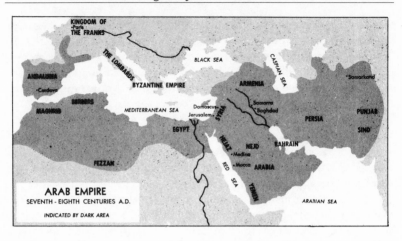

ARAB EMPIRE
SEVENTH - EIGHTH CENTURIES A.D.
INDICATED BY DARK AREA

nians. The Arab forces, moreover, were split by tribal and ultimately geographic interests. The conquered peoples, attracted by Islam but repelled by the Arab government, were drawn to movements of protest within Islam.

Finally, in 747 a revolt broke out in eastern Iran. Picking up adherents, the insurgents turned it into a full-scale revolutionary war in which they defeated the Umayyads and killed the caliph. For a while it was not clear in whose name this revolt had been fought, but after some months another branch of the Prophet's family, called, after his uncle Abbas, the Abbasids, emerged as leaders of the victorious forces of revolution.

The Abbasid revolution has often been portrayed as a Persian reaction to Arab rule. There is much truth in this. The revolt began in Khorasan, or eastern Iran, and many of its partisans were Persian converts to Islam, but the new ruling house, the bulk of the army, the language, and the religion were Arab. What had changed was the political matrix: the new dynasty could not impose itself upon the empire as an Arab kingdom. The Abbasids had to find a new base of authority and build a new structure of power. The Arab warrior caste was deposed from its privileged position because it was no longer strong enough to justify that position. In an attempt to find a replacement for the cohesive force of the tribal confederations and the Meccan oligarchy, the rulers allowed a new class of scribes to become a bureaucracy. The easterners, both Arabs and Arabized Persians, infused into the government elements of Oriental magnificence and mystery. The armies became less and less Arab and more like those of the Sassanian Empire, comprised in large part of contingents of mercenaries and foreigners. Yet emphasis on Islam, in the ruling group still defined as Orthodox or Sunni Islam, was heightened, for it had acquired a new popularity among the citizens of the empire.

The vast size of the empire influenced its politics and economic life. The richness of its far-flung provinces and the relative peace and stability they enjoyed in early Abbasid times supplied ample wherewithal for a brilliant and cultured urban civilization in the new metropolis of Baghdad which became the capital of the empire in 762. Apparently the original idea had been to lay out a garrison and administrative center, but rapidly a city collected around these and in the ninth century Baghdad had become perhaps the largest city in the world outside of China.

The world of the "Good Caliph Harun ar-Rashid" as it has come to the West in the *Thousand and One Nights* is a part of the treasure of legends of both East and West. In many ways it does mark the height of Islamic pomp and circumstance. But precisely because history is here so incrusted by the jeweled glitter of legend and fancy, it has exercised a powerful attraction on later ages of Arabs. So hypnotic, indeed, has this become as to immobilize the many for whom its greatness, learning, and wealth could never be matched. Arabs have found an escape from subsequent weakness, ignorance, and poverty in daydreams of this past instead of galvanizing themselves for efforts in their own times. Even today, the typical Arabic history book is a "heroic harangue," as a prominent modern Arab-American historian has written, in which "modern historians have addressed themselves almost exclusively to the glorious aspects of Arab and Islamic history, depicting them in bright colors and skipping over the many dark spots and inglorious episodes [or] to a mere listing of personalities, theories, works which were translated into European languages, Western scholars who were influenced by them, and orientalists who sang their praises."* This makes it useful to know both the myth and the reality.

The myth is perhaps best spelled out in the dozens of stories in the *Thousand and One Nights* or in Hollywood movies—enjoying record-breaking runs in many Arab cinemas—which rightly depict the Arab Empire as the bright light of civilization during the European Dark Ages. The Arabic contribution to world culture was not solely associated with the Abbasid caliphate but even more with successor governments and with the rival caliphates in Egypt and Spain, but the nationalist myth of Arab grandeur makes few distinctions, so here it will be treated as a whole.

The major contribution made by the Arabs was in keeping alive,

* Nabih Amin Faris in *Middle East Journal,* 8(1954):157–159.

during the long period of European ignorance, the substance and some of the spirit of inquiry which had been the gift of classical civilization. Translations from Greek and other languages into Arabic were actually begun under the Umayyads but were officially encouraged by the Abbasid government. Moreover, the Islamic men of learning were able to draw upon other civilizations they encountered. From the Indians they got their system of numbers—an innovation which made possible mathematics as we know it—and from China that great tool of our civilization, paper. The concept of zero; basic work on optics, in which the classical notion of Euclid and Ptolemy that the eye emitted a beam of light was upset; advanced work in mathematics, including the development of algebra, geometry, and trigonometry; and significant contributions in astronomy came from the members and clients of the Muslim-Arab Empire. The fact that many of the contributors were neither Arab nor Muslim is a great tribute to the tolerance and receptivity of that civilization. This great contribution was to be transmitted to and to stimulate Europe at a time in which, hungering for knowledge, it emerged into the beginnings of the Renaissance. Indeed, from the recapture by the Christians of Toledo in 1085 Muslim learning was available to all who wished to study it in Europe. The names of such of its philosophers, scientists, and doctors as ar-Razi (d. 925), Ibn Sina (d. 1037) and al-Biruni (d. 1048) fill medieval texts. But in the Islamic world itself from about the twelfth century onward invasions, massacres, neglect, misuse of resources, and the subdivision of the Empire, combined with the loss of confidence which had been based on power, prosperity, and success, encouraged religious leaders to narrow the scope of the intellectual life. As the scholarly and economic lights dimmed, a Dark Age came to Islam, as it had to Europe.

At the time of Harun ar-Rashid the central administration of the state was in the capable hands of a family known as the Barmakids, who also figure prominently in the *Thousand and One Nights* as the boon companions of Harun. This family, to whom much of the stability and richness of the empire was owing, was descended from a Buddhist temple guardian in the city of Balkh. For reasons which are so obscure as themselves to be sources of many legends, after seventeen years Harun dismissed the Barmakids and confiscated their wealth. Thereafter, his reign was a disaster. Upon Harun's death in 829 the empire, at his instructions, was divided between his two sons. The result of this division—in which one got the army and the other the capital—was a civil war which so weakened the central authority as to accelerate the process of disintegration. Province after province peeled off from the central core.

Within itself the caliphate ever had great capabilities for growth and equal susceptibility to destruction; what it always lacked was a basis of stability. Never had it managed to integrate its rural base into its civilization; ever was it exploitive of its resources. Neglect and decay are fatal to a system of irrigation, which was the wealth of Iraq and Egypt, and ruinous taxation makes refugees of productive peasants. Both were features of Abbasid rule. One of the more quaint and yet horrifying records of the Abbasid caliphate is the *Tabletalk of a Mesopotamian Judge,* but it is by no means unique in retailing the frivolous way the ruling elite squandered the resources of the empire.

The very success of the empire in conquering so much of the known world undermined it in two ways. First, so vast were the expanses of territory to be covered and so slow the means of communication, that decentralization of power began almost from the inception of the empire. And second, the *élan* of the empire could not be sustained: neither the original quest for loot nor the opposition to rival world empires sufficed. Looting had to be stopped if the government was to function, and Byzantium, the other side in the "Cold War" of that era, was too distant to pose a threat credible and immediate enough to cause men to rally around their flag. Rather, politics was played on less grand stages as provincial governors, petty officials, and army commanders performed vivisection on the body politic.

Within the ruling group itself sufficient manpower was lacking to staff the bureaucracy and the army. The bureaucracy, the virtual creation of the Barmakid family, improved and diffused by study of Persian court ritual, managed to develop a degree of a tradition of the service but not sufficient to survive in a basically hostile environment which lacked the public and governmental forces necessary both to sustain and to tame a bureaucracy. The army was always a problem. As the opportunities for conquests were dissipated in building an empire, other means had to be found to employ the army's energies. The Arabs increasingly withdrew from the military or were thrust away from it by suspicious caliphs, and were replaced by praetorians of many nations. As long as these contingents balanced and checked one another peace could be maintained, but outside of sheer force there were no balancing factors. So, as we shall see, those hired to act as the guardians of the state became its tyrants.

5

The Alien Empires: Arab Exclusion from Rule

T
HE ARABS were always a small minority in their vast empire, as they are today in the world of Islam, and even this small minority was rent by schisms. Tribe opposed tribe, one geographical area contested another, and Arabs were attracted not only to different religions but also to different sects within Islam. Moreover, these various religions and political groups attracted non-Arabs as their adherents and partisans. Thus, the exercise of centralized authority became more and more difficult as the establishment of a principle of allegiance and identity, which most people today seek in nationality, became impossible. More immediately significant, lack of political consensus produced such turmoil as to induce the caliphs to seek politically neutral agents of power. It was thus that the last Umayyad caliph, Marwan II, came to rely upon Armenian mercenaries and the early Abbasids created separate guard regiments of "foreigners" from eastern Persia, Central Asia, and North Africa.

As they found their way to power in the military and civil bureaucracy blocked, the original elite, the Muslim Arabs, began a process of withdrawal. In some provinces, notably in north Syria, Arabs remained supreme, but this was the exception. Elsewhere, tribal groups returned to nomadism, and urban Arabs began to detach themselves from the politico-military functions of the state to specialize, almost as a caste, in the legal-religious aspects of Islamic society. These divisions—the politico-military and legal-religious—come the closest to matching the division of Church and State in Western society. Thus, long before the fall of Baghdad the exercise of authority passed out of Arab hands and was not to return for many centuries.

The principal disadvantage of the alien bodyguards of the early Abbasids was that they tended to become Arabized too quickly and involved themselves in Baghdad politics. This was partly because among the "foreigners" of eastern Iran and North Africa were many Arabs. This "conflict of interest" made these regiments dangerous, or at least compromised, in a system in which the caliph sought to hold the balance of power between rival groups in his capital. It was the Caliph Mutasim (833–842) who took the fateful step of creating a praetorian guard of truly alien Turkomans from the lands beyond the Oxus River in Central Asia. Prior to Mutasim's time some Turkomans had been in the guard, but under him the guard as a whole, including its commanders, became Turkoman.

Troubles with the Baghdad mob and plots within the other regiments of the guard caused the Caliph Mutasim to move from Baghdad to Samarra where he established the new capital in 836. This city, a sort of Arab Versailles, was laid out on a vast scale with separate quarters for the divisions of the army. The caliph's hope was that there he would be safe from the Arab politics of Baghdad. His hope was realized but at the cost of upsetting the delicate balance of power on which his freedom of action was contingent. Isolated in the magnificence of Samarra, with its vast gardens, palaces, and a mosque three times the size of St. Peter's Cathedral, the caliph was at the mercy of his guardsmen. The outward magnificence contrasted violently, suddenly, and tragically with the near collapse of the caliphate. The Caliph Mutawakkil was murdered in 861. Then, in rapid succession came—and went—four caliphs, mere puppets of the Turkish generals, who inspired the satirical poem

A caliph in a cage, between [Generals] Wasif and Bugha,
  Who says what they say to him, just like a parrot echoes.
Kha-li-fa-tun fi qa-fa-sin baina Wa-sif wa Bu-gha
  Ya-qu-lu ma qa-la la-hu ka ma ta-qu-lu al-ba-ba-gha.

Mutawakkil's first successor was poisoned in six months, the second and the third were stabbed and the fourth was killed in battle against his guard. During this decade of chaos the outer provinces of the empire defected. In the south of Iraq, the home province, black slaves, originally from Zanzibar, who worked the salt deposits revolted and set up a revolutionary state. In Egypt the Turkish governor began to lay the foundations of what became an empire within the larger Abbasid empire, and in Iran the Saffavids carved out another kingdom. Meanwhile, the Arab tribes, who had even in the time of Harun been "bad neighbors" to the caliphate, espoused dissident religious movements under whose banners they were to sack Basra in 923, Kufa in 926, and Mecca in 930.

In Spain, at about the same time, a similar train of events had been set in motion. Abdur Rahman, a grandson of the tenth Umayyad caliph of Damascus, had established himself in Cordova in 755, and his descendants managed to recapture in Spain something of the grandeur of the Umayyads. Abdur Rahman III (912–961) carried Spanish Islam to its apogee and assumed the title of caliph in 929. Like the Abbasids, he brought in slaves and mercenaries to overawe his fellow countrymen; the main difference was that in Spain it was the *Saqalibah* or Slavs who were the praetorians.

In Egypt the governors since 858 had been Turks. The greatest of them, Ahmad ibn Tulun, who ruled Egypt from 868 to 884, best remembered for the great mosque he built in Cairo, was a sort of shogun, ruling Egypt, Syria, and much of Anatolia under the nominal suzerainty of the Abbasid caliph in Baghdad. Following him, Egypt was ruled by other Turks, an Abyssinian, and a motley crowd of rival bands of mercenaries, slave warriors, and bureaucrats who jostled one another for power and revenues. None was strong enough to win or establish a dynasty. But their rivalries so disrupted the life of the country as to attract the aggressive attention of the Arab-Berber dynasty of the Fatimids who had risen to power in North Africa.

After an initial failure in 914 the Fatimids conquered Egypt in 969. Laying out their capital under the guidance of the astrologers when Mars (al-Qahirah) was in the ascendant, they named it Cairo (al-Qahirah), and proclaimed a new era of Egyptian power and prestige. Legend has it that when the fourth Fatimid, the conqueror of Egypt, was questioned on his claim to be a descendant of Fatimah, the daughter of the Prophet Muhammad, he assembled the learned men and jurists of Egypt, unsheathed his sword, and said, "here is my pedigree."

Unlike the other Arab-Muslim dynasties, the Umayyads and the Abbasids, the Fatimids were bolstered by a religious movement, the Ismailis, an offshoot of Shii Islam. This gave them wide influence throughout the Middle East, and at one time they appeared on the point of absorbing the Abbasid caliphate, but it raised against them powerful counterforces of Orthodox Muslims. It was not the Fatimid religious mission but Egypt's rich Nile Valley and strategic central location in East-West trade that carried the new dynasty into a brief golden age. Their great mosque-university al-Azhar, founded in 970, still embellishes Cairo and stands today as the oldest university in the world.

But the Fatimids, however much they were favored by their location, the richness of Egypt, and their religious mission, were unable to consolidate a base of authority. Like the Spanish Umayyads and the Iraqi Abbasids they were forced to rely upon alien mercenary troops to whom they gradually lost power. By the time the fourteenth Fatimid caliph died in 1171 the Fatimid empire had lost its former grandeur.

In Baghdad, meanwhile, the caliphate had, after the bitter and tragic period of praetorian violence, managed to restore some of its former power. But, as in the later Roman Empire, the cost was great. From 870 to 908 the empire was reconquered, rebels destroyed, and tribute reassessed, but the effort virtually exhausted the dynasty and again the praetorian guard intervened, extorting and pillaging the citizenry, so that by the third decade of the tenth century the empire had virtually collapsed financially. Province after province broke away and refused to pay its tribute—it has been estimated that the revenue for the year 900 was about 3-4 percent of that of a century before. Men of influence in the bureaucracy and army commanders carved out estates for themselves even in the home province of Iraq and evaded all taxes. Smaller owners and men of little influence, on whom the remainder of the taxes had to fall, were ruined, abandoned their lands, or made over their titles to those rich enough to defend them. Lacking real power, the central government needed more, not less, revenue to buy allies and friends; moreover, it proved incapable of deflating the bloated administrative structure which had grown, sporelike, through all of the changes of Abbasid fortune. Even the imperial court, now ruling only a memory of an empire, continued to live on a lavish scale. It was as though the Abbasids could pretend to rule an empire only so long as they sat in an imperial court—even if it were supported only by a single, misgoverned, impoverished province.

In their desperation the Abbasids created yet new pieces of bureaucracy with the frank and honest names of the "Office of Bribes" and the "Office of Confiscations." Judging from the chronicles, these were staffed by the hardest-working bureaucrats in Baghdad. Increasingly, as money became difficult to get, officials came to be paid for their services in land or, if their assignments were of limited tenure, in rights to the revenue of certain estates for given periods of time. This, apparently, was the origin of the system of fiefs which was later to become common.

Finally, in 945, a Persian dynasty of Shiis, the Buwaihids, put an end to the pitiful pretence that was the caliphate. Under the new ruler, self-styled as *sultan* or holder of temporal power, the caliph became little more than a court functionary to be brought out on ceremonial occasions and discarded when troublesome or tiresome. At one point three former caliphs who had been blinded (and thus made legally unfit to hold office) by order of the sultan were alive in Baghdad, and one had to beg in the streets.

Only in Mosul (from 929 to 991) and Aleppo (944–1003) had an Arab dynasty, the Hamdanids, who were charged with guarding the Byzantine marches, managed to survive. But, ultimately, they too succumbed. As their great poet laureate al-Mutanabbi sang,

> Men from their kings alone their worth derive
> But Arabs ruled by aliens cannot thrive:
> Boors without culture, without noble fame,
> Who know not loyalty and honour's name.
> Go where thou wilt, thou seest in every land
> Folk driven like cattle by a serville band.*

In their turn the Buwaihids fought amongst themselves, and by the end of the eleventh century anarchy again prevailed throughout their empire.

Meanwhile, at the other side of the Asian land mass, in China, the Turkomans played a similar role in the affairs of the late Tang Dynasty. It was a Turkish general who ended the Tang Dynasty in 907 and Turkish officers who established the "Five Dynasties" which preceded the Sung. The re-establishment of a strong, centralized rule in China in 960 closed the northeastern frontier to further Turkish tribal incursions. Blocked by the Chinese and by a Mongol dynasty, the Liao or Ch'i-tan, bands of Turkoman tribesmen turned westward.

What distinguished the Turkish incursions of this period was that they came not as individuals to serve in the praetorian guards of Arab rulers, but in tribes, under their own leaders, knowing that they could not return. One of these groups, now known by the name of their chieftain Seljuk, was moving ever westward, bringing a new future to the Islamic Middle East. By 1040 the grandson of Seljuk had conquered eastern Iran, and in 1055 he captured Baghdad. Gathering Turkish bands as he went, the Seljuk Sultan Alp Arslan invaded Anatolia and in the battle of Manzikert in 1071 defeated and captured the Byzantine emperor. Anatolia was now open to Turkish migration and settlement. His successor, Sultan Malik Shah, and the famous vi-

---

* Translated by R. Nicholson in *Literary History of the Arabs* (Cambridge University Press, Cambridge and New York, 1953).

zier, Nizamu'l-Mulk, brought the Seljuk empire to the crest of its power and completed the conversion of what had been a money economy in the Middle East into one based on fiefs in land.

In Egypt at this time the Fatimid caliphate was dying out, and Syria was divided between several petty states. The Middle Eastern Islamic world was suffering, on the political level, from that sense of confusion and drift which is symptomatic of physical and emotional decay of civilizations. It was at this time, in 1096, that the First Crusade was launched against the Muslims in the Holy Land.

After a long march through the Balkans, the Crusaders were urged rapidly forward by anxious and mistrusting Byzantine officials. As they moved down the Levant coast, the Crusaders were relatively unopposed and were able to capture each town on their route. Finally, on the evening of June 7, 1099, they encamped before "Jerusalem the Golden."

The native Christians, perhaps having heard of the treatment of their cousins along the coast by these crude barbarians, who were interested in little but loot and cared not a whit for the religion of its former owner, were not pleased to see the Crusaders. But the Fatimid governor of Jerusalem took no chances on the enlightened self-interest of his Christian subjects or their loyalty to his empire and expelled them from the city. The Jews and Muslims resisted the invaders and after the Crusaders broke into the city were massacred. Most of the Jews were burned alive in their chief synagogue, in which they had taken refuge. Even those Jews and Muslims who surrendered were cut down in an orgy of blood, plunder, and religious ecstasy.

The state founded by the Crusaders, gradually tamed and softened by the balmy climate and easy ways of Palestine, lived, as it were, in the schisms of the Islamic world. With Syria divided between Aleppo and Damascus and Egypt under a weak and decayed regime, the Crusaders could survive. No sooner, however, were the Muslims to gain even a semblance of unity than the Crusaders were expelled. This was the work of the great Kurdish leader Saladin, who in 1171 put an end to the Fatimid caliphate, assumed all power, and set out to reunite Egypt and Syria. In 1187 he was able to muster just enough strength—and no more—to reconquer Jerusalem and most of Palestine. Upon his death in 1193, however, his state was shattered.

Again, the scene must shift far beyond the Arab lands to Central Asia where Genghis Khan (1155–1227) was putting together the most powerful military empire the world had ever seen. In 1215 the Mongol armies invaded China and took Yenching (modern Peiping), in 1219 they advanced into Korea, and in 1221 made their first raids into Russia and invaded Iran. The death of Genghis Khan temporarily slowed the Mongol advance, but soon Mongol armies were masters of most of Asia. In 1238 they took Moscow and two years later Kiev. A grandson of Genghis, Hulagu Khan, resumed the westward march in the Middle East and in 1258 captured Baghdad, killed the last, the thirty-seventh, Abbasid caliph, and abolished the caliphate. Pushing still westward, the Mongols reached Palestine where in 1260 they were finally stopped by forces of the Turkish "slave-rulers," the Mamluks, who had been established in Cairo after the death of the last of Saladin's heirs in 1260.

By this time the rapid turnover of masters had long since ceased to concern the subject Arab population. Deprived of their old military functions, excluded from authority, mere servants of those who exercised rule, the Arabs turned increasingly to the preservation of the institutions of Islam. For Islam itself this was an era of external expansion. Muslim traders spread Islam deep into Africa and eastward into south and southeast Asia. Even the Mongols, who had wiped out the remains of the political power of the Arab Muslims, were converted in large numbers, so that Islam became in the full sense a world religion. But in the realm of Islamic learning, as in Europe during the Dark Ages, scholars devoted themselves to the task of preserving the pale glow of a great civilization with little hope of rekindling its fire or adding to the former blaze, never daring to experiment or tamper for fear of snuffing out what little remained.

Further devastation, pestilence, and flood followed the sack of Baghdad in 1258. The remnants of the city population shrank within its walls. The peasants tried desperately to avoid contact with all outside their villages. Only the bedouin, who had already withdrawn from the empire, remained virtually untouched. The dreary chronicle of this period would net us little. Men clung to niches as we have imagined some might in the aftermath of nuclear war, desperately trying to survive, not daring to hope to live as they or their fathers had in former times. Then, in 1400–01 Tamerlane led another invasion of the Arab Middle East in which he sacked Baghdad, Aleppo, and Damascus. As the English historian Stephen Longrigg has written, "If the scenes and losses were less dreadful than those of the ruin of the Khalifate, it was that Baghdad in 1401 had not the same pride to be humbled, the same materials for atrocity." Part of Tamerlane's spoils in Damascus were the learned men and artisans whom he took back to his Central Asian capital and so dealt yet another blow to the civilization of the Middle East.

In Anatolia the petty states left by the decay of the Seljuk Empire struggled with Byzantium and with one another; gradually one of them, the House of Osman, the Ottomans, prevailed over the others and began to grow. In 1361 the Ottomans seized Adrianople and then moved into the Balkans. Their plan to capture Constantinople in the last years of the fourteenth century was delayed as they tried to ward off the attacks of Tamerlane who in 1402 captured the Ottoman sultan. But this was only a temporary setback. Finally in 1453 the Ottomans had recovered and were able to take Constantinople. For half a century their attentions were turned to Europe, but in 1514 Sultan Salim took Tabriz in a war with the Persian Empire. The problem of securing his flanks led him to conquer Kurdistan in the next year, and the following year his forces clashed near Aleppo with the Turko-Circassian Mamluk forces of Egypt. The great victory of the Ottomans encouraged them to seize Cairo, which they did in 1517. Rapidly they spread over the whole Middle East. A Turkish fleet was in the Persian Gulf in 1529. And in 1533, having just failed in their second attempt to seize Vienna, Ottoman forces took Baghdad.

Initially, the Turks made few efforts to change what they found. Often they confirmed the governments, as they did in the Lebanon, or merely imposed a chief functionary over the existing structure as they did in Egypt. Even when they sought changes, the great distances and slow communications of the empire made for a large degree of local autonomy. By the end of the sixteenth century the empire was in its more central parts a kingdom but further afield more of a federation, as local chieftains, the "lords of the valleys," exercised the functions of government while paying allegiance to the sultan. The vast desert and steppe lands, of course, were never effectively a part of the empire. And frontier provinces were often under a state of siege. Baghdad, which had been reconquered by Persia, was again besieged, sacked, and massacred in 1630. By 1704 Baghdad had recovered sufficiently to become the seat of a dynasty of pashas who were, for all practical purposes, independent. In Egypt, meanwhile, the Ottoman pasha had become little more than a figurehead; real power was in the hands of the landed Turkish aristocracy, the Mamluks. What is now Israel, Lebanon, Jordan, and part of Syria became in the middle of the eighteenth century an autonomous state, which in 1775 came under the rule of a Bosnian adventurer named Ahmad Jazzar, whose importance in Western history is that he was to give Napoleon one of his few defeats.

All over this vast expanse of empire the common people, tribesmen, peasants, and townsmen, lived their lives much as they always had. In religious brotherhoods, craft guilds, neighborhood associations, village councils, and tribal kinship, they found meaningful social life. Economically, they needed little as their standards of life and their expectations were minimal. Matters of their personal status, even transactions in land, taxes, and religious and civic expression, were governed by custom and legal codes which had little or no relationship to secular government. Their judges and religious leaders were not dependent upon their governors either for appointments to office or for salaries. Between the government and the people was a gulf defined not alone by language, culture, and temperament but in that the spheres of life were different. So total had this withdrawal become that it resembled a caste system: Turks were governors; Arabs were governed. Turks were warriors; Arabs were peasants or men of Islamic learning. In the colorful analogy to be drawn from Turkish terminology, the Turks were the shepherds and the Arabs the flocks.

PART 3

The Impact of the West

6

First Encounters: Point Counterpoint

TOWARD the end of the eighteenth century the Arab areas of the Middle East, although under the suzerainty of the Ottoman Empire, were in fact ruled by local dynasties or alien slave, military bureaucracies. The Arab population was not only small—with perhaps two million in Egypt and two million each in the Levant and the Arabian peninsula—but widely scattered and economically, administratively, and culturally isolated from all but near neighbors. Groups of towns, villages, and nearby clans of nomads or semi-nomads tended to cluster together as autarkic units. Few towns were large, but many which later became insignificant were in this period important trade centers. Even such widely scattered towns as Sidon, Kuwait, Jiddah, and Mokha carried on a wide-ranging and relatively prosperous trade. In some of the larger cities—Cairo, Aleppo, Damascus—as well as in a number of towns, medieval industrial crafts were practiced on a large scale.

Where men were favored by nature, as in the mountains of Lebanon, Palestine, Syria, and the north of Iraq and in the deserts of Arabia, they achieved a considerable degree of autonomy and freedom. Mount Lebanon, the most protected of these areas, not only had a high degree of village self-government, with secure land tenure, but an established and officially recognized "national" government which, at times, even carried on a separate foreign policy. Baron de Boislecomte, traveling about 1830, noted in his *Mission* that in many places the "cultivated valleys, separated from one another by the mountains and the great stretches of desert, form themselves into small republics." Writing of the bedouin "nations" in the Great Syrian Desert, Burckhardt observed that they were for all practical purposes autonomous states.

Bedouin tribes covered much of the land that is now agricultural. In the summer, for example, the valleys of Lebanon and Palestine and areas virtually within the shadow of the walls of Aleppo and Baghdad, were dotted with bedouin tents. In fact, as has been suggested above, a true picture of the Middle East at this period can be depicted in analogy to the sea: the agricultural areas and oases were the coast and islands in a vast sandy desert. Only occasionally could the people of the settled areas "go to sea," but the bedouin—merchantmen, privateers, fishermen—came and went at will. The sand sea was their natural element and in it they were safe from government tax collectors. Only rarely and temporarily could they be brought to heel by the forces of the government; in fact, they often are recorded as raiding and plundering the armed forces of the government whose valuable weapons were more targets than shields.

Between the tribes and the urban government, as between the upper and nether grindstone, was the peasant, accessible and defenseless, himself a domesticated animal, humbly submitting to the shears of the tax collector and the "brotherhood" extortion of the nomad. Where he could not defend himself, in the great river deltas of Egypt and Iraq or on the Syrian steppe lands, he paid the bill for both the town and the desert. Few families lived their entire lives in a single village. Great areas of agricultural lands had been abandoned and the so-called "frontier of settlement" had receded toward more protected areas. The Frenchman C. F. Volney remarked in his *Voyages,* "the peasant lives therefore in great distress; but at least he does not enrich his tyrant and the avarice of despotism is its own punishment."

Wherever possible towns were walled, and every man was a part-time soldier. Travel was expensive since each town, jealous of its autonomy and needing funds to pay taxes and hire guards, charged customs duties—in some cases little different from ransom—on entrants. Where the governor was strong, as in the city of Acre, he was really an autonomous prince although nominally an official of the empire. If he took a short-sighted view of his position he merely gathered as much treasure as he could, paid out to the empire or his overlords as little as possible, and retired to Constantinople. Jean Joseph Poujoulat, recounting his visit to Gaza, observed that the pashas looked upon themselves as travelers, camping out in their posts, never bothering to invest or repair. But this was not always the case. The pashas of the walled city of Acre encouraged the production of goods, both agricultural and industrial, which they monopolized, and taxed but tolerated the foreign merchant communities who settled in their midst. In some respects, Acre resembled a medieval Italian city-state.

With travel insecure and expensive, men moved mainly in caravans after careful preparation and along established routes. Some of these caravans were vast affairs. From Damascus, a city of 100,000, the Mecca caravan of 2000 camels departed once a year with 40,000 pilgrims; the Baghdad caravan of roughly a thousand camels made two or three round trips yearly. Ten to twelve thousand pilgrims yearly visited Jerusalem, then a city of 20,000.

Also because of the expense of travel, men tried to satisfy their wants locally. It is surprising to read the long lists of manufacturing establishments of such little villages as Gaza, Dair al-Qamar, Homs, and Zubair. The important fact, however, is not the *scale* of economic life but the fact that for centuries men had accommodated to it and had found in it a satisfying pattern. Woven into their commerce, social organization, military service, and family life were their religious beliefs and their expectations from life. In a man's family, clan, or neighborhood was the seat of his loyalty. City dwellers found in trade and religious guilds what tribal life gave to the bedouin, a social matrix for individual life. Desires were limited because horizons were narrow. Weapons had changed little in centuries and they were usually inherited from relatives or made locally; the principal luxury item of clothing was the Kashmiri shawl and this too lasted at least one lifetime. Agricultural implements were made by the farmers—the hoe and the "stick plow" were the whole range—while those of the artisan in the town required little more investment of time and resources. Food was not more exotic or expensive. The staples were cracked wheat, vegetables, and yogurt. Meat was a luxury for the agricultural and urban population.

The elements of society interacted and met one another's requirements. The bedouin provided the villager with a market for his crops and sold him animal products; the towns brought the products of bedouin and peasant, fashioned them into leather, soap, cloth, and luxuries, and sent them out to the world on the backs of bedouin camels. The economic machine was a simple one which by modern standards was slow and inefficient, but it worked. The breakdown of this machine, even if it is to be or in some instances has been replaced by a vastly superior though much more complex and expensive one, is what is ascribed to the "impact of the West."

European contacts with the Middle East had never totally ceased in the Middle Ages. Venice and Genoa, even in decline, maintained merchants' "factories" along the Levant and Egyptian coasts. The Portuguese, reaching the Indian Ocean in the sixteenth century, rapidly established similar factories on the Persian Gulf. Gradually, as the British and French aspired to world empires, they too created, took over, or inherited centers of trade and influence. Even the most remote areas of the empire were visited by the traveler and the merchant. The French monopoly port of Marseilles and the British East India Company developed vested interests in the politics of the area for not only was trade with and within the Middle East of importance, but the Middle East was the road to India.

In France plans for the conquest of Egypt had been discussed since the reign of Louis XIV. Behind them were motives more often romantic than practical, but Egypt did offer a shorter route to India than the Cape of Good Hope. This became of great moment to the French government when, in the last years of the eighteenth century, it entered a mortal struggle with the British Empire. Not only, it was thought, was Egypt capable of becoming the granary of France and a market for French goods, but from the port of Suez a French army could reach India in six weeks. This idea was first discussed by Napoleon in his correspondence with the Directory in the summer of 1797. With his customary dispatch he was ready to depart the following spring.

On July 1, 1798, a French army of 38,000 men disembarked from an armada of 280 ships off Alexandria. In a few hours Alexandria fell to the French force. The Egypt he found must have come as something of a shock to Napoleon. The population, living in the midst of the relics of ancient grandeur, was small and poor. It was, to the advantage of the French, divided into several, compartmented sections. The rulers, nominally Ottoman Turks but in practice the Turko-Circassian Mamluks, spoke a different language from the native population. The natives themselves were divided by religion, class, and education. The peasants, cut off alike from Islamic learning and from political experience, were, like the peasants of the rest of the Middle East, more objects than actors. The Copts, "Franks," Greeks, and Jews were the scribes, merchants, and tax collectors. And the literate, educated, Arabic-speaking Muslims tended to all matters of personal status and law. It was to them that Napoleon was to address his impassioned, nationalistic pleas for understanding and support. "People of Egypt, you are told that I come to destroy your religion. Do not believe it. Reply that I come to restore your rights, punish the usurpers and that I respect, more than the Mamluks, God, his Prophet and the Quran . . . Tell the people that we are friends of True Muslims. Is it not we who have destroyed the Pope who wanted to make war on Muslims? Is it not we who have destroyed the Knights of Malta because they believed that God wanted them to make war on the Muslims? Is it not we who have been throughout the centuries the friends of the Sultan (may God grant him favor) and the enemy of his enemies?" All Egyptians, Napoleon proclaimed, "are called upon to fill all the posts; the wisest, best educated and most virtuous will govern and the people will be happy."

In the Egypt of that time these were such outlandish notions as simply to be incomprehensible to the Egyptians. Indeed, even generations later the notion that the Egyptians were peasants, that rule was not their function or calling but rather was that of the Turks, was firmly held by very large numbers of people. The habit of centuries of foreign rule had deeply scored the Egyptian character. Their withdrawal from politics was to be incomprehensible to Napoleon throughout his stay in Egypt.

Much more startling to Egyptians was the ease with which Napoleon marched to Cairo with his large, disciplined, and modern force and in the famous Battle of the Pyramids, on July 21, in the space of an afternoon, utterly destroyed the colorful, dashing medieval army of the Mamluks. The next day the French army entered Cairo.

For Napoleon Egypt was a way station on the road of Alexander the Great to the Orient, but, realizing the necessity of consolidating this forward base, he entrusted to the Commission des Sciences et Arts the task of organizing an administration, surveying the country, regulating taxes and expenditures, in short, of performing all of the functions of a military government. For the most part the personnel and practices of the past were retained by the government; the major innovation, and the major failure, was Napoleon's attempt to enlist in the service of the government a council of native Egyptians. On October 21 the population of Cairo, led by the very men whose favor Napoleon had courted, the native Muslim, Arabic-speaking Egyptians, rose in revolt to throw out the French. Though they failed, they did shatter the liberation image of the French occupation.

Like most of the strong rulers of Egypt before him, Napoleon realized the importance to the security of Egypt of control over the Levant coast, and so early in 1799 he set out on the expedition to conquer Palestine and Syria and perhaps to open the route to the East. At the walled fortress-city of Acre he was handicapped by an English naval blockade and the outbreak of the plague. After an unsuccessful, fever-ridden siege, Napoleon turned back to Egypt in which, since it now was a jumping-off place to nowhere, he quickly lost interest.

After one more major battle against an Anglo-Turkish force, in which he demonstrated again the tremendous superiority of his army, Napoleon left Egypt on August 23.

Napoleon's invasion, and the long-range threat it posed to British interests in India, marked a great turning point in the history of the Middle East. The impact, however, was initially less in the Arab East itself—changes there have been greatly exaggerated by writers caught up in the romantic image of Napoleon and provided with superb propaganda in the publications of the expedition—than in the policies of the great powers. The French, pushed out militarily from the East, never lost their aspirations to play a major role in the East. The Ottoman government, surprised by the tremendous superiority of modern armies, accelerated its own programs of modernization and of the reimposition of authority over its huge but anomalous empire. Lastly, and more importantly, the British, frightened by the possible loss of their Indian empire, redoubled their efforts to drive the French out of India and, by a deep involvement in the affairs of the Middle East, to block any future moves from Europe toward southern Asia. A British army assisted in the expulsion of the French from Egypt in 1801, and in the Persian Gulf, Iraq, Mount Lebanon, and Egypt itself the English presence, whether the consul, the merchant, or the traveler, began to be felt.

The major if somewhat delayed impact of Napoleon's expedition was that made on one of the great figures of the nineteenth century, Mehmet Ali Pasha, a Turkish soldier of fortune who had nearly lost his life fighting the French.

Mehmet Ali Pasha, born in the Macedonian port town of Kavalla in 1769, the son of a police officer, orphaned young, a man whose energy was matched only by his ambition, was fond of remarking, "I was born in the same year as Napoleon in the land of Alexander." Throughout Mehmet Ali's life Napoleon and the expedition to Egypt were to exercise a profound influence on him. Like Napoleon he was a foreigner in the country he was to make his own; like Napoleon he was to win a vast empire; like Napoleon he was a superb opportunist. He realized, as few in the East in his time, wherein lay the real strength of the French, and his life was spent in attempting to acquire the modernization, the industrial and materials base, and the organization which had made a Napoleon possible.

By 1805 Mehmet Ali emerged as the leader of the most powerful faction within the Ottoman forces in Egypt and was able to seize power. He had his seizure of power ratified locally in Egypt rather than from the Ottoman Empire, by an assemblage of notables in

Cairo—itself rather an unusual move—and then negotiated with the empire as to how his position could be confirmed. Confirmation as governor came in 1806. But the political situation was still very unstable in Egypt, where rivals watched as hungry wolves the leader of their pack. The attempted British invasion of Egypt in 1807, which ended disastrously for the British at the Battle of Rosetta, came at a dangerous point for Mehmet Ali and his "victory" was not of his design or execution but was due to peasant xenophobia, poor British planning, and thirst.

In this period the necessity for reform in Egypt was recognized by everyone. Napoleon's military force had so easily destroyed the flower of Mamluk cavalry as to produce a profound impression on the whole Middle East. The Mamluk beys themselves, particularly the two who emerged as Mehmet Ali's major opponents in these years, aped French uniforms, had their troops drilled in French style, and attempted to gain modern French power by appearing, insofar as they knew how, French. The first Ottoman governor against whom Mehmet Ali contended for power, Khusrev Pasha, who was later to be grand vizier, enlisted French officers to train a Sudanese regiment on the French system. So it took no unique insight on the part of Mehmet Ali to realize where the new road of power lay. Each contender for power recognized that if he were to survive in the kind of situation which had been created by Napoleon's challenge to Egypt, he must create a modern army. Mehmet Ali won partly by his reforms and largely by luck. But, having won locally, he knew he could survive only by a combination of modernization and expansion.

In 1815 he tried to introduce into Egypt the *Nizam Jadid,* the new-style army. But the opposition on the part of his own army was such that he was forced to drop this program, and it was not until a lengthy war in Arabia against the Wahhabis had virtually killed off the veterans of his existing force that he was able to undertake the imposition of a modernized military system. It happened that just about the time the political situation was ready in Egypt for the introduction of this system, a former French army officer, then a captain, by the name of Sève, who subsequently became known as Sulaiman Pasha, arrived in Egypt and offered his services.

Mehmet Ali ordered Sève to introduce into Egypt several schools for the training of soldiers on the French system. At first these schools were largely made up of Turkish and Mamluk young men. Subsequently, Sudanese were enlisted in the Egyptian army, and ultimately, apparently at the suggestion of a French adviser, Egyptian peasants, for the first time in many centuries, were conscripted into the army. The wars of Mehmet Ali made further and further demands for a larger and larger military machine. By 1833 there were about 190,000 men in the Egyptian army and auxiliary forces, and by 1839 one out of every ten Egyptians was in one way or another involved in the army. (This compares with only one in each 160 in 1967 and one in each 45 in 1973.)

It was the genius of Mehmet Ali that he recognized that it was not simply a matter of numbers, or of the drill, or the style of uniforms, or equipment of troops which made power in the new sense. It was rather the control over the *means of production* both of modern weapons and of modern soldiers which differentiated him from his rivals. He recognized that he could not rely on Europe for either but had to open schools to train soldiers and factories to equip them. Therefore he set out to build in Egypt factories to produce guns, ammunition, and uniforms; arsenals to equip the army and the fleet; and ultimately shipyards to produce the fleet itself. The production of these things required not only a handful of technicians who could be hired in Europe, but also an intricate bureaucracy, a large number of literate, qualified, capable people, to run and organize all of the myriad services that a modern government required.

Mehmet Ali began quite early in his career to train his people abroad. In 1809 the first man was sent from Egypt to Europe for training, and in almost every year thereafter a new mission of students would be sent abroad. Very few of these were sent for what we would call "higher education"; most were sent for rudimentary technical training. Workers were sent to Italy to learn about the textile industry; others were sent to learn how to manufacture guns and equipment. Others were sent to military schools to learn not only tactics but engineering, medicine, and logistics. Although he apparently had not intended to do so, Mehmet Ali created a new generation, which was to come to the fore in Egypt after his death, of men who had begun to learn about the inner nature of European civilization.

Perhaps the most famous of these men was one who was sent to Europe not as a student but as the imam, or chaplain, of a group of students in 1824. This was Rifaa Rafi, who was born in the little Egyptian town of Tahta, where his father had been a fairly wealthy local landlord. So struck was Rifaa with the new world he discovered that while in Paris he set about writing a book which was intended to explain to the Egyptians what life was like in France. This book, called *The Journey* and published in 1834, went through three Arabic editions and a Turkish edition and was the most widely read of any book produced in the Middle East in the first half of the nineteenth century. It and that great classic of European description E. W. Lane's *Manners and Customs of the Modern Egyptians* present the most fascinating contrast of the intellectual contact between Europe and the Middle East produced in the nineteenth century.

When each Egyptian student returned from Europe, he was placed in the Citadel in Cairo and told to translate the textbook that he had been studying in France. So, somewhat casually, individual students made available to their confreres the works upon which they had relied during their European exposure. Ultimately, a special bureau was set up to translate a great corpus of European literature into Arabic. As manuals gave way to belles lettres the intellectual foundations of subsequent Egyptian history were laid.

The third aspect of Mehmet Ali's creation of power in Egypt lay in the field of economics. He recognized that it was necessary for the government to centralize agricultural, financial, industrial, and commercial control just as it had centralized military and political control. This was not the result of a sudden decision to undertake a new program. It was not comparable with the sort of decisions that are made in modern planning but came about as a purely pragmatic solution to a problem. Mehmet Ali had effectively eliminated his rivals, one by one, and finally in 1811 had massacred the Mamluk opponents of his regime and confiscated a great deal of their property. In 1816 he formalized the trend in centralization by subsuming land rights over all of Egypt. What these rights had amounted to was administrative control over a given area of land. The holder of this right (*iltizam*) would agree to pay to the central government a specified sum of money yearly in return for which he would be allowed to tax the people who lived on the land. He did not himself own, *de jure,* the land. The land was theoretically owned by the Empire. What Mehmet Ali did in broad outline was to take fiscal control over the land to himself and subdivide the rights to use the land among other people—in the main, peasants—who after 1816 produced crops for and paid taxes directly to the government.

Similarly, in the realm of urban finance, commerce, and industry, Mehmet Ali established a monopoly in 1816. Anyone desiring to buy Egyptian produce had to do so through a government agency. Ultimately, Mehmet Ali came to recognize that the government must undertake the stimulation of industrial growth. For this purpose the government sent industrial workers and students to Europe for training, hired European industrial workers and technicians to come to Egypt, furnished capital and raw materials, set production goals, purchased all finished goods, and paid the operating costs of the industry Mehmet Ali thought Egypt needed.

In Egypt in the 1820's, as in America at a later date, the textile industry formed the major thrust of the industrial transformation. Between 1818 and 1828 thirty cotton textile factories were opened. Additional woolen factories were built to provide uniforms for the army. Textiles continued to be the pace setter in Egypt and as late as 1952 accounted for 36 percent of the labor force in establishments of ten or more workers. Other industries lagged far behind textiles as Egypt lacked iron and coal. Here again there is continuity: in 1952 mining and manufacturing, of which textiles and food processing accounted for the bulk, still amounted to only 8 percent of the gross national product.

But in the time of Mehmet Ali as later, noneconomic factors caused the government to industrialize. In the 1820's and 1830's the Egyptian military machine, with about 130,000 men under arms, required the manufacture of artillery, small arms, powder, and other munitions. The growing navy demanded and got a rapid acceleration in the manufacture of naval vessels and stores in Alexandria. Troops and those who supported them had to be fed and supplied, so sugar refineries, dye works, glass-blowing factories, tanneries, paper mills, and chemical works were set up throughout the country.

All of these factories were supervised, financed, and controlled by the government. Many were under the immediate jurisdiction of foreign technicians but even in them Egyptians or other Orientals were trained to fill, ultimately, all the jobs. All of the personnel, including the directors, were government employees. The products were marketed by the government and all raw materials were procured by the government. Perhaps this government monopoly was necessary, as the growing and already far larger industries of Europe could swamp the area with their cheaper products, but the system, as the perceptive Egyptian writer Moustafa Fahmy has pointed out, did not permit the entry of a single capitalist or entrepreneur into industrial or, at times and in certain fields, commercial activity. This was to have profound social, economic, and political implications in later times.

In order to train the new personnel required by the government for its bureaucracy and its various other technical and military activities, Mehmet Ali also began a new venture or, more correctly, series of new adventures in education. Ultimately, over 10,000 students were enrolled in various government institutions, where they were given lodging, food, and stipends at a total yearly expenditure of approximately £150,000 or 5 percent of the then gross national product of Egypt.

In the enrollments one can see the obviously utilitarian aims. A school of languages, to train translators, was opened for 225 students; a school of secretarial service for clerks was opened for 300; a polytechnic institute had 300 pupils; artillery and medical schools had

300 each; a school for infantry officers enrolled 800; and a veterinary medical school, to minister to the cavalry, absorbed 120 young men. Upon graduation each young man was immediately taken into government service. Uniformly, and this was to remain a feature of the system until recently, education led directly to service in the government.

The number of salaried, permanent workers in factories reached approximately 30,000 in the 1830's and over a quarter of a million others worked in smaller establishments, or at their homes, on the government account. It has been estimated that between 1816 and 1850 the total number of industrial workers was at least 400,000.

At this same time rapid transformations were in process in Syria, which came under Egyptian rule in 1832. The population of the Syrian hinterland and coast was 1.3 million, of whom half were urban. In this area as in Egypt, commerce had always been an element in the economic life but relatively a secondary element. Following the French Revolution and during the French invasion of Egypt the violent and greedy rule of the Ottoman pashas based in Acre and Sidon caused a sharp decline in the international trade of the Levant. The French trading establishments were closed, the British had not at that time interested themselves in the Levant, and the American effort was then minor. On the eve of the Egyptian invasion even the British consul could not establish himself in Damascus so restrictive and xenophobic were its people. The people, as mentioned above, were content with the small world they knew and feared outsiders would destroy it. They grew, built, or inherited most of what they needed; and what little they got from outside was mainly from the Far East rather than from the West.

The effect of the Egyptian invasion of 1832 was to "open" the Levant to Western influence. This is a process which the author has described in detail elsewhere.* Here it is useful to point out that a change in tastes and technology distinguished the Egyptian period, as old ways, old tools, and old weapons were quickly judged to be outmoded. Cheap Western goods, the products of the new and booming industry of Europe, flowed into the Syrian market. Syrian handicraft industry was doomed. In the one year of 1833 an estimated 10,000 workers, mainly in textiles, were thrown out of work in Damascus and Aleppo. The smaller towns, which had to some degree specialized in particular local products, could no longer market their goods. Even the old caravan trade was hurt as clothing styles changed. The people of Damascus who would not allow the entry of one British official in

---

* *The Opening of South Lebanon* (Cambridge, Mass., 1963).

1830 were patronizing 107 shops retailing British goods in 1838. Even the great tribal groups in the deserts were affected as they found they could buy their headdresses and gowns from factories at Birmingham at less cost than they could weave them. Within a few years even the chief moneylenders of Damascus and other towns were British. The flood gates, once opened by the Egyptians, were never again closed.

In Syria, as in Egypt, the army was the principal agent fostering change. The soldiers were major purchasers. Officers were important investors. For the first time in Syrian history since Byzantine times the government, that is, the army, undertook public works projects and gave security to the roads thereby encouraging trade and travel. As a direct result the Levant began to be tied to the world market on a massive scale and to acquire a taste for the goods and disquieting new ideas of the West. As the British agent John Bowring wrote in 1839, "The soldiery became protectors instead of destroyers of property; they formed part of a structure of social improvement, which, with some attendant evils, brought an incomparably great portion of benefits. The effect of this better organization has been immense. Even in the populous parts of Egypt, before the time of Mahomet Ali, there was little security for life or property; in the Desert, none whatever . . . the Desert has been made as safe and secure as the high road of the Nile."

It is difficult to say what might have happened in Syria—or in Egypt itself—had Egyptian rule in Syria continued. This was not to be. At the height of his powers, after a series of campaigns that had taken his armies into Africa to conquer the Sudan, into Europe to attempt to retain Greece in the Ottoman Empire, and into Asia where they had conquered Arabia, Palestine, Lebanon, Syria, and half of Anatolia, Mehmet Ali had routed the forces of the Ottoman army and assumed control over the Ottoman fleet. The major Western powers were increasingly alarmed that the threat posed by Mehmet Ali to the empire would force the sultan into the arms of Russia. The English realized that they must weaken Mehmet Ali to get the sultan, and his prized Straits, away from the Russian grasp. Specifically, they must get the Egyptians out of Syria. Moreover, industrial England was actively in quest of markets and the restrictive practices of Mehmet Ali were frustrating British commerce. Mehmet Ali refused to allow the Commercial Code of 1838—which, having been negotiated with a weakened sultan, was extremely favorable to foreigners—to be applied in Egyptian-controlled areas, rightly seeing in it the ruin of Egyptian industry and the denationalization of commerce. "Monopoly," in free-trade England, was almost as damning a word as "Communism" is today. So, when the Egyptians had made themselves thoroughly unpopular and were in the midst of a civil war, the British assisted the sultan in driving them out of Syria, and forced Mehmet Ali to reduce his standing armed forces from over 130,000 to 18,000. With the *raison d'être* of the reform program removed, Mehmet Ali lost interest in the sweeping changes he had set in motion.

7

The High Cost of Modernization: Coming of the West

THE residual effects of Mehmet Ali's rule, both in Syria and in Egypt, were to be felt strongly by future generations. Mehmet Ali had created, albeit for his own limited purposes, the first of the successive groups of "new men" who were to come forward in Arab society over the next century.

What Mehmet Ali did was to unleash forces of economic change which had long-term but slowly maturing social consequences. He once referred to himself as "the armed missionary of European civilization in Arabia," trying to accomplish there what England was doing in India and what France was to try in Algeria. But Egypt lacked the power to sustain the effort, to control the process of change, or to replace older social institutions.

In 1824 Damascus alone had bought twice as much from the Orient (brought by the Baghdad caravan) as all Syria bought from Europe. When Egypt opened the Levant to Western trade, this situation changed drastically: by 1838 urban men were wearing fezes imported from France and drinking from glass made in Bohemia. By 1854 the French and Austrian steamers, plying the coastal Levant towns, had in the words of the British consul "annihilated the local carrying trade." New ideas from the West changed clothing styles, so that the key luxury import from the East, the Kashmiri shawl, went out of fashion. By 1857 the old Baghdad-Damascus caravan was finished.

Routes of trade were either forgotten or reversed: Aleppo traditionally had got its coffee from Yemen but began to get it from Santo Domingo via France; pepper, which had come to Beirut from the East via Baghdad, was, after the advent of steam, sent to Baghdad via Beirut.

Specialization in the produce of the area led to entry into the world markets. This in turn led to the necessity of cultivating certain kinds of crops and of processing these in a way suitable for European use. Silk, long the staple export of Lebanon, had been reeled by hand, but by 1850 the requirements of the European industry had brought a drastic change in methods. Silk thread reeled by hand fetched only a quarter as much as silk reeled by steam power. This opened a new market for European investors who constructed large-scale filatures in Lebanon. Cotton, which was introduced on a national scale by Mehmet Ali in Egypt in 1831, was likewise affected by the European market. The short-staple cotton of Syria was useful only for producing wicks, while that of Egypt commanded a wider market.

However, cotton and other large-scale crops were affected by the vagaries of the world market. The Crimean War caused a rapid rise in prices but the return of peace in 1856 caused a fall of 50 percent in prices of cotton and other local produce in the Middle East. In 1860 the United States supplied over 80 percent of the cotton used in European industry; thus, when the outbreak of the Civil War cut the source of supply, a "famine" was caused in textile mills, which were the heart of British industry. In the year 1861–62 the price of raw cotton quadrupled and attention was attracted to alternate sources of supply, of which Egypt was the most promising. British purchases from Egypt increased from £8 to £22 million between 1861 and 1865. Such smart operators as Ismail Pasha, who was to become khedive of Egypt in 1866, made their fortunes in this period (Ismail is reputed personally to have made £1 million). But the slump which followed ruined many who had overinvested in lands and equipment.

Thus, the units of society began to change both absolutely and relatively. The bedouin alone held out, relatively unaffected by the slow pace of the new social revolution. But incursions into the nomad's sanctuary were made. Relentlessly the line of settlement was pushed out into the steppe and modernized armies became more efficient in hunting him down.

British and French consular dispatches of the 1840's and 1850's are filled with references to Ottoman punitive expeditions against the bedouin. Since the Ottoman administrators regarded the bedouin as pirates, they tried to drive them back into the desert, cut them off from trade with the towns, and where possible to kill them. Fairly typical of their efforts was a campaign in 1864. It was, wrote the British consul in Aleppo, "successful as far as regards the numerous tribes of settled Arabs, all of which have confirmed their submission to the authorities and consented to pay their annual taxes. The [nomadic] Anezi tribes, however, are during this season in the plains of Nejd or Central Arabia whither they withdraw regularly for the winter." The Ottoman policy, in short, was similar to the American policy toward the Indians, but whereas the Americans were a numerous and pioneer people, backed by a mobile army, the Ottoman government was represented by tax-collecting pashas with small and usually immobile military forces. Their proper target was the land-bound peasant, not the elusive nomad. It was only as the bedouin could be induced to settle and invest in immovable objects that they could be controlled.

Settlement of the bedouin had been one of the most interesting aspects of the Egyptian occupation of Syria. The Egyptians had a large and relatively mobile army which could overwhelm the nomads if necessary, but continual warfare was expensive. Moréover the Egyptians needed more agricultural production. So the Egyptian governor hit upon the solution of inducing tribes to settle. Purchase of land was made extremely easy, bedouin and peasants were assisted with government loans, and a ready market existed for the produce. In this way a great deal of land was brought into cultivation on the Syrian steppe. But following the Egyptian withdrawal the market for agricultural produce declined. A return to government exploitive practices induced many peasants to abandon their newly acquired lands and return to nomadic life. The British consul in Damascus reported the complete failure of the policy of settlement of the tribes when, in 1863, he noted that the bedouin "are being pursued by the Government troops in every direction without any reason other than they are nomadic tribes." It was not until the able and wise Ottoman Governor Midhat Pasha went to Baghdad in 1869 that the policy of inducing settlement was again tried and with some more success.

In Lebanon one of the principal effects of the Egyptian occupation had been the upset in the traditional relationship between the Christians and the Muslims and Druze. Lebanon, set apart by its mountains from the surrounding areas, had always been able to live an independent life. The position there of the Christians and other minorities was always stronger than that of their confreres in other areas. But at least in the southern half of Lebanon the Christians were second-class citizens in 1830. Often they were the clients and peasants of the Druze warrior class. Favored by a tolerant or even superficially pro-Christian Egyptian government, the Christians of Lebanon emerged in 1840 as landlords and creditors of their former masters. The Druze attempted when the Egyptians were driven out to regain their former possessions but were thwarted not only by the Christians, against whom they probably could have won a war, but by the European powers who undertook either to protect the Christians (in the case of France) or to hold the peace (as in the case of Great Britain). When the Christians invaded a Druze area, they were defeated, but the British and French stopped the Druze from following up their advantages. When Druze shaikhs tried to collect rents from their properties, their agents were killed by townsmen whose arms were conveyed to them by priests under French diplomatic protection. Indeed, the first Ottoman governor referred to the "innumerable French Missionaries . . . [as] the Pope's Light Irregular Cavalry Established in Lebanon, who under the garb of priests were in fact political Agents and Perturbators of the Public Peace."

Friction between the Christian and Druze communities invited outside intervention and led to a series of crises which culminated in the 1860–61 civil war during which the French sent a military expedition to restore the peace. Finally in 1864 Lebanon's unique character was enshrined in a *reglement organique* which acknowledged Lebanese autonomy under a Christian governor appointed by the Ottoman sultan but approved by the great powers. This was the formalization of Lebanon as a Christian and Western-oriented enclave which it has been to this day.

Foreign religious activity in the Middle East was facilitated by the organization of non-Muslim subjects of the Ottoman Empire into self-governing millets or "nations" on the basis of religion. Most of these had long existed. The separation from the rest of society and the relative internal cohesion engendered both by a common concern in community affairs and the existence of a single hierarchy or ethnarchy, which controlled not only matters of personal status but also the rate of taxation, made each millet a receptive partner for foreign political, missionary, and economic activity.

Lebanon—a land protected by its mountainous chain, relatively isolated from the East but open by sea to the West, whose population included religious minorities with a long tradition of contacts with the West—was an ideal place for early Western Christian missionary activity. The first American missionaries came to Lebanon in 1823, but it was not until 1831 that the mission was firmly established. Faced as they were by hostile Christians in long-established churches (until 1871 the Protestants were hampered by not being recognized as a separate millet with their own institutions), and unable to make overt efforts to convert Muslims, the Americans turned to educational activities. To succeed in these, they had to learn Arabic. Having done this, they were able to establish ties with local men of letters, some of whom became converts and in cooperation with whom they translated numbers of Western books and the New Testament. Gradually, they spread a network of schools over the Middle East and in 1866 founded the Syrian Protestant College, now known as the American University of Beirut. The French opened the Jesuit Université St. Joseph, and by the eve of the First World War the Levant coast had over three hundred foreign schools educating more than twenty-five thousand students.

Foreign intervention in the life of the Middle East characterized the second half of the nineteenth century. Whereas in 1830 a British consul had been unable to enter the city of Damascus, in 1840 another British consul actually picked the man who was to be governor of Lebanon. British consuls intervened even in the most minute political affairs of remote areas. For example, in 1854 in the port of Beirut a native and a foreign ship collided. No court then constituted could try the case. It was the British consul not the Ottoman governor whose powers were adjudged most nearly able to meet the requirements of the situation, and he constituted a mixed commission to assess damages and responsibility.

The commercial code of 1838 gave to European merchants great advantages over their native competitors, and they used these with the full support of their governments. The "capitulations" removed them from the jurisdiction of local courts. Capitulations had long existed. Originally, they were granted by the Byzantine Empire to encourage trade by allowing merchants to follow their own customs and laws while temporarily residing in the empire. This fit easily with the Islamic notion that nations or groups of people with a common religion should have corporate institutions of their own. The Ottoman rulers granted this privilege to the French in 1535, to the Austrians in 1567, and to the English in 1592. However, in the decline of the empire the capitulations became both a symptom and a cause of the degeneration of Ottoman sovereignty. By the middle of the nineteenth century all foreigners enjoyed more privileges than do modern diplomats.

Foreigners on criminal charges could appeal their cases to courts in their native lands; even when their crimes involved natives, the local government was powerless to punish them. So flagrant were the abuses possible under this system that it was to be regarded as one of the great triumphs of Egyptian nationalism to get the great powers to recognize and participate in the creation and functioning of "mixed courts," in which Egyptian judges, though a permanent minority, could have a voice in the decision of cases involving their countrymen with Europeans. It was not until 1937 that Egypt was able to get the capitulations abolished.

The great stimulus to European investment in the Middle East in the nineteenth century was, of course, the huge Suez Canal project. This was the lifework of Ferdinand de Lesseps, who in 1854 was able to convince the Egyptian governor to grant him a concession to dig a canal to link the Mediterranean with the Red Sea. Lesseps was as ruthless, shameless, patient, and brilliant an entrepreneur as lived in a century of Morgans, Guggenheims, Rockefellers, and Rothschilds. The terms under which he began his operations in Egypt were almost the antithesis of those under which modern concessionaires work: The Egyptian governor was to purchase over half of the stock of Lesseps' company, but the stock gave him few rights and was held under various restrictions. Egypt was to get 15 percent of the net profits of the company but was to furnish a labor force of nearly 20,000 men to dig the canal. Then, as the company needed new sources of revenue, the Egyptian treasury was literally plundered of "untold amounts . . . for indemnities, fraudulent and semi-fraudulent claims, exorbitant prices to purveyors and contractors, and all manner of bribes designed to buy cheap honours or simply respite from harassment," writes David Landes. In 1869 Lesseps was especially hard pressed for money, and this, in Landes' words,

forced the ingenious entrepreneur to find other pretexts for an assault on the treasury. He found them without delay (the company cashbox did not admit of procrastination) in a catch-all of rubbish that was either no longer of use to the company or never belonged to it in the first place. By agreement of July 1869, the canal sold to the Egyptian government those barracks, hospitals and other structures built to serve during construction and no longer required; a stone quarry that the company had been *allowed* to exploit for purposes of building and maintaining the waterway . . . divers other imaginary "rights"; and, most important for Egypt, a renunciation by the company of any further claims . . . The Egyptian government paid 30 million francs for the package. Since it had no cash, it abandoned its rights to interest and dividends on its shares in the company for a period of twenty-five years. Lesseps in turn issued at 260 francs 120,000 assignment bonds covering the detached coupons; the gross yield to the company on the transaction was therefore almost 60 millions, while the purchasers of the assignments could hope for a total of about 110 million francs in interest alone during the period in question. As though this were insufficient, the Egyptian government also agreed to share with the company the proceeds of future sales of improved land along the canal, in spite of the fact that the Emperor's arbitration had specifically enjoined the company from seeking any profit from this source.*

The governor of Egypt, Ismail, made the opening of the canal in 1869 an occasion for Egypt to gain a sort of diplomatic recognition of independence from the Ottoman Empire. At vast expense he prepared a gala ceremony for the crowned heads of Europe, built palaces to accommodate them during their visits to Egypt, and commissioned Verdi to write an opera extolling the grandeur of Egypt—thereby giving us *Aïda*.

To meet the financial obligations he had undertaken, to buy his autonomy from the Ottoman Empire, and to satisfy his own wishes for luxury and for the development of Egypt, Ismail began contracting ever larger loans from the great European banking firms. It was this, wrote the later British proconsul Lord Cromer, that brought the British to control over Egypt. When Said Pasha died in 1863, the external debt of Egypt was £3.3 million; thirteen years later the debt totaled £94 million. Lord Cromer, who rarely minced words, wrote that "for all practical purposes it may be said that the whole of the borrowed money, except £16,000,000 spent on the Suez Canal, was squandered."

However, a contemporary English author, J. Seymour Keay, in a widely sold pamphlet called *Spoiling the Egyptians, A Tale of Shame,* and later historians have pointed out that of the vast debt, "only about 45,500,000 [pounds] were even nominally received" and on some loans the rate of interest was over 26 percent; indeed, one loan of £9 million was paid over to the Egyptians in defaulted bonds. Typical of the debts contracted was one in 1865 for £3 million. The Egyptians received £2.2 million and had to repay £4.1 million plus various fees and penalties. European sharp practice in Egypt was paralleled by European treatment of the Ottoman Empire, which between 1854 and 1875 borrowed the equivalent of $900 million of which it actually received not much more than $600 million.

Ismail did "waste" a great deal of money—the festivities at the opening of the Suez Canal, for example, cost £1.3 million—but his big outlays were to the Ottoman Empire, an obligation forced upon him by the fact that Europe had refused to allow Egypt to become independent, to the European creditors whose pressures he could not resist once he was caught in the web of usury, and for the development of Egypt. During his reign the new basis of the Egyptian economy was laid. Apart from the Suez Canal Ismail Pasha constructed over 8000 miles of canals, 900 miles of railroads, 5000 miles of tele-

---

* *Bankers and Pashas* (Cambridge, Mass., 1958), p. 316.

graphs, 430 bridges, the harbor of Alexandria, mills, factories, and lighthouses and reclaimed about 1.25 million acres of land. During this period Egypt's exports tripled in value.

By 1875 Egypt had sold its shares in the Suez Canal through the offices of Rothschild to Disraeli's government for a mere £4 million and had ceded to its creditors control over the collection of taxes and duties in large parts of the Egyptian economy. By 1877 about two thirds of the revenues of the Egyptian government were devoted to the debt, and Egypt was in effect placed in receivership by its European creditors and their governments. Finally in 1879 Ismail was deposed at the instigation of the European powers and replaced by a weak and vacillating ruler who could be little more than a front for the Europeans who controlled Egypt.

As a part of the economy drive the new governor allowed an international liquidation convention to force him to issue a "liquidation law." Then he cut the pay of the native officers, newcomers to high command, in the Egyptian army. This brought on a rebellion led by a triumvirate of officers—the first Egyptians to rise to the rank of colonel—of whom the principal was Arabi Pasha. In 1882, to maintain his throne, the discredited ruler called upon the great powers and both Great Britain and France sent warships to Alexandria. On July 11 the British bombarded Alexandria, while the French withdrew. In September a British force invaded Egypt by way of the Suez Canal, routed the Egyptian troops at the battle of Tal al-Kabir, captured Cairo, and arrested Arabi Pasha.

Retrospectively Arabi Pasha has been magnified as a great national figure who tried to protect the independence of Egypt and who sought to enhance the position of the native Egyptians in the face of a corrupt, alien aristocracy. But in his own time Arabi was not a popular man; his limited intelligence and lofty pride were not solid foundations for national leadership, and the Egyptian people had not yet firmly grasped the concept of nationalism. In large part nationalism was to be a by-product of the British occupation.

The British seizure of power in Egypt was almost embarrassingly easy. The official justification for it, the bankruptcy of Egypt, could not be satisfied by an early withdrawal. Thus, though Britain immediately announced that it was planning to withdraw, British officials set about the reorganization of the country. Once involved in this program they found it more and more difficult to leave. The last British troops did not, in fact, leave until 1956.

The underlying reason for Britain's interest in Egypt was the one which took Napoleon there—Egypt dominated the route to India. It might, indeed, be argued that the construction of the Suez Canal made inevitable in an age of unblushing imperialism, as Mehmet Ali had predicted it would, the occupation of Egypt by some one or a consortium of European powers. It should be noted that 80 percent of the ships using the Suez Canal in 1882 were British. Thus it was that when the two immediate causes of the invasion were satisfied—Arabi was overthrown and the finances of the country restored, as they were by 1890—the British remained in Egypt. There was always some compelling reason to stay a bit longer. As Lord Cromer put it, "England did not want to possess Egypt, but it was essential to British interests that the country should not fall into the hands of any other European power . . . British diplomacy, which may at times have been mistaken, but which was certainly honest, did its best to throw off the Egyptian burden. But circumstances were too strong to be arrested by diplomatic action."

Having acquired a position in Egypt and built a cadre of able administrators there, Britain was inexorably drawn into all of the Middle Eastern affairs which had been the traditional concerns of rulers of Egypt. The affairs of the Sudan could not be neglected, so an Anglo-Egyptian force reconquered it from its native ruler in 1898 and established in it a new administration. The affairs of the Levant coast and Arabia, to which thousands of Egyptians went yearly on pilgrimage, became the concerns of the British. As a buffer to Egypt, the British government required the Ottoman Empire to cede the Sinai Peninsula to Egypt in 1906. During the First World War these area-wide concerns forced the British government to take a commanding role in the whole Middle East even at the expense of a partial estrangement from its principal wartime ally, France. The occupation of Egypt, then, may be said to have begun the political phase of the impact of the West while it set a seal on the first efforts of the Arabs to find their own way into the modern era.

The "impact of the West," whether the result of actions by Europeans or by modernizing Middle Easterners, resulted more in the destruction of institutions and old balances between resources and expectations than in the creation of new institutions and balances. But, of course, it was long before intellectuals in the Middle East were able to formulate their fears of this disruption. Essentially the question posed to those who would protect their way of life was how to recoup the strength of the East in order to protect it from the West.

Answers to that question could be found in many ways. There was some flickering interest in "love of homeland," as expressed in the *wataniyat* poetry of the middle of the nineteenth century, but this amounted to little. In Egypt at least, Islam seemed to be the best ral-

lying point and found two able spokesmen in Jamal ad-Din al-Afghani, who spent the years 1871–1879 in Egypt, and Muhammad
Abdu, who eventually became grand mufti.

Jamal ad-Din, the subject of intense suspicion and recent investigation, a person who, to escape being classed as a Shii in the Sunni
Muslim world, claimed to be born near Kabul, Afghanistan, in 1839,
was the great promoter of anti-Western movements. He traveled
widely in the Islamic world and professed to find in Islam itself and in
the community of the Islamic peoples the best hope of the East to defend itself. During his stay in Egypt, Jamal inspired a new generation
of Egyptians with his interpretation of Islam and so gained the disfavor of the British and their Egyptian friends. In September 1879 the
new pro-British khedive expelled Jamal from Egypt, as one of the first
acts of his government.

Some of those associated with Jamal took part in the Arabi rising
in 1881–82, and his foremost student, Muhammad Abdu, joined
Jamal in Paris, where he was living in exile. In 1884 the two began
publication of a weekly newspaper in Arabic called *al-Urwah al-
Wuthqah* (the Unbreakable Bond) in which they urged Muslims
everywhere to unite to save themselves from Western domination.
The paper was short-lived, issuing only eighteen numbers, and was
banned in Egypt and India. Nevertheless it had a profound influence
on a generation which had begun to search for a means of identification and defense.

Secular nationalism was more difficult to project into popular concern. The government and all political figures were men of the well-
to-do classes of the city, were cut off from the life of the people in the
countryside, and were themselves too caught up in the process of
modernization and Westernization to oppose it effectively. Indeed,
such seemed to be the case all over Asia. To the Egyptians it came as
a major shock to learn of modernizing Japan and particularly of its
victory over Russia in 1905. Thus it was natural that the principal
leader of the secular nationalist movement at the turn of the century
in Egypt should have written a book called *The Rising Sun*.

Still, this was rather intellectual and esoteric fare. The average
Egyptian peasant had benefited from British rule, and whether his
benefit was due to investments made by the Khedive Ismail in the
1870's or to honest government under Lord Cromer in the 1890's
mattered little. It was not until the 1906 Denshawai incident that
public opinion was crystallized against the British on a mass emotional basis. The incident itself was small, resulting from a dispute
between British officers and villagers during a pigeon shoot near the
village of Denshawai, but the violent, unfair, and bullying response,

in which the British-controlled government sentenced three Egyptians to be hanged and others to be flogged and thrown into prison, shattered the mask of benevolence to reveal the face of imperial power. The Egyptians were never again able to focus on the benevolence, despite the best efforts of the British to play down their power. This new aspect of imperialism was to captivate Egyptian thought and lead them to revolt in 1920.

Though it was Egypt that was the main threat to British interests in the area in 1800 and the main base of British activity in the Middle East at the end of the century, Britain's major holding in Asia was India, and it was India that set the stamp on British endeavor throughout the Middle East. This concern tended to draw British activity into areas other than those of even long-term interest to Egypt. Prime among these was the Persian Gulf.

From the time of Napoleon the British were obsessed with the thought that another European power—first France, then Russia, then Germany, and then Russia again—might use the Euphrates River–Persian Gulf route to attack India. This concept was most clearly stated in the House of Lords in 1911 when Lord Curzon said, "the Gulf is part of the maritime frontier of India, and . . . in the politics of the Gulf are involved the security, integrity and peace of India itself." But as early as 1798 the British Secretary of War wrote that "Bonaparte will, as much as possible avoid the dangers of the Sea, which is not his element, but . . . by marching to Aleppo, cross the Euphrates, and following the example of Alexander, by following the River Euphrates and the Tigris, and descending to the Persian Gulf will march on India." The walls of Acre and the Royal Navy blockade stopped Napoleon but the memory of the real or imagined danger remained fresh in the minds of successive British and British Indian statesmen.

Moreover, communications were vital to the retention of control over the Indian empire. Before the advent of steam the Red Sea was regarded as a dangerous route, and the Isthmus of Suez was until 1882 in the hands of a potentially hostile or untrustworthy power. The route around Africa was excessively long for the carrying of government communications.

An alternative and rapid route was, therefore, what in modern policy pronouncements would be labeled a "vital national interest." Usually such a communication route was available on the Tatar post of the Ottoman Empire, but it was unreliable and was often subject to interference by agents of other European powers. Therefore, it was early realized that Britain must create its own service, the "British

Dromedary Post," protected by the agents and consuls established at Basra (in 1764) and Baghdad (in 1798). One undertaking led to the next as the very mechanics of the problems of communications drew the British deeper into Middle Eastern affairs. A governor general of India complained in 1800 that "in the present year I was nearly *seven months* without receiving one line of authentic intelligence from England ... Speedy, authentic, and regular intelligence from Europe is essential to the conduct of the trade and government of this empire." The Persian Gulf, although cleared of European rivals by the seizure of Hormuz in 1622, was still endangered by the pirates of Muscat. Indeed, these pirates raided India and the eastern African coast as far south as Zanzibar. After several expeditions the British established control over the gulf by 1820, suppressed piracy, and entered into treaty relations with the shaikhs of the "Pirate" (renamed "Trucial") Coast.

The desire to improve this route, and fear of Russian penetration, led the British government to send Lt. Francis Chesney to explore the Euphrates River with a view to establishing on it a steamboat service in 1830. In 1834 Chesney had two steamers on the river. Though the whole plan he had conceived did not prove feasible, he left behind a private company which operated a steamer on the Tigris River between Basra and Baghdad and provided the basis of British commercial penetration and development in Iraq.

If steamers were not the answer, the advent of the railroad seemed to offer renewed hope. The desert route itself was still in use by camel riders as late as 1886. A Euphrates valley railroad scheme was first discussed in 1840, but the British government lost interest. By 1888 Constantinople was linked by rail to Europe. France, the principal banker of the empire after 1854, also led the way in railroad development; by 1914 French investors had 500 million francs in Ottoman railroads. But as early as 1872 an Austrian engineer, serving as a consultant to the Ottoman sultan, had recommended that a rail net link Basra with the capital. As the land was then sparsely populated, and such a project was not economically feasible, the engineer suggested that two million Germans be settled along the route to develop the resources of the empire. Although relatively latecomers to Turkey, the Germans plunged rapidly ahead. Several German authors urged that ancient Babylonia was a proper area of German colonization; expansion of trade was vigorously fostered; and through military missions, Germany entered deeply into the affairs of the Ottoman Empire.

The actual concession to build a railway was given by the sultan in 1899 to a German company. By the outbreak of the war in 1914, 1200 miles from Constantinople to Baghdad were completed. In 1901 the Germans began the construction of the railway from Damascus south to the Hejaz, to take pilgrims to Mecca. Everywhere the Germans seemed to be pushing southward. After 1890 German trade increased dramatically, and by 1910 it ranked just behind that of England and India.

The British felt secure south of Basra where they had agreements with the native rulers not to deal with foreign governments. In 1869 the first of these had been negotiated with the Trucial shaikhdoms. Similar agreements were made with Bahrain in 1880 and Muscat and Qatar in 1891. In 1898 the British used their influence to deny to the French a coaling station in Muscat. In 1899 the British and the Shaikh of Kuwait agreed to prevent other foreign influence there. So, when a visiting German ship arrived shortly thereafter in Kuwait, the shaikh did not receive its captain, and when in 1900 a commission arrived to survey Kuwait as a possible terminus for a railway, it was turned back.

The British interest could have been accomplished by holding the line at Kuwait except for two developments which drew the British deeper into Iraq. The first was the discovery of huge deposits of oil in Persia (Iran) to the east of Abadan in 1907. The increasing production from this field stimulated interest in possible fields in Iraq—who had not heard of the "fiery Furnace"?—on which the British secured a concession on the eve of the First World War. The conversion of the Royal Navy to oil-powered ships and the rapid development of Persian oil led the British government to purchase control of the oil company operating in Persia just six days prior to the outbreak of the war. So important was this to become that Curzon was to say that "the Allies floated to victory on a wave of oil."

The second development was the growth of a belief in Europe that "Babylonia" could become the farm of Europe and a residence for the surplus and hungry population of India. The English expert on irrigation Sir William Wilcocks wrote glowingly in 1910 of the possibilities of agriculture in the Tigris-Euphrates valley to meet the wheat and cotton requirements of England and India. A few years later he wrote that "the delta of the two rivers would attain a fertility of which history has no record." A popular book of the period was J. T. Parfit's *Mesopotamia: Key to the Future*. And a senior British official, reflecting on this Garden of Eden, wrote that "there is no doubt that the land is the richest in the world."

8

The First World War:
Midwife of Nationalism

THE years before the First World War were filled with contests between the European powers, principally Britain, France, and Germany, for concessions and points of influence, but this rivalry in the Middle East had little to do with the actual outbreak of the war. Until the eve of the war itself the Middle Eastern issues seemed on the road to accommodation, particularly in the new oil industry, through the development of international consortia. Indeed, the Anglo-German Turkish Petroleum Company received its concession in Iraq as late as June 28, 1914. Like the causes so most of the events of the war were acted in other theaters. Here, four aspects of the war are of lasting concern, however: the situation on the eve of the war; the course of the war in the two separate and contrasting Arab theaters, the Arabian Peninsula–Syrian area and Iraq; the wartime arrangements, promises, and declarations of the participants which have left such a strong imprint on subsequent history; and the immediate aftermath.

But first a word of caution. The First World War ended one era and began another. It began seventy years ago, yet even today a satisfying perspective is difficult to achieve, so embedded are the politics of our own times in the events of these years. And even if a clear and logical perspective is achieved, it will be profoundly unreal. A too-precise systematization of events and pronouncements results in a pattern which, though true in hindsight, distorts the context in which each decision was taken and each event occurred. In the midst of that vast and protracted crisis, the events were confused, the future obscure, and the actors imperfectly informed. It is, therefore, difficult and necessary to keep in mind but separate both the events and their subsequent implication.

It is now fashionable to inveigh against the Ottoman Empire as the corrupt, tyrannical, "sick man" of Europe, which lived by exploiting the sullen, resentful, and uniformly hostile non-Turkish population of Asia, and thwarted all progress in the East. The facts are otherwise. The government of the empire, with few resources in trained people or a developed economy, chronically insolvent, and hard pressed by foes and well-wishers alike, was able to control inexpensively a vast, heterogeneous area—a feat beyond the capacities of its richer successors—while retaining the *essential* loyalty of the several nations who were its subjects. The secret of its success was its toleration of *other* loyalties. To see what happened in the Arab areas, at least, it is useful to understand what these loyalties were and what they were not.

There was, first of all, no clear sense of territorial loyalty. The empire was divided into administrative districts, but these were in no sense nation-states and were not separated from one another by frontiers, linguistic barriers, or infrastructure patterns. Only Egypt, over which a British protectorate was declared in December 1914, had a discrete identity. There was no "Syria" or "Iraq" except in a geographic sense, as one might refer to an American Midwest or to the eastern seaboard. The "Syrian" moved easily to Baghdad, Mecca, or Cairo and felt no more alien than an American from Kansas City would in Los Angeles.

Such loyalties as transcended the family, clan, and tribe centered mainly on one's religious "nation" or millet, and this concept had no geographic expression. Members of the several Christian millets and of the Jewish millet were scattered all over the empire. The millet system did not divide Turks from Arabs and Kurds as most of each group were Muslims. And, by extension, the millet of the Muslims was the empire itself.

Dissatisfaction with this conception of a polyglot, multinational, universal empire had grown gradually except in the Balkans, where it was accelerated in the nineteenth century as the Greeks (from 1821–27), the Bulgarians (in 1879), the Rumanians (in 1881), and others won recognition of their distinct nationalities. But even in the Balkans nationalism was often equated with religion—the Bulgarians, for example, won recognition in 1870 for a separate national church to distinguish themselves from the Greeks.

It was the Armenians who brought into the heartland of the empire, Anatolia, the notion of nationalism in the new, ethnic sense in
the last years of the nineteenth century. This, in turn, stimulated the
Turkish element in the empire to probe its own historical legacy for
what came to be called Turkism. This new sense of particularism was
a part of the drive in the Young Turk revolution of 1908. As the
Young Turks assumed power they forced upon the empire their Turk-
ishness in a way never before attempted by an Ottoman government.
School systems throughout the empire began to teach in Turkish and
to emphasize the virtues of the Turks. This new exclusiveness of the
Turks compelled the Arabs to seek for themselves an identity which
was different from Ottoman and different from Muslim.

From about 1890 onward Egypt was the cultural center of the Arabic-speaking Middle East. There, of course, *the* national enemy was
the West as represented by Great Britain. Most Egyptians who sought
a means of defense against this enemy turned to Islam as represented
in part by the Ottoman sultan-caliph. Unaffected by the growth of
Turkism, since the British posed a barrier between the Ottoman Turkish suzerain and their administration and school system, the Egyptians followed a different drummer than did the literate, vigorous,
and modernizing Arabs of the Levant and Iraq, who were in contact
with the new Turkish administration.

What the Syrians and Iraqis found exciting was that in Beirut, particularly at the American University, a sort of literary revival of Arabic was in process. This literary revival had meager origins and was of
small influence. Much has been written to make it seem otherwise,
but the intellectual archaeology of nationalist writers makes rather
pitiful reading for the dispassionate foreigner.

Even the most friendly foreign observers have found little Arab nationalism before the advent of the Young Turks. However, the core of
such a movement was there and its elements were clear. The major
stimulus came from the ideas of Europe and America; religion was
excluded as a prime differential since the Turks were also Muslim
while many of the best Arab thinkers were Christian. It was to the
rich, pre-Islamic heritage of the Arabic language itself that these
Arabs turned for the basis of national identity.

In 1905 a young Syrian Christian Arab, who subsequently published a book in French called *Le Réveil de la Nation Arabe,* issued a
manifesto deploring the alien rule of the Arabs. "Encouraged by our
servility, the Turks pretend to preserve the remaining independent
tribes of the Arab nation. [But they plan to dominate all Arab lands]
where they wish to construct railways ... And what is even more degrading, they plan to do it with our money and our labor so that we

ourselves will forge the chains of our own servitude." But, although the author claimed to speak for a vast network of secret organizations throughout the Middle East, few were interested.

In the first blush of the excitement of the Young Turk revolution of 1908 the Arabs had cooperated and even formed "Ottoman Arab" organizations to participate. When the Young Turks suppressed this form of organization, the Arabs retreated first to "literary" societies and then to secret societies. These, though very small in number, attracted the younger, active, literate Arab element in the Ottoman civil and military service. But the Arabs had no spokesman. None among their group had a "national" reputation, and, of course, no one transcended the religious barrier which divided their community. An early manifesto reflects this problem: "Muslim Arabs, this despotic state is not Muslim. Christian and Jewish Arabs, unite with your Muslim brothers. Those who say that they prefer the Turks-without-faith to you are imposters and enemies of our race." Ultimately, however, it was a quasi-religious official of the empire, the sharif of Mecca, to whom the Arabs turned for leadership. But even if the young Arabs could have agreed among themselves on their ultimate objective, which they could not, they had little of any substance to offer the sharif, that cautious and skilled figure who had lived most of his sixty years under the close supervision of the sultan's police. It was not the Arabs but the British who tempted him to act on a grander stage.

We have seen how the impact of the West altered the traditional social relationships and created new aspirations in the more advanced parts of the Ottoman Empire. It would be a mistake, however, to exaggerate the size and influence of the groups who, on the eve of the First World War, had already been led to sedition by these changes. Nevertheless, some overtures to outside powers had been made. In 1913 a group of Arabs toured the European capitals to seek support for reforms in the empire, a tactic used by the Armenians before them, while another group visited Cairo to suggest that the British annex Syria. More important, Amir Abdullah, a son of the sharif of Mecca and a man whose name figures prominently in subsequent Arab history until his assassination in 1951, contacted Lord Kitchener in Cairo and laid the foundation of subsequent British-Arab negotiations.

These negotiations, and others with the French, led the Turks to warn their military governor in Syria, on the outbreak of the war, that "the news from Syria points to general disturbance in the country and great activity on the part of the revolutionary Arabs." This intelligence was confirmed when the Turks seized the papers of the French consulate in Damascus.

What distinguished this surge of resentment against the empire was the fact that the outbreak of a world war provided the opportunity for a revolt sparked by the growth of both Arab and Turkish national consciousness. Yet, it is notable that many Arabs continued to be loyal to the empire and to serve in its armed forces throughout the war.

The outbreak of the war in Europe in August 1914 was not immediately followed by war in the Middle East. It was not until November 5 that Great Britain and France declared war on Turkey. Great Britain then annexed Cyprus and on December 18, after nearly deciding on annexation, proclaimed a protectorate over Egypt. But in October, before the declaration of war, British troops and ships from India had sailed into the confluence of the Tigris and Euphrates rivers. In return for aid given by the shaikh of Kuwait, Great Britain recognized its independence under British protection on November 3. On November 6, the Anglo-Indian force seized the town of Fao in what is now Iraq.

The British and French governments were profoundly worried at that time about the effect on the large Muslim populations in India and North Africa of the proclamation of a holy war by the sultan-caliph of the Ottoman Empire. Pan-Islam was then credited by Europeans with great popular appeal and the dangers of a massive Muslim revolt, in the midst of the war, were never far from the minds of the British policy planners. On November 14 the sultan-caliph did, in fact, issue a call to holy war but the sharif of Mecca, who should have joined in the appeal, kept his silence. The British now hoped that the sharif could be persuaded to espouse the Allied cause, which would at least mitigate the threat of a Muslim revolt. This was the basic aim behind the correspondence between the British government on the one hand and on the other the sharif of Mecca, the so-called Husain-McMahon Correspondence, which set the terms upon which some of the Arabs entered the war on the Allied side.

It is important to remember that the First World War was a hard and bitter contest, fought over vast distances by huge armies from many nations, and that the issue was in doubt until almost the very end. The battle plans for Europe had been conceived in great detail years before the war, but the fighting brought a revolution in military tactics. Early in the war the British considered making the Middle East a major front, to attempt to bring the Balkan states into the war on the Allied side. Had this been done, not only Middle Eastern history but also the course of Russian history might have been pro-foundly changed. In a sort of compromise, in April 1915, a British in-vasion force landed at Gallipoli, but the Turks held firm. Russia re-mained effectively cut off from Allied assistance. It seems possible, from what is now known, that had this force landed on the Syrian coast, a native uprising might have assisted it to bring the war in the East to a more speedy close. The Turkish military governor, who should have known, later wrote that after finding in the French con-sular records evidence of Arab plans to revolt he had quickly shifted the local Arab units in the Turkish army away from Syria. He was, he said, "certain that to the executions [of Arabs suspected of nationalist sedition in 1915 and 1916] alone do we owe the fact that there was no rising in Syria."

In the history of what was rather than what might have been, Syria did not revolt and the Turkish armies on all fronts fought deter-minedly and bravely. In February 1915 a Turkish force reached the Suez Canal and in the same month pro-Turkish tribesmen in western Iran cut the oil pipeline from the fields to the port; the threat thus posed at both ends of the British holdings in the Middle East required the British to garrison large armed forces in the Middle East throughout the war. In August 1915 the British army in southern Iraq attempted to push northward, to capture Baghdad, and so to relieve the pressure on the oil fields. Just south of Baghdad, however, they ran into a strong Turkish force which turned them back with heavy losses and ran them to ground in the town of Kut in December. There, after a siege of four months, in which the attempts to relieve the besieged garrison cost the British over 7000 casualties, the 13,309 men of the garrison surrendered. It was not until March 1917, after a bitter struggle in which 40 percent of the 40,000 attacking British and Indian soldiers were casualties, that Baghdad was taken. On the Egyptian front, likewise, the fighting was hard. The British would not agree to American suggestions to urge the Turks to make an honor-able peace. It was December 1917 before the British took Jerusalem and October 1918 when they took Damascus.

Of course, at the beginning of the war the British could not have known how hard-fought it would be, but prudence alone would have encouraged them to seek all the local support they could muster. And thus it was that on October 31, 1914, the British government offered Sharif Husain of Mecca a conditional guarantee of independence.

As a result of these factors—probable Turkish might, supposed Muslim restiveness, and actual Russian hunger—the Allies, led by Britain, entered into a series of agreements of a "tactical" nature to contribute to victory. Within two years Britain had made three major (and several lesser) commitments or proclamations of intent. To one of these the Arab allies were to rally as the fount of their rights in the Middle East. To another Zionists pinned their hopes; and on yet a third the French based their claims to realize their traditional desires for a French enclave in the Levant.

First in point of time came the letters exchanged between the Arab Sharif Husain of Mecca, who was than an official in the Ottoman administration, and the British high commissioner of Egypt, Sir Henry McMahon. This is the Husain-McMahon Correspondence, which contains the terms upon which the Arabs revolted and entered the war on the Allied side.

In the first letter in the series of eight, dated July 14, 1915, Sharif Husain demanded British recognition of the independence of the Arab provinces in an area now divided between Syria, Iraq, Jordan, Israel, Saudi Arabia, and a part of Turkey. These demands were countered in a letter from McMahon, dated October 24, 1915, which excluded as not "purely Arab" the districts of Mersin and Alexandretta and portions of Syria lying to the west of the districts of Damascus, Homs, Hama, and Aleppo. The British also reserved their position, established by treaty, with other Arab chiefs and in Basra and Baghdad. Further restrictions were made in the series of letters to protect the interests of France. The last letter was dated January 30, 1916, and the Arab Revolt began on June 5, 1916.

The Husain-McMahon Correspondence has been the object of detailed and searching criticism. The letters were not officially published until 1939, when a special Anglo-Arab committee was set up to evaluate their importance to Palestine. The existence of the exchange was known, however, and the terms had been printed in part in 1919, in the Paris newspaper *Le Temps;* but, in spite of the subsequent urging of Earl Grey, who was Foreign Minister during this period, the British government refused for twenty strife-torn years to publish the full text.

At the close of war a dispute arose over the phrase excluding from the area promised to the Arabs the land to the west of the "districts" (*wilayat;* the Arabic plural) of Aleppo, Hama, Homs, and Damascus. The later British contention was that *wilayat* meant here both "town" in the cases of Aleppo, Hama, and Homs and the Turkish administrative district known as a vilayet in the case of Damascus. If the word means the same in all four instances, then it must mean only town or township, since the towns of Hama and Homs were in the same vilayet and only the sea is to the west of the vilayet of Aleppo. West of the district of Damascus is Mount Lebanon. If by the *wilayah* (the Arabic singular) of Damascus was meant the whole of the vilayet of Syria, then excluded from the Arab area was the whole Levant coast including Palestine. Summing up the British government opinion in 1939, the Lord Chancellor said he had

> been impressed by some of the arguments brought forward in regard to the exclusion of Palestine under the phrase "portions of Syria lying to the west of the districts of Damascus, Homs, Hama and Aleppo." He considers that the Arab point of view as regards this aspect of the question has been shown to have greater force than has appeared hitherto, although he does not agree that it is impossible to regard Palestine as covered by the phrase.

The vilayet of Baghdad was, likewise, left until the end of the war for disposition. Distinct from the British pledge were agreements with other Arab chiefs. These included Kuwait, the Idrisi Sayyid of Sabya in Asir and the Amir Ibn Saud of Riyadh, who later founded the Kingdom of Saudi Arabia.

At the same time, in Europe, negotiations were begun with France to clarify postwar aims. These were spelled out in an agreement, known for its drafters as the Sykes-Picot Agreement, in which parts of the Middle East here under consideration were divided into five parts: (1) the Levant Coast which the French claimed; (2) the Syrian hinterland which the French would assist (the word used is *soutenir*); (3) a zone in Palestine which would be internationalized; (4) British-protected Arab areas of Transjordan and much of Iraq; and (5) British-controlled areas of Baghdad and Basra.

The Arabs had heard of the agreement by way of diplomatic hints before, but it was not until the Bolshevik government published the Russian Foreign Office Archives late in 1917 that the Arabs knew the full extent of the agreements. This information was obligingly passed by the German General Staff to the Turks, who relayed it, with an offer of a separate peace, to Husain. To his credit, Husain turned the message over to his British ally with a request for an explanation. In reply the British informed him that the Sykes-Picot Agreement was merely a series of exchanges of views which in any case no longer represented the situation because of the Russian withdrawal from the war. It was, however, put into effect at the end of the war in Syria.

The second, and much more important, European undertaking was the Balfour Declaration of November 2, 1917. During the subsequent thirty years this was to the Zionists what the Husain-McMahon Correspondence was to the Arabs: the final rallying point in the struggle for supremacy over British policy on Palestine. The declaration is disarmingly simple and delicately balanced in phraseology; is

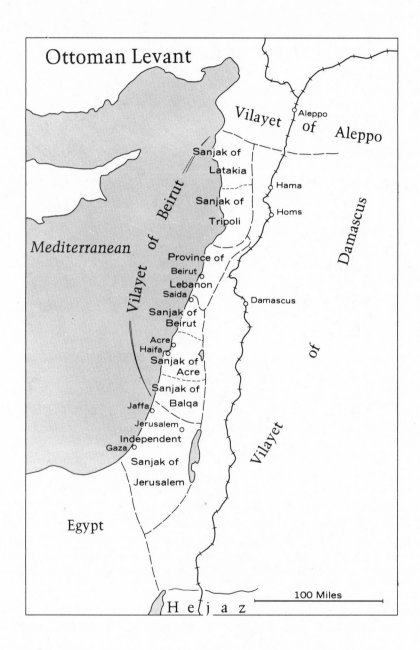

Ottoman Levant

Vilayet of Aleppo

Aleppo

Damascus

Sanjak of Latakia

Hama

Sanjak of Tripoli

Homs

Mediterranean

Vilayet of Beirut

Province of Beirut

Beirut

Lebanon

Saida

Damascus

Sanjak of Beirut

Acre

Haifa

Sanjak of Acre

of

Sanjak of Balqa

Jaffa

Vilayet

Jerusalem

Independent

Gaza

Sanjak of

Jerusalem

Egypt

100 Miles

H e j a z

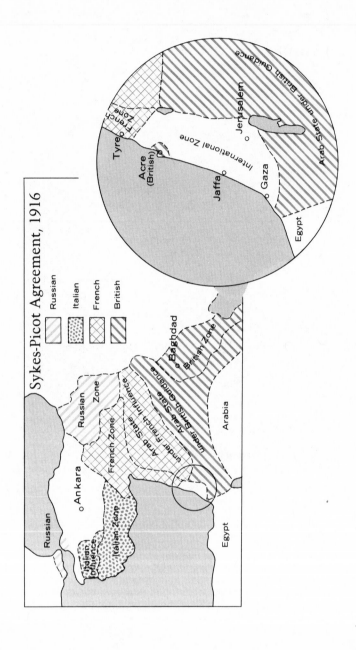

Sykes-Picot Agreement, 1916

Russian

Italian

French

British

described as an "expression of sympathy"; and is only sixty-eight words long. Yet, it was the result of months of discussion in the British cabinet and was carefully and deliberately constructed to thread the thinnest rail on the fence of political indecision. Like the pledges to the Arabs, it must be seen in context.

The key figure among the group of advocates of Zionism in England, Chaim Weizmann, supported by the Secretary of the War Cabinet on Middle Eastern Affairs, Mark Sykes, and others, made a concerted effort to convince the government of the value to Britain of a pro-Zionist declaration. Their efforts could not have come at a more favorable moment. In the first place, European Jewry was naturally suspicious of the Entente, for the same reason that the Turks were hostile to it: tsarist Russia was a member. To the Turks, Russia was the aggressor par excellence; and to the Jews, it was the land of the pogrom. Russian oppression had displaced many East European Jews—including Weizmann himself—and sent them into the West, where some had reached positions of influence. Thus, to a considerable extent Great Britain and France labored under the bad reputation of their ally. Germany, on the other hand, then had perhaps the best record in Europe of treatment of the Jews. There Jews found not mere toleration but acceptance. Many Jews had achieved national prominence, and the Jewish community as a whole was more assimilated than in almost any other European country. Germany had not yet had her pogroms or even her equivalent of the Dreyfus case. When World War I broke out, the Zionist Organization declared itself neutral but retained an office in Germany.

The Russian Revolution somewhat reversed the situation in Russia by bringing a number of Jews into key positions. The strong sentiment in Russia for leaving the war was an important element in the Revolution, and both the British Foreign Office and the German General Staff thought that Jews in Russia were leaders of this move. To encourage this feeling and to win over those who wavered, the Germans put pressure on their Turkish ally to grant concessions to Jews wanting to colonize Palestine. Turkey delayed, perhaps fearing to antagonize those Arabs who had remained on her side in the war, but eventually, as her armies were being pushed out of Palestine, granted the Zionists a concession there similar to the Balfour Declaration.

At the time the Germans were making a determined effort to win Jewish support, Britain was worried both about keeping Russia in the war and about American neutrality. In both cases British statesmen came to the conclusion that Jewish support could greatly aid British policy. As early as March 1916 Lord Grey had suggested to the Russian and French governments the utility of a pro-Zionist arrangement on Palestine to "bring over to our side the Jewish forces in America, the East and elsewhere which are now largely, if not preponderately, hostile to us." Mark Sykes was alarmed by the American position and thought pro-German Jews to be the cause. And Prime Minister Lloyd George noted that "their [the Jews'] aid in this respect [financial affairs] would have a special value when the Allies had almost exhausted the gold and marketable securities available for American purchases." Consequently, Lord Robert Cecil encouraged the English Zionists to request a British-Jewish Palestine. It thus would appear likely that the Balfour Declaration is rightly to be regarded as a declaration *through* rather than *to* English Jews, many of whom were opposed to Zionism. The real audiences were in Russia, Germany, and America. To inform them of the Balfour Declaration millions of leaflets were dropped by air, circulated by land, and printed in the press.

A leaflet in Yiddish was spread among German and Austrian troops proclaiming that "Jerusalem has fallen! The hour of Jewish redemption has arrived . . . Palestine must be the national home of the Jewish people once more . . . The Allies are giving the Land of Israel to the people of Israel. Every local Jewish heart is now filled with joy for this great victory. Will you join them and help to build a Jewish homeland in Palestine? . . . Stop fighting the Allies, who are fighting for you, for all Jews, for the freedom of all the small nations. Remember! An Allied victory means the Jewish people's return to Zion . . ."* In the Middle East, however, the declaration was withheld by military censorship until May 1, 1919, when it was read in Nablus, Palestine, by Allenby's successor.

The Declaration reads as follows:

> I [Balfour] have much pleasure in conveying to you [Lord Rothschild] on behalf of His Majesty's Government the following declaration of sympathy with Jewish Zionist aspirations, which has been submitted to and approved by the Cabinet:
>
> "His Majesty's Government view with favour the establishment in Palestine of a National Home for the Jewish People, and will use their best endeavors to facilitate the achievement of this object, it being clearly understood that nothing shall be done which may prejudice the civil and religious rights of existing non-Jewish communities in Palestine, or the rights and political status enjoyed by Jews in any other country."
>
> I should be grateful if you would bring this declaration to the knowledge of the Zionist Federation.

* Text in Doreen Ingrams, *Palestine Papers, 1917–1922* (London, 1972), p. 19.

In this form the declaration was approved, before issue, by President Wilson and subsequently was endorsed by the French and Italian governments. It was reaffirmed at the San Remo Conference in 1920, was written into the Mandate instrument for Palestine and so passed by the Council of the League of Nations, was unanimously passed by both Houses of the American Congress, and was approved by the Vatican. In 1922 the British Colonial Office declared it to be the basis of policy in Palestine and as such "not susceptible to change."

It was to prove a most difficult sentence to divide by a comma.

Among the less famous Allied commitments are the following. 1) The proclamation of General Maude (also written by Sir Mark Sykes) upon the capture of Baghdad, in which the British government set out its aim in grand but imprecise phrases, "that the Arab race may rise once more to greatness and renown amongst the peoples of the earth and that it shall bind itself to this end in unity and concord ... Therefore, I am commanded to invite you, through your Nobles and Elders and Representatives, to participate in the management of your civil affairs in collaboration with the Political Representatives of Great Britain who accompany the British Army so that you may unite with your kinsmen in the North, East, South and West in realizing the aspirations of your race."

2) In January 1918 the British government ordered Commander Hogarth to deliver a message to Sharif (then King) Husain which stated that "The Entente Powers are determined that the Arab race shall be given full opportunity of once again forming a nation in the world. This can only be achieved by the Arabs themselves uniting, and Great Britain and her Allies will pursue a policy with this ultimate unity in view." Continuing, the message embodied some of the language of the Balfour Declaration and urged the Arabs to consider that "the friendship of world Jewry to the Arab cause is equivalent to support in all States where Jews have a political influence. The leaders of the movement are determined to bring about the success of Zionism by friendship and cooperation with the Arabs, and such an offer is not one to be lightly thrown aside."

3) The June 1918 "Declaration to the Seven" was a statement on British policy addressed to seven Syrian Arab leaders then living in Cairo. It affirmed that British policy was to "recognize the complete and sovereign independence of the Arabs" inhabiting areas free before the war and those liberated by Arabs during the war "and support them in their struggle for freedom." In regard to areas liberated by the Allies, the declaration reaffirmed the proclamations issued at Baghdad and Jerusalem by the occupying armies which stated that

"It is the wish and desire of His Majesty's Government that the future government of these regions should be based on the principle of the consent of the governed and this policy has and will continue to have the support of His Majesty's Government."

4) Sir Edmund (later Field Marshal Lord) Allenby officially assured Amir Faisal, the Arab leader in Syria, that all military government arrangements were provisional and would not prejudice a final settlement. "I reminded the Amir Faisal that the Allies were in honour bound to endeavour to reach a settlement in accordance with the wishes of the peoples concerned and urged him to place his trust whole-heartedly in their good faith."

5) A joint Anglo-French Declaration of November 7, 1918, affirmed a policy for "the establishment of national governments and administrations deriving their authority from the initiative and free choice of the indigenous populations . . . Far from wishing to impose on the populations of these regions any particular institutions they are only concerned to ensure by their support and by adequate assistance the regular working of Governments and administrations freely chosen by the populations themselves."

These pronouncements were, with official encouragement, given extremely wide distribution in the press and on handbills. It seems highly probable in retrospect that without this official encouragement the population would have settled for far less, but with encouragement their aspirations soared.

Balfour, in a confidential memorandum to the Foreign Office, wrote on August 11, 1919:

> France, England, and America have got themselves into a position over the Syrian problem so inextricably confused that no really neat and satisfactory issue is now possible for any of them.
>
> The situation is affected by five documents . . . Each can be quoted by Frenchmen and Englishmen, Americans and Arabs when it happens to suit their purpose. Doubtless each will be so quoted before we come to a final arrangement about the Middle East.
>
> . . . The four Great Powers are committed to Zionism. And Zionism, be it right or wrong, good or bad, is rooted in age-long traditions, in present needs, in future hopes, of far profounder import than the desires and prejudices of the 700,000 Arabs who now inhabit that ancient land . . . Whatever deference should be paid to the views of those who live there, the Powers in their selection of a mandatory do not propose, as I understood the matter, to consult them. In short, so far as Palestine is concerned, the Powers have made no statement of fact which is not admittedly wrong, and no declaration of policy which, at least in letter, they have not always intended to violate.

It is easy to exaggerate the part played by the Arabs in the war. The glittering romance of Lawrence of Arabia is far more real to most people—both Arab and non-Arab—than is the murky reality of the war. *If* the Allies had landed at a Levant port instead of Gallipoli, the Arabs of Syria *might* have risen in revolt. But the British did not. As a result the Syrians suffered through the war in hunger and disease but did little to win their freedom.

In the desert the Amir Faisal's Arab army did isolate Yemen, capture most of Arabia, and harass the Turkish supply lines in what is now Saudi Arabia, Jordan, and Syria. By British consent they captured Damascus. (This was in accord with General Allenby's interpretation of the Sykes-Picot and Husain-McMahon agreements.) But probably the most important contribution made by the Arabs was as Muslims in deflecting the threat of a religiously inspired insurrection against the Allies on the part of their huge Muslim colonial populations.

When the war ended, there was a profound contrast between British-occupied Iraq, where the population was hostile and still quite pro-Turkish or at least anti-Western; Syria, where an Arab government had been installed at least nominally by Arab arms; and Palestine and Lebanon, where foreign armies of occupation were greeted as liberators by the inhabitants.

In the East the war came to an end with the Armistice of Mudros on October 30, 1918. Subsequently, however, the British forced the Turks to evacuate Mosul, in north Iraq, which they still held. The armistice was ultimately formalized in the Treaty of Lausanne which was signed on July 24, 1923.

The war in the East had been costly. Typhus, smallpox, and starvation had taken a heavy toll in the areas long under blockade. The British had committed almost 1.5 million men and had spent about £750 million (of which £6 million were used to subsidize the Arab Revolt). The French had relatively little part in the war in the East but had, of course, borne the brunt of the war in Europe and, at the end, demanded that their rights under the Sykes-Picot Agreement be honored on this basis. The British were not eager and the Arabs were strongly opposed, but it was a French naval unit which occupied Beirut and its hinterland.

In Iraq, little of value could be drawn from Ottoman precedent for the empire had vanished, records were packed and taken away, and the administrative personnel was gone forever. Necessity was the mother of the new government. The job of supporting an army makes harsh and immediate demands. Shortage of shipping space made it imperative to grow produce, especially cereals, locally. India, then facing another famine, could feed its army in Iraq only with the greatest difficulty, and every ton of shipping space that could be saved was vital. So the occupation force was immediately faced with nonmilitary demands in a situation in which it had the assistance of neither local personnel nor guides. If necessity was the mother, India was the father. Since the British forces came from India, it was not only natural but inevitable that British India would become the exemplar of Iraq. Large numbers of Indian laborers and clerks from the civil service and soldiers from the army were brought into Iraq. Moreover, the officers of the army and civil service were either directly trained in the Indian service or inspired by men who were. Many of these made distinguished careers for themselves and played a key role in the events over the next two generations.

In Egypt the war had brought prosperity and, at last, independence from the Ottoman Empire in name as well as in fact. Egypt became the farm for vast armies in Europe and the Middle East, and the peasants grew rich. But the political life of the country was stifled by a powerful and determined military government which, with a war to be won, could not be bothered with immature nationalism. What had been intended to be a request for volunteer help ended as confiscation and enforced labor. Thus, the Egyptians came out of the war, as did many new nations, embittered and determined to achieve independence.

So it was that a former protégé of Lord Cromer, Saad Zaghlul, approached the British Residency, the seat of power, on November 13, 1918, at the head of a delegation (Arabic: *wafd*) to demand the right to petition for freedom in London and Paris. When he was refused, Zaghlul organized committees throughout Egypt, circulating petitions calling for an end to British rule. These committees grew into the Wafd party. This was in violation of martial law, and the British authorities, who always held a low opinion of Egyptian will and daring, warned Zaghlul to stop his activities. When he refused, he was deported to Malta on April 7, 1919.

Few then realized the strength of the nationalist movement or the bitterness which years of wartime suppression and social contempt had engendered in the Egyptians. On the day after Zaghlul's arrest Egyptian students, in the first of their forays into the streets of violence, began what was to become a full-scale national rebellion.

In Syria the war had ended on strident notes of national liberation but muted voices of national organization. Everyone was restive with new aspirations, but among the Arabs there were few with the so-

phistication to move to the grand stage of Europe where the future
was being decided.

Amir Faisal, who had led the Arab Revolt, was then thirty-five
years old but quite inexperienced in international politics. He knew
his limitations but thought he had some hope, as he put it himself,
with Zionist money, connections, and *savoir-faire.* It was immediately
evident that the Zionists had these. The Zionist Organization had secured the appointment of a pro-Zionist as the chief political officer in
the Arab area, had the support of Lord Balfour and other senior British officials, and had a powerful American delegation, close to President Wilson, led by Justice Louis Brandeis. During Faisal's visit the
British officer closest to him, Colonel Cornwallis, reported, "I understand that Dr. Weizmann, in return for the Emir's help in Palestine
towards realization of Zionist aspirations, proposes to give money and
advisers, if required, to the Arab Government and claims that the
Zionists can persuade the French Government to waive their claims
of influence in the interior." At a dinner given by Lord Rothschild,
Faisal himself was reported to have said to a Jewish audience:

> Dr. Weizmann's ideals are ours, and we will expect you, without our
> asking to help us in return. No state can be built up in the Near East
> without the goodwill of the Great Powers, but it requires more than
> that. It requires the borrowing from Europe of ideals and materials and
> knowledge and experience. To make these fit for us, we must translate
> them from European shape to Arab shape—and what intermediary
> could we find in the world more suitable than you? For you have all the
> knowledge of Europe and are cousins by blood.

It is clear that at this period Faisal was far more worried about
French intervention in the Levant than he was about any possible future clash with Zionism. France had laid claim to most of the Levant
coast. Faisal realized before he left the Middle East, that even if the
French chose not to push into the interior their geographical position
would give them a stranglehold on the Arab state. The British Foreign Office seemed to want to set aside the Sykes-Picot Agreement, on
which France's claims rested, but seemed equally firm on insisting
that the Balfour Declaration must stand. Faisal realized, as few Arabs
have since, that in these circumstances politics is indeed the science of
the possible. So he came to a provisional agreement with Dr. Weizmann. The agreement was written up as a formal document in eleven
articles. In brief, the two recognized the need to work together to
achieve mutual aims, to give effect to the Balfour Declaration, to facilitate Jewish immigration provided the rights of the Arab peasant

and tenant farmers be protected, to ensure freedom of worship and protection of the Holy Places, to provide Jewish economic help to the Arabs, and to constitute the British government as their arbiter. To this agreement Faisal appended in Arabic, above his signature, the following condition: "Provided the Arabs obtained their independence as demanded in my Memorandum dated the 4th of January, 1919, to the Foreign Office of the Government of Great Britain, I shall concur in the above article. But if the slightest modification or departure were to be made I shall not then be bound by a single word of the present Agreement which shall be deemed void and of no account or validity, and I shall not be answerable in any way whatsoever."

Faisal realized that the local population of Palestine strongly opposed the creation of a Jewish state, but he thought he could act on his own, compromising as necessary in order to save his state from the French. Like other figures at the Peace Conference, Faisal lost touch with the mood of his countrymen. In Palestine itself, the visit of the first Zionist commission had roused the strongest antagonism and fears in the population. The British political officer in Jerusalem warned in August 1919 that "if we mean to carry out any sort of Zionist policy we must do so with military force."

Faisal was not alone in being confused as to the desires of the population. The Middle East was far away from Western Europe and America, unknown save as the Bible Land to all but a few, and even that small band violently disagreed. The American and British delegations were in favor of an international commission to ascertain the wishes of the natives, in the spirit of the various wartime statements on self-determination issued in the names of all the Allied governments. The French were opposed to a commission unless it were understood, as the senior French representative in the Levant put it, that its purpose was "to keep Faisal in the dark while partition of Syria is being arranged." British forces then held the north of Iraq and Palestine, large parts of which areas had been promised to the French under the wartime Sykes-Picot Agreement. At the Paris Peace Conference, France demanded that the commitment be honored, but the British, aware of the need to control the north of Iraq to make the Iraqi state viable and of the need for more territory than the area around the port of Acre-Haifa to honor the Balfour Declaration, refused to go by the letter of the Sykes-Picot Agreement. After a serious diplomatic crisis between the two countries, the issue was resolved in September 1919 by Prime Minister Lloyd George and Premier Clemenceau. It was agreed that Mosul should be given to Iraq, Palestine should come under British control, the British should withdraw from

Syria, which would come under French control, and France should share in the exploitation of Middle Eastern oil.

French accusations that the British were trying to make it impossible for the French to enter Syria embarrassed the British and caused them to give up urging the appointment of an investigating commission. But President Wilson unilaterally appointed his own, the King-Crane Commission. It visited the Middle East in the summer of 1919 but its report was probably never read by President Wilson and was not published for nearly four years. The report was, however, reproduced in British diplomatic reports. Essentially, the King-Crane Commission found that the population of Syria was strongly opposed to a French mandate, wanted, above all, independence and unity, but would settle for an American or British mandate. Its methods of gathering impressions have often been criticized (mainly by those who were unhappy at the results) but its findings are borne out by investigations of all the experienced British political officers then resident in the Middle East.

Meanwhile, Faisal's popularity was slipping badly in Syria. He had made no progress in keeping out the French, who were massing forces on the Levant coast, and he had been reported to have virtually given away Palestine to the Zionists. His understanding with the Zionists was in the words of the political officer in Jerusalem, "a noose about Faisal's neck . . . he is in favour with [the Arabs only] so long as he embodies Arab nationalism and represents their views." Indeed, the Arab congress at Damascus did repudiate the substance of his agreement with Weizmann.

When he returned to London in September, Faisal informed the Zionists that he could agree only to limited immigration and that he had intended that the Jewish homeland be thought of as a province of the larger Arab state. "I quite understand," he said, "the desire of Jews to acquire a country, a homeland. But so far as Palestine is concerned . . . it must be subject to the right and aspirations of the sentiments of the present possessors of the land." Jewish rights he brushed aside as the sort which would give the Arabs a right to take over Spain, which they had ruled for as long as the Jews had Palestine.

Another trip to Europe was equally fruitless. The French were determined to extract their pound of Syrian flesh and the British bluntly informed Faisal that he must go to Paris and make his terms. As Lord Balfour later told the chief political officer, "We had not been honest with either French or Arab, but it was now preferable to quarrel with the Arab rather than the French, if there was to be a quarrel at all." British troops gradually pulled out of Syria and Lebanon, turning over their positions to the French on the coast and to the

Arabs in the interior; the British monthly subsidy of £150,000 (upon which Faisal's state depended) was halved ostensibly on the basis that the French would then begin to contribute £75,000. Faisal, meanwhile, was not allowed to build up his army or police force and received no new equipment; his own position was by then so compromised that in the north of Syria a strong movement was begun to recreate the Ottoman Empire and the army passed into the control of Arab officers whose sympathies and service had been on the Ottoman side during the war.

At the eleventh hour Faisal recognized that there was no future in his course of moderation. Since he could expect nothing but sympathy from the British and obviously nothing from the Americans who, due to the illness of President Wilson, had virtually dropped out of the Peace Conference, Faisal threw himself into the ranks of the nationalists. He completely repudiated his understanding with the Zionists—which had always been conditional upon the granting of Syrian independence—and in March 1920 had himself proclaimed King of Syria and Palestine by the Arab congress at Damascus; he was not recognized as such either by the French or the British. The San Remo Conference in April awarded a mandate over Syria to France. The French army at this time had concentrated some 90,000 troops on the coast. A minor incident in July led to a French ultimatum that the mandate be accepted, the outbreak of hostilities, an invasion of Syria by the French, and the overthrow of the Arab government. The seeds were sown for a harvest of hatred of the French which was to be reaped yearly for a quarter of a century.

PART 4

Development of the Arab States

9

The Mandates: Iraq, Syria, Lebanon, and Transjordan

EITHER in Lebanon, which benefited from French protection and favor, nor in Transjordan, whose primarily nomadic population was loosely governed, was much opposition initially expressed to the mandates. Both in Iraq and Syria the mandate period began badly. In both, significant portions of the population regarded the mandates, as did many European statesmen, as "a substitute for old imperialism."

In Syria the tone of the whole mandate period was set in the initial contacts between the French and the Arabs. As we have seen, Amir Faisal, as head of a state, had participated in some phases of the Paris Peace Conference, had negotiated with the British and French governments, had accepted the title of king from the General Syrian Congress on March 7, 1920, and was in control of the government in Damascus. The French, at the same time, were in control in Lebanon and had gradually built up strong military forces there. After their long, frustrating, and bitter contest with the British at the Paris Peace Conference, at Sèvres, and at San Remo over the division of spoils in the Middle East, the French were not prepared to be stopped by a motley crowd of semi-savages, as they regarded the Arabs, and on July 14, 1920, issued an ultimatum to Faisal. Among the demands listed were reduction of the Syrian army, acceptance of the French mandate, punishment of those who had opposed France, acceptance of the French-controlled currency, permission to station French garrisons in most Syrian cities and important towns, and prior acceptance of other, then undisclosed, demands which the French might make later. Three days were allowed for compliance.

Recognizing his inability to resist, Faisal tried to temporize but finally on July 20 agreed to submit. At this point Arab mobs attacked the government and demanded that it fight for national independence. Whether for this reason or others, the telegram of capitulation from the Syrian government to the French high commissioner General Gouraud took seven hours to reach Lebanon. When it arrived the French troops had already marched. To the Arab negotiator who tried to get the invasion stopped, the French set forth a new schedule of demands. Clearly, the French were intent upon a definitive assumption of power, unhampered by any conditions or restraints. On July 24, after a skirmish at Maisalun, the French moved toward Damascus whose occupation they completed on July 25. Faisal tried to compromise, even at that point, but was rebuffed and on July 29 went into exile in the British zone of what is now Jordan.

Meeting much hostility in the interior of Syria, primarily from the Muslim Syrians, the French acted to create for themselves a more pro-French and more powerful Lebanon. On August 31 General Gouraud issued a proclamation which recast the frontiers of "Greater Lebanon" so that it became about four times as large as the Lebanon which had existed prior to World War I. Though this move made some of the Lebanese more pro-French, it accentuated the divisions both between the religious groups in Lebanon and between Christian Lebanon and Muslim Syria, divisions which underlay the 1958 Lebanese civil war and which even today are the source of bitterness. In the short run the French policy appeared successful, but, ironically, the inclusion of large areas wherein the population was predominantly Muslim has made Lebanon less secure as a Christian state.

The rest of Syria was dismembered also. The coastal area north of Lebanon, centering on the port of Latakia, was split off and put under a separate administration and even, in 1922, temporarily made a separate state. Alexandretta, on October 20, 1921, was separated and put under a special administration which eventually resulted in its incorporation in Turkey. Jabal ad-Druze, south of Damascus, was made autonomous under the mandate. Finally, Aleppo and Damascus were separated with each as capital of an autonomous area. From an administrative point of view these attempts to divide and control local opposition were so expensive that within a year the French rejoined three of the areas in a federation.

Throughout the French mandate period, although one administrative division after another was tried, the threat of violence was never far behind the outward face of events. Damascus, invaded in 1920, was bombarded in 1925, 1926, and 1945, and martial law was enforced periodically until the very end of the mandate. Constitutions were tried and suspended and independence was proclaimed or promised time after time until finally gained in 1945. Divisions between religious groups and districts were certainly not created by French policy, but were as certainly magnified by it. It would be fair to categorize the mandate period as less a school in government than one in administration wherein tendencies toward unrest, rather than being corrected by political means, were temporarily restrained but ultimately increased in violence. The bitter harvest is still being reaped.

In Iraq the situation was quite different. As we have seen, between November 22, 1914, and October 30, 1918, the British were in the process of capturing Iraq from the Turks. During this period they were forced to lay the base for what became the state they helped to create. Efficient military government was necessary to the conduct of war: lack of sufficient shipping space required the maximum amount of local production, especially of cereals, and the maintenance of forces required the construction and management of such facilities as ports and railroads. Above all, public security had to be established and maintained. Half a government was clearly impossible. Moreover, the British, unlike the French in their subsequent efforts in Syria, had a workable model in the Indian empire. Cadres of men familiar with problems of public security on the Northwest Frontier and in the Persian Gulf were imported into Iraq to handle analogous problems. In the caliber of these men is one of the most striking contrasts to the French in Syria. Included in the British forces were many of the Englishmen who, for a generation, dominated Western writings on the Arabs and who became legends in their own rights. But having said this, one must also say that their overt paternal system could not and did not work.

Sir Arnold Wilson was the very personification of the government of Iraq. Highly intelligent, well educated—his two-volume memories of his difficult years in Iraq is a model of its genre—strongly principled, inspiring, and personally liberal, he was an authority on the Persian Gulf area. Under his control the government was honest, efficient, and paternal. His aim was order and economy. He tended to divide the country into three groups: the bedouin and the Kurds, who composed the first, were the noble savages; the second, the peasantry, were pitiful and in desperate need of succor; but the third, the urban literati—the "town Arabs"—were deceitful, dangerous, pompous, inept, and best kept out of all affairs. If let into government, the town Arabs would only strip the bedouin of his nobility and would complete the ruin of the peasant. Neither the peasant nor the bedouin could rule; so the British must. Any other view was simply naïve and irresponsible.

Naïve and dangerous was Sir Arnold's description of the "romantic" policies which had flowed from President Wilson's declarations on self-determination and from the British promises to the Arabs. Without these Britain and France could rationally have carved out spheres of interest, and Britain's share would have been of great value to its empire in India. Wilson's bête noire was Colonel T. E. Lawrence, a flamboyant newcomer to the area who had captured the public imagination and the ear of senior British officials in London. But it was not Lawrence so much as a tired and nearly bankrupt England on which the plan for a greater Indian empire went aground.

Lacking the force to garrison the whole of Iraq while they also fought the determined and brave Turks, the British tried to create order in the countryside by "promoting" the shaikhs of clans or sections of tribes, the largest *effective* units of tribal life, to paramount status, making them responsible to the government for public order. To keep an eye on the shaikhs and their tribesmen, political officers with small detachments of locally levied police forces were stationed throughout the country. Since communications were often unreliable and always slow, the political officer relied largely upon his personal daring and bluff to maintain his authority.

Announcement in Iraq, at the end of the war, that Britain intended to assume the mandate for Iraq led to widespread popular discontent. Pro-Ottoman sentiment was not dead, and the Syrian government had dispatched a small group of nationalists who, calling themselves the Northern Iraq Army, had tried to capture Mosul in May 1920. Agitation against the government, particularly because of its measures of taxation and its friends among the new tribal paramount chiefs, increased during the summer. Finally, on June 30, a minor incident set off the great tribal rising which spread all over southern Iraq. As railroads were cut and trains derailed, the scattered and partly immobile British force was unable to act promptly to relieve the outlying detachments. For a while, indeed, only the area immediately surrounding Baghdad was secure. Not until mid-October, after the loss of 1654 British men, the expenditure of £40 million—or more than six times the total given to the Arab Revolt in the First World War—and the infuriation of the war-weary and impoverished English government, was order restored.

In a letter to the London Sunday *Times* in August 1920, T. E. Lawrence stung Wilson's imperial policies where the hurt was worst, the purse: "Our government is worse than the old Turkish system.

They kept fourteen thousand local conscripts embodied, and killed a yearly average of two hundred Arabs in maintaining peace. We keep ninety thousand men, with aeroplanes, armoured cars, gunboats and armoured trains. We killed about ten thousand Arabs in this rising this summer. We cannot hope to maintain such an average: it is a poor country, sparsely peopled. But Abd el Hamid would applaud his masters, if he saw us working . . . How long will we permit millions of pounds, thousands of imperial troops, and tens of thousands of Arabs to be sacrificed on behalf of a form of colonial administration which can benefit nobody but its administrators?"

It was the power of the purse that moved Iraq toward freedom. To the great credit of the British, they recognized, after a severe shock of tribal war, that they could not afford to govern Iraq directly as a colony, and they found a less overt system, with English advisers behind an Arab façade, which was more economical. In recognition of this fact, Sir Arnold Wilson was withdrawn from Iraq.

On October 21, 1920, the newly arrived civil commissioner, Sir Percy Cox, announced the formation of a provisional government under Arab ministers with British advisers. Meanwhile, the British sought a head of state. As provisional president of the Council of Ministers, they chose an old and venerated religious leader under the umbrella of whose prestige they set about organizing a government and administration. As the tribes submitted they were amnestied. At this time about 250 of Amir Faisal's supporters, many of whom had served in the Turkish forces, but who were born in the area which had become Iraq, petitioned to return. Wisely, the British decided to make them into an asset. In the first group, which returned early the following year, was Nuri Said, who was to serve as prime minister many times until his assassination in 1958.

At Cairo, in March 1921, Winston Churchill met with senior British advisers and worked out, essentially, the administrative arrangements that were to endure for the next forty years. Recognizing the need to cut expenditures and the fact that the mandate was unpopular in Iraq, Churchill decided to negotiate a treaty with Iraq, parallel to that between Britain and Egypt, which would, bilaterally and in name at least, end the mandate (although in the eyes of the League Iraq remained a mandate) and give Iraq that degree of nominal independence which would lessen the danger of hostilities or civil war. Recognizing also that Britain's position in Iraq would, in large part, depend upon the selection of a ruler, Churchill decided to move vigorously for the selection of Amir Faisal, so lately king of Syria. To this end, a program was worked out to ensure his election in the forthcoming referendum. "Popular" support was mobilized and Faisal's only serious opponent was arrested and deported on vague charges of sedition. Faisal arrived in Iraq in June 1921, met with a disappointingly cool reception, but was declared king on July 11, 1921.

Thus the British imported into Iraq, to make possible their indirect rule, the very man whom the French had at the cost of an invasion expelled to make possible their direct rule. Herein lay an essential contrast in methods. Throughout their period in the Arab East, the British sought the cheap ways of rule, making virtues of necessities and assets of rivals, while the French plunged on, often into unnecessary and costly clashes with nationalism. Whereas the French never consolidated their position, the British success is striking: reductions in British personnel in the Iraq government reached such proportions that by 1927 they controlled the country with only a handful of civil servants and small detachments of the Royal Air Force.

Like Lebanon, Transjordan was created as a separate unit without serious opposition by the local population. Transjordan was the product of Churchill's Cairo Conference. Its territory had been originally a part of the mandate of Palestine, as approved by the League of Nations, but was always administered under a separate regime and on May 26, 1923, was formally separated. Since April 1, 1921, it had been controlled by the Amir Abdullah, brother of King Faisal, who agreed to give up his plan to attack the French in Syria, to avenge his brother, if he were given control over Transjordan. The British, whose relations with France were still strained, agreed. They also had another reason. The British declared that Transjordan as constituted, was not subject to the Balfour Declaration and that Jews were forbidden to buy land there; thus the British could feel that in Transjordan they had honored their wartime promises to the Sharif Husain.

It is not important for our present purposes to follow in detail most of the developments of the mandates in the four countries. Major trends in the control of the hinterland, in the development of national markets, in the development of organizational cadres of the new states, and in the rise of education are, however, of such a formative influence on the area and the people of today as to require close attention.

Possibly the most significant aspect of the mandate period in Jordan, Iraq, and Syria was the spread of urban control over rural and desert areas. From time to time, under powerful and able governors, public security had been secured, but normally, as one left the Mediterranean coast it steadily declined. As we have seen, the nomadic tribes were autonomous "nation-states" which lived beyond the reach of urban government. As long as they were mobile, the tribes constituted a danger to public security; only when they had invested in immovable objects, particularly land, could they be brought to heel.

The great tribal rebellion of 1920 was the rock on which the British dream of empire had broken: it simply was far too costly to retain Iraq as the imperialists within the British government wanted. To cope with the tribes, the British relied upon two methods. On the one hand, they made clear that they had the power and the will to enforce public security in those areas of importance to them; and on the other, they appointed responsible chiefs to whom they gave incentives to control the tribes. Since all of the other clan chiefs would conspire against the government-appointed paramount chief, the British high commissioner, in a report to the League of Nations, reckoned that "as the authority of the central government increases, the problem [of security] should be logically solved by the gradual dissolution of the tribal bond." The first job, however, was to cope with the tribes militarily.

The British at the end of the First World War, like Egyptians in Lebanon in 1832, profited from a revolution in arms technology. Between 1840 and 1918 the Turks lacked a clear superiority in arms. The rifles they used were about the same as those used by the tribes. Their position was not dissimilar from that of the American army when the American Indians began acquiring repeating rifles. The First World War introduced several new sorts of weapons. The first was the armored riverboat which enabled the British to bombard fortified towns in the Tigris-Euphrates delta. The stunned Arabs whose mud forts crumbled had to surrender, lamenting that, in the words of one old warrior, "but this is not war." A second weapon and perhaps the most striking of all was the airplane. The rapid development of the airplane came just at the end of the war in Europe and air power got its first major test in the Middle East.

To control the vast expanses of steppe and desert, both the British and the French came speedily to rely on air power. For example, in 1924 occurred the last of the great tribal raids out of Arabia. In this raid, which was not unlike the original Arab invasion after the rise of Islam, some 26,000 sheep were seized and taken from southern Iraq and Syria to Arabia. The devastating effect on the tribes within Iraq and Syria, which had been more or less brought under government control by that time, was immediately recognized by officials. The Royal Air Force in Iraq was then called upon to police the vast frontier land of the great Syrian desert. Thereafter, the RAF patrolled the frontiers so that a bedouin tribe would be spotted as it got anywhere near the frontier area. If an "invader" were seen, the plane would radio to alert ground troops who rushed in the area in "armed Fords." The armed Ford was simply a truck with a machine gun mounted on the top, but between it and the camel was a gulf as wide as that between a Jenny and a jet. This combination of air power and mobile ground units gave the government the ability to reach out into the desert as no government ever had in the past.

In a report from the high commissioner of Iraq in 1923 the effect of this new power is vividly described: "a main factor in the pacification of the country has been the Royal Air Force. By prompt demonstrations on the first sign of trouble carried out over any area affected, however distant, tribal insubordination has been calmed before it could grow dangerous ... In earlier times punitive columns would have to struggle towards their objectives across deserts or through difficult defiles, compelled by the necessities of their preparations and marching to give time for their opponents to gain strength. But now, almost before the would-be rebel has formulated his plans, the droning of the aeroplanes is heard overhead, and in the majority of cases their mere appearance is enough. By its means (air power), it has been possible to achieve a highly centralized yet widely understanding intelligence which is the essence of wise and economical control."

The building of roads and the rapid rise of public transport made it unnecessary for notables to retain expensive bands of retainers. The local political officer in Kurdistan remarked in a report to the League in 1928 that in the town of Sulaimaniya one could see a good example of the pacifying influence of the motorcar. "Formerly, a tribal chief from the vicinity of the Persian border having business at administrative headquarters would make the two days' journey accompanied by a large escort of armed horsemen. Following the construction of a pioneer motor road, with police posts, from Sulaimaniya to [one of the administrative posts], a regular taxi service has sprung up. The tribal chief, finding that he could take a seat for three rupees and perform the journey without fatigue in two hours, ceases to entertain large bodies of expensive armed retainers. The practice of carrying arms thus tends to grow less." Thus, not only was it possible for the central government to move more rapidly and dramatically against rebellious people, but the people gave up a part of their means of rebelling.

The opening of roads tended to bring about the creation of national markets. This trend had been stimulated by the wartime conditions. Since shipping was everywhere at a premium and supply of large numbers of troops was difficult, the military administrations tried to organize sufficient production to meet local needs. The demands of war forced the administration to create a cash crop economy to replace the honeycomb cells of largely autarkic groups of villages and to encourage production of cereals needed by the army. This was a trend which the settlement of tribes, the building of roads, and the creation of an export market in the following decade was greatly to extend.

Moreover, British troops brought with them the desire for, and small supplies of, the accouterments of Western civilization: kerosene lamps, flashlights, pocket knives, cheap cotton cloth, automobiles, and trucks. These became objects of intense desire for the wealthier civilians not only for their utility but, no doubt, as status symbols of a civilization that was so obviously powerful and successful. The British army was not, however, able or willing to supply such things to the local inhabitants. So it was natural that a new commercial class should spring up on the foundation of large-scale purchases by the army and casual spending by troopers which had pumped money into the economy. New styles were introduced as influenced by the army: sandals to headdress, the Iraqi shed his Arab dress for Western. His Syrian cousin was not far behind.

As roads were built across the desert from Damascus to Baghdad along the Euphrates route and connecting the various Iraqi cities, the areas which had been largely autarkic, which had supported themselves and had a considerable degree of economic autonomy, came to sell their goods one to the other and to buy from central points those things which they could not produce as economically. The Kurds in the northern area of Iraq, for example, who had prior to this time bought very little from the outside world, began to buy cotton goods from England or India, chinaware from Japan, cigarettes from Baghdad. As they acquired new tastes, locally produced goods were no longer satisfying to them, and they were anxious to move in and out of the places like Baghdad and to acquire the accouterments of European life. Markets grew in strategic locations throughout the country and more and more people were drawn into the system which the state itself represented. Thus, more and more people came to have a stake in supporting the political existence of the state. It is interesting that Basra and Beirut, where this commerce developed earlier and most rapidly, saw almost none of the armed unrest that some of the northern areas of Iraq and Syria witnessed.

As the city governments extended their control over the countryside, townsmen extended the limits of their cultivation far beyond what had been considered relatively safe in Ottoman times. Of course, this meant that townsmen took over many of the watering places and extensively used farming lands of the seminomadic and nomadic tribes. Particularly in Iraq, something comparable to the "enclosures" of eighteenth century England or the changes brought about on the American range by the advent of cheap barbed wire happened during the first decade of the mandate.

In all of the mandates, but particularly in Iraq, the development of the economy was dependent upon security in the rural areas. Not only physical security, of the sort that could be supplied by military means, but also security of investment was essential to get money out of strong boxes and into the land.

As early as the enactment of the new land code in 1858 the Ottoman government had recognized the utility of the security of tenure. In 1869, during his short stay in Iraq, Midhat Pasha, the greatest of the Ottoman governors of the nineteenth century, tried to bring order into the system of land tenure. Similar efforts were made in Lebanon in the decade of the 1850's and in Palestine somewhat later. The details of the Ottoman system are complex, but the general purpose was twofold: to give sufficient title to those who would invest in the land and hire others to farm it, and to give the nomadic tribes lands on which to settle.

Before this time the Ottoman governments had concentrated their efforts in the towns and left the countryside to itself until the harvest, when tax collectors, accompanied by military escorts, collected what they could from the unwilling peasants. The effective law of the countryside, except when taxes were collected, was local custom. Peasants cared little what the records in the distant cities might say; they knew who owned the land. Even when encouraged to register their lands, they feared to do so since they suspected that land registration might be a government ruse to raise their taxes or to conscript their sons into the army.

Profiting from this disaffection from government of the peasant and the tribesman, the larger merchants and officials obtained formal rights to vast tracts of tribal and village lands. Later, when the Iraqi land system was studied by Sir Ernest Dowson, he found that "with the introduction of tapu tenure many village areas appear to have been wholly or partially registered as the personal possessions of local notables, without any consideration of the immemorial rights of those who had regularly occupied and tilled the land or pastured the flocks thereon. The pinch in these cases seems to have been mainly felt when the lands were pledged, and forfeited, to town-dwelling merchants for debt."*

*Sir Ernest Dowson, *An Inquiry into Land Tenure and Related Questions* (printed for the Iraqi government by the Garden City Press, Ltd., Letchworth, Eng. [1932]), p. 20.

As to tribal lands themselves, the Turks regarded them as government-owned, merely being used by the tribes with no rights of ownership. Taking up the Turkish definitions of ownership and the Turkish records, the Iraqi courts according to the high commissioner's report to the League for 1925, reached the momentous decision that "all lands excluding urban *mulk* (freehold) properties belong primarily to the State and that good title to such lands can only be obtained in consequence of alienation by Government ... acquisition of title to lands by long and undisturbed possession, is a legal impossibility in Iraq." This one blow placed the tribes on the danger list. Their lands could be encroached upon at will by city dwellers who could arrange with the government to buy or lease land. The tribesmen involved were forced to emigrate or to settle. Whereas in Turkish times they had been able to keep their lands by making it impossible for others to take possession, in 1925, under the droning of the airplane, they were powerless.

During the period 1920 to 1932 great tracts of land along the rivers which had in the past been lightly used by semi-nomadic and nomadic tribes as grazing, water, and winter-wheat areas became regularly cultivated private property. In 1921 along the Iraqi rivers were 140 water pumps, irrigating a total of 72 square miles; by 1929 the number of pumps had risen to over 2000 and the area irrigated to over 2670 square miles. In the three years from 1927 to 1930 some 1057 new pumps were installed with a substantial increase in the size of the area cultivated. The pumps were mostly owned by city men who expected to get from the government rights to the land. And, in fact, according to the lands sales of the period, they did. In the year 1927, for example, the government sold 7917 pieces of government land and 448 pieces of mortgaged land. As the report to the League of that year described the development, a gradual transition to an enclosure of arable land was being promoted. "The prospective pump-owner is usually an enterprising capitalist townsman, lacking land and anxious to develop a portion of the Domains already subject to tribal occupation."

The policy of the government was to grant a limited term tenure to the shaikh as the representative of the tribe, but in practice title to the land often passed to the shaikh, so that what had been in fact tribal land became in law his land. This, and the large investment necessary for irrigation, tended to produce a heavy concentration of land. Ultimately nearly 70 percent of the arable land of Iraq was held in blocks of over 250 acres. In southern Iraq the concentration was even more impressive. In one province 75 percent of the land was in units in excess of 2500 acres and only 6 percent in units less than 125 acres.

Shortly after achieving independence in 1933 the new national government passed a law which virtually converted the formerly free tribesmen into serfs. The key to the relationship between the owner and the tenant in the new land was debt. So widely was it defined that it is almost inconceivable that any peasant could ever be out of debt. The peasant incurred a debt for any work done by the owner, any seed advanced, any work *not* done by the peasant. If the peasant tried to leave the land, the owner was entitled to call out the armed forces of the government to have him brought back. Then he was blacklisted so that he could get no other job.

The shaikh who in the time of the peasant's father or grandfather had been the honored elder, the generous host who dared not inflict the most trifling punishment on the poorest man in the tribe, had become an absolute master, perhaps a member of Parliament, who lived far away in the city and who had all of the power of the government behind his word. This was nothing less than a social revolution, one whose legacy was to have profound—and violent—influence in the midst of the Iraqi revolution of 1958–59 and, perhaps, will again. At the least, it has been largely responsible for the creation of those vast concentric rings of slums which lean on Arab cities.

In all four mandates the governments were pressed to organize relatively cheap means of control. In general they sought to recruit local people to work for the government so that the more expensive Europeans would be required only for senior positions. This was particularly evident in the area of public security. Britain, as we have seen, was strongly opposed to the continued outlay of large amounts of money on public security and demanded a cut in the size of the British garrison in Iraq. Transjordan never had more than a handful of British officers and no sizable force.

The French, to the contrary, thoughout their tenure in Syria and Lebanon were compelled to retain very large military establishments. In 1921 the French had over 50,000 troops in Syria and shortly after the two-year rebellion of 1925–27 sent in even more. Additionally, from 1921 the French began recruiting Syrian and Lebanese auxiliaries and by 1925 had over 7000 of these under arms. Ten years later, at the high point, these *troupes spéciales* totaled 14,000. Until the bitter end of French rule in Syria in 1945, when they formed the basis of the incipient Lebanese and Syrian armies, the French were to retain control of these troops. To patrol the steppe and desert, they also formed in 1921 camel companies under French officers. But French efforts were always expensive since they could not entrust any significant role to the Arabs of Syria.

The British position was quite different. After the 1920 Iraqi revolt, the more settled areas of Iraq were relatively peaceful. Only in Kurdistan and in the desert areas was public security seriously threatened. Security in these areas, after the inauguration of the government of King Faisal, was the concern of the government of Iraq, with which the British had treaty relations (although under the terms of the League they formally exercised a mandate). This government had primary responsibility and was assisted to create and sustain its own military force under British guidance.

In 1926 the mandate government organized an "armed Ford police unit" to control the great bedouin tribe of the Shammar, and in 1928 a similar group was created in the south of Iraq. So successful was it that it became the model for changes in all the frontier guard forces organized in the area. In Transjordan the former commander of the Egyptian camel corps had formed a desert patrol in 1920 to fend off tribal raids from across the border and to bring a degree of security to the desert. The force, however, was not entirely successful as it could not gain the cooperation of the bedouin and had to meet raiders on their own ground with their own weapons. It was the scheme of enlisting bedouin into a special highly mobile desert force that made John B. Glubb (Glubb Pasha) famous and brought order and security never before imagined into the desert.

In Iraq the British had formed units of Assyrian and Kurdish levies to assist in the garrisoning of the country during the war. These forces proved loyal to the British during the 1920 revolt and by 1925 reached a strength of 7500. Since they were under British officers, paid by the British, and drawn from the non-Arab minorities, it was decided that they could not be a proper nucleus for an Iraqi army. However, throughout the mandate period they matched or overshadowed the young Iraqi army. The Iraqi army, itself, was formed in 1921 under the command of former officers of the Ottoman army of whom the chief was Nuri Said, later to be prime minister. A military college was also opened. By 1925 this force had reached 7500 (just matched by the levies 7500) and was able to replace departing British ground units.

The young Iraqi army was impelled into politics sooner than any of the other forces of the mandates since it had early "tasted blood" in the Kurdish revolt and then in 1933 had attacked and massacred large numbers of Assyrians whom the British had used as the base of their power in Iraq. In the 1930's, as later, the Iraqi army was always close to or involved in political power. Seven times between 1936 and

1941, it made or supported coups d'etat. The reason is not difficult to find. The army was by all odds the most efficient organization in the country. Its dedication and discipline contrasted as sharply with the often self-seeking politicians and their merchant allies as did its ability to communicate and move with the rest of the population. Moreover, it was used and permitted itself to be used by the government as "a valuable means of fostering a true National Spirit." From this position in the mid-twenties was no great step to the military coups of the mid-thirties.

One can argue that what happened in Iraq in the mid-1930's occurred twenty years later in Syria, delayed by the nature of the French-controlled military structure there. In the late 1950's the Syrian army began to intervene decisively in politics. This is a phenomenon which came to distinguish virtually all of the Arab countries by 1960.

With the exception of Syria, which had existed as an independent kingdom, though with uncertain frontiers and a rudimentary administration for two years until the French invasion, and to a lesser extent Lebanon, whose nucleus of Mount Lebanon had enjoyed autonomy for several centuries, the new mandate states did not exist even in the minds of the leaders of Arab nationalism in 1920. Tribal groups were divided—often bitterly—amongst themselves and held both their urban cousins and members of the minority groups in contempt. In Iraq the Shii community was politically attached to Iran, dependent upon its charities and culturally Persian. In northern Syria pro-Turkish sentiment was sufficiently strong to allow Turkish guerrilla bands a free hand. In Lebanon the several groups whose religions divided them still thought of their churches as their "nations." And in Transjordan statehood was a mockery, opposed by the Palestinians, both Arab and Jewish, scorned by the bedouin, and referred to by the British as "Churchill's inspiration."

It was long before any of these governments was to achieve a sense of identity. Even today the issue of nationality—whether a man of Damascus is a Syrian or an Arab or, if both, which is the object of his deepest loyalty—is unresolved. Even King Faisal, the hero of the Arab Revolt and the popular victim of French tyranny in Damascus, was far from accepted. A British report to the League of Nations for the year 1922–23 admitted that "Faisal and his government could not be maintained without British support and friendship." The real job of the mandate period, then, was the schooling of the Arabs in the requirements of statehood.

The creation of states, each distinct from its neighbors, was in large part a mechanical process. The growth of administration created jobs and careers; to travel a man had to have a passport which bore the name of his country; the forms and procedures of daily life developed in different patterns. Linguistic differences resulted from the fact that technical vocabularies, created to give instruction in fixing trucks or filling out government papers, were patterned on different models. The Iraqi army manual was unintelligible to the Syrian gendarme. Even the goods available from Europe differed as each copied the European metropole—the French radio using 110-volt electrical current would not work in Baghdad where the British installed 220. And, at least as important, each area developed its own enemy: The Syrians carried an abiding hatred of the French but remembered Britain with some favor, while the Iraqis who had never seen the French but who were captivated by stories of Paris felt no anger toward the French but were resentful of the British. Transjordanians, on the contrary, rather liked the British and, at least in the early days, admired the gallant band of Englishmen who knew the desert and the bedouin like the best of Arabs. The Lebanese, profiting from French benevolence and attracted by French culture while fearing Syrian nationalism, threw themselves almost wholeheartedly to the French. So, on the "new politics" the Arabs of Beirut, Damascus, Amman, and Baghdad literally had no common language.

From this to statehood, however, is a long jump.

Many small impulses contributed to that jump but none was more important than education. As an American educational consultant informed the Iraqi government some years later, "Without a public school system it is obvious to everyone that an independent nationality could not be maintained even if established."

Education in the Turkish era had been directed toward government service. Special schools were established to enroll the sons of tribal shaikhs—with the double purpose of impressing the young men with the power of the empire and holding them hostage for their fathers' conduct. Those of the city men who did not go abroad and wanted more than the religious schools could offer were obliged to learn Turkish. With little developed native industry or commerce, moreover, the roads of advancement led through government civil or military service. Most of those who achieved prominence in government service in the generation after the First World War had been Ottoman army officers. It was a principle of the British administration, but not of the French administration, to bring these young men right into responsible posts as early as possible.

Since the Ottoman craft of state aimed at creating essential public security, raising tax revenues, and maintaining territorial integrity at minimum cost, it is not surprising to find that little was done in the field of education. The few schools which Iraq had were mostly on the primary level and all, after the Young Turk revolt, offered courses in Turkish. In 1913 about 6000 students were registered but probably most of these were only part-time and very few got beyond the first two or three years of classes. Religious schools taught recitation of the Koran and literary Arabic; weak and unimpressive as they were, they did preserve in Iraq some unity of form in Islam and, for a very small part of the population, a standard of the written language.

When the British surveyed the educational system, they found little other than the buildings to be of any use. Most of the relatively modern teachers were not qualified to teach in Arabic while those who could teach in Arabic did not know the subjects needed by the class of clerks and administrators the British wanted to staff the mandate government and business enterprises. In 1920 less than one half of one percent of the population was registered and in attendance in the schools. In that year the government opened two secondary schools—one with seven and the other with twenty-seven students. The British viewed education in highly specific and utilitarian terms. In its 1923–24 report to the League of Nations the mandate government stated its view that "in this country, it is neither desirable nor practicable to provide Secondary education except for the select few."

In that same year some 15,000 students were in Iraq's 300 religious schools and about 5000 adults were enrolled in anti-illiteracy classes. But pressure of necessity forced the government gradually to increase its outlay from 3 percent to 8 percent of the budget in the field of education. However, even as late as 1932, when the mandate ended, the average rural school child got only two years of schooling, and of the 154 existing government schools only 14 had as many as six grades. Whole districts of Iraq had no schools with six grades.

In Syria the situation was similar but for different reasons. The French defined their mandate as an obligation to bring European, that is, French, culture to the benighted natives; it made little difference that the natives were Arabs, with a vast literary heritage. That heritage was eschewed to the extent possible. Students were encouraged to study French and the best among them found their ways to French universities and insitutes. But caution was the keynote. Since the French attempted to retain for themselves a far larger share of administrative and political power than did the British, they regarded education as a dangerous fuel for the fires of nationalism.

It is significant that the number of students in school rapidly increased when Iraq obtained its independence. By the end of the British mandate Iraq had 19 secondary schools with 129 teachers and

2082 students; within three years the number of students doubled, and by the eve of World War II it had reached nearly 14,000. But even more significant was the change in the materials of instruction: school books became increasingly directed at fostering nationalist feeling. The function of these schools, as seen by the Iraqi government, was to "select and train leaders for all the essential phases of life of [the] nation."

The British educational adviser was not rehired and the example of Germany came increasingly to attract Iraqi educators. Education, always considered as a means to the end of national betterment in the larger sense, became so in all points of detail. For example, the aim of teaching history was to "strengthen the 'national and patriotic feeling' in the hearts of the pupils." This was to be accomplished in Iraq, as in the Palestine school system of the same period, by means of study of Arabic literature and with "stories about famous Arabs and their qualities . . . taught in such a way [as] would lead to the growth of national feelings."* This was a difficult task, for far from burning with a sense of national mission, the students were apathetic. An American consultant wrote that "there is evident among teachers and pupils no great patriotic fervor for their new nationalism . . . Somehow the youth of the secondary school and their teachers must get a vision of what the nation demands of them and an inspiration from these new possibilities of national culture and political achievement. These things they do not seem to have, nor does the school experience contribute in any extent to them."†

This lack of purposefulness in what they were doing and disappointment with their much advertised new "democracy" were to be of great significance in the troubled days of the 1930's. As in Europe so in Iraq, the failure of democracy to put the meat of practice on the bone of pronouncement left the educated elite with little more than whetted appetites and sore teeth.

Consciousness of the apathy of the Iraqi people and shame at the weakness of the nation before Europe was a potent political mixture in the 1930's in Iraq. Despairing of adults, the government encouraged the rise of paramilitary youth groups. Even the Boy Scouts were involved and grew by 1930 to 12,000 members. But the most significant was the *Futuwah*—the name evoked the memory of the efforts of the last Abbasid caliph to restore his regime to its former glory on

* Matta Akrawi (later director general of education of Iraq), *Curriculum Construction in Economic, Social Hygienic and Educational Conditions and Problems of the Country* (New York, 1942), pp. 186–187.

† Paul Monroe, *et al., Report of the Educational Inquiry Commission* (Government Press, Baghdad, 1932), p. 37.

the eve of the Mongol conquest, but the spirit was more akin to the fascist youth movements of Europe—whose director urged Iraqi youth to "get tough for ease spoils virtue." "That nation," he admonished Iraqi high school students in 1933, the first year of independence, "which does not master the art of death with steel and fire will be trampled to death [shamefully] under the hooves of cavalry and the boots of foreign soldiers." Essentially, this "art of death" was an attempt to state in a modern and national form the famous pre-Islamic verse memorized by generation after generation of school children: "Who holds not his foe away from his cistern with sword and spear, it is broken and spoiled: who uses not roughness, him shall men wrong." This inculcation of pre-Islamic values, which ultimately made up the whole syllabus of the humanities in the public school system of all the mandates, was in part an attempt to find a national image which could transcend the bitter and divisive religious problems of the Sunnis and the Shiis, of the Christians, Jews, and Muslims.

Education was the road to advancement through government service, but few wanted to get their hands dirty in the process of building the nation. The law college, the high road to government, prospered, but in the agricultural state of Iraq in 1930 an agricultural college was closed for lack of students. The glittering lure in the educational system was a tour abroad. To imbibe Western learning at its source was to be on the road to success in Iraq.

In a broad sense the entire mandate system was conceived as a sort of giant school in self-government. In no sense had the Turkish government aimed at such tutelage. And, as in any school, the "students" eagerly pressed for graduation.

In its report to the League of Nations in 1928 the mandate government noted that "From the beginning, the idea of a mandate has been abhorrent to nearly all educated elements in the country, and it was this fact which, in 1922, caused the British Government to negotiate with the 'Iraq Government a Treaty of Alliance to define Great Britain's relations with 'Iraq. It was not long, however, before the view became prevalent in 'Iraq that the Treaty of Alliance was in effect only the mandate in another form and it was approved by the Constituent Assembly in 1924 on condition that negotiations should be opened with a view to amending it."

Iraq achieved its formal independence in 1932 when it joined the League of Nations. The Syrians, remembering with pride their prior independence, pressed for their freedom, and it was only with great difficulty, at considerable cost in lives and property, that the French were able to hang on. Ironically, Syria was economically a losing proposition for them since it was British trade which always predominated in the Syrian market and French administration was always expensive. A full-scale civil war raged in and around Damascus in 1924–25. Damascus and other Syrian towns were bombarded three times during the mandate. Finally, after another outbreak in 1944, Syria and Lebanon achieved their independence.

Many of the problems which the mandate system was designed to solve were merely deferred and still form a part of the Middle Eastern scene.

10

Arabia and Egypt:
Isolation or Humiliation

EGYPT and the Arabian Peninsula present a
sharp contrast in their development in the
twentieth century. In their experience with the West, this contrast is
particularly instructive and illustrates another aspect of "the impact
of the West." Egypt profited in its relations with the West by gaining
the most advanced Arab economy and by passing rapidly into the
modern era, but has paid a heavy price in the psychological scars so
evident in its political life. Arabia, unscarred, was also unassisted and
unorganized by imperialism. While enjoying what has been termed
"the ancient and comfortable right to be let alone," the states of Arabia have paid for their seclusion. None of the infrastructure associated
with the mandate system or Western tutelage was created, and, especially in those areas of the peninsula where oil was not found—in
Yemen, for example—the people suffer from material and cultural
backwardness.

The geography of Egypt is an invitation to invasion; and the regulation of the Nile irrigation system requires strong, centralized authority. These two facts have dominated Egyptian history. After suffering a series of invasions by the so-called Hyksos in the midst of its
classical period, Egypt was invaded by the Persians in 525 B.C. and
then conquered by Alexander the Great in 332 B.C. Never again, until
after the First World War, when Egypt attained formal indepen-

dence, or, as many Egyptians aver, after the Second World War, when the British troops were evacuated, did Egypt live under Egyptian rule. Its rulers were Greeks, Romans, Arabs, Armenians, Abyssinians, Turks, Circassians, French, and British. So deeply ingrained was the notion that it was not the métier of Egyptians to rule that, as we have seen, Napoleon's attempt to get native Egyptians to accept official responsibility was violently rejected. Forty years later, in the midst of the rule of Mehmet Ali Pasha, Egyptians told visitors that they were unsuited to rule themselves, that rule was the profession of others while they, the Egyptians, excelled in the law of Islam and in arts, crafts, and agriculture.

Egypt to Mehmet Ali Pasha and his successors was a base of power, not a homeland. Thus, though Mehmet Ali's dynasty rid themselves of the Albanian, Circassian, and other foreign slave or mercenary troops, they did so because these men refused to modernize, were expensive and unreliable; though they recruited native Egyptians, they did so because the Sudanese did not perform well and the Egyptians were available. Yet, Mehmet Ali Pasha and his more vigorous successors were personally if not nationally vitally interested in the growth of Egyptian power and in the achievement of Egyptian independence.

Twice during his long rule, Mehmet Ali had the Ottoman Empire in his grasp but both times the European powers forced him to let go. European statesmen realized, during most of the nineteenth century, that the sudden and dramatic breakup of the Ottoman Empire would endanger European peace and stability in a way unacceptable to them all. Thus, as has been said, British policy aimed at keeping the Ottoman Empire strong enough to withstand Russian pressure in the north but not so strong in the south as to constitute a barrier to the thrust of British commerce or imperialism. Russia wanted either no Ottoman Empire or one amenable to Russian policy; therefore, it alternated a policy of aggression with one of support against the aggression of others. France lacked such a clear conception of its national interests. Napoleon III sent an expedition to Lebanon in 1860 but withdrew, and in 1882 the French sent ships to Alexandria with the Royal Navy but took no part in the bombardment or the invasion of Egypt which established British power there. In general France tried to maintain friendship with the empire and its rivals, suffusing both with French culture and assisting in the development of both through commercial loans and entrepreneurial activity.

Mehmet Ali realized that his only security of tenure rested on his military power. Other rebels before his time in Egypt and elsewhere throughout the Ottoman Empire had gained a measure of autonomy only to lose their heads on the executioner's block. Safety lay in the acquisition of such power as to rival or replace that of the empire itself. Therefore, Mehmet Ali undertook his program of modernization of the army and the economy. To gain foreign exchange, he introduced cotton, encouraged agriculture, built and manned factories, sent missions of students and technicians abroad for training, and hired foreign specialists. Recognizing the geographic facts of Egypt, he instituted a strong, centralized regime, becoming himself the "landlord" of Egypt to get the most out of the country, and invaded surrounding areas to protect the open, defenseless Nile Valley. At the peak of his power, he ruled much of the Middle East and had armed forces totaling nearly 10 percent of the population of Egypt.

After the British-led invasion of Syria and the retreat of the Egyptian army in 1841, Mehmet Ali was forced to cut his army to 18,000 men, to give up a large part of his fiscal policy, particularly the monopoly system which sustained his industry and prevented the influx of cheap European manufactured goods, and to forgo the attempt to rival the Ottoman Empire. With his road to independence blocked and in declining health, Mehmet Ali lost interest in his reforms. In his last years and under his successors Egypt, in the words of an Egyptian historian, "was going slowly to sleep again."

But if this was true of the government, it was not true of the country as a whole. The growth of export agriculture, particularly in cotton, had tied the Egyptian to the world market. Even more significant was the intellectual ferment, at first affecting very few people, occasioned by the creation of a group of men who had been exposed to European culture and who, upon their return, infused their fellow countrymen with information and curiosity concerning Europe. In the shock of discovery of Europe, Egypt came, gradually, painfully, and partially, to recognize itself. Avant-garde Egyptian writers began to speak of the nation, love of the homeland, and nationalism as something Egyptian. It was long, however, before the seeds thus planted were to take hold and grow in the soil of Egypt.

Meanwhile, Egypt had much to learn of the power and influence of Europe. The lesson began in earnest in 1854 when the ruler of Egypt granted to Ferdinand de Lesseps a concession to dig the Suez Canal. The sorry story of this episode, in which the Suez Canal Company, backed by a powerful consortium of Europeans and uncontrolled by inexperienced or venal Egyptians, committed grand larceny, has been told above. Oriental delight in pomp and circumstance and the genuine need to develop the Egyptian economy led the ruler of Egypt deeper and deeper into the trap of the great European banks. And the refusal of the European powers to allow Egypt to break loose from the

Ottoman Empire saddled it with additional expenses. Prime Minister Disraeli announced to the House of Commons on March 23, 1876, that the khedive had requested that the report of an inquiry into Egyptian finances be suppressed. This was the coup de grace to the unsound finances of the country. Ultimately, Egypt was literally placed in receivership with its government under the control of a debt commission. This sparked native resentment against the weak Egyptian government and its European masters. A coup against the Egyptian government by a group of Egyptian army officers was put down by a British invasion and Egypt became in fact though not yet in name a British protectorate.

Immediately after their assumption of power over Egypt, the British announced that "although a British force remains in Egypt for the preservation of public tranquility, Her Majesty's Government are desirous of withdrawing it as soon as the state of the country and the organization of proper means for the maintenance of the Khedive's authority will admit of it." As the years went by the British government, according to a British historian, promised some 66 times to evacuate the country. Britain finally withdrew its last base in 1956 only to attempt later in that year to invade the country again.

British administration of Egypt was always a curious arrangement. The British did not claim possession or even protection over Egypt for three decades, the senior British official was the "consul general," and Egypt remained a part of the Ottoman Empire. Essentially, British rule over Egypt was the quintessence of enlightened imperialism: It was the international version of government by a city manager. Under Consul-General Lord Cromer, who ruled Egypt from 1883 until 1907, improvements in irrigation, notably the completion of the first Aswan Dam in 1902, made possible an increase in the cropped area from 4.7 million to 7.7 million acres, debts were repaid to the full face value, and many substantial improvements were made in the government. Following the reconquest of the Sudan in 1898, Egypt was made a nominal partner in the Anglo-Egyptian Condominium established to rule it. Egyptians have complained, and rightly, that little was done in the field of education and that they were excluded from participation in social as well as administrative affairs.

But Egyptians, having acquired a better educated minority, stirred by a native religious revival which at the least encouraged a belief that in the Arabic-Islamic past there was much of which to be proud, and watching the national assertiveness of Japan and Turkey, aspired to a larger control over their own destiny. Political parties espoused the slogan, common in sentiment to others in many parts of the world, "Egypt to the Egyptians." To some degree the British found this political agitation useful to keep the ruler, the khedive, more dependent upon them. In any case the nationalists posed no serious threat as they were merely a small group of urban professional and trades people without much popular backing. It was not until the Denshawai incident of 1906 that hatred of foreign rule stirred the average Egyptian.

Successors to Lord Cromer were somewhat more willing than he to allow Egyptian participation in government or, at least, expression on political affairs. In 1907 the first national congress was held, and more encouragement was given to education. Again, however, the government tightened down on public demonstrations, enacting a press censorship law in 1909 and instituting exile as a punishment for undesirable politics. Thwarted resentment found an outlet in the assassination of the Coptic prime minister Butros Ghali, whom many regarded as a puppet of the British.

Egypt had become more prosperous. The government had been extremely frugal and had managed to cut most taxes and duties to the bone. Yet income increased as more lands were brought under cultivation as a result of the Aswan Dam, and the population increased by nearly 30 percent. By the First World War exports had increased 30 percent over Lord Cromer's best year.

When the First World War broke out, both the khedive and the British agent were out of the country—the khedive in Constantinople and Lord Kitchener in London. In November, when Britain declared war on Turkey, Kitchener joined the British war cabinet. The cabinet voted to annex Egypt, but British officials resident in Cairo were opposed. In December Egypt was declared a protectorate, with all ties to the Ottoman Empire severed, and its pro-Ottoman khedive deposed.

Ironically, it was to be Lord Cromer's protégé, Saad Zaghlul, who was to lead the charge against the British. Zaghlul, picked to be minister of education in 1906, was commended to the Egyptian people by Cromer as one who "possesses all the qualities necessary to serve his country."

We have noted above Zaghlul's petition to the British, and how, when he was refused, Zaghlul set about organizing committees throughout Egypt and circulating petitions for an end to British rule. The arrest and deportation of Zaghlul led in March 1919 to nearly a month of violence in which the British won all the battles, but the Egyptians won the war. Caught, as in Iraq, between expensive civil strife and frugal war-weariness, the British invited the Egyptians to submit proposals for reform and announced in April that Zaghlul was to be released. A state of tension continued with one prime minister after another resigning, so the British government appointed a commission of inquiry to investigate the causes of the disturbance and to plan for a more peaceful future.

On its arrival in Cairo in December 1919 the commission met with a silent boycott from all Egyptians outside the palace since its terms of reference had restricted it to modification of arrangements *within* the protectorate rather than allowing it to consider independence. Again the pace of violence was stepped up, with a steady procession of terrorist attacks on British soldiers and on those Egyptians who cooperated with the British.

Zaghlul, who had failed to achieve anything in Paris, then approached the commission of inquiry in London and attempted to negotiate with the British for what he had failed to get in Paris. A memorandum was drawn up to show what the British were prepared to accept, but Zaghlul, impelled by now by the very public emotion he had helped to create, found consideration of any proposal short of outright British evacuation impossible.

The main items in the British proposal called for Egyptian independence, a mutual defense treaty between Great Britain and Egypt, British right to maintain military forces in Egypt, Egyptian assumption of control over financial affairs, centralization of the capitulations under British control, and Egyptian right to discharge foreigners employed by the Egyptian government at a future date. These points are important both in that they indicate how far Egypt was from true independence and in that they form the base line for all future Anglo-Egyptian negotiations. The very fact that Britain was willing to negotiate thus with a man who had no official standing in Egypt—Zaghlul was not then even a member of the government— was itself tantamount to a British admission that the government of Egypt was a sham. This served to strengthen the nationalist movement and to concentrate still further the leadership in Zaghlul's hands.

Failing to work out an acceptable pact with the nationalists, the British government agreed in December 1921 to negotiate Egyptian independence. To ensure that events went smoothly, the British again arrested and deported Zaghlul. But at this point the British government, despite the urgent pleas and even threats to resign by its able high commissioner, Lord Allenby, again delayed. Again Egypt was torn by violence. Finally, on February 28, 1922, London unilaterally announced the independence of Egypt, leaving "absolutely reserved" four areas: British imperial communications, Egyptian defense, protection of the minorities and foreign interests, and the Sudan, over which, in theory, Britain and Egypt exercised a condominium.

It is a part of the tragedy of the contrast between the ruler and the ruled, the powerful and the powerless, the donor and the recipient, that events which appear to the one in one guise do not so appear to the other. As the British saw it, after frustrating and often infuriating negotiations, undertaken in good faith by the British but punctuated by violence in Egypt, the Egyptians, acting with the encouragement if not under the direct leadership of the very men carrying out the negotiations, refused a reasonable and logical solution in which Britain agreed to independence, reserving for itself only those matters of vital national interest or international moral concern.

From the perspective of the Egyptians, the events appeared quite the contrary: In the midst of a great war, ostensibly and vocally proclaimed to be for freedom—so ringingly announced by President Wilson—the great powers showed, under their thin new masks, the old faces of greed, oppression, and cunning. At the Peace Conference in Paris when it suited their purposes they dealt with half-savages or phony representatives, but would not meet the legitimate demands of representatives of such advanced and civilized peoples as the Egyptians for self-determination. After so constituting all the "legitimate" avenues to power as to exclude the true representatives of the people, they accused these of breaking the law when they resorted to the course of true patriotism in the face of tyranny. Finally, when violence became too costly, they gave in, but did so with such cunning as to produce a stillborn state with matters of integral national concern like self-defense, maintenance of public security, and control over the headwaters of the Nile withheld. If any lesson had been learned, it was that Britain respected only force. Such was the Egyptian view.

Zaghlul was allowed to return to Egypt in September 1923. In the elections for the new parliament, the first conducted on a mass basis, he won an overwhelming victory with 190 out of 214 seats. Zaghlul was asked to form the cabinet and was invited by the British to negotiate a new treaty; he agreed to form a cabinet but refused to enter negotiations with the British unless there were no "absolutely reserved" points. On this, negotiations again broke down, and Zaghlul, flushed with what he thought was the proximity of victory, threw his Wafd into demonstrations in Egypt and the Sudan. In the atmosphere of hostility and passion the British officer who was commander of the Egyptian army and governor-general of the Sudan, Sir Lee Stack, was assassinated in Cairo on November 19.

The British reacted in a white fury, presenting an ultimatum to the Egyptian government which, after stating that "this murder, which holds up Egypt as at present governed to the contempt of civilized peoples, is the natural outcome of a campaign of hostility to British rights and British subjects in Egypt and the Sudan, founded upon a heedless ingratitude for benefits conferred by Great Britain," demanded "ample apology," "condign punishment" for the criminals, suppression of all "popular political demonstrations," payment of a fine of £500,000, withdrawal of all Egyptian officers from the Sudan within twenty-four hours, and notification of the Sudanese (that is, British) government that it could draw unlimited water from the Nile—thus appearing to strike at the jugular vein of Egypt. Moreover, Egypt was to "withdraw all opposition in the respects hereafter specified to the wishes of His Majesty's Government concerning the protection of foreign interests in Egypt."

The Egyptian government immediately agreed to apologize amply, to punish the criminals, and to pay the fine, but refused the other demands. In reply the British instructed the Sudan government forcibly to eject the Egyptians there and to renounce restrictions on its use of Nile waters. The British seized a part of the Alexandria customs to ensure Egyptian fulfillment of conditions. Further, the high commissioner suggested that hostages should be taken to be shot in the event of further assassinations.

Powerless to react but too proud to remain, Zaghlul resigned as prime minister and was replaced by a government that was little more than a British puppet. In December Parliament was dissolved and new, carefully rigged, elections were staged, but even in these the Wafd won almost half the seats. So Parliament was again dissolved. In yet another election the Wafd won 144 out of 201 seats but a British show of force, fear of palace intrigue, and, probably, weariness caused the 67-year-old Zaghlul to take a moderate position until the end of his life in 1927.

Once again, the Wafd took power in 1928 but was dismissed on charges of corruption and scandal—often more potent political weapons than gunboats—and in confusion, the Egyptian nationalist movement seemed itself in danger of being as discredited as were the very institutions of popular participation in government, the Parliament and the ministries. It appeared that long before it had reached its goals, the Wafd "sold out." Indeed, the man who followed Zaghlul as leader of the nationalists, Nahhas Pasha, was deeply involved in the scandals and corruption which so divided his party.

So Egypt faltered through the early 1930's, having lost all the élan of its nationalist period, led by men with an increasing stake in the status quo, dissatisfied but apparently, even in seeming victory, unable to achieve real independence. By 1936 the government was ready to sign a treaty with Great Britain which gave Britain essentially what she had asked for in 1922, military control, joint participation in British control over the Sudan, and British endeavors to end the privileged position of other foreign powers in Egypt. In 1937 on this basis Egypt was able to join the League of Nations.

Egyptian frustration and anguish is perhaps best documented in the rise of such extremists as fascist youth groups and the Muslim Brotherhood. The Egyptians, now really leaderless and with uncertain or complex goals, were unable to find a path to their future. Although formally independent they did not find themselves to be free.

As we have learned more about the process of development in the years after World War II, we gain a new perspective on the problems of Egypt under British occupation. The lack of spirit or a sense of inability to assume control over their own destiny may have cost the Egyptians even more than we have realized. It remained tragically "underdeveloped" despite the fact that it already possessed, even prior to World War I, the major economic "infrastructure" which is usually regarded as a crucial ingredient in development. In 1913, as Charles Issawi has pointed out, the 12 million Egyptians had a per capita income "higher than that of Japan, more than twice that of India, about 1/2 that of Italy, almost 1/4 that of France, 1/5 that of Britain, and 1/8 that of the United States. . . ."*

But Egypt remained relatively stagnant as Japan, the European countries, and North America forged ahead. Issawi believes that the problem was what he calls the asymmetry between economic and intellectual development. As he writes, "Egypt felt the impact of the Industrial Revolution before being influenced by the cultural, social, and economic movements that characterized the Renaissance and the Enlightenment, whereas in Latin America, Eastern Europe, Russia, and even Japan the sequence was reversed. In this respect Egypt was typical of the vast majority of countries of non-European culture; what is remarkable however is, on the one hand, the degree of its cultural isolation before about 1820 and, on the other, the swiftness of its economic advance and the slowness of its social progress after that date."

Issawi is right but I believe at least part of the explanation may lie elsewhere: in what may be called the psychology of development. The Egyptians had become accustomed to having others make their decisions and were so often told that they were weak, inefficient, "oriental," that they almost stopped aspiring to what may be the most crucial of all elements in the development process, the ability to work with and trust one another. This has become a ghost which has

* William R. Polk and Richard L. Chambers, eds., *Beginnings of Modernization in the Middle East* (Chicago, 1968), p. 383.

haunted successive generations of Egyptians up to the present time.

Egypt broke diplomatic relations with Germany when World War II began and with Italy when Italy entered the war in the summer of 1940, but did not declare war. The country became a huge armed camp for the British Eighth Army as the western desert became a major theater of operations, and in the exigencies of the situation such freedom of action as was possessed by Egypt was quickly subordinated to the demands of the British military. Egyptian reticence or sympathy for the Axis, widely shared in the Arab world, was overcome by a coup de main in which British forces surrounded the palace of King Farouk in February 1942 and threatened to depose the king unless he named a prime minister of their choosing. Ironically, the government so installed was of the Wafd, long since tamed and friendly to the British.

Even those who have criticized the British admit that they acted under the most extreme conditions, with the war apparently being lost in most theaters and the beginnings of a German drive in North Africa which would bring Field Marshal Rommel's tanks to a point within 70 miles of Alexandria. But British actions in Egypt as in Iraq and elsewhere did lend reality to the contention of nationalists that so long as British forces remained on Egyptian soil, Egypt was a good deal less than fully independent.

Perhaps as potent a factor in Egyptian thought as any that could be adduced in economics or politics was the scar tissue caused by the blatantly evident and utter scorn felt by many Europeans for the Egyptians. "Wog"—Wily Oriental Gentleman—and "Gypo" became soldiers' taunts; the words of the Egyptian national anthem were redrafted as a smutty joke on the Egyptian king and queen. The typical English-Arabic phrase book always prominently featured the words "Get out," *imshee,* and "Beat it," *yalla,* and were largely restricted to those words used by an impolite patron to a waiter. But perhaps most of all, the central and most inviting piece of real estate of Cairo, the island in the middle of the Nile, was largely taken up by a sporting club which was restricted to Englishmen and, toward the end, to acceptable Europeans and Americans. Even the king of the country was unwelcome. Later there was to be no prouder victory of nationalism, even the Egyptianization of the Suez Canal or the National Bank of Egypt, than the capturing of the board of directors of the Gazira Sporting Club.

As the tides of war changed, after the battles of El Alamein and Stalingrad, the British position eased considerably. Britain not only was prepared to allow more autonomy within Egypt itself but encouraged Egypt and other Arab states to move toward the realization of at least a part of their aspirations for some form of federation. It was in Alexandria in October 1944 that the Arab Unity Conference was assembled under the chairmanship of Egypt. And, in order to be allowed to join the United Nations, Egypt in February 1945 finally declared war on Japan and Germany.

Once again, Egypt emerged from a war with appetite whetted for real independence. Students and members of the Muslim Brotherhood and other groups dominated the streets of Cairo for some months. The Egyptians were able to begin negotiations with the new Labour government on a revision of the 1936 treaty, but the Wafd, attempting to recapture its faded youthful vigor and purity, refused to be bound by the negotiations or to take part in them. In beginning the negotiations Great Britain agreed to evacuate all of Egypt except for the Suez Canal Zone, which became the major British base in the Middle East, but the future of the Sudan, which the Egyptians regarded as a part of Egypt since, at least, the 1899 convention establishing the condominium, led to a break in the talks. Egypt then took to the United Nations her case against the 1936 treaty, which she held was negotiated under duress, and against British moves to alienate the Sudan, but the Security Council was unwilling to do more than urge continued discussions between the two parties.

Almost immediately upon the heels of the defeat at the United Nations came the Palestine War in which Egyptian forces, after glowing speeches by leaders of the Egyptian government, were defeated. The bitter consequences of this humiliation were not long delayed for a government by now almost devoid of the respect of its people.

The Arabian Peninsula, where Islam was born, ceased to be the major stage of Islam in the time of the fourth caliph, Ali, when the capital of the empire was shifted to Kufa in what is now Iraq. But Arabia, with Mecca as the target of prayer and goal of pilgrimage and Medina, the birthplace of the Islamic state, never lost its sentimental and religious hold on Muslims. Particularly after the bedouin "defected" from the caliphate, returning to their pre-Islamic ways, in the second century of Islam, Arabia remained the "blood bank" of Arab civilization. From it all but Arabs were excluded and to it the faithful sent their pious donations to support religious and cultural institutions. Indeed, as the routes of commerce and the centers of industry were concentrated elsewhere, religion became the major "business" of Arabia. Little scope existed for agriculture, for few areas other than Yemen and the southeastern coast had sufficient rainfall or springs—Arabia has no rivers—to support more than occasional farming, and until this century no other significant resources were exploited.

Periodically in Islamic history, a reform movement has come from Arabia, paralleling the rise of Islam. The last, and greatest, of these is the Wahhabi revival of fundamentalism.

A successor in spirit if not in fact to other attempts to return to the bases of the faith, Wahhabism was begun in Arabia in the eighteenth century when a religious reformer, Muhammad Abdu'l-Wahhab, made common cause with the shaikh of the princely tribal family of Saud. The classic Islamic combination of the "Book and the Sword" which thus resulted led to a wave of conquest and tribal raids into Syria, Iraq, and all parts of Arabia in the early nineteenth century. Temporarily suppressed in the second decade of the nineteenth century by the Egyptian armies of Mehmet Ali, Wahhabism survived in the highlands of Nejd and on the eastern shores of Arabia. Its influence was, however, contained by the rise of a rival Arabian dynasty, the Rashidis of Hail, and by the Ottoman protection and support given to the office of the sharif of Mecca. In 1890 the Rashidis forced the Sauds to flee from the Nejd, to seek safety under the protection of the shaikh of Kuwait. In 1902 the late Abdu'l-Aziz ibn Saud, with a small band of Kuwaiti and Nejdi retainers, in a predawn coup de main, recaptured Riyadh. The Rashidis, weakened by internal disputes, were unable to cope with the revival of Wahhabi power not only in the Nejd but also in the Ottoman province of al-Hasa which the Saudi forces captured in 1913.

In December 1915 the British government signed a treaty in which it agreed to recognize Ibn Saud as sultan of the Nejd and to grant him a subsidy of £5000 monthly. Essentially, the British were interested in keeping Arabia quiet internally so that the Arabs under the influence of the sharif of Mecca, the British chosen instrument, could carry the war to the Turks in the Hejaz and in what is now Jordan and Syria.

The British were at the same time negotiating with Sharif Husain on the terms under which *his* Arabs would enter the war. In the Husain-McMahon Correspondence the British had specifically undertaken to restrict his activities from interference with other Arab rulers with whom they had treaties. Consequently, the British refused to recognize Husain's claim to be "King of the Arabs." Meanwhile, an Arabian force under Husain's son Faisal captured Damascus and took over Syria.

However, in Arabia supporters of Husain and Ibn Saud clashed in 1918, and Ibn Saud decisively defeated the Hejazis in 1919. Preoccupied with his Rashidi rivals until 1921 when he overcame their last resistance, Ibn Saud made no move against the Hejaz until 1924. In that year, after the abdication of Husain in favor of his eldest son Ali, the Hejazi forces were defeated again and both Taif and Mecca taken. A year later, in December 1925, Ibn Saud completed the conquest of the Hejaz, taking Jiddah, and King Ali went into exile. In 1927, in the Treaty of Jiddah, Great Britain recognized Ibn Saud as King of the Hejaz in return for his recognition of Faisal as King of Iraq, Abdullah as Amir of Transjordan, and the special status of the British-protected shaikhdoms on the Persian Gulf. Except for a brief Saudi war with Yemen in 1936 the Arabian Peninsula was at peace from 1927 to 1961 when a coup d'état in Yemen developed first into a civil war and then a "civil war with outside intervention" as Egyptian troops landed in Yemen and the Saudis assisted the Yemeni royalists.

The British and the Ottoman Turks were almost the only foreigners in Arabia until the end of World War I, when interest in the possibility of oil brought in Americans. The major British interest in Arabia, until the discovery of oil in this century, has been the route to India. The Persian Gulf was a link in the Euphrates-Mediterranean route and so involved vital communications. We have seen that one effect of Napoleon's invasion of Egypt was to accentuate the importance of securing the northern Persian Gulf gate of the route, Kuwait, just as an earlier rivalry with the Portuguese and then the Dutch had brought the British to the lower end of the gulf and the Island of Hormuz in 1622. By 1639 the British had secured rights to open a trading post at Basra, and by 1764 had a consul there. By the end of the century the British placed a resident in Baghdad to superintend the post route to Europe. By 1820 they had established complete control over the Gulf, suppressed piracy, and entered into treaty arrangements with the shaikhs of the "Pirate" (renamed "Trucial") Coast.

From the time of Napoleon the British were deeply worried about the use by other powers of the Euphrates–Persian Gulf route to attack India. At first Russia was thought to pose such a danger and then Germany. One after another the petty shaikhdoms came under increasing British influence and protection. In 1869 the Trucial shaikhdoms agreed not to deal with foreign governments except through Great Britain; this was extended to Bahrain in 1880, Muscat in 1891, and Qatar in 1916. Kuwait, from the middle of the nineteenth century the key port on the gulf, was originally planned as the Persian Gulf terminus of the Berlin–Baghdad–Persian Gulf railway; but in 1898 it was effectively removed from the Ottoman Empire when, finding that the Russians intended to establish a logistics base there,

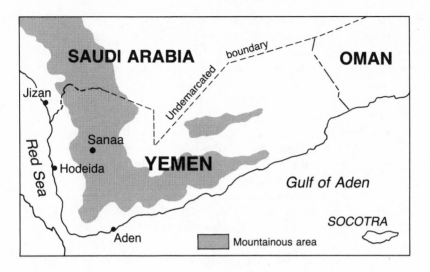

the British entered into treaty arrangements similar to the others concluded with the gulf shaikhdoms in previous years.

The shaikh of Kuwait was recognized by Great Britain to be independent under British protection on November 3, 1914. On April 30, 1915, the Idrisi Sayyid of Sabya in Asir was recognized similarly. These areas were backwaters in the general war effort, which was concentrated in western Arabia, in the Hejaz, where Sharif Husain initiated the Arab Revolt. But they were areas of immediate concern to the government of India and consequently their special status was reserved in the British commitment to Husain.

Southwest Arabia differs markedly both geographically and culturally from the rest of the Arab Middle East. Dominated by an extension of the hill and mountain range of western Arabia, the area has been strongly influenced culturally by Ethiopia, Iran, and India, all three of which were relatively easily accessible by sea. In ancient times, southwest Arabia supported non-Arab or at least not *north* Arab civilizations. The Minaeans and Sabaeans built modest, early agricultural and commercial civilizations based on the export trade of frankincense, which have left significant remains for archaeologists and somewhat more vague but still evocative memories for politicians. Yemen was also a stronghold of Jewish influence before the rise of Islam and, until the tragic 1948–49 Arab-Israeli war, was the seat of a thriving if backward Jewish community. Christianity, in its Nestorian guise, held a foothold until the rise of Islam.

Within the new idiom of Islam, southwest Arabia continued to

147

express its differences and dissidence by espousing unorthodox cults. Even within the lifetime of Muhammad, Yemen produced a rival prophet. Subsequently, Yemenis maintained their separateness and even hostility to orthodox Islam under the Ottoman Empire and in the face of the Wahhabi revival in Arabia. Yemen, like Kurdistan and Lebanon, drew on its natural endowment, the mountains, to protect unorthodoxy.

Relatively more exposed than the highlands, and more useful because of its magnificent port, Aden was the first area subjected to major western influence. Deeply disturbed by the thrust of Napoleon toward India, the British sent a small force in 1799 to occupy the island of Perim which forms a sort of stopper in the mouth of the Red Sea. In 1802 Britain signed a treaty of friendship and commerce with the sultan of Lahej. But almost immediately, the impetus behind the British move faded as Napoleon's threat to India receded. Little attention was paid to South Arabia until 1838 when the British, again concerned by an apparent threat from the Nile Valley, this time by Mehmet Ali, used the excuse of a raid on a wrecked Indian ship, flying the British flag, to capture and annex Aden.

Aden gained in value to the British as a refueling depot as steamships became important for commerce and war. Whether or not trade follows the flag, Aden offers an example of administration following the flag. Once having seized Aden, the British were inexorably drawn into protecting its frontiers and that meant, obviously, intervening in the affairs of the neighboring areas. It proved impossible to stay in the town of Aden without being concerned with tribal confederations which appeared to lurk almost immediately beyond its gates in what came to be called the Aden Protectorate. Five times before 1857 the town came under attack. Perim Island was again occupied in 1857; Socotra was brought into the Protectorate in 1886; the Kuria Muria Islands in 1854, while treaties of protection were negotiated with the motley collection of sultanates, shaikhdoms, and amirates during the course of the rest of the nineteenth century.

Yemen, "Arabia Felix" of the classical writers, the second largest of the states of the Arabian peninsula, remained relatively impervious to this process. Yemen was nominally conquered by the Ottoman Empire in 1517, but more effective threats to the autonomy of the country came from Europeans, mainly the Portuguese, who alternated trade with piracy and imperialism. Invaded in the nineteenth century by the Egyptians, who drove out the Wahhabi-led tribes of Arabia, restored the Imamate, and re-established Ottoman suzerainty, Yemen became, effectively, by the early years of the twentieth century, an Ottoman province. The Turks made little attempt to modernize its administration or even to collect taxes but were content to manipulate the often bloody and bitter division between the Shafii Muslims of the coastal plains and the Zaidi Shii sect of the hill regions to assure themselves a commanding position. In 1903, the then imam revolted and a series of clashes and truces, of bewildering complexity and inconclusive results, occupied the Yemenis until the outbreak of the First World War.

Ironically, Yemen elected to remain loyal to the Ottoman Empire throughout that war. Its loyalty enabled the Turks not only to maintain a significant base in Yemen, cut off as they were by the Arab revolt in the Hejaz from their supply lines, but even to make modest encroachments on the British position in Aden until the collapse of the Ottoman Empire in 1918.

Then, in the absence of a master, Yemen drifted almost unnoticed into independence. This was doubly ironic since it had not fought for independence but remained the least touched by nationalism or modernization of any of the Arab countries. What it had were those most precious assets in the struggle of independence, an inhospitable terrain and poverty. Of further irony: Yemen, perhaps the most conservative country on earth, entered into treaty relations with the Soviet Union, then perhaps the most radical country, in 1928, but was not recognized by the United States until 1946.

Meanwhile, in the Aden protectorate, the British managed at remarkably little cost to function as peacemakers and caretakers.

When the "impact of the West" came in Arabia, it came not in the uniform of the soldier, in the ledger of the European banker, or with the humiliating attitude of the imperialist, but with the magic wand of the oil drilling rig. Far from refusing to let the Arab into its posh clubs, the oil industry was delighted to sit as a guest in the bedouin tent or to build for the Arab Western, air-conditioned cities, railroads, schools, and hospitals in return for the privilege of being allowed to drill in the desert wastes for oil. Undreamed of wealth poured into the peninsula. The sudden infusion of wealth was initially intoxicating. Lacking the institutions or the trained people to manage the new income, the petty states wasted much. However, some, notably Kuwait, have not only learned rapidly to invest productively at home and abroad but also have created funds to assist in the overall development of the Middle East.

What the Arabian peninsula lost in missing the colonial period—training, building of infrastructure, and the imposition of constitutional institutions—was, at least in part, compensated for by what it also missed in the trauma of the deep wounds of national humiliation. The pride that the poorest of bedouins has retained is only now being regained, at great cost and effort, by the richest of the Egyptians.

11

Libya and the Sudan: Undisguised Imperialism

THE *Bilad as-Sudan* or Land of the Blacks was in the beginning of the nineteenth century a vaguely defined attenuation of Upper Egypt along the Nile. More an object than an actor in Middle Eastern history, it was particularly important for the Egyptians as a hunting ground for slaves and, of course, as the conduit or source—no one knew which—of the Nile floods upon which the life of Egypt was wholly dependent. Nevertheless, it would be a serious mistake to look upon the Sudan merely as a reservoir for slaves and water. There as elsewhere in Africa, both the angle of our vision and the poverty of source materials have kept us in partial ignorance of a surprisingly eventful history.

Despite enormous distances and extreme difficulty of travel, Arab merchants had brought the Islamic religion and the Arabic language into the area north of the modern city of Khartoum. By the nineteenth century, the whole of the north was Muslim and Arabic-speaking. The southern areas near the heart of Africa, which were grafted onto the Muslim north during the last century, have remained pagan or, under Western missionary influence, become Christian. The Southern peoples, the Shilluk, the Dinka, the Azande, and the Nuer have never been successfully "nationalized."

Like other inhabitants of the Middle East, the Sudanese were partly nomadic and partly settled. Until the harnessing of the Nile, most of the settled farmers lived in the narrow river valley north of

151

Khartoum. Nomadic peoples roamed widely through the central Sudan and, further south, the predominant mode of subsistence was a combination of farming and hunting which probably closely resembled that of the ancient Egyptians and Mesopotamians.

The historical antecedent to the modern state of the Sudan was the Funj Sultanate which was established at Sennar, near modern Khartoum, in A.D. 1504. Themselves converts, the Funj extended Islam throughout the Sudan. Like the Arabs and Turks to the north, the Funj sultans relied on slave armies which, in the Sudan, were drawn from the south.

In the early years of the nineteenth century, the Swiss traveler John Lewis Burckhardt estimated that Egypt had approximately 40,000 slaves. "I have reason to believe, however," he wrote, "that the number exported from Soudan to Egypt and Arabia, bears only a small proportion to those kept by the Mussalmans of the southern countries themselves, or in other words to the whole number yearly derived by purchase, or by force, from the nations in the interior of Africa . . ."*

Tragic and degrading as was east African slaving, it was on a small scale in comparison to west Africa which may have exported up to 50 million human beings in the sixteenth, seventeenth and eighteenth centuries. Moreover, in the east conversion often brought manumission and slaves were more often treated as "family." Slave holdings were small and slaves were seldom used for agricultural work. Indeed, as armed soldiers many had status in contrast to their positions on vast Western plantations. In addition to describing the slave trade in the Sudan, a topic which always fascinated European travelers, Burckhardt informs us that even in that corner of darkest Africa the people spoke an excellent Arabic and the town of Damer was a moderately flourishing center for the study of Islamic law.

In 1820, Mehmet Ali decided to invade and conquer Sudan. His motives sprang from pure imperialism—to secure a cheap source of slaves, with whom he was experimenting as soldiers for his growing army, and various products either originating in the Sudan or transiting its territory, notably gold. The military encounter was as unequal as that between Napoleon and the Mamluks a generation before. While Mehmet Ali's army had not yet achieved a particularly high level of performance, it was contested only by tribesmen armed with hippopotamus-hide shields, clothed in coats of mail, and carrying wooden lances and swords. The real enemies were disease and distance. Almost imperceptibly, the military campaign merged into a slave hunt. To make their task easier, the Egyptians sought to acquire

* *Travels in Nubia* (London, 1819), pp. 343–344.

slaves already owned by levying a slave tax so heavy, in an economy so short of currency, as to force the Sudanese owners to turn over a large percentage of their slaves to the occupational government. The Sudanese rose in revolt, less to save their *patria* than their patrimony, the slaves. The revolt was bloody but its outcome was never really in doubt. The real question was how much holding the Sudan was worth to Egypt. The Egyptians found an inexpensive answer: by creating an army of Sudanese slaves to act as their proxy.

As the trauma of the revolt ended, in 1825, the Sudan was gradually converted into a reasonably peaceful if poor province of Egypt. To increase revenue, the government encouraged the settlement of new lands and brought back as many as it could of those farmers who fled during the rebellion. Curiously, given the authoritarian nature of the regime in Egypt itself, governors of the Sudan sought, like Napoleon in his brief period in Cairo, to bring into being native councils. The aim was to head off possible revolts and to make administration and taxation more efficient. This "echo" of the Napoleonic expedition to Egypt is symbolic: Egypt attempted to institute in the Sudan what it understood to be a modern, centralized, and economically profitable control over an intrinsically valuable area which might possibly also be a stepping stone to other conquest, especially Ethiopia.

As the attention of Mehmet Ali Pasha was diverted in the aftermath of his catastrophic defeat in 1840 in Lebanon, the Sudan fell into a generation of imperial lassitude. It was not until the advent of Ismail Pasha in the 1860's that an attempt was made to return to the vigorous ways of Mehmet Ali. Like his grandfather, Khedive Ismail was sensitive to European pressures and thus vigorously pursued a previously announced but unsuccessful policy of suppressing the slave trade. Indeed it was partly in order to suppress the slave trade that Ismail ordered an expansion of Egyptian rule westward and southward along the Nile. The province of Fashoda was established in 1863, the Equatorial Province in 1871, the Bahr al-Ghazal in 1873 and Darfur in 1874. To avoid relying on the always bribable provincial officials and slave-collecting tribal chiefs and merchants, Ismail hired several foreigners as key officials. Two of these were English and partly because of that were particularly important in the ensuing events. Sir Samuel Baker was sent to the Sudan in 1869 to extend the khedive's dominion to the upper reaches of the Nile and was followed by General Charles George Gordon (of Khartoum) in 1874. Although a man of tremendous energy and personal courage, Gordon was severely hampered by his lack of knowledge of Arabic, inattention to local customs, and vociferous espousal of Christianity. Yet, ironically, it was not his faults which precipitated the Mahdist revolt of 1881 but his removal. When the vigorous Khedive Ismail was replaced as ruler of Egypt in 1879 by his weak son Mohammed Tawfiq, his commander Gordon resigned. That removed the lid from the pent-up anxieties, hatred, and ambitions in the Sudan.

In 1881, there arose in the Sudan one of those figures too difficult for those of another culture and another age fully to comprehend, a figure who managed to personify the inchoate or unarticulated yearnings of his fellow men in a symbolic language which transcended reason but tapped the deeper sentiments of religion and culture. Such a man was Mohammed Ahmad Ibn Abdullah who proclaimed himself to be the *Mahdi,* one sent by God to rectify injustices and unrighteousness and return his contemporaries to the true path of belief and justice. Such figures defy easy categorization as they are at once unworldly, impractical, and impolitic yet determined, unnaturally brave, and almost hypnotic in their hold over their followers. Logically, it was not only pretentious but preposterous that this forty-year-old recluse on the island of Aba about 100 miles south of Khartoum should issue a series of manifestos enjoining the leaders of the Sudanese tribes to accept him as their leader. Like Mohammed the Prophet at Mecca a millennium before, Mohammed the Mahdi had no powerful tribe and was supported merely by a small band, almost devoid of worldly experience, without riches and powerful connections.

Indeed, the disparity between his proclaimed aims and apparent capacity worked initially to the Mahdi's advantage since the government did not take his pretensions seriously. In the face of their half-hearted attempt to suppress his isolated little band of rebels, the Mahdi was able to score a surprising if modest victory. This enabled him to assemble a larger force of discontented nomads, villagers and tradesmen. Several small engagements followed and each resulted in a moderately important real, but tremendously important symbolic, victory. In the course of these clashes the Mahdi was able to organize a regular if rudimentary military force composed primarily of those Sudanese who had served in the Egyptian army. A major battle against a mixed British-Egyptian unit in September 1883 appeared to crown with triumph the mission of the Mahdi. The British, concerned with the shaky state of Egyptian finances, insisted in the winter of 1884 on evacuation.

General Gordon, the one available "expert," was sent to figure out how to get out with the least loss but his orders were vague and he was, after all, *the* expert, so when the compromise he offered the Mahdi was rejected, he set about organizing for war. Lacking much real power, he undertook an energetic campaign of propaganda. This had less effect in Khartoum or Cairo than in London. The British government had made no plans to assist him and, horrified that he had so far exceeded his instructions, determined that it could not then do so. As garrison after garrison fell, Khartoum was isolated. Under pressure of public opinion, the British government finally began, in fall of 1884, to organize a relief column which set out in January 1885. This move forced the Mahdi's hand and in an attack on the 26th of January, 1885, he took Khartoum by storm. Gordon fell in the fighting. Two days later, the British relief column arrived. Too late, it was immediately withdrawn. Four months later, his kingdom come, the Mahdi died.

Following the death of the Mahdi, his close friend and supporter, Abdallahi was designated Caliph (or *Khalifa:* successor). Abdallahi's rule was neither so heroic nor so tumultuous as the Mahdi's. Indeed, it was a holding operation: his principal task was to stay in power once the messianic justification for rule was gone.

In 1896, primarily because of European diplomatic considerations, the British Government ordered Egyptian forces into position near the Sudanese provinces contiguous with Egypt. On April 8, 1898, General Kitchener attacked the Sudanese army. There, and at the Battle of Omdurman on September 1, the Anglo-Egyptian force virtually annihilated the Sudanese army. The Sudan lay prostrate. Its disposition was in large part dictated by events which fall outside of Sudanese history: the British were intent that other European powers not enter into the Nile Valley as the French then appeared to be doing at Fashoda. Consequently, Lord Cromer, the de facto British ruler of Egypt laid out a scheme, embodied in the Anglo-Egyptian Conventions of 1899, to create a "condominium" over which the Egyptian and British flags were to be flown side by side, administered by a governor general who was to be appointed by the khedive of Egypt on the nomination of the British government. Essentially, the Sudan would be governed by Britain. Shortly to be created in the Sudan was a new civil service, patterned on the Indian civil service and drawn primarily from among athletes ("Blues") from Cambridge University. This gave rise to perhaps the truest, most succinct description of the Sudanese government for the next 50 years; "the rule of the Blacks by the Blues." This is the system, with certain minor alterations, under which the Sudan was governed until 1955.

Libya is Egypt without the Nile. Its sole cultivated area, other than scattered oases, is comprised of two coastal strips divided by the barren coast of the Gulf of Sirte. The Gulf, a great bite out of Africa, is more than a geographical area; historically it has separated Libya into two dependencies, the one, Tripolitania, looking toward Tunisia to the west and the other, Cyrenaica, toward Egypt to the east. Like Tunisia, Tripolitania first comes onto the stage of history as a Phoenician colony whereas Cyrenaica was settled by Greeks. Culturally and socially, the two areas have had different evolutions. Cyrenaica has been Arabian in culture and society for a millennium while Tripolitania has been Levantine. The one area is composed primarily of nomadic tribes and the other of agricultural laborers and townsmen.

Libya was conquered by the Arabs in A.D. 642 but not really Arabized until the eleventh century. The Normans managed to hold Tripoli for a dozen years in the middle of the twelfth century. Then, for the next 350 years, the country was divided between the rival North African caliphates of Fez and Cairo. For 40 years in the sixteenth century, the Spaniards and the Knights of St. John held Tripoli until they were thrown out in 1551 by the Ottoman armies of Sultan Sulaiman the Magnificent.

Thereafter, the history of Tripoli resembles that of the petty governorates of the Levant Coast. It was ruled nominally in the name of the sultan but in fact for the benefit of the local strongmen who were often renegades of Christian origin. Like Baghdad, Damascus, Acre, and Egypt in the eighteenth century, Tripoli fell under the rule of an independent dynasty in 1711. It was a later member of this dynasty who had the distinction of declaring war on the United States, in 1801. Although costly to the new republic, especially in the loss in 1803 of the Frigate Philadelphia with a crew of 300, the war sounds in our memory today as echo in the Marine Corps anthem ". . . to the shores of Tripoli." (Libyans might object to the choice of words on geographical grounds since in fact the Marines stopped 1,000 miles short of their objective!)

Like the Sudan and Arabia, Libya was to have its great religious revival in the nineteenth century.

The Sanussi movement of Libya was founded by Mohammed Ibn Ali as-Sanussi who was born in Algeria around 1790 in a family which claimed descent from the Prophet through his daughter, Fatima. After eight years of study in Fez he returned to Algeria where he acquired local fame as a pious man. After a short period at the Azhar University in Cairo, Mohammed made the pilgrimage to Mecca and spent some years studying, teaching, and performing missionary activities in Arabia among both natives and pilgrims. In 1840, he attempted to return to Algeria to reestablish his religious base but was prevented from doing so by the French invasion. He thus settled in Cyrenaica and, in 1843, established the first "lodge" of what was gradually becoming his new religious order within Islam. By the time of his death in 1859, he had built a secure base within Cyrenaica and had adherents in many parts of the Islamic world.

The Sanussi Brotherhood was puritanical but combined its puritanism with mysticism. Of great practical importance was the fact that Mohammed found a way to work within the pattern of bedouin society and to offer the bedouin a means of beneficially transcending the tribal divisions. Under his son and his successor, Mohammed al-Mahdi, the Sanussi order enrolled perhaps two million "brothers." But, despite its attractive message, the spread of its doctrines, and zeal of its adherents, the Order was unable to forge effective links with the other Islamic reformist movements in Arabia, in the Sudan, and in Egypt. Differences in lifestyle, identification of enemies and choice of means of defense of Islam were simply too deep and wide.

It was upon this deeply divided country, sparsely populated on an immense stretch of land, but strongly imbued with an Islamic revivalist organization and heritage, that the Italians—fearing to miss the wave of European imperialism—launched their attack on Tripoli in October 1911.

On October 3, 1911, the Italian fleet bombarded the Turkish forts surrounding Tripoli and on October 5 an Italian landing force occupied Tripoli. It made no attempt, however, to take on the Turkish forces in battle and they retreated inland to join tribal groups. Within three weeks, the Turks and the Libyans counterattacked and pinned down the Italians at the port, where they could be backed by naval guns. The Italians kept bringing in troops and soon had three divisions supported by 250 warships and transports. This was the first engagement in which the airplane was given complete battle test. The bomber was born in Libya on November 1, 1911 when an Italian pilot tossed a hand grenade out of his cockpit at tribesmen.

On November 5, 1911, the Italian King proclaimed Tripolitania and Cyrenaica parts of the Italian kingdom. Italy, at long last, had joined the general European march through Africa. Its share was the offal and bones of imperialism; the poor, barren, and narrow fringe of Libya. It was not much good but nothing better remained. Moreover, ironically, it was more prepared to fight for its freedom than almost any of the other African colonies. From the European vantage point, the Italian move was not regarded with disfavor except by the Germans who were increasingly concerned with their growing alliance with the Turks and saw in the Italian advance on Libya an opportunity to show the Turks the tangible benefits of their friendship. The British, the Austrians, and the Russians, on the contrary, saw the Italian action as either of no consequence or as potentially useful in stopping what otherwise might be a German move for what looked, superficially from the map, like a narrow waist of the Mediterranean. Italy chose the moment to move well since many of the Turkish forces, normally stationed in Libya, had been sent to South Arabia. Despite this, however, the Italians were not able to move fast enough and European public sentiment swung to support of the Libyans and the Turks, particularly in France and England. The Italian expectation of popular acquiescence in their invasion was soon disabused and the Turks, although unable to undertake formal or large-scale war against the Italians, were able to send crucial quantities of arms and such capable leaders, soon to play major roles on the world stage, as Enver and Mustafa Kemal (Ataturk). From having been the test ground of aerial warfare, Libya quickly became a school of guerrilla warfare. Even more than guerrilla warfare, Libya was a political school for Enver and other Turkish officers who, profoundly shocked and disillusioned by the willingness of the sultan to make peace with Italy, became even more determined to overthrow him.

Fighting swayed back and forth in Libya. After an initial, apparently victorious march, the Italians were driven back to the seacoast by tribesmen who, after Italy joined the war on the Allied side, were increasingly aided by the Ottoman Empire, Germany, and Austria. At this point, however, the Libyans took to squabbling among themselves and split into at least three major factions. Pushed by the Germans and Turks, the followers of the Sanussi made an attack on Egypt which, failing near the famous World War II site of El Alamein, finally exhausted the Libyan will to war.

As World War I ended, the Italians found themselves nominal victors but, in Libya, with an extremely weak position. A confused and desultory period follows in which the Libyans lost a major opportunity to strike for independence. Then, in July 1921, the Italians rightly gauged the temper of the times and decided to destroy all opposition to their rule in Libya. This bitter and destructive colonial war lasted, intermittently and in various parts of the country, until 1932 when Marshal Rodolfo Graziani, who may claim to be the inventor of the "regroupment" concept, finally starved out armed opposition by putting virtually the whole population behind barbed wire. Interpretation of this period illustrates how much history depends upon audience. To the generation of the 1940's, it conveyed merely the banality of evil; what could one expect of fascists but bullying. To the generation of the 1960's, its message if remembered was more complex: the clash of Asia and the West, poor and rich, weak and strong.

The fascist state hoped that Libya would become a new frontier for

Italy's overpopulated countryside. Colonization, however, proved costly and unprofitable. Even under fascism, it was difficult to get Italian peasants to migrate to Africa and, consequently, everything possible was done to make the venture attractive. The arriving peasant proprietors found houses built, furniture installed, fields laid out and crops planted in what must have been the most comfortable pioneering episode known in history. Still, only about 40,000 went. Even they, for all the help given, hardly put down roots.

To protect them and keep control of the country, Italy maintained large forces in Libya and so when Italy entered the Second World War in June 1940, it was able to launch an almost immediate attack with 250,000 men on the 86,000 troops Britain had in Egypt. During the next two and a half years, Cyrenaica was a scene of perhaps the most famous panzer warfare of World War II as the German Afrikakorps and Italian Ariete battled the British VIII Army.

This time, the principal Sanussi leader chose the winning side. Before El Alamein, as fighting swung from Alexandria to Tripoli, his people collaborated with the most romantic units on the Allied side, the Long Range Desert Group and the Special Air Services, in T. E. Lawrence-like raids on supply depots, airfields and even Rommel's headquarters. But the British felt themselves bound to honor the rules of war: military administration did not sanction sweeping changes in the governmental structure of the former Italian colony. So in victory the British were administering a modified (for the better, to be sure) colonial fascist state.

Finally, in 1945 the Great Powers met and determined the fate of the former Italian colonies. Their views could hardly have been more different. Secretary of State James Byrnes wanted a United Nations trusteeship; the Soviet Union, anxious to break out of Eastern Europe, claimed the right to become the trustee itself; France wanted to return Libya to Italian rule; Britain refused. In the ensuing months, as the Cold War began to be codified, the British Labor government, curiously, adopted the French position, and agreed for a renewal of Italian rule.

Again, a historical echo: the foreign ministers decided that a Four-Power commission should attempt to ascertain the wishes of the unrepresented inhabitants as the King-Crane Commission had attempted to do in the confusing aftermath of World War I in Palestine. The results were similar. Libyans expressed themselves quite clearly but the Commissioners had their reports prepared before they visited the disputed area. The report of the Commissioners was a jumble of contradictions. Each Commissioner left his ears in his own capital. The dispute was turned over to the United Nations General

Assembly. Finally, as all compromise measures failed, the Political Committee of the General Assembly decided that Libya should become independent no later than January 1, 1952. To assist Libya in moving toward independence, a United Nations Commissioner was sent out in the first part of 1950. The work was nominally completed by the end of 1951, just a few days before the United Nations Mandate was due to end. The United Kingdom of Libya under the rule of Sayyid Mohammed Idris as-Sanussi was proclaimed on December 24, 1951. It was the first state to emerge under United Nations auspices.

Emerging into statehood after 30 years of brutal Italian colonial rule, several years of war, privation, several more years of postwar uncertainty, Libya was almost totally unprepared for the new tasks it faced. Virtually every function in the previous years had been performed by Italian immigrants and as most of these had left, there were few Libyans who could perform any of the functions required in a modern state. Money was extremely scarce and regional animosities, encouraged by the Italians, were strong. The King and the royal household were avaricious, ignorant, and high-handed; their opponents were not less so. The future boded little good.

12

Palestine: The Promised Land

ON FEBRUARY 18, 1947, the British government announced to the world what had been evident to many long before, that "there is no prospect of resolving this conflict [in the Palestine mandate] by any settlement negotiated between the parties ... We have ... reached the conclusion that the only course now open to us is to submit the problem to the judgment of the United Nations."

As with so many simple and straightforward statements in international relations, behind the words lies a complex, emotion-fraught, and bitter story, many of whose ramifications lie far outside the scope of this book, yet one whose influence permeates the whole history of the modern Middle East—and the world—and which, therefore, commands our greatest and most sensitive attention. It is not incumbent upon the author or the reader to join the emotional fray—quite enough authors and readers have already done this—but it is essential for anyone who aspires to understand the Middle East today to know the sources, the extent, and the depth of those emotions in order to be the better able to cope with the events and men they have so profoundly affected.

The history of the Palestine problem is a long and spotty one; for the present purposes, only a few things need to be said about it: (1) though Palestine remained the emotional center of Zion, the Jewish population was almost totally expelled or drawn away from Palestine under the Roman Empire; (2) the Arab invasion in A.D. 636 brought relatively few new people to Palestine, so that the ancestors of most of today's "Arabs" were actually converted (either to Islam or to use of the Arabic language) over the centuries of Arab and Turkish rule; and (3) the immigration of Jews, other than the small number who came for religious reasons over the centuries, began in the late nineteenth century and was the result of persecution in Europe.

During the First World War, as we have seen, much or all of what subsequently became the Palestine mandate, entrusted to Great Britain under the League of Nations by the Paris Peace Conference in April 1920, was promised to France under the May 1916 Sykes-Picot agreement, to the Jews for "the establishment in Palestine of a National Home for the Jewish people" in the November 1917 Balfour Declaration, and, at least under one reasonable reading, to the Arabs by the Husain-McMahon Correspondence of 1915–16. The war ended with Great Britain in control of the area and the other three contenders attempting to secure their rights. A serious diplomatic clash with France over what the French regarded as British bad faith on the issues of Palestine, Syria, and Mosul was settled in Paris. This left two contenders, the Zionists and the Arabs, with the British holding an uneasy and unstable balance for nearly thirty years.

Initially, as we have seen, the Arabs were less concerned with opposition to the Zionists than to the French. The Arab leader Amir Faisal thought that if he came to terms with the Zionists, they could persuade the French government to waive their claims of influence in Syria. In a formal understanding with Dr. Weizmann, Faisal agreed, on behalf of the Arabs, to work together with the Zionists to achieve their mutual aims, to give effect to the Balfour Declaration, to facilitate Jewish immigration provided the rights of the Arab peasants and tenant farmers be protected, to insure freedom of worship and protection of the Holy Places, and to constitute the British government as their arbiter, provided the Arabs achieved their independence. Also a part of this agreement was Jewish economic aid to the Arabs. But the Arab Congress at Damascus repudiated the essence of Faisal's agreement with Weizmann, saying: "We regard their claims as a grave menace to our national, political and economic life. Our Jewish fellow-citizens shall continue to enjoy the rights and bear the responsibilities which are ours in common."

Faisal, himself, had little more time on the world stage as spokesman for the Arabs of the Levant. On July 14, 1920, French troops invaded Syria and, after routing the small Arab forces sent to oppose them, seized Damascus and overthrew the Arab government. Never again were the Arabs of Palestine to find a spokesman of international stature, and not for years were they to be represented by an Arab state with even the shadowy authority enjoyed by Faisal's Syrian kingdom.

Meanwhile, events in the occupied territory of Palestine had begun to assume, as they had in Iraq, a shape of their own. As in Iraq, so in Palestine, it was discovered that the administration was in a state of chaos. This was particularly evident in Palestine in questions of land ownership. Not only had the retreating Turks taken with them most of the administrative personnel but also had either taken or destroyed official registers of land holdings. Confusion was compounded. In Palestine, due to the Turkish ban on foreign ownership of property, dual sets of land ownership records had been maintained since the middle years of the nineteenth century. The many foreigners who had bought land registered it in the name of a subject of the empire. Over the years the land might have been sold or inherited several times. Moreover, since the Ottoman land tenure system was superimposed on local usage, rights of various sorts were often exercised by different parties in any given piece of land. In some instances land cases begun in the immediate postwar years were hardly settled by the end of the Palestine mandate.

The first chief administrator of Palestine urged that the Zionist program be dropped as inimical to public security in Palestine. The King-Crane Commission, which President Wilson sent to the Middle East to ascertain the wishes of the population, of which about 10 percent was Jewish, reported an overwhelming rejection by the population of Zionist aspirations. But before the end of the military administration and the inauguration of the mandate, upwards of 5000 Jewish immigrants were allowed to enter the country, and Hebrew was adopted as one of the official languages.

Meanwhile on July 1, 1920, authority in Palestine was handed to Sir Herbert Samuel as the first high commissioner of the mandatory government. But it was not until 1923 that Palestine legally ceased to be a part of the Ottoman Empire and became a mandate of the League of Nations. A little over a month after taking power the new civil government issued the land transfer ordinance which reopened the registry office so that lands once more could be bought and sold. The first major purchase of land, by the Jewish National Fund and the Palestine Land Development Company, Ltd., encompassed seven Arab villages in Galilee.

At the same time Sir Herbert Samuel, who had been a principal supporter of Zionism in England during the war, set the quota for the first year's immigration of Jews at 16,500. Just before the publication of the quota on immigration, occurred the second of what was to become a series of Arab-Jewish clashes. In the following year, in May 1921, immigration was suspended after another series of Arab attacks on Jews and Jewish settlements. Everyone, even among the Arab moderates, feared that sooner or later a Zionist state would be created if a sufficiently large number of Jews had moved to Palestine. This was the finding of an investigation commission. However, immigration was allowed to continue the following month with fewer restrictions than prior to the outbreak.

Thus, in 1921 two precedents were set by the government which were to be followed for the next quarter century. In the first place, in the face of acts of violence, the government *did* temporarily accede to the aims of those committing the acts of violence: it did temporarily suspend immigration. In the second place, after the situation had been brought under control and an investigating commission had studied the underlying causes of the trouble, the government *did not* address the identified causes in its subsequent policy.

In 1922, after further Arab outbursts against Zionism, the high commissioner requested that the Colonial Office define exactly the meaning of the phrase "a National Home." The then Colonial Secretary, Winston Churchill, replied with a statement of policy. After affirming that the Balfour Declaration was to remain the bedrock of British policy, he restricted, more narrowly than any senior British offical had to that date, what was meant in the Balfour Declaration: "Unauthorized statements have been made to the effect that the purpose in view is to create a wholly Jewish Palestine. Phrases have been used such as that Palestine is to become 'as Jewish as England is English'. His Majesty's Government regard any such expectation as impracticable and have no such aim in view ... They would draw attention to the fact that the terms of the Declaration referred to do not contemplate that Palestine as a whole should be converted into a Jewish National Home, but that such a Home should be founded in Palestine."

In 1922 the British government decided to separate Transjordan legally from the mandate of Palestine. Transjordan, said the British government, was not included in the Balfour Declaration and Jews were forbidden to buy land there. This move satisfied no one. The Zionists felt that if their historic claim was justified in principle, it was justified in its particulars; so they argued at that time, as they had previously argued at the Peace Conference, that Transjordan was necessary for the development of their National Home. The Arabs, in their turn, argued that Britain's act tended to weaken the position of

164

those who lived in the Palestine mandate by appearing to settle the Arab claim to the dubious benefit of the small number of nomadic tribesmen moving about in the Jordan desert. Further, they pointed out, this action gave a larger degree of independence and self-government to Arabs far less advanced than they, and so sapped the idea of tutelage in statecraft inherent in mandate conception.

In Palestine itself the high commissioner tried in 1922 to establish a government agency in which Arabs would have a voice—at least in lesser issues of policy. The plan called for a council of twenty-three members, including the high commissioner. Ten of the other twenty-two would be official appointees; of the remaining twelve elected positions, two would be Christian, two Jews, and eight Muslims. The Arabs opposed the plan since they would have only ten votes—a permanent minority—on such matters as land policy, immigration, and Zionism. In the face of Arab hostility the high commissioner dropped the whole project. The following year he suggested that the Arabs form "an Arab Agency" analogous to the Jewish Agency, so that the Palestine Arab community would have voice in the affairs of government. This also the Arabs refused.

There can be no doubt that the Arabs were mistaken in not accepting this proposal, for their refusal deprived them of all effective concentration of their activities in the Palestine mandate. Again and again in the following years the Arabs refused to be involved responsibly in political affairs. They argued to themselves that if they accepted responsibility for any part of the affairs of the mandate they would thereby acquiesce in the basic policy of creating a Jewish National Home and would become actually, as the mandate suggested they were politically, but a single part of the population of Palestine.

In Palestine, as in the other mandate states, noteworthy developments in education, public works, health, and other "social overhead" facilities took place. In the excitement of the developmental activity so evident within the mandate, the political questions appeared briefly in the 1920's to have been shelved.

This is true to a certain extent because the worst fears of the Arabs had not been realized. The country had not been "swamped" by Jews, a Jewish state seemed no nearer to establishment than in 1922, and as long as times were good, everyone was prepared to deal in the present and leave the future worries for bad times. Then, somewhat curiously, the arrival of a sharp economic depression, which resulted partly from a collapse of the Polish currency, instead of increasing Arab discontent tended to lessen Arab fears. From 1925 to 1928 no meetings of the Palestine Arab Congress were held, and no protests were voiced over Jewish immigration. The immigration figures themselves provide an index.

The year 1925, when a series of Arab protests were made to the mandate authority, was the largest immigration year to that date, with a net Jewish immigration increase of 31,650. In the next year, however, only about one sixth as large a net immigration was recorded. The Arabs reached the conclusion that with their high birth rate they were not in danger of losing their majority of the population. In 1927 the Jewish community had 2358 more emigrants than immigrants. By the Arabs this was taken as a sign that the National Home had failed, the Jews were leaving, and the Arabs could relax in victory. In the following year, however, the trend was reversed; a very slight net gain was made. And in 1929 the net gain was 3503. The optimism of the Arabs was shattered. They also observed that the Zionist crisis had tended to heal the breach between the Zionist and non-Zionist Jews and even led to an enlarging of the Jewish Agency.

The relative calm of the middle years of the 1920's was ended by a riot in 1929, begun when a number of Zionists organized a demonstration at the Wailing Wall in Jerusalem in the course of which the Zionist flag was raised and the Zionist anthem sung. Within two weeks of violence 472 Jews and 268 Arabs were among the casualties. The commission which investigated the disturbances noted: "The Arabs have come to see in the Jewish immigrant not only a menace to their livelihood but a possible overlord of the future . . . and the result of Jewish enterprise and penetration have been such as to confirm that they will be excluded from this soil."

After questions were raised in the League of Nations Permanent Mandate Commission, the British government decided in May 1930 to appoint a special commission under Sir John Hope-Simpson of the League of Nations Refugee Settlement Commission for Greece, and formerly of the Indian Civil Service, to investigate the underlying causes of the recent disturbances. The Hope-Simpson report recommended an immediate halt to immigration, but suggested that it might become possible again on a limited scale in future years.

The British government accepted the report and on the basis of it issued the Passfield White Paper which went even further toward granting Arab desires than did John Hope-Simpson's report. Jewish reaction was both immediate and effective. Zionist leaders protested to the Colonial Office, and the president of the Jewish Agency, Chaim Weizmann, resigned in protest. From a wide variety of public figures, including the leadership of the opposition Conservative party, protests flowed in. In hasty retreat, the British government took the unusual step of redefining its action in a letter published in *The Times* in which the prime minister denied that the government intended to stop the development of the National Home. Subsequent speeches in Parliament and statements to the press further modified the intent of the Passfield White Paper. In February 1931 the British prime minister, in a letter to Weizmann which was published in *The Times,* proclaimed that immigration "can be fulfilled without prejudices to the rights and positions of other sections of the population of Palestine," and so repudiated the Passfield White Paper.

Coming as this letter did, only as the result of protests by one group in Palestine and their supporters, without benefit of another government study or commission, it was naturally taken by the Arabs as concession to political pressures. They called it, in bitter jest, the "Black Letter" which canceled the White Paper. For the first time Arab hostility began to be directed at the government rather than toward the incoming Jews.

The immediate result was an Arab boycott and a refusal to work together with the Jewish community on civic affairs. But on a positive program, the Arabs spoke with many voices when they spoke at all. Lacking a constituted representative, as the Jews possessed in the Jewish Agency, the Arabs divided into a number of mutually hostile groups which were ineffective in expressing their desires to the government. Moreover, the minimum Arab program was independence, end of immigration, and restriction of land sales. On these terms the government had shown itself unwilling, if not unable, to negotiate. As a result, moderate Arabs could have no concrete and positive program to urge upon the government.

Meanwhile, with the rise to power in Germany of the Nazis in 1932, a new sense of urgency and, eventually, desperation was felt by the Zionist organization, and its ability to act was stiffened by the increasing scale of immigration from Germany. Between 1932 and 1933 the number of immigrants tripled. As the subsequent royal commission pointed out: "As the National Home expanded from 1933 onwards, so the Arab hate and fear have increased." The attitude of the Arab leaders became more hostile toward the government, and the tone of the Arab press more bitter. In the autumn of 1934 the Arab executive submitted to the high commissioner a formal expression of its view that the safeguards for Arab interests embodied in the mandate had broken down. In the single year of 1935, 61,854 Jewish immigrants arrived. This figure was as large as the total immigration of the first five years of the mandate, and in the four years from 1932 to 1936 the Jewish population of Palestine quadrupled.

Meanwhile, in other Arab countries, notably Egypt and Syria, the

British and French governments appeared to give way before violence and nationalist demonstrations. So once again, the Palestine Arab community resorted to direct and violent action. On April 13, 1936, a series of terrorists attacks began throughout the country. Violence bred further violence between the Jewish and Arab communities. Throughout Palestine committees were formed in the Arab towns to demand the establishment of a representative government, prohibition of sales of land to Jews, and end of Jewish immigration. The normally mutually hostile Arab political leaders were forced by their rank-and-file supporters to form a united front and call for a general strike. This time, the government refused to submit to pressure and on May 18 issued an immigration schedule which was somewhat higher than in any previous year. The general strike quickly developed into a civil war. Two trains were derailed, a bridge blown up, and guerrilla bands which included soldiers from Syria and Iraq began to operate in the hill country. On May 23 mass arrests of Arab leaders were made, and in June members of the Arab Higher Committee were interned in a concentration camp.

In June 1936, 137 Arab senior officials and judges in the Palestine government presented a memorandum in which they set out their contention that the disturbances were caused by the fact that

the Arab population of all classes, creeds and occupations is animated by a profound sense of injustice done to them. They feel that insufficient regard has been paid in the past to their legitimate grievances, even though those grievances had been inquired into by qualified and impartial official investigators, and to a large extent vindicated by those inquiries. As a result, the Arabs have been driven into a state verging on despair; and the present unrest is no more than an expression of that despair.

The fact must be faced that that feeling of despair is largely to be traced to loss of faith on the part of the Arabs in the value of official pledges and assurances for the future, and to the fact that they are genuinely alarmed at the extent to which His Majesty's Government have from time to time given way to Zionist pressure. Their confidence was severely shaken as far back as 1931, when the Prime Minister's letter to Dr. Weizmann was issued as an interpretation of the White Paper of 1930. But more recently, when the projects regarding the Legislative Council and the restriction on sales of land were hotly challenged in Parliament, their loss of confidence turned to despair.

Coming as this did from the most moderate, committed, and responsible members of the Arab community, the memorandum made a considerable impression both on the government and on the royal

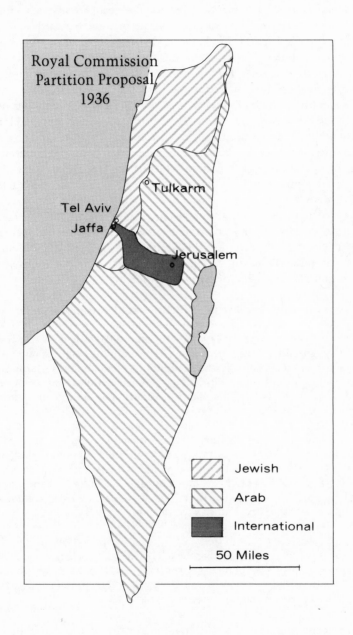

Royal Commission
Partition Proposal
1936

Tulkarm

Tel Aviv
Jaffa

Jerusalem

Jewish

Arab

International

50 Miles

commission which was subsequently sent to investigate the cause of the disturbance.

By September 1936 some 20,000 regular troops had been sent to Palestine to try to reestablish public security. Severe punishment, including the destruction of villages and the quartering of troops, was meted out to those accused of harboring rebels. Arab casualties amounted to over 1000. Both Amir Abdullah of Transjordan and the prime minister of Iraq offered to mediate, but the British government could not allow mediation to include the issues of any of the terms of the mandate or the goal of the establishment of a National Home. Their offer of mediation having been refused, the rulers of the other Arab states advised the Arabs of Palestine "to rely on the good intentions of our friend Great Britain who has declared that she will do justice." By mid-October the strike had ended and the Arab bands had dispersed.

A royal commission, appointed to investigate the underlying causes of the disturbance, arrived in Palestine in November 1936. After careful study of the situation the commission decided that the mandate was unworkable in its existing form. Their conclusions, published in 1937, are still worthy of attention.

An irrepressible conflict has arisen between two national communities within the narrow bounds of one small country. About 1,000,000 Arabs are in strife, open or latent, with some 400,000 Jews. There is no common ground between them. The Arab community is predominantly Asiatic in character, the Jewish community predominantly European. They differ in religion and in language. Their cultural and social life, their ways of thought and conduct, are as incompatible as their national aspirations. These last are the greatest bar to peace . . . The War and its sequel have inspired all Arabs with the hope of reviving in a free and united Arab world the traditions of the Arab golden age. The Jews similarly are inspired by their historic past . . . In the Arab picture the Jews could only occupy the place they occupied in Arab Egypt or Arab Spain. The Arabs would be as much outside the Jewish picture as the Canaanites in the old land of Israel. The National Home . . . cannot be half-national . . . This conflict was inherent in the situation from the outset. The terms of the Mandate tended to confirm it [and] the conflict has grown steadily more bitter . . . In the earlier period hostility to the Jews was not widespread among the fellaheen. It is now general . . . The intensification of the conflict will continue . . . it seems probable that the situation, bad as it now is, will grow worse. The conflict will go on, the gulf between Arabs and Jews will widen.

The recommendation of the royal commission was that Palestine be partitioned between the two communities since the only alternative appeared to be a rule of repression which would lead nowhere. The British government accepted the royal commission's report and issued a White Paper announcing that partition would be the basis of British policy. In the debate in the House of Lords, however, Lord Samuel, the first high commissioner, pointed out that the Jewish state, as small as it necessarily would be, would contain a population of Arabs almost equal to that of the Jews. Later he wrote that "the Commission seems to have picked out all the most awkward provisions of the Peace Treaty of Versailles, and to have put a Saar, a Polish corridor, and a half a dozen Dansigs and Mamels into a country the size of Wales." Such a monstrosity, he warned, would be impossible either to administer or to defend. After an initial cool reaction, the hostility of all parties to the conflict hardened against the plan. The Zionist Congress refused it outright. The League of Nations was not in favor but, in the final analysis, could do little but accept the advice of the British government. Those Arabs whose districts would be lost to the Jewish state brought pressure on their leaders to oppose the plan. To see if a better redrawing of the map of Palestine might not be possible, a partition commission was appointed and sent to Palestine.

Meanwhile, in September 1937 the acting district commissioner of Galilee, which under the royal commission proposal would have been given to the Jewish state, was murdered by Arab terrorists. On October 1, a week after the assassination, the government outlawed the Arab Higher Committee and all national committees, ordered the arrest and deportation of six leading Arab figures, and froze the funds of the Pious Foundation which had supported Arab political activity. Almost 1000 people were interned. During the year, 438 attacks with bombs or fire arms were made on police posts, Jewish settlements, and Arab houses.

When the partition commission arrived in Palestine in April 1938, the leaders of the Arab community were for the most part under detention, but the community itself was united as never before and not one Arab collaborated with the commission. To counter Arab hostility, the government armed nearly 5000 Jews as active and reserve police, but the period of Zionist cooperation with the government was short-lived. Following the June 1938 hanging of a Jewish revisionist terrorist convicted of firing on an Arab bus, the Jews attacked government buildings and bombed Arab markets. In one such attack in Haifa 74 Arabs were killed and 129 others wounded.

During 1938 the government reported 5708 "incidents of violence" including over 1000 attacks on troops or government facilities. Some

2500 people, almost all Arab, were interned, and it was estimated that at least 1000 rebels had been killed by the police and army.

The partition commission published its recommendations in November 1938. After admitting that "the Arabs remain inflexibly hardened to partition" and that "it is impossible to divide a country of its size and configuration into areas the frontiers of which, having regard to the conditions of modern warfare, will have any real military significance," the commission presented three plans for partition. The unsolved dilemma was simply the need to create a Jewish state of sufficient size as to be economically viable and yet one which would not have an Arab majority.

The ensuing government White Paper admitted that "the political, administrative and financial difficulties involved in the proposal . . . are so great that this solution to the problem is impracticable."

The next British move was to summon yet another conference— this time only of the more moderate Arab leaders and those of the Jewish community—to London in February 1939. There, the government decided to review the basis of the Arab case including the Husain-McMahon Correspondence which, for the first time, was made public. A committee was established to evaluate the correspondence as it related to Palestine. Though this committee was not able to agree, the British government representative admitted that the Arab condition was found to be stronger than was thought before. The conference adjourned without having reached any agreement, and with both Jews and Arabs resolved to resist any limitation on their rights. The Arab rebellion continued in the hills of Palestine with covert and overt support from Arabs in surrounding countries. At the same time Jewish legal and illegal immigration was greatly accelerated.

To cope with the dilemma in which it found itself, the British government decided to issue a new statement of policy in which it proposed to adhere to *its* original contention that Palestine was not included in the area promised to the Arabs, but that neither was it the intent of the Balfour Declaration to convert Palestine into a Jewish state against the will of the Arab population. Therefore, the British government offered a plan whereby Palestine would, if possible, within ten years, be given representative institutions and a constitution. After five years Jewish immigration would cease, and Arab land sales would be permitted only within selected areas. The White Paper ended with a plea that both Jews and Arabs take note of the reverence "of many millions of Muslims, Jews and Christians throughout the world who pray for peace in Palestine and for the happiness of her people."

In Palestine the Jewish community was outraged. The transmission lines of the broadcasting station were cut so that announcement of the White Paper was delayed. Government offices were burned or sacked, police were stoned, and shops looted. The government thus found itself under attack from both the Arab and Jewish communities at once.

Meanwhile, in Europe the lights were dimming, and on September 1 the Second World War began with the march of the German army into Poland.

In Palestine reactions to the war were mixed as members of both communities rallied to support the British government against the Germans. Altogether some 21,000 Jews and 8000 Arabs served in branches of the British armed forces. However, both Jews and Arabs did maintain their opposition to the local government, and demonstrations and terrorist attacks never ceased throughout the war. Shortly after the immediate German threat to the Middle East was ended with the British victory at El Alamein in 1942, public manifestations of hostility increased. Members of the Stern Gang clashed with the police in a number of instances. On August 8, 1944, a Jewish attempt was made to assassinate the high commissioner, government installations were raided and looted, and the commander-in-chief of the British forces in the Middle East was moved to issue a communiqué pointing out that the "active and passive sympathizers of the terrorists are directly impeding the war effort of Great Britain and assisting the enemy." On November 6, 1944, the British minister of state resident in Cairo, Lord Moyne, was murdered by two members of the Stern Gang. In the late spring of 1945 the incidence of attacks on the government and on British army units greatly increased. Raids were made with great precision on arms dumps, banks, and communication facilities. As Europe emerged from the war, Palestine took up war in earnest.

As the full horror of the war in Europe and Nazi massive murder of Jews came to the public attention, the already critical situation was inevitably further inflamed in Palestine. The British government was blamed, because of the restrictions on immigration which followed the 1939 White Paper, for the death of hundreds of thousands of Jews who failed to escape from Europe.

With an unbroken record of failures in its attempts to settle the Palestine problem the British government asked the United States to participate in one further inquiry. The resulting Anglo-American committee of inquiry had as a key part of its terms of reference instructions to inquire into the *European* Jewish community's needs. So it was at the assembly points for the survivors of Nazi bestiality that the Anglo-American committee began its short life. The heart-rending tour was an emotional gauntlet for the committee members who eloquently described in the report "the depths of human suffering there endured."

In Palestine the committee found the observations of the royal commission to be valid, as valid in 1946 as in 1936. Hostility of the Arabs to Zionism was unanimous. The major difference between the two dates was the new and increasing power of the Jewish Agency with its unofficial army, the Haganah, then estimated at 60,000. The committee's description of Palestine will be recognized by all who saw it in those violent days. "Army tents, tanks, a grim fort and barracks overlook the waters of the Sea of Galilee. Blockhouses, road barriers manned by soldiers, barbed wire entanglements, tanks in the streets, pre-emptory searches, seizures and arrests on suspicion, bombings by gangsters and shots in the night are now characteristic."

While awaiting the report of the Anglo-American committee the government of Palestine had set the immigration quota at 1500 monthly and tightened up on penalties for armed attack, possession of firearms, and membership in terrorist groups. These police measures did little to calm the situation.

On the night of June 16 the paramilitary activity in Palestine became more concentrated as the commando group of the Haganah, the Palmach, destroyed nine bridges in different parts of the country. The next night the Stern Gang attacked railway installations in Haifa, and on the eighteenth the Irgun kidnapped six British army officers and held them as hostages. The government published a series of intercepted telegrams which showed that the Jewish Agency was involved in the activities of the terrorist groups as well as of its own army, the Haganah. On June 29 the government arrested a number of key figures in the Jewish Agency and occupied its headquarters long enough to seize a part of its files. Twenty-seven hundred people were arrested, of whom about seven hundred were detained after questioning. Most of the personnel of Palmach was included among those arrested, and large supplies of arms were discovered and seized by the British troops. In reprisal the Irgun blew up the King David Hotel, where the senior staff of the government of Palestine was housed, on July 22.

Meanwhile, in London, American and British officials discussed the possibility of solving the problem of Palestine in a way which went far beyond the cunning of Solomon. The proposal was to divide the Jews and Arabs into separate zones or provinces but to leave these provinces as autonomous members of one state. This was actually a contingency plan worked out some years before by the Colonial Office as a last resort. The plan was considered in London by representatives of the Arab states, who rejected it. Neither Palestine Jews nor Arabs even accepted the British government invitation to discuss the plan. The Arab position remained that Palestine should become an independent state ruled by its native majority with due protection for the rights of the minority. The Zionist position likewise was familiar: Palestine should be a Jewish commonwealth, open to Jewish immigration as controlled by the Jewish Agency.

As yet another attempt at compromise, the British government suggested in February 1947 that Palestine be administered for five years as a trusteeship with substantial local autonomy in areas with Jewish or Arab majorities, the protection of the minority being the responsibility of the British high commissioner, with provision for nearly 100,000 refugees to enter the country in the first two years. This proposal was rejected by both the Arabs (including the Arab Higher Committee) and the Jewish Agency.

In these circumstances, failure, heavy expenditure of men and money, and what the British regarded as American irresponsibility— in 1946 both the Democratic and Republican parties attempted to win Jewish electoral support by declarations favoring mass immigration into Palestine—Britain decided to turn the problem over to the United Nations. Speaking in the House of Commons on February 18, 1947, Ernest Bevin said the government had "been faced with an irreconcilable conflict of principles. There are in Palestine about 1,200,-000 Arabs and 600,000 Jews. For the Jews, the essential point of principle is the creation of a sovereign Jewish State. For the Arabs, the essential point of principle is to resist to the last the establishment of Jewish sovereignty in any part of Palestine. The discussions of the last month have quite clearly shown that there is no prospect of resolving this conflict by any settlement negotiated between the parties . . . We have, therefore, reached the conclusion that the only course now open to us is to submit the problem to the judgment of the United Nations . . . We shall then ask the United Nations . . . to recommend a settlement of the problem. We do not intend ourselves to recommend any particular solution."

The United Nations had previously taken official recognition of the problem of Palestine, in the Security Council and General Assembly, but it had not itself investigated the situation. On May 15, 1947, the General Assembly voted to create a Special Committee on Palestine (UNSCOP), to submit not later than September 1, 1947, "such proposals as it may consider appropriate for the solution of the problem of Palestine."

UNSCOP members arrived in Jerusalem on June 14. Once again

the Arab Higher Committee showed itself inflexible by refusing to participate in the meetings of the special committee. The Arab states, however, did make their views known by repeating arguments they had previously advanced.

The Jewish Agency, to the contrary, cooperated in full with UN-SCOP and provided its members with extensive documentation and appeals. Even the Irgun, then engaged in a game of hide-and-seek with the whole of the British forces in Palestine and not always on friendly terms with the Haganah, managed to hold a lengthy meeting with the chairman of the committee.

The committee found little that was different from what its predecessors had reported. It pointed out that Palestine was a small country and of its limited extent of somewhat over 10,000 square miles, only about half was inhabitable by settled people, although the country was principally agricultural—65 percent of the population gained a living directly from agriculture—some 50 percent of the cereals used by the population had to be imported. Palestine, it noted, "is exceedingly poor" in all of the resources needed for modern industry. The population was then 1,203,000 Arabs to 608,000 Jews or about 2 to 1. Since the Arab birth rate was much higher than the Jewish, by 1960 these figures would probably become by natural increase, if immigration were stopped, 1,533,000 to 664,000—or almost 5 to 2. Lastly, to complicate the problem of any sort of partition, UNSCOP found that there "is no clear territorial separation of Jews and Arabs by large contiguous areas." "Jews are more than 40 percent of the total population in the districts of Jaffa (which includes Tel-Aviv), Haifa and Jerusalem. In the northern inland areas of Tiberias and Beisan, they are between 25 and 34 percent of the total population. In the inland northern districts of Safad and Nazareth and the coastal districts of Tulkarm and Ramle, Jews form between 10 and 25 percent of the total population, while in the central districts and the districts south of Jerusalem they constitute not more than 5 percent of the total."

Unquestionably the problems involved in partition were great, yet the urgency of the problem was even greater than in the previous year. Some 17,873 illegal immigrants were under detention and 820 Palestinians were under arrest for security reasons; if anything the situation reported by the Anglo-American committee had worsened. "The atmosphere in Palestine today is one of profound tension . . . In the streets of Jerusalem and other key areas barbed wire defenses, road blocks, machine gun posts and constant armoured car patrols are routine measures. In areas of doubtful security, Administration officials and the military forces live within strictly policed security zones and work within fortified and closely-guarded buildings."

The British administration found that virtually its whole energies had to be devoted to public security and eventually, in all truth, to self-defense. "The right of any community to use force as a means of gaining its political ends is not admitted in the British Commonwealth. Since the beginning of 1945 the Jews have implicitly claimed this right and have supported by an organized campaign of lawlessness, murder and sabotage their contention that, whatever other interests might be concerned, nothing should be allowed to stand in the way of a Jewish State and free Jewish immigration into Palestine."

This being the situation, UNSCOP recommended that the mandate be terminated "at the earliest practicable date," that independence be granted, and that until independence the United Nations assume responsibility. It further recommended that the international community assume *its* responsibilities in assisting the 250,000 Jewish refugees assembled in Europe so as to relieve the pressure on Palestine. Finally the committee urged that whatever other divisions be made in Palestine, it be preserved as an economic unit. The majority of UNSCOP voted to approve a plan of partition with economic union. The states thus created would have the following populations: Arab state, 10,000 Jews and 725,000 Arabs and others; Jewish state, 498,000 Jews and 407,000 Arabs and others; internationalized district of Jerusalem, 100,000 Jews and 105,000 Arabs and others.

This was about the best UNSCOP felt it could do. The Arab state would contain a 1½ percent Jewish minority but the Jewish state would contain a 45 percent minority of Arabs (not including an estimated 90,000 bedouin). In the international zone there would be an almost 1 to 1 equality. The United Nations Secretariat estimated on the basis of past returns for the various districts of Palestine that the Jewish state would have a revenue three times larger than the Arab.

A minority of the committee—India, Iran, Yugoslavia—proposed that a federal state be created. The major motive behind this solution was to "avoid an acceleration of the separatism which now characterizes the relations of Arabs and Jews in the Near East, and to avoid laying the foundations of a dangerous irredentism there, which would be inevitable consequences of partition in whatever form." Moreover, the UNSCOP minority pointed out that the vast majority of both Jews and Arabs opposed partition. The Arab and Jewish states within the federal state should have full powers of self-government under the federal constitution. The boundaries suggested differed slightly from those proposed by the majority.

At the United Nations, before the proposals of UNSCOP were published, Soviet delegate Andrei Gromyko expressed the Russian position on the Palestine issue. He stressed the "bankruptcy of the mandatory system of administration of Palestine." In this he agreed (except, perhaps, in choice of words) with almost every observer of the problem from the royal commission onward. He then went on to support the "aspirations of the Jews to establish their own State." However, he agreed with the Arabs that the responsibility for this state of affairs was European, was due to the "fact that no western European State has been able to ensure the defense of the elementary rights of the Jewish people." Finally he supported the sort of dual state proposed in the minority UNSCOP report. The British and American delegates wanted to avoid discussing the possible solutions until the UNSCOP report was available and clearly wanted to avoid any approach to solution that might involve Russian entry into the Middle Eastern sphere.

When the UNSCOP proposals were published, the British government announced its intention to remove its military installations from the Palestine–Suez Canal area deep into central Africa, to an area which then seemed relatively quiet, Kenya. In effect, Britain was getting ready to wash its hands of Palestine. As desperately as everyone had wished this in the past, there was an immediate realization that such action would precipitate a grim and bloody struggle, that as violently condemned as the British had been, they had exercised the only existing restraint.

The Jewish Agency could be satisfied in having gained recognition of its early claim to independence and a much larger slice of territory than ever before offered, except in the limited "National Home" sense suggested in the Balfour Declaration. The Arabs felt that they had lost everything, and they publicly announced that they intended to resist the implementation of UNSCOP's proposals by force. The Egyptian newspaper *al-Ahram* predicted in September 1947 that "the Palestine Arabs will launch a relentless war to repel this attack on their country, especially as they know that all the Arab countries will back and assist them, supplying them with men, money, and ammunition."

The rival communities prepared for war, the Arabs in two— rival—paramilitary organizations neither of which proved to amount to much when tested. The Jews of course had large cadres of men who had served in the British army or the American army and air force during the war, and they already had standing, if concealed, armies in the Haganah, its Palmach elite corps, the Irgun, and the smaller

Stern Gang. Quantities of equipment and ammunition were being seized from British stores and soon the Jewish purchasing agents were able to send into Palestine considerable amounts of American and Czech equipment.

At the United Nations both the United States and the Soviet Union supported partition, and by agreement, arrived at on November 10, decided that the British mandate should end May 1, 1948, and that the two states would be established by July 1. The British delegate announced that the British army would have evacuated the country by August 1, and that Britain would thereafter not participate in whatever efforts were made to police partition. When the General Assembly met on November 26, Sir Alexander Cadogan announced that Britain wanted to make quite certain that the General Assembly realized it could not count upon British forces to impose its decisions on either Jews or Arabs.

In the Middle East outside of Palestine itself, the growth of anti–Zionism among the Arabs had reached a fever pitch. Ugly demonstrations broke out in many points all over the Middle East. In points as widely scattered as Aden, Libya, and Baghdad a growing feeling of anger over Palestine which could not be expressed against the distant Palestine Jewish community was vented locally upon Jews who in most cases had little or no contact with Zionism. The Jewish communities in their turn recoiled in fear from the nations in which many of them had participated, often at the highest levels of government. This ugly situation in the ensuing months led to a large-scale migration from Iraq and Yemen which further increased the immigration pressure upon Palestine.

After study by various subcommittees and lengthy debates on the floor at the United Nations, a proposal was made to partition Palestine, in general according to UNSCOP's recommendations with minor frontier changes (the main feature being to include Jaffa within the Arab state). Finally on November 29 the partition proposal was passed by a vote of 33 to 13 with 10 abstentions. The end of the mandate was in sight.

In Palestine the Arabs managed to gain a semblance of unity by reverting to their 1936 model of local national committees. The first of these was established in Jaffa just before the United Nations voted partition. Arab attacks on Jews and Jewish settlements and Jewish reprisals and attacks on Arabs began at the end of November and rapidly gained in intensity. In January 1948 Arab volunteers from other states began to enter Palestine. The Arab leader of the 1936 revolt was again in Palestine with about 5000 volunteers in scattered and uncoordinated bands. The streets of all towns and many villages were already forests of barbed wire, and only the foolhardy and the combatants moved about at night.

As the British troops exposed themselves less and less and began to withdraw from remote positions, Arab bands raided settlements and even managed to cut the road from Tel Aviv to Jerusalem, but they soon showed they were no match for the Jewish military units. Both Jews and Arabs set up shadow governments by drawing on the personnel of the mandate government and their respective organizations. In the Jewish Agency, of course, the Jewish community had a ready-made government. The Arabs were more restricted in their experience. They never had an organization comparable to the Jewish Agency, and even their few leaders had been absent for a decade.

The day-to-day events in Palestine from December 1947 to May 1948 belie the arbitrary classifications of peace and war. There were 5000 casualties—one in every 350 people in the country—in this five-month period, and the damage to property may be estimated in the millions of dollars. In some days as many as fifty "incidents" were reported all over Palestine. Trains were blown up, banks robbed, government offices attacked, convoys ambushed, and mobs and gangs looted, burned, and clashed with troops or rival mobs.

The surrounding Arab states prepared for war, and their presses proclaimed in lurid and strident tones that they would resist to the death the UN decision. However, on March 21, the political committee of the Arab League unexpectedly made a bid for a compromise peace. It decided to insist that the original British proposal, which the American government was also considering, be enforced. This would have Palestine under a temporary trusteeship. The committee further urged that the Jews then on Cyprus be accepted into the several Arab states as immigrants and that those in Palestine be assured of their rights as a minority in an Arab state. If the proposal was in earnest, it was certainly too little and too late. Psychologically no one could retreat, least of all the Arab governments.

On the surface the Arabs appeared infinitely stronger. After all, the whole Arab world was publicly pledged to intervene in the war. Egypt, Iraq, Syria, Lebanon, and Transjordan all had standing armies and were receiving surplus British or French equipment. Public enthusiasm, especially among students and the middle class, was high. Yet, it was already evident how weak the Arab governments were. None of the governments was "popular" in its own home, and subsequent events proved that corruption was not only prevalent but existed to such an extent as to all but incapacitate most of the Arab forces. The army commands proved inefficient particularly in logis-

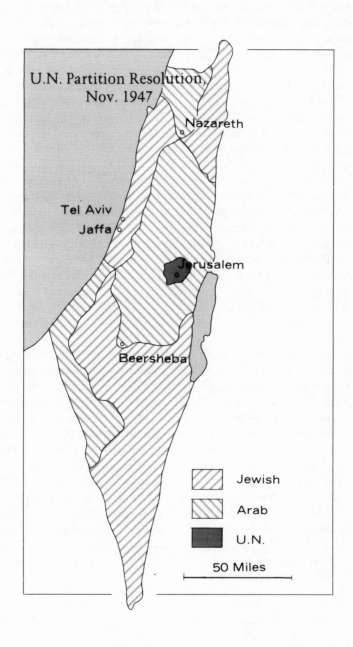

U.N. Partition Resolution,
Nov. 1947

Nazareth

Tel Aviv
Jaffa

Jerusalem

Beersheba

Jewish

Arab

U.N.

50 Miles

tics but lacked initiative in tactics as well. The troops were poorly trained and often poorly led. And finally, even in dire need, the Arab governments proved that their jealousies and personal quarrels were of much more importance to them than their declared interest in Palestine. None of the Arabs, Palestinian or other, except the Arab Legion of Transjordan, could begin to match the level of technical competence of the Jewish forces. Moreover, among the Arabs of Palestine, they found little support. These had been virtually leaderless since 1938 and had never really recovered from their rebellion of 1936–38. By the end of the mandate, they had become terrorized, psychologically defeated mobs, fleeing in all directions.

Early in April the pattern of events began to assume some shape. British forces had been steadily pulling out of the country. The March 20 statement by the Secretary General of the Arab League, that the Arabs would accept a truce and limited trusteeship for Palestine if the Jewish Agency would agree, was rejected out of hand by David Ben-Gurion "for even the shortest time." Fighting raged over most of Palestine. On March 27 Jewish aircraft had begun to participate in the fighting for the first time. Then on April 8 the most active and popular Arab leader, Abd el-Qadir Huseini (who was then chief of the Arab national guard) was killed. On April 10 the Irgun with the help of the Haganah attacked and took the village of Deir Yasin. After the Haganah left, the Irgun, in a deliberate attempt to promote terror among the general Arab population, massacred all the village inhabitants and widely publicized its action. Arab attacks on settlements and Jewish areas began to be beaten off and on April 15 the Haganah launched a major counterattack against the main Arab army under Fawzi el-Qawaqchi. From then on the Arab forces began to fail in their attempts and to assume the defensive. On April 19 the Haganah took Tiberias as the British evacuated its Arab population. April 21 saw the Irgun and Haganah offensive on Haifa, which surrendered and was evacuated by the Arab population. Early in May Jaffa was declared an open city under Haganah control, and on May 14 the Haganah captured Acre. Staggering from these defeats, Arabs were pouring out of the country by every road. On May 14 in the afternoon at Tel Aviv, David Ben-Gurion proclaimed the establishment of the State of Israel.

The mandate had ended.

PART 5

The Independent Arab States

13

Formal Independence: A Short Flight on Fledgling Wings

THE end of World War II marked the close of a period of overt and covert guidance and restraint by the West and the emergence of the Arab states into the community of nations. On the surface this statement is simple enough. However, the precise definition of the time framework and the realities of power which lie behind it pose the key issues of Arab politics of the last generation.

Though no part of the Arabian Peninsula was under Western domination or tutelage, the entire economic life of that area was financed, managed, and developed according to the decisions of the international petroleum industry, and—rightly or wrongly, in scorn or envy—Arabs then as now ascribe to that area something less than full independence. More significant and more measurable, however, was the Western impact on the political history of the other, more advanced, and more populated Arab states.

Egypt, which had been declared a protectorate at the outbreak of World War I, entered into a treaty with Great Britain in 1922 which gave it formal independence with four "absolutely reserved" areas of British control. In 1936 this treaty was revised so that Egypt got more independence of action, and in 1937 she joined the League of Nations. However, British troops remained in Egypt, and from the perspective of Egyptians they were the trump card which made the British the final arbiters of Egyptian affairs. In 1942 the British did, *in extremis,* use their military power to impose upon the Egyptians a prime minister of their choosing. At the end of World War II Egypt finally declared war on the Axis, joined the United Nations, and got the British to agree to withdraw their troops from Cairo and to restrict their military presence to the Suez Canal Zone. It was not until 1954 that the bulk of the British troops withdrew from the Suez Canal, and in 1956 the British and French made an effort forcibly to re-enter Egyptian affairs.

In Iraq the story was similar with a few changes in dates and names. After a costly attempt to rule Iraq as a province, loosely attached to the Indian empire, the British organized a national government in 1921, installed a less than popular monarch of their choosing, and accepted a mandate from the League of Nations. The mandate was, however, so unpopular in Iraq that while maintaining it vis-à-vis the League Great Britain negotiated a treaty in 1922 in which Iraq's special status was recognized. In 1930 a new treaty was negotiated which gave to Iraq sufficient independence for it to join the League of Nations in 1932. The British continued to maintain garrisons there. These made no attempt to intervene in the political unrest of the mid-1930's, but when in 1941 a pro-Axis government came to power, the British and their Arab allies invaded the country to replace the government with one composed of Britain's friends. Iraq declared war on the Axis in 1943 and joined the United Nations. An attempt to negotiate a new treaty in 1946 (the Portsmouth Treaty) led to an outbreak of riots in Baghdad. The treaty was dropped, but behind the shield of the monarchy and the astute political leadership of Nuri Said, British interests remained safe. As Iraq joined the Baghdad Pact in 1955, the British relinquished more of the form of their special position.

Transjordan, which had been separated from the Palestine mandate in 1922 and placed under the rule of Amir Abdullah, remained a client state of Britain. In 1946 it was declared independent but was in fact dependent upon Britain for financial support and for the leadership of its army. Growing resentment at the recognition of this dependence led to the ousting of Glubb Pasha, the British general who commanded the Arab Legion from 1939 to 1956 and to attempts to find other sources of revenue, including Egypt and Saudi Arabia and, after the failure of these, the United States.

Lebanon, which had benefited from French favor in 1920, when its area was multiplied in size, became in that year a French mandate. In 1926 it was given a constitution, but this was amended twice and suspended in 1932. After a period of direct French rule the Lebanese government was restored but with strictly limited powers. The constitution was reestablished in 1937. The period before and immediately after the outbreak of war saw French power retained but operating behind a façade of Lebanese political activity. Then, following the Franco-German armistice in June 1940, Lebanon and Syria went under the Vichy government, and a year later both were invaded by a British–Free French military force. At that time Lebanese independence was promised, and this promise was repeated and reaffirmed in various forms until in 1945 when the British ordered the French to evacuate their military forces. At that point Lebanon joined the United Nations.

In Syria the story parallels that of Lebanon, but the actions were at each stage considerably more bitter. Syria was not augmented by the French in 1920 but rather was invaded and then divided into a collection of petty states. In 1924–25 the Druze and others revolted against French rule, and the French retaliated by bombing villages and shelling Damascus on two separate occasions, in October 1925 and May 1926. In 1928 a constituent assembly was convened in Damascus, and the constitution was put into effect in 1930 but suspended in 1932. In 1936 Syria was rent by a general strike, attended by considerable violence and national agitation, which the French met with an attempt to negotiate a treaty, patterned on those the British had made in Iraq and Egypt. If concluded, this would have made Syria a member of the League of Nations with certain military facilities left in French hands. But the French government refused to ratify the treaty.

Syria, like Lebanon, was invaded by the British and Free French forces in 1941 and received the same assurances of independence. Continued delays in the implementation of these assurances created an atmosphere of smoldering resentment which burst into flame in May 1945 when, after a general strike and sporadic outbursts of violence, the French shelled and bombed Damascus and other Syrian cities. On June 1, 1945, the British ordered the French to cease all military actions and to withdraw all their forces. Syria at last achieved de facto independence which was symbolized by participation in the San Francisco Conference of the United Nations.

As a move toward the realization of the generally held aspiration of Arab unity, the Arab states, with the encouragement of Great Britain, in 1945 formed the Arab League. Actually, as early as May 29, 1941, alarmed by the pro-German activities of the Iraqi government, Anthony Eden, in a widely publicized speech at Mansion House, encouraged the Arabs to look to Britain as a friend of Arab unity aspirations. "This country has a long tradition of friendship with the Arabs . . . It seems to me both natural and right the cultural and economic ties between the Arab countries, and the political ties too, should be strengthened. His Majesty's Government for their part will give their full support to any scheme that commands general approval." Taking up this encouragement, Nahhas Pasha as leader of the Wafd and Prime minister of Egypt spoke of "the bonds which bind us to the Arab and Eastern peoples [as] many beyond numbering and strong beyond sundering . . . with Egypt in the forefront [they will build] a powerful and cohesive bloc." Somewhat later, in January 1943, in announcing the Iraqi declaration of war on the Axis, toward which, as the enemy of Britain, many Iraqis were still sympathetic, Prime Minister Nuri Said proposed the formation of a new state, composed of Syria, Lebanon, Transjordan, and Palestine—"Greater Syria"— with which Iraq would join to form an Arab League. Finally, after consultations and negotiations among all of the Arab leaders, delegates of the several Arab states and the Palestine Arab community met in September 1944 at Alexandria and agreed to form a League of Arab States.

Thus, it may be said that the end of World War II marked a real beginning of independence and self-assertion in the Arab countries. With the departure or the formal "nationalization" of the military and paramilitary forces which had been created in the mandate states, national governments had more real power but also accepted more real responsibility than ever before.

At this point the old objects of national struggle became irrelevant: little merit attached to anti-French activity in Syria when the French had departed. A single new issue of nationalism took the center of the Arab stage, an issue for which all of the Arab governments eagerly sought responsibility and to which they turned all of their suppressed energy and ardor of nationalism. That issue was Palestine.

Not only through the Arab League, whose attentions were largely devoted to the Palestine problem during the immediate postwar period, but singly each Arab government became deeply involved in the issue in consultation with the British government, at the United Nations forums, and in virtually all public media in the Arab countries. Even the religious leaders of the Mosque-University of al-Azhar declared a Holy War. An irregular "Arab Liberation Army," financed and condoned by the Arab governments, of some six or seven thousand men, infiltrated into the Palestine mandate. As the mandate drew to a violent close, the Arab radio and press publicized the plight of the Palestine Arab community, particularly the massacre at Deir Yasin in which almost the entire village population was killed, and thereby stimulated Arabs everywhere to demand action by their governments.

On May 14, 1948, when the mandate ended, the Arab governments had to try to implement their decision to intervene. However, no government was really prepared to act. The most effective force, that of Transjordan, consisted of only four battalions with very little ammunition or other supplies and was under the command of British officers. It had virtually no logistical base or transport. The other Arab armies were ill-equipped and ill-trained. Their commands, moreover, were timid and mutually antagonistic. The governments behind them were suspicious of one another. The Egyptians, fearing King Abdullah's ambition to take over Palestine, deliberately took action to undercut Transjordanian effectiveness by seizing military supplies destined for Transjordan.

Military forces of Egypt, Transjordan, Syria, Lebanon, and Iraq were sent to Palestine. After a month of fighting the Arab states agreed to a truce which the United Nations undertook to monitor. This period, which lasted just a month, was used to bolster the fighting capacities of both forces, but truly herculean efforts on the part of the Israelis enabled them to emerge at the end of the truce far stronger than they were before. However, the public announcements by the Arab governments led their peoples to expect an early victory and the Arab governments refused to extend the truce.

Fighting broke out again on July 8 but the Arab armies were hopelessly disorganized and had no common plan of action. Israeli forces used the next ten days before the second truce greatly to enlarge their area of occupation. During the truce itself, an "Arab Government of All Palestine" was proclaimed in September, recognized by all the Arab governments except Transjordan, which organized a rival "National Congress." The open split between the governments of Kings Farouk and Abdullah encouraged the Israeli military command to concentrate all their strength against the Egyptian forces, and after winning air superiority the Israelis captured the southern area of the former mandate in October. Yet another cease-fire was proclaimed on October 22 in the south, but on that day fighting which spilled over into Lebanese territory broke out in the north. Meanwhile Abdullah had been declared by his supporters to be King of Palestine, and this led to violent reactions in the other Arab countries. Again the Israelis hit the Egyptians on December 22 and penetrated Egyptian territory.

In Cairo public outcries, at first directed against foreigners, quickly turned against the government whose ineffectiveness, despite propaganda and censorship efforts, had become clear. On December 28 a member of the militant Muslim Brotherhood assassinated the prime minister. At this point, seeing that hostilities threatened its interests, Great Britain announced that it would invoke the 1936 treaty to intervene unless Israel withdrew her forces from Egyptian territory and some stability were achieved in Egypt. The Egyptian government wished to avoid British intervention above all, and notified the United Nations that it was prepared to discuss an armistice.

Armistice agreements were negotiated bilaterally between the Israelis and the *separate* Arab countries in the early months of 1949. In the midst of the negotiations the Iraqi government withdrew its forces and so exposed the Transjordanian forces' flank; consequently the Transjordanian government, under threat of a resumption of the war, was forced to cede to Israel additional territory. The Syrian government was unable seriously to undertake armistice negotiations until April, when the others had been concluded, due first to violent public demonstrations leading to a fall of the government and then to a military coup. The latter almost caused Iraqi and Jordanian military intervention in Syria and further split the Arab governments.

The fact, however dressed up or explained, was simply that the Arab states were beaten in the Palestine War.

Fairly uniformly, there was the realization that below the façade of government and authority little real power existed. "But how could this be" was the implicit question behind the outpourings of the critics. The governments of the Arabs who created Islam, who conquered half the world, whose caliphate shone with the bright glow of civilization while Europe slept in the ignorance of the Dark Ages, and whose vast corpus of literature and rich language were admired all over the world, were spotlighted as impotent, backward, corrupt bombasts. The shock of this discovery created a trauma from which Arabic society suffered for a decade. Many sought excuses—the governments, mere puppets left behind in the wake of imperialism were rotten; the arms furnished the Arab armies were worthless; Israel was a front for a combine of the great powers and of course the Arabs were not able to defeat this combine. Radio propaganda warfare, with each state blaming the "other" Arabs for the defeat in Palestine, started in late 1948 and was increased in violence in 1949. Throughout the 1950's and 1960's, it remained a regular feature of the Middle Eastern scene. Many Arabs blamed the West: Israel was the "last stage" of imperialism, was the stepchild of the West, was the way Westerners, shamed by the horrors of the Nazi "final solution," sought to repay the Jews (at the expense of the Arabs), and so forth.

Other Arabs sought the causes in more complex problems of Arab society and politics. A bitter critic of the failure of the Arabs, the former ambassador of Syria to the United States and president of the National University in Damascus, Constantine Zurayq, wrote immediately after the events in 1949, in *The Meaning of the Disaster,* "Seven Arab states declare war on Zionism in Palestine, stop impotent before it, and then turn on their heels. The representatives of the Arabs deliver fiery speeches in the highest international forums, warning what the Arab states and peoples will do if this or that decision be enacted. Declarations fall like bombs from the mouths of officials at the meetings of the Arab League, but when action becomes necessary, the fire is still and quiet, the steel and iron are rusted and twisted, quick to bend and disintegrate. The bombs are hollow and empty. They cause no damage and kill no one." Equally bitter was the statement by the Palestinian Musa Alami, who had helped to found the Arab League. "In the face of the enemy the Arabs were not a state, but petty states; groups, not a nation; each fearing and anxiously watching the other and intriguing against it. What concerned them most and guided their policy was not to win the war and save Palestine from the enemy, but what would happen after the struggle, who would be predominant in Palestine, or annex it to themselves, and how they could achieve their own ambitions. Their announced aim was the salvation of Palestine, and they said that afterward its destiny should be left to its people. This was said with the tongue only. In their hearts all wished it for themselves; and most of them were hurrying to prevent their neighbors from being predominant, even though nothing remained except the offal and bones."*

Most Arabs found it hard to disagree and the press was filled with bitter reproach against the Arab governments. In an oft-quoted passage, from his *Philosophy of the Revolution,* Gamal Abdul Nasser later wrote: "In Palestine I met only friends that shared the work for Egypt, but there I also discovered the thoughts that shed their light on the road ahead. I remember the days I spent in trenches pondering over our problems. Falougha was then besieged and the enemy had concentrated his guns and aircraft heavily and terribly upon it. Often have I said to myself, 'here we are in these underground holes besieged. How we were cheated into a war unprepared and how our destinies have been the plaything of passions, plots and greed. Here we lay under fire unarmed.' As I reached that stage in my thinking my feelings would suddenly jump across the battlefront, across frontiers to Egypt. I found myself saying, 'What is happening in Palestine is but a miniature picture of what was happening in Egypt. Our Mother-Country has been likewise besieged by difficulties as well as

* *Middle East Journal,* 3(1949):385.

ravaged by an enemy. She was cheated and pushed to fight unprepared. Greed, intrigue and passion have toyed with it and left it under fire.' "

The events of the period from the winter of 1948, when it was obvious that the war was lost, onward make clear how widespread was the feeling of malaise in the Arab world. To take Egypt as an example: On November 9 an attempt was made to kill former prime minister Nahhas; on November 13 the printing plant of the major European-language Egyptian newspapers was blown up; on November 28 the leaders of the Muslim Brotherhood were arrested; and on the same day police opened fire on a demonstration in a provincial city; on December 4 the Cairo chief of police was killed by a hand grenade; on December 28 the prime minister was assassinated; and on February 12 the leader of the Muslim Brotherhood was killed. Riots, attempted bombings, and threats were almost daily occurrences. Minor episodes were the divorce by the unloved King Farouk of his popular wife and the bitter, degrading, but revealing fight in the Egyptian parliament over passage of Egypt's first progressive income tax in February 1949.

The first government to collapse, however, was not in Egypt but in Syria where on March 30, 1949, a Kurdish colonel seized power in a bloodless and rapid coup. In all likelihood the coup was "popular" since the public was sick of the failures and ashamed of the weakness of the old regime. But the Syrian parliament refused to legalize the new government and was dismissed. Dismissal of a discredited parliament was not enough and the new government could not build a base of popular support; on August 14, in his turn, the colonel was arrested, tried, and shot by another military clique. The ensuing government was greeted with less warmth than apathy by the Syrian public. This government, in turn, was overthrown by an army lieutenant colonel on December 19, 1950.

Egypt in January 1950 held general elections, won by the Wafd party, which had been out of office during the Palestine War and which now promised a program of basic reforms. Education in particular was to be brought to the whole people as never before, but the government also promised to modernize the army and industrialize the country. These were bold programs and deeply stirred the Egyptian public, for the Wafd, despite many tales of corruption, still had a powerful organization and, comparatively, some luster of its nationalist days in the 1920's.

Recognition that more was wrong with Arab society than a government, or a collection of governments, was made manifest in the United Nations–sponsored conference on social welfare in Cairo in November 1950. Explicit was the notion that poverty and backwardness were direct results of structural defects in Arab society, and implicit was the notion that governments could act to remedy these if they had the will and the intelligence. Titles of many of the papers given at the conference centered on "How should a . . . project" be undertaken or "The practical steps which can be undertaken."

In concluding the conference its chairman, the Egyptian minister of social affairs, said: "This [giving of needed social services and raising the standard of living of the mass of the population] is their right from the State. The time is passed in which social services were rendered as a form of charity. The responsibility of the States has developed; it is no longer confined to matters of order, security, defence and the like, but its prime duty is to secure the welfare of its people, by providing possibilities of employment and adequate wages for a decent living, together with social services including education, medical care, suitable housing, and so forth . . . This is the prime responsibility of the States." This admission, not particularly important in itself, was typical of many which all of the Arab governments made either explicitly as here or implicitly in beginning programs of development as Iraq did in 1950.

Once made, the admission of responsibility, and possibility, raised further questions: If development is, in fact, possible and if the well-being of the citizenry is the "prime responsibility of the States," then does not the blame for past weakness, misery, lack of development, and humiliation fall upon those same states? If development is possible now, was it not possible before? And if it is now possible, is it not possible faster and more fundamentally? Is the development going to be real or merely the subject of wordy conferences? Can it be carried out by parliaments which represent those groups in society—landlords and tribal shaikhs—most firmly and obviously opposed to change? These were the questions of political discussion in the press, where it was free, in the army officers' messes, the coffee houses, and in every gathering of students.

As if in partial answer to the feelings behind such questions, the Wafd government had passed in July 1950 a law making journalists liable to a year in prison and a fine for publishing even innocent information on the biggest Egyptian landlord, the royal family, without government consent. Censorship, fear of confiscation or retaliatory action, caused the press to moderate its attacks, except on the "fair game"—governments in neighboring states. But throughout the area discontent was seething. No one who visited Egypt could miss it. As Sir Malcolm Darling wrote in the Manchester *Guardian* on December 7, 1950, "In the village ignorance may not be bliss, but it is some protection against discontent. Now, however, a new wind blows. With the greatly increased facilities of communication and the steady if very gradual spread of education the seed of new ideas, of new hopes, is carried from town to village. Ignorance of the outer world is no longer universal, but almost universal poverty remains. Herein lies the danger. Poverty and ignorance can lie down more or less happily together, but not poverty and education. That nowadays is likely to be an explosive mixture."

The peasants, themselves, did nothing to overturn the regime, but in the ruling class a split rapidly became manifest. The students, as they often had, led the revolt. Street demonstrations were common during this period, and the government retaliated by cracking down on the students. The Wafd government, originally a product and benefactor of student violence, imposed fines and jail sentences on anyone who incited students to demonstrate. Even professional men had to be banned from striking. By suppression of legitimate protest and itself stimulating the desires of the people for reform, the government contributed to the rise of violence. By December 1950 the press reported agitation in the army of a group known as "The Free Officers."

Meanwhile, the Egyptian government proved unable to win any concessions from the British government on a revision of the 1936 treaty, but encouraged the activity of paramilitary groups against the British army in the Suez Canal Zone. When the British refused Egyptian demands, however, the government turned on those who had supported its anti-British program.

Caught between its own nationalist propaganda, its weakness in dealing with the British forces, and the militancy of its own people, the Egyptian government faltered and fumbled from one mistake to another. While continuing its violent verbal attacks on the British, it ordered the police to fire on demonstrators who repeated its slogans and closed schools and universities where the agitation was carried on. Encouraging a belief that reform was possible and publicly condemning senior officers of the army and even members of the royal family for corruption in supplying faulty arms to the Egyptian forces in the Palestine War, it failed to produce any tangible results of reform or progress.

In July 1951 King Abdullah of Jordan was assassinated by a Palestinian Arab in Jerusalem. This was an act of violence which ripped away the already thin and tattered veil of kingship which had held at least some of the rulers aloof from the sorry plight of their peoples and what an increasing number of army officers and students regarded as the sordid gluttony of the politicians. Revealed were weak men with tarnished scepters. At once they were pulled knee-deep into the muck of corruption and intrigue.

Finally, on January 26, 1952, "Black Friday," anti-Western and anti-privileged-class mobs raced through Cairo, burning, pillaging, and killing. Among the casualties was the world-famous Shepheard's Hotel in Cairo. The Wafd government fell, only to be replaced by a series of weak and less popular teams of ministers. Just hours after the last of these was announced, the army led by the "Free Officers" seized power on July 23, arrested many senior officials, and forced King Farouk to abdicate and leave the country.

14

Coups, Conflicts, and Conferences

THE coup of July 23, 1952, in Egypt was an event of the greatest significance in the Arab countries. Even at its inception, it was viewed by other Arabs as qualitatively different from the coups which had punctuated Iraqi politics in the 1930's or Syrian politics in 1948–50. To many it seemed, from its beginnings, the most needed reform—total abolition of the old regime—before real progress could be made.

In a mood of jubilation other Arabs demanded revolution à *l'Egyptienne.* Even in Lebanon, where cooler heads have created a tradition of commercial shrewdness since the time of the Phoenicians, editorials called for a "complete revolution" which would sweep away the past and all its memories, to bring immediately power, progress, and above all dignity. Plagued by scandals of truly epic proportions, threatened by general strikes, and not supported by the army, the president of Lebanon resigned on September 19, 1952. The chief of staff of the army became prime minister *ad interim,* and a new president was elected by the Chamber of Deputies on September 23. In Lebanon, however, the army refused to stay in politics; in fact, so quickly was power turned back to civilian politicians that the new president had to come to terms with the very forces and vested interests, as represented in the parliament, he presumably had come to office to supplant. The poisonous plant of discontent, so vigorous in the

Lebanon of 1952, was pruned but not extirpated; it was to grow again and to bear the bitter fruit of civil war in 1958.

In Iraq, meanwhile, the process of development had begun under the development board formed in 1950. The rather sudden infusion into the economy of massive oil royalties, as both production and profits soared in the early 1950's, produced a shock to the whole society. The vista of a real and proximate new world seemed to open ahead. Everything appeared ready to sail forward on a wave of change. Yet, the current was neither uniform nor rapid enough to suit many.

Young women, held apart from society more strictly than their cousins in the Levant or Egypt, suddenly emerged into educated society. They, like their brothers, began to win government fellowships for study abroad, and they were "liberated" from the long black gown, the *abba,* which had symbolized their confinement and social disability. But the end of confinement, in some spheres, led to great emotional stress, to the accentuation of a sense of doubt, loneliness, frustration, and fear which haunted and distorted Iraqi intellectual life in the 1950's. In the spring of 1952 a young Iraqi woman was expelled from her college for writing a short story depicting a young woman's hunger for meaning in a time of "tasteless emptiness" in which an "ignorant, leaderless people" still clung to "crippling and immoral social mores." She spoke for too many.

Similarly, the Iraqi young men returning from long periods of education abroad ran head-on into the roadblocks of Iraqi society and bureaucracy. The backward Iraq to which they returned both embarrassed them and spurned them. They were prevented from putting into effect their new learning and felt themselves to be aliens in their own homes. A best seller in those years was an Arabic translation of Turgenev's *Fathers and Sons,* which was set in a Russia of comparable anguish and dislocation. But, in the early 1950's the number of able, energetic, and uncommitted people in Iraq was very small; by the end of the decade it had become powerful. In 1951–52, for example, Iraq had only five native mechanical engineers, but so many of Iraq's more able people were abroad studying that by 1958 it had over a hundred mechanical engineers. Changes of proportional magnitude were in train in all the professions and in other parts of the society as well.

Movement and change were "in the air" in Baghdad. At first each individual rushed headlong toward a better future. There was no focus to the obvious discontent. Times were clearly better. But the "new men" of Iraq were mesmerized by the contrast of a potential future and an actual present. It was only as the government got more efficient and devoted more resources to the development program that its end was hastened. The irony of Iraq lies precisely in this fact: Iraq had the resources and the capital and was developing the people for the inevitable overthrow of the government. If it lacked any of these, the old regime might have lasted years longer.

The government was led by Nuri Said, a wise and experienced stalwart, trained in the Ottoman army, who had fought in the Arab Revolt. He had weathered many a storm and three times fled for his life from (and returned to vanquish) more powerful enemies than what he regarded as mere children of indifferent education. Nuri guided the Iraqi government with a sure hand. Even his enemies respected him, and so popular—or so accepted—was he that his most bitter opponents admitted that he would have won even a free election. He knew what he wanted and how to get it. But Nuri's government was creating a new Iraq in which he and men of the old school would have no place. Great economic and social change was unmatched in political life, which, like a dam, held back the forces of protest. Pressures built steadily until 1958.

The military officers who had engineered the coup in Egypt in July 23, 1952, were clearly unsure what to do with their power. They *were* sure they had to destroy the power of the monarchy and so forced King Farouk to abdicate and leave the country within a few days. It was eleven months, however, before the monarchy was formally abolished. The relationship of the older politicians to the new order was more open-ended. First the government was entrusted to a "clean" politician of the old regime, but the officers also moved to destroy both public recognition of the old elite, by abolishing titles connected with the monarchy, and the base of its power, the ownership of huge tracts of fertile, irrigated lands along the Nile. On September 7 the army took over formal power as General Nagib, the figurehead of the "Free Officers," became prime minister. Most of the ministers, however, were civilian, and as late as March 1954 the officers were still flirting with a return to civilian rule.

It appears clear, in retrospect, that the Free Officers really did not have any precise notion of the structure of the new Egypt they sought. They wanted to abolish much of the old structure, but just how much was determined more by the events of the first two years after they seized power than by any preconceived ideas. For example, it appears that the land distribution program was suggested to the Free Officers *after* the coup as a popular move, one needed for any real progress in the country and the sure way to sap the foundations of their potential opponents, the men of the old order. They did not seize power to carry out land reform, but having seized power set about learning what they could do to improve their chances of staying in power and of uplifting the country. Similar was their attitude toward civilian politicians. It was not until the Muslim Brotherhood militants had tried to assassinate Gamal Abdul Nasser on October 26, 1954, that rival political groups began to be suppressed. And in pressing to get the Sudan recognized as a part of Egypt and to get the British to evacuate Egypt, the new government was carrying forward, more vigorously perhaps, policies espoused by Egyptian governments for over half a century.

Nasser has stated that he never thought his group would have to build a new regime, but that he conceived of his job as one of destroying the old. In his *Philosophy of the Revolution* he speaks bluntly of his "shock," "sorrow," and "bitterness" at the lack of support for the coup. "Prior to that date I imagined that the whole nation was on tip-toes and prepared for action, that it awaited the advance of the vanguard and the storming of the outside walls for it to pour down in a solid phalanx marching faithfully to the great goal . . . After July 23rd I was shocked by the reality. The vanguard performed its task; it stormed the walls of the fort of tyranny; it forced Farouk to abdicate and stood by expecting the mass formations to arrive at their ultimate object. It waited and waited. Endless crowds showed up, but how different is the reality from the vision! The multitudes that arrived were dispersed followers . . . We needed discipline but found chaos behind our lines. We needed unity but found dissensions. We needed action but found nothing but surrender and idleness . . . Personal and persistent selfishness was the rule of the day. The word 'I' was on every tongue."

It is not really necessary to question whether or not the military had always intended to retain power: even if they wished to turn it back to another group, the Free Officers could hardly have done so safely, for having seized the tiger by the tail they had to hang on or be eaten themselves. The question was not whether to retain power but who would exercise it and for what ends. This brought to the surface a power struggle between General Nagib and Lieutenant Colonel Nasser which involved the army, the Muslim Brotherhood, and civilian politicians. Ultimately, after much covert and some overt struggle and maneuver, Nagib was ousted from power and placed under house arrest on November 1, 1954. But the regime was still very far from having an established and agreed policy on domestic issues. Up to that time its energies had largely been absorbed in consolidating power.

The most emotion-laden and popularly watched if not important issue with which the new regime had dealt grew out of its relations with Great Britain. When the British evacuated Cairo in 1945–6, the bulk of their forces, at times as large as 80,000 men, moved to bases in the area of the Suez Canal. Successive Egyptian governments tried to get them to leave Egypt but to no avail. Appeals to the United Nations were unsuccessful. As we have seen, the inability of the last series of precoup governments to satisfy nationalist goals, in large part stimulated by the same governments, was a major factor in their being discredited. After lengthy negotiations the new government achieved this aim in the October 1954 Anglo-Egyptian treaty. By April 14, 1956, the British had evacuated the last of their Suez installations.

The regime was less successful in its attempt to reunite the Sudan and Egypt. The importance of the Sudan to Egypt had long been recognized: it was the conduit through which the Nile River passed and from which Egypt historically derived cheap labor. The Sudan was conquered by the forces of Mehmet Ali Pasha in 1821 and indifferently ruled until it revolted in 1881. When the British came to Egypt, they and the Egyptians reconquered the Sudan in the battle of Omdurman in 1898. After 1899, when it was administratively separated from Egypt, the Sudan was ruled as an Anglo-Egyptian Condominium. Reacting to the nationalist agitation following World War I, when Sir Lee Stack was assassinated in Cairo, the British almost totally excluded the Egyptians from participation in the Sudanese government.

Thus, while Egyptian cultural contacts, particularly through the spread of Islamic teaching from Cairo's Azhar Mosque-University, remained strong, the Sudan began to develop a separate system of administration, to deal directly with Great Britain, and to achieve some sense of separate national identity. Economic activity was sparked by the creation of a rich cotton-growing agricultural area at the confluence of the Blue and White Niles. This brought a degree of prosperity to the Sudan but raised two problems in Sudanese-Egyptian relations: was the amount of water taken from the Nile for use in the Sudan harmful to Egyptian agriculture and was the amount of cotton grown in the Sudan a threat to Egyptian exports. These issues were debated regularly in the press and in various intergovernmental conferences up to 1952 when Britain decided to allow the Sudanese self-determination.

At that time the Egyptians made a determined effort to woo the Sudanese into a union with Egypt. The British and the Egyptians agreed to allow the Sudanese to elect a provisional government which would, after a three-year period, decide whether or not to join Egypt.

It is easy to see why this was a serious tactical mistake for the Egyptians: once the Sudanese had tasted the sweet fruit of self-government, they were unwilling to give it up.

Syria also was unable to achieve a sense of identity or national cohesion. The sequence of coups of 1959 was followed by an interlude in which a civilian government served as a façade for military power. Then Lieutenant Colonel Adib Shishakli openly took power in December 1951, became president in July 1953, only to be ousted from power in February 1954. A civilian government returned to office but the real nature of its power was probably only the relative exhaustion of the many rivals.

Whether Syria was to be an independent state, a part of "Greater Syria," in union with Iraq and/or Jordan, or ultimately a part of a larger Arab state was a question for which Syrians found no answer in the 1950's or 1960's.

The issue which pointed this up most clearly was the Western attempt, particularly from 1953 to 1955, to get the Arab World into an area defense pact. Following the Korean War the United States sought to forge a "shield" of interlocking alliances from Europe to the Far East. It was United States policy to encourage its allies to take the leadership wherever possible in forging these alliances. Since the Middle East was an area of British influence and expertise, Britain's advice and leadership were sought. In British thinking Egypt was the center of military power. Britain's base at Suez contained the major military facilities for the whole area. Therefore, Britain sought, as early as 1951, to bring Egypt into an alliance. But London was unwilling to meet Egyptian demands on the Sudan and the weak and corrupt government of Nahhas Pasha could not compromise on this issue.

American thinking on Middle Eastern defense turned increasingly to what came to be called "the Northern tier," Greece, Turkey, and Iran. This resulted in United States military assistance programs and bilateral military pacts between Turkey and Pakistan in the spring of 1954. At that time the United States began giving military aid to Iraq, but the suggestion that Iraq might join such a pact was strongly attacked by Egypt. Throughout the summer of 1954 it appeared that Egypt might, itself, be receptive to some sort of alliance with Turkey, but her incentive was sharply reduced when Britain, unilaterally, agreed to withdraw from Suez. By December it was clear that Egypt was opposed to other members of the Arab League joining any Western-oriented military pact.

In Iraq, however, the motivations of the government were quite different. Nuri Said, whether in the government or working behind the scenes, was firmly committed to a pro-Western orientation. Iraq, moreover, had begun to benefit by United States military assistance and was on the eve of its great "leap forward" through the development plan, with which it needed Western help. Iraq had its "Suez" also. It sought to get the British to terminate the 1930 Anglo-Iraqi treaty. Great Britain agreed to do this if Iraq joined in an open-ended collective security pact with Turkey. So in February 1955 the Baghdad Pact was born, and in April Britain terminated the 1930 treaty. This led to a violent outburst from Egypt, which accused Iraq of having betrayed the quest for Arab unity. In riposte Egypt sought compensatory stronger ties with Syria and Saudi Arabia and, for a time with Jordan.

The whole relationship of Arabs one to another remains the key unresolved issue in Arab politics. The ideological basis of this problem is discussed below but here it should be pointed out that moves toward some degree of Arab federation or unity had been made or talked about since 1919 when Sharif Husain of Mecca proclaimed himself "King of the Arabs." During the latter phases of World War II, as described above, the Arab states had founded an Arab League. But the Arab League was always as much a cockpit as a coordinating committee. It had effect on the policies of its members only on key issues and then only sporadically. It tried to achieve a coordinated approach to the Palestine War, but it failed. Its attempts to establish what sort of entity "Arab Palestine" should be only high-lighted the profound differences between Kings Farouk and Abdullah. Subsequently, as King Farouk was ousted and Egypt acquired a militant, reforming government of young men while Iraq and Saudi Arabia remained under the control of what the Egyptians regarded as old regimes, the lack of accord became painfully obvious.

As Tom Little, the *Economist* Middle Eastern correspondent, wrote of the October 1955 meeting of the Arab League in Cairo "The Arab League met in Cairo in October in 'an atmosphere of cordiality.' To judge by reports of every meeting it has held in the eleven years in its existence, it has never done otherwise ... the simple fact that the League met at all, after the violent polemics between Egypt and Iraq during the first nine months of 1955, was enough to warrant satisfaction of the Arab statesmen ... Arab unity does not exist. I question whether it has ever existed ... The Arab League revealed from the outset this historical condition of the Arabs: their persistent inability to unite politically but their abiding belief that union is a natural condition of their peoples which only required political formulation. In the Arab League, the Arabs trod a little too heavily upon their own dreams."

Meanwhile, the Palestine problem continued to occupy the attentions of the Arabs and others. When Secretary of State John Foster Dulles visited the Middle East in 1953, he found that whenever he attempted to discuss the Communist menace, his Arab counterparts rejoined with what they considered the more immediate danger of Israel.

Peace, indeed, had never really come to the Middle East. Despite the armistice of the Spring of 1949, the borders of Israel were fronts rather than frontiers. Raids and counterraids, intelligence probes, commando attacks, or foraging expeditions were the order of the day, almost every day. Shootings back and forth across the Syrian-Israeli, Jordanian-Israeli, and Egyptian-Israeli frontiers were normal operating procedure. The United Nations Mixed Armistice Commissions were kept busy sorting out conflicting claims and charges and passing judgment, or recommending censure by the Security Council, for acts of aggression. Between 1949 and 1955 thousands of incidents occurred.

Armistice lines, drawn to fit a haphazard pattern of military events rather than to meet economic, social, or even strategic criteria, make notoriously bad frontiers. In this case they cut off from their normal means of earning a living, either their places of employment or their fields, an estimated 150,000 Arabs. These people, technically not refugees since they still retained their dwellings, were the most grievously hurt of all of those who lost in the Palestine War. As such, they constituted an angry, hungry, and desperate element in the political life of Jordan where most lived.

The others, the legally certified refugees, almost a million strong, were scattered in the surrounding Arab countries. The bulk were in refugee camps maintained by an agency of the United Nations at a cost per person—including everything they got—of less than $2 monthly. That gave them medical attention and food measured at 1600 calories daily. But they were idle, miserable, and sustained by intoxicating memories of an idealized past and enervating dreams of an unlikely future. Idleness became the dry rot of character. As more "refugees" were born each year and the older refugees died off, the number who had ever known a life outside the confines of the camps declined. Able to do little for themselves—few had any skills to sell while most fell into that already saturated economic category of landless agricultural laborers—they bitterly reproached their Arab hosts for their plight. It was a refugee who killed the Arab statesman regarded by non-Arabs as the "most sensible" and realistic on the Palestine issue, King Abdullah. This lesson was not lost on the public figures in the other countries. Everywhere, even if inarticulate, passive, and humbled, the refugee was a reminder of the Arab humiliation and shame in the war and a living indictment of those who had promised to protect him.

Israel had embarked upon a policy of "massive retaliation" for Arab border violations. Demonstrations of this policy came in Israeli raids with regular army units against Nahhalin, Jordan, in March 1954 and Gaza in February 1955. In the latter case the Gaza headquarters of the Egyptian army was the target, and there were sixty-nine Egyptian casualties. Apparently that raid alarmed the Egyptians as no previous raid had and made obvious to them their need for better equipment. When this was not forthcoming from the Western powers on the schedule, on the terms and in the amounts desired, Egypt decided to explore other sources. In September 1955 Nasser announced that Czechoslovakia would supply large quantities of late-model military equipment to Egypt on terms not then known.

It speedily became apparent that the United States viewed this development with alarm, for it appeared that the "northern tier" had been hurdled. But the Arabs, still conscious of a long and often unhappy history of relations with the West, were gleeful. Nasser had done what no other Arab had thought possible. He had used the Cold War to internationalize Arab affairs and so, apparently, gained a lever to extract better terms from both the West and the East.

Meanwhile border friction grew rather than lessened. Israeli forces attacked Syrian positions on October 22, Egyptian positions on November 2, and Syrian outposts on December 11. For these attacks Israel was censured by the Security Council. For its impartiality in voting for censure, the United States got less credit than an outsider would have thought due. The Arabs regarded Israel as a Western state, and Arab, particularly Egyptian, propaganda grew more bitterly anti-Western. In Jordan demonstrations were held in December against the pro-Western government and the Baghdad Pact. The government fell and violence continued well into 1956 until finally, on March 2, the British officer who commanded the Jordanian military forces, Glubb Pasha, was discharged by King Husain in what was perhaps the most popular move made by a Jordanian government. In his place the king named a young Jordanian Arab nationalist. Putting aside the colorful bedouin headgear of the Legionnaires, he dressed them in the drab but "modern" caps of Western armies.

In Iraq, in a bid to win more popularity, the government decided in April 1956 that it would shift its development emphasis from massive but remote and unseen projects, such as it had undertaken, to "impact" projects in the populated areas. But the Iraqi government remained politically and emotionally isolated from the currents of change in the Arab world—for example, in June 1956 it banned a visit by a popular Arab hero, the young Algerian nationalist leader Ahmad ben Bella.

Worsening relations between Egypt and the West induced Secretary of State Dulles to announce on July 20, 1956, that the United States would withdraw an offer to lend Egypt $200 million toward the construction of the Aswan "High Dam." In riposte Nasser nationalized the Suez Canal on July 26.

Western reaction was swift and noisy. The foreign ministers of Britain and France and the American secretary of state met in London on August 2 and organized the first conference of "user states" for August 16. This group sent a mission to Cairo in the first week of September to attempt to work out a compromise solution. None proved possible. Egypt continued to run the canal despite the removal of most of the pilots. Threats and the freezing of Egyptian assets abroad failed to move Nasser. Egypt offered to pay compensation to shareholders in the company but insisted that the canal had been and would continue to be Egyptian. After various moves and pronouncements by all the parties, which will be described in Chapter 17, Israel attacked Egypt on October 29, despite warnings from the United States. Great Britain and France issued an ultimatum ostensibly to both sides and then on October 31 bombed Egypt and on November 2 invaded the canal zone. On November 5 the Anglo-French force captured Port Said but agreed to a United Nations–ordered ceasefire on November 7.

Insofar as there had been careful Allied planning, it presumably had as an immediate object the fall of Nasser. That did not happen. The Egyptians—particularly the guerrilla and paramilitary forces— fought better than had been expected, and there was no attempt at a palace coup.

As the dust settled it was clear that major changes had taken place in the Middle Eastern scene. Suez was going to remain Egyptian; Egypt was going to pay any price to get what it regarded as adequate arms to prevent another defeat; the Jewish, English, and French communities of Egypt, as minority communities always do in such circumstances, paid the price for the acts of those associated with them, had their property sequestered, and for the most part left Egypt; and Israel gained one objective, unhindered passage through the Straits of Tiran to her port in the Gulf of Aqaba, Elath. The failure to enshrine this new situation in a treaty and the subsequent assertion, by Egypt, of its right to close what it regarded as territorial waters to Israeli shipping, was a major contributory cause to the outbreak of fighting a decade later in June, 1967. The United Nations was brought into even closer contact with the Palestine problem as a United Nations Emergency Force (UNEF) was established to monitor the withdrawal of Israeli troops. Again, while this arrangement was to last for a decade and was generally successful in preventing the outbreak of fighting between Egypt and Israel, failures in its initial implementation were to have profound consequences. First, Israel's refusal to allow UN troops on the Israeli side of the frontier exposed the Egyptians to the taunt that "they were hiding behind the skirts of the United Nations." Moreover, while the UN force did act as a buffer, its creation was retrogressive in the sense that the Mixed Armistice Commissions had involved Egyptians and Israelis in daily negotiations. However, for Egypt, the withdrawal of British and French forces symbolized the end of a century of foreign interference—one of the first things Egyptian troops did upon entering Suez was to blow up the statue of Ferdinand de Lesseps.

The Suez crisis had made Nasser an Arab hero. Before his nationalization of the Suez Canal Company and his purchase of arms from the Soviet Bloc, Nasser had been regarded by many Arabs as a strong but colorless modernizer, but weighed in Arab scales, Suez was Stalingrad, El Alamein, and the Battle of Britain rolled into one. In the Arab view Egypt had stopped Britain, France, and Israel and Nasser had defied the world and won. In expression of support for the Egyptians, the Lebanese cut the oil pipeline at Tripoli and the Syrians blew up the Iraq Petroleum Company pipelines. ARAMCO, as an American company, was unharmed. So strongly, in fact, did this emotional wave of pro-Nasser feeling carry the Arabs that young King Husain of Jordan, believing he was about to lose his throne to it, himself struck against the more extreme nationalists in April 1957, dismissing his prime minister and the chief of his army and installing a government in the style of his grandfather, King Abdullah.

Continued Syrian instability led, in February 1958, to a merger of Syria with Egypt to form the United Arab Republic. Moves toward some sort of closer association between the two countries were begun in 1956. In January of that year the new Egyptian constitution proclaimed that the Egyptians were "a part of the Arab nation," and the Syrian parliament, in July, voted to set up a negotiating committee to explore plans for a federal union with Egypt. After an interval of some months, November 1957, a joint parliamentary session was held in Damascus. This group urged further steps toward a federal union. Finally in February, when the Syrians grew alarmed at the rise of Communist power in Syria, the formation of the United Arab Republic was announced. Other Arab states were invited to join in a larger union called the United Arab States. Rather curiously, Yemen, alone among the other Arab states, decided to adhere to this new, and largely theoretical, entity.

Stung by the challenge the formation of the UAR seemed to offer to their security, integrity, and pride, the governments of Iraq and Jordan speedily, on February 14, formed the Arab Union, taking as their flag the banner of the Arab Revolt. Little that had made them separate states was actually affected. It was clear that the initiative and the leadership were in the hands of President Nasser of the United Arab Republic, and the Arab Union aroused few patriotic sentiments.

In Saudi Arabia, where the sudden and vast inflow of riches had produced something like an Arabian nights dream come true, mounting criticism of extravagance, corruption, and decadence led, in April 1958, to a gentle, intrafamily palace coup in which King Saud, the son of King Abdul Aziz, who had died in 1953, handed over power to his brother Crown Prince Faisal.

Just a month later the political and religious factions of Lebanon, which had been at one another's throats since the 1830's, broke into open warfare again. The issue this time was the extent to which Lebanon should be overtly committed to the West, through the Eisenhower Doctrine, or be attached to the major powers of the Arab World, particularly Egypt and Syria. These and other issues tended to divide the country along religious lines with the Christians, in general, favoring closer ties with the West, and the Muslims, with the Arab countries. In these troubled waters the Egyptians and others were fishing. The president of Lebanon, himself a product of the coup of 1952, sought to retain office beyond the constitutional limit and invited the help of the United Nations and ultimately of the United States to this end. All eyes were upon Lebanon when, suddenly and with no apparent warning, the Iraqi army overthrew the government of Nuri Said.

The American reaction was quick and powerful: within hours the first contingents of American marines began landing from the Sixth Fleet. And Britain put air units into Jordan. Unlike Suez, this intervention came at the request of the government and came promptly. But like Suez, it was harder to stop than to begin, more complex to withdraw than to mount. What ultimately made possible a graceful American withdrawal was a Lebanese compromise by which the commander of the Lebanese army, General Fuad Shihab, agreed to become president of the country, and the incumbent agreed to step down.

In Iraq Abdul-Karim Qasim's new government, born of a violent coup and conceived in a social revolution, differed markedly from

207

that of Nasser in Egypt. The king, the crown prince, and the prime minister were hunted down and shot, amid scenes of great brutality and mob hysteria. The military forces which had seized power quickly split among themselves. The moderate, nationalist forces which had set the tone of the movement in the fall and early winter were replaced in 1959 by groups which moved more and more to the radical left. A counter-coup was tried in the spring of 1959; when this failed, it was followed by a savage repression in Mosul and Kirkuk. The government became paralyzed, and the development program ground to a near standstill as the government failed to move on new contracts and defaulted on previous engagements.

The Kurdish followers of Mullah Mustafa Barzani rose against the Iraqi government in the late summer of 1961, rapidly seized the whole of the mountainous area of northeastern Iraq (Kurdistan), and prevented government forces from moving off the plains. In reply, Qasim's government bombed Kurdish villages and issued an endless stream of communiqués announcing that the revolt had been completely crushed, or soon would be, or both. In August 1962, to show the world—and the Iraqi people—their power, the Kurds blew up the oil pipeline which connected Iraq to the Mediterranean. The inability of the Iraqi army to put down the revolt reflected both the lack of trust in the line officers on the part of Qasim, who insisted on controlling all operations, and the inability of his regime to act decisively. Finally, this issue, in conjunction with the other mistakes he had made, precipitated a coup, which on February 8, 1963, resulted in the fall of Qasim's government and his own execution. These events will be treated in detail in Chapter 21, which discusses the Kurdish involvement in Iraqi-Iranian fighting.

In Syria, the United Arab Republic was not destined to last as originally planned. The centrifugal forces were simply too strong. Personal ambitions, regional particularism, and Egyptian insensitivity all played a part. On September 28, 1961, a junta of army officers revolted, established a national government, and ordered all Egyptians to leave the country. On October 19 Syria was readmitted to the Arab League. On December 1 a general election was held, but on March 28, 1962, the new government was overthrown and yet another was installed.

Events in Aden in the 1940's and 1950's were a replay of those in Iraq in the 1920's and 1930's; in both, the British Empire made its strength felt in rural areas through the Royal Air Force and on the townsmen through the manipulation of the trappings of representative government. Inherent in this dualistic policy were bitter conflict and the demise of first British and subsequently all Western influence. Virtually no serious attempt was undertaken to modernize, educate, or unify and, through force of circumstance, the already existing split between the rural and urban areas was widened and deepened.

In southwest Arabia, Aden Port grew into a relatively prosperous and organized enclave of western technology and trade. The growth of the oil industry, the increase of shipping and the shift southward of the fulcrum of British Middle East strategy enriched Aden Port while the tribal areas of what came to be called the Federation were little affected and were, indeed, purposefully left apart. In the distance, beyond the control of the British, Yemen remained a somber, glowering, and unhappy neighbor. Yet, at the end, it was neither the Yemenis nor the wild tribesmen of the hinterland, with whom the British fought Kiplingesque battles, but the sophisticated and relatively pampered, unionized workers of Aden Town who were to destroy the British Empire's position in southwest Arabia.

Formally, Aden became a Crown Colony in 1937 and in 1947 a fully appointed legislative council was created. Half the council were members of the Governor's staff. Even that tame and hand-selected group had no real power because the governor was not compelled to submit questions of public policy to it nor to accept its recommendations. The impossibility of bringing about change through such a group was a prime cause of dissidence among better educated, ambitious younger people. Little was done to take note of their unhappiness. Not until 1955—by which time the Egyptian revolution was already three years old and a new wind was blowing in the Arab Middle East—were a few of the positions on the legislative council made elective. Nor was much attention paid to the growing industrial labor force. In March of 1956, over 6,000 workers struck in Aden. The strike was partly successful and the Commission of Inquiry opined that it was largely justified. But in October, following the Anglo-French-Israeli invasion, the Suez Canal was blocked and Aden Port was virtually shut down. This brought about a severe trade and financial slump and a rise in unemployment among the newly organized workers.

Meanwhile, the Soviet Union, recognizing a new Cold War opportunity, offered arms assistance to Yemen. The equipment and the personnel were utilized by the Yemenis in frontier skirmishes with the British during the early months of 1957. These, in turn, encouraged both the tribesmen who were, among other things, bored by the imposed British peace, and the now strongly disaffected urban radicals of Aden. But these events, real enough in themselves, would probably not have been particularly significant except for what was, ironically, the very caricature of a meaningless political event, the decision of archaic, royalist Yemen to adhere, in an undefined and certainly unimplementable manner to the United Arab Republic which was proclaimed in February 1958. The Imam of Yemen probably hoped that in some yet undetermined way this would help to push the British out of Aden. He was right, but with consequences which would have horrified him. The real result of this incongruous paper creation was that in remote and unsophisticated villages, the aura of President Gamal Abdel Nasser began to penetrate. His charismatic personality proved to be the one missing ingredient in the smoldering anti-British sentiment in southwest Arabia. By the middle of 1958 what had been sporadic and uncoordinated acts of terrorism blossomed into a costly and formless insurrection before which the British decided to bury the problems of Aden Port in the sand of traditional, more favorable, less sophisticated hinterland. This became known as the Federation of the Emirates of the South and was proclaimed on February 11, 1959. The Federation was as outrageous as the Union of Yemen and Egypt. It was seen by the urban Adenis as a "shotgun wedding." The spectre of the union, and particularly the inconclusiveness with which it was approached by the British government, plunged Aden into a turmoil and speedily into a guerrilla war.

All of these issues were thrown into a new light when, on September 9, 1962, the Imam Ahmad of Yemen died and was succeeded by his son, Badr, an irresolute and weak young man who wavered between reaction and reform, liberalization and repression, cruelty and timidity. In less than three weeks after his father's death, the new Imam was overturned by a clumsy and ultimately abortive coup led by his protégé, army chief Abdullah as-Sallal.

Sallal proclaimed himself a field marshal, prime minister, and a leader of the new revolution. He was none of these. But finding this out cost Yemen, Egypt, the British, the Americans, and the Saudi Arabians years, lives, and treasure.

Of minor importance in itself, the Yemen coup precipitated a significant international crisis by affording an occasion for Egypt to establish a dominant position in southwest Arabia. Unsure of itself, the new Yemen government appealed to Cairo for assistance and Cairo quickly but modestly responded. In time, the force of Egyptian troops and advisers grew to about 70,000. Yemen became Egypt's Vietnam, complete with strategic bombing, close air support, paratroop drops, and armor-formation sweeps against an elusive guerrilla force.

The British, already concerned by strident and almost incessant radio attacks over the Cairo-based Voice of the Arabs on its role in Aden, were alarmed. The United States was increasingly concerned with the impact of the Egyptian intervention on the stability of pro-royalist Saudi Arabia whose production of oil was then judged to be vital to the maintenance of the American position in Western Europe. The Egyptians regarded the Yemen revolution, although not of their making, as an opportunity to spread, and therefore protect, the Egyptian revolution against its many enemies. President Nasser told Western diplomats that regardless of the Egyptian assessment of the Yemen revolution (which was not very high), Egypt had to help those who had proclaimed revolution in the name of the principles which guided the Egyptian revolution itself.

Soon the Egyptians had virtually occupied the country and, as the Yemen government proved unable to carry out most of the tasks necessary for the successful prosecution of the war, came to constitute a second and predominant government.

It was natural, perhaps even inevitable, that once the revolution in Yemen had been contested by the royalists, their British and Saudi supporters would come under Egyptian attack. In this unpleasant situation, the United States equivocated, turning a blind eye to Saudi arms and British volunteers for the royalists, and sternly lecturing Nasser on the risks he ran in bombing Saudi Arabia and attempting to subvert Aden, while withholding recognition from the republicans. When, after a long delay, it half-heartedly recognized the Yemen government, America antagonized Saudi Arabia and Britain without gaining new "leverage" in Cairo or Sanaa.

Assassinations, bombings, and terrorist attacks punctuated the southwest Arabian calendar in the next few years. But, for all the sound and fury, the results were inconclusive. No great victory could be announced by either side but gradually the British government realized that it could not "win" and therefore had no reason convincing to its taxpayers why it should expend more men and treasure for "security" in Aden. By early 1967, the British knew the game was up. How to get out gracefully became the central question. The answer was at hand: the United Nations which played no part in the decisions leading to the failure could be the cosmetic to disguise it. A UN mission, like those to Libya and Palestine, arrived in the midst of a general strike; indeed so pervasive was the violence that its members had to travel about Aden Town by helicopter. Its predicted failure was the last nail in the coffin of British rule. By August, the British were withdrawing the last of their troops.

On November 29, the People's Republic of South Yemen was proclaimed in Aden and its citizens, now proficient in the use of the instruments of war, inexperienced in the use of the tools of government, and bitterly divided over the meaning of their revolution turned upon one another. The moderates, tarred by the British brush, were quickly shunted aside and each power struggle carried the government further to the left until South Yemen became perhaps the most radical of the Arab states.

Meanwhile in the other Yemen, the war began to run out of gas. Meeting in the Khartoum "summit" conference of August 1967, Egypt and Saudi Arabia agreed to withdraw support from their proxies. Imam Badr characteristically sulked in exile while Sallal furiously denounced the Egyptians, purged hundreds of "peaceniks," had his minister of the interior shot, and set out for Baghdad to try to recruit a new patron. The republicans seized the occasion to depose him and the royalists, now seeing an opportunity, deposed Badr and tried to get the war underway again. Peace negotiations were tried but proved as inconclusive as the military encounters. The war lingered on, a forgotten event, an anti-climax to which there was no formal conclusion—finally almost everyone just went home.

In other parts of the Arab World, political legitimacy proved elusive. Frequently, indeed, force seemed to have constituted the only really effective claim to legitimacy. Coups were attempted in virtually all the Arab lands. In Iraq and Syria, they came with monotonous regularity. In the Sudan and Libya, they were a new experience.

Just two and a half years after the Sudan achieved independence, on Janary 1, 1956, the army intervened. The coup of November 17, 1958 was bloodless and generally popular but it excited hopes beyond its capacity and the victors were, in turn, overthrown on October 21, 1964 by a remarkable civilian demonstration which paralyzed the country. A series of civilian coalition governments ruled the country until 1969. The slowdown of the national economy, increased dissidence in the south, and failure to agree on national objectives and the constitution of the state led to yet another army intervention on May 25, 1969, under the leadership of a small group of officers under Jafar Numairi. In its turn, this government underwent a violent coup, engineered by the Sudanese Communist Party in July 1971, but after a few tense days in prison, Numairi was returned to power. His position was codified in October 1971 when he was elected president. The Communists were firmly suppressed. Thus, in the few years of its independence, the Sudan has seen one-party rule, coalition, right-wing military rule, a civilian coup, two military coups, a Communist Party takeover, a successful countercoup and the "civilianization" of a military government.

In Libya, the government of King Idris was always a poor compromise in the eyes of most residents of the western provinces. Libya almost stumbled into independence after World War II. Despite its long and desperate struggle before the war, it had failed to galvanize as a nation, except over the issue of anti-Italian colonialism. But to outsiders Libya seemed to matter little. Even inside the pace of change was slow. Libya was essentially untouched by the forces of modernization. Poor and backward, it was only a more accessible Yemen. Then came the golden touch of oil. From modest beginnings in 1959, when it was first discovered, oil began to enrich the government and awaken the people during the 1960's. That proved a heady combination and popular dissatisfaction mounted.

At the same time an unrelated force was set in motion. The American Air Force had focused the training program of its NATO command at Wheelus Field just outside of Tripoli. As part payment for the use of the clear skies and desert gunnery ranges of Libya, the Americans began to train Libyan pilots. To buy time and win friends, the Air Force turned over a few jet trainers and a small piece of the airfield to the Libyans. There the young officers could watch scores of expensive, sophisticated American fighters and bombers flash in and out of the field and roar over the city. What the officers learned in America, what they saw at the airbase and what they envied and despised in the royal government finally coalesced. On September 1, 1969, a group of junior officers, led by Muammar al-Qaddafi followed the lead of their Egyptian model, President Nasser, and abolished the royal regime, proclaiming the Libyan Arab Republic and moving to establish what has been variously termed a "radical," socialist, Islamic, or "purist" regime. Qaddafi speedily became the wealthy *enfant terrible* of the Arab world.

Jaded but not educated, the first generation of the "new era" of Arab freedom, neutrality, and assertiveness ended with the major questions of national life yet to be answered.

15

The Third Round: The Six-Day War of June 1967

HISTORIANS occasionally err by knowing too much and understanding too little of the unfolding of crises. The diplomatic documents, even when they finally emerge in full, tend to foreshorten and distort the decision-making process as well as to focus and clarify the sequences of events. Beneath articulated rationales lie reasons which even if inarticulate are often compelling. Indeed, the phases of unfolding of the major international crises of the twentieth century are so similar as to suggest an almost biological pattern. Pronouncements and events, the foreplay of the crisis, create a tension and excitement that impels men and nations seemingly inevitably toward a climax. In the growth of the passion of the crisis, strong and rational men are easily swept away by the apparent logic and even necessity of each step in a progression which they neither desire nor can control. Having taken steps A, B, and C, statesmen find it difficult, even illogical, to avoid step D—even when step D is not desirable.

It is fortunate that President Kennedy and other American leaders read and pondered Barbara Tuchman's excellent study of the outbreak of World War I, *The Guns of August,* before the onset of the Cuba missile week. No such warning had been read or, if read, appreciated in the Middle East. There, as we shall see, once the events of May 1967, got under way, they, much like the sequence of moves in a passionate love affair, overcame the calculating realism of statesmen and drew them inevitably toward a climactic encounter.

As in all affairs, the beginnings of the crisis were tentative, even unimpressive and fragile. In their early phases, events might have taken a different direction or might have stopped. To understand why they did not, it is as important to know the situation of the participants as it is the individual events.

There was a general propensity on the part of the Arabs and the Israelis to believe the worst about one another. The Arabs were sure that Israel, which they regarded as the last example of imperialism and knew to be a powerful, modernized Western society in their midst, would be impelled by the logic of its situation to attack them if and when it needed more land or concluded that the Arabs were gaining significantly in power. The Israelis, on their side, assumed and were repeatedly warned—by strident public statements of the Arab leaders, by the constant din of the Arab press, and by the bitter invective of the Arab radios—that they were Middle East Public Enemy Number One. At some point in the future, they were constantly told, they would be expelled from the Middle East and their state would be destroyed. The dreary encounters of forty years confirmed the beliefs and assumptions of both parties. It was a fact that the Arabs had lost few opportunities to make the life of the Israelis dangerous or uncomfortable and to arm themselves for what was anticipated to be the final showdown. Conversely, it was a fact that Israel had consorted with Great Britain and France, despite repeated denials of all three powers, to attack Egypt in 1956, and based its security policy on massive retaliation and preventive war.

Thus, when in early May the Soviet, the Syrian, and other intelligence forces asserted that Israel appeared to be on the point of launching a massive raid against Syria, the Arabs were quick to credit the reports. Indeed, they had ample reason to believe that such an attack was justified in terms of Israel's stated policy of retaliation, because the Syrian government had for two years sponsored, equipped, and paid the paramilitary force of al-Fatah to raid northern Israel. Beginning in September 1966, the Israeli government continuously warned the Syrian government of retaliatory action. One of these warnings, made by Israeli Prime Minister Levi Eshkol, came on May 12, 1967, and appeared to confirm intelligence warnings that a large-scale Israeli attack was planned on Syria. The Israelis were, within bounds, not unhappy that the Arabs should believe that such an attack was likely unless Syria stopped supporting the guerrillas. However, the pace of events rapidly got beyond that anticipated by either party.

On May 14, the United Arab Republic Chief of Staff flew to Damascus, and, on the following day, the Egyptian army, in an obvious parade of strength, began to deploy through Cairo toward the Sinai Peninsula. Up to this point, all moves by the Syrian, Israeli, and Egyptian armies may be regarded at least in part as designed for domestic consumption—to show their respective populations that each government was doing its duty in preparing to defend its people. But at this point, events began to take control of men: in every Arab city demonstrations broke out in the belief that the moment of vengeance had come. Even distant and sober Kuwait placed its forces under the nominal command of the United Arab Republic. Old enmities, even those as bitter as that between King Faisal and President Nasser, appeared submerged. By May 27, 1967, the Arab League had unanimously declared the solidarity of the Arab world with the United Arab Republic against the expected Israeli attack.

In this situation, President Nasser once again found himself catapulted into a position of leadership and the recipient of almost universal acclaim—a startling contrast to the scorn dealt him by the Syrians and Jordanians only a few weeks before. A rational approach to the situation at this point would have raised such questions as the ability of the Arabs to match the Israeli army in the field—especially with a large part of Egypt's army still in Yemen—or the ability to stop short of "the brink" if war were to be avoided. Skilled and sober planners would have urged the clear definition of goals and objectives short of the brink and of the means of avoiding miscalculation. There is evidence that some Egyptians attempted to make such calculations. However, even with the most sophisticated intelligence and national security apparatus, "brinksmanship" is a dangerous and crude game. When one confronts another "eyeball-to-eyeball," he must run the risk not only of blinking but of getting a finger in his eye. There are limits to the "game," and the Egyptians, even if they had the will, probably lacked the skill or the power to control events in the required manner. In this circumstance, they seemed hardly to have tried.

The next logical step in the buildup of pressure against Israel was unhindered troop concentration in the Sinai Peninsula. There, the United Nations Emergency Force, UNEF, behind which President Nasser's rivals had constantly accused him of seeking shelter, patrolled the frontier and occupied Sharm ash-Shaikh at the Straits of Tiran. Between May 16 and 18, Egyptian troops forced the withdrawal of UN forces from strategic positions and requested that UN

Secretary General Thant withdraw all UNEF forces "as soon as possible". The Secretary General complied with the request at a speed which subsequently caused him to be criticized by Israel and the Western countries. In his defense, the Secretary General subsequently said "it is entirely unrealistic to maintain that the conflict would have been solved, or its consequences prevented, if a greater effort had been made to maintain UNEF's presence in the area against the will of the government of the United Arab Republic." Two of the seven governments supplying troops to the contingent, he pointed out, had already notified the United Nations that they were withdrawing their troops. Moreover, he stressed, when a member government requested the withdrawal, no legal or political base remained for the continued presence of UN troops. Illustrative of this point is the fact that Israel, as late as May 18, refused to allow UNEF to be stationed on Israeli territory in a last-minute attempt to retain their peace-keeping role. Lastly, U Thant and others pointed out, the UNEF was a symbolic rather than a serious military unit. It was not only small but unarmed.

By May 23, UNEF units were withdrawn from the Straits of Tiran and this posed the ultimate question—would Egypt close the Straits to Israeli shipping, an act which Israel had clearly warned would be taken as a cause of war?

> This is the question all Arabs are asking: Will Egypt restore its batteries and guns and close its territorial waters in the Tiran Strait to the enemy? Logic, wisdom, and nationalism make it incumbent upon Egypt to do so . . . if she fails to do so what value would there be in military demonstrations?

This was the contribution of Amman Radio in those critical days. The answer which President Nasser gave was clear:

> Under no circumstances will we allow the Israeli flag to pass through the Gulf of Aqaba. The Jews threaten war. We tell them you are welcome. We are ready for war, but under no circumstances will we abandon any of our rights. This water is ours.

In retrospect it appears clear that then the die was cast. It would have been almost impossible for Nasser to back down from his public statements although there is some reason to believe that he hoped, even at this stage, that Israel would acquiesce in the "blockade" (which, ironically, was never enforced) and would agree to submit the case to the World Court.

During these hectic days, the United States government was making intensive efforts to calm the Middle Eastern situation and to find some means of compromise. But for the strenuous urging of the United States, the Israelis probably would have attacked almost immediately. In the more public aspects of its diplomatic action, the American government issued a statement emphasizing that "the United States considers the Gulf to be an international waterway and feels that a blockade of Israeli shipping is illegal and potentially disastrous to the cause of peace." The British government took a similar public position and, presumably, as a result of British government initiatives, the Soviet Ambassador dramatically awakened President Nasser in the early hours of the morning of May 26 to deliver a Soviet demarche counseling restraint. In a curious echo from the events of 1956, the British Foreign Secretary called for a "maritime declaration" to marshal multilateral support for an end to the Gulf of Aqaba blockade.

Meanwhile, so long as President Nasser was embarked on a straight and clear anti-Israeli course, no Arab leader could gainsay him. It appeared just barely possible that the last-minute breakdown of Arab unity, the ruptured diplomatic relations between Jordan and Syria on May 23, would serve to divert the forces which had appeared so clearly on a collision course. But, dramatically, on May 30 Jordan's King Husain flew to Cairo to embrace Egypt's President and his policy. The two rulers signed a mutual defense pact and organized a defense council and joint high command under the Chief of Staff of the Egyptian armed forces. Thus, only seven days after the rupture of diplomatic relations between Jordan and Syria the outline of a unified military organization had been drafted. Within a few days, Iraq joined the new military alliance and token units of Egyptian and Iraqi forces moved into Jordan.

In almost continuous behind-the-scenes negotiations, the United States government had used intensive pressure on the Israeli government to forestall immediate military action. It had not, however, been able to devise any peaceful scheme which appeared likely to bring to a halt the Arab military preparations or to reopen the Straits of Tiran. In its last move, the American government had arranged to bring the Egyptian Vice President to Washington for urgent talks. The decision was made on Saturday, June 3, and the Egyptian Vice President was due to arrive on Wednesday, June 7, in what was an almost classic example of "too little and too late."

While the full record is not yet—and will not for many years—become public, four aspects of the crisis are now known. First, President Johnson, after consultation with former President Eisenhower, was prepared to use American naval power to break the blockade of the Straits of Tiran. Second, Israeli Prime Minister Levi Eshkol told the

American government in the last few days of May that Israel would hold off military action for two weeks to give the Americans a chance to prevent war. It was in this context that the Egyptian and American presidents decided to send their vice presidents to exchange visits in Cairo and Washington to offer a face-saving way out of the crisis. Third, King Husain's sudden visit to Cairo—where he had been publicly excoriated as a traitor to the Arab cause—on May 30, appears to have jolted the Israeli government more severely than outsiders realized and was probably the major precipitating cause of the Israeli attack. And, fourth, Israel made the decision to go to war at least as early as June 2. At least as late as the late evening of June 3, however, the American government believed that the crisis was subsiding and that Israel would not attack.

Two hours after dawn on Monday, June 5, fighter bombers of the Israeli Air Force caught on the ground and largely destroyed the bulk of the Egyptian Air Force.

The events of the six-day war were predicted. They are vividly described in a deluge of books, articles, and press dispatches. Briefly, the Israeli army, having acquired mastery of the air, defeated the Egyptian army in Sinai, in a series of classic tank and artillery duels, and established itself on the East Bank of the Suez Canal. Meanwhile, Jordan opened hostilities in and around Jerusalem, as presumably required by the five-day-old mutual defense pact. The Israeli government tried to get the Jordan government to cease fighting, offering a sort of informal separate peace; but no Jordanian government could have accepted and survived. Consequently, the Jordanian forces were driven, in some of the fiercest fighting of the war, back across the Jordan River. Iraq, Saudi Arabia, and Lebanon did not take direct or meaningful parts in the war. Lastly, Syria was the object of a furious frontal assault which cleared the Golan Heights and destroyed the Syrian army's combat capability.

The Israelis had demonstrated conclusively that a modern nation can muster and deploy power on a different scale of effectiveness and quality than can underdeveloped countries. Its soldiers were not supermen but were highly motivated, well trained, and excellently led. Against this order of battle of a modern people, all the Migs and tanks were, as all serious critics knew, largely irrelevant. The six-day war was not a replay of Napoleon's Battle of the Pyramids, but there were similarities.

This war of June 1967 was extremely costly to the Arab countries. The extent of material damage and loss of life in the military is

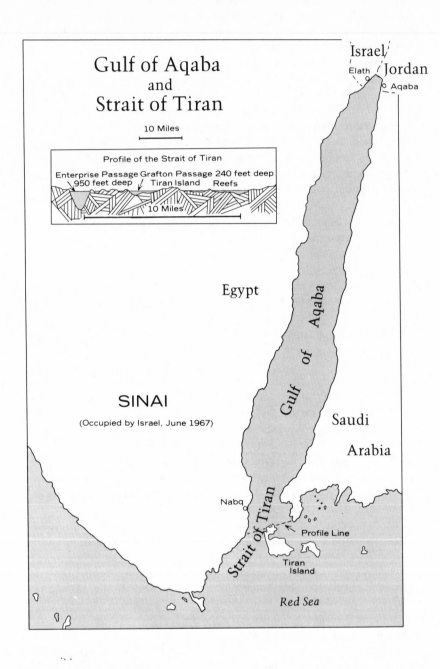

Gulf of Aqaba
and
Strait of Tiran

10 Miles

Profile of the Strait of Tiran

Enterprise Passage Grafton Passage 240 feet deep
950 feet deep / Tiran Island Reefs

10 Miles

Israel

Elath Jordan

Aqaba

Egypt

Gulf of Aqaba

SINAI

(Occupied by Israel, June 1967)

Saudi

Arabia

Nabq

Strait of Tiran

Profile Line

Tiran
Island

Red Sea

known, but the meaning behind the statistics is more difficult to assess. The loss, for example, of 25,000 to 30,000 able-bodied, disciplined, relatively well-trained men amounts to losing perhaps five percent of the then modernized labor force of the Arab countries. In terms of a rough comparison with the United States, this would be a loss of approximately five million men. In fact, the loss may be even greater, because the proportional expenditure of skilled personnel and resources to train these men was much higher than would be a similar task in a developed country.

The most serious blow was psychological. While difficult to measure, the effect was pervasive, distorting, and crippling. Not only did Arab leaders find thought or planning on the urgent tasks of development more difficult but defeat appeared to turn the prewar euphoria into a sullen and tenacious hatred.

The third aspect of the loss was economic. A United Nations survey indicates that Israeli occupation of the West Bank of the Jordan River deprived Jordan of approximately 38 percent of her productive capacity. In certain sectors the decline was even more stunning: tourism declined 85 percent and 80 percent of the olive crop was lost.

Lebanon, which managed to stay out of the war, lost approximately 26 percent of its tourist revenue, and Saudi Arabia, unaffected directly, lost 9 percent of its oil revenues and felt obliged to contribute heavily to emergency funds for Jordan and Egypt. The losses in Egypt included oil production in the Sinai Peninsula and revenues from the Suez Canal and from the oil refineries along the Canal. The large-scale destruction of cities along the canal made the recovery problem all the more difficult. Additional burdens were imposed by swarms of refugees pouring into the underdeveloped and damaged Arab economies from the battle zones and occupied areas.

Collectively, these events severely undercut development programs even in those countries not directly affected by the war. The true cost may be measured in the slowdown of national development programs. Egypt, for example, fell from an average rate of growth of about 6 percent in the period 1960 to 1965 to an average of about 3 percent from 1965 to 1970. The 50 percent drop does not give a true or full picture, for when considered in the context of the rise of population, it meant that there was no per capita growth at all.

When the dust settled, the map of the Middle East was found to be profoundly altered. Israel controlled vast new pieces of territory carved out of the states of Syria, Jordan, and Egypt in which about one and a half million Arabs lived. In the euphoria of victory, the nature of the new dilemma gradually became visible: however attractive appeared the acquisition of new territory, providing more "secure" frontiers, further from Israeli settlements, what about the conquered peoples?

In a perceptive account shortly after the end of the fighting, prepared by the Institute for Strategic Studies, Michael Howard and Robert Hunter prophesied that

> the Israelis may well look back with regret to the days when Israel was almost as homogeneous a Jewish state as its Zionist founders intended; for it will never be that again. Two and a half million Jews now control territory containing nearly a million and a half Arabs, and whatever settlement is made on the West Bank, Arabs are likely in future to make up at least a quarter of Israel's population. Israel will be confronted with all the problems of a multi-racial society, in which the minority group is potentially hostile and sustained by powerful consanguineous supporters beyond the frontier.

Arab terrorists proved effective, as have practically all terrorist movements in carrying out sporadic attacks. While these attacks fell far short of the obvious aim of disrupting the Israeli state, they produced one major result: the polarization of society. Whatever attempts the Israelis made to defuse the Palestine national movement, at least among those Arabs under their control, they were thwarted by such events as that reported by the *New York Times* on September 4, 1968. This instance was a bombing which caused only moderate immediate damage but a predictably ugly mob reaction. Gangs of young men from the Jewish community attacked and severely beat Israeli Arab peddlers, shopkeepers, and other innocent bystanders. The long-term reaction of the beaten and innocent bystanders was one of fear, alienation, and hatred toward those who beat them. Even if they personally felt angry about the individuals who carried out the bombing, and disagreed with their aims, they could not escape being "polarized" as Arabs.

Toward them, Israeli policy was complex. Israel really did not, of course, want them. Even those Israelis who wanted to keep the conquered territories, wanted them empty. Like the early Zionists who had hoped for a "Land without a People for a People without a Land," the Israeli leaders of the period after the 1967 war found the reality hard to accept. They had, in fact, acquired about one and a half million Arabs.

Although cut off from political participation in the events of the Arab countries, even among the Palestine refugees who will be discussed in the next chapter, the Arabs of the occupied areas were an issue in Arab politics and a few notes on their situation are necessary here.

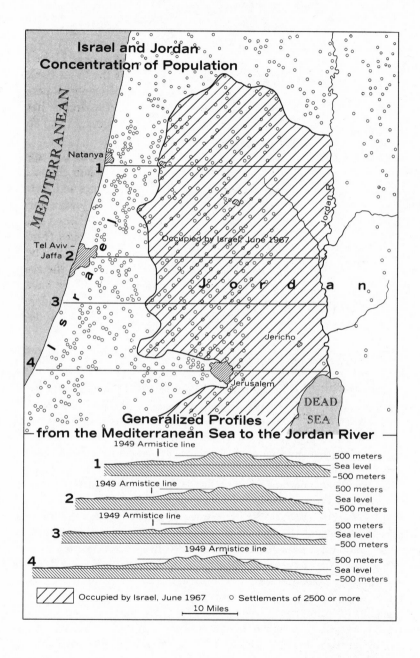

Israel and Jordan
Concentration of Population

MEDITERRANEAN

Natanya

1

Tel Aviv – Jaffa

2

3

4

Occupied by Israel June 1967

Jordan

Jericho

Jerusalem

DEAD SEA

Generalized Profiles
from the Mediterranean Sea to the Jordan River

1949 Armistice line

1   500 meters / Sea level / –500 meters

1949 Armistice line

2   500 meters / Sea level / –500 meters

1949 Armistice line

3   500 meters / Sea level / –500 meters

1949 Armistice line

4   500 meters / Sea level / –500 meters

Occupied by Israel, June 1967   ○ Settlements of 2500 or more

10 Miles

In the immediate aftermath of the war, each challenge to the government or hostile act was ruthlessly put down. Harboring guerrillas or being identified with them subjected houseowners to destruction of their houses, imprisonment, or deportation. Large areas were cleared. Several villages were then completely razed. The Arab population of sensitive areas was moved and Jews have been placed in their stead. This was most evident in the Golan Heights, Sinai, and Jerusalem.

In defiance of the United Nations Security Council resolution and despite objections by the United States, Israel rushed completion of a project to settle what was Arab Jerusalem with Jewish inhabitants. "The object of the settlement," the Israeli Mayor was quoted as saying, in the *New York Times* of July 3, 1968, "is to insure that all of Jerusalem remains forever a part of Israel. If this city is to be our capitol, then we have to make it an integral part of our country and we need Jewish inhabitants to do that." To accomplish this purpose, the Israelis initially expropriated over 800 acres in the Arab city.

The most serious obstacle faced by Israel in its attempt to neutralize the Arab community living within Israel—both those Arabs who were Israeli citizens and those living under occupation—was the fact that Israel has always proclaimed itself to be a Jewish state, a state to which Jews all over the world have a special relationship and in which Jewish immigrants can automatically become citizens, a state whose flag is the Star of David and whose national anthem is the Hatikvah. While some Arabs managed to assimilate, including upwards of a thousand who married Jewish women, most suffered the dark fears reported in the Peel Commission Report in 1937: that in a Jewish state they would be little better than the Canaanites of old, "hewers of wood and bearers of water."

The most dangerous spot, in terms of physical security, was the Gaza strip. The huge refugee population was under the control of the guerrilla organizations' local emissaries, themselves in only tenuous contact with the main organizations in Amman and Beirut. There Israeli military forces, after a number of months of virtual siege, struck in a "search and destroy" type of operation and successfully hunted down and killed or captured all the guerrillas.

What to do with the Palestinians remained the issue. Gradually, the issue seemed to resolve itself as the attractiveness of the Arabs as a cheap labor force became evident. In increasing numbers, the Arabs were daily driven into Israel from Gaza and the West Bank to work. Not allowed to remain overnight, they became the Middle Eastern equivalent to the Chicanos in America, the Turks in Germany, the Pakistanis in England, the Algerians in France, or even the blacks in South Africa. Many in Israel were disturbed at the erosion of the original Zionist ideal but the pragmatic attractions were difficult to deny: Israel had much to do, the Arabs were in need of work, and perhaps a closer exposure to the reality of life in Israel would calm Arab fears and heal Arab hate. This, at least, Israeli "doves" hoped.

It is true that major efforts have been made by the Israeli government and by particular individuals within it to find methods of political compromise. The Mayor of Jerusalem made significant efforts after the expropriations to show his desire to be regarded as the Mayor of all Jerusalem. Even General Moshe Dayan, then the leading representative of the Israeli "hawks," went out of his way to try to build "bridges" with the Arab community.

Although they have few ways to express themselves, the Arabs appear to have remained unmoved. It would be remarkable if they were won over for what they were offered could not meet their national aspirations in any sense. Neither Israeli doves nor hawks wanted a binational state and merely by working in Israeli projects, the Arabs could not become Jews. So the Arabs sat and waited, happy to have money, but struggling with a sense of guilt in taking it. Realizing that they could only get hurt, they gave little support to the guerrillas but similarly abstained from participating, as in the Jerusalem elections of 1969, in Israeli political affairs. By the spring of 1973, even Israeli doves conceded that the bridges to the east remained down.*

As the booklet prepared by the Institute for Strategic Studies ends, "Israel thus faces a dilemma to which her military talents provide no solution, and to which even nuclear weapons will be irrelevant. A strategically secure frontier, in the South and the East, will give her a strategically insecure population."

Throughout the Middle East crisis, the American government had organized itself to keep in the closest possible touch with events but had maintained a posture of distant reserve. This was in part enforced upon the government by the fact that the Arab states, charging that the American military units had assisted Israel in the surprise air attack of June 5, 1967, had broken diplomatic relations. More significant, however, was the belief of President Johnson and his close advisers that there was little or nothing that the United States could do under the circumstances and that it was best, perhaps, to let events in the Middle East take their course. This latter contention was based in part upon the belief that the Soviet Union had suffered a serious setback in its Middle Eastern policy because of its unwillingness to intervene on the Arab side but more significantly because Israel, having won the war, had apparently created a new Middle East which was at least not worse than the Middle East with which American policy makers had struggled unsuccessfully for twenty years.

The first major presidential intervention in the Middle East crisis came on June 19, 1967, when President Johnson enunciated five "great principles of peace in the region." These were

(1) "Every nation in the area has a fundamental right to live and to have this right respected by its neighbors."

(2) "Justice for the refugees." "There will be no peace for any party in the Middle East unless this problem is attacked with new energy by all and, certainly, primarily by those who are immediately concerned."

(3) "A third lesson from this last month is that maritime rights must be respected . . . the right of innocent maritime passage must be preserved for all nations."

(4) "Now the waste and futility of the arms race must be apparent to all the peoples of the world. And now there is another moment of

* See the article by Jim Hoagland, "Israeli Sentiment: Keep Land But Not Arabs," *International Herald Tribune,* June 29, 1973.

choice. The United States of America, for its part, will use every resource of diplomacy and every counsel of reason and prudence to try to find a better course."

(5) "Fifth, the crisis underlines the importance of respect for political independence and territorial integrity of all the states of the area."

Rhetoric aside, the American government had already reached the decision by June 8, 1967, that peace with an Egypt led by President Nasser was unacceptable. Nasser's accusation that America had intervened in the war and breaking of diplomatic relations was accepted in cold anger. President Johnson was content to let Nasser live with his words and deeds.

Desiring to keep the problems of the Middle East at arm's length, the United States joined with other nations in a series of debates and resolutions aimed at constituting the United Nations as the focus of diplomatic activity. Thus, when Nasser sent an emissary to the United States in early November to work out an approach to peace, he was rebuffed. The United States supported but did not take the lead in drafting or urging adoption of a British-sponsored resolution aimed at setting forth a basis for peace. Adopted by the Security Council on November 22, Resolution 242 has become a pivotal document. Like the Balfour Declaration with which the Palestine story began, so to speak, it is short and every word and phrase is the result of hours of consultation, compromise, and debate. Drafted by British Minister of State for Foreign Affairs Lord Caradon, it reads as follows:

The Security Council,

Expressing its continuing concern with the grave situation in the Middle East,

Emphasizing the inadmissibility of the acquisition of territory by war and the need to work for a just and lasting peace in which every State in the area can live in security,

Emphasizing further that all Member States in their acceptance of the Charter of the United Nations have undertaken a commitment to act in accordance with Article 2 of the Charter,

1. *Affirms* that the fulfilment of Charter principles requires the establishment of a just and lasting peace in the Middle East which should include the application of both the following principles:

(i) Withdrawal of Israeli armed forces from territories* occupied in the recent conflict;

* The article "the" before "territories" was purposely left out of the English version but is included in the French version. The distinction, which could not be expressed in French, allowed for future compromise on whether [all] the territories or merely [some] territories would be returned. It was on this basis that the vote was unanimous. The ambiguity has, obviously, given rise to great controversy ever since.

(ii) Termination of all claims or states of belligerency and respect for and acknowledgement of the sovereignty, territorial integrity and political independence of every State in the area and their right to live in peace within secure and recognized boundaries free from threats or acts of force;

2. *Affirms further* the necessity

(a) For guaranteeing freedom of navigation through international waterways in the area;

(b) For achieving a just settlement of the refugee problem;

(c) For guaranteeing the territorial inviolability and political independence of every State in the area, through measures including the establishment of demilitarized zones;

3. *Requests* the Secretary-General to designate a Special Representative to proceed to the Middle East to establish and maintain contacts with the States concerned in order to promote agreement and assist efforts to achieve a peaceful and accepted settlement in accordance with the provisions and principles in this resolution;

4. *Requests* the Secretary-General to report to the Security Council on the progress of the efforts of the Special Representative as soon as possible.

In addition to declaring that the acquisition of territory by warfare was inadmissible, the resolution set out a series of principles for the establishment of peace. Included among these were Israeli withdrawal from Arab territory, an end to the state of belligerency, respect for the integrity of each state in the area, freedom from threats or acts of violence, freedom of navigation through international waterways, and reaffirmation of the rights of refugees. The resolution required that the Secretary General designate a representative to arbitrate the dispute in the area. On November 23, therefore, Swedish Ambassador Gunnar Jarring was appointed the Security Council's representative.

Ambassador Jarring undertook his assignment in most difficult circumstances. The Israeli government informed him at the first meeting that it did not agree to his mission. A settlement, the government of Israel asserted, "could be reached only through direct negotiations between the parties culminating in a peace treaty and ... there could be no question of withdrawal of ... forces prior to such a settlement." Israel proposed a face-to-face meeting to discuss an agenda. Jordan and the United Arab Republic (Egypt) refused to discuss even an agenda until Israeli forces had withdrawn to the June 4, 1967 frontiers. Both sides continued to affirm their acceptance of their interpretations of Resolution 242 but were adamant on the sequence of steps leading to its implementation: Israel, negotiations first; Egypt and Jordan, withdrawal first. There, despite numerous meetings with Ambassador Jarring, both sides remained.

But the situation was far from static. First, the war gave a powerful impetus to the Palestinian political-guerrilla groups. (This development will be the subject of the next chapter.) Second, it was an enormous setback for President Nasser. After a theatrical gesture of threatening to resign on June 9 Nasser suffered a severe recurrence of his diabetes. Told that one or both legs might have to be amputated, Nasser went off to the Soviet Union for medical treatment and rest. His vice-president and the man most personally implicated in the events leading to the war, Field Marshal Abdul Hakim Amr, was arrested on September 4 along with some 50 senior military officers, and allegedly committed suicide on September 14. The Egyptian regime appeared profoundly shaken but no serious internal challenger appeared.

Externally, Egypt was able to use the war to heal its breach with the conservative, oil-producing countries of the Arabian peninsula. Toward the end of August, a "summit" conference was held in Khartoum to attempt to settle outstanding problems and to rally support for those most wounded by the war. For Egypt, the conference was a major success. Not only was the issue of Yemen, in which a sizable portion of the Egyptian army was still bogged down, settled in an Egyptian-Saudi accord, but the oil-producing states agreed to give Egypt and Jordan approximately $350 million yearly to make up for their loss of revenue with the decline of tourism and the closure of the Suez Canal.

Meanwhile, on the Suez front, "no war, no peace" was established as the normal situation. Great artillery exchanges became the order of the day. By late October, the cities of the Suez Canal had been reduced to smoking, vacant ruins.

On the eastern fronts, military actions were less massive but no less bitter. On January 8, 1968 a full-scale engagement of tanks, jets, and artillery took place and on March 21, 12,000 Israeli troops attacked Jordan along a 200-mile front. Partly because it was condemned by the Security Council for this action on March 24, Israel began to employ smaller commando units in punitive raids and counter-guerrilla strikes. While Syria stood sullenly but quietly aloof, Lebanon suffered heavily in prestige when, on December 28, an Israeli commando unit attacked Beirut International Airport, in retaliation for a guerrilla attack, and destroyed 13 commercial jet airliners belonging to Lebanese companies.

While these clashes always threatened to lead to large-scale war and were economically costly and psychologically enervating, they were even more important in that they both required and justified large and increasing budgets for arms. The Jordanian defense budget jumped almost 25 percent to approximately $80 million while Syria's outlay reached $140 million: whereas the Jordanians got their new jets and tanks from American suppliers, the Syrians got theirs from the Soviet Union. In both Egypt and Israel, military expenditures reached over 20 percent of Gross National Product. Both not only replaced the equipment lost in the war but acquired larger inventories of even more destructive and sophisticated matériel. Thus, far from securing a reduction in military expenditure, Israel found itself on the morrow of its smashing victory spending the highest proportion of GNP on "security" of any country on earth.

In the context of the weakness of the Arab governments, their inability to accept defeat, the anger of their more militant citizens at the "shame" of their performance in the June 1967 war, and the failure of the Jarring Mission and other moves toward peace, the stage was nearly set for a Fourth Round. But, at this point the action shifted, or appeared to shift, from the governments and states to the displaced Palestinians who were trying to form their own state in exile.

16

The Palestine Arab Diaspora

URING the past sixty years, the Arabic-speaking inhabitants of Palestine have attempted
to coalesce into a nation and to create national institutions. On both
scores they have failed to meet the challenges they have faced. To
date, Palestinians have not managed to achieve territorial, social, or
political unity or to agree upon either institutions or leaders. Their
attempts and failures are wellsprings of some of the diffusion, disorga-
nization, and despair so evident in recent Middle Eastern history.

In the Balfour Declaration, the Palestinians were referred to as the
"existing non-Jewish communities."* With unintended irony this
curious phrase grouped Christian, Muslim, Druze, and others in a
subordinate category and implicitly denied that newly conquered
Palestine constituted a coherent nation capable of statehood.

The major contemporary characteristics of the "existing non-Jewish communities" were language, religion, occupation, and sense of
origin. Virtually all "existing non-Jewish communities" spoke Arabic.
They were divided, however, into several Christian and Muslim sects.
These religious differentiations were not only more profound but

* Fifty years later, Israeli Premier Golda Meir was widely quoted as saying
"There was no such thing as Palestinians." Now few responsible Israelis would
support that view but it had a profound effect on the already desperate Palestinians.

231

more pervasive than those with which Westerners are familiar. Religion, in the Ottoman Empire, was regarded as the basis of "community." Each community (Turkish: *millet*) was allowed a high degree of autonomy in precisely those areas which in Western law constitute the distinguishing characteristics of the state: military service, taxation, family status (marriage, divorce), property transference, and inheritance. The religious leader of each community was deputized by the state to perform a broad spectrum of political, social, and religious functions. His community was largely autonomous vis-à-vis the central government, and formally unrelated, politically and administratively, to other communities.

In addition to language and religion, the third significant division of the "existing non-Jewish communities" was occupational and/or geographical. Most of the Arabic-speaking population lived in villages and engaged in agricultural or agriculture-related crafts and trades. The village communities acquired a high degree of cultural, political, and fiscal independence from the state and from one another. Almost all marriages were contracted within villages and property was rarely farmed by "foreigners." Villages asserted rights of corporate self defense, customs collection, communal assets such as wells and streams; they marched under village flags, mounted village militias, paid taxes as a unit, and assessed these taxes amongst themselves. In short, the effective political unit in most of the country was the village. The wider world was unknown, the Ottoman government was the tax collecting enemy, and the concept of a Palestinian nation-state was unimagined.

Despite the challenge of Zionism and some training in civil administration, Arabic speakers were unable to overcome their divisions in the Mandate era. They did, increasingly, develop a sense of common origin. But defeat (by the British) in the rebellion of 1936 to 1939 and removal of the incipient national leadership in its aftermath, wartime martial law, and defeat and migration in the 1948–49 war shattered what little unity had painfully and slowly evolved. Although extensively a small-scale affair in comparison to European wars, the 1948–49 war was intensively one of the most disruptive in modern times. Upwards of 80 percent—about 800,000—of the Arab population of Palestine lost their homes, lands, and country. In the summer of 1950, the UN Agency established to care for them estimated that 896,690 Palestinians were living as refugees on a UN dole. Thirty-one thousand were in Israel and the rest scattered and largely cut off from one another in widely separated camps in Lebanon, Syria, Jordan, and the Gaza Strip.

In the camps the refugees lived in a "deplorable material and moral situation." The most employable, the best educated, and the lucky found temporary or permanent homes in Iraq, Kuwait, Saudi Arabia, Libya, or further afield; those who remained in the camps lived in a limbo in which they initially gave up trying to control their destiny. Their condition was beyond desperation—desperation is, after all, an emotion of one who still actively tries to control his fate. Most of the refugees grew to adulthood or into old age in ragged tents, some in caves, and many in public buildings converted into dormitories by burlap drapes. Less than $27 per capita per annum for medical care, food, shelter, and clothing was the total spent by UNRWA. The monthly individual food ration was valued on the local market at $1.80 and was estimated to provide a daily intake of 1600 calories.

If the material diet was insipid, it was sustaining. The emotional diet was fatty and noxious. It consisted of a blend of exaggerated memories and unrealistic hopes. Idleness was a dry rot in adults and camp life a stultifying atmosphere for the young. And the young predominated. A decade after the end of the war, over 50 percent of the refugees had not lived as much as ten years outside of the refugee camps.

Like Moses' sojourn in the desert, the refugees' sojourn in the camps saw the rise of a new generation. The first refugee generation, primarily composed of former peasant farmers, conserved the mores, political context, and culture—indeed virtually recreated the "neighborhood"—of their villages, and increasingly found itself cut off from the hopes and fears of the young. Never having known life outside the camps, the younger men and women, the "pure refugees," differed radically from the elders. Their worlds were narrow and confined, their experiences and loyalties were centered in the camps. Each camp became a world unto itself. Divided from one another by national frontiers and economic barriers, they grew up in an atmosphere even more fractured and disorganized than that of their fathers. The more desperately they longed for and strove after national coherence, the more frustratingly and completely it eluded them.

Dependent upon the United Nations for a monthly dole, they depended upon the inhabitants of the "host country" for everything else. Jobs were few and payment exploitative. Both pitied and resented, they competed for the available jobs and were a constant reminder of Arab weakness. Those in the camps in Lebanon needed but hated—and were used by but annoyed—the Lebanese. Those in Syria suffered a similar grateful-resentful relationship with the Syri-

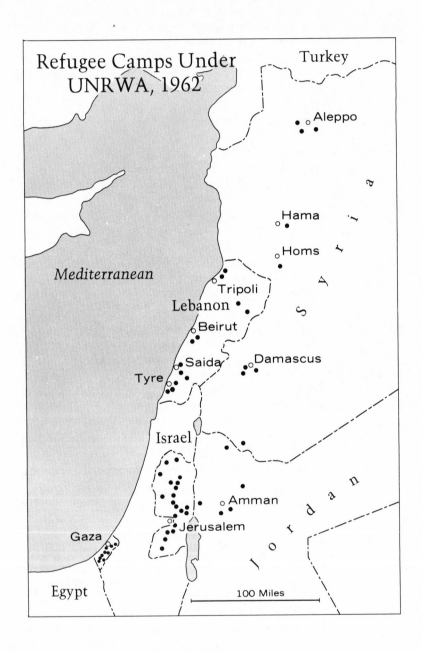

Refugee Camps Under
UNRWA, 1962

Turkey

Aleppo

S y r i a

Hama

Homs

Mediterranean

Tripoli

Lebanon

Beirut

Saida

Damascus

Tyre

Israel

J o r d a n

Amman

Gaza

Jerusalem

Egypt

100 Miles

ans. Those in Gaza were totally cut off from Egyptian society. The Jordanian-Palestinian relationship was easier. Palestinians automatically were given Jordanian citizenship and the more prosperous, better educated, and least damaged by the war were able to begin new lives in the private sector or the Jordanian bureaucracy. Others scattered to the Arabian Peninsula, North Africa, and further afield.

In the early "post war" years, the Palestinians were treated as "raw materials" for inter-Arab politics. The Muslim Brotherhood, and the Baath, and the *Harakat al-Qawmiyin al-Arab* (The Arab Nationalist Movement) each built Palestinian branches as a part of their pan-Arab movements. This dependence of Palestinians on other Arab parties and governments set a pattern: espousal by the several Arab governments of rival representatives of the Palestinian community, and refugee identification with and dependence upon different governments and leaders.

While it is always difficult to trace the origins of political movements, such evidence as exists indicates that the Palestinians remained politically passive until about 1962. The first stirrings were military. Commandos operating from Egypt attacked southern Israel during March 1955; a few months later groups apparently operating from Jordan managed to mount sabotage raids into Israel. Shortly thereafter raiders struck northern Israel from Lebanon. These groups apparently were uncoordinated but little is known of them. The groups operating from Gaza were described by a later Palestine Liberation Organization publication as "not based on, connected to, or part of any political organization, but were trained and led by Egyptian army officers . . . (and) were disbanded after the 1956 Tripartite aggression on Suez."

Limited in purpose, cut off from one another, and clandestine, the groups defy the assemblage of an historical account. No documentary records give a view of their gradual transformation into political organizations. Indeed, we must look essentially to Arabic literature, to poetry and fiction to get some "feel" of the genesis of what later became the guerrilla movement. Put simply, what appears to have occurred is that the young, raised on blurred memory of childhood, the tales of the elders, the sorrow, privation, and humiliation of refugee life, came to feel a new sense of romantic nationalism. One of their poets, echoing the sentiment of the psalmist, wrote,

O lost paradise! You were never too small for us,
But now vast countries are indeed too small.

Torn asunder your people,
Wandering under every star,*

What was it that brought into a single focus this nostalgia and partisan warfare? The most convincing answer, I think, was the distantly perceived example of Algeria.

The Algerian Revolution was adopted as a case study by those Franz Fanon called "The Wretched of the Earth"—and by those who opposed them. Fanon's own book became a clarion cry for radical organizations just as Colonel Roger Trinquier's *La Guerre Moderne* became a guidebook on counter-insurgency warfare. In the Algerian resistance movement, then apparently also disaffected, leaderless, inchoate, and powerless, but beginning to achieve a kind of heroism, the Palestinians found a family resemblance.

From extraordinarily unpromising beginnings, the Algerians achieved by 1961–62 an almost miraculous success. Their national revolutionary movement was begun by only a dozen angry young men. It made its major mistakes: it attempted to engage in static warfare with the French forces. It splintered. It contained its share of double agents and traitors. It was forced to rely on the fickle, lukewarm support of the surrounding Arab countries. But finally, it was driven back upon its own resources. (Here, the Palestinians saw not only the family resemblance but the elements of a program.) With less than 13,000 armed combatants, the Algerians faced up to approximately 485,000 French troops, helped by a million Europeans, and won. In their program, the Palestinians thought, there must be some secret, some master plan, which if identified and followed would bring success to them also. Algerian songs, Algerian uniforms, Algerian instructors were indiscriminately sought out as the propaganda, the symbols, and the guides. The Algerians were not slow to respond. Flattered and confident of their own background, if less sure of their peacetime tasks, they basked in the adulation and willingly gave advice on how to form, administer, and win with armed political organizations.

The two most important early organizations were *Harakat at-Tahrir al-Falastini* (whose letters form, in reverse, the acronym Fatah; in Arabic: to conquer) and the Palestine Liberation Organization (PLO). These two organizations were ultimately to become the quasi-official representatives of the Palestinian people, but they were very different in character. The first in point of origin was Fatah.

* A. L. Tibawi, "Visions of the Return: The Palestine Arab Refugees in Arabic Poetry and Art," *Middle East Journal,* 17 (1963): 507–526. See also Trevor J. LeGassick, "Some War-Related Arabic Fiction," *Middle East Journal,* 25 (1971): 491–505.

As a clandestine organization, Fatah's beginnings remain somewhat hazy and it was not until 1965 that it emerged more or less in the open as an identifiable organization. Although begun somewhat later, PLO was the first to become generally recognized; more remote from the refugee camp experience, it was essentially the creation, by the Arab states, of a kind of Arab Agency. The project grew out of a "summit" conference in Alexandria on September 15, 1963, and was financed by the Arab League. The next spring, some 400 Palestinians, forming the Palestine National Congress, met in Jerusalem, with the ceremony opened by King Husain and resolved to establish a Palestine Liberation Organization (PLO) and to open camps to train guerrillas.

The PLO was considered by the other Palestinian organizations to be an "establishment institution," was ridiculed as a "Ministry of Foreign Affairs without any state," and was feared as a "sponge to soak up Palestinians" and so prevent them from acting effectively. PLO formed an armed force, the Palestine Liberation Army, as a standing army, completely different from the Algerian (internal) guerrilla model. PLO Chairman Ahmad Shuqairi was a poor choice as leader—such reputation as he had in the Palestinian community in post war years he acquired as a member of the Saudi Arabian diplomatic service. Yet, for all of these weaknesses in the PLO, the Palestinians had come closer to having a recognized political spokesman. PLO conferences in Jerusalem (1964), Cairo (1965), Gaza (1966), and Cairo (1968), attracted considerable international attention and produced manifestos, press releases, and other propaganda.

Wholly different in origin, spirit, and relationship with the Palestinian community was Fatah.

The most significant of the Fatah leaders was Yasir Arafat. Unlike Shuqairi, he was not the "chosen instrument" of any Arab government. Of a poorer background, he had drunk the dregs of the bitter cup of sorrow and humiliation. Able and energetic, he managed to acquire an education and to escape the camp life. Like many of the Fatah personnel, he was technically qualified (as an engineer) but had not risen to a position of prominence in another Arab country.

As Gerard Chaliand observed, the Fatah leaders were not only of a different class but had troubled relations with the leaders of the Arab states:

The Union of Palestinian Students in Cairo was one of the principal sources of recruitment. The future general staff of El Fatah were students or lower-middle class Palestinians who were gradually becoming aware that the Palestinian people would have to take on the responsibility for fighting their own battles. The initial impetus was weak, and went against the current trend. In fact Arab aspirations toward unity, particularly under the leadership of Nasser, began to take noticeable effect in the years 1957–58, and finally resulted in the Syrio-Egyptian unification and the base for the United Arab Republic. Only Kassem's Iraq showed favour to the Palestinian national idea, to the extent that it seemed to Kassem a development directed against Nasserite interests. Between 1958 and 1962, Palestinians suspected of nationalism were refused permits, so that they were unable to travel, and in certain Arab countries some were even imprisoned until 1967.*

It was the 1967 Arab-Israeli war which gave Arafat and Fatah their opportunity. In the fighting, 175,000 refugees were moved once again and 350,000 more Palestinians were turned into refugees. In 1968, 1,375,915 were registered with UNRWA. More important, it was clear that a wholly new situation had arisen on the Arab side. Weighed in scales of their own propaganda, none of the Arab governments appeared strong or capable; the formal military structure of the Arab countries had proved unequal to Israel; then, other, non-Palestinian Arabs had to suffer the bitter life of defeat and migration.

Israel's very victory appeared to create a special new vulnerability. Having battled for a strategically secure frontier, it had also acquired a strategically insecure population. In short, what might be termed the Algerian alternative, with the guerrilla replacing both the commando and the soldier, appeared relatively promising. Indeed, guerrilla activity seemed to pose the only viable alternative between outright surrender to Israeli proclamations that all the conquered areas would be retained and further battle with ill-equipped, demoralized and shattered armies. "The old slogan that Arab unity was the end to the liberations of Palestine," writes William Quant, "was reversed to read that the liberation of Palestine would be the path to Arab unity. This renewed sense of Palestinian self-respect and determined activism contrasted with the low state of morale in other Arab countries after the June defeat and provided a focus for political activity, especially among Palestinians in Jordan and Lebanon."†

Of course, the guerrilla groups were not alone in aspiring to the leadership of the Palestinian community. "Community," indeed, is still at this stage too strong a word. The old lines of division remained strong. The older generation still deferred to its traditional leadership. Where village communities had been maintained, as on the West Bank of the Jordan, provincial loyalties were still paramount.

* The *Palestinian Resistance* (Harmondsworth, 1972), p. 57.
† William Quant, Fuad Jabber, and Ann Mosely Lesch, *The Politics of Palestinian Nationalism* (Berkeley, 1973), p. 52.

Where the refugees lived in camps, the camps had become extended villages with their own leadership, their own interests, and their own arrangements with local authorities. Ironically, these very factors—which hindered the development of a national constituency—played into the hands of the guerrillas in that they, alone, moved easily from village to village and camp to camp and across frontiers. Where they were favored by government, they alone had relatively large financial resources and in their concentration on propaganda, education, and agitation, they captured the imagination even if not fully the loyalty of younger people. But, they were not only deeply split among themselves but almost chameleon-like in their camouflage.

The creation of new refugee politico-military groups, the coalescence of old ones, and the struggle for dominance is shrouded in the shadow of clandestine life. Guerrillas and revolutionaries survive only if they obscure their trails: to accumulate archives is to court disaster and death. Michael Hudson summarizes the little that is publicly known when he writes that:

> While the Arab states were still reeling from the June 1967 defeat, Fatah was beginning to expand and other groups were coming into existence. Of the several dozen other groups that emerged, two were of particular importance—Sa'iqah, a commando movement reportedly closely directed by the Syrian army, and active on the Syrian and Jordan River fronts, and the Popular Front for the Liberation of Palestine. The Popular Front grew out of the merger of three small groups, the most important of which was the Arab Nationalist Movement. Galvanized by the 1948 defeat, a Christian Palestinian, George Habbash, founded the ANM to recover Palestine and realize the long-standing ideal of one Arab nation. The ANM decided that the recovery of Palestine—the heart of the Arab nation—could be achieved through prior unification of the existing Arab regimes. Thus it supported Jamal 'Abd al-Nasir in the middle 1950's as the strongest available unifier, but it eventually moved ideologically to the left of Nasir. Through the Popular Front the ANM returned to the problem of recovering Palestine; but it returned with a radical socialist ideology it did not have in 1948 and which its comrades-in-arms in Fatah and the PLO do not share.*

By the end of 1967, Fatah had begun to attract relatively large numbers of young men to its ranks in Jordan. Although tightly restricted by the Jordanian government in its scope of operations, it began to receive fairly large-scale financial support from other Arab governments. Unable to establish itself in the Israeli-occupied territories,

* "The Palestinian Arab Resistance Movement: Its Significance in the Middle East Crisis," *The Middle East Journal,* 23 (1969): 297–298.

Fatah engaged in several successful military ventures along the Jordan River. In riposte, the Israeli army attacked Karamah village and a commando staging area on March 21, 1968. Militarily, the Israelis won but the fight was a hard one and Fatah managed to turn it into an important political-psychological victory. Fatah's relatively good showing in the battle caused President Nasser to shift some of the Egyptian support for the Palestinians to Fatah.

The alliance between the Egyptians and the Palestinians was always a marriage of convenience. The Egyptians encouraged the Palestinians both to put pressure on King Husain to support Egyptian policies and to relieve some of the Israeli pressure on the Egyptian positions at the Suez Canal. However, as in Yemen, the Egyptians were comfortable only when in control. Moreover, there was a clear if mute divergence of interest between the Arab states and the Palestinians. Insofar as they agreed on anything, the Palestinians sought to reclaim Palestine. If necessary, they were willing to tear down the political edifice of the Middle East in the process. For their part, the Jordanians, acutely conscious of their exposed position and their relative weakness, wanted to perform the minimum possible anti-Israeli activity consistent with maintaining their position in the Arab national camp. The Egyptians sought to get the Israelis out of occupied Egyptian territory but feared another military disaster.

These conflicting priorities made relations between the Palestinians and the Egyptians and Jordanians extremely fragile. Even when praised by one or the other of the governments, the always wary Palestinians often reacted with public scorn. But the guerrillas recognized that in order to increase their bargaining position vis-à-vis governments, they needed to set their own house in order. To this end, they convened a new Palestine National Council in May 1968. No longer was the old leadership of PLO accorded overwhelming power. Fatah pushed its way into the organization and was given over one third of the seats. Fatah, however, was no longer the only claimant to the role of an activist guerrilla organization.

As an aspect of their own ideological struggle with the Egyptians, the Syrian Baathist regime determined to sponsor its own group of Palestinians. The decision was made in the fall of 1967 and during the early part of 1968, a group known as *Sa'iqa* or the Vanguard of the Popular Liberation War was brought into being. Not to be outdone, the Iraqi Baath Party set up and funded its group of Palestinians as The Arab Liberation Front.

To the left in the immediate aftermath of the 1967 war, a number of tiny cliques and committees had coalesced into what came to be called the Popular Front for the Liberation of Palestine (the PFLP).

One of these cliques was the Arab Nationalist Movement (ANM) which sought a pan-Arab rather than a Palestinian identification. A part of this nebulous political organization was centered at the American University of Beirut and it was in this company that Dr. George Habbash, later leader of the PFLP, gained his first political experience. The ANM was, in fact, little more than a debating society but for a short while the Egyptian government appears to have thought it would be a useful adjunct to the Arab Socialist Union with which it was seeking to underpin its own political influence abroad.

Yet another splinter group, partly associated with the ANM, called itself "the Vengeance Youth" and also was associated with the American University of Beirut through its leader, Nayif Hawatmah. Another component, led by Ahmad Jabril, who had served in the Syrian army, was named the Palestinian Liberation Front. Finally, the "Heroes of the Return" (*Abtal al-Awda*), led by Wajih al-Madani, established some links with the PFLP. About six months after the June 1967 war, all of those groups "almost merged," agreeing to accept the leadership of George Habbash, but retaining their somewhat separate identity and sources of support.

Then, just as some clarity seems to have been achieved, the picture fades: shortly after the PFLP was founded, the new leader, George Habbash, was forced to flee from Jordan to Syria where he was arrested and imprisoned for nearly eight months. While he was out of circulation, esoteric ideological quarrels between the "left" and the "right," concerning, among other things, the theoretical role of the "petite bourgeoisie," terrorism, and mass political education in the revolutionary struggle, as well as a struggle for leadership, tore the Front back into its component parts. One faction, led by Ahmad Jabril, had already begun to experiment with various forms of paramilitary activities. Through him, the guerrillas stumbled onto the tactic, which increasingly dominated newspaper headlines, of hijacking aircraft. It was Jabril's splinter group which had been responsible for hijacking an Israeli plane to Algiers in the summer of 1968. Such activities required small, tightly knit, and well-financed organizations rather than broad political fronts. The already fractured nature of the Palestinian population was thus further exacerbated by the very nature of the combat. The ever present fear of double agents led to a determined quest for organizational or ideological purity. This, in turn, reinforced natural disagreements on tactics and political philosophy and encouraged the separate and conflicting ambitions of political leaders.

When George Habbash managed to escape from the Syrian prison in November of 1968, his attempt to reassert his leadership brought him into immediate conflict with his de facto successor, Nayif Hawatmah. By the early months of 1969, the guerrillas came to realize that they were committing political suicide through their internal clashes. A determined new effort was made, not so much for unity—now viewed as unobtainable—but for tolerance. The various groups entered into a sort of passive agreement to live and let live within the refugee camps. The separate status of Hawatmah's organization was recognized and the new group, dubbed the Popular Democratic Front for the Liberation of Palestine, PDFLP, was recognized as a formal constituent part of the PLO.

Yet other splits continued to occur, even within tiny, obscure, even ephemeral fringe organizations,* but enough has been said to indicate the extraordinary complexity, diffusion, and dissidence within the Palestinian community.

By July 1968, at the fourth PLO Congress in Cairo, Fatah decided that the time was coming for it to assume leadership of the movement. After months of negotiation with the other guerrilla organizations, Fatah called for a fifth congress. For the meeting, to be held in Cairo in February of 1969, Fatah was allotted 33 of the 105 seats on the Palestine National Council while Sa'iqa received 12. Although the conference was boycotted by the PFLP, which had been offered only 12 seats, Fatah emerged with what on paper appeared to approach the status of a government in exile. It established regional committees in all the refugee populated areas and equipped itself with all the paraphernalia of a clandestine political-military organization—cells, code names, security procedures, communication links, couriers—all reporting to a central committee and a political bureau. Dependent upon the bounty of the Arab countries for its finances and needing the quasi-diplomatic support of their governments, it sought to maintain its independence as a Palestine entity while not fatally antagonizing its hosts or bringing about further internal splits. It sought, in short, to use the armed struggle against Israel as a means to bring about unity within the Palestinian community rather than seeking through ideological or other means a unity which could be imposed upon the struggle. Fatah's Yasir Arafat was elected chairman of the Palestine Liberation Organization and the eleven-men executive committee fell under the control of Fatah members and sympathizers.

Immediately after becoming chairman, Arafat created the Pales-

---

* Yehoshafat Harkabi, "Fedayeen Action and Arab Strategy," *Adelphi Papers* (December 1968) No. 53, Institute for Strategic Studies, London.

tine Armed Struggle Command to attempt to coordinate the military activities of the member groups. By the summer of 1969, eight guerrilla organizations were represented, but notably the PFLP remained aloof. It boycotted the September National Congress meeting and it was not until hostilities broke out between the various guerrilla organizations and the Jordanian armed forces in February of 1970 that the PFLP was forced to cooperate with other groups in the Palestine Armed Struggle Command. Its cooperation, however, was half-hearted. It refused to abide by the tactical directives of the overall group, insisting on retaining separate clandestine organizations, separate codes, separate security systems, and maintaining its right of "independent action."

At least on paper, the May 1970 Congress was the high point of the moves toward Palestinian unification. The powerful brew of unity was going to everyone's head. The guerrillas thought themselves near the long-sought achievement of effective political community. The last obstacle appeared to be the Jordanian monarchy. The monarchy agreed to this assessment and a collision was inevitable. It came in two stages, called by the Palestinians "Green June" and "Black September."

Relations with Jordan had, of course, always been tense. The basic political tenet of all guerrilla groups was that the Palestinians constituted a discrete community whereas Jordan's government regarded Palestinians resident in Jordan (including the West Bank) as Jordanians. Ideologically, adminstratively, and personally the government of Jordan and the various guerrilla organizations were not only different but were anxious to exaggerate their differences. The guerrillas did this not only with stirring proclamations but with bullets. Rightly or wrongly, the Jordanian government believed that the guerrillas tried to assassinate King Husain on June 9, but that was only one of many "incidents" during those tense days. The royal palace and the radio station were attacked by rockets from one of the guerrilla organizations and the radical PFLP occupied the two main Amman hotels and took the sixty occupants hostage to attract world press attention. Rapidly, the central aim of the guerrillas became clear; to create a pliant Jordanian government agreeable to its long-range plans but still "orthodox" enough to prevent total breakdown and so invite Israeli invasion of Jordan.

As a first step, the guerrillas demanded the arrest and dismissal of the king's uncle, who was commander of the armed forces, and other senior royalist officials. To legitimize and somewhat defuse the confrontation, the PLO asked the other Arab governments to intervene as negotiators. To the surprise of many, probably including the guerrilla leaders, King Husain went a long way toward accepting their demands. On Jordan's radio station on June 11, he announced dismissal of his uncle and other officials but warned that this concession was his last. A further guerrilla push, he said, would result in civil war. Their appetites whetted, however, the guerrillas did not believe him. As the *New York Times* correspondent reported the next day, "The pact King Hussein has signed with guerrilla leader Yasser Arafat comes close to granting the Palestinian militants full partnership in Jordanian affairs."

Despite their attempt to utilize the model of Algeria, the Palestinians in fact operated under very different circumstances. Not only were they severely divided among themselves; they were largely cut off from that form of activity which had, in fact, made all the different in Algeria. Despite the relatively more glamorous and large-scale cadres of what the Algerians called the "external" army, the real politico-military tasks were performed in Algeria by guerrillas whom the French were never able to expel. In the Palestine clash, to the contrary, virtually everything was external. Because the Jewish Israelis were not, like the French in Algeria, an "enclave" society, the Arab guerrillas were largely precluded from politically significant activities within Israeli occupied territory. On the West Bank, no guerrilla organization managed to establish a secure base of operations or an effective following, while in Gaza, after initially succeeding militarily, the guerrillas failed politically and administratively. There, with a combination of "search and destroy," "community action," and economic incentives, the Israelis destroyed the opportunity for the guerrillas.* This tended, consequently, to force the guerrillas into less profitable commando-type operations. In these, even the Algerians had never been successful. The casualty figures document the failure. The total number of Israeli casualties at the peak of the guerrilla activity from 1968 to 1970 were less than 300. By the end of 1970, Israel claimed to have killed over 1800 and held another 2500 Palestinian activists in prison.

Unlike the Algerians, who had ruthlessly purged their organization of dissidents and who had managed to achieve an effective if not total degree of unity, the Palestinians remained vulnerable to effective counter-intelligence operations. The Israelis exploited these differ-

* See detailed reports by John de St Jorre and Walter Schwarz in *The Observer* of August 1, 1971.

ences fully* to hamstring or uncover planned operations before they could take place, and by destroying villages and regrouping populations they removed potentially vulnerable spots in their armor.

During the summer of 1970, when the United States was attempting to bring about the "Rogers Plan," Israel independently made discreet inquiries about the possibility of a cease fire in the war of attrition. President Nasser, then in Moscow, cautiously accepted the result if not the form of the overture. As a result of confidential, informal, third-party negotiations, one of the guerrilla groups, the Action Organization for the Liberation of Palestine, determined to accept the cease fire. When President Nasser announced Egypt's acceptance on the anniversary of the Egyptian revolution, Egypt and Nasser personally were bitterly criticized by the PLO's radio program which was then broadcast over the Egyptian Voice of the Arabs. In riposte, President Nasser ordered that no further broadcasting would be done from Cairo.

Once again, the Palestine guerrilla movement seemed on the rocks. Formally spurned by the Egyptian government, it lived in an increasingly hostile and bitter atmosphere in Jordan. Always restricted in its activity in Syria, it was distrustful of an ideologically committed regime which sought to use rather than to be used by it. Unwanted and feared in Lebanon, which in any event did not have the resources to support it, it found itself in a delicate and dangerous position. Israel's overtures for a cease fire, dangerous enough in themselves, appeared merely to be the harbinger of a sellout of the Palestine cause.

In August 1970 the level of tension in Amman had reached a high point. Everyone was armed. Members of the various guerrilla organizations, sporting the prized symbol of wars of national liberation, the Kalashnikov automatic rifle, wearing their camouflage paratroop jumpsuits, *a l'Algerienne,* swaggered past the sullen Jordanian soldiers, drably clad and carrying World War II surplus American rifles. Uneasy confrontations occurred at every street corner, every finger was on a trigger and in each voice a slogan or a taunt. It needed only a spark to ignite the country.

The spark was provided, ironically, by the most successful and most flamboyant action of the guerrillas, the hijacking of a gaggle of jets—a Swissair DC-8, a TWA 707 and a Pan American 747 on September 7 and on September 9, a BOAC VC 10—by the PFLP. Except for the Pan American plane, all were flown to an abandoned World

---

* See E. D. Hodgkin (Foreign Editor), *The Times* (London) October 28, 1969, and David Leitch, *The Sunday Times,* November 23, 1969.

War II fighter strip near Mafraq in northern Jordan and the passengers and crews held hostage. Proclaiming that the area was under the control of the PFLP and "belonged to no one (else)," the guerrillas not only asserted their ability to carry the war to the world community but their right to do so irrespective of Jordan's government. The Jordanian army, both the representative and the symbol of the government, was rendered impotent by the guerrillas' threat to blow up both passengers and planes if any attempt were made to free them.

Thus, the guerrilla movement found itself poised both at the pinnacle of its power and at the brink of its destruction in those first days of "Black September." Embarrassed and humiliated, the king had decided that he must destroy the guerrillas or watch his regime bleed to death. Indeed, it now seems probable that he had no choice: had he not moved, the army might have moved without him. On September 15, Husain appointed a military government "to restore order and impose the State's authority." Given its head, the army moved rapidly, using every weapon it had, including heavy cannon against those parts of the capital city housing the refugees, and swept through the refugee encampments. Estimates of casualties varied widely. Sudanese President Numairi guessed as many as 25,000 may have been killed, but the number was probably between 5,000 and 10,000. The bulk of the fighting was over on the 26th and King Husain flew to Cairo to sign a truce with Arafat. The back of the guerrilla movement in Jordan was broken but the next six months were to be spent in mop-up operations.

Driven to new depths of despair, frustrated in their principal political objectives, both the already identified and new clandestine groups continued to commit often spectacular deeds—an Israeli-owned oil tanker was attacked in June 1971, the American-owned pipeline from the Arabian oil fields was sabotaged five times in 1971, and the Jordanian prime minister was assassinated in November. In 1972, terrorist attacks continued and became somewhat more successful against Israeli targets. The two most publicized events were the PFLP-affiliated Japanese attack on Lod Airport on May 30 and the September 5 abduction and murder of eleven members of the Israeli Olympic team. World opinion was not so much mobilized as horrified. These acts were seen as the lunges of desperate, defeated men who had failed in their central political purpose.

Driven from Jordan, the guerrillas fell back perforce upon Lebanon where some 300,000 refugees were encamped. At this point, Israel intervened dramatically to make the guerrilla sanctuary costly for Lebanon. That strategy proved not very difficult. Lebanon had already experienced the iron fist of Israel's military force in the attack on Beirut International Airport in December 1968 and further large-scale operations in 1969 and 1972. In the latter, the Israeli army occupied much of south Lebanon. Thus, when the Lebanese were warned, as they were publicly on February 24, 1973 by the Israeli chief of staff to expect reprisals, they forced Fatah to agree to suspend attacks on Israel from Lebanon. In April Israeli commandos made a spectacular day-long raid on Beirut in which they hunted down and murdered three leaders of the resistance movement. Outraged, the guerrillas accused the Lebanese of cowardice or collusion and kidnapped two Lebanese soldiers. In "massive" retaliation, the government used this as an occasion to replay, on a much smaller but still spectacular scale, "Black September."

Thus, from its high water mark of June 1970, the Palestine Armed Struggle Movement found itself, apparently, in May 1973 at a low ebb in Lebanon. Precluded from meaningful action in Israel, unable to assert political or administrative hegemony over any part of the occupied territories, violently opposed in two crucial Arab countries, grudgingly tolerated in others, and "kept" in Iraq, Syria and Egypt, unable to achieve effective internal unity, the Palestinians were indeed living in a diaspora. All that they had been able to prove was that peace could not be made secure without their participation. But how, when, and by whom were questions hardly even posed much less answered. Indeed, the issue of the Palestinians was left an unresolved item on an unformed agenda, to be discussed without a native spokesman at whatever forum can be created to attempt to bring a settlement between the Arab states and Israel. In default, the action turns again to the states.

17

The Fourth Round: The October 1973 War

J UST at the end of the bitter "Black September" clash between the Palestinian guerrillas and the government of Jordan, on September 28, 1970, President Nasser suddenly died in Cairo. All Arab eyes and ears turned to Cairo. In their shock and grief, his mourners—who in death included even old and bitter enemies—fell back on the solace of Islam and for a day the usually strident Voice of the Arabs chanted the litany of the Koran. Nasser's funeral was one of the most massive popular demonstrations ever witnessed anywhere. To it flocked hundreds of thousands who had been foes, alongside friends. And in the mind of everyone was the same question: who could step into his shoes as leader of the Arab cause?

The very politics of Nasser's life seemed to preclude an answer. A jealous and vindictive guardian of power, he shared little of its trappings with others. While his regime was noted for the kindness with which it treated most of his fallen rivals—paid retirement at the golf and tennis clubs of Cairo—it was also noted for the frequency with which they were retired. Most of the "old guard," the original members of the Revolutionary Command Council, were golfers or under polite house arrest and even the ranks of their protégés had been thinned by purges. Outside these groups no potential leaders had survived or come to the fore in eighteen years of Nasser's regime. The old regime was dead, the Wafd Party but a memory, the Muslim Brotherhood a phantom, and the Communist Party, a spectre.

At Nasser's funeral, Soviet Premier Alexei Kosygin commented that "it is relatively unimportant who succeeds Nasser. The essential thing is to hold the regime together at a time when part of your country is occupied by foreign troops." From the Soviet perspective that may have been true, but to those on the spot such detachment was both personally and politically unthinkable. But, as a practical matter, who was available?

Only three possible candidates pushed forward. First, the efficient but authoritarian former Vice-President Zakhariya Muhiaddin, sometime leader of the "pro-American" wing of Nasser's entourage. But Muhiaddin was feared for his un-Egyptian ruthlessness by friend and foe alike.

The second was the ambitious, bright, and shrewd leader of the "pro-Soviet" wing of Nasser's entourage, former Vice-President Ali Sabri. Teamed with Ali Sabri were several powerful members of the governing apparatus at the time of Nasser's death—that being a time of relatively pro-Soviet Egyptian leanings. They included the former Governor of Alexandria and Minister of the Interior, Sharawy Gomaa; Minister of War, General Mohammed Fawzi (an Egyptian "hawk"); and one of the most brilliant and well-trained intelligence managers in the Middle East, Sami Sharaf. Having benefited with fine impartiality from careful training by both the CIA and the KGB, Sharaf had become chief of the entire apparatus of Nasser's intelligence and was Minister of State for Presidential Affairs. Covertly, these men received a good deal of encouragement from the Soviet Union. On the surface, they appeared overwhelmingly powerful but they well and rightly gauged the unpopularity of their cause and decided to delay somewhat before pushing it. The third candidate appeared to give them this option.

Known as an amiable, unambitious man, Anwar Sadat had been the butt of many a Cairo political joke. Nasser had treated him with evident and well-publicized scorn and Sadat made no overt attempt to build a circle of allies. Little known among the general public, he was more a figure of levity than of charisma and, although the titular vice-president, was without intimate knowledge of the often tortuous and always secret diplomacy of the Nasser regime. In the shoes of Nasser, that proven nationalist, revolutionary leader, popular hero, and master of Third World politics, Sadat was thought to be Charlie Chaplin playing James Bond. It was precisely for these qualities that he was picked as the compromise candidate. No one suspected that he would last long, and meanwhile the real rivals would be gathering their forces for an appropriate showdown.

When Anwar Sadat took office, the Egyptian presidency's inheritance consisted of a rather shaky possession of the keys to a Pandora's box of woes. Egypt had lost the 1967 war catastrophically, its major cities along the Suez Canal then were in ruins, the war of attrition had hurt Egypt more than its enemy, and the war in Yemen had ended in complete embarrassment of Egypt's policy, while diplomatic efforts among the other Arab countries had resulted in the breakdown of Egypt's relationship with the Palestinian guerrilla organization but with virtually no improvement in its relations with the Jordanian monarchy. The Egyptian economy was prostrate and the Egyptian population continued growing at an alarming rate. It took all of Nasser's skill, adroitness and charisma to hold the box shut. It seemed unthinkable that Sadat could do so.

In misjudging Sadat himself, the cabal miscalculated even more the potential of the presidency in Egypt. Beset it was, surrounded by would-be heirs, certainly; isolated by a vast and self-serving bureaucracy, undoubtedly. Yet these very defects in combination were its strength. And they enabled Sadat to survive in the first critical months and finally to outlast his rivals. On May 13, 1971, when they made an ill-conceived and clumsy move against him, there was no response from the general public or the army and Sadat was able simply to order their arrest and trial.* He had survived and by default was the real ruler of Egypt. His struggle to retain his position and to sort out Egypt's problems formed the critical elements in the backdrop to the October 1973 war and demand our attention at this time.

While the Palestinian aspects of the Arab-Israeli conflict received the most public attention in 1972 and 1973, the dilemma facing the Arab states' governments, particularly the Egyptian government, was growing. Such incidents as the Israeli raid on Lebanon in January 1972, the Arab terrorist attack on the Israeli Olympic team in Munich in September 1972, the Israeli shooting down of a Libyan airliner with 108 passengers in February 1973, and the Israeli commando attack on Beirut in April 1973, made the maintenance of the 1970 truce increasingly difficult for the Arab governments.

The Jarring Mission had failed and the Rogers Plan, put forward by the American Secretary of State,† resulted merely in a cease fire which Sadat rapidly came to realize was the worst of the various options before his government. Egypt was increasingly dependent upon the Soviet Union for the maintenance of its expensive military force

---

* Eric Rouleau, "Sadat Consolidates His Position," in *Le Monde Weekly,* May 20–26, 1971.

† See Chapter 23 below.

but the Soviet Union was decreasingly responsive to Egyptian demands for replacements, more sophisticated material, and further training. The Israelis appeared to be unwilling to make any concessions. The United States, cool and distant, constantly and concretely supported Israel. To Sadat, the reason appeared to be increasingly clear. "[Secretary of State] Rogers thought we would never fight. The Israelis thought they could never be surprised. The West thought we were poor soldiers without good generals."*

Always uncomfortable with the Palestinian guerrilla organizations, the Egyptians found that the strains of the cease fire were giving birth to even more radical terrorist groups. One, known as Black September, gunned down the visiting prime minister of Jordan in the lobby of Cairo's best hotel on November 29, 1971. Unity among the Arab governments, always highly problematical, was put to even greater strains. For a time, both Syria and Egypt again severed diplomatic relations with Jordan. Moreover, the "truce" appeared to be becoming increasingly set in concrete as Israeli settlements were created in the conquered areas of Syria, Jordan, the Gaza strip, and Sinai, and were formally justified by the Israeli Foreign Minister as being in areas which were to be included within Israel permanently. General Dayan's Plan was called "Creeping Annexation" in the Israeli and Western press.

Internally in Egypt there was great dissatisfaction with the government. Those who had disapproved of President Nasser's policies were effectively held in check during his lifetime but their pent-up dissatisfactions exploded against Sadat. The charisma of Nasser's leadership had appeared to satisfy some if not all of the ambitions of radical Egyptian youth but Sadat found that he had inherited a presidential image which his reputation and personality appeared unable to fulfill. Moreover, the Egyptian economy was increasingly running down. The cost of the maintenance of "security" was enormous. Probably as much as 25 percent of Egypt's national income was devoted to its armed forces and large numbers of its best educated and most productive young people were pulled out of the economy into the army. The Suez Canal remained closed and the once prosperous and industrialized area along the Canal was literally a no-man's-land. Egypt's major oil field was under Israeli domination and producing for the Israeli, not the Egyptian, economy. Hard-currency laden tourists were frightened away from this potential war zone. The danger of a military coup d'etat, never to be completely discounted in any developing country, had increased. By the opening of 1973, indeed, two

* Insight team of the Sunday Times, *Insight on the Middle East War* (London, 1974), p. 29.

unsuccessful attempts had already occurred. Increasingly, critics—especially among the radical youth, but also those who knew the answer—asked why, with an enormous and massively equipped army, the government acquiesced in the occupation of 26,000 square miles of Egypt less than 100 miles from its capital city.

To maintain even this uncomfortable situation required constant supplication to foreigners. First, there were the oil-producing Arab countries on whose yearly dole Egypt absolutely depended. Second, and more important, was the Soviet Union. From Russia Egypt had acquired virtually all of the military equipment it possessed. Upon future Soviet largesse Egypt's "security" depended. The nearly fifteen thousand Russian military personnel living in Egypt to advise the Egyptian armed forces also manned the anti-aircraft defenses and were, like all foreign military experts, frequently high-handed and universally unpopular.

While the Russians were obviously anxious to use their position in Egypt to influence the whole Afro-Asian world, they were unwilling to do so to such an extent as to jeopardize the growing detente with the United States or to allow the Egyptians to risk a hot war in which they might have to become involved. Thus, when President Sadat visited Moscow in February 1972, he was rebuffed in his request for new armaments. His second visit, in April, was apparently more favorably received by the Russians but arms, in the quantities and marks desired by the Egyptians, were not forthcoming. Another visit, by the Egyptian Prime Minister, Dr. Aziz Sidqi in July was also a failure. Two days after Sidqi's return, on July 15, either in anger or as a signal of desperation, President Sadat ordered the immediate withdrawal of Soviet military personnel and dependents, in all some 40,000 people, and sent Egyptian army units to take control of Soviet bases and equipment. In an hour-and-a-half radio broadcast Sadat said that, while he hoped that a new stage of Soviet Egyptian relations could be introduced, Egypt would assume responsibility for its destiny. The world was agog—was a secret deal in the making with the West? This was hinted in Western press articles which bore all the signs of deliberate leaks to test American reactions. As the *Washington Post* put it, "Sadat had pledged to Rogers in 1971 that within three months after Israel began a phased withdrawal from the Sinai Peninsula, Sadat would remove Soviet advisers from Egypt . . . Sadat has shown that he can deliver . . . has in fact already delivered. Now it is time to look at what America can do."

But, in fact, America chose to do nothing. The Israeli leaders thus thought they saw the triumph of their hard-line policy. The sentiment behind that policy got a further fillip from the September 5

Munich massacre, and on September 10 *The Sunday Times* (of London) reported that Israel was further stiffening the terms for peace. Mrs. Meir, the Israeli Prime Minister, set out five points as Israel's basis for settlement:

> ... total retention of the Golan Heights in Syria; retention of rule over West Bank areas with a minimum Arab population living there; free access to the Mediterranean for Jordan which would have the use of the Israeli ports of Haifa and Gaza; retention of the Gaza Strip; and, finally, retention of Sharm El Sheikh, plus "a broad strip" linking it to Israel.

> Evidence is growing that Israel is not interested in negotiating a settlement at all, and nothing that has emerged from the Israeli side has come near acceptability for Egypt.

Whatever the motives, the Soviet withdrawal and Israel's shift toward a harder line faced the Egyptian government with a dilemma to which there were three possible alternatives. It is worth examining these precisely because the Egyptian government contemplated or tried each in turn.

The first option was to sit tight, continuing on the policy laid down by the August 1967 Arab summit conference at Khartoum, neither (full scale) war nor peace. This was in practice not a stationary policy for it cost Egypt about 25 to 30 percent of its total income. Statistics aside, any observer could see that Egypt was becoming increasingly shabby. While the Egyptian people are remarkably passive and enduring and so were unlikely to cause any unrest serious enough to trouble the regime, the Egyptian leaders were aware that the population was rapidly growing, that water-borne diseases, always appalling, were spreading as an aftereffect of the High Dam, that the High Dam had not "worked" and that there was no new potential for development efforts of that magnitude. Moreover, the policy was, at best, merely a holding action.

The second option was surrender. To accept the Israeli "hard line" terms would probably have brought about a coup d'etat. While much of the army was still licking the wounds of the June war, important fighting formations had been stationed in Yemen during the debacle and were unbloodied. Since the army was conscript and on relatively short service periods, most private soldiers had not experienced combat. Moreover, during the six years since 1967, a natural turnover had occurred in the officer corps. So the army of 1973 was not that of 1967. It would not sympathize with a humiliating deal. Probably it would not permit one. At best, "surrender" would bring an end to the subsidies from the other Arab countries, replaceable only at some unknown price and, presumably, after a moneyless interval, by perhaps lesser subsidies from the West. Moreover, Israeli peace terms would open Egypt to massive economic inroads from the better organized Israeli industry.

The third option was a "forward policy." One form of the "forward policy" was diplomatic. In September 1972 Egypt began a diplomatic "offensive" to take its case to the United Nations. This was to grow and diversify in the months ahead. On December 8, 1972, the UN General Assembly voted 86 to 7 to urge member states to provide no funds to Israel which would help it to hold conquered territories, but the United States, source of most of the funds, voted against the measure and disregarded it in practice.

It was necessary, of course, even if Egypt planned to resort only to diplomatic activities, to hold open the option of warfare, the other form of a "forward policy." A number of leaks from the Egyptian government to the press indicated that increasing attention was being given to war preparedness. Sadat proclaimed 1972 "the Year of Decision." In October 1972 General Ahmed Ismail was appointed Minister of War and Commander in Chief of the army and an intensive training program was publicly begun under Egyptian Chief of Staff Lieutenant General Saad Shazli who was widely regarded as Egypt's most able and aggressive combat leader. At the end of the year, intensive negotiations were undertaken with Syria and Libya to create a unified command structure under General Ismail. These activities were largely discounted by outside observers. They were too public, too flamboyant, too frequently announced to be credited.

Special diplomatic emissaries were sent from Cairo in February 1973 to virtually every major capital throughout Europe, Africa, Asia, and North America. At the United Nations Egypt's Foreign Minister, Mohammed Zayat, attempted to draw a parallel between Egypt's position in 1973 and Ethiopia's position in the 1930's: more was at stake, he asserted, than merely the survival of the Egyptian government or even of the nation; the whole structure of the international system was threatened, he asserted, by Israel's occupation of Egyptian national territory in defiance of worldwide sentiment and United Nations resolutions. The apparent success of the diplomatic initiatives was gratifying. Everywhere the Egyptian emissaries went, they were greeted by words of sympathy. But, as *Observer* diplomatic correspondent Robert Stephens reported on April 8, 1973:

Egypt is in a mood of bleak frustration after six years of "no peace, no war," in the Middle East and after the apparent international indifference to her Government's latest attempts to break the deadlock by diplomatic means. Consequently President Sadat has now embarked on a difficult and dangerous political operation. He is trying to convince his own skeptical people and the outside world that he is both reasonable and desperate, that he is serious when he talks of war as well as of peace . . .

Sadat clearly does not want to start a general war and hopes that the mere threat of a small one might be enough to produce international action. But if the threat is serious enough to be effective, it could also provoke an Israeli pre-emptive strike, as in 1967. Sadat's advisers are aware of this danger, but they say that Egypt is now being pushed too close against the wall; that she may soon have no alternative but to hit out, whatever the risk.

The Israeli reaction to the Egyptian diplomatic offensive was to put forward a firm and even hardening line. As Jim Hoagland reported in the *International Herald Tribune* on June 29, "If the Arabs wait longer to make peace with us, they will lose even more, Israel's deputy prime minister Yigal Allon told American newsmen recently . . . 'Keep land but not Arabs' is clearly the drift of the national mood in Israel's 25th anniversary year, which is also an election year . . . More than a quarter of a million acres of West Bank land are estimated to have already been expropriated by the Israeli government."

This policy of pushing the Egyptians into a corner was openly avowed by the Israeli government and was clearly perceived by the Egyptian president. In an interview with *Newsweek* editor Arnaud de Borchgrave in March, Sadat had lamented that "every door I have opened has been slammed in my face—with American blessings."

In talks in Israel in June with the author of this book, General (later to become Prime Minister) Itzhak Rabin defined "peace" more expansively than ever before, to include four items: i) "reconciliation" to the existence of a Jewish independent state; ii) absolute insistence on face-to-face negotiations, justified as the only way to prove the existence of reconciliation; iii) open boundaries, that is, free trade, economic competition, travel, etc.; and iv) "viable, tangible defense capabilities for Israel" defined to mean continued overwhelming Israeli military force but the absence of international peace keeping forces.

All the Israelis with whom I spoke (including General Rabin) recognized that the objectives so stated then created an "unbridgeable gap" to peace. Consequently, their policy emphasized a negative aspect: to *frustrate* hopes in Arab force, in Soviet protection of the Arabs, and in the possibility of effective United Nations intervention. Only if the Arabs were completely blocked and forced into a corner, thought the Israeli government, would they recognize the inevitability of dealing with Israel on Israeli terms.

Feeling that this was *politically* impossible even if *strategically* logical for any conceivable Egyptian government, I was convinced that war was inevitable within a few months. This observation was shared by knowledgeable observers throughout the Middle East and in the Soviet Union. Indeed, in the warming glow of detente, Soviet officials privately warned their American counterparts of the drift to war.* The only real question appeared to be when war would come and at what cost it would be fought.

Ironically, the more evident the Egyptian preparation became, and the more President Sadat openly spoke of it, the more it was discounted. The best form of military deception turned out to be complete frankness.

The culmination of the diplomatic offensive came in July when 13 of the 15 member nations of the Security Council voted to deplore Israel's continued occupation of the Arab territories. China, abstaining, found the resolution too mild while the United States voted in opposition and so vetoed the resolution. To the Arabs, it appeared that the diplomatic option had been closed and that their capacity to force implementation of resolution 242 would always sunder on the rocks of an American veto.

As David Holden reported in the *London Observer* (July 29, 1973): "The Israelis . . . argue—and the Americans now appear to support them—that if only the Arabs are deprived of all the other options, military or political, including the illusion of international pressure on their behalf, they will swallow their medicine along with their pride and accept the reality of Israel's superior power."†

Meanwhile, arms supplies from the Soviet Union had begun to pick new momentum. Syria received a promise in May of a large number of MIG-21 fighters and complementary batteries of surface-to-air missiles. All in all, Syria received in the first half of 1973 about $200 million worth of arms, a rate of supply almost double that of the previous year. Quietly, Yugoslavia also began to furnish Egypt a new anti-tank missile.

By the end of June, President Sadat and President Assad of Syria had formed a rough plan of battle, Operation Badr. Egypt was to be the senior partner and Syria was to limit its objectives in order to act

* Leslie H. Gelb, "Russian Says U.S. Was Warned of Mideast War," *New York Times* (December 21, 1973).

† Also see Walter Laqueur, *Confrontation: The Middle East and World Politics* (New York, 1974), pp. 34–43.

in consonance with Cairo. Already, the Egyptians had picked October 6 as their "D-Day." Not only was that night one in which the weather and moon conditions were expected to be perfect for their plan, but it had symbolic religious importance as well. The tenth day of the Muslim month of Ramadan (which corresponded to October 6 in 1973) was the day on which the Prophet Muhammad began his preparations for the most significant early battle in Islam, the battle of Badr which set up the conquest of Mecca and which his small and persecuted community took to be the sign of divine approbation. Also, as the Jewish Yom Kippur, October 6 obviously offered the most likely time of Israeli inactivity and inattention.

King Husain, together with President Assad of Syria, met with President Sadat in Cairo on September 10 and apparently agreed upon the broad outlines of the Arab strategy. Essentially, their agreement called for a series of last-ditch efforts to cajole the Great Powers into bringing pressure on Israel to withdraw from the conquered territories. They were expected to fail. King Husain was probably kept in the dark about the extent and certainly about the timing of the October war.

On September 13, units of the Israel Air Force provoked an air battle off the Syrian coast and shot down at least eight Syrian aircraft. For President Assad, this appears to have been a critical turning point. He is said to have immediately called President Sadat agreeing to all of the Egyptian conditions provided that war was initiated soon.

Around September 25, American intelligence ascertain that Egypt had mounted division-size maneuvers. Large stockpiles of ammunition were spotted in the process of being assembled and field communication networks were monitored in greatly elaborated activity. Under the provisions of the intelligence exchange relations then in effect, American officials warned the Israelis of these signs of impending war. To those "in the know" there was an ominous parallel to the events of June 1967 except that the shoe now appeared to be on the other foot. On September 28, President Sadat warned that war was imminent in a public speech. In a surprisingly low-keyed voice, he said, "I only say that the liberation of the land, as I have told you, is the first and main task facing us. God willing, we shall achieve this task."

In retrospect, it is astonishing how many clues there were that war was about to break out. Forty-eight hours before fighting began, the Russians evacuated their advisers from both Damascus and Cairo. The Israeli army was put on "the highest state of military prepared-

MAIN WEAPONS SYSTEMS OF MIDEAST COMBATANTS COMPARED*
As of beginning of hostilities on October 6, 1973

	TANKS			AIRPLANES				MISSILES	
	WEIGHT	CROSS-COUNTRY SPEED	MAIN GUN		MAXIMUM BOMB LOAD AND ARMS	SPEED	LOADED RANGE		RANGE
ISRAEL	600 Centurions (British)	56.9 tons	12–15 m.p.h.	105 mm.	95 F-4E (U.S.)	8 tons One 20-mm. multiple barrel, 4 Sidewinder	1,320 m.p.h.	900–2,000 miles	416 Hawk (Surface-to-air U.S.)	22 miles
	250 Ben Gurions (Adapted Centurions)	56.9 tons	12–15 m.p.h.	105 m.m.	35 Mirage III B/C (French)	2 tons, 4 Sidewinder air-to-air missile	1,419 m.p.h.	745 miles	Jericho (surface-to-surface, Israeli)	280
	100 T-67 (Rebuilt captured T-54/55's)	55 tons	15–19 m.p.h.	100 mm.	160 A-4E/H Skyhawks (U.S.)	4.1 tons, two 20-mm.	675 m.p.h.	2,000 miles	SS-10 (Surface-to-air, low altitude, U.S.)	

	Tanks	Weight	Speed	Caliber	Aircraft	Armament	Speed	Range	Missiles	Range
EGYPT	1,650 T-54/55 (Soviet)	38.5 tons	14–21 m.p.h.	100 mm.						
	100 T-62 (Soviet)	41.8 tons	15–21 m.p.h.							
					24 Tu-16 bombers (Soviet)	10 tons	575 m.p.h.	3,975 miles	SA-2 Guideline (High altitude)	25 miles
					210 MIG-21 interceptors (Soviet)	Two 30-mm. plus two Atoll air-to-air missiles	1,320 m.p.h.	375 miles	SA-3 Goa (Low altitude) SA-6 Gainful (Low altitude and mobile)	15 / 15
					80 SU-7 Fitter fighter-bombers (Soviet)	Two rocket pods or two 30-mm.	1,055 m.p.h.	500–600 miles	Frog 3 (Surface-to-surface) Frog 7	20–30 / 40–50
SYRIA	900 T-54/55				300 Su-7 Fitter fighter bombers 200 MIG-21 interceptors				SA 2, 3 and 6 Frog 7	
IRAQ	900 T-54/55				60 Tu-16 bombers 90 MIG-21's				SA 2 and 3 (Others unknown)	

Reprinted by permission from the *New York Times* (October 12, 1973).

* Both sides in war also had tanks and planes not shown on chart. In case of missiles, information on totals is unavailable in most cases.

ness" and the Israeli Air Force reserves and senior officers were called back to their posts.

War broke out, virtually simultaneously, on the Syrian and Egyptian fronts at about 2 P.M., local time, on Saturday October 6. The war in Syria began with air and tank attacks on the Israeli front lines and on the Suez front with a commando amphibious landing across the Canal.

In the fighting on the first evening, the Egyptians managed to penetrate Israeli defenses at three points and to prepare the way for five Egyptian divisions to get across the Canal on hurriedly constructed bridges. The principal Israeli defense "weapon," a system of pipes designed to cover the Canal with a sheet of oil which would then be set afire to incinerate the advancing Egyptian troops, was knocked out by commando raids the night before the main attack. Using high pressure water hoses, the Egyptians washed away a huge sand barrier, constructed by Israeli bulldozers, on the east bank. Every step of the invasion route had been meticulously planned and the first wave of troops had not only been fully briefed but repeatedly trained on simulation courses which reproduced the Israeli Bar-Lev Fortified Line. New Soviet equipment, particularly the "Sagger" wire-guided anti-tank missile played havoc with the Israeli tanks while the SAM-6 batteries and the VSU-23 anti-aircraft guns prevented the Israelis from full utilization of their tactical air force. These weapons, together with the infantry-borne SAM-7s were to cost Israel over 100 aircraft.

Meanwhile, on the Syrian front, massive formations of tanks plowed into the prepared Israeli defense line. The carnage was appalling. Hundreds of Syrian tanks were destroyed and perhaps as many as 8,000 infantrymen were killed. Both Syria and Israel escalated the fighting: the Syrians fired about a dozen "Frog" missiles into northern Israel—the only attack in the whole war on Israel proper—and the Israeli Air Force struck Damascus, killing 200 civilians including foreign diplomats. Then the Israeli Air Force turned to oil refineries, fuel tanks, and other industrial structures throughout Syria. The oil port of Banias was devastated. And, although Lebanon had remained neutral, the Israeli Air Force bombed a radar station there on the 9th of October.

The Egyptian strategy remained throughout the war one of limited engagement. What the Egyptians sought was to create a war of sufficient proportions to force the Great Powers to intervene and solve a crisis that had become too dangerous for their national interests. The military action was seen merely as a means to require effective (on the Israelis) and responsive (to the Arabs) diplomatic effort. Consequently, the Egyptian plan of action was highly limited in scope.* It never involved, for example, attacks on Israel proper; and after the first push beyond the Bar-Lev Line, the Egyptian army stopped and dug into defensive positions. It was, indeed, almost the military undoing of Egypt that this strategy was so exactly followed. At a time when Egypt could have pushed forward to seize or at least block the openings of the three passes connecting Israel with the front, the Egyptian army stopped. The Egyptian front was only ten miles deep across the Canal, too little for effective maneuver or defense, and this afforded the Israeli army the opportunity to group for a major counter-attack which ultimately pinned the Egyptian Third Corps to the southern part of the Suez Canal.

It appears clear that throughout the planning for the military operations in the October war, the Egyptians were under no illusions about their capacity to defeat Israel. The fundamental disparity between the Arabs and Israelis, which had pertained since 1948, still remained: Israel was a modern, industrialized state and the Arabs were poor, backward, and underdeveloped. The important thing, which Ismail clearly understood, was to fight creditably enough to win political flexibility and to force the Great Powers to intervene.

Some observers believe that Egyptians had these objectives well within their reach early in the October war. Based on extensive interviews in the Middle East, Europe, and the United States, the *Sunday Times* team arrived at the following analysis: "Kissinger wanted a limited Israeli defeat. The nicety lay in calculating the optimum scale of this defeat: big enough to satisfy the Arabs; modest enough to preclude a propaganda triumph for the Russians; sobering enough to bring Israel to the conference table; bearable enough to avoid the collapse of Mrs. Meir's government and its replacement by rightwing intransigents."†

On October 16, Sadat set out his terms for peace.

> First: We have fought and we shall go on fighting to liberate our land which was seized by Israeli occupation in 1967, and to find the means towards the restoration and respect of the legitimate rights of the Palestinian people. In this respect, we accept our commitment to the decisions of the United Nations, the General Assembly and the Security Council.
>
> Second: We are prepared to accept a ceasefire on condition that the Israeli forces withdraw forthwith from all the occupied territories to the pre-June 5, 1967 lines, under international supervision.

* Walter Laqueur, *Confrontation,* p. 127.
† Insight team, *Insight,* p. 132.

Third: We are ready, once the withdrawal from all these territories has been carried out, to attend an international peace conference at the United Nations. I shall try to persuade my colleagues, the Arab leaders, who are directly responsible for leading the conflict with our enemy. I will also do my best to convince the representatives of the Palestinian people to participate with us and with the whole international community in laying down rules and measures for peace in the area based on the respect of the legitimate rights of all the people in the area.

Fourth: We are willing, at this hour and at this very moment, to start clearing the Suez Canal and opening it to international navigation so as to contribute, once again, to world welfare and prosperity. I have in fact given the order to the head of the Suez Canal Authority to start this task immediately after the liberation of the eastern bank . . .

Fifth: Throughout all this we are not prepared to accept ambiguous promises or flexible expressions which lend themselves to various interpretations, draining our time needlessly and returning our cause to the stalemate . . .*

Unknown to Sadat, a small tank force under General Arik Sharon had already begun to attack through a weak point on the Egyptian lines seeking to cross the Canal south of Ismailia and cut off the Egyptian Third Corps. By October 17, Israel was well on the way to a stunning tactical defeat of the Egyptian forces in the south.

It was at this point that the second stage of the Arab offensive was brought into gear with the announcement of the so-called "oil weapon."

On October 17 in Kuwait, the Persian Gulf members of the Organization of Oil Exporting Countries (OPEC) met to discuss their reaction to the Middle East crisis. The representative of Iran, a major supplier of petroleum to Israel, chaired the meeting. While Iran was certainly not in favor of any form of boycott, it urged a dramatic rise in price and managed to reach immediate accord with its Arab neighbors on this point. Minus the Iranian chairman, who then left the meeting, the Arab delegates voted to suspend oil shipments until Security Council Resolution 242 was implemented.

During the previous decade, the American government had been aware of the prime importance of oil shipments on reasonable terms to Europe. It was assumed throughout the late 1950's and early 1960's that upon provision of relatively cheap oil, rested the prosperity of Europe. This, in turn, enhanced the solidity of the NATO alliance. Toward the end of the 1960's, however, the general assumption in Washington was that the European nations were then strong enough to fend for themselves and that American action to underpin their

* Insight team, *Insight,* p. 157.

economies was no longer as crucial as previously. When the second edition of this book was prepared in 1968, consequently, the importance of petroleum to the United States was regarded as being somewhat diminished. Between 1968 and 1973, however, European and Japanese dependence upon Middle Eastern petroleum dramatically increased and the United States, having steadily increased its own oil and petrochemical consumption, had itself come to depend upon petroleum imports much more than in the past. Consequently, the "oil weapon" proved extremely powerful. Japan, England, Italy, and Germany were hard hit. The poorer nations of Africa and Asia saw the Iranian-led move to raise oil prices as the virtual death knell of their development efforts.

The Saudi Arabian government argued, throughout the early phases of the crisis, for moderation, particularly in its relations to the United States. Only Holland and Japan, as major trading partners and friends of Israel, and Portugal, as a major opponent of African nationalism, were singled out for harsh treatment. But "any friendly state which has extended or shall extend effective material assistance to the Arabs" would not be affected. The United States was assured that it would have some time to react before it was directly affected. King Faisal called in the American ambassador and sent his Foreign Minister, Omar Saqqaf, to see President Nixon to urge American action to bring about a settlement in the Middle East. But, the day after Saqqaf met with Nixon, the White House requested that Congress appropriate $2.2 billion for military materiel for the Israeli armed forces.* King Faisal obviously regarded this as a personal affront and a rejection of his overture and on October 20 suspended all oil shipments to the United States.

The escalation of the economic and diplomatic confrontation with the Great Powers and the continuous erosion of the Egyptian military position convinced both the Soviet Union and the United States to intervene to bring a halt to the fighting. The American aspects of this truce-seeking will be described in more detail in Chapter 24 below. Here, it should be stated merely that the United States and the Soviet Union jointly sponsored Security Council Resolution 338 calling on the parties to terminate all military activity immediately and to begin immediately the implementation of Security Council Resolution 242. Further, it demanded that the interested parties begin negotiations to establish a just and durable peace. With China abstaining, the vote was 14 to 0.

The "first" cease-fire for all intents and purposes did not take effect,

* The U.S. Air Force airlifted 22,300 tons of equipment in 33 days to Israeli forces.

and during the two days from sundown October 22 to midnight October 24, the Israeli military forces completed the envelopment of the Egyptian Third Corps near Suez City. At that point the second cease-fire, called for by Security Council Resolution 339, more or less came into effect and the war on the Egyptian front gradually died down.

On the Syrian front, however, the fighting was to continue intermittently and then with growing intensity, not only in the days but in the weeks and months ahead. Cease-fire was not to be achieved there until May 31, 1974.

The cost of the war was shocking. Israel suffered somewhat fewer casualties than either Egypt or Syria (5,000 in comparison to roughly 8,000 each for the Egyptians and Syrians), and lost about 800 tanks and 200 aircraft, compared to 2,000 tanks and 450 airplanes for the Arabs. The dollar cost was staggering: three weeks of the war had cost nearly $750 million a day, or a total of perhaps $15 billion, divided among the three participants.

Then, soberly, everyone realized that it could have been much worse. Had the Great Powers not stopped the Israelis, they might have annihilated a large part of the Egyptian army; had the war not been stopped, the Soviet Union might have been forced to intervene; had that happened, the United States would probably have been forced to intervene. At some stage the weapons would have been nuclear; and the issue, survival of the planet.

As it was, despite the horrible cost in lives, treasure, and developmental hopes, there were some compensations. The most important of these was that the war lanced, at least on the Egyptian side, the boil of national humiliation. With the war, a page of Arab history had been turned. And at last, the Arabs appeared able, without the disfiguring weight of humiliation of their past weakness, to turn to their economic, social, and intellectual problems and prospects.

At least it appeared so at the time. But, as we shall see, below the surface discontent was growing. This discontent was not just with the government of President Sadat, although he became its first major victim, but against the very process of "development" (as we in the West conceived it) or "Westernization" (as its Middle Eastern critics envisaged it). It is to this complex process, still by no means worked out in 1990, that we must now turn.

PART 6

The Matrix of the New Arab

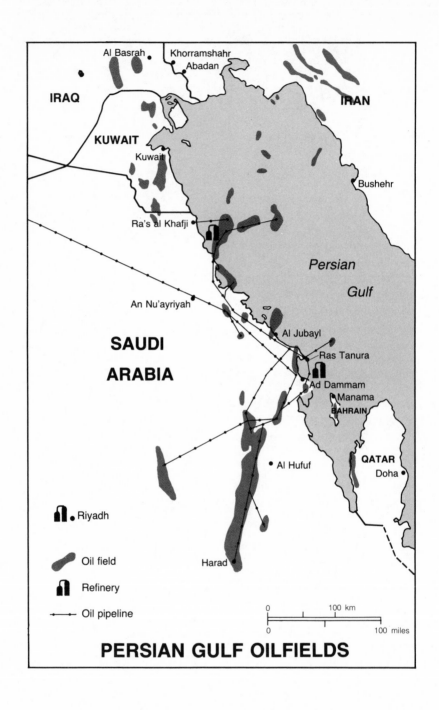

PERSIAN GULF OILFIELDS

18

The Economy of the
Arab World

THE economy of the Arab world is profoundly
affected by international politics and can be
understood only in this perspective. The Middle East is an area
of scarce rainfall, few natural resources, and great vicissitudes of
climate. However, lying athwart the trade and communication
routes joining Europe, Asia, and Africa, with important religious
and cultural influence in Africa and Asia, with an agricultural season different from Europe's, and with its vast deposits of oil discovered in the twentieth century, the Middle East has been of great
strategic value to others. Until recently, these factors have worked
to the disadvantage of the Arabs. Now they have become a major
asset and a major source of hope for the Arabs' future.

In recent years, some of the advanced, industrialized nations
have felt obliged to assist the poorer or less developed nations in
their efforts to modernize. To this end, substantial amounts of
credit have been made available bilaterally and through the World
Bank, and teams of experts have offered advice on virtually every
aspect of the modernization process. Despite disappointments and
shortfalls, the Americans and Europeans can take considerable
credit for statesmanship and generosity. But it was not always so.
Like their neighbors in other parts of Asia and Africa, the Middle
Easterners retained bitter memories of the greed, exploitation, and
humiliation visited upon them by the rich commercial nations of

267

Europe, who grew to strength in the wake of the Industrial Revolution.

In many ways, the symbol of the past was the Suez Canal. Located on Egyptian territory, the Canal was dug by Egyptian labor and largely paid for by Egyptian capital, yet gave Egypt almost no return for the first sixty years of its operation. Indeed, its very existence was a prime reason for the British invasion of 1882 and the Anglo-French-Israeli invasion of 1956. Nationalized in 1956, it began to produce significant revenues for Egypt. By June 1967, immediately before the outbreak of Arab-Israeli fighting, the Canal was yielding Egypt $250 million annually in hard currencies. Closure from June 1967 to January 1974 cost the world, primarily the Europeans, South Asians, and Africans, an estimated $10 billion in extra shipping charges, raised prices, and loss of revenue. In that decade a revolution occurred in shipbuilding. Although only 12 meters deep, the Canal accommodated ships of up to 60,000 tons. Nowadays, having been deepened in the late 1970's, the Canal accommodates all but the very largest supertankers and remains an important source of revenue for Egypt.

In contrast to this symbol of the past, the symbol of the new age is oil. Foreign companies have paid vast treasures simply for the privilege of being allowed to explore some of the most inhospitable and barren land on this planet. In petroleum, neither the labor, nor the capital, nor the technology was originally the contribution of the Arabs. From modest beginnings in the 1930's, the oil industry has grown into the most important single asset of the Middle East. Saudi Arabia, which earned upward of $60 billion in 1990, had revenues of only $4 million from all sources in 1934, just before oil began to be exploited. Income increased very gradually as its oil fields were brought into production around the time of World War II, so that in 1950, after sixteen years of development, sales yielded only $57 million. The reason was that the price of oil remained low. In the 1960's a barrel of oil sold for approximately $1.80. It increased slowly by the end of the 1960's and then, during the crisis created by the Middle Eastern war of 1973, advanced rapidly. During 1974 some high-quality Middle Eastern oil was sold for $17 a barrel. That seemed incredible, but in 1979 the U.S. government itself sold oil to Japan for $40 a barrel.

In 1982, the oil revenues of Saudi Arabia, Kuwait, and the UAE reached $186 billion. Then, in the mid-1980's, traders spoke of an "oil glut" and both prices and demand fell. The same three countries saw their combined revenues decline to about $57.6 billion in

1985. This fall caused major cuts in development programs, declines in imports, and a growing sense that the "boom" would be followed by a "bust." In America, the Carter administration's efforts to find means to cut energy use and to develop alternative sources of energy were phased out by the Reagan administration. The price of oil fell to an average of about $14 a barrel. Expressed in terms of 1989 dollars (that is, adjusted for inflation), the price of oil was roughly $30 a barrel from 1974 to 1978; it hit a peak of $50 a barrel from 1980 to 1981; and then it fell gradually to roughly $14 a barrel in 1986.

In 1989, the United States was using about 16.5 million barrels a day, of which about half was imported. Saudi Arabia, Iraq, and Kuwait supplied about 27 percent. Japan, which derived somewhat more than 11 percent of its energy from nuclear power, obtained roughly half of its oil imports from the UAE, Saudi Arabia, and Kuwait. In August 1990, Kuwait and Iraq (with combined production of roughly 4.5 million barrels a day) were forced out of the world's oil market, and the price of crude oil more than doubled. Saudi Arabia announced plans to increase its production to make up about half of the loss of Kuwait and Iraq, or roughly 2.2 million barrels a day. At the higher prices, Saudi Arabia stands to earn roughly $4 billion a month more than it had projected before the

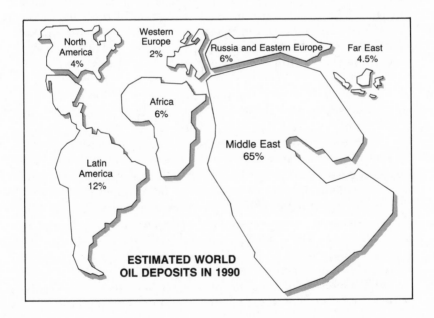

North America 4%
Western Europe 2%
Russia and Eastern Europe 6%
Far East 4.5%
Africa 6%
Middle East 65%
Latin America 12%

ESTIMATED WORLD OIL DEPOSITS IN 1990

crisis. The impact of this in the West was shown on September 14, when the United States announced plans to sell Saudi Arabia $20 billion worth of weapons. But it was also shown when, for the first time, the United States announced plans to begin drawing down its strategic reserve of petroleum.

Four facts about Middle Eastern oil are fundamental. First, it is available in vast concentrations, so that its fields are cheaper to exploit and will last longer than those in most other areas. Second, unlike oil from fields in North America, Europe, and Russia, it is relatively little used locally. Third, it involves the transfer of vast revenues from the industrial nations to the Middle East; to date, such transfer probably has amounted to about $1 trillion in goods, services, and capital. And, fourth, since oil exists in finite quantities and has been actively sought throughout the world for more than a century, it is unlikely that major new fields will be found outside the Middle East, except, perhaps, in Siberia. Thus, until alternative sources of power are refined and/or energy requirements are cut, Middle Eastern oil will continue to be regarded by the industrial world as a vital resource. Yet it is sobering to consider that of the Middle Eastern oil fields, only those in Iran, Iraq, Kuwait, and Saudi Arabia are expected to remain in production for another twenty-five years.

What is the impact of these considerations on the Middle East? Again, the Suez Canal and petroleum offer a convenient index of change. Mehmet Ali had opposed the digging of the Suez Canal because he rightly perceived that it would make foreign domination of Egypt inevitable. His attempt to industrialize Egypt was opposed by those European powers which sought markets for their own produce. Ultimately, European bankers and merchants committed what amounted to grand larceny against Egypt. As described above, Egypt was subjected to sharp practice and fraud on a scale rarely if ever met in international relations. Today, the Great Powers compete to assist the Arab countries with grants, loans, special trade arrangements, and technical assistance on an unprecedented scale. They also give or sell great quantities of military equipment. The strategic value of the Middle East has now become its major natural resource. Whereas the Egyptians of the nineteenth century were occasionally forced to purchase defaulted bonds and regularly paid up to 20 percent interest on loans, the Arabs of today have received billions of dollars in grants and loans on concessionary terms.

The combination of these factors has enabled the whole Middle Eastern area to undertake a major program of development.

The domestic resources of the Arab world, as we have seen, are extremely meager. Only in a few places—mainly in the north of Syria and Iraq—does sufficient rain fall to sustain agriculture. On the Arabian Peninsula, which is a fifth the size of the United States, only one tenth of one percent of the land—an area about twice the size of Long Island—is arable. Egypt, as Herodotus said, is the "gift of the Nile": without the Nile, the arable land would be as barren as the 97 percent which is now desert. Iraq owes most of its agriculture to the Tigris and Euphrates rivers, which rise in the Turkish and Kurdish highlands where more than eight inches of rain falls annually. Elsewhere, agricultural areas are islands in a vast, waterless sandy "sea."

The economy of the Arab countries of the Middle East has gone through three discernible stages and is now in a fourth, characterized by major efforts at development. In the first, which lasted until the 1820's in Egypt, the 1830's in Syria, and perhaps the 1860's in Iraq and the 1930's in Arabia, the economy was largely fragmented into clusters of villages and tribal groups which, in the main, were self-sufficient and in which a balance existed between nomadism, agricultural life, and small-scale urban industry. This first phase was followed by a second, characterized by the rapid introduction of cheaper Western goods and more attractive Western styles as a result of the European Industrial Revolution, of the development of public security, and of the weakness of the Ottoman sultans, who, according to the commercial code of 1838, virtually turned over to Europeans the commerce of the empire.

In the third phase—which began in Egypt at the end of the First World War, somewhat later in Iraq, Syria, and Lebanon, and in Arabia only in the 1970's—the Arabs set about creating an industrial base. Beginning with early and failed attempts in Egypt, the feeling has never died that until the Arab world has its own industrial base, it will be nothing more than a "country cousin" of Europe. Moreover, it was clearly not acceptable in terms of national self-respect merely to have industry *in* the Middle East. Arabs felt strongly that the institutions of modern capitalism must be native.

Egyptian industry never was able to match Egyptian agriculture in competition for private capital, however. Cotton was king. Any Egyptian with money put it into land. Egyptian industry was new and untried, and with international commitments preventing the government from creating tariff barriers, infant industry was not an attractive investment. By 1927 only about 5 percent of Egyptian gross national product came from industry and mining. In the 1930's, however, the collapse of cotton prices and the continued rise in Egyptian population without compensatory rises in agricultural area or production led to a renewed interest in industrialization.

Textiles were the front runner in Egyptian industrial growth. Production increased from 9 million square yards at the end of World War I to 20 million in 1931 and 159 million in 1939. A major part of the activity of Egyptian industry was stimulated by the Misr Bank, which participated in the founding of some twenty-seven companies. But the bank was always short of capital.

It was not really until the Axis blockade during World War II and the presence of a huge Allied army—whose expenditures totaled 25 percent of Egyptian national income—that the major stimulus to local production was felt. In Egypt 80,000 skilled and semi-skilled workers were employed to supply the British Eighth Army.

The Iraq government began in 1927 to allow the import of industrial equipment without duty, and in 1929 passed a law to encourage industry by granting some tax exemptions if the industry to be started was above a certain size and used power-driven rather than hand-powered equipment. In 1933 Iraq imposed high tariffs on those industrial goods which could be supplied locally. And in 1936 the Agricultural and Industrial Bank was formed to initiate industrial schemes.

The war made a major impact on Iraq, as elsewhere. The military expenditures of the Allied forces there in 1943 were about three times the size of the government budget for that year. The existence of ready cash and the lack of imported goods caused a wartime spurt of industrial activity.

Not only was the war a short-term stimulus to industrial activity in the Arab countries; even more significant was the long-term impact it left by means of a "school" in fiscal and commercial control. This "school" was the Middle East Supply Centre. The Supply Centre was established by the British government in 1941 (and made a joint Anglo-American project in 1942) to ensure that the population of the Middle Eastern countries would continue to get essential supplies despite the wartime shortages of goods and shipping space. Essentially, the Allies sought to cut imports. The principal means of accomplishing this reduction was to expand local production. Since the major bulk imports were agricultural and the primary danger was famine, a premium was put on agricultural development. The most lasting results, however, lay in the second major means available to the wartime military authority: government regulation of industry, commerce, and agriculture. As elsewhere, in the Middle East the war provided a justification and a need for forms of government activity which were continued long after the war ended. All imported goods had to be licensed, currencies were controlled, and elaborate plans and machinery were established to allocate goods and services. Even for those who assumed that the purpose of the Middle East Supply Centre was to exercise foreign control over the area's economies and that its heavy emphasis on agriculture was motivated by a desire to keep the Middle East backward, the principle of central control was not abhorrent.

In Iraq, Syria, and Lebanon, meanwhile, little industry had been started until the end of World War II. Characteristically, textiles led the way. In Iraq the oldest plants processed cotton and wool, which were sold in large part to the government for army use. What little industry there was in Syria before World War II was primarily handicraft, but the shortages and high prices of the war and immediate postwar years served as a stimulus to the development of native industry. This, in turn, was encouraged by the newly independent government as a means of achieving economic independence to match political independence. Protective tariffs were introduced in 1949 alongside low-interest, state-guaranteed loans for industry. In 1952 the importation of a number of articles that could be manufactured in Syria was prohibited, and import quotas were imposed on others.

The problem faced immediately in Syria and Iraq was how to create industry in the general absence of capital or skills in the population. Whereas in Egypt both had evolved over a number of decades, Syria and Iraq wanted to find short cuts to catch up with the West. In Syria the government was further hampered by the fact that the little capital it had was channeled through the Banque de Syrie et du Liban, then controlled by France.

But everywhere in the Arab countries, industry was a small part of the economy. Just what it amounted to prior to recent years, in terms of gross national product of the several countries, is at best a guess. In fact, relatively little was known of the economy of the Middle East as a whole, despite the efforts of the Middle East Supply Centre, until the Palestine War posed, in the displacement of nearly a million Arab refugees, economic problems of such magnitude and immediacy that a special United Nations Economic Survey Mission, the Clapp Commission, was created to study the problem.

The report of the commission, published in December 1949, pointed out that "the solution of the problem of the poverty and unemployment of the refugees is . . . inseparable from a solution of the problem of poverty and hunger as that already affects a large section of the population of the Middle East." Apparently reacting to their talks with officials of the newly independent governments, the commissioners commented that

a higher living standard cannot be bestowed by one upon another like a gift. An improved economy does not come in a neat package to be sold or given away in the market place . . . The highly developed nations of the world did not make their way by wishing. By work and risk they forced the earth, the soil, the forest and the rivers to yield them riches. They pooled their energy and resources by taxation and mutual enterprise . . . There is no substitute for the application of work and local enterprise to each country's own resources. Help to those who have the will to help themselves should be the primary policy guiding and restraining the desire of the more developed areas of the world to help the less developed lands.

The report pointed out that the area is, "and for a long time to come will remain, agricultural." The first requirement was said to be the Middle East's need to develop its potential to feed its people and increase export crops. Only limited industry was seen to be immediately required. Needs apart, large-scale projects were confronted with many obstacles. "The region is not ready, the projects are not ready, the people and Governments are not ready, for large-scale development." The conclusion was that pilot projects should be begun, with international assistance, while governments of the area organized themselves to mobilize their resources and focus their talents on national development plans and agencies.

The advice given to the Arab governments had two immediate effects, one good and one not. On the one hand, the report pointed out the potentials of the area and indicated a road toward their realization; it encouraged local enterprise and promised external help; and, avoiding impractical and unrealistic aims, it underlined projects that could be undertaken immediately. On the other hand, the mission was viewed with a jaundiced eye by the critical and suspicious Arabs, suffering from the humiliation of the Palestine War. In their eyes, the West was providing external assistance so as to salve its conscience for the fate of the Arab refugees, and it was emphasizing agricultural development in order to keep the Middle East merely a "farm" for Europe.

The first country to profit from the advice offered by the Clapp Commission was Iraq, which in 1950 created a Development Board charged with the planning and execution of schemes to develop the country. To carry out its projects, the board was to receive 70 percent of the government's revenue from oil. At that time this sum was only $12 million. Recognizing its lack of skilled planners, Iraq asked the World Bank to send a team to study its prospects. The first development plan (for the period 1951–1956) was based on the report of this group.

Iraq also asked the United States government for technical advice, and commissioned various consultants to prepare reports. Indeed, planning became virtually an end in itself, as the Development Board commissioned whole teams of contractors to design facilities which required or catered to talents and personnel not then available in Iraq.

But Iraq was fortunately situated between the two extremes of the Arab countries: those with dense population and a shortage of capital, led by Egypt, and those with proportionally vast capital resources but few alternatives for investing it locally, typified by Kuwait.

Among the many problems associated with development is how to acquire sufficient foreign exchange to buy the equipment or hire the skills needed to build the physical plant and train the personnel for modern economic activity. In the Middle East, during the past three decades, oil has been the magic source of this foreign exchange.

Used on a small scale for thousands of years wherever it bubbled to the surface, as at Nebuchadnezzar's "fiery furnace" near Kirkuk, oil was first discovered in commercial quantities in Iran in 1908. Since at that time the Royal Navy was changing from coal- to oil-burning ships, the British government, at the insistence of Winston Churchill, on the eve of the First World War acquired 51 percent of the stock of the corporation set up to exploit Persian oil production. (In large part it was the existence of the Iranian oil fields and the need to protect them from the Turks that led to the establishment of Kuwait and to the Anglo-Indian invasion of Iraq in November 1914.) While American and other companies acquired leases in the Ottoman Empire, the government of India arranged with the Arabian shaikhdoms under its protection to withhold concession rights from any but British nationals. An Anglo-German enterprise, the Turkish Petroleum Company, acquired a concession in Iraq on June 28, 1914.

After the war, it was in part the desire of the Turkish Petroleum Company to control the areas around Mosul that led the British government to get French agreement to a revision of the Sykes-Picot Agreement, which had awarded Mosul to French-controlled Syria. In return for the inclusion of Mosul in Iraq and transit rights across Syria for oil, the British agreed in the San Remo Conference to let French interests take up a part, later reduced to roughly one fourth, of the combine which later became the Iraq Petroleum Company. Turkish acquiescence to the inclusion of Mosul in Iraq was purchased for a consideration of 10 percent of Iraq's oil revenue for a twenty-five-year period.

In America, at this time, there was a panic over oil, with talk of American reserves being depleted in four to six years; the government was, in fact, so alarmed that it considered entering the oil business itself, as the British government had done. But American companies, some of which had concessions from the now defunct Ottoman regime, were excluded from areas of British and French influence. After long and somewhat acrimonious diplomatic negotiations, the British agreed to let American companies operate in the Middle East, and in 1925 American companies took roughly a fourth of the stock of the Iraq Petroleum Company. With the major oil interests included, in 1928 a monopoly area of the Middle East was created for the Iraq Petroleum Company alone.

American companies that had not participated in the 1928 agreement tried to get concessions in the Arab areas. In 1932 the Standard Oil Company of California, having found a loophole in British restriction on foreign enterprise in the Persian Gulf by establishing a Canadian company, struck oil on Bahrain Island. Stirred by this enterprise, it acquired a concession in Saudi Arabia in 1933. Joined by the Texas Company, which had a stronger market for oil, it struck oil in Saudi Arabia, near Dhahran, in 1938. Meanwhile, in 1933, the Gulf Oil Company in partnership with the Anglo-Iranian Oil Company, which held the concession in Iran, acquired a concession in Kuwait. In 1938 it struck what was immediately recognized as the world's richest single oil field, the Burgan Sands, which was a short distance from the coast, about eighty square kilometers in area, and less than a thousand meters deep. It was the oil prospector's dream field.

World War II interrupted the development of Kuwait's oil before it had achieved commercial production. The real stimulus came in 1951 when Anglo-Iranian Oil lost its concession in Iran and turned to Kuwait in search of another source of supply. From

1950 to 1954 Kuwait production tripled and additional oil was discovered.

In 1972, Kuwait produced 3 million barrels of oil a day, for a total of 151.2 million tons yearly. (By way of comparison, this was at that time 5.8 percent of the world's oil production, or equivalent to 19 percent of America's consumption.)

These factors made Kuwait a golden land. With proven reserves of about 100 billion barrels of extremely high-quality petroleum, costing only about $0.10 a barrel to pump to the nearby sea lanes, Kuwait has made the Arabian Nights a modern reality. In 1939, in the old days (now nearly forgotten), Kuwait earned less than $300,000 a year from pearl fishing and trading. By 1979 Kuwait had a GNP of $12.8 billion, and by 1990 it had built up reserves and investments abroad in excess of $100 billion. Individual Kuwaitis rapidly became the landlords of Cairo, Beirut, and Lausanne, and Kuwaiti deposits in London became an important factor in the stability of the pound sterling.

Kuwait quickly came under heavy criticism among the Arabs for its inability to spend its vast riches to their satisfaction. Iraq, in serious financial trouble, in 1958 resurrected the claims made repeatedly by successive Iraqi governments that Kuwait was a part of Iraq. In the face of a threat to invade the country, Britain rushed in troops and equipment in 1961, until the Arab League took action to replace them with a mixed Arab force. For the Kuwait government the lesson was clear: it must give other Arabs collectively a stake in its security. Hence, in 1961 Kuwait created the Kuwait Fund for Arab Development. Originally the fund's assets were about $170 million. They grew rapidly as the Kuwait government came to view the fund as a way to create a shared and balanced interest in its independence among the other members of the Arab community. By 1987, the fund stood at $6.75 billion; by 1985, it had participated in projects worth more than $1.3 trillion to sixty-four countries.*

The Iraq Petroleum Company was one of the world's great cartels. Among its owners were Royal Dutch Shell, British Petroleum (which was 56 percent owned by the British government), the Compagnie Française des Pétroles (35 percent owned by the French government), and a consortium of American petroleum "giants." The Arabian American Oil Company was jointly owned

* See Walid Moubarak, "The Kuwait Fund," *Middle East Journal*, 41 (1987):538ff.

by California Standard, the Texas Company, Standard Oil of New Jersey, and Socony; the Kuwait Oil Company was jointly owned by Gulf and British Petroleum. The maze of interlocking and separate research, refining, marketing, shipping, production, and exploration companies controlled by these groups and their vast assets and armies of employees made them virtually empires within the petty states of the Middle East and silhouetted them bleakly against the simple economic horizons of the countries in which they operated. Irrespective of the enormous contributions to Middle Eastern development and the usually enlightened public relations policies of the companies, this fact created a highly charged political atmosphere both for the governments and the companies.

As the governments began to develop cadres of men with some knowledge of the petroleum industry, they naturally aspired to control and exploit this single national resource of worldwide importance. They found that the companies usually could afford to pay almost any demand, after a decent period of bargaining, because the stakes were so enormous: the goose was hard to kill and the golden eggs seemed unlimited. Oil royalties went up from token payments in the 1930's to a fifty-fifty split, to joint ownership, and finally to nationalization. The Arabs have concerted with the other members of the Organization of Petroleum-Exporting Countries (OPEC) to find ways further to increase their income from petroleum. A favorite idea of some Arabs is that fully integrated companies—extending "from the well head to the gas station pump"—should exist to give the Arabs a share of profits at each stage of the operation.

Most of the producing countries' governments now own the oil companies. As their younger citizens acquire proper training and experience, some are managing all and most are managing some of the production and refining facilities in their territories.

Aside from the oil boom, the traditional economy of the Middle East has been agricultural. Until quite recently, roughly two out of each three people were directly dependent upon agriculture for their living. Moreover, most of the foreign currency earned by non-oil countries was from agriculture. Agriculture still accounts for substantial portions of the income of Iraq, Syria, Jordan, and Egypt.

Arabs traditionally have despised the menial lot of the peasant, and the constituency of today's governments is urban, young, and modernizing. Consequently, we should not be surprised to find

278

that the national development programs have favored industry over agriculture. As we examine the Middle Eastern economies, country by country, the trend away from agriculture is clear. Uniformly, we see reasons for this: the prestige of technology, the inability to upgrade the skills of the peasantry, the paucity of water, the poor quality of most of the land, the frequent weakness in the commodities market, and the close relationship between modernizing governments and their urban constituencies.

The economic and political situation of the Arab countries is dynamic: yesterday's dream is today's norm and tomorrow's failure. The "revolution of expectations" is continuing and accelerating. The "new man" in part brings about and in part is a result of the growth of industry.

Improvement in agricultural output and marketing, therefore, is vital to the success of the development effort. How possible is it? The answer cannot be given in purely economic terms.

For many centuries the *fellah,* or peasant, had been treated as a domestic animal, a part of the sultan's flock, to be shorn of his yearly produce by tax collectors, usurers, and casual robbers under various titles. His attitude toward government was one of sullen hatred, fear, and—when one of his many ruses succeeded— contempt. For him, as for the very rich, the best government was the least government. In no way did the government benefit him. Regulation of his personal affairs, guidance in matters of law, and what little succor or education he received came from the religious establishment, from the village custom and its council of elders, or from his own numerous kindred.

The villager and many of his city cousins lived apart from government and according to rules different from its formal laws. In the eyes of the government, the village lands belonged to the state; the villager enjoyed an insecure tenure upon payment of various sorts of taxes and fees to someone rich or powerful enough to contract with the government for the right to a tax farm (*iltizam*). The tax farmer obligated himself to pay a fixed fee or render military service to the government in return for the right to extract anything he could from the peasants.

Let us take Egypt as the example, since the history there is the most precise. When Mehmet Ali became pasha of Egypt in 1805, he was in conflict with the previous ruling group, the Mamluks, and proceeded to undercut their authority in various ways. One way was in the abolition of the *iltizam* titles. As in his military reforms, he had to move somewhat slowly, and it was not until after his massacre of the Mamluks in 1811–1812 that he was able to destroy the system.

Lands were then turned over to village communities, which became responsible for the payment of taxes. What the individual "owned" was the right to cultivate certain plots of land, and this right was passed from father to son. The government hoped to stimulate production, but, more important, to undercut the power of the only social group able to challenge it. This event was to be copied, unconsciously, in 1952.

Having destroyed the "feudal" class and established a direct relationship between the state and the land, Mehmet Ali began in 1829 to encourage the development of uncultivated lands by granting tenure to army officers, merchants, and others willing to invest in them. Apparently, he also sought in this way to create a new landed aristocracy. Gradually, over the years, as the role of the state in the economy declined, laws and decrees converted tenure rights into something approximating full ownership.

Meanwhile, great improvements in land productivity were made. After the introduction of cotton in 1821, the rich lands of Egypt became golden. The American Civil War, which took American cotton off the world market and produced a financial panic in industrial England, made Egypt prosperous and lured to the land large amounts of capital. Finally, even a peasant could own and sell or mortgage his lands.

What effect this had on the peasant is clear: he achieved more mobility, but his ties to the land were weakened so that in bad years he risked losing both his new title and his age-old usufruct. In the slump following the end of the American Civil War, the smaller operators in Egypt went heavily into debt or lost their lands to larger companies. As the government became desperate for revenue, particularly in the days of Ismail Pasha, it was willing to play fast and loose with law and tenure, so that the wealthy were able to buy titles to land, and rights over the peasants on it, by the payment of back taxes.

Foreigners were encouraged even in the time of Mehmet Ali to invest in the land of Egypt, and by 1901 they individually and through land companies had acquired about 11 percent of the agricultural land of the country.

As dams and canals were built by the state, marginal lands came into production and passed into the hands of larger capitalists and land companies.

The amount of land devoted to agriculture increased from

19,425 square kilometers in 1893 to 21,862 square kilometers in 1906. It has undergone little lateral expansion since: to 26,710 square kilometers, after the completion of the High Dam. More control over flooding and irrigation has meant that progressively larger amounts of land could be double-cropped. Today, this "vertical expansion" gives Egypt 43,320 square kilometers of "cropped" land. In twenty years of land reclamation efforts, less than 15 percent has been added horizontally to Egyptian arable land—and most of that has been of marginal quality. Once the granary of the Middle East, Egypt is now importing half of its food. It is, ironically, the largest customer for American millers.

The completion of Lake Nasser, formed by water backed up by the High Dam, has given Egypt a reserve approximately five times the size of Lake Mead on the Colorado River. This is the equivalent of approximately two and a half times the yearly Nile flow and is, of course, a stupendous engineering and irrigation feat. The impact on industry is similarly great, through the provision of cheap electrical power. However, the dam is not without its disadvantages. The silt which yearly renewed the fertility of the Nile Delta has now been stopped, and Egypt must use much heavier amounts of expensive fertilizer than before. Waterlogging of the delta has diminished crop production in some areas and increased salting problems. The debilitating disease of bilharziasis and various sicknesses carried by flies and mosquitoes have spread. Ironically, Egypt could significantly increase the produce of its land if it used less rather than more water. A study of the agricultural potential of the Middle East suggested that buried drains might increase crop yields up to 50 percent.*

Of course, there is no single technique that will magically enhance agricultural production in the Middle East. To a certain extent the Egyptian government built the High Dam because it realized it did not have the potential rapidly to educate and uplift the Egyptian peasantry. However massive and expensive, the dam was a discrete, doable project; in contrast, the scattered, poor, ill-educated, tenaciously traditional Egyptian peasantry had successfully defied all efforts at change in their basic pattern of life for more than 5,000 years.

Recent experience suggests that any serious improvement must be considered a long-term investment and that the tools to be employed are complex. They involve not only improved seed, more

* Marion Clawson et al., *The Agricultural Potential of the Middle East* (New York, 1971).

fertilizers and pesticides, control of water, and adequate drainage, but also massive programs in rural education. This requires a fundamental transformation for which "nearly all of the ingredients . . . must come from *within* the region. To be sure, outside help will be of value. Especially in the initial phase, new technology and new plant and livestock material from abroad will be indispensable; capital limitations may be eased by foreign grants or loans; and technical expertise may fill in shortages in locally available manpower. These aids are not to be underestimated. But basically, agricultural progress will either capture the imagination of the government and people of the country itself, or it will not take place."*

At the present time, agricultural yields in the Arab countries not only are low but show no discernible improvement. "The Arab farmer is efficient in the sense that he expends little on his output; but he is extremely inefficient because, spending little, he produces little." With production per acre low, it is clear that the potential is very great. "Potential grain production, perhaps the single most significant measure for a region in which grain is the staff of life, could rise from its present 11 million tons to 50. At that rate of output, the region would be a net exporter of grain in a volume that raises questions of export outlets. Production of other crops could rise similarly, in some instances perhaps even more sharply."†

The problem in Syria and Jordan is substantially different from that of Egypt. Both countries have attempted to extend their agricultural lands horizontally. As a consequence, they have brought into production marginal lands. Of Syria's 185,000 square kilometers, about 65,000 are now cultivated, but roughly half lie fallow every year and only 5,000 square kilometers are irrigated. As Bent Hansen has written, "Syrian agriculture in the post-War period is almost a Ricardian textbook case of marginal returns decreasing with the extension of the margin of cultivation. This is the key to understanding the stagnation of agriculture."‡

Syria, like Egypt, is pinning its hopes on major irrigation and hydroelectric projects. A dam across the Euphrates River at Tabqa will generate 2.5 billion kilowatt-hours of electricity and irrigate about 1.5 million acres of land. Like all reservoir projects, however,

---

* Clawson et al., *Agricultural Potential*, p. 4.
† Ibid.
‡ Charles A. Cooper et al., *Economic Development and Population Growth in the Middle East* (New York, 1971), p. 343.

this has been very expensive. Not only has it cost Syria approximately $400 million, most of which has been borrowed from the Soviet Union, but it has displaced approximately 70,000 people, whose farms will be flooded. Of major importance is that it offers a means to even out the statistical rollercoaster of Syrian production. Heavily dependent upon rain, Syrian grain production varies between 600,000 and 1,800,000 tons yearly. The Euphrates dam should not only increase production but should provide a more secure and stable base for Syrian economic development.

Jordan is even more tightly constrained than Syria. It has little water, and only about 10 percent of its 22 million acres is regarded as "agricultural." Only on the western fringe, toward the Mediterranean, does annual rainfall allow for steady use, but much of the soil there is heavily eroded and of low quality.

The situation is even more extreme, of course, in Libya and the Arabian Peninsula, where relatively small amounts of land can be brought under cultivation by natural sources of water. Both countries are now experimenting with desalination and with exotic food crop production techniques. To date, these have proved prohibitively expensive. In addition they have tried deep wellcenter pivot irrigation systems, which deplete water reservoirs and lower the water table, thus killing natural vegetation and making the area unsuitable for most animals.

Iraq and the Sudan appear to have the greatest agricultural potential in the Middle East.

Iraq has 435,000 square kilometers, of which roughly 35,000 are tilled by rain-fed agriculture and approximately the same number are irrigated. Using its oil resources, Iraq has managed to make significant inroads on its problems of flood control and adequate drainage. Unlike the generally predictable Nile, the Tigris-Euphrates complex is highly erratic and frequently destructive. Consequently, flood control was judged an even greater priority than the provision of new irrigation water, and the early hydrological work in Iraq in the 1950's was aimed less at utilizing the potential of the rivers than at keeping them from destroying existing agricultural lands.

As the waters of the Tigris-Euphrates and various tributaries flow toward the Persian Gulf, they become increasingly saline. The intensity of the Iraqi heat, and the multiple use of water for irrigation and drainage purposes en route, pose an ever-increasing burden of drainage. In the past, this problem was solved by simply abandoning lands as they salted up. Since this process has been normal operating procedure for more than a thousand years, Iraq today must pay a heavy price for the lack of investment in drainage facilities and lack of careful control over crop rotation. There is, however, a bright side to this dismal legacy: the Iraqi peasantry is by no means so fixed in its ways as the Egyptian peasantry and can more easily be induced to use modern, higher-potential methods. Indeed, it has been suggested that a carefully directed program of education, as well as better seed, more fertilizer, and, above all, better drainage, could cause a tenfold rise in Iraqi agricultural production.

The Sudan has a vast area, 2.5 million square kilometers, watered by the Nile and its tributaries. In the far south is the great swamp, *as-Sudd,* and in the north the even vaster deserts. All told, the Sudan has about 125,000 square kilometers in agricultural use. Most of this, however, can be only lightly used, due to the shortage of water. The most intensive use of land is in the 8,000-square-kilometer Gezira plantation. Begun in 1911, Gezira is one of the few success stories of large-scale agricultural development. Today, it works as a modified state enterprise, with 100,000 farmers who receive 49 percent of their crops and form the stable agricultural backbone of the country.

The Sudan now has under planning a new agricultural project, roughly half the size of the Gezira scheme, which it intends to devote primarily to food production. The Sudan already suffers from extensive overgrazing in its western provinces, and the work that is now under way to drain the swamplands in the south may have disastrous ecological consequences for the whole of Africa.

Industry is the aspiration of the Third World. All underdeveloped countries have come to believe that the acquisition of modern technology, the creation of an industrial labor force, and the building of factories is not only the road to modernization but indeed its very embodiment. In the first phase of industrial expansion, many countries attempted to create the heavy industry which they believed essential to development. The outstanding example was the Helwan steel mill in Egypt. Increasingly, however, governments have come to understand that light industry, particularly one related to the production of textiles, made more profitable use of their limited hard currencies and, because it is relatively labor intensive, facilitated the social transformation they sought to bring about. The results have naturally been most striking where power and money were relatively abundant. This has been particularly notable in Kuwait, which since 1952 has created an industrial society.

Industry still lags behind agriculture as a source of national income. In Syria, for example, during the 1960's, industry accounted for approximately 14 percent of net domestic product, whereas agriculture accounted for approximately 26 percent. Almost everywhere, investment in industry has been regarded as essentially unattractive to potential entrepreneurs, so that government has taken an increasingly large share of the lead. Indeed, in Syria, Iraq, and Egypt the governments have virtually stifled all private initiative in this field.

As we shall see in the next chapter, this industrial transformation has resulted in and been stimulated by a rapid rise of urban population and an impressive growth in the industrial labor force.

Where goods sold abroad did not suffice, money was borrowed. By 1972, Egypt had contracted a foreign debt of £5 billion, with obligations to pay more than two thirds of the cotton crop to the Soviet Union. Some measure of the transformation of the last century can be gauged by a comparison of Egypt's debt levels in 1972 and 1882. The yearly service charge alone in 1972 was almost three fourths of the total debt in 1882. In 1984, debt servicing alone was costing Egypt $536 million a year, an amount almost equivalent to the yearly infusions of hard-currency aid.

Today, there is reason for guarded optimism. The record of the past has not been bad. In Egypt, for example, between 1939 and 1947 the value of industrial production rose 50 percent; from 1947 to 1954, 40 percent; and from 1954 to 1960, a further 50 percent. During the early 1960's, the national income of Egypt rose approximately 5 percent yearly. Tragically, this thrust at modernization was blunted by the diversion of Egyptian resources to the Yemen war and by the Arab-Israeli war of June 1967. In the 1970's, because of the development of oil, because of the increase of remittances from Egyptian workers abroad from $200 million in 1974 to $1.9 billion in 1979, and because of a rise of tourism and foreign aid, the economy grew statistically at a rate of 8 percent. In the 1980's, the growth rate fell again to less than 5 percent. Continuing population growth led to a density of over 4,000 people per square mile of arable land. Yet Egypt has achieved a per capita income of $700 per year.

19

Social Change and the New Men

IN the Arab world there are many divisions. All mankind has traditionally been visualized as a pyramid of kindred, from the family to the clan to the tribe to the races descending from the sons of Noah. Traditionally, in Arabic society, as in medieval European, Byzantine, and Japanese society, women were largely secluded in the home. Society was thought of in terms of men. In the Koran, men are divided by religion and by language. We in the modern West tend to think of divisions by income and class. But in analyzing the nature of the social revolution in the Arab countries, it is more useful to distinguish men of the traditional society from the "new men."

Both the new men and the traditional men can be seen in all social, religious, and economic groups and at all levels of society. The new men form a sort of "vertical" society, composed of all classes. They have an inner similarity and share certain values, despite the obvious differences in economic, educational, and political attainments of their members.

The growth of this core within Middle Eastern society is one of the most significant changes in recent years. But viewed historically, what we observe today can be seen as but a recent phase in a much older process.

The traditional society is not, of course, completely static. Contemporary hallmarks of conservatism were, in the traditional society, often marks of social or aesthetic advance. This is as true of social values as of such superficial signs of social usage as the wearing of a fez or tarbush. Regarded by recent reformers as the very symbol of reaction, the fez was a revolutionary innovation when introduced in the third decade of the nineteenth century to replace the more cumbersome and time-consuming turban. When the Lebanese Amir Bashir put aside his turban and donned the fez, he was symbolizing his entry into a new age; when the Egyptians later banned the fez, they meant this as a symbolic step toward secular modernization.

Like the tastes and the ideas, so the new men of each generation tend to fade into traditional society as they are overtaken and surpassed by a new generation. This is not, necessarily, to say that their role as modernizers has ended; some have come to be appreciated only long after their times. Moreover, some of the most significant innovations in the Middle East have been brought about by men who were, personally, deeply committed to the old order.

Writing in the first half of the nineteenth century, that remarkable observer and student of Egyptian life E. W. Lane echoed the thoughts of many previous writers when he pointed to lethargy as a hallmark of the people of the Nile. Since the three or four million people then living in Egypt could so easily support themselves on their fertile land, lacked a major incentive to devote themselves to industry, and found their simple and often crude products satisfactory, they could afford the luxury of backwardness. The picture painted by Lane and others is of a people whose lives were minutely regulated by established custom and who as yet had no appetite for the new and the exotic produce of the Industrial Revolution, and for the stimulating if disquieting ideas of the Renaissance, the Reformation, or the Enlightenment.

In the Syrian hinterland and the Iraqi basin, likewise, the people had accepted traditional approaches to life. Everyone had his place in society. If that place was not entirely satisfying, it was God-ordained. To attempt to change it was unnatural. Indeed, even the word "change" (*ghaiyara*) carried the implication of "to corrupt" or "change for the worse." What was, was right, and the limits of acceptable human endeavor were narrow. As Joseph Schacht wrote in *The Arab Nation* (Washington, D.C., 1961, p. 21): "One ancient Arab idea, arising from the very core of the mental endowment of the Arabs . . . became the central concept of Islamic religious law and theology . . . The Arabs were, and are, bound by tradition and precedent; they were, and are, dominated by the past . . . Whatever was customary, was right and proper; whatever their forefathers had done, deserved to be imitated."

The facts of life lent weight to this natural bent toward conservatism. The bedouin already had a highly sophisticated approach to a most difficult environment. To change his pattern of life, the bedouin would be required to change his environment. Only by nomadism can the extensive resources of the desert be utilized. Significantly, one of the Arabic words meaning "to settle" (*qantara*) also means "to possess a hundredweight," for when a man becomes acquisitive, he must settle.

The villager, tilling a small plot of land, consuming most of what he produced, in need of only the most rudimentary weapons, tools, and consumables, and fearful of outside influences, was content within his small world. Surrounded by kinsmen with whom he shared his means of livelihood, the villager was intent on *protecting* his water rights, marketplaces, and common pasturage. Deeply wedded to his land, the villager married within his village and called it his "nation" (*watan*). Oppressed or ravaged on one side by the rapacious nomad and on the other by the equally rapacious tax collector, the villager sought to retain and enjoy rather than to expand his means of livelihood. Seldom did he attempt to market his produce or to communicate with people outside the small autarkic clusters of villages which were the limits of his world.

The city dweller, likewise, was enmeshed in a world of narrow scope but known satisfactions. The mosque was his school, his club, and his parliament. In craft and religious guilds and brotherhoods, his relations with his fellows were drawn tightly together. His neighbors, like those of his village cousin, were often his kinsmen. They and he were segregated from other neighborhoods by walls and were ruled internally by men at least partly of their choosing. In the city as in the village or the tribe, people were never isolated but were able to find a stable, understood, and reasonably satisfying pattern of life.

The government was distant and its local agents were often foreigners, partaking of little of the local life and adding less to it. The government agent was himself a sort of nomad, camped in his headquarters, but little concerned with the life around him except in the collection of taxes.

More exposed, less secure, and less integrated were the minority groups. Some of these groups shared religions or languages with foreigners. Those who were most open to change, therefore, were not the Muslims but the members of the minorities.

The British agent Dr. John Bowring, in his report entitled "Commercial Statistics of Syria" in 1839, said that he found the

Muslims to be the most backward as a group, since they "accumulate little capital and fail to practice the arts progressively," whereas "most of the commercial establishments . . . [were] in the hands of the Christian or Jewish population." The merchant, he wrote, "is rarely an honored being—the power of the sword and the authority of the book—the warrior and the Ulema (religious leadership) are the two really distinguished races of society. All productive labour—all usefully employed capital is regarded as belonging to something mean and secondary."

The Christians, particularly of the Levant, had been in contact with European missionaries, and many had studied European languages. The Jews were less aided by European powers or organizations but were freed from many of the inhibitions of Islamic politics and were somewhat affected by European contacts. Moreover, the Christians and Jews were able to enter into professions that the Muslims despised. In the Levant, for example, Jews and Christians were moneylenders. The men who served as the equivalent of ministers of finance to the pashas of Saida were Jews and Christians, and the prevalence of such names as Katib, Haddad, Najjar ("scribe," "blacksmith," and "carpenter") among the Christians testifies to their economic activity. The rulers of Egypt traditionally used the Copts as their tax collectors and as the cadres of their civil service. As late as 1910, almost half of the civil service of Egypt was drawn from the Coptic minority, which made up only 15 percent of the population.

Traditionally, in Islamic countries, education was a function not of the state but of the Islamic institutions. In Egypt, it was not until 1869 that the government tried even to inspect the schools, and only in 1925 did the state open half-day primary schools.

Egypt has been a pacesetter for the Arab countries in recent generations—even today half the literate Arabs are Egyptians—so it is instructive to observe trends there in some detail.

Between 1913 and 1945, school attendance in Egypt rose among boys from 206,000 to 477,000 and among girls from 26,500 to 418,000. In 1931 six public schools catered to 2,500 secondary students, of whom none were girls, whereas in 1945 fifty-three schools enrolled 33,000 boys and 3,000 girls. During the same period the number of private schools increased from five to seventy-four. Higher schools increased their enrollment during that period from 1,500 to 15,000. In 1952 only 45 percent of the children of proper ages attended schools, but following the 1952 revolution the figure rose to 65 percent, and facilities for all children were created by 1969. Total enrollment in 1950–1951 was 1.5 million; by 1960–1961 it had reached 3.1 million; in 1979 it reached 7 million. During that same period, university-level technical students almost tripled in number, and the secondary schools graduated more students yearly than the total enrollment in 1945–1946.

In Iraq, one of the key factors when the British established their control in the last stages of World War I was the need to create a sufficiently large cadre of skilled men to administer the country and to work its industry. Particularly after the expensive revolt of 1920 had raised serious protests in London, it was decided that parsimony must be the rule. Therefore, the British were anxious to replace their relatively expensive foreign personnel as rapidly as possible. The Indian clerical help the British had imported during the war was, for political reasons, not regarded as a feasible alternative. However, India could be taken as a model for the small core of senior British officials who set policy for Iraq and supervised its execution by a local staff.

In Iraq as in India, the British faced what ultimately was an insolvable dilemma: they needed a skilled bureaucracy but deeply distrusted the urban literati who were its only native source. They felt that if this superficially Westernized group were allowed to gain control, it would corrupt the simple nobility of the "good Arabs," the bedouin, and would further impoverish the miserable peasantry. In any event, British interests would suffer. Consequently, a fine line had to be drawn between training for bureaucracy and education for government. The British, therefore, put major emphasis on primary schools. Their plan was to restrict secondary education to the "select few" needed by the administration.

In Kuwait, the coming of oil can be seen graphically in the rise of the education budget from $90,000 in 1942 to $33 million in 1960, $95 million in 1972, and $510 million in 1979. Yet this expenditure did not solve Kuwait's need for skilled manpower. Even in 1984, 58 percent of the total population and 77 percent of the labor force was foreign. Though proportionally smaller, the actual numbers in Saudi Arabia were even larger, since millions of Koreans, Philippinos, Yemenis, Egyptians, and others were employed at every level.

During the 1960's, enrollment in preparatory and secondary vocational schools in four countries grew as follows.

	Schools		Students	
	1960	1970	1960	1970
Egypt	181	261	114,693	274,688
Iraq	34	48	6,732	9,995
Jordan	14	12	1.281	2,088
Syria	32	94	6,830	8,991

These figures do not include trainees in industry or apprentices. Occasionally, this kind of training has been on a massive scale. Even when, as in Saudi Arabia today, use of expatriate labor is extensive, much of the labor is drawn from other Arab countries (Yemen, Jordan, and Egypt) and is trained on the job or in special courses.

Today the emphasis placed on science and technology, both in and outside the schools, has greatly increased as several countries have set out to industrialize. It was estimated in 1961, by the Higher Council for the Sciences, that 38,000 Egyptians had graduated in the natural sciences and technology from Egyptian faculties. Of these, 10,000 were engineers, 9,700 were agronomists, 9,000 were physicians, and 5,000 were scientists. In 1970–1971, 86,412 students were enrolled in these fields, and over 22,000 were graduating annually.

In addition to the more formal education in schools, there was, of course, a major if less formal educational development— namely, an increasing awareness of the outer world. This awareness was fostered by the presence in Iraq, Lebanon, Syria, Jordan, the Palestine Mandate, and Egypt of large numbers of foreigners, who brought with them distinctive habits.

Impressive though these strides have been, we see that by the middle of the 1970's, the proportion of the work force that remained in the "traditional" sector was over 50 percent in Egypt, about 65 percent in the Sudan, 47 percent in Syria, and 55 percent in Yemen. Jordan showed great improvement: a decline to 13 percent. When the "informal" sector, which more or less equates to the old cottage-industry category, is added, these percentages increase by 7–14 percent. In short, the modern sectors remain small, particularly in the poorer countries.

It is instructive to compare the former mandates and the colonial countries of the Middle East and other areas with those which have not had the disruption and benefits of foreign rule. A wound has been inflicted in the former colonial and mandate states' "national psyche." On the other hand, such countries as Yemen, in which there has been no outside rule, have missed the beneficial aspects of foreign tutelage. Foreign powers did leave a sense of "structure" or organization and set styles for the new men, who alone could run them.

In Iraq, there was an early recognition that the army was a school of nationalism. In its report to the League of Nations in 1926, the mandate government noted that "the army is proving a valuable means of fostering a true national spirit." Even the paramilitary groups, including the Boy Scouts, played an important part in the growth of national identity on the new model.

It was this same spirit which subsequently caused an Egyptian army officer to declare that "military life is the school of the people; it is an advanced school in public, social and national aspects of life, for the first lesson that a young soldier learns is self-denial and to exert all his efforts toward a noble cause. It is the repudiation of personal interests in favor of the public interest. The individual becomes a sound ideal citizen."*

It was logical that modernizers should assign this role to the army. We have seen that in the time of Mehmet Ali, the army was in fact a vehicle as well as a reason for reform.

Today in many of the Middle Eastern countries the army is viewed as the guardian of national virtue, the sole force capable of and interested in pushing forward those reforms which alone will give dignity, strength, and justice. In part the army and modernization programs fulfill the role of creating the "image" which the military modernizers would like to project to the world—an industrialized, militarily powerful state, respected in the world community.

Traditionally, of course, this was not the case. The military establishment, as we have seen, was restricted to a very narrow stratum of society. In Egypt it was an alien force which did not even share the language or customs and certainly thought little of the well-being of the population. Egyptians only gradually won admission to its service, and then, in the time of Mehmet Ali Pasha, usually as common soldiers. Indeed, it was not until 1936 that the Egyptian government opened the military academy to all social ranks. The nature of the change in the social composition of the army, as it

* Quoted in Morroe Berger, *Military Elite and Social Change* (Princeton, 1960), p. 25.

grew larger and more "national," has been described as one "from Praetorian Guard to Advance Guard." The armies were the only institutions organized along nationalist, modern, and secular lines without commitments to the past. The military alone had a defined code, a clear line of command, channels of communication, mobility, force, and, ultimately, will. The better an instrument of the state it became, the less committed it was to the state. As Manfred Halpern in his *Politics of Social Change* has perceived: "The more the army was modernized, the more its composition, organization, spirit, capabilities, and purpose constituted a radical criticism of the existing political system . . . In civilian politics, corruption, nepotism, and bribery loomed much larger. Within the army, a sense of national mission transcending parochial, regional, or economic interests, or kinship ties, seemed to be much more clearly defined than anywhere else in society . . . As the army became modernized and professionalized, the traditionalist elements within the civilian sector found army service less to their taste."

Whereas in Western society the army has tended to be equated, at least until the Vietnam War, with the middle class, in the Middle East until recently this has not been the case. In the first place what we would call, on economic grounds, the middle class was often in large part composed of non-Muslims or even of alien minority communities. This was particularly the case in Egypt, where the Copts and large foreign communities of Greeks, Italians, and others predominated in the middle reaches of the economy and society. The Egyptian middle class in 1947 was estimated to comprise only about 6 percent of the population, or half a million people. Of these about 51 percent were thought to be merchants, 26 percent clerks, 19 percent professionals, and only 4 percent businessmen. Very few were the new men who sought to remake the country.

In part, at least, the role taken upon itself by the Egyptian army has been to *create* a modernizing cadre. The new cadre, composed of managers, administrators, teachers, engineers, journalists, scientists, lawyers, and army officers comprises, for the most part, employees of the state. Where new state organs have been established, they are often staffed by men who were recently army officers. This is true of the Suez Canal Authority, the oil refinery, and many of the nationalized business concerns.

The middle class in the modern Middle East is rather different in several ways from the Western middle classes we associate with the Industrial Revolution and democratic government. It is not distinguished by a dedication to private ownership, rights of self-expression, or a particular political credo. It uses and agrees to be used by the state, for whose well-being it strives. And the new middle class is highly pragmatic in its approach—espousing "socialism" or whatever seems to offer solutions to baffling social problems. In these ways it differs significantly from the traditional sector, which shares its "middleness" in economic terms with, for example, the landlords and merchants.

Today the lack of a technical education effectively blocks the progress of men even within the middle class. Men who are well trained but trained in the traditional subjects do not have the assets to move upward socially and economically. Significantly, the acquisition of a foreign education (preferably at the source, in a Western university), not a man's social rank or wealth, is the surest passport to advancement. This is the field of education in which one can note the most spectacular progress in the years since World War I, in several Middle Eastern countries.

To take Iraq as an example, in 1921 nine Iraqis were sent abroad to acquire a Western education; by 1928 the number had risen to 93; by 1939 it had reached 238. By 1931 over 200 young men had spent periods of study abroad and had returned; by 1950 the number had reached almost 2,000. In the one year of 1962 nearly 7,000 men and women were abroad at Western schools, colleges, and universities. As increased numbers were sent, and as governments committed higher proportions of money to education, on both the lower and the higher levels, the young men and women were drawn from more humble social strata. Thus, in education as in the army, social class origins became less important. And, perhaps more significantly, whereas education *inside* an Arab country involved a limited exposure to the West in an Eastern context, the student on a mission abroad might spend upwards of eight years living in the West, acquiring new habits of life and far higher expectations; upon return, a sense of bitterness, extreme criticism, and frustration were common.

Curiously, this sort of contact with an alien society seems to have affected the humble more strongly than those at the top of the social ladder. Perhaps it was partly that the young man from a humble family could more fully commit himself to a new life and, because less bound, more readily accept its ways and values, and partly that upon his return from a relatively comfortable, well-paid, and challenging experience, he viewed his own former position more bitterly, having less means of action and less protection—in family and money—from a harsh adjustment.

But those who went abroad and learned, at the prestigious source, a profession or new technical field were able to move ahead economically, politically, and socially more rapidly than those who stayed behind. Thus, even men of wealth and family who stayed behind gradually became socially inferior to those of more humble origin who went abroad and returned with a marketable skill. Graduates of a Baghdad college were destined for inferior jobs, perhaps as primary or secondary schoolteachers, whereas graduates from Oxford or Harvard could teach in the colleges, practice their profession, or take a responsible government position. Here it is possible to see the very sharp differentiation between the new men and the more traditional.

At the high point of the oil boom, students flooded into Western universities. In the United States alone, there were 3,080 Libyans, 1,860 Egyptians, 790 Sudanese, 10,440 Saudis, 6,770 Lebanese, 6,140 Jordanians, 2,990 Kuwaitis, 1,460 Iraqis, and 1,150 Syrians. There were also 810 students from the UAE, 620 from Qatar, 250 from Oman, 260 from Bahrain, and 250 from Yemen. Upon their return, especially to the smaller countries, these Western-trained men and women constituted nearly a social class.

In some of the more conservative countries, precisely those with the most disposable income, women continued, even after acquiring educations and living in relatively open societies, to play a minor and highly restricted role. Almost the only positions open to them in Saudi Arabia, for example, were those in education for other women. Women could not even work as secretaries in government offices. In the more radical countries, on the contrary, women were allowed to serve even in the army. On balance, however, it can be said that throughout the generation from 1960 to the end of the 1980's, the role of women was highly restricted and they were unable to play a major role in the development or politics of their countries.

One can also observe differentiation among the groups which we would categorize as lower-class. In their study *Human Resources for Development in Egypt* (New York, 1958), F. Harbison and I. Ibrahim distinguished several groups of workers. The largest was unskilled, landless, and without capital. The second, much smaller, consisted of skilled or semiskilled traditional artisans who, with the advent of larger-scale production and power-driven machines, became technologically outmoded. The third group, very small at the time of the study, increased rapidly in the 1960's and 1970's. It is made up of men—and gradually of women—with some degree of modern skills. Although all would be lower-class because of the sharp contrast they present to men of the rest of the social order, they are clearly distinguished from one another by salary, regularity of employment, and morale. In Egypt, where, as in most countries of the underdeveloped world, unemployment and underemployment are common, a mechanic, for example, earns three times as much per diem as a day laborer and is assured of continual employment—so his real wages may be many times that of the day laborer. Everywhere the differential has been very high, and apparently the aim of a number of the Arab governments is to increase it.

The degree of urbanization in the Arab countries is striking. Jordan, for example, is 47 percent urban; Iraq, 39 percent; Syria, 38 percent. In Lebanon, 40 percent of the total population lives in the city of Beirut. The latest available figures showed manufacturing labor forces on the order of 750,000 in the Sudan, 250,000 in Jordan, 60,000 in Lebanon, and 800,000 in Syria. Egypt towered above the rest, with an industrial labor force of about three million.

Aware that a technologically backward and poor population is unable to form a solid base for the growth of national dignity and power, the two cherished goals of the modernizers of the Middle East, the Iraqi and Egyptian governments in the 1950's embarked upon programs to create new men not only in the cities but also in the countryside. This was the essence of the "Liberation Province" scheme in Egypt and the resettlement and housing experiments in Iraq.

Roundly, and perhaps rightly, criticized as an economic fiasco or as an example of ambitious political planning without the requisite technological and economic foundation, Liberation Province does show how the government felt about the need to build a new Egyptian. In the words of M. Gamal Zaki, who was then director of the Social Affairs Department:

Settlers are selected scientifically on social, medical, psychological tests. As social qualifications, applicants must possess one wife, no dependents except children, and no property; they must have been married only once, and must have finished their military service. Of 1,100 applicants so far, all have the right social qualifications, but only 382 families were accepted medically, because while most of the men were healthy enough, the women and children fell far short of the standard. Only 180 families survived the psychological test . . . Of these, 132 are now undergoing a six-month training, which included a three-month proba-

tion period. We must consider both people and land to be under reclamation.*

The new man of Liberation Province was marked off from the
traditional Egyptian peasant by a new standardized uniform in
place of the traditional gown (the new version of the fez for the
turban or the cap for the fez), by a much higher caloric intake of
food, and by a salary four times the average rate in Upper Egypt.
In addition, the workers were to put their children into a boarding
school, as the Israelis put their children in kibbutzim, which presumably would enable teachers to ensure a better and modern
upbringing for the children. Moreover, like the rest of Egypt, Liberation Province was to become a mixed rural and industrial economy, with factories interspersed throughout the agricultural area.

Liberation Province had a stormy career and certainly fell far
short of the goals intended for it, but the purpose was clear, and
one may see this purpose, if less clearly specified, perhaps much
more uniformly carried out, in certain other ways. For example,
as mentioned above, the army has long been regarded as a school
in civic virtues. In addition, the army became a school to impart
modern skills, a hospital to cure the ills of society and turn out
healthier men, and a source of discipline. Each year in the 1960's,
approximately 20,000 Egyptians—and by the end of the decade
nearly 100,000 Egyptians—were inducted into the army for three-
year enlistments; in Syria, approximately as many are called up
for two years. From 1957 to 1963, perhaps as many as 130,000
Egyptians passed out of the armed forces into civilian life. When
one considers that larger-scale, modern Egyptian industry in 1961
employed roughly 250,000 workers—in 1970 the number in modern industry was only about twice as high, about 500,000—the
impact of the former soldiers can be appreciated.

Little is known about these new men when they return to civilian
life. It is clear, however, that they are possessed of a rudimentary
technical training, a sense of discipline, an indoctrination in nationalism, and certainly a far higher standard of health than are those
who have not had army experience. All of these things are rare
and prized possessions in a rapidly evolving and industrializing
society.

* Quoted in Doreen Warriner, *Land Reform and Development in the Middle East*
(London, 1957), pp. 50–51.

At the upper echelons, the former army officer is the "doer" of the new order. He may aspire to cabinet rank, or take a key managerial job in the apparatus of government-run industry or commerce. As a factory manager or a senior bureaucrat, he will play a dominant role in modernizing the country. In the middle levels, it is probable that the former noncommissioned army officers and junior officers take on lower-level administrative and industrial functions, and former private soldiers are probably readily absorbed into industry. It is doubtful that many return to village communities, where their skills are not in demand and where the life they have learned to lead, or at least aspire to, is impossible. As yet little is known in specific terms, but, in the round, it is possible to see that in the making is a multiclass, nontraditionalist, as yet politically or philosophically uncommitted, pragmatic, disciplined, privileged core of new men.

In all of the Middle Eastern countries, revolutionary and conservative alike, it is the aim of governments to increase both absolutely and proportionately the sector of the "new men." This is the political constituency of the modernizing governments and is the group upon which all governments, conservative as well as modernizing, must depend for the development of national power. With the rapid growth of the school system and the perpetuation of conscript armies, it seems likely that the influence of this group will conclusively permeate each country. These relatively more effective citizens will ensure that their interests are represented in government, and, as their absolute numbers increase, the outlines of a different kind of society will become—are even now becoming—more apparent.

20

The Arabs and the World:
A Quest for
Identity and Dignity

ARAB politicians and thinkers have set out to answer two basic questions: "who are we?" and "how can we get the world to respect us?" These have been implicit in most of the speeches, books, and actions of the Arab leaders since the end of World War I, and are still burning issues today. It was not very long ago that they were explicitly stated in all significant Arabic-language books. Most began with an attempt to define who the Arabs are: Are Egyptians to be considered Arabs? If so, to the same degree as men of Arabia? Are Christians *really* Arab or must an Arab be a Muslim? Is a man of Damascus more an Arab or more a Syrian? How does the Westernized Lebanese compare in "Arabness" to the isolated Yemeni? Is there *one* Arab nation despite the obvious diversity and conflict of the several Arab states? And, if so, how can the Arabs so express this nation in political, economic, and social terms as to give it reality?

The political experience of the several Arab countries, as we have seen, have been remarkably different. This fact has profoundly colored both Arab reactions to the situations in which they found themselves and their intellectual formulations of their goals. The surer road to understanding starts from a description of the Arab situation than from an analysis of the ideas. Many of the ideas were borrowed from Europe and are, in reality, more in the nature of flags of convenience than precise ideological formulations.

Egypt was geographically and culturally the most coherent of the Arab states. Compressed into the Nile Valley, cut off from the other Arabs by great distance, and after 1805 ruled by a strong national, if not Arab, government and after 1882 by a British government, Egypt was subjected to intense, beneficial but intellectually disquieting Western influence. Thus it was to achieve, more surely and easily than the other Arab states, an awareness of itself as a separate entity. Not only were other Arabs far away and living at least economically very differently from the Nile dwellers but the Egyptians, living in the shadow of monuments of their ancient grandeur, developed a sort of Aïda complex. Egypt as Egypt, rather than as an Arab country, had a continuous and recorded history for 4000 years, and whatever changes the successive invaders had made, each layer of foreign influence was built on the same Nilotic core. In contemporary squalor and weakness before foreigners, Egyptians were awed by the majesty of the past, their past, a non-Arab past. These feelings were accentuated by the exciting archaeological discoveries of the late eighteenth and the nineteenth centuries, particularly when the decipherment of hieroglyphics suddenly opened a wide window on the ancient civilization.

Nevertheless Mehmet Ali's attempt to create an Egyptian power failed in 1841 when the European powers forced Egypt to give up its military machine and the economic organization which had sustained it. Thereafter, Egypt "slowly went to sleep again" as Europeans took over more and more aspects of the national economic and cultural life and the more energetic and better educated Egyptians competed in becoming European.

By the 1870's Egypt had no real "line of defense" against the West in political, economic, or even cultural affairs. While each reform was, in itself, of some value, the whole seldom was the equal of its parts. Rather, it was less. There remained, consequently, the nagging belief that some intrinsic, inner thing was still lacking. What was the "spirit" or "inner value" of the culture? Was not that core, after all, both the thing to be defended against the Europeans and what alone made a successful defense possible?

For most of the nineteenth century and in the minds of most of the people, this "spirit" was not "the nation." It was, instead, some largely undefinable or, perhaps more accurately, variously defined, conception of a way of life. As seen from the outside, this sense of difference from others expressed itself simply in xenophobia. The real quality of this feeling obviously differed among classes and groups of the society. The minorities and the upper class were much more open to Western influences than the lower and Muslim classes. Within each class or group certain categories of thought and action were more sacrosanct than others. Issues of religion were more impervious to outside influence than were those of technology; family life was more protected from changes of mores than was male organization; and, linguistically speaking, the cultural core, as expressed in the "classical" language, was more treasured and guarded by Arabic speakers than was the vernacular.

Along with a growing receptivity to the byproducts of the Western intrusion came a growing self-consciousness about certain aspects of Middle Eastern identity.

Briefly, and at the risk of oversimplification, it may be said that the quest for identity took two separate but overlapping forms. On the one hand, the reaction was in terms of religion. Throughout the nineteenth century, the society of the predominant population of Egypt continued to define itself chiefly in religious terms. As intellectual life quickened, in part because of the stimulus of the West, there was a renewed interest in Islam itself and a consequent attempt to strip away the later medieval accretions of Islamic society to get at the sources. In large part, this was an attempt to recapture the vigor and sureness of early Islam. The relative backwardness of contemporary Middle Eastern society was equated with the long "sleep" of the later Middle Ages, in which it was assumed (as we now know, erroneously) that the religious life had ceased to offer an intellectual stimulus. It was at that time that Jamal ad-Din al-Afghani came to Egypt, inspiring all he met with the notion that Islam could offer a coherent and powerful identification and means of defense. As a result of his influence and that of his Egyptian disciple Muhammad Abdu, the hope of a revival of Islam and the identification of Egypt as a part of the enduring Islamic civilization became cardinal elements in successive Egyptian efforts to achieve a sense of identification and dignity.

On the other hand, speakers of Arabic, Christian and Muslim alike, sought to recover the sources of their suprareligious culture. The speakers of Arabic found language, even more than Islamic religion, on which they disagreed, to be the core of their culture. The centrality of language, the fascination with the word, the concern with the medium rather than the message has long been seen as a distinctive Semitic characteristic. Language is not *an* art form, it is *the* art of the Arabs. The threat of its obsolescence, corruption, or even loss was profundly disquieting. Far more than the speakers of French, Spanish, Russian, or other national-cultural-political languages, Arabic speakers sought to tighten the bonds of their language and to identify means of preserving its classical form, as well as its utility, in the modern world.

Two courses of action appeared possible. The first was to reassert the uniqueness, unity, and perfection of the language. While antiquarian in form, this movement represented a considerable gain over the torpid, imitative, and lazy approach to language of recent centuries. To those concerned with a reaction to Western penetration, the Arabic "purist" revival appeared a very attractive option.

Conversely, the introduction of Western individuals, forms, mores, goods, and services seemed to demand a wholly different linguistic thrust. Vulgarly, language became bifurcated. The literary language, restricted to the classical subjects, was treasured by all the educated groups, while the uneducated, those with educations oriented toward the West, and the general public moved practically and unsystematically toward the development of linguistic forms more suited to their current needs. Reconciliation of these two divergent trends—both linguistically and philosophically—lies at the heart of the problem of modern Arabic intellectual life.

It is easy for speakers of English, secure in the imperialism or even colonialism of their language—conquering and settling, as it were, whole vocabularies of German, French, Latin, and even Arabic—to scorn what appear to be puerile or at least pedantic defensive linguistics. Secure in the far-flung domain of our language, we cannot really understand the desperate defensiveness of those who stand against us. Is not language, after all, merely a means of communication, and, as such, to be judged solely in these pragmatic terms? If a better means is available, should it not be adopted? Can there be any real virtue in maintaining inefficient, obsolescent, or even obsolete languages? Surely serious men of affairs have more important tasks than to worry about the origins of words, their esoteric meanings, their linguistic "purity."

To the defenders of other languages, the case appears quite different. Not the Arabs alone but the speakers of dozens of other languages have found in their languages not merely a means of communication but the genius of their nationhood. And not only among the non-European languages has this been the case. We have only to remember the enormous influence of the brothers Grimm upon the rise of German nationalism or the flowering of Russian literature in mid-nineteenth century to appreciate the relationship.

A contrary force was evident, however, in the extensive Westernization of urban Egypt. This was evident in the political movements before World War I and was codified, in the 1930's, by the Egyptian scholar, novelist, and statesman Taha Husain, who stressed the Mediterranean base of Egyptian civilization and urged Egyptians to think of themselves as having a culture in common with Europe rather than with Africa or Asia. Even on the eve of the foundation of the Arab League, Egyptian statesmen echoed this sentiment and described the role of Egypt as a bridge between East and West. But the East was not exclusively the Arab East. If East and West could not meet in Kipling's Suez, they might in Taha Husain's Cairo, which was, in fact, a remarkably cosmopolitan city in a remarkably discrete land. This tendency in modern thought was in the main stream of the urban, polyglot, tolerant, cosmopolitan tradition of the golden age of Islam.

In Syria the environment was quite different. In the first place, before World War I the government was the Ottoman Empire, an Islamic state, so that Islam offered no means of achieving a separate identity. Moreover, a number of the pioneers of nationalism were Christians. Obviously, the Christian minorities could not hope, except to a limited extent in Lebanon, to achieve power or even security as Christians. The only things which they shared with their Muslim neighbors were the Arabic heritage and Syrian residence. In historical memory the shared residence achieved major importance only as the seat of the Umayyad Arab kingdom. That kingdom was not only little associated with Islam but was viewed by many Muslims almost as a secular, indeed as a pre-Islamic, pagan Arab state. The post-Umayyad Arab heritage had, of course, become intertwined with Islam. Thus to avoid the divisive religious issue and to capitalize on such elements of Syrian "nationalism" as existed in the Arabic heritage, modern Syrians had to go back to pre-Islamic Arabism to find a common base. That base could only be the notion of folk nationalism (*qawmiyah*) with a glorification of Arabism (*Arabiyah*).

In Iraq, for reasons quite different from those in Syria, the emphasis was also placed on Arabism. Like Egypt, Iraq had a rich and long past; unlike the Egyptians, however, the Iraqis were not so conscious of their pre-Islamic, pre-Arab past as to find in it the basis of a separatist nationalism. Like the Syrians, the Iraqis could not oppose the government, the Ottoman Empire, in the name of Islam since the Ottoman sultan was also the Muslim caliph. Unlike the Syrians and the Egyptians, however, the Iraqis had not one but two Islams: whereas the Syrians and Egyptians were almost exclusively Sunni or Orthodox Muslims, the Iraqis were divided between the Sunnis and the Shiis. Many of the Shiis were Persian or culturally oriented toward Iran and differed profoundly from the Sunni Arabs, who, in turn, differed significantly from the Sunni Kurds. Iraq also had a sizable Jewish population, some of whose leaders were active in the process of building the state—a good deal of the prosperity of the Iraqi state was due to the wisdom of a Jewish minister of finance—before the violent clash between the Arabs and Zionists after World War II. All of these factors tended, as in Syria and Lebanon, to de-emphasize religion as a basis of national identity. Consequently, as in Syria, nationalism came to have an ethnic and cultural coloration.

Arab nationalism received its first major challenge in the Middle East in Palestine; there a competing ethnic nationalism, Zionism, was the challenger. Impressed as they were by the vigor of this challenger, Arab writers, particularly of the 1930's, sought to meet the strengths of Zionism point by point in a revival of Arabism. And it was just at this time that the spread of public education, made possible in large part by the mandate system, required authentic Arabic cultural materials to form a humanities program for the increasing numbers of students. What could this program be? It could not, with Western notions of the separation of Church and State and with serious religious cleavage within the Arabic-speaking population, be Islamic. Whereas Islamic schools had taught pupils to read by reciting the Koran, public schools could not. There was no modern literature. The only acceptable answer was, therefore, pre-Islamic. This was the classical basis of the culture of all Arabic-speaking peoples of whatever religion or whatever region. Thus it was, with little thought of the political consequences, that the public school system injected into the population on a mass basis the elements of pre-Islamic, pan-Arab values as embodied in classical Arabic literature.

Meanwhile, inhabitants of the Arabian Peninsula, cut off from the disturbing intrusions of foreign thought, relatively secure from the tyranny of the Ottoman Empire and the imperialism of the European powers, and almost completely Sunni Muslim, were little concerned with what the outside world thought of their culture. They knew themselves to be tribal, Muslim Arabs and, like members of a small club, never were concerned with identifying badges.

The mandate system posed new barriers between the separate units of the Arab World. The young man of Iraq acquired English as a second language and was influenced by European formulations of ideas and information as these were filtered through English thought and institutions. The Syrian, to the contrary, viewed the world through a French window. The Egyptian either attended one of his own national universities, the first founded in the Arabic-speaking areas, or picked freely from Italian, French, English, German, or American institutions. Culturally he was apt to be influenced by France, but politically he dealt with the English. The Saudi Arabian usually went to an American school, often under the sponsorship of an American oil company, but was less motivated to learn foreign ways than his Iraqi, Syrian, or Egyptian cousin since, he discovered, his oil made foreigners willing to learn his own difficult language and to respect his customs. The Libyan was not encouraged either to learn Italian or to keep Arabic; for him Arabic was the medium of his religious nationalism which alone sustained him.

Ironically, in this diversity was a force for unity. Arab students meeting in London or Paris were impressed by their foreignness from the English and the French and with their common identity as Arabs. Measured by their cultural distance from the Europeans, their differences from one another as Syrians, Iraqis, Saudis, or Egyptians paled into relative insignificance.

Meeting in Brussels in December 1938, a group of Arab students tried to reach an agreed definition of "Arab" and "Arab Homeland." The very cumbersomeness of their definition provides an index to the seriousness of their problem. An Arab, they decided, is anyone "who is Arab in language, culture and *wilā*'," the last term being defined in a footnote as one who has "nationalist sentiments" (*ash-shu'ūr al-Qawmi*) while nationalism (*qawmiyah*) is defined as "sensitivity to the existing necessity of liberating and unifying the inhabitants of the Arab lands in view of the unity of the homeland and language and culture and history." Interestingly, a decade later the Syrian Baath party, in many ways the most ideological of the Arab political movements, had not got much further with an attempt at definition. It regarded as Arab one who lives in an Arab country, speaks Arabic, and believes in his connection with the Arab nation.

The desire on the part of the several Arab governments to cater to the popular sentiment for some degree of Arab unification, added to their determination to improve their own bargaining position, impelled the Arabs to organize the Arab League during the later phases of World War II. The principal test of that organization came in the Palestine conflict, and that test, as we have seen, was a trauma for the whole Arab body politic. The Palestine War severely challenged the previously acceptable concept of separate states in a loose confederation; consequently, great stress came to be placed upon the unity of the Arabs. Disunity was branded as a holdover from the bad old days of Western colonialism.

Yet long after the departure from the Middle East of instruments of Western influence and power and even after the overthrow of the government of Nuri Said in Iraq and the withdrawal of Iraq from the

Baghdad Pact, unity was still unattained. The union of Egypt and Syria was short-lived, and its disintegration clearly had nothing to do with Western policy or pressures.

The fact is that the "artificial" states into which the Arabs have been divided have their separate existence enshrined in the whole complexity of Middle Eastern life. Consequently, however profoundly united the Arabs may feel themselves to be culturally, they have not been able to formulate even intellectually an acceptable basis of political or administrative unity.

There can be no simple answer to the question "what is an Arab?" or, as phrased in the beginning of this chapter, "is a man of Damascus more an Arab or more a Syrian?" In his political acts he shows himself to be both—and many other things, which impinge upon the precise frontiers he would put around *his* Arabness.

In his book on the Egyptian coup of 1952, *Egypt's Destiny,* Muhammad Nagib, the first president of Egypt, said, "We seized power because we could no longer endure the humiliation to which we, along with the rest of the Egyptian people, were being subjected." Anwar Sadat, later to be President of Egypt, wrote, similarly, in his *Revolt on the Nile* that "the humiliation, frustration and anger aroused by the incompetence of the men who had led Egypt to defeat instead of victory, provoked a passionate desire to overthrow a régime which had once again demonstrated its complete impotence."

Remarks of this sort filled the press in the Arab states in the aftermath of the Palestine War. It had been clear to some intellectuals since World War I that the West had not taken the Arabs seriously. Periodically—as in Egypt following the murder of Sir Lee Stack in 1923, or in Iraq in putting down an anti-British government in 1941, or in Syria in bombarding the capital city in 1925 and 1945—the new national pride of the Arabs was wounded. But it was in countless smaller ways that Westerners hurt the Arab pride the most. The facts that Egyptians were not allowed in the British sporting club in Cairo and were subjected to continuous and biting satire in cartoons, songs, and books were particulary galling.

The "quest for dignity" has, therefore, been at the heart of virtually every political movement in the area. But what gives dignity to a people? Obviously, there are many answers. No one answer is acceptable to all Arabs. But, there are three points on which there is a striking degree of agreement. One is negative and the others positive.

First, none of the modernizers of the Arab lands is prepared to accept the coherence of traditional society as the source of dignity. The "dignity" of a village elder or a Muslim shaikh or the haughty pride of a bedouin, so often admired by Western visitors, seems to the modernizer a consequence of ignorance. The attitude of the Westerner toward these people, moreover, seems to the modernizer to be compounded more of condescension than admiration. In short, the modernizers regard the "colorful bedouin" or the "quaint villager" in the same light as American Negroes regard "Uncle Toms."

Second, the Arabs must be united in order to achieve the strength and coherence which causes others to respect them. This was the lesson of the Palestine conflict. Unity is a complex quality, however obvious may be the manifestations of disunity. The failure of the union of Egypt and Syria showed just how fragile the elements of unity were. Clearly, the lack of unity was not simply a factor of foreign opposition or the lack of agreement between Arab rulers—although both are believed by Arabs to be significant—but depended in part on many other factors: economic organization, political orientation, trade, military doctrine, relations with outside powers, and so forth. It seemed manifest, after the breakup of the union of Egypt and Syria, that only when the Arabs became united in a myriad of cultural, economic, social, political, and military ways could this unity be expressed in a governmental form, and that the expression of the form would not necessarily give reality to unity. Thus, while all Arabs remain vocally committed to union, they differ on questions of the terms, the leadership, and the speed and the profundity of the measures.

Third, most if not all of the modernizers are willing to use the full apparatus of the state to carry their reforms into effect. This does not, in the Middle Eastern context, imply the same sort of ideological commitment as it would in Western Europe. It is not, as some observers aver, pragmatism—a willingness to experiment with various answers to problems—but is a commitment to use all available power. It is this which links Mehmet Ali Pasha to Gamal Abdul Nasser. On this basic point there is no significant ideological disagreement.

Why should this be so?

We in the West are so conscious of our own norms as often to seek to use these too precisely as measures for the actions of others in different cultural patterns. The split we find to be normal between Church and State, for example, we do not find in quite the same form in Arab society. Nor has there been in the political and economic spheres of life in Arab society the sharp distinction between the state and individual endeavor. It is important to be clear about this.

In the great river basin economies of the Near East, the role of the state in economic life was not only predominant but both minute and active. The state controlled water, the state set the standard in taxation and rent of land, the state decided what should be planted and when; in industry, the state owned the factories, bought the raw materials, employed the worker, set output quotas, and collected and distributed the production; in commerce, the state was often the sole merchant, monopolizing virtually all distribution of imports and exports. This was a pattern common to the ancient pharaohs, the Mamluks, and Mehmet Ali and is today the pattern adopted by "Arab socialism."

In this pattern there is no major role for the initiative of the individual, except as he operates within the state machinery, and no respect for or toleration of separate bases of power. Private property is not deeply rooted in either the Islamic or the Middle Eastern past: men have traditionally had usufruct of income producers but the state retained ownership. Land, for example, was the possession (*mulk*) of the state even though individuals either as favorites, payers of taxes, or holders of office, ex officio, had rights to some of the revenue of the land.

Property, per se, was regarded as exploitive rather than creative. It was what God did, through rain and sun, that made land yield under the hand of the peasant, himself virtually a "natural resource," rather than what a manager or investor did that gave value.

In nomadic society the land was the gift of the superhuman forces which control the fall of rain and the changes of the seasons. Herds of animals depended upon teams of men, the clans, for their guidance and protection. No man could accumulate very much because he could neither protect nor use more than a certain amount. For the individual real wealth and power came from membership in a rich and powerful "nation-state," his clan.

The peasant often had an understanding with his fellows on allocation of resources for he, like the nomad, could not exploit or profit from more than a certain amount of land and water. Even less than the nomad could he protect wealth. Consequently, in many parts of the Arab World, as in the Russian village commune, the *mir,* land was periodically reallocated. It was less in a particular plot of land than in a village community that the farmer had a share. He had, of course, no major incentive to invest in the particular plot that was his this year and might be someone else's next. When he had to invest, as on the mountain sides of Lebanon and Yemen where terrace walls had to be built and maintained, property tended not to be reallocated and tenure to be clearly defined.

The landlord, similarly, could not count on possession of land for long periods. The estate which he "owned" came to him primarily in his capacity as tax collector for the government or to give him an income while he exercised an office or supplied soldiers. His relationship to the land was thus that of an exploiter rather than an investor or entrepreneur.

Finally, the merchant and manufacturer lived on the bounty and at the whim of the governor. It was essentially the control of competition, through the customs and marketing outlets, that decided success or failure of a venture. The business man, therefore, became a sort of agent of the ruler rather than an independent contributor to public prosperity.

Thus, as tolerant as Islam and pre-Islamic society have been of religious or kindred diversity, they never found congenial the notion that ownership of property or creation of wealth alone entitled men to any special toleration. Nor did they understand or condone the division between the individual and society or the individual and the state in ways familiar to us. These are factors of major importance in understanding the Arab Middle East of today.

Two other factors contribute to the emphasis on the role of the state in economic affairs. On the one hand, the modernizers in Egypt, Syria, and Iraq, particularly, came to power to speed up the modernization process. Their competitors for power were the men of the existing regimes, and these men, under the liberalizing influences of European mandate or guidance, had tried to diminish the role of the state and to foster the rise of private business initiative. Ownership of property had not yet created a vigorous, reforming "middle class," but had been adopted as a protection of privilege by the old power elite. The landlords of Iraq and Egypt and Syria had seized control of parliaments and had used their power to evade taxation and to tighten their control on the rural areas; to break their power the revolutionary regimes logically as well as sentimentally turned to programs of land distribution and sequestration of property.

Secondly, the "new men" wanted to move quickly and dramatically to catch up with the industrialized West and to solve problems of unemployment. They needed investment of a sort that private capitalists were unwilling to make. What the nation needed, in the eyes of the new men, was not necessarily, or even probably, going to have a good investment-profit ratio. What Egyptian capitalist could be Egypt's Carnegie to build the Helwan steel mill? With Iraq's oil fields already farmed out to the international consortium, the Iraq Petroleum Company, Iraq had no scope for a Rockefeller.

Moreover, if the Arabs are to catch up with the industrial areas of the world, they are going to have to make massive investments quickly in "social overhead" facilities which are traditionally, even in Western society, the domain of the state. Schools, hospitals, dams, and bridges are a felt need for the present, and in most of the Arab countries these have virtually been begun from the start in the last generation. Not only was the state, therefore, the organizer and motive force but it had to operate on a scale and in a period of time which made it preponderant: the Arab World has not had time for an Oxford, much less a Harvard or even such a new university as a Stanford, to evolve; what it needed, it needed quickly and on a huge scale. Over the course of sixty years, for example, the Egyptian educational system has moved from no government schools to a system which, by 1979, enrolled 7 million students, from the first grade to postdoctoral work in nuclear energy. Only the state could make such progress; in this, men as different from one another as Lord Cromer and President Nasser have agreed.

Contributing to this emphasis on the role of the state, also, was the other major impulse of the modern Arab scene, the need to acquire military power. Clearly, this was a proper role for the state. Private armies did exist in Egypt until about 1805, and, in a sense, still today exist in Saudi Arabia, but these guards units and "White armies" do not and cannot command the plethora of expensive and complex equipment which distinguish modern armies. Only a state can afford to buy and maintain a Mig-25 or a T-72 tank. But, as Mehmet Ali realized long ago to own the machine is very different from having power. Power comes from control over production of the machines, the generation of economic capability to sustain them, and the training of men to use them. Thus, the growth of military establishments has led most of the Arab states into the myriad of associated problems of logistics, creation of maintenance facilities, and, ultimately, the development of factories to make all the tools of modern armies and air forces. These efforts have led the state into many activities which in earlier, less complex times in the West contributed to the establishment of a sphere of economic activity in which the state played a lesser, more detached role. There is, therefore, no place for a Du Pont, a Krupp, or a Nobel in the Arab World today.

On this basic point of the role of the state there is today very little difference between any of the Arab governments, whether monarchies or revolutionary "new men." What then are the principal points of difference?

The major differences are in the tactics to be adopted to achieve agreed aims: the speed and control of the modernization process and the political involvement of the individual in the state. On these points there are profound differences of emphasis and direction particularly between the "postrevolutionary" or "intrarevolutionary" states of Iraq, Syria, and South Yemen (and Algeria in North Africa) on the one hand and on the other the more conservative, nonrevolutionary states of Lebanon, Jordan, Kuwait, North Yemen, and Saudi Arabia (Tunisia and Morocco in North Africa). Neither group feels safe as long as the other continues its programs and both have made strenuous efforts to persuade or force the other to adopt its model.

Involvement with outside powers likewise distinguishes the Arab states. From membership in the Baghdad Pact in the spring of 1958, Iraq swung very close to the Soviet Bloc in the spring of 1959; Saudi Arabia and Jordan depend heavily upon the West; Lebanon and Kuwait are usually able to set their own terms, but each has ultimately shown to all that its security rested upon Western protectiveness. Egypt and post-Qasim Iraq charted a more or less middle course, which was termed, by President Nasser, "positive neutralism." Essentially, this involved two elements: maintenance of political independence, and extraction of all possible aid and assistance from both sides in the Cold War. Egypt, before 1973, managed to get nearly $6 billion worth of arms and $3 billion worth of economic assistance from the USSR while banning the Communist party in Egypt. While nationalizing foreign and domestically owned industry, it convinced the United States between 1975 and 1990 to give it $15 billion to further the American national interest. Neutralism has exercised a strong attraction not only in the Arab world but all over the Tropical belt of modernizing nations.

In oil, the Arab states believe that they have finally acquired a diplomatic "weapon" which will force the modern industrial nations to respect them. Industrial growth in Japan, Europe, and America, they understand, can be roughly equated with the availability of cheap power. The oil-producing countries, in a situation of rapidly increasing demand for power, literally control the industrial prosperity of the advanced nations. Thus, if the West would not listen to their pleas on the justness of their case, particularly on the Palestine issue, it could be brought to understanding and even sympathy (motivated by self-interest) by the consequences of an oil cutback. This was the reason behind the Saudi Arabian–led embargo on shipments to the United States following American provision of massive amounts of military equipment to Israel in the October 1973 war. In oil, the Arabs have found not only a diplomatic weapon but also, potentially, a new means of participating in Western industrial growth. Massive amounts of capital flow not only into the oil-producing countries but even into the poorer Arab countries, whose emigrant workers remit their earnings and whose governments receive aid from their neighbors and loans from the exporting industrial countries. A new pool of employable capital, probably at least equal in size to the Eurodollar market, is gathered and available for investment in Japan, Europe, and North America. Today, consequently, the Arabs find themselves not unlike the East Texas dirt farmer in the days of the American oil boom. From hardly being welcome in polite restaurants, he now finds himself royally received and courted by the captains of world industry. Thus, despite tremendous areas of disagreement among the Arab countries, there is basic agreement that *the* objective is the achievement of a place of dignity for the Arabs in the world and a growing recognition that oil has now provided at least one important means of achieving it.

PART 7

War, Fragmentation, and Uprising

21

The Iraq-Iran War

THE Iraq-Iran war was one of the most bitter, destructive, long-lasting, and yet enigmatic conflicts of modern times.

When the war began in September 1980, Iran had about 45 million people and Iraq about 14 million. During its course, at least 5 million people lost their homes and about 1.25 million were killed or gravely wounded. Whole cities have been wiped out. Some 546 ships were attacked, damaged, or sunk. The war calls for comparison with the American Civil War and World War I: the relative sizes of the two forces resembled those of the North and the South in the American Civil War (although the casualties and property damage were considerably worse), while the method of fighting along 1,169 kilometers of front resembled the ruthless, static trench warfare of World War I. Except at the very beginning, neither side moved significantly from its dug-in positions.

The war lasted a decade, was fully reported by the news media in Iraq and Iran and by foreign observers, and was marked by constant propaganda on both sides. Yet its beginnings are disputed, the objectives of each participant were never clear, and the end has been bizarre.

To attempt to understand it, I propose to look at the war from five perspectives: first, the age-old rivalry of the two peoples; second, the religious dimension; third, the Kurdish issue; fourth, the rivalry in this century of the two states over frontiers; and fifth, the military action. Let us begin with a bit of historical background and a note on geography.

Long before history was recorded, the areas which have become Iraq and Iran were settled by vigorous, progressive, and aggressive peoples. To them we owe some of the great inventions that made subsequent societies, including our own, possible. According to archaeologists, it was on or very near the sites of some of the most violent of the recent war's battles that the first experiments were made with irrigated agriculture. Not far away, early peoples undertook the first significant civil engineering projects—namely, the building of walls around their settlements—because they had already come to fear warlike enemies. Organizing for defense probably was a major incentive to form the first cities.

Fundamental to the continuity of the history of this area is the land itself. The only significant changes over the last 5,000 years have been in the location of river beds and in the boundary between river deltas and the Gulf. There is no evidence for major changes in climate. It was always hot and dry. The land and climate of today are as they have been throughout history.

To understand the recent war, or more ancient history, we must note that Iraq and Iran consist of *three,* not two, entities. Between the upland plateau of Iran and the flat, almost featureless plain of Iraq, composed of silt brought down from the northern mountains by the rivers, is a band of foothills and mountains known as the Zagros. Running northwest to southeast for about 400 kilometers, and roughly 200 kilometers wide, this zone has a distinctive culture and economy. With better water supplies and cooler temperatures than either the plains or plateau, its rugged hillsides and green valleys support and shelter the vigorous, warlike, and independent peoples we know today as the Kurds. Their struggle for self-determination is one of the many unresolved problems of the modern Middle East. Since their area extends northward into Turkey, they also involve Turkey in the affairs of Iran and Iraq, as we shall see.

Knowing that the ecology of this region had become established by early historical times, we should not be surprised to find that Iraqi, Iranian, and Kurdish social and political problems and disputes have followed repetitive patterns.

As early as 4,000 years ago, Iraq had become a predominantly Semitic country, sharing the language and culture which united Arabs, Hebrews, Egyptians, and Phoenicians. By roughly the same time, Iran had been invaded and dominated by Central Asians who spoke various dialects of the ancestor of most of today's European languages. Among their distant relatives were the Aryan invaders of India, the Hittites, the Greeks, the Romans, the Slavs, and the Germans. Iranian (or Persian, as we often call the language and the people—the name comes from the West's early familiarity with Fars, one of the provinces of medieval Iran) is thus grammatically and syntactically closer to English than to the Arabic language of Iraq.

Since language is the bearer of culture, each linguistic system brought distinctive religious beliefs, patterns of social organization, and ways of life. The Semites and Indo-Europeans have long stressed their differences. These differences have often been used, as they are today, by political leaders as propaganda weapons to galvanize popular hostilities. They are therefore both real and artificial. But it is beyond doubt that while the Iraqis and Iranians are neighbors, they regard one another as strangers. This duality— proximity and alienness—has given rise to many destructive wars.

Sumerians, Babylonians, Assyrians, and other ancient Iraqi societies fought more or less continuously with the inhabitants of the hills and mountains, most of whom we today call the Kurds. These people were often aided against the Iraqis by Iranians, and used by the Iraqis against the Iranians. That pattern, too, has been echoed in recent events.

In historical times, the balance of power tipped first to one side and then to the other. The ancient Assyrians conquered much of the Iranian plateau. Then in about 550 B.C. Cyrus the Great, the "father" of Iran, merged the "Medes and the Persians," as the contemporary Greek traveler and reporter Herodotus called them, and led them to conquer not only Assyria and Babylon but also most of the Middle East. The memory of this imperial past was heavily emphasized during the regime of the late shah of Iran.

Successors of Cyrus the Great employed Greek mercenary soldiers, whom Xenophon depicts in the *Anabasis,* in his stirring account of a fighting retreat through the Kurdish mountains. In later centuries Macedonians, Romans, Byzantines, and others fought Persians and Kurds along what is approximately the modern frontier. Then in A.D. 633 the Muslim Arabs burst upon the ancient world, destroying completely the empire of the Iranians and crippling Byzantium.

In announcing Islam, I must return to the subject of religion (discussed in Chapter 3) and look at it from a different perspective.

Religion in the Middle East has traditionally been both a cause for and an explanation of political action. Indeed, it is obvious even from today's newspapers that without an understanding of what religion means in the lives of the two peoples, we cannot hope to understand the Iraq-Iran war or politics in either country. To fully comprehend this force, we must dig beneath the "formal" religion of Islam to get at the ways in which religion is shaped by each country's experience, memories, and living tradition.

Let us begin with Iran. Essentially, the Iranian tradition is Indo-European and is therefore closely related to beliefs and practices that Westerners know best in classical Greece. The ancient Iranians worshiped a pantheon of gods who were likewise revered by the Greeks and the Indians. Iranians even today retain in disguised forms these traditions and beliefs, despite the overlay of Islam.

Prior to Islam the "national" religion of Iran was Zoroastrianism, which was an Iranian codification of ancient Indo-European belief and practice. It was founded by the prophet Zarathushtra (Zoroaster) sometime before the fifth century B.C. Its holy book, the *Avesta*, played a major role in spreading the classical Iranian language (Pahlavi) and culture. So alive was this culture—albeit transmuted by subsequent religious influences and political changes—that the dynasty of the last Shah chose "Pahlavi" as its reign name in an attempt to associate itself with national tradition.

To an even greater extent than its medium, namely the language, the religion bequeathed a legacy that profoundly affects modern Iranian religion and politics: a belief in mystery, other-worldliness, the duality of good and evil, and the transcendental powers of the "guides" (those who are divinely inspired or particularly learned). This religion survived the Muslim invasion and incorporated itself into Islam in remarkable and subtle ways.

In part, the old culture was able to survive because, when the Muslim Arabs conquered Iran, they were content to leave the natives more or less alone. Far from spreading Islam at the point of the sword, as myth has it, Muslims often sought to *prevent* conversion, since converts paid lower taxes than did adherents of other religions. Consequently, for hundreds of years Muslims remained a minority in the conquered areas. Indeed, Arab rulers forced their Arab subjects to live in garrison towns apart from the natives. (Basra in modern Iraq, the Gulf war's Stalingrad, derives from one such garrison.) As increasing numbers of natives converted to Islam, they brought ideas and practices from the older religion into their new faith. In short, as they became Muslim, they did so in ways that symbolized and expressed *in the "idiom" of Islam* the differences between them and their conquerors.

The converts found a means to draw the distinction they sought in materials already at hand, stemming from early Islamic history. Briefly put, the materials derived from the issue of succession to the Prophet Muhammad.

When Muhammad died in A.D. 632, just eleven years after his flight from Mecca, he had barely had time to sketch the outlines of the Islamic community. His followers were stunned by his death and by the political crisis it created. In a slightly forced modern analogy, we might say that Muhammad had been both Islam's chief executive and its chief administrator; his early Arab followers apparently believed that no one could take his place as chief executive, shaper of policy, but that his lesser functions, *administering* what God had already decreed, could be passed on.

And so, Islamic sources tell us, his close companions got together and selected one among themselves to be *khalifa* (caliph). In the sense in which they meant this term, there was no precedent for the role, so that conflict over its precise nature has been one of the most profound and pervasive problems in Islamic political thought. It lies at the very heart of the Iranian revolution today, just as it lay at the heart of the first revolution, more than a thousand years ago.

The revolution in which the Islamic polity was established is one of those few moments that become divorced from time and hover above history, like a stationary satellite beneath which generation after generation passes in procession. For each generation it is immediately overhead, a fixed and present point, and a means of communication with contemporaries. Just as the Russian revolutionaries in the early twentieth century spoke and thought in terms of the French Revolution, as a sort of syllabus of their politics, so the Iranian revolutionaries today are often guided by and think in terms of analogies to events and personalities in that earlier Islamic revolution.

Among the closest companions of Muhammad were four who had major roles in the rise of the fledgling Islamic community. One (a father-in-law) had been designated by Muhammad, during his absences, to lead public prayer. That was the closest thing to a delegation of powers known in the community, and the father-in-law was chosen as the first caliph. An old man, he died after only two years in office. Again the inner group chose one of themselves, another father-in-law of Muhammad, as caliph. The second caliph ruled for ten years, until he was stabbed to death by an Iranian captive. Again, the young community was faced with the problem of choosing a caliph. This time a somewhat larger "election committee" picked a man who today would be called a compromise candidate: he was the weakest of the group, then seventy-four and infirm. Unlike the first two caliphs, he had close kinship ties to the old Meccan oligarchy against which Muhammad had struggled.

In each of these "elections" Muhammad's cousin and son-in-law, Ali, was passed over. Because of his close relationship to the Prophet and his personal merits, Ali *may* have hoped to become caliph, but if so he did not openly object to the elections. Indeed, he withdrew from what we might loosely call "public life" for almost a generation, while the great events of the conquest unfolded and the nature of the Islamic community was dramatically altered.

This decision would be of merely academic interest, were it not for the fact that the members of one wing of Islam, led until recently in Iran by Ayatullah Ruhullah Khumaini (Ayatolla Rohallah Khomeini), identify themselves as the "Partisans [Arabic: *Shiis*] of Ali." Thus, however remote from contemporary events those distant happenings may seem to outsiders, they constitute a sort of benchmark from which some of the most important of the divisions and passions of the Islamic world are measured.

During that generation of Ali's withdrawal, the shrewd merchants of the Meccan oligarchy were desperately eager to profit from the opportunities available in the conquered provinces. Finally, with the election of a kinsman as the third caliph, they seized their opportunity. Corruption and profiteering quickly reached monumental levels.

In the eyes of some of Muhammad's original band, the evils of pagan Mecca, so deplored by Muhammad, were thus being exported and made universal in the name of Islam. In place of the Meccan poor, whose plight had so disturbed Muhammad, whole nations (including Iran) had become the proletariat of the new Arab state. To some Muslims it seemed that everything Muhammad had stood for was being traduced by the old pagans, who had wrapped themselves opportunistically in the mantle of the prophet.

Their anger, of course, was echoed and magnified not only by the conquered but particularly by those among the conquerors who felt that they had not received their fair share of the spoils. Six years after his election, during a lull in the wars when the Arab soldiers were temporarily idle, and so free to brood on grievances, a group of them came to Medina and assassinated the third caliph.

Knowing that they would be held to account under Islamic law and tribal custom, they sought to protect themselves by forcing Ali to accept *their* election of him as caliph, much as rebellious Roman armies forced the election of emperors. Their act was the first of what has become a long tradition of coups d'état in the Arab world, and it immediately split the small Muslim state. The legal issue hinged on the question of whether or not the caliph had been killed legally, as a "tyrant" (a term we shall encounter again in connection with modern Iran) who had condoned the perversion of Muhammad's teaching. If so, then Ali's election as the fourth caliph acquired a certain validity; if not, then he was only a usurper.

While believers debated this legal point, the old Meccan oligarchy rallied around the governor of Syria, who claimed the traditional Arab right of vengeance against his kinsman's murderers. Against them, Ali was a reluctant leader. Although he had been disaffected by his predecessor's actions, Ali could not bring himself to condone the murder. In the ensuing civil war, he was forced to fight against both the conservatives and the radicals. The radicals, members of his own camp, he defeated, but in doing so fatally undermined his power. The first civil war did not last long, and ended in his defeat and death in 661.

The next act in the drama was played by his son Husain (Persian: Hosain) nineteen years after Ali's death. Encouraged by the people of Iraq, Husain led a rebellion against the Arab caliphate, then headquartered in Damascus. But although they had encouraged him, the Iraqis gave him little practical support. Those on whom he had counted stood aside and left him to his fate. Surrounded and cut off from food and supplies, he and his little band of followers were butchered by government troops. Around his "martyrdom" in 680 has been woven what might be regarded as the political-religious mythology of Iran. A saga elaborated by generations of storytellers, it is reenacted each year as a passion play before hundreds of thousands of Shia Muslims.

The Shia Passion Play is a vast public display of sorrow, shame, and personal abasement. Usually it takes the form of a parade through a city or town toward a field where the last battle of Husain is reenacted. Whole populations take part as participants and witnesses, weeping, beating their breasts, and rending their garments, while scores or hundreds of men parade past, whipping themselves with chains, mutilating themselves with daggers and swords, smeared with blood from their wounds, and screaming with pain and fury.

The Passion Play is an emotional orgy which people in our jaded age, at least in the more or less secular West, cannot comprehend. Perhaps it could have been appreciated by the so-called flagellants of medieval Europe, but it bears little resemblance to the relatively passionless Christian Passion Play. It is literally stunning to observers and participants. As it is performed, each generation takes upon itself the sins of the ancestors who stood aside and allowed the Imam Husain to be killed, so that each witness recreates the experience for himself with unparalleled personal immediacy.

We might achieve a "translation" of the event if we imagined that each year thousands of citizens of Munich walked barefoot to Dachau, dressed in concentration camp uniforms, gaunt and haggard from days of self-imposed starvation, performing punishments on their bodies like those the inmates had suffered, while the rest of the population lined the roads to weep in an ecstasy of shame and remorse.

Such a scene is virtually unimaginable. Yet in the Shia world such scenes occur each year. They are enacted not only in the great cities but in every village and hamlet. They are particularly "popular" in Iran, eastern Iraq, and southern Lebanon. Moreover, they do not consist merely of a single day's outpouring of grief. They are experienced—"performed" is too limiting a word, since there is no clear emotional division between actors and audience— publicly, day after day, during the first part of the Islamic month of Muharram, and climaxing on the tenth.

Indeed, throughout the year on holidays and special occasions, the events are retold by storytellers and poets before weeping gatherings of the faithful in private homes. For hundreds of years, foreign witnesses have attested to the power of the emotional experience of such performances. Through them Shiis are "programmed" with an intimacy of the past and with current beliefs, in a way that is virtually unique among modern peoples.

In the Passion Play are revealed the most fundamental distinctions between the Shia, Sunni, and secular communities. The differences we find are in part explainable in ethnic terms, but only in part. And the distinctions are not crudely or simply drawn. The martyred Husain was himself, of course, an Arab, but he is exalted beyond any ethnic designation. As portrayed, he is, at least to some extent, a recreation of an ancient, pre-Islamic Persian hero whose shameful betrayal was similarly lamented in popular Zoroastrianism. Thus, the circumstance, the format, and the occasion of the Passion Play touch deep and unconscious Iranian memories.

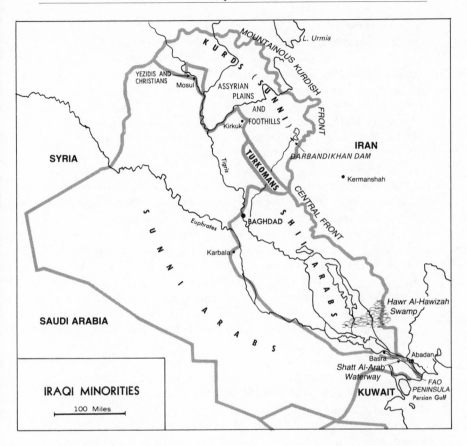

But, equally obviously, the mixture of Iranian and Arab and of pre-Islamic and Islamic elements is complex, with connections and divisions of a highly subtle nature. At its simplest, we can see that the Shia community comprises virtually all of Iran but also about half of Iraq, as well as significant numbers of Arabs in Lebanon, Saudi Arabia, Oman, and Yemen. What is more complex, we see that the roles in the Passion Play are not stereotypes of "good guys and bad guys." True, the killers are the Sunni Arab oppressors, but the particularly shameful villains, for whom atonement is sought and to whom the "audience" relates, are Shiis. They are, in two senses, both Arab and Iranian: mythically and culturally they hark back to an ancient Iranian prototype; historically they were the dispossessed, fringe groups of early Islamic Iraq—Arabized Iranians and mixtures of Arabs and Iranians. Even today, the lines are blurred. Begin with the fact that the holiest Shia shrines are in

323

Iraq. To these sites, in the last centuries, a steady stream of Persians has migrated, so that the Iraqi population is mixed ethnically as well as culturally. Thus, however we may seek to dissect the Iranian-Arab, Iranian-Iraqi, Sunni-Shii mixtures in order to analyze them, we must remain aware that, as living cultures, religions, and peoples, they cannot be neatly divided. We shall observe some of these ambiguities in the war and its conclusion.

In the Passion Play, our attention is focused on Husain, the hero who is inevitably the martyr. But beyond the drama looms the more fundamental issue of role. *What* is the figure who suffers and dies? As in Greek theater, which also was profoundly religious and moral in original intent, the hero cannot be merely Everyman; he must be worthy of the great events that befall him. Husain is not merely the rebellious son of a former caliph; he is the anointed of God. And here we delve deeply into the emotional, political, and religious meaning of Shiism.

In Shiism, Ali, the father of Husain, has been lifted beyond his Sunni-approved station as one among four close and "rightly guided" successors of the Prophet Muhammad to a position which, in some senses, transcends even that of Muhammad. Ali is thought of as the first of the imams: leaders, descended from Ali and a daughter of Muhammad, whom Shiis recognize as divinely ordained. In this tradition, we see both a non-Arab emphasis on inheritance of role and a non-Sunni definition of the mission of Muhammad's successors.

Whereas the Sunni Muslims, who in this respect follow the Arab custom, hold that the leadership of the Islamic community is not necessarily passed from father to son, the Shiis believe that it must be. The Sunnis argue that it matters not so much *who* exercises power on earth but whether the ruler acts according to the forms established by God through Muhammad. For the Sunnis, consequently, religious thought has tended to become legalistic. To the Shiis the issues appear otherwise. Both Sunnis and Shiis believe that God appointed Muhammad as His "messenger," to bring his Book to mankind. Both also hold that Muhammad was more than merely a messenger, since what he did, under God's inspiration, established a standard and model for his followers. God had to have Muhammad do more than merely deliver the message because what he conveyed was, by definition, all-embracing. Here the Sunnis and the Shiis begin to part company. The Sunnis believe that the combination of "the Book" (the Koran) and the traditions of Muhammad's actions and comments suffices to enable scholars and lawyers to comprehend God's message. Shiis disagree. They believe that the message is too subtle and complex to be understood by ordinary men. Even the most pious and learned, they stress, are hampered by minds whose perception has been warped by earthly weaknesses and sins. In attempting to read God's will, even the learned and the pious can understand only the superficial aspects. But the Shiis go further. They assert that the legacy itself may be quite different from the one we observe. Beyond, or in the Arabic expression "within" (*batin*) the written and obvious text of the Koran is, they believe, another and perhaps quite different message. To get at *that* message requires transcendental powers which can be acquired only by divine conferment.

The Shiis believe that God obviously wanted mankind to understand, and that therefore He could not have given these powers of understanding to Muhammad alone, since in his mission the message had not been fully illuminated. The task was ongoing and required for its performance a succession of guides, or imams.

Who could such guides be? Obviously not people elected or recognized by some sort of democratic consensus. Ordinary Muslims would have no way of knowing who had such powers, since they themselves had no access to esoteric lore. Nor could any form of worldly success or power be the criterion, such manifestations being subject to human foibles. It was conceivable, even probable, that God's real purposes would not be made manifest through so trivial and ephemeral an endowment as earthly power. For reasons beyond the understanding of mankind, the true leader might be a person who, in the eyes of contemporaries, was an improbable figure. The only reasonable guide to God's will turned out to be an old Iranian tradition: appointment by the already anointed. In this fashion, the Shiis believe, true guides have been successively appointed through the line of Ali.

It follows that those who opposed or were not guided by the dictates and actions of Ali and his progeny were illegitimate. This is the case not only for all Sunnis, who (Shiis hold) do not understand the real meaning of God's commands, the "inner" meaning of the Koran, but also for all secular governments, *both* those of the Sunnis (as the Persians regard the government of Iraq) and those (like the government of the late shah) ruling over Shia societies but not organized according to Shia law and ritual. Withdrawal from politics, when that alone is possible, or rebellion, when that becomes feasible, are legitimate and, indeed, obligatory. The thread leading to revolution in modern Iran is clear.

Clear, but not unbroken. Like most dynasties, the line of the divinely sanctioned successors finally ran out. The three main sects among the Shiis recognize only a limited number of imams (the Shiis of Iran and Iraq recognize twelve), of whom the last is said to have "disappeared" in A.D. 872 or 873. He is expected to return on Resurrection Day.

In the meantime, holding restricted but still extensive powers and acting on his behalf, another category of religious leaders has come to the fore. By their study of the thoughts and their emulation of the acts of the imams, these people have acquired superior wisdom. They gradually have formed themselves into a self-perpetuating religious establishment, of which Ayatullah Ruhullah Khumaini (Khomeini) is the most famous contemporary representative.

This religious establishment was and still is rooted in what we may think of as scholastic institutions, the first of which was founded nearly a thousand years ago in the Iraqi city of Najaf. Like medieval Western universities, they were centers of learning outside the mainstream of civil and political life. Those within them formed a self-perpetuating community, attracting outsiders and converting them into scholars in the mold of the community, generation after generation.

But in contrast to savants at both modern and medieval Western universities, Shia scholars always prepared themselves to rule. This is not to say that they studied or taught administration or "policy studies," but rather to say that they studied an interpretation of the will of God which they believed should be made manifest on earth. They believed that questions of the *means* appropriate or even apparently necessary to effect God's will were trivial, when weighed in this scale; in due course God would create a way, and, at that time, those who were deserving and properly educated would be ready to establish His policy and rule in accordance with it.

In the meantime, the religious establishment performed a number of tasks and derived various benefits which in other societies are functions of government. It acquired vast wealth through tax collection, control of pious foundations, and donations. Until half a century ago, it staffed and controlled virtually the entire educational system, whose curriculum consisted of its materials. It judged law cases and affirmed or denied government ordinances, rather in the fashion of a supreme court, and its approval was often actively courted by kings, whose legitimacy in part depended upon the attitude of the religious authorities. Through its close ties with the mercantile and artisan communities, it was able to confront government with strikes, boycotts, and propaganda which were difficult for any ruler to withstand. From time to time, it enlisted the strongmen of each district as a sort of militia (in Iran called the *lutis*), and it had a final weapon in its ability to motivate its followers to assassinate even the most powerful public figures.

Historically in Iran, as well as in theory elsewhere, the Shia scholastic-religious bureaucracy has constituted a shadow government. No other force—shah, parliament, political parties, or army—measured up to the religious establishment in the Iranian mind. So obvious was this potential role to all Iranians that in the first days of the revolution, government officials throughout Iran, including even the shah's police and army, spontaneously turned over authority to the clergy. We shall see that something of this fanaticism (as it seems to us) is also evident in Lebanon, where the Shiis act with a fervor and singleness of purpose that stuns their opponents.

For much of their history and in most places, the Shiis have been subject to persecution. Not only were their beliefs abhorrent to many of the orthodox clergy, but their actions were regarded as seditious by the rulers. Consequently, Shiis learned to hide their beliefs through dissimulation (Arabic: *taqiyah;* Persian: *kitman*). They thus practiced what might be thought of as both a civic and a personal "withdrawal" from the dominant society, while asserting that they were its only true members.

In a broad sense, we may say that the Shiis take a stance comparable to that of the early Christian fundamentalists, who held that the established churches had distorted the true religion. It is for this reason that Western orientalists have occasionally suggested that we think of the Shiis as "Protestants" and the Sunnis as "Catholics." When opportunity arose, as it did for the Protestants in northern Europe several centuries ago and as it has for the Shiis in contemporary Iran, they enforced their beliefs in uncompromising detail. The Puritans were no more tolerant of Catholics or other Protestants than the established church had been of them in England or the Shiis of Iran are today of those who differ from them. They seek to sweep away the debris of a hated past and in their attempt, they have taken over the whole apparatus of state power. They use it unflinchingly and without pity.

Their seizure of government raises a third issue in the Shia experience that is usually overlooked: disappointment with all temporal power. Each time the Shiis approached or assumed power they ended in disappointment, failure, and often violent suppression. Even in Iran, Shiis fared little better than in the Arab countries. While paying lip service to Shiism, the last three Iranian dynasties, the Safavids (1502–1736), the Qajars (1794–1925), and, especially and recently, the Pahlavis, have either traduced or failed to uphold Shiism. Experience has shown that Shiism has never long coexisted harmoniously or securely with government.

So pervasive is this experience that many Shiis do not believe they can, or even should try to, establish their perfect society until the return of the Hidden Imam. Others, including the current leadership of Iran, obviously disagree. For them, the bad experiences of the past cannot be allowed to deter this generation from doing their utmost to effect in all spheres of life what they believe to be God's ordinances. However it may appear to outsiders, to Iranians, or even to fellow members of the religious establishment, the followers of Ayatullah Khumaini are sure that they are right, believe that they are acting under divine inspiration, and are unmoved by human opposition or suffering. Nor are they to be seen marching to the drumbeat of opportunism. For them, the difference between success and failure is not measured in the same scales Westerners use. All this has been made painfully manifest in the Iraq-Iran war and in the curious peace that has followed it.

As nonorthodox (or, in their belief, uniquely orthodox), withdrawn, essentially extra-institutional, and often "outsider" societies, the Shiis have been most successful and most comfortable engaging in covert opposition to existing regimes. They have spread for the most part "underground," along informal pathways among the disaffected. As we learn more of medieval Islamic history, we are finding that a great many people living in supposedly Sunni lands were Shiis but were either out of touch with the ruling institutions or hid their Shia faith. We may find in the coming decade that many in Sunni or secular lands would welcome a similar return to this kind of Islam. (We surely will find that the way we glibly speak of whole societies—"the Egyptians approve" or "the Syrians oppose"—uses comparable oversimplifications.)

Not surprisingly, since they felt themselves to be outlaws—that is, outside the law of the dominant Sunni society—and since they consequently had no access to "legitimate" forms of power, Shia groups often resorted to violence to attain their ends. Perhaps the most famous of the Shia sects has given the Western world the word "assassin," which derives from the Arabic word *hashishin* and stems from the belief that the "hit men" of the sect were sent on their missions under the influence of narcotics. Because today we are so painfully concerned with terrorism, and because we have found the Shiis of Iran and Lebanon able and willing to employ it, this sense of being literally an outlaw, of not being a part of the legal system of the existing societies, is another thread in the complex Shia fabric.

The majority of Iranians and of the Arabs of Iraq are Shiis, but, at least for the present, Iraq has been able to persuade its population to act like Sunni or secular Arabs. It has found this an exhausting and not very productive task. Although the population has not rebelled, it has been far less enthusiastic in support of the regime and the war than the Shiis of Iran have of their regime and its part in the war. Both governments are tyrannies and both have been cruel to their peoples, so the reason for this reluctance must lie elsewhere. Part of it, I suspect, consists in the fact that the Iraqi regime is ambivalent about its identity. Originally, it proclaimed its Arabism. *Baath* is the Arabic word for "resurrection," and the resurrection referred to is that of the Arab nation. But, both because it regards Arab Syria as an enemy nearly equal to Iran and because many of its people are not of Arab extraction, the Iraqi regime has flirted with an identity based on other grounds. One of these is its pre-Arab, "Babylonian" past. Another is Islam itself. In recent years, President Saddam Husain has identified himself to his people repeatedly as a descendant of the imam Ali.

Iran has no such identity crisis. Despite a failed economy, great personal suffering, oppression, and the virtual annihilation of a whole generation of its youth, it displays obvious support, even ecstatic devotion, for the regime of the ayatullahs.

Within the Iranian religious establishment, however, assumption of power has not been universally approved. While most outside observers focus their attention on the involvement of "the clergy" in government, many conservative members have, from the outset of the revolution, strongly opposed such involvement and have withdrawn from participation. This comes not so much from disagreement over programs, certainly not disagreement over the attempt to enforce the religious law, as from religious or philosophical conviction. Many fear that assumption of power before the return of the Hidden Imam will cause the religious establishment to become corrupted by tyranny and worldly vanity. I expect that, with the death of Ayatullah Khumaini, this trend will become more

329

pronounced, both because the clergy will want it and because Khumaini's successors, who lack his religious standing, will find it attractive.

In summary, the picture we derive of Shiism is highly complex and involuted. We can see manifestations in the way the Iranians have fought for their cause, often virtually barehanded with incredible courage and ferocity, and yet also in the way they have allowed the war just to "wither away"; in the bitterness of the assault on the Iraqis, and yet also in the sudden achievement of accord between them; in their violent quest for political power, and yet also in their apparent feeling that it is a vanity to be despised. We see it in their disdain both for "world opinion" and for practicalities. Above all, we see elements of it in their shared perception of what they believe to be the American danger. This they evaluate not so much in terms of money or tanks or aircraft as in terms of mode of life, materialism, and human fate. In these matters, they are willing not only to defy the entire world but even to give it up.

With these observations, which at least acknowledge the peculiar religious framework of Shiism, I turn to the third aspect of the war, the involvement of the Kurdish people.

The Kurds have never achieved, and have rarely sought, either political union or statehood. Their homeland, divided as it is among high, almost inaccessible valleys, has never fostered large-scale political organization. Yet in recent times, painfully, often bloodily aware of the hostility of the Iranians and Iraqis, the Kurds have sought to find some means of coalescing into a defensible entity. In the twentieth century, such an entity had to be a nation-state. Thus, while there is little reason to believe that the Kurds were "infected" by the virus of nationalism, as were most of the other Middle Eastern peoples, they nevertheless have sought some form of coalition larger than their traditional tribes and villages. They got their first major chance at the end of World War II, when the Russians were occupying northern Iran and sought some local group to help perpetuate their control. These quite separate, even contradictory objectives—the attempt at foreign control and the desire for local autonomy—gave rise to the short-lived Kurdish Republic of Mahabad. When the Russians withdrew, the Iranians quickly suppressed even the memory of this embryonic state. For years, the Iranians (like the Turks) even denied the Kurds' existence as a separate people.

So long as the Kurds were divided and weak, the Iraqis and

Iranians were content to leave them more or less alone. But each party tried to use the Kurds against the other. And the Kurds sought to use each opportunity to increase their autonomy or to achieve their dream of independence. Both of these trends were made manifest in the 1960's. Finding war profitless and dangerous, the Iraqi regime under General Qasim offered the Kurds an amnesty in 1962 and 1963. Divided among themselves as usual, the Kurds could not agree on a price for peace and so did not accept the offer. Failure to end this expensive, unpopular war contributed, in turn, to the fall of Qasim.

Reading the message, the next Iraqi government offered the Kurds a larger measure of autonomy than ever before. But the Kurds, now feeling their power, pushed for independence. The Baghdad regime, frightened at the prospect of the breakup of Iraq and with the lesson of Qasim's fall in mind, replied with a military offensive.

In these troubled waters, Iran, the United States, and Israel (which had identified Iraq as a dangerous Arab enemy) began to fish. Each established covert links and began to supply military equipment, communications support, and other intelligence services to the Kurds in attempts to "destabilize" the Iraqi regime. With this help and encouragement, the Kurds living in Iraq hardened their stand and engaged in sporadic and sometimes relatively large-scale fighting with the government. But no one really wanted the Kurds to win. Iran and Turkey certainly were not anxious to have a Kurdish state that would encourage their own Kurdish citizens toward independence, nor did the United States want a new Kurdish Republic that, like the earlier one, might be subject to Soviet influence. So the support was almost enough to cause trouble but not enough to really swing the balance. And as the Iraqis were likewise halfhearted, the fighting dragged on. In time, it became clear to the Iraqis that the game was not worth the candle and that, probably, they could not ever achieve complete mastery in the forbidding Kurdish mountains. The Kurds, starved, bombed, thwarted, also lost their taste for battle. So in 1966 a new cease-fire was achieved. To judge from the written agreement, Iraq appeared to be moving toward binational statehood.

Given the nature of the Kurdish nation and its homeland, cease-fires and settlements could be only temporary, and the issue of what Kurdistan was and how it related to Iraq remained open when the Baath Party seized power in Iraq in 1968. Immediately after assuming power, the Baath leaders began to seek some sort of accommodation. By 1970 they thought they had worked out a deal with the traditional Kurdish leader, Mullah Mustafa Barzani, under which the Iraqi Kurds would remain Iraqi but would be granted autonomy.

For nearly four years, relations remained relatively good. Then fundamental disagreements surfaced among the Kurds themselves over social policy, leadership, and the relationship with Iran. Barzani favored a close relationship with Iran, while a young, leftist party opposed the shah's regime and urged radical reform. This caused a split with the Iraqis in 1974. Again, the mountains were the scene of sporadic warfare.

The Kurds then came to be seen as useful tools in a quite different strategic problem—a problem that was, in fact, distant from Kurdistan: it concerned the nature of the two regimes and their precise frontier. To put this issue in perspective, we must go back a few years.

Iraq was, as we saw in Chapter 9, created by the British from three provinces of the Ottoman Empire at the end of World War I. Iran had long disputed and occasionally fought with the Ottoman Empire over the control of Iraq, and still aspired to bring it under control. It was not until 1929 that Iran even recognized Iraq as a separate state. Ultimately Iran more or less gave up the idea of taking over the whole country, and in the 1937 Saadabad Pact settled (at least temporarily) for a revision of the frontier in its favor.

World War II, British and Russian occupation, the deposition of the old shah, and other matters deflected the government of the new shah, Muhammad Reza Pahlavi, but by 1958 he felt himself strong enough to assert memories of empire. His first target was at the head of the Gulf. There the confluence of the Tigris and Euphrates, known as the Shatt al-Arab, provides access to the Iranian oil facilities at Abadan, opposite the Iraqi city of Basra. This waterway is the modern frontier between Iraq and Iran, but precisely where the frontier falls has been the subject of repeated negotiations. The first took place in 1847. When the shipping of oil came to be important in the early twentieth century, this agreement was modified in favor of Iran; at that time the British were eager to help Iran because they wanted to be able to load their tankers more easily at their new oil refinery at Abadan. When Iraq became formally independent—though still, of course, under British control—this agreement was confirmed. When the Iranian government nationalized the oil fields and refinery, the British became less enthusiastic. Iraq then became the British favorite.

In 1958, the pro-British royal government of Iraq was overthrown, and the Iranians felt free to assert new demands. In 1959, the shah menacingly moved troops to the frontier and stopped paying the tolls set by the treaty for use of the waterway. He also began to encourage, bribe, and arm the Kurds against the Iraqi regime. No resolution was reached in the dispute. In 1969, a year after the seizure of power by the current (Baathi) regime in Iraq, the shah stepped up his pressure, giving large quantities of arms to the Kurds, and announced that Iran was unilaterally abrogating the existing treaty. Fighting broke out between Iraqi and Iranian forces in April 1971, whereupon Iraq severed diplomatic relations. At about the same time, Iran seized three islands in the Gulf, near the Straits of Hormuz. Tiny and barren in themselves, these islands appeared capable of acting as stationary aircraft carriers and boat docks, and thus of giving Iran the capacity to close Iraq's only maritime outlet. The shah followed these actions with well-publicized "covert" military assistance to Oman, which included the stationing of Iranian army combat units there. While Iran's apparent purpose was to fight insurgents from South Yemen, the strategic implication was clear: Iran planned to make the Persian Gulf an Iranian lake and so achieve a vise grip on Iraq. Whatever else he may have intended, the shah made it clear that Iran aspired to paramount power in the Middle East and, eventually, as oil revenue and development gave him the capacity, to great-power status.

The shah was playing his cards close to his chest. One card was the Kurdish aspiration for statehood. With considerable Iranian help, the Kurds threw themselves into what soon became a full-scale war. In bitter fighting, the Iraqi army was forced to retreat and took heavy casualties. Iraq took the issue to the UN Security Council. Then it struck back against the Kurds with about six divisions. Inexorably the Iraqis advanced and drove many of the Kurds into Iran. But the war was costly for Iraq, and "softened" its regime for a deal. The pressure exerted by the shah had helped him achieve his goal. He let it be known that he wanted to negotiate. With Algeria as an intermediary, discussions began that led to a compromise: in February 1975, at the OPEC meeting in Algiers, Iran and Iraq signed a bilateral agreement.

The deal was that Iraq would yield to Iranian demands on the waterway, give up all of its long-standing claims to the Arabic-speaking province of Khuzistan (also known as Arabistan), and recognize Iranian sovereignty over the three islands Iran had occupied in the Gulf; in return, Iran agreed, to put it baldly, to sell the

Kurds "down the river." Iran abruptly stopped supplying the Kurds with arms and other supplies, including food, so that their revolt collapsed. The old Kurdish leader, Mustafa Barzani, broken and dispirited, died in exile in America, bitter more at the treachery of his friends than the bullets of his enemies.

The days of the shah were likewise numbered. His nemesis was then in exile in Iraq. The shah had expelled Ayatullah Khumaini in 1965, and the redoubtable ayatullah had found haven in the Shia city of Najaf. There he was to live for fourteen years. At first, Khumaini was allowed complete liberty and used this to build his revolutionary organization and to propagandize his Iranian followers. To press an analogy, Khumaini was Iraq's "Kurd." When the Baath government assumed power in 1968, it was not averse to letting this thorn fester in the side of the hostile Iranians. This lasted until 1975, when the government struck its deal with Iran in Algiers. Then Khumaini began to become an embarrassment. And as the religious community in Iran became more forceful in its opposition to the government, the shah began to see its leaders as a possible threat. In 1978, he asked the Iraqis to clamp down on Khumaini. In the new spirit of cooperation, the Iraqis first curtailed Khumaini's movements, then placed him under house arrest, and finally expelled him. (He tried first to go to Kuwait but was refused entry, and subsequently made his way to France.)

For this cooperation with Iran, a domestic price had to be paid. The Iraqi Shiis, many of whom already had found reason not to like the Baath regime, were angered by the treatment of this famous religious leader. The gap widened between the regime and the Shia community. While not particularly hostile to the Shiis as such, the Baathis were opposed to the use of religion in politics and were jealous of the Shiis' power. We do not yet know the precise circumstances, but it is clear that as early as 1974 they began to arrest and execute leaders of the Shia community.

Angry over the fate of his colleagues, embittered by his experience in Iraq, and associating its secular Baathi government with that of the shah, Khumaini, who was then living in Paris, came to see the Baathis as the third of his four categories of enemies—the Shah, the United States, Iraq, and Israel. So, when his followers overthrew the shah in January 1979 and attacked various American targets, Khumaini was ready to mount his campaign against Iraq.

Through various propaganda channels, the revolutionary regime began to attack the Baathis, claiming that they were pawns of the shah, tools of Israel, anti-Muslims, atheists, and so on, and calling openly and repeatedly for the assassination of Saddam Husain. The Iranians clamored for a Shia march on Baghdad to oust the Baathis. Covertly, they began to arm and pay Iraqi Shiis to bomb Iraq government buildings and to assassinate Iraqi officials. A number of the latter were in fact killed, and the Iraqi foreign minister, a Christian, narrowly escaped an attempt on his life. Remarkably, during this time the Iraqis continued to conciliate the new Iranian regime. The underground war grew bitter and dirty. In downtown Baghdad, small fortresses sprouted around government buildings and the residences of officials. Even more ominously, the Iranians resumed arms shipments, suspended in 1975, to the Kurds. In riposte, in June 1979 Iraq arrested, tried, and shot the leader of the Iraqi Shia community. The Iranians redoubled their denunciation, calling for the Iraqi army to rebel. Bombings increased, and in the early months of 1980 the Iraqis expelled more than 15,000 Iranian nationals then living in Iraq. Many were the descendants of Persian families who had lived in Iraq for generations. Iraq also hit hard at the Iraqi Shia (Dawah al-Islamiyah) party, and is alleged to have executed about 500 of its members.

In an attempt to split the Shia ranks, Saddam Husain not only imprisoned and shot whatever prominent Shiis he could catch, but also offered the Shia community incentives to support his regime. Some were merely symbolic. Among other things, he made the birthday of the fourth caliph, Imam Ali, a national holiday, rebuilt various mosques and pilgrimage facilities, and in a number of public speeches asserted his own descent from the house of Ali. He also promoted many young Shiis through the ranks of the Baath Party, so that its membership became more truly representative of the country.

In its relations with Iran, Iraq tightened the diplomatic screws by demanding full implementation of the 1975 treaty, which had never been completely effected; Iran refused. There were a number of "incidents," including artillery exchanges, and on September 22, 1980, the Iraqis launched an invasion. The background of the hostility was certainly clear, and to both the Iraqis and Iranians it was compelling. Only the timing of the outbreak of war was circumstantial.

The opportunity that the Iraqis seized was the disintegration of the Iranian army. No sooner had the new Iranian regime assumed power in February 1979 than it began an extensive purge of the American-trained army. Virtually the entire officer corps was killed, imprisoned, or driven into exile. When I visited the Iraqi battle front some time afterward, I was told by the Iraqi commanding general that when in the early days of the war an Iranian brigade had been cut off and forced to surrender, it was found to have only one professional officer. The air force was almost totally destroyed in this manner. Amazingly, shortly after Iraq attacked and appeared about to conquer Iran in September and October 1980, the Iranians let a number of officers out of prison (where some were awaiting execution) and sent them to the front in commanding positions. Clearly, Khumaini was the most effective enemy of his own army.

After their initial successes against this essentially leaderless army, the Iraqis bogged down. They did not have the manpower to "win." In this, as I have suggested, Iraq resembled the Confederacy in the American Civil War. It could not reach the centers of its opponent's power; they were quite simply out of its reach. It had no candidate for a national leader if it managed to topple Khumaini. It does not even seem to have given much consideration to taking over strategic Iranian assets such as oil fields. At most, it may have hoped (although even this is not clear) to establish more favorable frontiers. One is left with the thought that, rather simplistically, having found the door open, the Iraqis simply decided to walk in. Then on December 15, 1981, Saddam Husain, not liking what he found, and having tripped over the doorsill, offered to end the war if Iran would recognize the old frontiers. Iran, by this time beginning to win some victories on the ground against the faltering Iraqi army, and nursing old grudges, refused.

During 1981 a second sobering event shook Saddam Husain. On June 7, the Israeli air force carried out a strike against the Iraqi nuclear center outside of Baghdad. The raid, which involved a flight over about 1,000 kilometers of Jordanian, Ṣaudi, and Iraqi territory, was unopposed. That was sobering enough, but worse was the fact that it was the culmination of two years of successful anti-Iraqi acts of espionage, including the murder of a senior scientist and the destruction of much equipment. It was widely believed that Israel was responsible for these acts. The espionage and air raid temporarily halted the Iraqi nuclear program. They may also, however, have convinced the Iraqis both that peace with Israel was unlikely and that Iraq should seek other means, perhaps especially chemical weapons and rockets, to defend itself. Certainly, Iraq began to invest more heavily in these programs following the air raid.

By 1982 the Iranians had regrouped into three distinct organizations: what was left of the old army, the *pasdaran* (roughly, the "revolutionary national guard"), and the lightly armed and more or less informal *basij* (or people's militia). In the spring and summer they counterattacked and drove the Iraqis back behind the old international frontier. No sooner had they achieved this victory than the Iranians began again to purge their officer corps. Probably as many as 10,000 officers were executed or imprisoned.

The effect on their army was, of course, predictable. It lost cohesion and all sense of strategy. Particularly on the central front, tens of thousands of soldiers were butchered by the Iraqis. But the Iranians seemed not to care. Expendable young boys were pushed ahead in human waves to clear paths through mine fields for the more precious tanks. Each "martyr" was promised his reward in heaven. The spirit of the Iranian troops was breathtaking—and sickening—to behold. But gradually the Iranians managed to build a professional, highly motivated, and fiercely loyal force (the *pasdaran*), separate from the regular army. Those officers of the regular army who were still alive and in military command were made subordinate to religious leaders. The government backed both the regular army and the *pasdaran* with a militia, the *basij*. Before the end of the war, despite its massive casualties, Iran had about 2.2 million soldiers.

Iraq, similarly, had three echelons of troops: a regular army of about half a million; a Popular Militia, also comprising about half a million, created by the Baath party in 1970; and a reserve of somewhat less than 100,000. Iraq had overwhelmingly superior equipment, which was controlled by a general staff that had benefited from Russian training. Yet the Iraqi army never really had its heart in the fight. From my personal observation during two trips along the central front, where conditions were most favorable to the Iraqi form of fighting, I can attest that the army was bored by the war. Deeply and comfortably dug in, it was reluctant to stir itself to fight. At no time did it match the courage or élan of the Iranians.

In 1982, after Iraq's initial offensive had failed and Iran had plunged across the border, killing large numbers of Iraqi soldiers and destroying much equipment, the Iraqi army seemed on the brink of collapse. At that point, Iraq decided to use what has been called "the poor country's nuclear bomb": chemical weapons. It appears that the Iraqis made this decision in desperation and used the weapons, at least initially, only when they feared a catastrophe on the battlefield.

By 1984, profiting from a major infusion of Soviet equipment and French training, particularly of its air force, Iraq reorganized its front-line forces. Taking advantage of its road and rail network and its short lines of communication, it began to employ its armor and infantry to envelop and destroy Iranian units. These tactics worked particularly well on the dry, flat central front. At that point, faced with the same pressures that Iraq had earlier felt, the Iranians likewise equipped themselves with chemical weapons and began to use them as soon as they could. Again, the comparison with World War I is striking.

During this time, Iran wisely shifted its line of attack from the central front, where it was at a major disadvantage and where it was suffering massive casualties, to the marshes of the southern area around Basra and the mountainous Kurdish area to the north.

In the north, fighting spilled over into Turkey, which also had a large population of Kurds, whom the Turks called "mountain Turks." Traditionally, the Turks had ruled "their" Kurds with an iron fist, sometimes using search-and-destroy missions and what amount to scorched-earth tactics, and keeping them more or less permanently under martial law. Turkey was no more willing than Iraq to allow the Kurds scope for any sort of national movement; and so, in October 1984, it worked out an extraordinary agreement with the Iraqis under which the armed forces of either side could operate against the Kurds on the territory of the other. The agreement led to frequent and sometimes large-scale military operations in the mountainous junction of Iraq, Iran, and Turkey.

The October agreement with Turkey, in itself a psychological boost to Iraq, was followed a month later by a meeting between U.S. president Ronald Reagan and Iraqi foreign minister Tariq Aziz in Washington. There the two countries announced that they were resuming diplomatic relations, after a break of seventeen years.

In the south, troops waged what became nearly an amphibious war on the vast Hawr al-Hawizah swamp. Wave after human wave was thrown against Iraqi defenses in an attempt to overwhelm them. Casualties, as in World War I along the trenches, were obscenely high. But the Iraqis were gradually worn down and dispirited. Then, in February 1986, the Iranians tried new tactics. In small groups, swimming and floating, they circled around the Iraqi defenses and took the Fao peninsula on the Persian Gulf. (The Iraqis publicly blamed the United States, from whom they had regularly been receiving intelligence, including, apparently, satellite photographs, for giving them incorrect information on Iranian movements. The United States denied the charge.)

Strategically the Iranian campaign was an Iraqi disaster: had they been able to hold the Fao peninsula, the Iranians would have effectively cut off Iraq from most of its petroleum markets. Tactically it was almost worse, since the Iranians had made an end run around the carefully prepared Iraqi defensive lines. The Iraqis could not easily adjust to the new challenge. Only at great cost were they able to counterattack and drive the Iranians back. Iraq had survived its worst danger in the war. From that point onward in the central and southern fronts, the advantage lay with the Iraqis.

In the spring of 1988 the Iranians turned to the more or less neglected northern front. There, in mountains pierced by few roads and divided by deep valleys, the main advantages of the Iraqi army, heavy equipment and division-scale tactics, were difficult to employ. So the relatively lightly armed Iranians were able to strike close to one of the most critical Iraqi targets: the Darbandikhan dam, which supplies hydroelectric power to Baghdad. In panic, the Iraqis again employed gas on a large scale, with devastating effects on the civilian Kurdish population as well as on the attacking Iranians. With this terrible weapon, they stabilized the front.

From an economic perspective, the war went through similar phases. During the early years of the war, Iran appeared to have a great advantage. Because Iran could interdict Iraqi oil shipments in the Persian Gulf and because its Arab ally, Syria, cut off the Iraqi pipeline to the Mediterranean, Iraq was forced to ship oil by truck through Jordan. Its exports fell to less than 750,000 barrels a day. Iran, meanwhile, able to move in the Gulf, raised its exports to about three million barrels a day. For some time, the only Iraqi answer to this situation was to beg or borrow money from Kuwait, the UAE, and Saudi Arabia. It is estimated that about $50 billion came to Iraq in such credits and gifts.

By 1986, however, the advantage had swung to Iraq. By then, Iraq had opened or rebuilt pipelines through Saudi Arabia and Turkey, so that it was able to export about two million barrels a day. More pointedly, the Iraqis began to attack Iran's oil installations and its tankers in the Gulf, particularly on Kharg Island; these attacks did not stop Iranian exports, but they served to make them more dangerous and expensive. The result was a reduction in tonnage, to about half the amount sold abroad earlier. And as the world oil market softened and the price of oil dropped, the real effect on Iran was more like a 75 percent loss of revenue.

As Iran became more desperate, it began to come into conflict with Kuwait (it bombed the country and threatened its tankers, causing the U.S. government to "reflag" them as American), with Saudi Arabia and, eventually, through its mining of the Gulf, directly with the United States. Characteristically, a key element in the attack against Saudi Arabia was a demonstration at the great mosque in Mecca on July 31, 1987, which killed many people and electrified the Islamic world, raising again and in violent terms the question of the status of the Shia community.

For reasons that are still not clear but may be related to its own Muslim minority problems, the Soviet Union decided at roughly this time that Iranian military actions and propaganda endangered its interests. Whatever may have caused its disenchantment with the Iranian revolution, the cause was apparently not the Islamic regime's attacks on Iran's Communist Party; Khumaini had violently attacked that party, jailing and eventually executing most of its leadership, almost from the day he took power. To these measures, the Russian government made few and feeble protests. But by the spring of 1988, Soviet officials had begun, quietly, to act in concert with, or at least not to oppose or denounce, such American actions as the April 18 air strike on an Iranian oil target.

So Iraq gained power, and Iran felt its resources melt away. Finally, on July 17, Saddam Husain set forth the Iraqi conditions for peace. A cease-fire, called for in United Nations Resolution 598, was accepted by the Iranian government. It was affirmed personally by Ayatullah Khumaini. Fighting continued, however, as both sides quibbled over the terms and commitments of the cease-fire. Not until August 20 did the cease-fire go into effect.

But the war had not exactly or conclusively ended: neither party was prepared for anything like a peace treaty. Both continued the war politically, off the battlefield. What changed was that the fighting, long triangular in nature, shifted in emphasis. Instead of emphasizing the Iraq-Iran front, the Iraqis decided to use the opportunity afforded by the cease-fire to liquidate, once and for all, what they regarded as the Kurdish threat to the Iraqi state. To general world condemnation, they turned their battle-hardened and now victorious army north into the mountains. The results were devastating. During August and September 1988, an estimated 56,377 Kurds fled or were driven into Turkey, and about 16,500 fled into Iran. More were to follow as the Iraqis—disdainful of world opinion, believing that both Turkey and Iran, whatever they might say, would secretly condone their action, and that both the United States and the Soviet Union were more or less neutralized—began to use chemical weapons against the Kurds. Probably as many as 15,000 were killed in the attacks. The Iraqis were correct in their beliefs: editorials in the foreign press condemned their actions, but no effective response was forthcoming. For the present, at least, Kurdistan is the real victim of the Iraq-Iran war.

A sort of "peace" born of exhaustion fell on the three neighbors. It was to continue, fitfully, until the American response to the Iraqi invasion of Kuwait in August 1990. Then, Iraq announced that it was pulling its military forces back from all the areas it had occupied in Iran, and the Iranian government announced that it had ended its hostility to Iraq. Local peace, in the eye of a gathering storm, had finally come.

22

Maelstrom in the Levant

A s the 1980's began, the document that set out the best guide to the Middle East's future (although not precisely in all the directions intended by its author) was one by an Israeli. General Ariel Sharon, then Israel's minister of defense, laid out his recommendations for Israel's strategy in a speech at Tel Aviv University on December 15, 1981. His program for the future, more than any other, set in motion the tragic events that were to characterize the maelstrom in the Levant throughout the 1980's, and it was Lebanon that he addressed in the first part of his plan.

So much has happened in so many troubled areas that it may be well briefly to refocus our memories on the complex issues that arose in Lebanon. Although these issues are of course interrelated in intricate ways, for analytical purposes I will divide them into the Lebanese polity, the Palestinian presence, the Syrian involvement, the Syrian-Palestinian relationship, the Syrian-Soviet alliance, Israeli strategy prior to June 1982, the Israeli invasion, the American involvement, and the aftermath in Lebanon. These events will take our narrative to the occupied territories and, finally, to the *Intifada* (or uprising against Israel), Israel's attempted repression, and the current situation. Let us begin with the evolution of Lebanon as a political entity.

Since the time it was a province of the Ottoman Empire, Mount

Lebanon (as it was then known) had been a loosely linked collection of primarily religiously defined communities. At the end of World War I, the French took over the Levantine provinces of the Ottoman Empire. The Syrians resisted this invasion, but the French were generally welcomed in Mount Lebanon. Since the Syrians were hostile to their rule, the French sought to provide themselves with a secure local ally. On the surface, the choice was obvious: Mount Lebanon should become the pro-French Christian counterpoise to unfriendly Muslim Syria.

Obvious but ultimately impossible. The French faced a dilemma at two levels. First, Mount Lebanon was not uniformly Christian. Even if we leave aside the large Druze minority, the Lebanese were Christians rather than Christian. The Maronite majority, itself divided by other loyalties, coexisted with Greek Orthodox and Greek Catholic communities, with a small but vocal Protestant community, and with other groups which, while Christian in religion, defined themselves in ethnic or linguistic terms.

Second, if Lebanon was to be big enough to be helpful to the French, it had to be more than the old Ottoman province of Mount Lebanon. So the French decided to add to the original province relatively large areas inhabited by Muslims and others. Thus, to gain importance as a whole, it had to cease being whole. The Lebanon that the French created and left as their legacy was a precariously balanced collection of economically and politically linked autonomous societies.

Under a firm French hand, these societies had managed to coexist with relatively little friction; then, as the French hold weakened, the leaders of the main groups found a sort of common cause, so long as their rights were respected by their neighbors and by the central government, and so long as each was relatively weak. During World War II, with considerable help from the British, who had pushed the (Vichy) French government out of the Levant, and with the approval of the United States, a new political order was negotiated in the so-called National Pact of 1943, which divided the responsibilities and offices of the emerging state essentially between the then-dominant Maronite and Sunni Muslim communities. The Maronites got the key office, the presidency, and the Sunnis the premiership. The other minorities got minor and provincial satisfaction, but they were not then regarded as strong enough to make their desires felt in the positions that counted. So the situation remained "frozen," particularly under strong Maronite presidents, until nearly the end of the 1960's, when the introduction of the Palestinians as a new community tilted the Lebanese political balance.

But while the political arrangements remained unchanged in the 1950's and 1960's the social conditions that had given rise to the national pact changed. A massive migration into Beirut brought the partly isolated communities into closer contact; each poor community acquired new wealth, aspirations, and self-esteem. They wanted "in." The Druze especially, led by the charismatic Kamal Junblatt, found the old division of benefits unfair and agitated for a larger share. But at this point the traditional Lebanese bargaining process broke down. The army intervened, and, in the name of efficiency, two authoritarian Maronite presidents effectively circumvented the political process which had assured civic tranquillity. Meanwhile, Beirut exploded with new wealth so that the divide between the new rich and the old poor widened. These trends built up tensions which were no longer being resolved.

Then, as a result of wars, waves of Palestinian refugees came into Lebanon. The last and most important influx followed the "Black September" of 1970, when the Jordanian government crushed an attempt by the Palestinians to take over its government. At that time, large numbers of politically active Palestinians entered Lebanon, thereafter constituting, in effect, another of its minority communities. Ultimately, they amounted to more than 15 percent of the Lebanese population. The Palestinians, invited to participate in Lebanese politics by the political "outs" (each group of whom wanted to claim them as *its* ally), took advantage of the opportunity to establish what became virtually a state within the Lebanese state. And within that state—since their ultimate objective was, as they proclaimed, the "return" to the homeland they had lost—the Palestinians built their own military force.

Lebanon offered them a haven in two crucial senses. On the most obvious level, being excluded from Israel, unable to operate in the occupied territories, and having failed in their attempt to make Jordan their base, they found Lebanon nearly vital to their movement. They believed it was their last redoubt. The leadership of their national organization, the Palestine Liberation Organization (PLO), found Lebanon crucial in another sense as well. They had learned that without a territorial base, the PLO could exist only in the fissures dividing the Arab states. Merely to stay politically alive, the PLO leader, Yasir Arafat, had to spend most of his time successively courting the Arab leaders and playing them against one another. That was bad enough, but worse was the fact that several of the Arab states, particularly Syria, Iraq, and Libya, were playing the same game. Each found one faction of the Palestinians more to its liking than the overall organization, so Arafat had also to jockey for prestige and influence among mutually hostile Palestinian splinter groups. For him, Lebanon offered the closest approximation possible in the circumstances to a unified political base.

Syria watched the trends in Lebanon with cold and calculating eyes. Syria had always felt that Lebanon had been "artificially" split away by the French and that it *really* remained a special part of Syria; no matter what treaties or constitutions might say, Lebanese ports were the natural outlet to the sea for the Syrian hinterland. More important, the Syrians were sensitive to the fact that Lebanon had been the "beachhead" on which the French had established their imperial base and the route of invasion to the interior. Syria was determined that Lebanon should never again be a source of mortal danger to it. Even if we leave aside these strategic considerations, the Lebanese economy was nearly vital to Syria. These facts had been recognized in the instruments that established Lebanese independence at the end of World War II. Syria's "rights" in Lebanon naturally have remained among its most sensitive national policy considerations.

Consequently, Syria was never far from deep involvement in Lebanese affairs. By 1976, according to the Syrians, the Palestinians were getting so strong that Lebanon was in danger of disintegrating, an event that would probably invite an Israeli invasion. For this reason, when requested to do so by the Maronite president, the Syrian army marched in. What was already a tense and dangerous situation rapidly turned into a devastating civil war.

In the fighting, the regular Lebanese army, itself as much a mosaic of ethnic and religious communities as the state it represented, speedily disintegrated. In place of the national—or, more accurately, multinational—Lebanese state army, each community began to train and arm its own militia. The most active and powerful Lebanese group was the Maronite Kataib, a distant echo of the kind of authoritarian, religious-military organization inspired by Georges Sorel and known in the 1920's and 1930's in Europe as the Falange (or Phalange). To oppose the Kataib, the smaller and less wealthy Druze community and other groups armed themselves. Each did what it could to ensure its own autonomy and security.

The Palestinians, of course, were involved, but since they viewed

Lebanon primarily as a way station in their long-range plan to "return" to Palestine, they used their growing military power, when they could, to attack Israeli targets.

The Syrians were not emotionally opposed to the Palestinians' hatred of Israel. They, too, feared and hated and mistrusted the Israelis, but they tempered their anger with a more detached view of strategy. They realized that their army was no match for the high-tech Israeli forces, which, with American help, seemed to be able always to short circuit or circumvent their attempts to apply their more raw power. So when they made a deal to stop the fighting on the Golan Heights, the Syrians scrupulously adhered to it. They avoided provocations at all points. For an entire decade the Syrian leader, Hafez al-Assad, sought repeatedly for a modus vivendi with Israel based on UN Resolutions 242 and 338. He chose to husband Syria's resources and where possible to augment them. Even when Israel announced on December 14, 1981, that it was annexing the Golan Heights (an action the United Nations denounced as illegal and against which the United States protested bilaterally), the Syrians denounced the move but in practice did nothing about it.

Among Syria's potential resources were, of course, the Palestinians. But to be of value for the Syrians, the Palestinians had to be brought under discipline. The attempt by Yasir Arafat to carve out an independent position for the PLO was thus anathema to Damascus. In the view of the Syrian leadership and particularly of Hafez al-Assad, the Palestinian leader was a "loose cannon" who had the ability to start a conflict with Israel but not the ability to win it. That calculation and a variety of personal issues made the two men into bitter enemies. It caused the Syrians at critical points to withhold support to the PLO even when—indeed, especially when—such help appeared to be a matter of life and death. Assad nearly always sided with the PLO's enemies.

Assad's calculation was grounded in reality. As a matter of both emotion and policy, the Israelis hit back at each attack or threat posed by the Palestinians. They even adopted a policy they termed "prospective retaliation," or "preemptive reprisals." In the Israeli retaliations, the Biblical injunction of "an eye for an eye" was inflated to more like "a hundred eyes for an eye." Often it was bystanders who got hurt. Given Lebanese geography, those who most frequently paid the price of Israeli vengeance were the Shia Muslim villagers along the Lebanese-Israeli frontier. For a long time, the Shiis were merely victims, and large numbers of them fled from the south northward; but during the long years of fighting, they were energized by a remarkable religious leader, Imam Musa al-Sadr. Drawing on their own traditions as an "outsider" community, they quickly developed the skills of violence. Ultimately, they coalesced into a potent military force known as *Amal* (Arabic for "hope").

Meanwhile, the Israelis, justly renowned for their intelligence activities, identified an opportunity to create a sort of pseudo-community to police southern Lebanon. Having no suitable local group, they found their instrument in a disaffected Lebanaese army officer, Major Saad Haddad, who, with their money, arms, and training, carved out a fiefdom along the Israeli frontier.

The Lebanese government, watching the whole country slide into chaos, judged that the point of greatest danger was in the south, where the Palestinians were provoking the Israelis by their attacks across the frontier. In an attempt to seal off that point of danger, what was left of the Lebanese army, then just a few thousand men, was moved south. The Palestinians were clearly not favorably disposed to having their freedom of action against Israel curtailed, but they did not oppose the redeployment of the Lebanese army. The main opponent was Major Haddad, who apparently feared court-martial if the Lebanese government forces managed to establish themselves in the south. His attacks halted them.

It would be pointless, and probably impossible, to recount all of the "incidents" that accumulated into the misery of Lebanon during these months. But one is important because it triggered the next escalation of fighting: in March 1978, a Palestinian guerrilla group carried out a raid on northern Israel in which a number of Israelis were killed. On March 15, 1978, the Israeli army invaded southern Lebanon. Important enough in itself, the invasion threatened the whole strategy of the Carter administration for the Middle East, coming as it did in the midst of the Camp David peace negotiations among Israel, Egypt, and the United States. So America took the issue of Lebanon to the United Nations and managed in just four days to get the United Nations to create yet another multinational peace-keeping force. This one, known as UNIFIL, was given the mission to oversee the Israeli withdrawal and to help restore Lebanese government control over the disputed area.

Nearly everyone, perhaps naturally, was cynical about the role and potential of UNIFIL. The Israelis even refused to allow it to control areas along the old international frontier, entrusting these instead to the Israeli-trained, -equipped, and -controlled Lebanese force under Major Haddad. UNIFIL itself worked, perhaps had to work, under a narrow interpretation of its role. It was not even armed for combat, and was ordered to use its light weapons only in self-defense. Charged with interdicting guerrilla attacks, it operated essentially "blind," without the elaborate (and expensive) communications intelligence apparatus that is the principal weapon against guerrillas. When it happened to catch armed infiltrators, it disarmed them, returned them to the north, and released them, since there was no constituted authority to which it could resort. Innocuous as this role certainly was, it was still not safe. UNIFIL was frequently attacked, presumably with Israeli approval, by the forces of Major Haddad. For their part, the Palestinians viewed UNIFIL as a sometimes useful screen against Israeli attack, but also as an unwelcome restraint on their actions. So, from the start, UNIFIL was essentially emasculated.

Syria, which by then occupied most of Lebanon, also found the situation in which it had deployed its troops uncomfortable and dangerous. It had intervened to help the Christian government, but it found that government, and the Maronite community as a whole, to be fickle friends. The Lebanese government maintained close and friendly relations, often quite openly, with the Israelis, with whom Syria was legally at war. And Syrian forces, necessarily scattered in small garrisons all over Lebanon, had ceased to be an "army." Thus, they could no longer carry out their primary function, namely to stop an Israeli attack on Syria.

The likelihood of an Israeli attack seemed to the Syrians very real, since Syria (like virtually all of the Arab states) interpreted the Camp David Accords as an American-Israeli ploy to remove from the Arab camp the largest Arab army, the Egyptian, and thus to leave Syria, the most militant of the "front-line" powers, open to preemptive attack. So in 1980 the Syrian government pulled back into the areas adjacent to Syria.

The Lebanese government used the apparent opportunity created by the Syrian withdrawal to attempt to reassert its sovereignty in the formerly occupied areas. Almost everywhere it met with resistance from the militias of the several communities. Still believing that the south was the area of greatest danger, the government was particularly eager to introduce its remaining army units into the south. It sought American help in dealing with the Israelis to make this possible. The Americans were assured that the Israeli army had sanctioned the move. But on the way to the agreed-upon positions, the Lebanese troops were attacked by Major Haddad's force with the approval of the Israeli army. Ironically, the Lebanese forces were able to remain in the south only under the UNIFIL umbrella.

Meanwhile, the Soviet Union had been essentially excluded from participation in Middle Eastern affairs. In the Nixon and Ford administrations, Secretary of State Kissinger had made every effort to prevent the Russians from playing even a positive role in the area. The Russians resented the American policy, both because they insisted on being treated as a great power and because they judged the Middle East to be an area of great strategic importance for their own interests. So they waited for an opportunity to reassert their influence. The opportunity came in the aftermath of the Camp David Accords. For the same reason that made them regroup their army, namely their fear of Israel, the Syrians welcomed Soviet offers of assistance. These were codified in September 1980 in a military treaty.

Meanwhile, with Israeli encouragement, the Maronite Kataib militia began undermining the Syrian position in the Biqa valley. Although they were happy to have the Syrians help them against the PLO, the Kataib wanted the Syrians out of Lebanon. Consequently, wherever they did not need the Syrians, they did what they could to make life difficult for them. In April 1981, the Syrians besieged the town of Zahle. Alarmed, the Kataib requested and got Israeli air support. Israeli aircraft shot down two Syrian air force helicopters. For a time Israel and Syria appeared to be on the brink of major hostilities. The crisis passed, however, as the Syrians recognized that they could not take on Israel alone. Nothing was resolved, but a sort of de facto peace took effect during most of the remainder of 1981.

This, in summary, was the context in which General Sharon laid out his vision of long-range Israeli strategy.

What Israel must do, Sharon argued, was to begin a multiphase program leading to great-power status. In round one, Israel would occupy the areas of southern Lebanon from which raids and rocket attacks had been launched against Israel. While there, it should aim to completely destroy the Palestine Liberation Organization. By this, he meant not only military destruction; but also, as the former deputy mayor of Jerusalem, Meron Benvenisti, wrote in the *New York Review of Books* (October 13, 1983): "The true objective of the war . . . was the destruction of the powerful political and intellectual center of Palestinian nationalism that had developed over the years in Beirut." In this way, the invasion would decapitate and demoralize the incipient resistance movement still living under Israeli occupation in Gaza and on the West Bank. Next the Israelis should install a Kataib-dominated Maronite government in Beirut, in return for which that government would sign a peace treaty with Israel. Next it should "encourage" the remaining Palestinians on the West Bank to abandon their homes and migrate into Jordan. Not only symbolically but also actually, this would make Jordan into "Palestine." No longer would there be a homeland to which the Arab Palestinians could aspire to return. As a result of such a large-scale move, of course, Jordan would be convulsed, since the Jordanian monarchy could hardly accept its demise passively. The ensuing chaos would, in turn, justify Israeli intervention to install a government that would likewise make peace with Israel. Syria would be isolated as the only remaining "front-line" state. And working through Jordan, Israel would become the neighbor of Saudi Arabia, which, faced with a powerful, modern state, would react with its traditional policy of accommodation. At the end of the road, Israel would be recognized as the predominant Afro-Asian power.*

The "doctrine" was certainly audacious, and while in office Sharon moved to implement the first step, the invasion of Lebanon. This took place on June 6, 1982, six months after his speech. Ironically, unlike the frequent Israeli raids, it came with no immediate provocation: in the previous year only one mortar attack on northern Israel from Lebanon had been reported, and the Syrian-Israeli frontier was absolutely quiet. Clearly, this particular invasion was not a riposte but the first step in Sharon's long-term strategy. Indeed, a senior Israeli official told a reporter for the London *Sunday Times* that Israel had been disappointed at the lack of PLO response to an Israeli air strike, because "we wanted the excuse to move in in a big way."† Some observers have concluded that the

---

* The full text was published as a press bulletin in Jerusalem, December 15, 1981. It is summarized in Robert G. Neumann, "Assad and the Future of the Middle East," *Foreign Affairs,* 62 (1983): 237ff. Also see Ze'ev Schiff, "Lebanon: Motivations and Interests in Israel's Policy," *Middle East Journal,* 38 (1984): 220ff.

† May 2, 1982, quoted in Jim Muir, "Lebanon: Arena of Conflict, Crucible of Peace," *Middle East Journal,* 38 (1984): 210–211. The Israeli official observed that "its overriding motivation had far more to do with the West Bank than it did with Lebanon or any strictly military PLO threat." As we shall see, the Syrians, Israelis, and Kataib all shared antipathy to the PLO; conversely each was willing to tolerate, and some even to work with, the more violent and extreme groups among the Palestinians because these posed no political threat. Thus, ironically, *both* the Abu Nidal faction and the "Jewish Armed Resistance" claimed to have murdered the PLO deputy director in Paris, on July 23, 1982.

timing resulted from Israeli fears that the United States was on the brink of a peace initiative which might have called into question Israel's ability to remain in the occupied territories. President Reagan said as much in his September 1 broadcast on his peace initiative. Having just secured the return of Sinai at the end of April, Secretary of State Alexander Haig had announced plans for a new American initiative and had dispatched Ambassador Philip Habib to the area. Had significant efforts then been made by the United States and accepted by the PLO, it would have been difficult for the Begin government to sustain its determined policy of holding onto the territories.

And this time the invasion was massive. In the first phase, the Israelis overran UNIFIL. Completely outgunned, the UN troops did not resist. But in New York, the Security Council immediately and unanimously passed a resolution demanding Israeli withdrawal and requesting the parties to observe the existing cease-fire. Ignoring the UN, the Israeli army then surged northward toward Beirut and arrived to within twenty-five kilometers of the capital by June 8. Their prime target was the PLO, but they were quickly engaged in combat also with the Syrians. In the next few days, the Israeli air force claimed to have shot down about fifty Syrian air force planes and wiped out the Syrian air defense system in Lebanon. Heavy fighting between the Syrians and the Israelis engulfed the area around Beirut and in the Biqa valley.

The U.S. government was duly alarmed at the prospect of Israel's occupying Beirut and, of course, at the probability that the war would become general throughout the Middle East. Even more, it worried that the Syrian-Soviet military treaty would be invoked. In direct démarches to Israel, it demanded an Israeli withdrawal but vetoed a UN resolution condemning the Israeli attack. In Europe, leaders of the European Economic Community "vigorously condemned" the Israeli invasion.

On June 11, the Israelis and Syrians agreed to the first of several cease-fires, but General Sharon excluded the PLO from this agreement. He was determined, as he had said in his speech, to completely destroy the PLO. Fighting on the ground and in the air continued and, indeed, became more bitter and destructive with each passing day.

Israeli actions then began to draw widespread criticism. The United States charged that Israel had illegally used American-supplied cluster bombs in the attack on civilian targets. Israel later admitted the charge; but upon receiving an Israeli promise not to enter Beirut (a promise General Sharon later denied that Israel had made), the United States rejected a request by the PLO for direct talks. At the UN, the General Assembly voted 127 to 2 (the two were the United States and Israel) calling for an immediate Israeli withdrawal and urged the Security Council to consider sanctions against Israel. The United States vetoed the Security Council resolution. And on July 2, some 50,000 to 70,000 Israeli citizens marched through Tel Aviv to protest the invasion. In an even more surprising move, an Israeli army colonel commanding a front-line regiment resigned his commission rather than participate in the attack on Beirut. Major leaders of the world Jewish organizations called for Israeli withdrawal and, with the approval of Yasir Arafat, urged Israel and the PLO to recognize each other. But on July 17, Israeli Prime Minister Menahem Begin took part in a massive rally, estimated at 200,000, in support of the invasion. Clearly, the Israeli government was unmoved by the opposition. In the current phrase, it was creating "facts" which, more than demonstrations, appeals, or resolutions, would determine the future course.

For the Israelis, Beirut proved no easy prize. The besieged Palestinians held out there for more than two months, despite merciless and often indiscriminate air and artillery bombardment. Having blockaded the city, the Israelis cut off electricity and even water. Tens of thousands of people were made homeless, were wounded, or were killed. Eventually, forced to withdraw and given American pledges for their own safety and that of the exposed inhabitants of the pitiful refugee camps, the Palestinian soldiers went out bearing their arms, many even proud that they had achieved a sort of political victory in military defeat. But the cost to the PLO was immense.*

As General Sharon had planned, the Israeli invasion destroyed the PLO's military potential: PLO soldiers were forced to leave Lebanon and were scattered in small contingents throughout the Arab countries. It also drove a new and even more dangerous wedge between the factions represented in the PLO. A major Israeli target was the "memory bank" created by the PLO to house what amounted to the national archives of the Palestinians. It was seized and shipped off to Israel. The cost to the civilians cannot, of course, be measured by any realistic calculation. The United Nations reported that at least 47,000 Palestinians lost their homes; how many Lebanese endured similar suffering is beyond reckon-

---

* See Eric Rouleau, "The Future of the PLO," *Foreign Affairs*, 62 (1983): 138ff.

ing. How many were killed or crippled will probably never be known.

When the Palestinians finally agreed to withdraw from Beirut, the United States proposed the creation of a new United Nations force to garrison the city. Israel refused, but accepted the second American proposal, on July 6, which was to create a multinational force composed of Americans, Frenchmen, and Italians to monitor the PLO withdrawal. The United States thus found itself again on the ground in Lebanon.

In these circumstances, President Reagan suspended delivery of advanced jet fighters to Israel until it withdrew from Lebanon, and former presidents Carter and Ford both denounced Israel's settlement policy. On the ground, in Lebanon, fighting lost all coherence as the various Lebanese factions battled one another, the Israelis, the Syrians, groups of newly introduced "Revolutionary Guards" from Iran, and, from time to time, the soldiers of the multinational force. As many as six factions were by then at war with one another.

On September 1, 1982, President Reagan announced his plan for Middle Eastern peace on American television. The plan was, in essence, simple: it called for the creation of a joint Palestinian-Jordanian state which would include the West Bank and Gaza. The president also sent a message to Prime Minister Begin that the United States would no longer support Israel's settlement policy. Begin reacted angrily both by denouncing the Reagan plan and by announcing the formation of new settlements. In the coming months, the Israeli government mounted an extensive press and advertising campaign to speed up and enlarge the settlements.* On the Arab side, despite Yasir Arafat's attempt to find elements in the Reagan plan he could support (an attempt which was to lead some PLO military officers to rebel against him), King Husain's efforts to find a common means of action with the PLO, and initial favorable response among the more conservative Arab governments, the plan was likewise rejected by the PLO. King Husain finally abandoned his efforts on April 10, 1983.

On September 9, 1982, Israel launched a large-scale attack on Syrian antiaircraft defenses in Lebanon.

With perhaps unintended irony, Jerusalem Radio reported a "secret" meeting between the Maronite Kataib leader, Bashir Gamael, who had been elected president of Lebanon on August 23,

* See Larry L. Fabian, "The Middle East: War Dangers and Receding Peace Prospects," *Foreign Affairs*, 62 (1983)): 632ff.

and Israeli prime minister Begin in northern Israel. A few days later, Bashir Gamayel was assassinated. On September 21, Bashir's brother Amin was elected to take his place as president.

The Israelis then entered Beirut in an uneasy coexistence with the multinational force. Despite unanimous Security Council condemnation, the Israelis took complete control of Beirut on September 16. Fighting continued in other parts of the country. The bitter events of the following weeks, bad as they were, suggest that the situation might have become much worse than it did. The American government quickly had second thoughts about the open-ended possibilities of its new commitment, and began to withdraw its Marines within two weeks.

The principal task of the multinational force had been to oversee the withdrawal of the main elements of the Palestine Liberation Organization from Beirut. No sooner was this accomplished and no sooner were the Israelis in control of Beirut than one of the worst of many vicious incidents occurred: the massacre on September 16–18 of hundreds of unarmed women and children (328 bodies were identified, and 991 people were still reported missing a month later) at the two Palestinian refugee camps of Sabra and Shatila just outside Beirut. These massacres were carried out by Kataib militiamen, but they and the camps they attacked were under Israeli military control and General Sharon admitted assisting the Kataib militiamen with flares to light up the camp at night.* The massacres so shocked the United States that it reintroduced its Marines into Lebanon; similarly, France and Italy extended the term and increased the number of their troops in the multinational force. In Tel Aviv, on September 25, an estimated 350,000 people protested the government's actions in Lebanon; the Israeli governor of the occupied West Bank, Menahem Milsen, resigned in protest; and 1,000 Israeli reservists formally requested that they not be assigned to Lebanon.

In the wearisome months that followed, U.S. Marines frequently clashed with Israeli forces, the Israelis threatened Syria with a preemptive attack, and the Soviet ambassador to Lebanon warned that the Soviet Union would intervene if Israel attacked Syria. In

* The massacres were investigated by a commission headed by Supreme Court Justice Yitzhak Kahan, whose report, published on February 8, 1983 (noted in the bibliography), recommended that three Israeli generals (including the chief of staff) be relieved of their command and that Defense Minister Sharon be removed from office. It also criticized the prime minister and foreign minister. Sharon refused to resign but was voted out by the cabinet.

December, the USSR also began a massive resupply of air defense equipment, so as to more than replace that destroyed by the Israelis, and stationed some 8,000 Soviet troops and technicians in the area to operate the equipment. Israeli troops fired on Arab protesters; Israeli settlers attacked Palestinians in the occupied West Bank; terrorists attacked Jewish targets in Europe; hundreds of people were shot, kidnapped, or beaten, and thousands were arrested and held without bail or even without charges in detention camps; and, in that explosive atmosphere and despite American urgings not to do so, Israel announced plans to establish nearly a hundred additional Jewish settlements in the occupied territories. Even at this distance, rereading the daily press accounts is a numbing emotional experience. There is little profit in following them in detail.

The year 1983 saw no prospect of the return to peace. Incident followed incident with dreary regularity. Many of these led to large-scale military confrontations. Particularly grim were fights in the Shuf mountains above Beirut between the Druze and Christian militias. Paradoxically, this fighting caused the U.S. government, in August 1983, to request that Israel *delay* its planned withdrawal. It also caused the American government to send 2,000 Marines into the Beirut area. When the Druze overcame the Christian forces and the Lebanese army, the U.S. Navy opened fire with sixteen-inch cannons on the little Druze village of Suq al-Garb, above Beirut. Then, on September 17–18, naval artillery fired on targets in Syrian-held areas; Syria threatened to fire back. France, America's main partner in the "peace-seeking" venture in Lebanon, was shocked into criticizing the U.S. action—a highly unusual move. Then, on the twenty-third of October, 241 U.S. Marines were killed in a suicide attack on their barracks in Beirut, and 58 soldiers were killed in a bomb attack on the French headquarters.

A few days later, the various Lebanese factions met in Geneva to try to work out a national reconciliation. The talks adjourned after two weeks, without progress. It was clear that the fears and hatreds, perhaps long latent, stirred by the invasion and the bitter fighting that followed it were by then too deep for compromise. And, as though these animosities were not enough, the Palestinians loyal to the PLO were attacked by those under the control of the Syrians, and American aircraft attacked Syrian positions. It appeared to some observers that the United States had adopted the tactics of Israel without the keen intelligence on Lebanese politics that usually guided these tactics.

355

By the beginning of 1984, the United States was taken to be a party to the conflict, and its troops and civilians were targets for attack and reprisal. On January 18, assassins gunned down Malcolm Kerr, a well-known scholar on the Arab world and the son of widely appreciated American medical missionaries. Kerr was then president of the American University of Beirut, which for a century had been the very symbol of American philanthropy in the Levant. His murder was clearly meant to signal that no American would be safe in Lebanon.

On February 7, President Reagan ordered the U.S. Marines to reboard their ships off the coast, and the other peace-keeping forces began their withdrawal. In what appeared an outburst of anger rather than an attempt to achieve anything in the conflict, the USS New Jersey fired 250 one-ton shells from its sixteen-inch cannons into positions held by the pro-Syrian Muslim militia near Beirut. By February 26, all American military personnel were out of Lebanon. And finally, on March 30, 1984, the Sixth Fleet sailed away.

Israel retained a strong intelligence and political liaison group in the Beirut area and, of course, occupied the south; but with the departure of the United States, and the removal of the most obvious part of the Israeli forces by June 6, 1985, only Syria remained much in evidence as an occupying power. What, one may ask, had been the core of the policy of each and the result of its implementation?

Surprisingly, the central contention of each power started out more or less the same: that Lebanon was essentially a *Maronite* state. The Syrians were first on the ground. They came into Lebanon initially to support the Maronites. With their help, they thought, the Maronites could recapture the unity and structure they had imposed on Lebanon in the late 1950's and 1960's. The Syrians seemed to want to promote order and stability so as to avoid giving a pretext to the Israelis or others to move in. They certainly understood the social or religious (the so-called confessional) complexity of Lebanon—Assad himself is a member of a Syrian minority community—but looked upon the Lebanese minorities as problems to be dealt with rather than as political forces to be incorporated. Although they opportunistically shifted their local alliances, the Syrians failed to achieve a firm basis for their policy, much less a consensus among the warring parties. Finally, their Maronite allies, who had originally invited their intervention, got tired of Syrian high-handedness and in due course were willing to swap their Syrian patrons for Israeli patrons.

The United States had no comparable clarity of objectives. Whereas the Syrians sought to dominate or at least protect from the Israelis their access to the Levant coast and the Israelis sought to consolidate their northern frontier and to achieve another break in the Arab front, American objectives were both less urgent and more diffuse. As will be discussed more fully in Chapter 27, they were essentially anti-Soviet rather than Middle Eastern. As he said in his statement of October 24, 1983, President Reagan regarded Syria as the Soviet "surrogate" in Lebanon. The Lebanese civil war was seen as an opportunity for Soviet involvement in the area. So, despite the depth of American experience in the Levant, the senior American leaders tended to overlook or neglect the issues, fears, ambitions that motivated the Syrians, Lebanese, and Israelis.

Israel's primary aim was the destruction of the PLO; all other issues were, at least initially, subordinated to that one. The Israelis were certainly well aware of the complexity of the Lebanese confessional or social mix, but chose to act as though it would be possible to impose, with its military force, a Maronite image or at least Maronite hegemony on the whole. Had that been accomplished, Israel would have had a price to exact: a formal Lebanese peace treaty on the model of the Camp David Accords. Israel began the military adventure, sure, at least, of its mutually beneficial relationship with the Maronites. At the end of the war, this relationship was badly frayed. Worse from the Israeli perspective, the Shiis, who at the start of the campaign hardly counted as a militant group and whom the Israelis had patronized as a counterpoise to the Palestinians, became the most determined of Israel's enemies. Israel later felt compelled to intervene time after time against them, and threatened them with a scorched-earth policy in 1985. And finally, as Israel withdrew in 1985, it took along thousands of young Lebanese, whom it claimed were not prisoners of war and so not protected by the Fourth Geneva Convention of 1949. Both the International Red Cross and the U.S. government claimed that as many as 1,100 of these young men were being held in Israeli detention camps in April 1985. Subsequent events make it clear that the men returned home with an abiding hatred of Israel.

Each of the three powers had contributed not only to the breakdown of what remained of national institutions—in fairness it can be said that little remained by the time the United States came on the scene—but also to the loss of any sense that there was a nation. Belief in the possibility of social affinity, despite the lack of consanguinity or religious accord, was the major casualty of their interventions: the minority communities, discovering that they were

excluded from what the intervening powers and their chosen instrument, the Maronites, meant by "Lebanese," fell back on surer,
simpler, more immediate forms of association. In this atmosphere,
there could be no respect for law, no belief in order.

So fighting raged among the various factions. The Muslims
fought the Maronites around Beirut, and the Druze fought them
in the mountains. The Druze produced evidence of another Kataib
massacre, this time of Druze in the Shuf mountains. Finally, judging that exhaustion had set in, President Gamayel convened another "national reconciliation" conference in Geneva on March 12
with the major Lebanese factions, which by then numbered eight.
The groups initially agreed to a cease-fire, but parted without
agreement on the fundamental issue of how to put Lebanon back
together again.

Even the physical damage to the country, which certainly ran to
the tens of billions of dollars, was not the crucial problem; nor,
arguably, was the sense of outrage—the "blood," as the Arabs
say—between the contending factions, although in the fighting
and manipulation, events had taken place that surely would be
spoken of for generations. A sort of rough and bloody balance was
achieved among the various groups, since no one had sufficient
power to establish hegemony over the rest, and, with the events of
the previous years behind them, no two appeared willing to work
together. Indeed, even the existing ethnic-religious factions often
spawned splinter groups, as those with special interests or hates
carried out their own vendettas. Not surprisingly in the circumstances, terrorist attacks and, above all, kidnappings became the
hallmark of subsequent years.

If it is conceivable that there could be something even worse, it
was the brutalization of a whole generation of young people. Children who in other circumstances would have argued over football
teams and carried in their arms nothing more lethal than a soccer
ball were growing up with Kalashnikov machine guns. Even the
most sympathetic observers could hardly imagine how the virus of
hate, having reached pandemic proportions, could be extirpated.

While these dismal events were unfolding in Lebanon, there
were continual outbreaks of violence in the occupied territories,
the West Bank, and Gaza. Since the Israeli occupation of these
areas in 1967, the gulf that separated Jews and Arabs had widened
and deepened. The gulf was not just a matter of power (although
the Israeli Jews were armed and the Palestinian Arabs were not),

or a matter of access to schools, medical care, courts, and other benefits of a modern state (although here, too, conditions were radically different for the two communities); it consisted also in the fact that their perceptions of each other and their appreciation of each other's ultimate objectives rendered them utterly alien. To understand the so-called *Intifada* (Arabic: "insurgency" or "uprising"), we will have to appreciate how wide this distance had become and look at the events leading up to the present situation.

In the 1967 war, Israeli forces occupied the Gaza strip (which had been garrisoned by Egypt), the West Bank of the Jordan River, and the Golan Heights (which was a part of Syria). Under generally accepted principles of international law, these territories could be administered by the victorious power but were entitled to keep their juridical status. Various attempts had been made since the Napoleonic wars in Europe to devise safeguards for civilian populations, and these had been codified in conventions (among others, the Hague Conventions of 1899 and 1907 and the Geneva Conventions of 1949), treaties, and decisions by the World Court. Although there were, obviously, many violations, the agreements were upheld at least in principle by most powers.

Israel immediately proclaimed that the situation it confronted was special because of its historical and religious claims to "the Land of Israel." So, in the immediate aftermath of the war, it dismantled the barriers between East and West Jerusalem and proclaimed that East Jerusalem was an integral part of Israel.

The government, then under the control of the Labor Party, also began a program of planting quasi-military colonies in strategic locations in the occupied territories, particularly on the West Bank. The beginning point was preoccupation with security: installations were established in areas where the Israelis felt danger lay. And in the kibbutz tradition, these installations were not just garrisons but were more or less self-supporting, usually agricultural colonies. To be effective, the colonies had to be sited adjacent to inhabited areas; and so, wherever such a measure was useful or necessary, land was confiscated from the local residents.

When criticized for its land requisitions, the Israeli government usually replied that the measures were "interim" and could be reconsidered when peace was achieved.

But in fact, they were not merely ad hoc decisions. The issue of land in Palestine was perhaps the oldest, most disputed, and most sensitive throughout the development of the Israeli state. Indeed, it long predates the formation of that state.

As we saw in Chapters 8 and 12, the early Zionists at the end of World War I claimed substantially more territory in Palestine than Jews then occupied. Their claims were set forth and evaluated in a number of ways: historical perspectives, religious imperatives, the need for stability, the strategy of the British Empire, its desire for a viable ally in the eastern Mediterranean, and so forth. When the British concluded that hostilities between Jews and Arabs were too expensive to be contained, they decided to do what had been done often at the end of World War I: to divide territory and populations, so as to reduce friction. In various studies, attempts were made to more or less relate territory to population, while making the incipient Jewish state large enough to survive. As Jewish migration from Europe increased, each proposal became more favorable to the Zionists; but still, in the Royal Commission's proposal of 1936 (see map on page 169), the British could not on any grounds justify making Israel very large. Unable to find an answer, the British kept redrawing maps. Meanwhile, the Zionists decided not to wait and fought what amounted to a guerrilla and terrorist war with the British from 1944 to 1947. Under great financial and other pressures, the British then turned over to the United Nations their failed mandate. The United Nations in turn studied the problem and came up with a partition resolution, which was adopted in 1947 and which established the state within the frontiers shown in the map on page 181.

Neither the Arabs nor the Zionists liked any of the proposals. The Zionists were prepared to accept the final proposal as an interim solution, but the surrounding Arab states, acting ostensibly on behalf of the Palestinians, tried to alter it by military force. Their efforts failed, and in the war of 1948–1949 Israel was able to conquer considerably more territory than it had been awarded. The new frontiers, indicated in the map on page 224, were recognized by the parties in peace treaties. Then in the 1967 Arab-Israeli war, Israel occupied Gaza and the West Bank, which was then inhabited solely by Arabs. The West Bank area that was occupied is shown in the map on page 223.

For years, the United States and other governments worked under the assumption that, ultimately, the occupied territories would become the residence, the homeland, and/or the state for the inhabitants, and perhaps in some fashion for the refugees then living "temporarily" in the surrounding areas, as shown in the map on page 234. However defined, this supposition has been the center point of each successive peace plan.

From the outset, the logic of the "moderates" with respect to the Palestine issue was summed up in the famous statement of the Royal Commission in 1936: "Half a loaf is better than no bread." Thus the English justified their decision that Palestine be divided between the two groups. But this logic was never accepted by either of the two parties, although the Arabs and the Zionists spoke often of compromise and occasionally even of cooperation.

When the British first publicized their desire to partition Palestine, the most outspoken opponent was the early Zionist activist Vladimir Jabotinsky, who was the spiritual father of the Likud Party of today and of the Irgun and Stern Gang of the 1940's. "A corner of Palestine, a 'canton'—how can we promise to be satisfied with it?" he asked rhetorically. "We cannot. We never can. Should we swear to you we would be satisfied, it would be a lie."

At the time, it was fashionable to dismiss the "revisionist" Jabotinsky as a fanatic, and his views were publicly disavowed by mainline Zionists. But in private, the logic of what he said was not only admitted but espoused. No more establishment figure than Ben Gurion existed. He told the Jewish Agency Executive in June 1938 that he favored the idea of partition because "after we constitute a large force following the establishment of the state, we will cancel the partition of the country and we will expand throughout the Land of Israel." It is true that at an earlier stage of his political career, just after World War I, Ben Gurion had said, "We do not intend to push the Arabs aside, to take their land, or to disinherit them"; but he changed his private position when he wrote that "we must expel the Arabs and take their places" (private letter, 1937). Then, in 1948, when the state was being formed, Ben Gurion privately told one of his assistants, "The Arabs of the land of Israel have only one function left to them, to run away."*

The reasons for private thoughts about a greater Israel were, in part, demographic: it is not possible to have a Jewish state with more or less representative institutions if a large and rapidly growing part of the population is Arab. Ben Gurion's policies, Arab panic, and the vainglory of the surrounding Arab states all combined to make the Israel of 1949 viable. But a new situation was created by the conquests of the 1967 war. Once again, as in 1936, there were just too many Arabs for the state to remain both Jewish and representative.

* Benny Morris: *The Birth of the Palestine Refugee Problem, 1947–1949* (Cambridge, 1987), pp. 25ff. The British and Israeli documents on which Morris's work is based were not available until recently.

Slightly more emotional than land ownership, and certainly a more concentrated issue, is the question of holy sites. In the generally secular contemporary West, religious fervor is often remote from our political calculations, but it has never been far from those of the inhabitants of the "Holy Land." And because the three monotheistic religions—Judaism, Christianity, and Islam—share veneration for prophets, saints, and other men of religion, the places associated with those men are also jointly venerated. The focal point is of course Jerusalem, where Temple Mount for the Jews becomes Haram ash-Sharif for the Muslims. The Jewish Wailing Wall and the Muslim al-Aqsa mosque are cheek-by-jowl in a small neighborhood containing many shrines, hospices, churches, and other places maintained and venerated by Christians. Long before Israel existed, officials in the British mandate government suffered with and tried to adjudicate among religious zealots—with striking lack not only of success but even of comprehension. And those were relatively calm times.

Today, of course, the problem is much worse. Religious fundamentalists and religious fervor are on the rise among both Jews and Muslims. Both feel embattled and both focus their anxieties, hopes, and fears on physical symbols. These often tiny pieces of real estate thus become symbolic and occasionally actual battlegrounds.

Frequently the struggle is muted, even bureaucratic. Much Christian and some Muslim resentment has been focused on Israeli "archaeological" removals in the Old City of Jerusalem and the construction of new buildings. Some anger has also been directed at Jewish attempts to rent or otherwise take over little-used or marginal buildings. But the primary issues are brought to a point on the question of the major shrines of the Jews and Muslims, located on the little hill overlooking Jerusalem (Temple Mount or the Haram ash-Sharif)—namely, the Dome of the Rock, the al-Aqsa mosque, and the Wailing Wall.

When Israel took over Jerusalem after the 1967 war, it banned Jewish worshipers from entering the Muslim holy area, which was administered by a committee of Muslim religious leaders. For some years, this arrangement appeared to work. But with the rise of Jewish religious zeal in Jerusalem, it began to break down about a decade ago. It seemed intolerable to some Jews that an Islamic mosque should be—tragically, as it turned out—just a "stone's throw away" from the Wailing Wall. Some religious zealots decided not to tolerate it. In April 1981 an American Jew was sentenced to life in prison by an Israeli court for shooting his way into the Islamic holy site, the Dome of the Rock; two years later, Israeli police arrested forty-one Jewish militants to prevent them from forming a "settlement" in the Haram ash-Sharif, and in November 1983 Jewish religious students went on a rampage against Islamic sites in the Old City. In 1984 the Israeli police arrested Rabbi Meir Kahane—assassinated in New York City in the fall of 1990 by an Egyptian emigré—for inciting attacks in Jerusalem. In April 1984, an Israeli court sentenced a number of Jews to jail for trying to blow up the Dome of the Rock mosque. Various other incidents followed. The impression spread in the Muslim community that one way or another the Israeli government was itself going to close down, or was going to allow others to destroy, what was Islam's original target of prayer and what is still one of its major religious sites.

Then came the tragic events of October 8, 1990, when Israeli police killed 21 Palestinians and wounded 140. Apparently (for the issue has still not been clarified in detail) a man by the name of Gershon Solomon, known as the leader of the radical "Temple Mount Faithful," who demand that the Muslim mosques be torn down, announced a few days before the outbreak that he would lead a demonstration into the Muslim sacred area. He did indeed go into the Muslim area from the Wailing Wall area and protested Muslim occupation of it. The Israeli police turned back his demonstrators, but the Palestinians who were gathered there for prayer, and who were already assuming the worst, felt under attack. What happened next is disputed, but it appears that tear gas was fired and obscured some of the area. Before or after the gas was fired, the Muslims began throwing stones, many of which fell in the heavily crowded Jewish prayer area by the Wailing Wall, and the Israeli police opened fire. At the United Nations, the Security Council unanimously passed Resolution 672 condemning Israel and calling for an inquiry by a commission appointed by the Secretary General. Israel refused to accept the U.N. commission (the Security Council again unanimously "deplored" the refusal) and sporadic violence has continued; Palestinians have murdered Israelis, and Israeli police and settlers have beaten to death Palestinians. It seems unlikely that the deep wells of religious passion which have been tapped can be recapped.

Curiously, the attention paid to the problem of peace in the Middle East was almost all directed toward *external* aspects: how the surrounding Arab states and Israel could coexist, and how the refugees living abroad could somehow be accommodated. This is the essence of UN Resolution 242, drafted by Lord Caradon, which forms the basis of most discussions on the possibility of a settlement. Very little attention was devoted to the Palestinians still living within the occupied territories.

Of course, this was a luxury or an oversight that Israel could not afford. Already, shortly after the 1967 war, a contingency plan was developed to force the Palestinians out of the occupied territories. Like so many disagreeable actions, this one was referred to with a euphemism: "transfer." The Arabs would be "transferred." Having progressed as far as they had along the road to statehood, both Israeli "hawks" and "doves" could do nothing but go forward. The logic of security was imperative. There really was no choice once the first step had been taken. We shall see that the differences between the "hawks" of the Likud Party (including Begin, Shamir, and General Sharon) and the "doves" of the Labor Party had more to do with political jockeying than with strategic considerations.

Let us turn now to the Arabs. It can be misleading to speak of *the* Arab side. In the first Arab rebellion against the British in the late 1930's, the Palestinians were on the way to becoming a coherent society, but World War II put a stop to their efforts before they had achieved their goal. In the events from 1944 to 1947, the Palestinians were simply brushed aside in the Zionist struggle with the British. Then, in the 1948–1949 war, the surrounding Arab states arrogated to themselves the right to speak for the Palestinians. And when they did so—ineptly, with actions that ranged from the avaricious to the cowardly—the Palestinians found themselves reeling in defeat out of Palestine toward the refugee camps to sit and wait. In the 1950's, as the Arab countries were convulsed by military coups, the Palestinians were presented with new self-proclaimed "saviors"; but in 1956 and again in 1967, their saviors proved to have feet of clay. It was not until the end of the 1960's that the Palestinian community, particularly in the camps, became politicized. Even then, indeed especially then, the process led to the community's fracturing into small, clandestine, and mutually hostile groups. The Palestinians, who already had been divided by their many villages and several religions, found themselves following rival drummers. And having no other means of action, they espoused the weapon of the weak: terrorism. Their misadventures are the subject of Chapter 16 above.

Meanwhile, the two other groups of Palestinians—those who had stayed in Israel and had become Israeli citizens, and those who lived in the occupied territories—were assumed to be politically quiescent. Wherever they benefited from Israeli rule, as they certainly did in Israel proper, they were assumed to be more or less immune to the virus of Arab nationalism. And wherever they were obviously disaffected, as they certainly were in the wretched camps of the Gaza strip, their motivation was usually thought of as the result of poor housing, inadequate sanitation, idleness, low wages, and outside agitation. If they could be moved out of the camps and into housing, as Ariel Sharon hoped, their living conditions could be improved and the level of their political disaffection would decline. At least, that is what most Israelis thought. But no one could be sure. And so, the Israelis kept the Palestinians under a harsh military occupation.

In those years, between roughly 1970 and 1980, three trends can be singled out. First, populations have expanded and pressures on land have increased. As the number of Jews in Israel grew and standards of living rose, people wanted new (and cheaper) living space, Similarly, the number of Palestinians has grown: the total today is about five times what it was in 1949, or about five million, of whom roughly 40 percent live in the occupied territories.

Second, the gulf between the two communities has widened as Israel has become a modern, technological, confident, victorious society, while the Palestinians in the occupied territories have, at least until recently, remained a refugee people, not unlike the European Jews of the immediate postwar period—dispirited, defeated, divided, and increasingly desperate. These facts have altered the perception of each people in the eyes of the other.

As hostilities between the Arab and Jewish communities have grown, emotions have become more crude. Many observers have commented on the fact that racial slurs are now common. For his extreme advocacy of racism, which is against Israeli law, the former leader of the Jewish Defense League Meir Kahane was evicted from the Knesset, and his party, Kach, which was gaining popularity, was banned from politics. But there is ample evidence that Israelis generally have come to regard Arabs as irredeemably alien. At one point in the 1980's, settlers in the new Israeli town of Ariel forced the local Palestinians to wear white badges inscribed with the Hebrew words for "Foreign Worker." When the Israeli press pointed out how bitterly Jews had resented being forced to wear identifying labels in Europe, the town changed the wording but kept the badges. As the *New York Times* reported on June 3, 1989, Ariel townsmen beat up three Israeli journalists who visited the town to investigate the matter, and the Israeli attorney general subsequently ordered an investigation to find out if the mayor of the town had violated the law against racism.

Throughout Israel and in the occupied territories, there are signs that Arabs and Jews no longer trust one another even on the individual level. Jews see Arabs as stone-throwing, knife-wielding fanatics and terrorists, while Palestinians believe that Israelis intend to deprive them completely of their lands and expel them from the occupied territories. Almost worse, extremists among the Jewish community have attacked Jews (such as members of the "Peace Now" movement) who sympathize with Arabs or oppose the settlement policy, and have even attacked such political figures as former prime minister Rabin. Meanwhile Palestinian extremists have murdered fellow Arabs whom they accuse of collaborating with the police or intelligence services. The gulf between the two communities is now very wide, and attitudes within each have hardened.

The *Washington Post* on June 17, 1989, quoted the Israeli chief of staff, General Shomron, as saying that the only ways open to end the uprising were "transfer, starvation or physical extermination—that is, genocide."

Third, the aims and objectives of the two sides have changed. The Palestinians by and large have come to the conclusion that there is no way they can recover their old homeland. True, the desire remains, and factions and individuals (particularly among the Muslims of Gaza) cling to unrealistic programs, but the more sober and intelligent realize that their dream is just that. They do not now, if they ever did, want merely a better standard of living. They want to be members of their own self-governing society. And they have shown themselves willing to die for that goal. The Israelis, too, have changed. They no longer are willing to give back the occupied territories.

In the immediate aftermath of the occupation in 1967, Israelis spoke of trading land for peace. In conference after conference, in bilateral government exchanges, in party programs, indeed almost universally, this was the Israeli program. But the formula proved elusive. Naturally, each side has blamed the other for the main failures to achieve progress toward peace. But regardless of cause, the fact is that no real progress was made. Meanwhile, the Israelis found that not only strategic but also other purposes could be served by the way in which Jews were settled. Jerusalem was the first example: as a part of the program to ensure that Jerusalem remained a single city, the Israelis designed and built (ironically, largely with Arab labor) a sort of wall of apartment complexes around the eastern approaches. What began there spread. Religious zealots, particularly the Gush Emunim, wanted to establish settlements in towns they identified as being of religious or historical significance. Their activities have been highly publicized, but, ultimately more important, the government concluded that it should turn the West Bank into a giant suburb for its major cities. As Jerusalem grew, the inhabitants, like American and European city-dwellers, have found it attractive to spill out of the congested areas into areas where land was cheaper.

And they were encouraged to do so. On February 2, 1982, the newspaper *Haaretz* published details of sixteen "presettlements," and on April 28 the government opened six new settlements, bringing the total then in operation to ninety-four. In a speech to the Knesset on May 3, Prime Minister Begin said that Israel would advance its claim to sovereignty after the expiration of the Camp David Accords interim period (he was then being criticized for having dismantled settlements in the Sinai as part of the Camp David Accords), and in reply the Knesset voted not to close the settlements, even as a function of peace negotiations. On July 27, 1989, the Chief Rabbinate declared that all territorial concessions were forbidden on religious grounds. These moves, as Israelis began to say, created "facts" to which everyone would have to accommodate.

Time after time, the United Nations General Assembly or the Security Council condemned Israel for violating international law by establishing settlements. Often, just after protesting to the Israeli government, the United States would veto a Security Council resolution (as it did on April 2, 1982); but occasionally (as in the case of Resolution 509), the United States would vote with the other members of the Security Council to demand Israeli withdrawal. Undeterred, the Israelis went right ahead with their programs. On November 30, 1982, for example, the government offered for sale 1,250 lots of land it had confiscated on the West Bank, making them available under a program that allocated $1.5 billion for resettlement and that offered low-cost mortgages and tax incentives for the settlers.

The Israeli settler is, in a sense, the creation of the Likud government. As the former deputy mayor of Jerusalem, Meron Benvenisti, argued, the Likud aimed not only to build settlements in areas densely populated by Arabs, and so to create "facts" in the international arena, but even more importantly aimed at "creating internal political facts"—that is, building a political constituency of Israelis with a stake in the land which it would not willingly give up. If enough people could be settled in the occupied territories, they would hold a veto over any future Israeli government that might wish to, or be pressured to, compromise on the issue of Greater Israel. (On July 20, 1987, the Likud leaders made this explicit in order to win the support of the small, right-wing Tehiya Party.) Thus, while the Labor Party wanted fortified villages for strategic purposes, the Likud wanted suburbs. The Likud today is committed to this legacy from Begin, and even in a Labor-led coalition "one can expect a change in style—an avoidance of extreme religious and historical claims—but not in substance." Benvenisti, who wrote these words, went on to comment:

> I doubt that the magic formula of "a freeze on settlements and territorial compromise," which many think is the key to renewed peace efforts, would produce practical results, even if it is finally uttered by a more moderate government [because] . . . there is a broad national consensus accepting the day-to-day transformation of the territories. Among those who are ideologically motivated, the old Zionist ethos is still powerful. Others, who lack ideological motivation, have strong materialistic motives. The morally troubling questions that have arisen since the Israeli occupation, the reports of violence, of arbitrary administrative actions, and of the dual system of law and personal status are, for the most part, swallowed up in a sea of indifference. (*New York Review of Books*, October 13, 1983, p. 13)

Figures vary according to source, but by 1986 Benvenisti estimated that about 52 percent of the occupied territories had been purchased or confiscated, or otherwise had passed into the hands of Israeli citizens or the government. Naturally, associated with these transfers has been a certain amount of sharp practice by speculators. This was confirmed in 1983, in a report by the Israeli government office of the comptroller. Prime Minister Yitzhak Shamir was quoted as having ordered the police not to look too deeply into West Bank land fraud cases, of which there were many in these years, since "a certain amount of sleight of hand" was needed to obtain land from the Arabs.* According to Israeli government plans, the Jewish population of the occupied territories would rise to about 100,000 by the end of 1990.

* Quoted in Robert I. Friedman, "The Settlers," *New York Review of Books*, June 15, 1989, p. 52, citing the *New York Times*.

Meanwhile, by natural increase, the Arab population of the occupied areas continued to grow. In 1988, Gaza was estimated to contain 650,000 people; 445,397 were refugees, of whom 244,416 lived in eight camps. Gaza consists of 350 square kilometers (about twice the area of Washington, D.C.), most of which is waterless desert. It was then the most densely populated area on earth. But the population is still rising rapidly, and, partly because the average age of the inhabitants is less than nineteen, it is predicted to reach over one million by the year 2000. The standard of living is relatively low; per capita income is only $555. The population of the West Bank is somewhat higher, today perhaps 700,000, and the per capita income is about double that of Gaza (roughly $1,037).

These figures mean that the occupied territories provide relatively cheap labor, which is attractive, indeed almost necessary, for the economy of Israel. The old Zionist imperative to refrain from "exploiting the natives" has long since been laid aside. But conscious of the security and political risks inherent in using Arabs, the Israelis have tried to make sure that incoming Arab labor returned to the occupied areas, usually at nightfall, and so remained insulated from Israel. Physically this worked reasonably well, but psychologically it could not. The Arabs who daily worked in Israel returned at night wanting to brighten their lives with what they had seen and participated in during the day. Curiously but understandably, the people on the West Bank and in Gaza grew more *like* the Israelis than any other Middle Eastern community. In particular, their emphasis on education is stronger than that of any other Arab community. This did not promote the cause of peace, however, since it made them even more aware of the unfair ways in which their lives and, above all, their legal status differed from those of the Israelis.

Recognizing this discontent, Israel ruled the occupied areas with an iron hand. Employing laws enacted by the British in colonial times, they sealed or blew up houses belonging to the families of rebels, arrested and detained people on administrative order for up to six months (later extended to one year) without legal charges, conducted searches and interrogations that violated concepts of justice held in Israel itself, confiscated land on a massive scale, closed institutions such as schools and even hospitals in the face of political opposition, demanded loyalty oaths specifically aimed at the PLO (the remaining Palestinian organization), administratively excluded perhaps 200,000 people from their former residences, and forcibly expelled suspected local leaders into other countries.

In these ways, the Israeli administration tried to "keep the lid on" discontent and gradually "created facts" that were no longer open for negotiation.

Watching this from afar, the United States and other governments protested from time to time. One issue that has been particularly prominent in the protests at the United Nations is deportation of inhabitants. This is a matter on which international legal precedent is clear: an occupying power is not legally allowed to deport inhabitants. Yet the Israelis have had a consistent program of deportations since the 1967 war. Immediately after that war, some 15,000 men from Gaza were arrested and trucked across Sinai to Egypt. A further 1,261 are known to have been deported since the 1967 war. By and large, Israel has ignored the protests. The Israeli security affairs writer Ze'ev Schiff commented that the "security people consider the deportation of Palestinian activists an extremely effective sanction."* Israel has sought to justify its policies by arguing that no progress had been made toward peace and that the Palestinians were represented by violent, irresponsible groups of terrorists with whom it was impossible to deal. And in the final analysis, no foreign country, whether European, American, or Arab, cared as much as the Israelis about the issue. The only people who did were, of course, the Palestinians.

The reaction to this evolution among the Palestinians varied over time and between groups. For years, most people in the refugee camps and on the West Bank and Gaza were subdued in their reactions. Their central concerns, apparently, were to live as securely and comfortably as possible. Fatalism is never far below the surface in Arab culture, and this was evident during most of the 1960's and 1970's. But increasingly, those who were better educated and more active found themselves at odds with the matrix that had been imposed on their lives. They also found that they had no legal means to do much about it. To write in the press or speak even in small groups often invited repression by the police; noncooperation frequently brought dismissal from jobs; and since it was held that the occupied territories were not legally a part of Israel, the political process was closed to the inhabitants. Anger and resentment were sublimated or suppressed, but from time to time broke out in sporadic acts of violence. The press contains

---

* On the numbers deported, see Helena Cobban, "The PLO and the *Intifada*," *Middle East Journal,* 44 (1990): 226ff. Schiff's comment appeared in *Haaretz,* September 8, 1989 (quoted in Cobban).

almost daily accounts of such outbreaks for many years before the actual rebellion.

As we attempt to evaluate these developments and to seek pathways toward peace, it is important that we see these events for what they are. The powerful view the weak as irresponsible, violent, untrustworthy, and illegal, and as either actual or potential terrorists, while the powerless see those in power as tyrants who are using the apparatus of the state and the law unfairly and mercilessly to strip them of their possessions, their security, indeed their very humanity.

Long before the actual outbreak of the *Intifada,* Israeli settlers in the new towns on the West Bank had formed themselves into vigilante "intervention forces." They were armed by the Israel Defense Force, or IDF (the army), and were allowed, even encouraged, to act as auxiliary police. They readily took up the habit of searching, raiding, and intimidating Arab villages near their settlements. More extreme groups formed themselves into terrorist squads, which the Israeli police monitored and, from time to time, arrested or broke up. On December 12, 1983, for example, the *Jerusalem Post* reported that the Israeli police had discovered such a group, known as "Terror against Terror," operating on the West Bank and had diffused five hand grenades placed at targets in Jerusalem. Scores of incidents of settler violence against Arab villages have been reported since. On the national level, the most active group consisted of the followers of Meir Kahane. On July 29, 1988, the *Wall Street Journal* reported that some twenty armed members of his organization were arrested by Israeli police for inciting unrest in Arab areas of Jerusalem. Particularly active was the Jewish Defense League, which, in addition to acts in the Middle East, murdered officials of the PLO in Rome and Paris.* Some of these groups of Jewish terrorists have begun to attack Israeli Jews (such as members of the "Peace Now" movement). A shadowy group known as Sicarayim, for example, on March 16, 1989, tried to burn the house of a prominent Jewish journalist and that of a MAPAM leader. Even such political figures as former prime minister Rabin have been threatened.

The Israeli army has, for the most part, succeeded in preventing the Palestinians from arming themselves. Their only weapons have been stones and knives. Most of these have been used by young

---

* The *New York Times* of June 18, 1982, reported the incident in Rome, and the *Washington Post* of July 24, 1982, reported the incident in Paris.

men against troops and settlers armed with Uzi submachine guns. So the casualties have been not only high but almost entirely Palestinian. Remarkably, the first Jewish casualty in what has become a savage internal war was not reported until March 20, 1988. In November and December of 1990, Muslim fanatics committed a number of apparently senseless and indiscriminate acts of terror against Jews. For the most part these were attacks with knives, and they set off a new shudder of fear and loathing in the Jewish community.

Particularly disturbing, of course, is the use of the organs of state power against prisoners. In one of the most famous cases, the Security Police beat to death two surrendered hijack suspects on April 12, 1982. In another case, in August 1988, the court acquitted four soldiers who had been charged with beating to death an Arab prisoner, saying that "so many soldiers had beaten him it is difficult to judge who actually killed him." The CBS network showed on American television pictures of Israeli soldiers breaking the bones of young men they had chased down. Their commander, Colonel Yehuda Meir, was sentenced only to a "severe reprimand" for ordering his soldiers to break the bones of Palestinians they arrested. In June 1988, the IDF admitted that it allowed teenage Jewish paramilitary trainees to beat Palestinian detainees. General Eitan, then chief of staff of the IDF, testified in February 1983 that he had given orders to troops to "harass" Palestinians on the West Bank. The government made few attempts to stop such abuses. On January 19, 1988, following an outbreak of international criticism, Minister of Defense Rabin (of the Labor Party) announced his support for a policy of "might, power, and beatings." Three days later, the respected Israeli newspaper *Haaretz* reported that since Rabin's statement, about 200 Palestinians had been treated for fractures as a result of beatings by soldiers. This policy has now been stopped.

Torture in prison was widely reported. Generally it was substantiated only when the detainee died, as did several in 1989. For example, in Gaza prison, a Palestinian died in the Shin Bet (internal security) interrogation room on March 6; and the *New York Times* reported on December 19 that a twenty-seven-year-old Palestinian had died in the same prison of internal bleeding caused by repeated blows on his abdomen. Particularly nauseating was the action of two Israeli soldiers who buried four Palestinian detainees alive, up to their necks, with, apparently, the intention of leaving them to die.

International observers, and many Israeli civil rights activists, protested these and other events. The International Red Cross deplored the "increasingly frequent use of firearms and acts of physical violence against defenseless civilians." Amnesty International and the American government likewise voiced strong objections. On February 7, 1989, the U.S. Department of State's annual report on civil liberties noted a "substantial increase in human rights violations" causing "many avoidable deaths and injuries." In the previous year, according to the report, some 366 Palestinians had been killed, more than 20,000 had been wounded, and 108 houses had been demolished. (Yet ten days later, the United States vetoed a Security Council resolution that deplored Israeli treatment and called for respect for human rights.) At roughly the same time, Amnesty International asserted that about 5,000 Palestinians (of the 13,000 then admitted to be in detention) were being held in prison camps without charges.

The IDF has frequently used tear gas against demonstrators. Although this gas is obviously not so deadly as nerve and mustard gas, it can be used in lethal concentrations—and it so often was, that at least eighty Palestinians had died from asphyxiation by August 30, 1989, according to the Israeli newspaper *Ha'olam Haze*. Israeli doctors have estimated that at least thirty miscarriages were caused in that year by the use of tear gas.

In more subtle ways, disparity in treatment became an issue in the Palestinian community. The Palestinians felt helpless not only because government-armed settlers, police, and soldiers were used without restraint against them, but also because courts and even hospitals were either closed to them or treated them with different standards. For example, the soldiers who were convicted of burying Palestinian prisoners alive were sentenced to a maximum of two and a half months in jail, whereas two weeks later a Palestinian was sentenced to five years for laying a telephone cable across a road to disrupt traffic. When a young Israeli girl was killed, presumably by Arabs, nearby settlers went on a rampage against Arab villagers. Then, when it was discovered that the girl had in fact been shot by an Israeli, and that no Arabs were involved, the army went ahead anyway with the demolition of fourteen houses belonging to Palestinians they *had* thought were involved. Even in cases where Israeli soldiers or civilians have been convicted and given sentences, the government has reduced their sentences. On July 10, 1985, the Israeli court found fifteen Jews guilty of attacks on Arabs, including murder; Prime Minister Shamir referred to them as "excellent boys who erred" and pardoned them. President Herzog has consistently used his powers to reduce the sentences of Jewish terrorists, as he did on May 20, 1988, in the case of three members of a group convicted of an assault on Hebron University in which three Arabs were killed.

What has been evident in the courts also became clear elsewhere. The *Washington Post* reported in January 1989 that Israel was denying Palestinians access to medical care in Israeli hospitals, while cutting the budgets of West Bank facilities. Six months earlier, military officials had doubled the cost of a night in a West Bank hospital to $175. Meanwhile, taxes have been increased for inhabitants of the occupied territories, to cover the costs of the insurrection.

Colleges and schools in the occupied territories were, of course, among the casualties of the *Intifada.* In 1988 and 1989, the whole educational system was shut down for sixteen months. University faculty members have been subject to arrest and intimidation, work permits have been withdrawn, and loyalty oaths required. Arabic-language newspapers were subjected to censorship and were, from time to time, closed down. Radio stations broadcasting from abroad in Arabic were often jammed.

Arguably, these measures have affected the civilian population less than curfews have. Frequently, general curfews were imposed on individual refugee camps or towns. On April 17, 1988, house curfews were imposed on fifteen camps. And on May 15, 1989, Prime Minister Rabin, facing a boycott of Israeli goods in Gaza, imposed an indefinite curfew; according to a statement attributed to him in the *Jerusalem Post* on May 15, 1989, the curfew was intended to let the residents of Gaza "know that we—and not some [clandestinely circulated nationalist] leaflet—decide when and how life should be disrupted."

The gross figures say much: in the first eighteen months of the uprising, 25,599 Palestinians were injured, at least 430 were killed, 48 were expelled, 176 houses were blown up or bulldozed by the IDF, and 6,599 Palestinians were imprisoned. Six months later, these figures had gone up: the Israeli newspaper *Ha'olam Haze* reported on August 31, 1989, that 514 had been shot to death by the IDF or settlers, 80 had died from asphyxiation, 50 from electrocutions and beatings, and 78 from other causes.

This record provokes two questions. Why was the rebellion not quelled? And given the legacy of these events, what is likely to happen now? It is, of course, difficult to find answers amid such violent confrontation; but various partial ones can be given. At the forefront of answers to both questions is the Palestinians' belief that they are the victims of a great injustice. One effect of this belief is the fact that the *Intifada* continues.

The Arabs have always been a fractious people, and the history of the Palestinian community, like that of all village communities, is full of internal quarrels. In the nineteenth century, the world of the Palestinians was bounded by their clan or village; outside these narrow parameters were foreigners and enemies. Some of the "frontiers" were religious and others were geographic, but both barriers were real. So, when faced with an invasion by the Egyptians in the 1830's, as I have recounted, the Palestinians could not draw together. A century later, in the face of what they perceived to be the danger of Zionism, they similarly failed to coalesce. And in the face of danger in 1948–1949, they tried to save themselves individually or in small groups. The assumption, as I have said, was that they would do the same in the 1980's. But they have not. Even without weapons, and subjected to the overwhelming power of a modern state, they have stubbornly resisted. In this they resemble various other peoples who, allegedly peaceful and nonviolent, similarly were forced together by events beyond their control. The consensus, including that of Israeli intelligence, is that the Palestinians perceive a common and mortal challenge of such magnitude that their reaction to it has forged them into a nation. In February 1989, this opinion was publicly stated by the chief of staff of the IDF.

A second reason for the Palestinians' continued resistance is the way detention has changed people, by putting prisoners in touch with one another. In the 1980's, detention camps became schools in which the politically active communicated their experiences and ideas to the new arrivals. And this is no small-scale operation. Walid al-Khalidi has noted that "in the extended family networks that prevail in the territories, only a minority will not include a relative who has been manhandled, humiliated, injured, imprisoned or exiled, or has had his home demolished." (*Foreign Affairs*, vol. 66, 1988). Even those people, particularly the very young, who have not been in prison will be influenced by kinship or acquaintanceship with those who have. As Robert I. Friedman has written, "Every refugee family I met in the occupied territories had at least one son in prison, in the hospital or dead" (*New York Review of Books*, March 29, 1990).

A third reason for the continuation of the Palestinian movement is the apparent unity behind the PLO, the sole "national" organization. Israel has absolutely refused to deal with the PLO and has done everything it could to destroy or at least discredit the organization. It has found curious allies in the Syrian government, which sponsors its own Palestinian organization, and in the more violent of the Palestinian terrorist groups, of which at least some have played a particularly intriguing role in the murky world of the underground. And, of course, the Israeli government has tried to cut off all contacts between the resident Palestinians and the distant headquarters of the PLO. Menahem Milsen, a promient Israeli Arabist and former governor of the occupied territories, argued for years that the PLO was really irrelevant to, or at least distant from, the politics of the Palestinians. Yet a remarkable survey based on 1,024 face-to-face interviews, conducted in the occupied territories by Mohammed Shadid and Rick Seltzer in 1986, before the *Intifada,* showed that 95 percent of the population regarded the PLO as the "sole and legitimate" representative of the Palestinian people.* (An earlier survey, commissioned by *Time* magazine in 1982, had yielded similar results.) Only 0.1 percent favored continued Israeli rule with provision for improving the quality of life, and no one favored the Israeli autonomy plan. Asked to pick their preferred Palestinian leader, 78.6 percent picked Arafat. The radical leader George Habbash was second, with 5.6 percent, and none of the rest received approval from as much as 2 percent.

These are remarkable results, given the isolation of the community, its presumed sense of being a daily victim while the leadership of the PLO lives in relative comfort and safety, and Arafat's much-publicized sequence of failures. How to explain it? No one can know, but the general opinion is that the Palestinians feel themselves to be, for the first time, a truly united people. Their suffering obviously has a central role in this: of those actually questioned in Shadid and Seltzer's survey, 22.7 percent said that they or a member of their immediate family had had their land expropriated by Israeli authorities. But there may be another reason for the support given to the PLO, namely that the PLO adapted itself to the *Intifada* and became its sole point of coordination. This is a crucial if so far not well-documented point.

The *Intifada* can be dated from an incident (one among many) on December 8, 1987, when a vehicle driven by an Israeli killed four Palestinians and wounded eight others in the Jabalya camp

---

* "Political Attitudes of Palestinians in the West Bank and Gaza Strip," *Middle East Journal,* 42 (1988): 16ff.

in Gaza. The outbreak that followed was spontaneous. The local Palestinians, pushed to their limit, struck back angrily at what they perceived to be deliberate murder. No one expected what then happened. As Professor Sari Nuseibeh of Bir Zayt University has written, "For two weeks the fire raged in almost unfathomable proportions. Even the local grassroots committees, activists, and leaders were caught off-guard."*

Normally, the Israelis took every precaution to isolate the various groups in the occupied territories. They also sought to build up weaker groups to undermine the stronger. Specifically in Gaza, they promoted the growth of the two Muslim organizations, the Muslim Brotherhood and Islamic Jihad, to offset the secular, nationalist PLO. They were disappointed in these ventures, as the two Muslim groups have by and large supported the PLO, deferring any disagreements, as the leaders of the Islamic Jihad put it, "until independence." Islamic Jihad was thought to have been involved in the deaths of a number of Israelis, and the Israeli government finally declared HAMAS, an outgrowth of the Muslim Brotherhood, a terrorist organization in May 1989.

Realizing their isolation and the danger of disruption, the Palestinians placed great value on communication. Denied access to the established media, they had to develop informal pathways. Within a month after the December 1987 outbreak, what has become a series of leaflets urging resistance began to appear. With Syrian help, a new radio station called al-Quds (Arabic: "Jerusalem") broadcast the message contained in the first leaflet. A week later, a similar station operating out of Baghdad repeated the next message. As message followed message, each came to be signed by the PLO. In each message, specific actions were requested on given days. Thus, for the first time, work stoppages, for example, took place throughout the territories at the same moment. But the authors of the messages took great care not to demand more from the Palestinians than they could sustain. This care and concern were evidently appreciated, and so trust grew.

Israeli authorities struck back. Radio al-Quds was jammed whenever possible. Time after time, every suspect in sight was arrested; repeatedly, Israeli authorities claimed to have rounded up the whole leadership. But apparently, there was no formal leadership. Whenever some were arrested, others took their places. The intelligence services tried various forms of black propaganda. For exam-

* "A True People's Revolution," *Middle East International*, December 15, 1989, quoted in Helena Cobban, "The PLO and the *Intifada*," *Middle East Journal*, 44 (1990): 208.

ple, undercover police used press credentials and pretended to be foreign correspondents to try to lure Palestinians into talking. In one particularly bizarre incident, a group of Israeli soldiers, dressed like Palestinians and shouting Arabic slogans, was actually shot at and wounded by Israeli border police; as mentioned above, the whole area of Gaza was put under curfew as a punishment. Then, in April 1988, a group of Israeli commandos and airmen attacked the distant headquarters of the PLO in Tunisia and murdered Khalil al-Wazir, the PLO official who was the designated contact with the *Intifada*; when protests and demonstrations broke out in the occupied territories, the IDF killed fourteen Palestinians. In despair, the Israelis even made attempts (one that occurred on July 7, 1988, was reported in the press) to issue their own versions of the leaflets and radio broadcasts, in an effort to sow confusion and discord.

The price paid for the *Intifada* in Gaza was terrible. In 1989, the Jabalya refugee camp, where the *Intifada* began, was 156 days under curfew. Some 78 children were killed in Gaza, and more than 11,000 Palestinians were wounded.

What is likely to happen now? There are, as I see them, four possible outcomes. First, the revolt may continue. The cost has been real for Israel, particularly in lost income from sales to the West Bank and Gaza, and in a fall in tourism. The Bank of Israel reported a $650 million loss of exports during the rebellion, and incalculable losses from deterred would-be investors. A 15 percent fall in tourism was reported for 1988, and a 50 percent fall in exports to the occupied territories (from $928 million to $650 million). But these are by no means crippling; and the actual cost in lives and property has been slight. Curiously, the *Intifada* has been the mirror image of the war in Lebanon: there, Israel faced a heavily armed, mutually hostile collection of foes and lost about 500 soldiers, whereas in the occupied territories it has faced a unified, unarmed group and has lost only a handful of people. To the charge that such a condition cannot long continue, I reply that history shows it can.

Second, it is possible the Israelis may find some form of compromise that will win the support of many Palestinians—enough so that the revolt will slowly die down. Various attempts have been made. Prime Minister Shamir and the leaders of the Labor Party have put their minds to several. One that has recently been discussed is the autonomy or "enclaves" plan. In this scheme, the Palestinian communities of the West Bank and Gaza would be regrouped into more or less autonomous areas separated from one another by Israeli settlements and military installations. This has the attraction for the Israeli government of not requiring any negative decision on the existing settlements. Its major disadvantage is that it probably will not work. The reason is that it meets none of the objectives of the Palestinians. Even if the various Arab communities were granted a relatively large degree of local autonomy, they would in no sense be collectively autonomous or constitute— even informally—a national identity. Nor would they own or control much of the land in the occupied territories. But, given increasingly desperate circumstances, this plan or some variant may still be tried.

The third possible outcome is that the Israeli government will force the "transfer" of the Palestinian population. Support for this apparent solution appears to be increasing in Israel. On August 12, 1989, the *Jerusalem Post* reported that 49 percent of adult Israelis thought forced expulsion would allow the democratic and Jewish nature of Israel to be maintained. A few months later, another poll indicated that 52 percent were prepared to consider deportation of the entire two million Palestinians from the occupied territories. Is this feasible? Yes, I think it is. We have seen similar vast exoduses in the past and, given such an opportunity as Saddam Husain tried to present, namely a war with the United States in which Arab forces struck against Israel as well, such an event is not beyond the imagination. Where would the people go? The answer is Jordan. How would they live there? I believe that, under favorable circumstances, the Israelis would say simply that this is not their problem. The Palestinians could be cared for by a greatly expanded UN relief organization.

The fourth possible outcome is that Israel would withdraw from most or all of the occupied territories, so that some form of national Palestinian entity can be created. On March 20, 1989, an Israeli intelligence report which was leaked to the press asserted that the *Intifada* could not be overcome in the near future militarily and urged that the only possible solution was political—in conference with the PLO.

Is this feasible? The Likud Party, as mentioned above, has done all in its power to make such a course as difficult as possible. There is now a constituency of more than 100,000 Israelis who would vigorously oppose it. And as many as 75,000 Soviet Jews are expected to settle in occupied territories in the next few years. So each day that passes makes it less likely. Neither any state nor the United Nations collectively is likely to be able to force such a solution on the Israelis. No country in the area has the power; the

United States is certainly unwilling and probably unable, and (as the president of the World Jewish Congress has remarked) has had a policy of "automatic vetoes of UN resolutions that Israel considers hostile"; the Soviet Union has shown little interest.* My hunch is that even those political leaders who believe such a move might be in Israel's long-run interest will not wish to pay the necessary political price to achieve it. Former Prime Minister Peres set out the Labor Party position as the "four noes." No negotiations with the PLO; no Palestinian state; no foreign armies in the territories; and no dismantling of settlements. Whatever Arafat may say or do, as in his declaration in December 1988 renouncing terrorism and agreeing to Israel's right to exist (and thus beginning a dialogue with the United States through the embassy in Tunis), is the Likud likely to do more? I think it is not.

Arafat has had to tread a narrow path, which in the Iraq war grew more tortuous. The Palestinians in the occupied territories followed Arafat both in eschewing the use of arms in their rebellion, which won them some approval by the United States government, but also in expressing support for Saddam Husain, which earned them the hostility of most Arab governments and of the United States. In the Iraq war, the Palestinians thus lost their financial and much of their political backing. While there are now signs of an American initiative to find some sort of modus vivendi and of a willingness by the Palestinians to at least discuss compromise, both the PLO and the residents of the occupied territories have indicated that they will not compromise on the issue of national self-determination, which the Israelis have repeatedly rejected. Secretary of State James Baker has said that the opportunity for peace has never been better, but whether there can be a settlement of the Palestinian problem or just an accommodation, on the Egyptian model, among the Arab states and Israel remains to be seen.

Thus, it seems likely to me that we are watching the last act of a long drama, a true tragedy, in which good people are locked in a struggle that, ultimately, will certainly severely harm and may even ruin them both.

* In the midst of the *Intifada*, Soviet Foreign Minister Shevardnadze promised to restore diplomatic relations (broken after the 1967 war) with Israel, provided it promised action on two issues of keen Soviet concern: reduction of long-range missiles and ratification of a nuclear treaty. The Palestinians were not crucial to the Soviet agenda.

The remarks by the president of the World Jewish Congress, Edgar Bronfman, can be found in his article on the peace process, *New York Times*, December 9, 1990.

PART 8

The United States and the Arab World

23

A Decade of Discovery

URING the period from 1945 to 1955, the main lines of American policy in the Middle East were established. As laid down in the Truman administration and elaborated in the Eisenhower administration, they still form the basis of most contemporary activities. In large part, they were inherited from Great Britain, transferred from other areas, or grew out of American domestic attitudes; only in small part were they adjusted to or in resonance with the hopes and fears of Middle Easterners. Therein lies much, but not all, of the cause of their shortfalls and disappointments. Too little did Americans perceive the Arabs and too little did the Arabs perceive Americans, to cushion our joint passage through the stormy postwar generation.

Unlike Latin America, Europe, and the Far East, the Middle East held little commercial or political interest for Americans in the nineteenth and early twentieth centuries. It was the missionary, for whom the Middle East was the Land of the Bible, who set the style of American involvement there. But the early missionary found its people so ignorant of their heritage and so borne down by the ills of this world as to be unwilling and unable to aspire to a higher calling. Consequently, starting in 1823, small bands of American missionaries began laying the foundations of what by the end of the century grew into a network of schools, colleges, and hospitals in Syria, Anatolia, and Egypt. In times of crisis, the Americans were sustained by British consuls. Rarely was much notice taken of them by the United States government except that it occasionally augmented its own small diplomatic corps by appointing missionaries as part-time consuls.

The United States did not declare war on the Ottoman Empire in World War I. But during the war President Wilson's declarations on self-determination led to a belief on the part of others that the United States would accept a large measure of responsibility for the achievement of a just and enduring peace in the Middle East, based upon the applications of its own domestic political ideals. There was a period in which the United States seemed to be moving in this direction. At one time it was deeply involved in the Armenian question. Suspicion of the intentions of Britain and France caused the United States government to send to the Middle East the King-Crane Commission to ascertain the desires of the native populations. At the Peace Conference an American Zionist delegation persuaded President Wilson to urge the application of the Balfour Declaration. But with the American return to isolationism, these efforts amounted to little. A bill urging an American protectorate for Armenia was killed in Congress; the report of the King-Crane Commission was probably never seen by Wilson, was not published in the United States until the end of 1922, and had no perceptible effect in the Middle East; and though the American Congress passed the first of several resolutions approving the Balfour Declaration, it was unprepared to commit the power of the United States to realize its terms.

The return to isolationalism was not, however, complete. Oil interests, already grown strong within America, were pressing for free entry into the new and promising field of the Middle East while their British, Dutch, and French competitors were anxious to keep these areas to themselves. In this case, for the first time, the American State Department took an active part in securing American access to the area. But the chief motivation behind the United States action, fear that American reserves were near exhaustion, was weakened by successive petroleum discoveries on the North American continent. Consequently, the United States government took little further part in Middle Eastern affairs until the coming of World War II.

During World War II, with the notable exceptions of stimulating Saudi Arabian oil production and establishing the Persian Gulf–Iran route to Russia, America took a decidedly secondary role in Middle Eastern activities; the area was British, and the United States was otherwise occupied. Where useful, the United States would associate with Great Britain, as in the Middle East Supply Centre or in the moves to evict France from Lebanon and Syria, but the United States remained, as it traditionally had been, far more concerned with other areas.

Yet, the fading memory of the past kept best preserved the benevolence of Americans. It was our schools and our hospitals men preferred to remember in their contemporary hostility to French or British commerce and dominion and, flattered, we fanned the glowing embers of our benevolence. Forgotten was our lust for oil, our isolationism, or our strategic priorities. Inherent were disappointments on both sides—the Arabs saw that as a nation-state, we were not merely missionary-teachers writ large; we, that the Arabs as nation-states were unwilling to be merely grateful student-patients.

At the end of the war the United States government resisted British attempts to draw it into a responsible position in Middle Eastern politics. With its own overseas might being severely contracted, its deep sense of involvement in the Far East and Europe, and its people's desire to return to their homes to enjoy the fruits of wartime prosperity, was joined the conviction that Great Britain had both the power and the experience to handle the problems of the Middle East. Few Americans in 1945 thought otherwise. Thus, though President Truman on April 6, 1946, warned of the area's weakness and instability and its importance to the West, he was willing to work only through the United Nations, as in the Iranian dispute, or to offer mediation, as through the Anglo-American Committee of Inquiry in Palestine. He was not willing to accept direct responsibility.

A situation was being created, however, which impelled America to intervene. The Soviet Union refused to participate in the supervision of elections in war-ravaged Greece in 1946 while the Greek Communist party led the rebels in civil war. Soviet territorial demands upon Turkey in 1945 and the prolonged stay of Russian troops in Iran into 1946, emphasized as these were by events in the Balkans, convinced the American government that America must—as Britain announced in February 1947 that it could not—counter Soviet pressure. As the President said: "If Greece should fall under the control of an armed minority, the effect upon its neighbor, Turkey, would be immediate and serious. Confusion and disorder might well spread throughout the entire Middle East."

It was because of its determination to "contain" the Soviet Union, then, that America first undertook direct and large-scale responsibility for events in the eastern Mediterranean. It did so in default of Great Britain, to whom it had preferred to leave responsibility for the area. And through its European commitments in Greece, America was drawn into an involvement in the Arab World.

A touchstone of American policy has remained its desire to keep the Soviet Union out of the Middle East.

Despite the intensity of interest which it had evoked, the Palestine problem was long in receiving a considered expression of official American policy. The Palestine problem has involved, more than any other of the overseas relations of the United States, an extension of domestic American politics. Both American Zionists, with well-directed, large-scale campaigns to influence the public, and American liberals, shocked and outraged by the brutality of the Nazis and fearful of future anti-Semitism in Europe and America, have taken to heart the issue of the settlement of Jews in Israel. This interest made itself felt only after the end of World War II. The problem of Palestine seemed to challenge no basic and vital American interest; whereas the United States government was not prepared to allow Greece or Turkey to slip into the Soviet orbit, it was prepared, within limits, to tolerate hostilities in Palestine.

When Great Britain indicated that it was unable to resolve the Palestine conflict and intended to turn it over to the United Nations, the United States played a major role in pushing through the General Assembly, in November 1947, a modification of the latest partition plan. However, the United States government felt unable to lend the United Nations the force which *might* have made partition possible without war. Its military establishment was depleted and those planning American policy believed that they could not count on congressional or party support for an active policy.

Unable to move forward with any confidence, the government on March 19, 1948, suggested at the UN that action on partition be suspended and that a trusteeship be established over all Palestine to delay final settlement. When this was refused, both by the Soviet Union and by Great Britain, the United States again strongly advocated partition and recognized the State of Israel within minutes after it was proclaimed. Meanwhile, the United States urged the creation of the UN Palestine Conciliation Commission. When the Commission was established in December 1948, the United States, in its first direct acceptance of responsibility in Palestine, agreed to serve as a member (along with France and Turkey). To support and to resettle the Arab refugees, the United States cooperated in the formation of the UN Relief for Palestine Refugees.

Outside of the United Nations, the United States joined Britain and France in issuing the May 25, 1950, Tripartite Declaration on the security of Middle Eastern frontiers, out of "the desire to promote the establishment and maintenance of peace and stability in the area and ... unalterable opposition to the use of force or threat of force between any of the states in that area." This remained American policy for fifteen years.

Returning from the Middle East in May 1953 Secretary Dulles said he had ascertained that the Arabs were "more fearful of Zionism than of the Communists" because they thought that "the United States will back the new State of Israel in aggressive expansion." The new administration clearly perceived that this fear, and the suspicion it promoted of pro-Israeli policies, inhibited American action in the Middle East.

Israel at this point of her statehood was dependent upon American governmental and private aid. Private aid was pouring into Israel in loans and U.S. income tax–deductible gifts. In the fiscal year 1953 American aid still accounted for an estimated 35 percent of all imports into Israel. The new administration saw this factor as one of considerable leverage in influencing Israeli policy and used it.

When, in the early summer of 1953, the Israeli government began to move its offices to Jerusalem from Tel Aviv the United States government protested that this violated the 1947 UN partition resolution which, inter alia, recognized Jerusalem as an international city. Shortly thereafter, the UN Truce Supervision Organization, acting on a Syrian protest, requested that Israel not undertake a hydroelectric project on the Jordan River at Banat Yaqub, but Israel in September refused to halt work. On October 14–15 the Israeli army raided the village of Qibiya and killed fifty-three Arabs. Joined by France and Great Britain, the United States brought this issue to the Security Council, and Secretary Dulles, noting that the United States had "played an essential part in creating the State of Israel," admonished Israel that "this was clearly an occasion to invoke the concept of decent respect for the opinion of mankind as represented by the United Nations." At the same time it was announced that since September 25 the United States had been withholding an aid allocation because Israel was acting in defiance of the UN. On October 27 Israel suspended work in the demilitarized zone, and the next day Secretary Dulles recommended a grant of $26,250,000 in economic aid for that fiscal year.

Plain speaking on the Palestine issue drew hostile comments from both Israel and the Arab states. Assistant Secretary Byroade in particular was criticized for setting out American policy in 1954 in the following terms:

> To the Israelis, I say that you should come to truly look upon yourselves as a Middle Eastern state and see your own future in that context rather than as a headquarters, or nucleus so to speak, or world-wide

groupings of peoples or a particular religious faith who must have special rights within and obligations to the Israeli state. You should drop the attitude of a conqueror and the conviction that force and a policy of retaliatory killings is the only policy that your neighbors will understand. You should make your deeds correspond to your frequent utterances of the desire for peace.

To the Arabs I say you should accept this state of Israel as an accomplished fact. I say further that you are deliberately attempting to maintain a state of affairs delicately suspended between peace and war, while at present desiring neither. This is a most dangerous policy and one which world opinion will increasingly condemn if you continue to resist any move to obtain at least a less dangerous *modus vivendi* with your neighbor.

In retrospect, we may see that officials in the Eisenhower administration perceived a clash of goals—the one, strategic, to contain Soviet influence, and the other, political, to aid a state with which powerful groups of Americans felt an intense emotional affinity. The clash could only be resolved if the Arabs and Israelis could become "sensible"—that is to say, could share the American strategic imperatives and eschew their own political impulses.

Border tension continued to increase with clandestine raids on the one side and on the other the announcement and fulfillment of Israel's policy of retaliation. The February 28, 1955, attack on Gaza was the high point of these clashes; for it, the Security Council censured Israel on March 29. Since the Gaza raid may be taken as the key event in the build-up to the Czech arms deal, it will be useful at this point to turn to the attempt by the United States government to improve the economies of the Middle Eastern states as a way of creating a more "rational," less political, climate.

The New Deal experiment with "pump priming" was perhaps the most extensive government economic endeavor in American experience. Moreover, wartime spending accustomed the public to large outlays by the government of funds and the use of these funds for the creation of new industries. The first major application to foreign affairs of government economic initiative was in the 1947 Marshall Plan for European Recovery. The basic ideas there were elaborated and carried a logical step forward in the famous Fourth Point of President Truman's inaugural address in 1949: "We must embark on a bold new program for making the benefits of our scientific advances and industrial progress available for the improvement and growth of underdeveloped areas . . . Our aim should be to help the free peoples of the world, through their own efforts, to produce more food, more clothing, more materials for housing, and more mechanical power to lighten their burdens."

Already, in fact, between 1945 and 1950 Export-Import Bank loans to Middle Eastern and Asian states had totaled $266,110,000. Also the United States had already undertaken a share in the responsibility for the Palestine refugees' economic future.

The American government realized, of course, that the Arab refugees could not be permanently supported on an international dole and that a capital investment would be required if they were to be reintegrated into the economy of the Middle East. To this end, the State Department urged the UN Conciliation Commission for Palestine to send to the Middle East an economic survey mission under the leadership of Gordon R. Clapp, the chairman of the Tennessee Valley Authority. Out of the Clapp Commission report came the establishment of the UN Relief and Works Agency and, not less important, a broad scheme for the economic development of the whole area due to the recognition that "solution of the problem of poverty and unemployment of the refugees is ... inseparable from a solution of the problem of poverty and hunger as that already affects a large section of the population of the Middle East."

The United States government undertook to assist in both programs. It contributed $45 million to the initial UN Relief and Works Agency and yearly thereafter met over one half of the agency's budget. The 1950 Act for International Development set aside $34.5 million for technical assistance, and the 1951 Mutual Security Appropriation Act set up a $160 million fund for technical and economic assistance and allocated $21.5 million for general Point IV aid. In addition the United States contributed $12 million to the UN technical assistance program for the eighteen months from July 1, 1950. By the end of the fiscal year 1963 the United States had advanced some $795 million in grants and $584 million in loans for economic and technical assistance. (During this period, the Soviet Union gave or lent approximately $1.2 billion to the Arabs.)

In presenting the argument for the Mutual Security Program for the fiscal year beginning July 1, 1952, the government stated that "Political unrest and intense nationalism characterize many of the countries in this area, and in part reflect deep-rooted social and economic ills ... The poverty resulting from these factors together with a disease and illiteracy contributing to them, form a vicious circle which we can help to break by the application of technical skills." Given this analysis, the policy of the United States was to "assist the people and governments of the area to achieve not only greater military security, through the Middle East Command and limited military assistance, but also to assist responsible leaders in getting under way orderly reform and development, in which the energies of the people can find constructive expansion. Our purpose is to demonstrate to these countries, by concrete cooperative effort, that they themselves can achieve their desires for economic and social progress as a part of the free world. People who have evidence of this will not turn in desperation to Communism."

Initial reception in the area was good: Israel, Libya, Egypt, Saudi Arabia, Lebanon, Jordan, and eventually Iraq entered into Point IV or subsequent aid agreements. But no one seriously questioned the suppositions or the objectives of this aid—and both were, at best, ill-considered. In the Middle East, as in the rest of the poor Afro-Asian world, the task was not that of the war-devastated Europe of the Marshall Plan, not to *rebuild* with a trained and experienced population, but to build from virgin soil with an untrained and uncomprehending population. The goals were either left to the imagination or were in obvious opposition—an Afro-Asian "Europe," *or* a docile and friendly because improving, poor area, *or* a depoliticized strategic base, *or* a Western-oriented bastion against Communism? These were only vaguely perceived; in no sense were they fully considered, much less answered.

The Middle East was not mentioned in President Eisenhower's Inaugural Address in January 1953. The tide of United States involvement ebbed in the Middle East but flowed in the Far East. Under the impact of the Korean War American thinking increasingly followed military paths in its quest for security, and American funds were forthcoming mainly for military projects. Of the $540 million proposed for 1953 for the Middle East, exclusive of economic assistance given to Greece and Turkey, $415 million was to be spent on military aid, mainly for Greece, Turkey, and Iran. Even at this date the government was clearly most concerned with the military aspects of what Secretary Dulles was later to call the "northern tier of nations," and in September and October invited Turkey and Greece to make arrangements to join in the military planning work of NATO. Both accepted and in the following September were invited to join as full members.

The rest of the Middle East presented a pact-maker's nightmare. Iran, already in serious financial troubles, was involved in the dispute which ended in the nationalization of the oil company and so in conflict with the British government. It was, therefore, a most unlikely partner in a British-led pact. Israel was an unlikely choice since its participation would automatically exclude the Arab states. The center of military strength at that time was at Suez, and in British thinking Egypt was the pivot of Middle Eastern power. Therefore, Egypt seemed to be the logical place to start. Consequently, on October 13, 1951, Great Britain, France, Turkey, and the United States invited Egypt to help found the Allied Middle East Command. If Egypt were prepared to join and to permit the use of her facilities, including the Suez base, Great Britain would agree to suppress the Anglo-Egyptian treaty of 1936 and would withdraw all British forces not assigned to the Allied Command. Britain made clear, however, that Egypt's demands on the Sudan would not be met.

Given the political climate in Egypt, neither the formula nor the time was propitious. Prime Minister Nahhas' weak government, under attack for domestic corruption, sought to protect itself with wordy patriotism. It was publicly committed to the "unity of the Nile Valley" and could hardly give its domestic enemies the weapon they could have fashioned from a Wafd deal with the British. Nahhas immediately rejected the proposal and then pressed a counterattack by abrogating, unilaterally, the 1936 treaty under which British troops were in Suez. Thus, not only did the West not get a better coordinated defense arrangement, but it seriously weakened, at least de jure, its existing position.

The United States government was not prepared to give up. Despite the Egyptian rejection and Soviet protests that the United States was trying to draw the Middle East into the "aggressive Atlantic bloc," the government tried to keep the project alive until the May 1953 visit of Secretary Dulles to the Middle East.

Returning from that trip, Dulles indicated that he had come to the conclusion that it was not then feasible to attempt to create a Middle East parallel to NATO. There was, he found, "a vague desire to have a collective security system, but no such system can be imposed from without. It should be designed and grow from within out of a sense of common destiny and common danger." No two senses could be further from the thoughts—and nerves—of the Arab states. Mr. Dulles found that American fear of Communism was paralleled by Arab fear of Israel. But in Greece, Turkey, and Iran, he took hope. The implications of this finding represented less of a new departure in American policy, which had throughout the period included heavy contributions to Greece, Turkey, and Iran, than a departure from the ideal strategic model of the British, based upon Suez, a concept, incidentally, upon which the Arab League Collective Security Pact has been partly based.

Extension of the "northern tier" concept into the Baghdad Pact was a development in which the United States government took the keenest interest without playing an overt part. It was thought in

Washington that however much use of the carrot and the stick were required, the states involved must seem to pull their own loads. By late 1953 the United States had begun to plan a military assistance agreement with Pakistan which materialized in May 1954; on April 2, 1954, Turkey and Pakistan signed a military pact. When Pakistan joined the Southeast Asia Collective Defense Treaty in September, it became obvious that the U.S. had created was a belt of defense treaties from Europe to the Far East. The United States extended military assistance to Iraq in April 1954. In February 1955 Turkey and Iraq signed the Mutual Cooperation Pact which was opened to all members of the Arab League and other states concerned with peace and security in the Middle East. The United Kingdom adhered to this agreement on April 4 and terminated the Anglo-Iraqi treaty of 1930; Pakistan joined on September 23 and Iran on October 11.

Since the new pact bypassed the Arab League and was based in Baghdad whose government was hostile to President Nasser, it brought about an immediate deterioration of American relations with those Arab states in which President Nasser then had strong influence, first Syria, then Saudi Arabia, and for a time Jordan. This development, coupled with the growing tensions along the Arab-Israeli frontier, with the United States' unwillingness to supply arms on terms acceptable to Egypt, and possibly with internal pressures in the Egyptian army, caused Nasser to conclude the arms purchase agreement with Czechoslovakia. President Nasser announced the arrangement on September 27, and on September 28 an American emissary was sent to Cairo to reactivate and make more acceptable the earlier American arms offer. The Egyptians were not swayed, but the American response to the Russian move set what President Nasser was to regard as a precedent—the key to American motivations—when he came to negotiate aid for the Aswan High Dam.

As the United States government saw the Czech arms deal, the terms upon which the arms were acquired would mortgage the Egyptian economy to the Soviet Union far into the future and bring the Cold War into Arab-American relations as never before. These arguments failed to impress the Egyptian government, which pointed out both that it had tried unsuccessfully to acquire arms from the West and that it thought the Czech deal was a good swap for Egyptian cotton. Syria and Saudi Arabia indicated their willingness to make similar arrangements. In the United States the fear grew that the "northern tier" had been hurdled.

The Palestine problem remained, as it remains today, a focal point of all the separate problems of the area and, therefore, of American efforts to assist in the achievement of peace and stability there. To the Council on Foreign Relations on August 26, 1955, Secretary of State Dulles had set out one possible approach to this complex issue. Dulles suggested that an international loan might enable "Israel to pay the compensation which is due and which would enable many of the refugees to find for themselves a better way of life." He further offered American assistance in determining satisfactory frontiers which the United States would then guarantee against aggression.

Eric Johnston had been appointed in 1953 as a special representative of the President to work on the problem of the Jordan River waters and was then in the midst of protracted negotiations with the Arab states and Israel. These did not produce any agreement but did lay the basis of American aid efforts. In effect, the United States indicated that it was willing to assist both the Arab states and Israel to complete projects which were in accord with the Johnston proposal; thus, though the Johnston Plan was not in principle accepted, it was in practice largely implemented.

But in the Arab states there was no appreciation of Western attempts to be impartial. Egyptian anti-Western propaganda grew in bitterness, and this propaganda played an important part in creating an atmosphere in which Great Britain lost its control over the Jordan army. In other Arab states responsible political leaders privately expressed their fears that President Nasser had found his model not in Arabi Pasha but in Mehmet Ali Pasha—that his aim was not liberation of Egypt but regency over the Arabs. To the American public and Congress Nasser began to assume the shape of a villain and the possible range of State Department actions in regard to him narrowed.

Meanwhile, the Egyptian government, anxious to secure the necessary hard-currency funds to construct the Aswan High Dam, had approached the International Bank for a loan. The bank had agreed, contingent upon British and American participation to the amount of $70 million, to lend Egypt $200 million. In December the United States had been prepared to agree to this, but Egypt did not at that time accept. When the president of the International Bank went to Cairo the rumor was "leaked" that agreement with the Soviet Union, on much better terms, was near. If this was a ploy to get the same reaction as in the Czech arms deal, the ploy did not work. The grant from the Soviet Union did not, at that time at least, materialize; then, when President Nasser tried to reopen discussions with the United States by sending an ambassador to Washington to close the agreement, he met with a sharp and, in Egyptian eyes, humiliating rebuff. Secretary Dulles, having already found, but not countered, opposition to such a loan in Congress, announced on July 20 that the United States could no longer consider participating. In its statement, moreover, the United States government questioned "the ability of Egypt to devote adequate resources to assure the project's success" and also indicated its unfavorable view of the increasingly close ties between Egypt and the Soviet Union. Infuriated by the "public insult," President Nasser struck out at the only available large target, the Suez Canal. In his Alexandria speech of July 26, he announced that the Universal Suez Maritime Canal Company had been nationalized.

Reaction to nationalization of the company was swift. The foreign ministers of the United States, Great Britain, and France met in London on August 2, and the first London Conference of the "user states" was held from August 16 to 23. It was there agreed that a five-man delegation be sent to Cairo to present to President Nasser the proposals agreed to by eighteen of the users. The delegation visited Cairo from September 3 to 9 but failed to reach any agreement. The United States froze Egyptian funds in the United States, on the plea that it must be able to indemnify shippers who, while paying tolls to the Egyptian government at Suez, might also be sued for tolls by the Canal Company in Europe.

Up to this point, the reaction had been so swift as to startle the Egyptian government. But already a fatal weakness appeared in the Western position. Greece refused to attend the conference, and there was, within the conference, obvious disagreement as to the ways to negotiate a settlement and on the extent of pressure to be applied to Egypt. The attitude of Sir Anthony Eden was unmistakable, but that of Mr. Dulles was overtly, at least, imprecise. The United States would not recommend to its citizens that they continue to serve in the canal, as other Westerners resigned from their posts, but it also would not urge its shipping lines, all highly susceptible to government pressure as the recipients of its subsidies, to boycott Suez. In these circumstances President Nasser made every effort to keep the canal in operation, so as to avoid charges of obstruction or incompetence, and waited for further disagreements to turn the de facto Egyptian control into one recognized as de jure.

On the eve of his departure for the Second London Conference Secretary Dulles took what must have been read in Europe as a threatening tone toward Egypt. He went on to outline his answer to the problem, the Canal Users Association, the precise nature of which was to become the major point of discussion at the Second London Conference. And at this conference Mr. Dulles issued a statement in which the main lines of American policy are clear—but clear in their exact emphasis, it must be admitted, only in retrospect. "Now we are faced here with a problem whereby great nations are faced with a great peril. It is a peril that they could readily remedy if they resorted to the methods which were lawful before this charter was adopted. Then, we wouldn't be sitting around here—perhaps somebody else wouldn't be sitting where he is, either. But those days, we hope, are past. There has been exercised, and is being exercised, a great restraint in the face of great peril. But you cannot expect that to go on indefinitely unless those of us who appreciate the problem, who are sympathetic with it, rally our forces to try to bring about a settlement in conformity with the principles of justice and international law."

On September 21 the United States subscribed to the Co-operative Association of Suez Canal Users which later was called the Suez Canal Users Association. Five days later the United States announced that it would back the United Kingdom and France in the forthcoming United Nations debate. In his press conference on that day Secretary Dulles commented that "the decision of the United States, at least, as I put it, [is] not to shoot its way through the canal." He went on to say that "there are pressures which gradually grow up, not artificially stimulated but as quite natural and inevitable . . . But I do not believe that the situation is such now as to call for any drastic action like going to war."

In the rush of events and in the circumstances, as now known, within the British government and the French government, these remarks did rather less than clarify exactly what the United States would agree to. The position of the United States was, in fact throughout opposed to the use of force, but each statement, such as that of Secretary Dulles on October 6, was so worded as always to hedge with a "But those who are concerned about peace ought to be equally concerned about justice." Dulles was, of course, playing "brinkmanship," which required the use of threat; what went wrong was that he spoke both to his adversary and to his—armed—allies.

Apparent indecision in the United States government was certainly matched by confusing moves by the British government; only the French and Israeli governments appear, at the beginning of October, to have had clear plans. On October 10–11, when Israeli forces attacked Qalqilya, the British government reaffirmed its treaty obligations to Jordan despite the fact that Jordan was obviously and rapidly moving in the direction of closer ties with Egypt. (On October 26 a unified military command of Jordan, Egypt, and Syria was established.) The British and French governments certainly did not, however, keep the United States informed of what plans they had. Former Secretary Acheson said bluntly in 1958, in his *Power and Diplomacy*, that "the British Government did not inform ours of its plans to use force. It is fair to go further and say that, at that stage, its conduct was deceitful." American alarm caused, for the first time, attempts by the C.I.A. to "penetrate" the British Government.

When reports of an Israeli mobilization reached President Eisenhower, he sent a personal message to Prime Minister Ben Gurion "expressing my grave concern and renewing a previous recommendation that no forcible initiative be taken which would endanger the peace." On October 28 the President again wrote to the Prime Minister. It is now known that already at that early date the United States was applying strong pressure on Israel not to act. But the Israeli army struck the next day; the following day came the Anglo-French ultimatum, and on the thirty-first, the Anglo-French invasion.

On the day of the ultimatum the United States took the issue to the Security Council (where its resolution was vetoed by Britain and France) and the President made a national television address on the Soviet attack on Hungary and the invasion of Egypt. In the course of his talk, Mr. Eisenhower said: "We believe these actions to have been taken in error . . . The actions taken can scarcely be reconciled with the principles and purposes of the United Nations to which we have all subscribed. And beyond this, we are forced to doubt even if resort to war will for long serve the permanent interests of the attacking nations . . . There can be no peace—without law. And there can be no law—if we were to invoke one code of international conduct for those who oppose us and another for our friends."

At the General Assembly, to which the United States had taken its vetoed resolution from the Security Council, Secretary Dulles on November 1 summed up, as perhaps no other statement he had ever made did more truly, the feelings of many Americans: "I doubt that any delegates ever spoke from this forum with as heavy a heart as I have brought here tonight. We speak on a matter of vital importance, where the United States finds itself unable to agree with three nations with whom it has ties, deep friendship, admiration, and respect, and two of whom constitute our oldest, most trusted and reliable allies."

The General Assembly adopted, 64–5, the United States resolution calling for an immediate cease-fire and withdrawal. But on November 3 this was rejected by France, Great Britain, and Israel. Negotiations were conducted by the UN Secretary General with Israel and Egypt, but both the United States and the Soviet Union took strong independent action. On November 4 the Soviet government delivered a note to the British government in which it "emphatically protests against these illegal actions by the United Kingdom and France and declares that the responsibility for all the possible consequences of those actions rests with the Governments of the United Kingdom and France." At the UN the United States supported a draft resolution introduced by Canada, Colombia, and Norway to establish the United Nations Emergency Force. On the same day Soviet Foreign Minister Shepilov sent a note to the UN Security Council president declaring its readiness to send to Egypt "the air and naval forces necessary to defend Egypt and repulse the aggressors." Soviet Premier Bulganin wrote at the same time to President Eisenhower proposing "joint and immediate use" of the naval and air forces of the two powers to end the attack. In a White House statement, the United States immediately rejected the proposal saying that "neither Soviet nor any other military forces should now enter the Middle East area except under United Nations mandate ... The introduction of new forces under these circumstances would violate the United Nations Charter, and it would be the duty of all United Nations members, including the United States, to oppose any such effort." The statement contrasted the Soviet attitude on Egypt with Soviet intervention in Hungary. Many in the American government felt that the Suez invasion gave the Soviet Union a free ticket to Hungary.

On October 7 Prime Minister Ben Gurion, far from indicating any fear of the Soviet attitude, which had included the withdrawing of the Soviet ambassador to Israel, spoke of the "glorious military operation ... an unprecedented feat in Jewish history and ... rare in the world's history." But on the same day the General Assembly once again called upon Israel to withdraw, and President Eisenhower again wrote to express his "deep concern" at the refusal of the Israeli government to withdraw its army from Egyptian territory. In reply, the following day, in the face of strong American pressure, Ben Gurion agreed to comply but indicated that the problem of the Sinai hostilities could not be separated from the context of the whole aftermath of the Palestine War. As Israel saw the steps toward peace, they must include, along with evacuation of Sinai, an end to the economic boycott of Israel, direct negotiations between Israel and the Arab states, and freedom of passage for Israeli ships through the Straits of Tiran and through Suez.

Israeli demands were regarded with sympathy in Washington since it was the opinion of the United States government that Egypt had done much to provoke the attack and that a return to the status quo ante was dangerous. Yet, the United States also was worried about the implications of a solution brought about by the use of force, for if the invasion could be reckoned a success, even indirectly, then the dangers of coups de main were certainly increased. Consequently, both in public and in private, the American government assured Is-

rael that it would do all in its power to settle the outstanding problems of the status quo ante, but that, as Ambassador Lodge said in
the General Assembly on several occasions and Secretary Dulles affirmed in dispatches to the Israeli government, the United States
agreed with the Secretary General that "withdrawal is a preliminary
and essential phase in a development through which a stable basis
may be laid for peaceful conditions in the area."

The United States government felt, possibly, less sympathy with
the British and French position, in that the actions of such close
allies—particularly in the context of NATO—put the United States
in a position of acute embarrassment. It was felt also that the Anglo-
French invasion had at least mitigated the effects of the brutal Soviet
repression of Hungary and was thus not only irresponsible but tragic.
Considerable relief was felt in Washington when the last of the
Anglo-French force was evacuated on December 23, and the United
Nations Emergency Force began their forward movement into Sinai.
The last Israeli troops left Egyptian territory on March 1, 1957.

It was at this point that the United States had to try to pick up the
tangled lines of its various alliances and to reassess the general context
of its foreign policy. If the United States was to attempt to hold together a broad and at times mutually hostile coalition of Europe and
Asia, it must have firm, clear, and definite policy assumptions and
goals by which crises could be controlled. The Eisenhower Doctrine
was an attempt to accomplish this purpose.

A part of the justification for the British intervention in Suez was
given in Commons on December 3 by Foreign Secretary Lloyd as a
response to "Soviet mischief making." "The large supply of Soviet
arms to Colonel Nasser," said Lloyd, "put him very much under Soviet influence. The Baghdad Pact gave a measure of security against
direct Soviet penetration from the North, but the arming of Syria and
Egypt, was no doubt intended to turn its flank also." It was this element which rapidly re-emerged from momentary eclipse in American
thought as the local crisis became manageable. On January 5, at a
time in which the United States was attempting at the United Nations and through direct pressure to bring about a withdrawal of Israeli forces in Egypt, President Eisenhower turned his attention back
to the threat of the Soviet Union in the Middle East. In the course of
his address to Congress the President said: "All this instability [in the
Middle East] has been heightened and, at times, manipulated by International Communism ... Russia's interest in the Middle East is
solely that of power politics. Considering her announced purpose of

Communizing the world, it is easy to understand her hope of dominating the Middle East ... [If this came about] Western Europe would be endangered just as though there had been no Marshall Plan, no North Atlantic Treaty Organization. The free nations of Asia and Africa, too, would be placed in serious jeopardy."

The UN, said President Eisenhower, had shown its abilities when faced by nations with a decent respect for the opinions of mankind, but in Hungary the situation was otherwise. Therefore, "a greater responsibility now devolves upon the United States. We have shown, so that none can doubt, our dedication to the principle that force shall not be used internationally for any aggressive purpose and that the integrity and independence of the nations of the Middle East should be inviolate. Seldom in history has a nation's dedication to principle been tested as severely as ours during recent weeks." The President went on to propose a joint congressional-presidential declaration embodying three features: (1) provision for the United States to cooperate with nations in the area to build up their economic strength; to this end $200 million yearly for the discretionary use of the President was requested; (2) greater flexibility for the President to use funds already allocated to assist any nation or group of nations desiring military assistance and cooperation; and (3) permission to use the "armed forces of the United States to secure and protect the territorial integrity and political independence of such nations, requesting such aid, against overt armed aggression from any nation controlled by International Communism."

Congress passed the Eisenhower Doctrine as a joint resolution on March 9, 1957, and on the same day the President appointed James P. Richards, former chairman of the House Foreign Affairs Committee, as his special assistant to carry the doctrine to the Middle East. Like the doctrine itself, the mission was largely redundant since all that it gained was public endorsement by those states that had already indicated their friendly attitude toward the same policy in a former guise. But upon his return Ambassador Richards spoke glowingly on June 13 to the House Foreign Affairs Committee of his mission. "This new departure, this entirely American line of action, evoked a heart-warming trust from the nations of the area." On his trip, Richards said, he had managed to give out $120 million. "International Communism," reads the first report of the Richards mission on August 5, 1957, "has been put on notice ... and the nations of the area are encouraged to help themselves."

The "Syrian crisis" of August and September was a clear test of the assumptions underlying the new doctrine. On August 6 the Soviet government agreed to provide large amounts of economic aid to Syria; on August 15 the Syrian chief of staff was replaced by a man regarded in Washington as pro-Soviet. Then officials of the United States embassy in Damascus were expelled, and in retaliation the Syrian ambassador was asked to leave Washington. United States arms shipments were announced to Jordan (by airlift), Lebanon, Iraq, and Saudi Arabia. These moves were followed by a statement from Secretary Dulles that "Turkey now faces growing military danger from the major build-up of arms in Syria." Nowhere in the Middle East was this taken at face value. Given the facts—the Syrian army contained only about 50,000 men, mostly lacking in battle experience, whose presence on the Israeli frontier was necessary, and whose equipment was new and for which they were poorly trained; the Turkish army of half a million men (the largest field force in NATO) had been armed and trained for a decade by the United States, and, in being able to rely upon NATO guarantees, were able to deploy on the Syrian frontier—it is not surprising that many in the Middle East thought that the United States was looking for an excuse to employ the Eisenhower Doctrine.

It quickly became clear that the United States was not prepared to act decisively to block the Soviet Union's offer of aid, but having given the impression that it intended to do so, had both to back down and to be damned for having opposed the good that might result from such aid. As it was, the actions of the United States government were both futile and damaging to its position.

But if the Syrian crisis of the fall showed the shortfalls of the Eisenhower Doctrine, the Lebanese crisis of the spring and summer showed its dangers. On May 8, 1958, the editor of a Beirut newspaper was shot, and this act touched off an already tense and smoldering atmosphere. The contributing causes of the tension were many and deeply rooted in history. A more recent element, of import here, was what many Lebanese regarded as an excessive identification of the government of Lebanon with United States policy to oppose President Nasser of Egypt. The Richards Mission had been interpreted in the Middle East as a demand that the Middle Eastern states leave the neutralist position, which many had found attractive, and "stand up to be counted," a posture for which the United States was prepared to pay cash. Thus, on May 10 the United States Information Service (USIS) library in Tripoli was sacked; on the twelfth Beirut was blockaded. On the fourteenth the United States said it was doubling the marine force with the Sixth Fleet; on the sixteenth announced that it would shortly send further military assistance to Lebanon; and on the seventeenth stated that it was considering sending troops to

Lebanon if requested. On the eighteenth the Soviet Union accused the United States of interfering in Lebanese domestic affairs. Great Britain and the United States agreed to joint action if needed and on the twenty-fifth the Royal Air Force delivered arms to Lebanon. By June 3 the last (the fifth) USIS center was closed.

As tensions mounted, all that was missing was a spark. This was struck on July 14 in Baghdad when the army overthrew the pro-Western government of Nuri Said, the host of CENTO, the Baghdad Pact, and so set alight the powder of the Eisenhower Doctrine. On the day after the coup, American Marines landed in Lebanon.

24

American Policies
of the 1960's

OLLOWING the death of John Foster Dulles, it was
clear that the United States had been unable to
enforce its wishes upon the Middle East. The intricate system of pacts
proved to be no more than paper and even the use of American military force, while more spectacular, proved no more effective. Consequently, in the last years of the Eisenhower administration, the
American government pulled back from its assertive policy and
began tentatively to grope toward the reestablishment of friendly ties
with the Arab countries. With the advent of the Kennedy administration in 1961, the opportunity naturally arose to reassess and rebuild.

The new administration came into office with the belief that a
great deal needed to be changed in policy and personnel. In the appointment of ambassadors in various parts of the world, it sought to
show its sympathy with and understanding of other peoples. The appointment of John Badeau as ambassador to Egypt was such a gesture, for he had been President of the American University of Cairo
and spoke Arabic. Yet there was more "image" than reality in the initial acts of the new administration. The fact was that the Kennedy
administration had come to power without any clearly conceived notions of foreign policy in the Middle East and, upon assuming control
over the government, was unsure what policies to implement and,
more pointedly, which to discard. Its councils were profoundly divided.

The new Secretary of State, Dean Rusk, had been an intimate

friend and adviser of John Foster Dulles and shared with him many of the conceptions of America's role in the world arena. As this view affected the Middle East, it became clear in one of his first significant acts as Secretary of State. In April 1961, Secretary Rusk announced that the United States would continue the policies of the previous administration in regard to the CENTO alliance. To emphasize the view he took of this alliance, Rusk himself, that same month, attended the meeting of the CENTO powers. Others pointed out that the CENTO alliance was not only anachronistic and of little or no value to the United States, but that it was a positive danger in that it emphasized a military role for America in the Middle East, aligned it with governments of dubious popular support, and might embroil it militarily in a situation similar to the Vietnamese conflict in Southeast Asia.

At the time, however, the reaffirmation of American support for CENTO appeared relatively small, even insignificant. The President decided that it was not worth the gesture of "disengagement" and considered Secretary Rusk's trip a sop to a moribund and irrelevant institution. Moreover, the implications of the move were not fully appreciated. Indeed, the issue of whether or not America should "get out" of CENTO was being debated long after the point of decision had been passed. In foreign affairs, as the Kennedy Administration was to learn, there is a relatively short period in which a new president, without massive resistance from those whose prestige or jobs are dependent upon a continuation of policy, could impose new policies. In those critical early months, much of the energies of the new administration were devoted to what appeared to be far more pressing issues in the Caribbean, Southeast Asia, and Europe. In fact, of course, CENTO played almost no discernible role in ensuing events but it did set the stage for America's posture in the area.

Policies which were inherited from the previous administration—such as attachment to CENTO—grew out of basic military and intelligence requirements. A major inhibition to changes in these policies was the realization that the non–Middle Eastern, essentially Cold War determinants remained the same as in the previous administration. While the U-2 flights no longer set aid and political standards for American policy in Pakistan and Turkey, continuation of other intelligence and military activities and facilities closely hedged in American policy in those areas, in Iran in the East, and in Libya and Morocco in the West. These activities and the commitments on which they were based were to have profound consequences for American policy in the Arab countries.

Moreover, the Department of State—both in the person of the Secretary and the officers at the "working level"—continued to hold the view of the American long-term interests and objectives in the Middle East which underlay the policy of the previous administration. The emphasis on military overflight rights, continuation of the flow of petroleum on acceptable terms to Europe, and, above all, prevention of the real or ostensible incursion of the Soviet Union into the Mediterranean area underlay the policies of both administrations.

It was only gradually and haltingly that the United States determined to try to achieve the same basic objectives through a slight modification of program. Accentuating the trend which had become manifest during Christian Herter's tenure as Secretary of State, the American government began to emphasize the economic aspects of its aid program and to develop a gradual rapprochement with the more radical Arab countries, notably the United Arab Republic.

The theory behind American policy in this period rested on two assumptions: that it might be possible to use American aid to encourage tendencies and people, even where regimes appeared hostile, to create a situation more favorable to American interest; and that the United States could tolerate, with safety to its fundamental objectives, a high level of "static" in Arab political activity. Emphasis was to be placed, planners hoped, on a longer-term strategy. Consequently the United States government was basically undisturbed, however much it might seek to moderate them, by a succession of crises and alarms in 1961.

When the Saudi Arabian government in April 1961, asked the United States to move its military units out of the Dhahran Airfield, the United States was quick to comply; so quick, in fact, as to surprise and apparently to disappoint the Saudi Arabian government. The American government was somewhat more disturbed by the claim advanced by General Qasim of Iraq in June to hegemony over Kuwait. Since, however, Kuwait was very much more important to the British than to the Americans, Great Britain undertook the initial steps to preserve Kuwaiti independence. Kuwait was learning to make itself important to a number of Arab states, so the British were able to bow out gracefully as their forces were replaced by a mixed Arab contingent. The breakup of the United Arab Republic in late September 1961, drew as the American response only the calm recognition that it was an intra-Arab affair of little concern to the United States. When the level of "static"—as when the Yemen war threatened to spill over into Saudi Arabia—grew so high that the United States government felt impelled to act, it made every effort to keep its intervention to minimal levels.

The longer term strategy of the United States was based on a growing appreciation of the fact that the Middle Eastern countries were involved in a basic social transformation and that this transformation was as evident where regimes were conservative as where they were radical. At the very heart of the modernization process was the creation of new capabilities, new forms of social organization, and "new men." Even before the nature of these transformations was understood, the United States was committed to their assistance through the greatly enlarged program of aid specified in Public Law 480.

Through all of the formulations of policy ran a central theme: that the United States should do everything in its power to accentuate those tendencies in transformation which appeared likely to be "constructive." The primary assumption behind this policy was that to the degree that the Middle Eastern Arab countries put their best efforts toward internal development, they would tend to de-emphasize those policies which were born of a sense of frustration, despair, and humiliation. The second assumption was that as the development process picked up momentum, it would create higher criteria of success. Central among these would be the fulfillment of ambitions of human well-being. It was thus anticipated that an ever increasing percentage of the population would win for itself representation in the civic culture and that this evolution would make it less possible for governments to act arbitrarily and irresponsibly in external and internal affairs. The third assumption, a much more debatable one, was that as more and more people became aware of their improving standard of living and of a widening horizon toward the future, they would become less prone to the violent, destructive lunges which appear, retrospectively, to typify the last generation of Middle Eastern politics. In short, if not the society as a whole, at least those members of it which were politically effective would develop a stake in peaceful and constructive evolution.

Public Law 480 offered the basic instrumentality of American foreign policy. It disposed of a surplus American commodity, primarily wheat, employed American citizens to process and ship it, enriched American ship-owners who transported it, gave the United States government some apparent "leverage" in foreign policy dealings and, at the recipients' end, was used to generate local currencies which could be committed at the option of the donor. Since the expenditure of monies tied up local currencies, the law had the effect of locking the recipient economy and government into development projects. It appeared that the United States had an almost perfect instrumentality to effect its *strategy* in the Middle East. Unfortunately, what was a perfect tool of strategy was mistakenly assumed to be an adequate tool of *tactics*. Governments could be rewarded or punished in visible ways, by the application or withdrawal of P. L. 480 wheat as their actions pleased or displeased Americans. For the most part they did not respond flexibly or overtly enough. And, as we shall see, both because of the worsening relationship between the United States and the Arab countries in 1966 and the fact that wheat was no longer a surplus commodity in the United States, the P. L. 480 instrumentality was largely given up.

One aspect of the problems of the Middle East was singled out for serious if cautious attention. This was the dilemma of Palestine. In September 1961, the President determined to try a new approach by arranging for the United Nations to send Dr. Joseph Johnson, the president of the Carnegie Foundation and a former member of the Policy Planning Staff, to consult with the governments in the area on means to settle the refugee problem. Despite strenuous efforts by Dr. Johnson, then and in the spring of 1962, the mission ended in a failure. As was predicted, the refugee problem proved to be both the most complex and intractable aspect of the Palestine issue.

Dr. Johnson's plan involved giving priority to the wishes of the refugees, within limited areas of choice, and under the active supervision of the United Nations. His plan called for the expression of preferences by the refugees on whether to "return" or not, then, under United Nations auspices, for the processing of individual refugee families through security clearances, travel to Israel, or payment of compensation for settlement outside of Israel.

As Dr. Johnson pointed out, "neither the Arabs nor Israel would get what they want. Both would have to give up something." Israel, he pointed out, "would have to take in some refugees she did not want, without any prior agreement on the number (which, parenthetically but most importantly, I am convinced would, under the procedures I propose, be very small, fewer than one-tenth of the total of true refugees and their descendants)." He subsequently pointed out, "if the [American] government—which of course means the President—decides to pursue such a course as I have proposed, it must at the same time anticipate and be prepared to meet a well-organized, efficient, determined, persistent, pervasive effort to alter that course." The American government was not willing to make such an effort, nor did either the Israeli government or the several Arab governments give the plan serious consideration as the means of settling the conflict.

Of course, the policies of the United States in the Arab world were only one part, and not necessarily the leading part, of the bilateral and multilateral relationships that constituted the United States' relations with the Arab world. As serious as was the failure of the new administration to make and utilize sophisticated analyses of the nature of the social transformation in the Middle East, even more serious was the failure of the leaders of the Arab countries to recognize the true nature of the revolutionary process they themselves had loosed upon their countries. At the heart of this failure was the incapability of the various Arab rulers, notably President Nasser of Egypt, to recognize the nature of modern power.

As we have noted above, one of the most striking characteristics of the early Egyptian modernizer and reformer, Mehmet Ali, was his perceptive analysis of power in his own time. He knew that it was not the appearance or even the implements of modernization which had made Napoleon capable of defeating France's enemies; rather, the French ability to mobilize and stimulate themselves to *produce* the implements and cadres of trained men set them apart from their contemporaries. In modern terms, President Nasser, during the 1960's, never appeared to be able to differentiate between the symbols and implements of modern power and the factors which made them employable. Throughout the early and middle years of the 1960's, he and other Arab leaders emphasized the accumulation of military hardware to such an extent as to preempt the skilled personnel and the production capabilities. The growth of military establishments thus tended to sap the energies and to slow down or distort the process of social change. In pursuing the mirage of Arab unity—even in far off Yemen—President Nasser resorted to violent and unsuccessful means. And these factors, the obviously aggressive bent of the government, the extremely hostile pronouncements, and the non-productive appropriation of resources, in turn, tended to operate as a brake on cooperative aspects of American foreign policy.

The Yemeni revolution brought the underlying suspicion and hostility to a head. As noted in Chapter 14, a military coup toppled the Imam's successor and the state appeared to have shattered in a tribal revolt. Thus, when the new leader, Abdullah Sallal, requested help from the Egyptians, President Nasser elected to intervene rather than see the modernizing forces crushed. Within a very short period, Egypt put 30,000 troops in Yemen. But, to the surprise of all observers, particularly the Egyptians, these troops proved insufficient to bring the fighting to an end. Indeed, their very presence may have helped to coalesce tribal opposition around the person of the deposed Imam. Yemen than entered into an almost classical military stalemate in which the Egyptians, using airpower, tanks, and other tools of modern warfare—including, on occasion, poison gas—proved unable to defeat the tribal guerrilla forces led by the Imam and assisted by technicians, money, supplies, and material from Saudi Arabia.

After three months' hesitation, the United States recognized the republican regime in December 1962, in circumstances which were rightly criticized as too late to win friends and too early to be safe. To ease the pressure on Saudi Arabia, the United States began a lengthy series of negotiations and demarches designed to effect an Egyptian troop withdrawal. The most visible aspect of this was a mission headed by Ambassador Ellsworth Bunker to Cairo and Riyadh in June and August of 1963. The efforts were ineffectual—mainly because the Egyptian withdrawal appeared certain to cause the collapse of Sallal's government—and more than 70,000 Egyptian troops were still in Yemen in 1967.

Egyptian reliance on Soviet equipment, military training, and in certain cases, personnel in its Yemen operation, a growing rift with the United States over the Yemen policy, Iraqi and Syrian hostility to the United States, and the ever tense Arab-Israeli situation combined to offer the Soviet Union what appeared to be a tactical advantage. The Soviet Union moved to use it. Employing essentially the same tools used by the United States, the Soviet Union offered massive amounts (estimated to be on the order of $2 billion worth) of military equipment and economic assistance to the various Arab countries. While the amounts of aid appear more or less equally balanced between civilian and military, the overall effect of the Soviet aid programs was to accentuate the militarization of Arab regimes. By catering to demands for the latest and most sophisticated military equipment, the Soviet Union built still further the dream of power which was so humiliatingly shattered in June 1967. What appeared to be an almost endless stream of tanks, self-propelled guns, naval armaments, and jet aircraft poured into Iraq, Syria, and Egypt.

Moreover, in order to increase its bargaining power with the Soviet Union and to accelerate the pace of its own military development, the Egyptian government hired large numbers of German technicians to engage in extremely expensive programs to develop surface-to-surface missiles (essentially a slightly modernized version of the World War II German V-2 missile), a jet-fighter plane, and certain other weapons. The former political affiliations of the technicians, perhaps more than the apparently dangerous nature of the weapons, increased the hostility toward Nasser's regime within the United States and Europe.

In response, the United States began to give certain categories of military equipment, notably the "balancing" Hawk missile and tanks, to Israel, and other items of conventional military equipment to Jordan and Saudi Arabia—two states which sought to remain outside the Egyptian-Syrian-Iraqi "radical" camp. The dynamics of the tactical policy of "balancing" the Soviet arms build-up, however important to the maintenance of peace, did encourage the militarization of these two societies and so undercut the longer-term American strategy. The policy of "balancing" was not, in any event, capable of sustaining the status quo. It merely assured that when the explosion came, it came with a bigger bang.

In the United States, growing tension with the "radical" Arab countries rapidly led to a congressional revolt against the policies of the Kennedy administration. In the debate on the Foreign Assistance Act of 1963, Congress inserted a restriction to withhold aid to any country "engaging in or preparing for aggressive military efforts" against other countries to which the United States also gave aid. President Kennedy opposed inclusion of this restriction but, after his death, it was passed by Congress. Its effect, predictably, was to diminish the already small *tactical* influence of the United States in the Arab countries. However, under the circumstances, it is more remarkable that the administration was given the latitude it had than that it was unable to sustain a sophisticated, long-range policy. In fact, the "static" in the Middle East had proven too loud.

Ironically, as the Western withdrawal from the Arab countries was completed, the Soviet Union appeared bent on recreating a situation for itself not dissimilar from that which Secretary Dulles had aimed at in the creation of CENTO, the acquisition of military bases and the build-up of the Sixth Fleet. At the time of the war, June 1967, the Soviet Union had created the equivalent of a Sixth Fleet—a military formation which the more sophisticated military thinkers in the United States had come to realize was obsolescent if not obsolete—and acquired the sort of military facilities which had proven so expensive and of such limited value to America. Thus, as those military strategists most concerned with the Cold War had predicted, the Soviet Union did what it could to enter what had always been thought of by geopolitical planners as a "power vacuum" in the Middle East.

25

Foreign Policy of the Nixon Administration

Two of the three great Middle Eastern themes of
the 1960's—the internal social revolutionary
change with its associated political turbulence, and the ebb and flow
of Soviet and Western policy initiative—have been accounted for.
The third major sequence, intimately associated with but overshadowing these two, was the diplomatic stalemate following the June
1967 war, finally causing the October 1973 war, and the ensuing diplomatic initiative aimed at bringing about peace between the Arab
states and Israel.

Before the Nixon Administration took office in 1969, the President-elect's new foreign affairs adviser, Henry Kissinger, established
an office in New York where he received a parade of friends, colleagues, and would-be advisers on virtually every aspect of American
foreign policy. Three great issues appeared to loom before the new
administration: the continuing Vietnam war, the dangerous and sour
relationship with the Soviet Union and the lack of relationship with
China. The Middle East appeared a most unpromising area for diplomatic initiatives. Nonetheless, Mr. Kissinger decided to try to find out
informally if there were any possibility of "give" on the part of the
Egyptians, with whom we still had no diplomatic relations, toward
some form of peace negotiation. The reply was disconcertingly forthcoming: President Nasser indicated that he would welcome negotiations aimed at reducing tensions in the Middle East and leading to-

ward the implementation of UN Security Council Resolution 242. Toward that end, he said, he was prepared to agree to demilitarization of the Sinai Peninsula, opening of the Suez Canal and, in due course, exchange of diplomatic representatives between Egypt and Israel.

For reasons which still have not been made public and can only be surmised, no attempt was made to follow up on this initiative. The political atmosphere was not conducive: Nasser's war of attrition had only just begun to take effect and the bitter memory of Nasser as the man who falsely accused the United States of initiating the air attack on Cairo in June 1967 still rankled in Washington. The Nixon Administration decided to keep as remote, and as unexposed as possible, an issue in which the odds always appeared unfavorable. Consequently, the United States opted for initiative limited to four-power discussions at the United Nations during 1969.

It was not until November 1969 that the State Department induced Secretary William Rogers to put forward a proposal, reaffirming United Nations Security Council Resolution 242, which proposed negotiations between the interested parties themselves. In a speech on December 9, Secretary Rogers reaffirmed the policy of the Johnson Administration opposing unilateral alteration of the status of Jerusalem by Israel,* and reaffirmed that "there can be no lasting peace without a just settlement of the problem of those Palestinians whom the wars of 1948 and 1967 had made homeless." These statements were widely taken as signs that the Republican Administration wanted better relations with the Arabs. They were followed by a slowdown in new arms sales to Israel. During the spring of 1970, the United States informed the Russians that it would like to encourage joint Soviet-American restraint on arms supply to bring about an end to the war of attrition. The war had taken an ominous new turn as in riposte to greater Israeli success along the Canal and deep penetration air raids against Egypt, the Soviet Union had begun to commit not only advisors but operational troops and air defense units for the first time outside Warsaw Pact countries. Not only was Israel no longer able to pursue its reprisal policy against Egypt with impunity but the United States watched with alarm as the Soviet Union consolidated an entirely new form of "presence" in the Middle East by acquiring bases, flying air patrols, and stationing heavily armed combat troops in an increasingly dependent state. Even without these dramatic developments, however, the war of attrition had been a costly under-

---

* U.S. Representative Arthur J. Goldberg US/UN Press Release 124, July 14, 1967; also see United Nations A/RES/2254 and 2253.

taking for all participants. For the Egyptians, the main cost was to be seen in the virtual immobilization of the economy as growth rates in population and national income canceled one another; for Israel, the war of attrition had claimed more casualties than the Six-Day War. In Jordan, meanwhile, the growing challenge of the Palestinian guerrilla organizations was leading rapidly and obviously toward civil war. Thus, everyone in the Middle East, with the exception of the Palestinians, was attentive if not fully receptive when Secretary of State Rogers put forward "The Rogers Plan" on June 25, 1970.

This was the first occasion when the Republican Administration's policy toward detente with the Soviet Union paid dividends. President Nasser was then in the Soviet Union and doubtlessly was influenced in the nature of his reply by his conversations with Soviet leaders. At the time, this seemed somewhat ironic because Kissinger was widely reported as having said "Washington wanted to 'expel' Soviet combat forces (from Egypt), though he made it clear that he hoped to achieve this as part of a peace settlement, not by force."*

The most tangible outcome of the Rogers Plan was the agreement, ultimately effected on August 7, 1970, for a 90-day cease fire.† The agreement called for a military standstill on the Suez front and the recommencement of talks with Ambassador Jarring on the basis of Security Council Resolution 242. The agreement was at the time regarded, at least by the Administration, as having made a significant contribution to peace in attaining both Egyptian and Jordanian public expression of consent to Israel's right to exist within secure and recognized borders, and Israeli commitment to accept Security Council Resolution 242 including the principle of indirect negotiations. The United States gave assurances to Israel that if the cease fire standstill terms were violated, the United States would act to compensate any disadvantage which Israel might suffer; to Egypt, the United States promised restraint in further delivery of military aircraft to Israel.

Unfortunately, almost immediately the various provisions of the agreement began to break down: Egypt immediately and flagrantly violated the standstill provisions and, in riposte, the Israelis took actions to improve their position along the Canal. The United States, feeling that Israel had been disadvantaged by this violation, and viewing with alarm the continued large-scale Soviet supply of equip-

---

* *International Herald Tribune,* July 18–19, 1970.

† *The Sunday Times,* London, August 2, 1970 gives an excellent background by Henry Brandon on the negotiations.

ment, stepped up its own delivery of military aircraft to Israel.* While the Egyptians and Jordanians accepted the Jarring Mission, the Israelis did not. The Mission lingered on for a number of months; in fact was never officially terminated, but it was no longer actively supported by any of the governments party to the Middle Eastern dispute. The cease fire, the one concrete development of the Rogers Plan, was renewed on November 6, 1970 and again in February, but was allowed to expire on March 7, 1971. De facto, however, the cease fire continued until the outbreak of the October 1973 war.

Once more, the Middle East issue seemed to disappear in 1971 from the Washington agenda and it was not until the October 1973 war that the issue was vigorously, indeed, brutally, thrust onto center stage.

Subsequent events in the Middle East would not be understandable if viewed solely within the context of American relations with the countries of the Middle East. Two other factors must be considered: U.S.-Soviet relations, and Egyptian relations with the Soviet Union. The latter were almost always tense and troubled. Observers of Egyptian politics have often noted that the Egyptian government, wavering uneasily between the Great Powers, no sooner appeared to make a serious commitment to one than it began to backpedal lest it be drawn too exclusively into the orbit of that power. Since Nasser's death, relations with the Soviet Union had deteriorated badly. This resulted, as described above in Chapter 17, in the expulsion of nearly 40,000 Soviet citizens, the takeover of Soviet-manned bases, and a slow-down in Soviet arms deliveries. Moreover, the Egyptian political faction most identified with the Soviet Union was purged from the government, the Arab Socialist Union, and the government-controlled press. Repeated overtures were made to the United States for easing of Egyptian-American relations and while these were rebuffed and while diplomatic relations were not reestablished, the Egyptian government remained hopeful and sensitive to this option.

Much more significant, however, was the growing detente between the United States and the Soviet Union. Symbolized by exchanges of visits between senior officials, highlighted by negotiations designed to reduce the momentum of the arms race and, perhaps most significantly, underpinned by massive economic deals involving the shipment of millions of tons of American agricultural produce and billions of dollars of industrial equipment, the detente was a major political gamble for both the Soviet and the American governments. Quite apart from the national strategic considerations, the leaders of each

* 1971 was the highwater mark of American military aid to Israel; $600 million worth, or seven times as much as ever given by the Johnson Administration.

government had a major personal stake in preventing such actions as might seriously embarrass them amongst their own harder-line constituents. When Brezhnev set out to visit the United States in June 1973, the question uppermost in the mind of Soviet Middle Eastern experts was whether or not events in the Middle East might result in an armed clash and so, possibly, abort his trip or bring about a sharp reversal of the trend toward better relationships between the Soviet Union and the United States. In short, both administrations were sensitive to the need to preserve the progress which had been made and to avoid actions by one another which might be used by their domestic opponents to criticize their previous pronouncements. Even more important, while both were anxious to hold onto the positions of advantage they had acquired in the Middle East, neither was willing to allow its local ally in the Middle East to take such actions as might undermine its relations with the other power. In short, the detente acquired a life of its own and served as a cushion on activities within the Middle East. When, at one point in the October 1973 war, the Soviet Union appeared temporarily to lose sight of the need for restraint, a "signal" was transmitted by the proclamation of a worldwide alert by the United States. The Soviet Union slowed down. At a later point, when the United States appeared to be shoving too hard against Soviet positions in the Middle East, the Soviet Union showed its capabilities to hold up progress toward a Syrian truce. The United States then took measures to assure the Soviet Union of its good intent.

In the United States, the laborious and painful unfolding of the Watergate scandal tended to weaken the presidency and to divert the President's attention from and undermine his interest in anything other than his political survival. Given his already close relationship with Henry Kissinger as his foreign affairs adviser, the President made no attempt, apparently, to continue to act, as most American presidents have, as in all but name his own Secretary of State. In his dual capacity as Chief of Staff of the National Security Council and Secretary of State, Mr. Kissinger acquired unprecedented bureaucratic power. In his personal popularity, in the approbation which followed his receipt of the Nobel Prize for his role in diminishing direct American combat involvement in Vietnam, and as a result of his widely recognized personal accomplishments, Secretary Kissinger was in a unique position to move effectively and authoritatively when an opportunity was afforded him in the Middle Eastern arena.

When the war broke out in October, the course of events lent themselves to truce-making initiatives. The Egyptians were ahead but on the brink of catastrophe. By the end of the third week of fighting, the Egyptian Third Corps was surrounded and cut off, its troops were low on ammunition, food, and water, and its morale was shattered. Its collapse would have been a stunning tactical victory for Israel, but a defeat of such magnitude for both the Egyptian and Soviet governments as to be "unacceptable." Further pressure at that time would almost certainly have brought about an escalation of the crisis. On their side, the Israelis had suffered and were suffering heavily from the war. In the three weeks of fighting, Israeli casualties, proportionally, were higher than those of America in the entire war in Vietnam. The Israeli economy had been brought to a virtual standstill, and the cost of the war had run to $6 billion. Further warfare on the scale then undertaken would virtually have bankrupted Israel. So for different reasons and however much they may have disagreed on the timing and terms of a cease fire, both the Egyptian and the Israeli governments recognized the need for an end to the war.

It was in this complex of Middle Eastern, American, and Russian contexts that Secretary Kissinger undertook what was to become a stunning virtuoso performance in Egypt and Israel in the winter and Syria and Israel in the spring. The history of the ensuing months was largely one of what came to be called "shuttle diplomacy" as the United States Department of State was crammed aboard a jet airplane.

The *New York Times* of November 11, 1973, gave its impressions: "As Secretary of State Henry Kissinger completed his breathless race through the capitals of Islam, two images came to mind. One is of a speeded-up Charlie Chaplin movie in which Charlie desperately rushes around a collapsing house trying to prop up one wall while the other threatens to fall. The other is of a jig-saw puzzle solver determined to fit or force together the pieces of a puzzle that defies solution."

Actually, a log of the travels not only of Secretary Kissinger but of senior officials of the Soviet, Egyptian, Israeli, Algerian, Syrian, Saudi Arabian, French, British, and Japanese governments is stunning commentary on the transformation of diplomacy over any previously known practice. The age of airborne diplomacy had arrived.

On October 20, Kissinger flew to Moscow to discuss with the Soviet leaders ideas on how to end the hostilities. Although he was not present, the vast investment in sophisticated communications equipment allowed the Secretary of State to keep in minute-by-minute contact with events in Washington and New York so that he was able to supervise American passage of Security Council Resolution 338, calling for a cease fire, on October 22. On that date, Kissinger arrived in Israel. The truce, although agreed to by both Israel and Egypt, was never really implemented; on October 24 President Sadat asked both the United States and the Soviet Union to furnish troops to police the cease fire. The United States refused while the Soviet Union accepted; the next morning at 3 A.M., the United States went on what was described as a "precautionary" worldwide alert and announced that it was adamantly opposed to the "unilateral introduction by any Great Power of forces into the Middle East in whatever guise." Later that day, the Security Council voted 14 to 0 to establish a Middle East Emergency Force.

At that point, the travel schedules of government leaders and diplomats became truly mind-boggling. The Egyptian Foreign Minister flew to Washington on October 28 and was followed by Mrs. Meir, Prime Minister of Israel, on the 31st. Presidents Sadat and Assad went to Kuwait and Saudi Arabia; Algerian President Boumedienne flew to Damascus; Soviet Deputy Foreign Minister Kuznetsov flew to Cairo and Damascus, and on November 5 Secretary Kissinger flew to Morocco while the Egyptian Foreign Minister flew to Paris. Meanwhile, Takeo Miki, Japanese Deputy Premier, toured the Arab countries.

Arriving once more in Cairo on November 6, Kissinger was able to work out an arrangement with President Sadat so that on November 7, the United States and Egypt announced resumption of diplomatic relations and Assistant Secretary of State Joseph Sisco was detached to Israel as "anchorman" of the armistice team. Secretary Kissinger then, on November 8, flew to Jordan to meet King Husain and on to Saudi Arabia to meet King Faisal. The next day, the United States communicated through the UN Secretary General Kurt Waldheim the text of an agreement which it indicated both Israel and Egypt were prepared to sign.

The agreement specified six points: cease fire; discussions to be initiated on the return to the October 22 cease fire line; emergency supplies were to be allowed to Suez City; non-military supplies were to be allowed for the Egyptian Third Corps; United Nations personnel was to replace Israeli personnel on checkpoints; and all prisoners of war were to be exchanged. The cease fire was signed at a tent 101 kilometers from Cairo—"Kilo one-o-one" entered the peacemakers' lexicon—on November 11 by Israeli General Yariv and Egyptian General Gamasi. Within four days the first prisoners of war had been exchanged.

The immediate danger of the escalation of the Middle East war into a world war had ended, and the Soviet Union credited the detente with creating an atmosphere in which the fighting could be halted. Obviously, Middle Easterners on both sides were very concerned about their relationships with the Great Powers. On November 19, the Palestinian leader, Yasir Arafat, flew to Moscow to be reassured by Soviet leaders on the implications of their policy toward the Palestinian issue. Arafat then proceeded to Algiers where on November 24 the Foreign Ministers of the Arab countries met preparatory to a summit meeting of the leaders of the Arab countries. On that occasion the Palestine Liberation Organization was declared to be the sole representative of the Palestinian people.

The "oil weapon" proved to be the most powerful and persuasive in the Arab arsenal. Despite warnings dating back several years, few in the United States realized the havoc which a cutback would cause not only in Japan and Western Europe, but also in the United States. A simple and often quoted phrase summarizes the importance of oil: Western technological advances in recent years are a direct result of cheap power. Even without the Middle Eastern war or the oil embargo, Western demand for oil was increasing at such a rate that a serious short fall could be expected soon. In 1973, before the October War, the United States imported either directly or through third countries, an average of 1,600,000 barrels daily. This amounted to 25 percent of all American oil imports or 10 percent of total oil consumption. Moreover, a further 300,000 barrels a day were supplied directly to military forces overseas. Taken together, U.S. direct losses of imports, losses of imports through third countries, and cutbacks in supplies from countries which needed to divert their own production, deprived the United States of approximately 3 million barrels of oil a day or about 17 percent of our estimated demand of 18.5 million barrels a day.

The situation was even worse in Japan which is wholly dependent upon imported oil for its daily consumption of 6.2 million barrels. Forty percent of that was supplied by the Arabs. The importance of these figures can be seen when it is realized that 70 percent of Japan's total energy consumption is from oil. Both Britain and France receive between 70 and 80 percent of their oil from Arab producers and both were hit with more than 10 percent short fall as a result of the Arab oil cutbacks. Germany, Europe's largest consumer, imported 3.2 million barrels a day of which 70 percent came from Arab producers. A further 20 percent was imported into Germany through Holland which was totally embargoed.

The Arab "oil weapon" was introduced on October 17 in Kuwait at a meeting of the Arab Petroleum Ministers in which they agreed to a 5 percent cutback each month until certain conditions had been met including the implementation of United Nations Security Council Resolution 242. On October 20, after the U.S. announced a $2.2 billion weapons program for Israel, Saudi Arabia banned the sale of oil to the United States and on the 21st the Persian Gulf oil-producing countries followed suit. On November 4 the Organization of Arab Petroleum Exporting Countries (OAPEC) raised the embargo quota to 25 percent. In riposte, Secretary of State Kissinger, on November 12, warned the Arabs that there would be no result of their oil embargo pressure and said that the United States was considering a mutual security treaty with Israel. Desultory negotiations followed, particularly with intermediaries from Europe and Japan, and on November 18 OAPEC canceled the cutback except for the United States and Holland. On November 21, Secretary of State Kissinger threatened countermeasures against the Arabs.

Then followed the major diplomatic breakthrough which set up the diplomatic conference in Geneva. The oil issue appeared to die down slightly in comparison to the more spectacular events of the cease fire and disengagement. However the oil embargo was not ended and on January 3, Secretary of State Kissinger announced that the United States was seeking a united front of oil consumers, a measure somewhat reminiscent of Secretary of State Dulles' plan for a Suez Canal Users Association during the crisis of 1956. On January 6, Secretary of Defense James Schlesinger warned the Arabs that they risked violence if they sought to use the oil weapon "to cripple the larger mass of the industrialized world." He followed this up the next day with a remark that there was a "risk" that the Arabs would impel the United States to consider the use of force. These threats drew a riposte from Kuwait Foreign Minister Shaikh Sabah that Kuwait would blow up its oil installations if invaded. On January 11, Secretary of State Kissinger suggested that both producing and consuming nations work together to find ways of meeting future petroleum needs. This was a considerably toned-down version of the original plan which called for a sort of consumer cooperative. It resulted, however, in a meeting of 13 nations in Washington (which France refused to attend) to put forward a joint proposal to be considered by the producing countries.

The real importance of the oil crisis was not, however, only in its immediate effect on the negotiations in the Middle East. Rather, there was a recognition of the long-term nature of Western dependence upon the Arab oil-producing countries.* This affected not only

---

* In 1972, the year before the oil crisis, Americans consumed about 17 million barrels daily or 776.2 million tons yearly. That was 8 percent more than in 1971. Production, meanwhile, had increased only 0.1 percent to 9.45 million barrels daily. U.S. reserves are 6.2 percent of the total world reserves, but U.S. consumption is 30 percent of the world total. The average American consumes 3.46 times as much energy as the Japanese; twice as much as the Englishman; 2.5 times as

the amounts of oil, the need for which was growing yearly at a staggering rate, roughly doubling each decade, but also the necessity to develop appropriate incentives to get the Arabs to produce oil. At one point in the crisis, Shaikh Zaki Yamani, the Saudi Arabian Minister of Oil, pointed out that the Arabs could cut production and still earn considerably more money than they could absorb. As a consequence of this, prices soared during the crisis. On December 11, Iran announced that oil prices had hit $17.40 per barrel and on December 23 the Gulf Oil Ministers posted the prices for their crude oil at $11.65 per barrel. While these prices softened somewhat during the ensuing months, it was clear that petroleum would be two to three times as expensive as in previous years. The consequences would be felt not only in the price of goods produced by the industrialized countries or in the availability of funds for developmental purposes in the poorer countries but in a massive shift of the world monetary structure.

Recognition of all these factors was certainly achieved early in the Middle Eastern crisis and was, undoubtedly, the major factor which forced the United States to intervene so dramatically and repeatedly in attempts to bring about a peaceful solution to the crisis.

Various behind-the-scenes diplomatic moves in late November and early December probed the question of resumption of oil supplies to the United States, but the oil-producing Arab countries were reluctant to move unless or until the war was wound down on satisfactory terms. Throughout this period, desultory fighting continued along the Egyptian front with often serious clashes between Egyptian and Israeli forces and, on one occasion, a fistfight between United Nations and Israeli troops.

Then, on December 13, Secretary Kissinger began his second whirlwind diplomatic tour in the Middle East by flying to Algiers where he met with President Boumedienne. He followed this by visits to Cairo and Riyadh on the 14th; Damascus and Amman on the 15th; and Israel on the 17th. The way was then prepared for the Geneva talks to open on December 21 under the titular auspices of United Nations Secretary General Kurt Waldheim.

On January 11, 1974, Kissinger began the third of his forays to the Middle East by flying to Aswan to meet with President Sadat. The

---

much as the Russian; and 37 times as much as the citizen of the less developed countries. The United States in 1979 produced approximately 78 percent of its energy requirements. To put it in terms of use, Americans *produce* more energy per capita than the advanced economies of Europe and Japan *consume* per capita. Yet the oil we import now accounts for over 20 percent of the energy we consume. Approximately two thirds of that is from the OPEC countries and roughly 15 percent is from Saudi Arabia.

next day he flew to Israel to meet with the Israeli cabinet and returned to Aswan on the 13th; back to Israel on the 14th and then to both Egypt and Israel on the 16th. He secured agreement between the governments so that the disengagement of forces was announced simultaneously in Jerusalem, Cairo, and Washington on January 17. It was signed the following day at the already famous tent 101 kilometers from Cairo and once more the key figures went off on frantic rounds of visits to explain their actions. President Sadat flew to Riyadh, then to Damascus and finally to Kuwait on January 19 while Secretary Kissinger flew to Jordan and Damascus on the 20th. Probably never in history had there been anything quite equal to the mobility of diplomacy between the end of October and the middle of January.

The question was, what had really happened?

The most important immediate consequence of "shuttle diplomacy" was that the military forces of Egypt and Israel were to be separated by a United Nations buffer zone more or less parallel to the Suez Canal and that both the Egyptian and Israeli forces were to remove themselves, except for limited men and military equipment, from the immediate vicinity of the buffer zone.

Less dramatic but certainly of much greater long-term importance was the fact that the Sadat regime had now committed itself to the cause of peace. This was so clearly recognized by the Israeli government that it was able to demobilize large parts of its army immediately. President Sadat was severely criticized by a number of his intimate friends and supporters, including the influential editor of the Egyptian newspaper *Ahram,* for relying too much on Secretary Kissinger's good will and for not even having secured the return of its major Egyptian economic asset in the Sinai Peninsula, the oil fields. This criticism impelled Sadat to move against his domestic critics and so thrust him even more firmly into a commitment to work with the United States. Various rumors circulated through the Middle East about a quid pro quo—the amount of aid which the United States would give to Egypt following a conclusion of peace. No authoritative figures were brought forward then but in May the administration put a request to the Congress for an appropriation of $250 million to assist in the restoration of the Suez Canal and other projects. Plans were made in January which also resulted in the transfer to Egypt of mine-clearing units of the United States Navy.

Even more important for the long term was the creation of what might be called "atmosphere of negotiation." It is a truism about international affairs that interim measures tend to become more or less permanent, and in the change of atmosphere which the disengage-

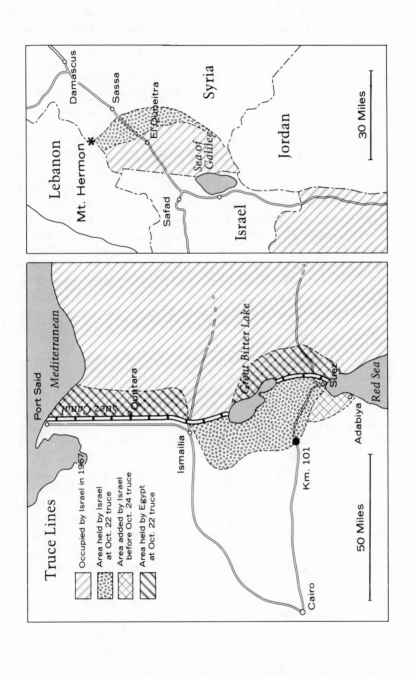

Truce Lines

Occupied by Israel in 1967

Area held by Israel at Oct. 22 truce

Area added by Israel before Oct. 24 truce

Area held by Egypt at Oct. 22 truce

Port Said

Mediterranean

Suez Canal

Qantara

Ismailia

Great Bitter Lake

Suez

Adabiya

Red Sea

Km. 101

Cairo

50 Miles

Lebanon

Mt. Hermon

Damascus

Sassa

El Quneitra

Safad

Syria

Sea of Galilee

Israel

Jordan

30 Miles

ment agreement typified, American and European businessmen flocked to the Middle East and were greeted with the encouraging news that Egypt planned substantially to liberalize its internal economic order to encourage a greater degree of foreign investment. The dramatic nature of the change in Egyptian-American relations was based, of course, primarily on hope and on the extraordinary personal rapport which President Sadat and Secretary of State Kissinger had established in their brief meetings.

Everything on the Egyptian front naturally hinged on whether or not fighting could be brought to a halt on the Syrian front, and there a considerably different situation pertained. Most important, the Syrians had not managed to retake any Syrian territory in the fighting. Indeed, from October 10, Israeli armored units advanced into Syria beyond the 1967 truce lines. The Syrians were bitter that the Egyptians had signed a separate cease fire leaving them to bear the full brunt of Israeli military force. Syria had lost heavily in the war, not only in its frontline army but from Israeli air action that damaged much of its industry and substantial parts of its major cities. These factors made negotiation very much more difficult for Syria than for Egypt. More ominously, the Soviet Union, feeling itself upstaged and elbowed aside by the American diplomatic onslaught, was anxious to prove that it was still a major factor in Middle Eastern politics. Consequently, it appears that the Soviet Union encouraged the Syrian "hawks" to stay in the war.* When the United States recognized the seriousness of the Soviet annoyance, Secretary Kissinger arranged to meet with the Soviet Foreign Minister Gromyko on Cyprus and, in various public statements, to reassure the Soviet Union that American intent was not to exclude it from an influential position in the Middle East.

Meanwhile, an election had taken place in Israel in which the militant right wing, the Likhud, had gained in strength. Israeli Prime Minister Meir was under increasing pressure not only from the Likhud but from members of her own party to take a hard line. Negotiation on the Syrian front depended more upon factors of Israeli domestic politics and particularly upon Mrs. Meir's willingness to "stay the course," than had been the case in the Israeli-Egyptian cease fire. The issue of the Golan Heights was a much more "domestic" and emotional issue in Israel than that of the Sinai Peninsula, and the degree of bitterness which had developed in the fighting on the Syrian front far exceeded that on the Egyptian front. Both the Israelis and

* The Soviet Union also supplied the Syrians with the nuclear-capable "Scud B" missile which has a range of 165 miles, in January 1974.

the Syrians accused one another of failing to give adequate medical attention to and even of torturing or killing prisoners of war. But, by the end of April, both the Israelis and the Syrians were ready to accede to pressure from the United States, with tacit agreement from the Soviet Union, to conclude a truce. Once again, Secretary of State Kissinger swung into action and for twenty-eight days shuttled back and forth between Jerusalem and Damascus conveying the opinion and demand of each side to the other and attempting to find a formula which would satisfy both. In all, he spent over 120 hours of conversation with the heads of state of Israel and Syria.

The agreement he reached at the end of May allowed the Syrians to regain almost all of the 300 square miles lost in the 1973–74 war and small but symbolic amounts of land lost in the 1967 war. Israel retained possession of the Golan Heights and a part of the natural observation tower of Mount Hermon. As on the Sinai front, the United Nations created a buffer zone, but in Syria an extremely narrow one—in places only two kilometers wide. The Syrians regained civil authority over the United Nations buffer zone and over the destroyed city of Quneitra. Four zones of "limited force" were also created. Closest to the United Nations buffer zone Israel and Syria were each allowed only 6,000 troops and 75 tanks. In the outer two limited zones each country was allowed 450 tanks and medium range artillery. No anti-aircraft batteries were allowed within 15 miles of the buffer zone. This complex and delicate exercise in map drawing was signed in Geneva at the Palais des Nations by Israeli General Shafir and Syrian General Tayara on May 31.

Good auguries seemed to appear everywhere. Syrian President Assad was said to have promised Israel that Syria would curb the activities of the Palestinians; Syria and Israel exchanged wounded prisoners (although both were accused by an international body, and each accused the other, of mistreating them); and the Security Council voted to set up a new military force to supervise the "separation of forces" on the Syrian-Israeli front. The very momentum of the diplomatic process seemed likely to carry the Arabs and the Israelis to a Geneva peace conference. But at that point the straightforward, if complex, military issues were replaced by the political heritage of the twentieth century.

Even the fundamental issue of who should attend a peace conference cut to the root of the area's problems. On the surface, the answer appeared simple enough: the participants in the war. They were the parties to the dispute. Moreover, they, unlike the Palestinians, were states, and thus by definition were members of the international com-

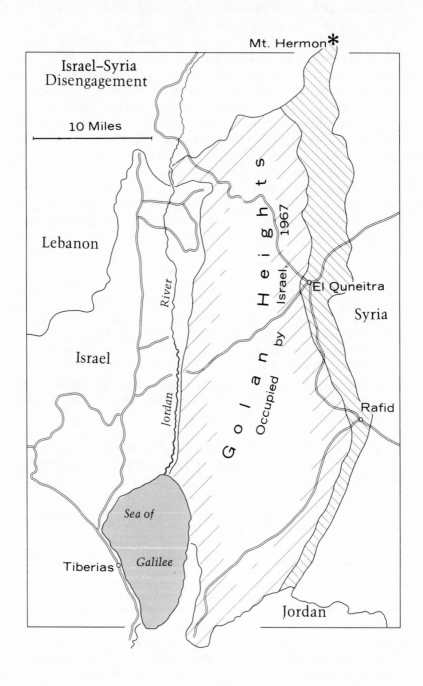

Israel–Syria
Disengagement

10 Miles

Mt. Hermon ✷

Lebanon

River

Jordan

Israel

G o l a n   H e i g h t s

Occupied by Israel, 1967

El Quneitra

Syria

Rafid

Sea of

Galilee

Tiberias

Jordan

424

munity. The Palestinians were still a nonstate and their "government," the Palestinian Liberation Organization, although obviously the de facto representative of the community, had not even been so designated by the Arab governments. (This was done at an Arab summit conference in Rabat on October 28.) And at that point Israel not only vigorously opposed any notion that the PLO was a government or that the Palestinians constituted a quasi-state, but Prime Minister Golda Meir was quoted as denying that they were even a "people." Secretary Kissinger found a position for the United States between these views. Although he professed some sympathy for the plight of the Palestinians, he took a formalistic view of the international system—a view according to which they could not be regarded as participants even though the decisions of any constituted peacemaking apparatus would determine their fate. International affairs, Kissinger believed, occurred among states, and whatever else they were the Palestinians were not a state.

Moreover, even to raise the issue of their participation would, in Kissinger's view, derail the process of peacemaking. No one had found answers to the Palestinian problem and he thought that no one would. To address that issue head on would prove sterile, and Kissinger—like Metternich, from whom he had learned so much of his diplomatic approach—believed in addressing only those issues on which one could succeed. These considerations led Kissinger to commit the United States to a "step-by-step" approach to peace.

The idea of doing things step by step was comfortable, pragmatic, familiar. It was similar to Israel's slogan, "A piece of territory for a piece of peace." It "kept the options open," allowed flexibility in timing and selection of subjects, and made possible the "one-to-one" personal diplomacy that Kissinger made his own. But, like many slogans, its surface simplicity disguised a complex situation and a fundamental decision. Essentially what the policy came to was a separate peace between Israel and Egypt, and this was, of course, evident to the participants from the start. Kissinger's argument was that once peace was made between Israel and Egypt, Syria would have to fall into line. (This was what had happened in the military disengagement.) Jordan would follow suit. Then Lebanon could be dealt with, and the Palestinians could be assigned their proper place in the scheme of things in the Middle East. Israel understood and approved. The process initially avoided the thorny issue of the Palestinians and broke the Arab bloc into manageable pieces. Of course, the Israelis disagreed with many points of timing and "equivalency" and with the amount of territories to be ceded, but regarding the main line of Kissinger's policy they had no serious disagreement. President Sadat understood and approved because the policy enabled him to achieve the immediate Egyptian aim, one that had preoccupied him throughout his adult life—that of getting the invader off Egyptian soil. Moreover, by going along with the American program, he had hopes of winning the massive American assistance that alone would give his government a chance of dealing with Egypt's social and economic ills. The policy had the additional advantages of putting some pressure on his Arab allies who were often slow or fickle in providing assistance. And he, like Kissinger, found the Palestinians uncomfortable bedfellows.

The Syrians, too, understood, but despite Secretary Kissinger's "leak to the press" that President Assad approved, they violently disagreed. They could not face Israel alone; the step-by-step policy would effectively remove the Egyptian army from their camp and set them up as a target. The Palestinians saw in the policy a mortal blow to their hopes of statehood. Without Egypt and Syria, their only weapon was terrorism. And in a decade of clandestine war, they had lost their base in Jordan, alienated many of the Arab governments, and lost the support of world public opinion. Far from avoiding the issue, in their view, Kissinger's policy was their national death warrant.

But although the main lines of the policy were evident, the steps were not easy. After the euphoria of his visit to Cairo on June 12, President Nixon was forced to resign as a result of the Watergate scandal, and for a while it appeared that Secretary Kissinger would follow him. The whole nation was caught up in the drama of the Senate hearings, and it was not until October that serious negotiations could begin again in the Middle East.

Meanwhile, resistance in Israel proved far stronger than had been anticipated. Israeli military leaders doubted the wisdom of giving up the Sinai Peninsula, which they thought of as a valuable buffer. In the years of their occupation, they had turned it into a fortress with airfields, military dumps, redoubts and, most important, a strategic concept. Their conclusion was arrived at, on other grounds, by the political right wing which opposed giving up any territory anywhere on any grounds. In the past, this position had been countered by the leadership of such men as Ben Gurion and the effective political power of the trade unions, but the disarray of political forces was increasing the power of the right and would shortly lead to a Likhud coalition electoral victory.

Negotiations continued until September 1, 1975, when Israel and Egypt were induced at last to sign an agreement involving an Israeli pullback of forces to the east of the Mitla and Gidi passes in Sinai. A new buffer area was to be patrolled by a special UN force, and the area that had proved most sensitive in the past was to be monitored by a civilian American team. Egypt was to allow nonmilitary Israeli ships to use the Suez Canal (which had been reopened on November 20, 1974). And American aid to Egypt was to be dramatically increased from $8.5 million in Fiscal Year 1974 to $250 million in the next year and $750 million in Fiscal Year 1976 and subsequent years. (The yearly amounts would nearly equal the aggregate aid given Egypt between 1946 and 1967.) Israel was promised $2.3 billion.

As anticipated, Egypt closed down the PLO broadcasting station in Egypt, and Israel showed itself in no hurry to negotiate with the Syrians now that it had neutralized Egypt. Meanwhile Israel continued its attacks on refugee camps and PLO sites in Lebanon in order, the Israeli authorities said on September 7, to keep the Palestinians off balance so they could not attempt to disrupt the Israeli-Egyptian accord.

Lebanon, almost a sideshow in the march of diplomatic events, was to be the tragic victim of the step-by-step approach. Already beset with historical social and religious problems and disfigured by the sudden infusion of wealth in the 1960's, it was the last redoubt of the Palestinians. Knowing that if they lost their position there, they were finished as a national movement, the Palestinians in desperation plunged into the simmering discontent; their presence, and the Israeli intervention it immediately brought about, turned this discontent and disturbance into a civil war. By the end of 1976 the war had cost an estimated 40,000 casualties, had made some 85,000 homeless, and had caused an estimated $10 billion worth of damages and loss of revenues.

Three issues came into focus during the war. First, Lebanon had not achieved a national consensus on what it was. The state had been created by the French in 1920 from the Ottoman province of Mount Lebanon, which was mainly Christian, and from other areas, about four times as large, which were mainly Muslim. The struggle for national independence heightened intercommunal tensions, since the Maronites favored French presence while the other communities opposed it; the Maronites looked back to Phoenician antecedents, whereas the Muslims sought Arab unity.

In 1943 the Lebanese political leaders had worked out a "national pact" that assigned to each community its share of the spoils of political power. But the system made no allowance for change, and Lebanon was changing. Whether or or not there had originally been a Christian majority (justifying the allocation of the presidency and leadership of the army to the Maronites), this majority disappeared

427

as the Muslim population grew faster. However, the relative wealth of the Christians increased. As money from the oil states poured into the free Lebanese economy in the 1950's and 1960's, the urban, commercial, primarily Christian population increased and the rural, primarily Muslim population decreased. The 13 percent of the population engaged in commerce contributed about 50 percent of the gross national product, whereas the 50 percent engaged in agriculture contributed about 13 percent. Strong governments in the 1950's and 1960's prevented challenges to the system but allowed no adjustments.

Into this volatile situation were injected the Palestinians. Originally, in 1948–1949 and until the mid-1960's, the Palestinians had been a poor, marginal social group, living in ragged camps and interacting with the Lebanese mainly as low-paid labor. The war in Jordan in 1970 changed this. The leadership of the Palestinians moved to Beirut and began to organize and energize the Palestinians, who by then constituted about 10 percent of the Lebanese population. Excluded from Jordan, tightly and oppressively controlled in Syria, and having no other base of operations, the Palestinian leaders looked upon Lebanon as their only hope. Thus, when the Lebanese Left, in danger of being defeated by the Christian Right, urged the Palestinians to intervene, they could not refuse. With their help, the Left began to predominate.

The Syrians and Egyptians, who had both favored the Left-Muslim faction, began to worry. The Syrians in particular realized that if a Left-Muslim-Palestinian coalition assumed control over Lebanon, the Israelis (who were already mounting almost daily air attacks on Lebanese targets) would invade. If the fighting ended in partition, as was being discussed by both factions, the Syrians feared that the Israelis would occupy the southern (Left-Palestinian) sector and cut them off from the sea. Thus, as the war became more serious in early 1976, Syria admonished the Left; when this did not work, they and the Egyptians began to give money and arms to the Christians. Finally, on June 5, Syria sent 20,000 troops and 450 tanks into Lebanon to reestablish a conservative, Christian, non-Palestinian government and to suppress and disarm its enemies and critics. Israel, disturbed by the possible victory of the side on which the Palestinians were so active, had already begun to arm and train on its territory (with American weapons) a new Christian army for service in Lebanon. Ironically, Israel found itself following a policy parallel to that of Syria against the Palestinian-Left-Muslim coalition. In the violence, Lebanon was torn apart—the real casualty of the step-by-step policy.

26

The Carter Administration

THE Democratic administration that came to power in January 1977 brought with it one political legacy and inherited another. Some of the ambiguity of its policy and the apparent ineptness in its actions arise from a conflict between what it brought and what it found in place.

On the one hand, President Carter was a self-proclaimed "outsider," viewing the "Washington Establishment" and its policies with suspicion, if not outright hostility. He had campaigned on promises to take the government back to the people, to decency, to the fundamentals of American populism. A deeply and publicly religious man, he gave every indication of being most comfortable with those who shared his beliefs and his background in rural Georgia. To such men, the Kissinger policy of *realpolitik* seemed both alien and immoral. Yet, on the other hand, Carter's key appointments gave little hint of a radical break with the Establishment. The new Secretary of State was a former Under Secretary of Defense and, like Secretary Dulles, a Wall Street lawyer. The new chief of staff of the National Security Council shared much of Kissinger's background and ideas. The Trilateral Commission, which he had headed and to which President Carter had belonged, was certainly a part of the Establishment. The first Assistant Secretary of State for the Near East and South Asia was a career Foreign Service officer; his replacement was a career civil servant who had been in the CIA under President Eisenhower, the White House under Presidents Kennedy and Johnson, and the State

Department under Presidents Nixon and Ford. Thus, although the President said that the issues were to be viewed afresh in the light of his principles, they were often addressed by the same or very similar men.

What *was* new was the extraordinary way in which the President and his wife appeared to encourage informal, private, personal contacts to sound out unofficial opinions and then to speak openly about their ideas without reference to the formal apparatus of government. The contrast was most striking with the Eisenhower administration, where nothing was said or done without elaborate, even stifling staff studies and papers prepared by the Operations Control Board. Determined to "be his own man," President Carter often shocked his staff by floating foreign-policy pronouncements before understanding their full implications, before attempting to reach a consensus among the government departments, or even before discussing them with his staff. This was especially evident in the Palestine problem.

The President realized that American Middle Eastern policy had hit a dead end with the conclusion of the Sinai Accord in September 1975 precisely because it had been designed to avoid the problem of the Palestinians. And, like President Kennedy with the Algerians in 1961, Carter had a remote sympathy for the Palestinians. What they said they wanted or he assumed they wanted made sense to Carter as a man concerned with human rights, whatever the experts told him about the rougher edges of their armed struggle. On this issue it was easy to discount the "experts" in government.

Normal diplomatic avenues of contact were closed to the PLO as they were to most other underground movements. Not only was the PLO a "nonstate," and so an anomaly in the international system, but it was difficult to locate bureaucratically in the American government.* The PLO was also at war with a favored and jealous ally. What followed was that it was virtually impossible for senior American government officials to talk, even privately, with representatives of the PLO. Indeed, an unauthorized conversation in a private house in New York, monitored by Israeli intelligence, led to US Ambassador Andrew Young's leaving his job in 1979 despite his warm friendship with the President and the political support of the American black community. The diplomatic problem was that, by custom, contact constitutes a degree of recognition. (There was also the issue of whether or not Young had reported his conversation to his superiors.) Recognition, of course, was an objective earnestly sought by the

---

* This was not a small point, as the problems of dealing with Algeria had earlier shown. The author was head of the Algerian "task force" in the Kennedy administration.

PLO and vigorously opposed by Israel.* Indeed, the Israeli government had extracted a written promise from former Secretary of State Kissinger precluding such meetings. Thus, by definition, the personnel in government most accessible to the new President were precluded from the intimate, personal involvements of the sort that on other issues was precisely what made them expert. Relatively speaking, on this issue the President was out of touch.

The Palestinian issue was one on which, apparently, President Carter felt a personal, even a religious, commitment. He had spoken of it often during his campaign, yet in his pronouncements there is no hint that he had informed himself in any detail of its history or complexity. He did, however, identify the Palestinians as poor and needy, and amelioration of their plight thus acquired for him a double moral imperative. In one of his first pronouncements on the Middle East, addressing the town meeting of Clinton, Massachusetts, on March 16, 1977, he said that there were three conditions for peace in the Middle East. The first two had often enough been stated: recognition of Israel's right to exist and the establishment of permanent frontiers. Then the President dropped a remarkable word, a "code" word that had taken on almost theological overtones since it had first been coined sixty years before as a substitute for "state" in the Balfour Declaration. The word was "homeland." The third condition for peace, he said, was "a homeland for the Palestinian refugees."

Why he said it, what he meant by it, and what he intended to do about it perplexed his own staff as much as it did the Arabs and Israelis. To compound the gesture, the next day, after addressing the United Nations, the President surprised delegates by shaking hands with the PLO observer. To many it seemed that a new wind was blowing. The Israelis were disturbed but the PLO was not appeased, feeling that the gesture was very little and very late. Three days later, the Palestine National Council voted overwhelmingly to continue its "armed struggle" against Israel. Although these episodes were not important in themselves, they illustrate a tendency in the administration: to make the decent, simple, human gesture expecting that somehow everything would thereafter be different, and then to be disappointed—even hurt—when it was not. It was at once the most

* Shortly after Israeli Foreign Minister Moshe Dayan vigorously protested Ambassador Young's meeting in New York, he met in Gaza with a leading Palestinian who had been chairman of the Parliament of the Liberation Organization in Gaza and a member of the Palestine National Council. As the London *Financial Times* commented, "Apparently indifferent to the irony of the situation, Mr. Dayan explained afterwards that he had sought the meeting 'to get some answers on how Israel and the Arabs can live together. You cannot get the Arab opinion by sitting and talking with the Jews,' he said" (August 31, 1979).

appealing and the most dangerously naive aspect of the administration.

But changes did seem to come. Spurred, perhaps, by Carter's gestures, West German Chancellor Helmut Schmidt publicly affirmed his government's position that the Palestinians must take part in the peace process. A few days later, President Sadat told Carter that the Palestinian problem was the "core and crux" of the Middle Eastern problem and that the Arab-Israeli conflict could not be resolved apart from it. But, as a practical matter, how could anyone do anything about it? Israel would not, at that time, admit that the Palestinians existed as a people and refused to have anything to do with the PLO. Although living under martial law, the inhabitants of the West Bank often rioted; there and elsewhere terrorist attacks (mostly against civilians) continued, to which the Israelis responded with military force and clandestine "hit man" squads murdering a number of prominent Palestinians and others. On that "front" there was no point of entry for the United States. And who was to speak for the Palestinians? Sadat did so to an extent, but in his demarches to the American government he naturally sought primarily Egyptian aims. Most of the other Arab governments were either discounted as hostile to the United States or were ambivalent in their acts and statements. The PLO, as Arafat put it to the United Nations, communicated at least as often with the gun as with the olive branch, and often did so in ways shocking to men of conscience. More crucial was the fact that Arafat could never speak directly to senior advisors of the President, much less to him personally as Sadat and Begin were to do with such effect. Although difficult to gauge precisely, the overall importance of these factors was great.

Another aspect of American policy inherited from the previous administration was the attempt to exclude the Soviet Union from the Middle East. Strategically the policy rested on the "two pillars": Iran, which the United States sold billions of dollars' worth of military equipment, and Saudi Arabia, from which the United States bought billions of dollars' worth of oil. Together they were assumed to guard the oil-producing areas of the Arabian peninsula and Persian Gulf. Whereas Iran had developed close, even friendly commercial and diplomatic ties with the Soviet Union, Saudi Arabia excluded it from all diplomatic contacts and allowed Soviet Muslim minorities into Arabia only on pilgrimage.

In other areas and on other issues, it was clear that the Middle East was not an American preserve. The 1973 war and its diplomatic aftermath had briefly allowed Secretary Kissinger to ignore this reality, but his policy could not be sustained and was in any event self-defeating. An excluded Soviet Union was an irresponsible critic and an available alternative. Moreover, if the United States wanted SALT II and hoped for a more normal general relationship, as clearly the Carter administration did, it had to make some gesture in the Middle East toward the Soviets. Even the Nixon and Ford administrations had found this useful; it was, indeed, their formula that the Carter administration used. After a series of meetings in the summer, the United States and the Soviet Union issued a joint declaration on October 1, 1977, more or less reaffirming the two 1974 summit meetings. But for those whose ears had grown accustomed to nuance in the vocabulary of Middle Eastern conflicts, a sign appeared: in referring to the Palestinians, the 1974 declaration had used the phrase "legitimate interests," and this in the 1977 declaration became "legitimate rights." Not a major change perhaps, but one that was read to mean a step toward statehood.

But joint declaration aside, it seemed that nothing much could be done about the Palestine issue. The day after the declaration, a bomb exploded in the Jerusalem bus station. A few days later an airliner was hijacked and more bombs went off; a West German team stormed the hijacked airliner when it finally came to rest in Somalia, after the hijackers had killed the pilot. There seemed no end to the violence. And around the President, most already felt the hostility later vented by National Security Adviser Zbigniew Brzezinski toward these apparently irresponsible, violent men.

Just at that moment the control of events—if ever it had been in Washington—shifted dramatically and suddenly to the Middle East and, in a profound sense, never returned. To understand how it happened, we must digress.

At about the time President Carter arrived in Washington to begin his administration, President Sadat was facing the most dangerous crisis of his presidency since the attempt to overthrow him in 1970. The euphoria of the October war had dissipated. The repeatedly proclaimed *infitah* or opening (to the West) was yielding the problems of development, but few evident benefits. Most noticeable was the ostentation of new wealth of the privileged few. Although statistically impressive—with a yearly rise in gross national product since 1974 of 6 to 7 percent and a per capita income of $350—the social reality was more somber. Well over half the Egyptians had incomes of less than $50 a year and participated in the new improvements only vicariously through radio and television. Even in such critical sectors as the army, the situation was grave: the army and air force had received essentially no new equipment or even spare parts since *before* the 1973 war—and yet the government was spending about 30 percent of Egypt's gross national product on the military. It is true that the United States had committed itself to giving Egypt money, but Egypt's capacity to absorb it was proving very limited and very slow. The Egyptian bureaucracy was the equivalent of Russia's "General Mud." Project after project was planned and announced but never completed. Being centralized, the economy depended upon decisions that never came, and those who might have been its entrepreneurs found wealth easier to obtain from government favor than from work. Over $1 billion in United States aid funds were unexpended, and the backlog was to increase by at least 50 percent during 1977. Sadat found his economy as elusive an issue as Carter found the Palestinians.

To the average Egyptian, that most patient of human beings, life remained tolerable. But in his desire to win support, Sadat had encouraged dreams that were impossible even to dream. The symbol of affluence to the Egyptian middle class was an automobile—an influence, no doubt, in part derived from seeing American films—yet the price of a medium-sized car equaled the total salary of a policeman for a century or an army general for a decade. To actually purchase a car, one had first to buy hard currency on the black market at nearly three times the official rate. So for the great majority of the people, what really mattered were the staples of life—bread, soap, sugar, tobacco, tea. The Egyptian government realized this and subsidized these items, while it heavily taxed some luxury goods. Subsidies, of course, were a continuation of the evils of bureaucracy, and enlightened policy makers thought they should be phased out. On other grounds, the International Monetary Fund was opposed to further financial help to Egypt so long as they were maintained.

In January 1977 Sadat announced that subsidies would be ended or drastically reduced, and that the prices of basic commodities would accordingly rise. On January 18 a truly remarkable popular demonstration broke out in Cairo. Unlike the rigged demonstrations one so often saw, it was virtually silent. Barred from the public media, the tens of thousands of demonstrators quickly set up informal chains of communication that spanned the entire Nile Delta. Martial law was declared and curfews imposed. Life came to a halt not only in Cairo but in small, relatively remote towns. Violence was minimal; the demonstrators directed their fury against Sadat personally and for a few tense days he remained out of sight. It was the army, entering the political arena for the first time in twenty-five years, which held firm and enabled the government to ride out the storm. The demonstrations ended and the government struck back quickly, arresting nine hundred people. But it restored the subsidies. The lesson was not lost on Sadat. The problem was, what could he do? During the course of 1977, the answer became clear: very little.

Sadat shuffled his government, rammed through the People's Assembly a ban on strikes, blamed the Communists and other enemies for the troubles. Every public-relations gambit imaginable was tried in order to demonstrate that progress was now being made. Hardly a day passed without some new announcement. But even a casual observer could see that little was being or could be accomplished. For twenty-five years no capital investment had been made in Egypt, and conservative estimates indicated that merely to catch up—assuming the economy could absorb the money—it would need about $25 billion. Subsidies from the Arab countries were small and slow in coming when judged according to the scale of need, and increasingly the Arab governments regarded Egypt as a bottomless pit. Inflation was spiraling, as was population growth. Cairo swarmed with a population over twice as large as ever had inhabited the whole of ancient Egypt. And the army, which had demonstrated itself to be the savior of the government, was desperate. In its best days, it had never matched the Israeli army. And in July a minor frontier clash with Libya showed how feeble it had become. The no-war, no-peace with Israel was seen to be a cancer wasting the Egyptian body politic.

In June, Israel got a new government. Even though it was thought to be more "hawkish" than the previous one, the faces at least were new. Sadat was known to be fascinated with the new premier, Menahem Begin, with whom he had shared certain experiences.* And in his memoirs Sadat says that he was told by the President of Rumania, Nicolae Ceausescu, that "Begin wants a solution." What effect this had or what effect private communications from President Carter had is difficult to say, but quite suddenly, with no notice to his staff, no prior planning, no "soundings" with the Israelis or consultations with the United States, Sadat announced on November 14, 1977, that he wished to visit Jerusalem.

The whole world was electrified. In Egypt, where almost everything had been done at least once before, Sadat had scored a first. The American government was, to put it mildly, surprised. And the Israeli government was thrown into a quandary. The chief of staff suspected a ruse to cover an attack and prepared for war, while the office of the Prime Minister was frantically preparing welcoming parties to receive the Egyptian president. American embassies were

* See William R. Polk, *The Elusive Peace* (London and New York, 1979), pp. 138 ff.

turned into messengers and armies of journalists descended upon Cairo and Jerusalem. Amid great fanfare and ceremony, Sadat arrived, almost alone, in Israel. Invited to address the Knesset, he spoke eloquently of his desire for "no more war," and in a whirlwind tour placed flowers on the monument to those who had fallen fighting his and other Arab armies. Even Woodrow Wilson would never have conceived of so open a diplomacy, so instant a public access, or so wide an audience. In the blaze of television lamps, diplomacy as theater had arrived.

Then Sadat went home. Inevitably the question arose: What had happened? Critics were quick to point out that Begin had listened but had said almost nothing. It was Sadat who had made the gesture. Merely by going to Jerusalem—which none of the Western powers including the United States then recognized as the capital of Israel and which under the United Nations resolutions was still partly "occupied territory"—Sadat had given away what most Arabs were determined to withhold until peace came: recognition. Apparently no staff work had been done, and Sadat had taken with him almost none of his official staff—his foreign minister had resigned when he had announced the trip. And if he had expected some grand Israeli gesture to match his own, he had not received it. His supporters did Egypt little good by attacking Sadat's Arab critics as "barefoot shepherds of Arabia . . . who were willing to fight to the last Egyptian." Within two weeks a new anti-Egyptian Arab front had come into being.

But neither Sadat nor, by then, the United States could allow the initiative simply to die. What to do next was not easy to decide. On Christmas Day 1977, Begin visited Sadat—but far from Cairo—and it was only then that the two leaders got down to thinking of what a peace might look like.

Begin's position was hard: the real Palestinians were the Jews, he said, and Israel would never negotiate with the PLO or cede Judaea and Samaria, which others chose to call "the West Bank." Return of Arab Jerusalem was simply unthinkable. And the large number of settlements already planted in the occupied territories—113 on the West Bank alone—would not only stay but grow in both number and density. (The new "technical" term came to be "thickened.") In his plan for the occupied territories, Begin foresaw unending military government even though some minor local autonomy might be considered.

Blocked in their bilateral talks, both leaders went to Washington to talk separately with Carter, but no real progress was made. Then in March 1978 Israel invaded Lebanon, and this seemed to some to be the deathknell of the Jerusalem initiative. A trip by Secretary of State Vance to the Middle East was, everyone admitted, a failure, and Sadat at that time must have been carefully considering his options. Prudence would have suggested that he return to the Arab fold as "the man of peace rebuffed." Perhaps the Arabs, needing the Egyptian army, would receive him with open arms and full purses. In a last-ditch effort to head off an Egyptian retreat, the American government held a conference at Leeds Castle in England on July 18. After only one day of meetings, the spokesmen reported merely that a "wide gap" still was evident between the positions of the Israelis and Egyptians. A few days later Sadat made a rare personal attack on Begin, and the next day Israel rejected an Egyptian request for a conciliatory gesture in the Sinai peninsula. If anything, the Israeli position seemed to be hardening, and on July 26 Egypt ordered the Israeli military mission to leave Cairo. Bilateral talks were completely broken off.

In August, Secretary Vance again visited Begin in Jerusalem and Sadat in Alexandria. He brought an invitation from President Carter for the three leaders to meet in September at the presidential retreat at Camp David, Maryland.

The Camp David meetings were perhaps the most remarkable diplomatic event of this century. Quite apart from the substance of the discussions, the fact that the heads of three states suspended all other activities for thirteen days was unprecedented. The informality of the meetings, encouraging the members of the delegations to visit one another throughout the day and night, contrasted sharply with the usual diplomatic interchange in which formality and protocol were nearly as important as substance. (No one could forget that in the meetings relating to Vietnam the shape of the table had occupied dozens of hours of frantic and heated discussion.) The three principals could make decisions on the spot, and in confronting one another necessarily brought great weight to their arguments. Although the records, scanty as they will probably be, are not yet available, it is known that President Carter in particular engaged in much late-night "arm twisting," and on at least two occasions prevented a breakdown of the meetings by his personal intervention.

On September 17, 1978, the three parties signed what are known as the Camp David Accords. Two documents emerged, followed by "letters" setting forth additional or supplementary understandings. Rumors persist, despite denials, that additional verbal or secret understandings were reached as well. The following is the main substance of the accords.

The first document was apparently drafted in large part by President Carter himself, and is a highly personal statement. It is termed a "framework for peace" and bases itself in part on UN Security Council resolution 242. (This resolution, drafted in 1967, had sought a "just solution to the *refugee problem*," [emphasis added], and not—as Sadat, Carter, and others claimed was needed in 1978—a solution to the problems of the *Palestinian people*. This discrepancy would arise later in further considerations of the meetings.) It then outlined a solution to the problem of the West Bank and Gaza in three stages stretching over a period of five years *beginning after* Israel, Jordan, and Egypt had agreed "on the modalities for establishing the elected self-governing authority in the West and Gaza" and *after* this authority had been established. In other words, the agreement was open-ended. It was agreed that at that distant point in the future, Israel would retain certain "security locations" and would engage in joint military patrols for an unspecified time.

During the transitional period, Israel and Jordan were to conclude a peace treaty, and negotiations would take place "to determine the final status of the West Bank and Gaza and its relationship with its neighbors." These negotiations were to be "based on all the provisions and principles of United Nations Security Council resolution 242 . . . The solution from the negotiations must also recognize the legitimate rights of the Palestinian people and their just requirements." The negotiations would be among Israel, Jordan, and Egypt but their agreement would be submitted to elected representatives of the inhabitants. In other words, there would be no referendum but opinion would be expressed through some form of elected assembly or assemblies. How they were to be chosen was not specified. The elected representatives would then decide how they should govern themselves, "consistent with the provisions of their agreement." But their new "authority" was described as an "administrative council." In other words, it was not to be a policy-making body.

These statements, obviously contain a thicket of modifying or contradictory clauses. As the *Washington Post* pointed out in an editorial on August 20, 1979:

> At Camp David, Israel had three lawyers, the United States had one (and he was out of the room for crucial hours) and Egypt had none. This is reflected in the outcome. On key issues, Camp David policy offers Palestinian autonomy "to the inhabitants"—not to the land. It defines the self-governing authority as an "administrative council" without legislative or judicial powers. It offers the Palestinians not self-determination but simply the chance to "participate in the determination of their own future." It makes no mention of Jerusalem. And so on. In brief, it is a Begin document to the letter. This is why Anwar Sadat

now appeals to the "spirit" of Camp David. This is why Jimmy Carter and his diplomats, realizing that Camp David restricts their current options—precisely as Israel planned—are squirming and trimming now.

John Campbell noted in *Foreign Affairs* that "the Plan was built on the structure of the Begin plan of the previous December." Carter and Sadat evidently paid no heed to the old British diplomatic maxim, "Never negotiate on the other fellow's draft." But perhaps this was the intent—to "Make the right noises" on the Palestine issue, hedging it so confusedly with provisions as to make it, in practice, meaningless, while the really serious job of making peace between Egypt and Israel could be accomplished. This was hinted at by former Israeli Foreign Minister Abba Eban in *Foreign Affairs* when he wrote, "The harsh truth is that on the most crucial and complex issue—that of the Palestinians and the West Bank—the Camp David signatories did little more than postpone their confrontation by the kind of semantic dexterity that is quick to wear out."

With that, the signatories did get on with the Israeli-Egyptian deal. There they reaffirmed Article 33 of the United Nations Charter (a much-abused statement), declaring that they would settle their dispute by peaceful means, and promised to conclude a peace treaty in three months. After setting forth various principles on the nature of peace, they turned to the second document, which had largely been agreed to before Camp David, entitled "Framework for an Egypt-Israel Peace Treaty." This agreement was fairly straightforward, calling for Israeli evacuation of the Sinai, which would return to Egyptian sovereignty; use of the Israeli airfields for civilian purposes only; free Israeli use of the Suez Canal; the opening of a highway between Egypt and Jordan; and a limit on military forces in the evacuated territory.

These were subsequently incorporated in the treaty, but this was many months in coming. What had been papered over had come unstuck. The Egyptians began to worry about the "linkage" between the various parts of the Camp David Accords. They were concerned about the growing hostility of their Arab "brothers"—nineteen Arab states (including Saudi Arabia) and the PLO, who met in Baghdad in November to disapprove of Sadat's action. A second Egyptian foreign minister resigned, and on November 6 the (Egyptian) Secretary General of the Arab League announced that the League was moving from Cairo.

In private, the Saudi Arabians were cautioning that the United States was gambling on long odds. They thought that Sadat was brave and, probably, well intentioned—in their view, certainly a great improvement over Nasser and, given the fickle nature of the Egyptians, about as good a leader as they were likely to get. But they did not believe he had or could hold a long-term consensus; American policy thus, as with the Shah, rested on the life and will of one man. Worse, they said, the United States had harmed, perhaps fatally, Sadat by encouraging him—even admitting that he needed little encouraging—to "stand up and be counted" on an American-favored policy. The Saudi Arabians argued that the United States had denationalized him and made him appear to most Arabs a Western puppet. Their conclusion was that the United States had polarized the Middle East in a new fashion, forcing a division among the Arabs, and thereby had given the Soviet Union its best opportunity in years.

Meanwhile, Israeli Foreign Minister Moshe Dayan announced to the UN General Assembly that Israel had resolved "never to compromise the unity of Jerusalem." In Jerusalem the Prime Minister announced that Israeli settlements on the West Bank would be expanded. These events happened at a time when U.S. Assistant Secretary of State Harold Saunders was meeting on the West Bank with Palestinian leaders to assure them that Israel had agreed to self-determination, and thus ultimately to statehood. When he reported the same understanding to King Husain, Prime Minister Begin protested to President Carter that this had never been agreed.

Misunderstandings filled the air. The United States protested to Israel over the settlements policy. Israel protested to the United States over the understanding on the Palestinians. Sadat and Begin disputed the fine points of their understanding and the war between Israel and the Palestinians continued. Ironically, it was at this point that Prime Minister Begin and President Sadat received the Nobel Peace Prize.

Behind the scenes, American envoys were meeting almost daily with Egypt and Israel to try to work out the final agreements. A second round of talks at the foreign-minister level was held at Camp David from February 21 to 25, 1979, but at the conclusion the Israeli cabinet announced that the American peace proposals were "inconsistent with the Camp David agreement." Begin returned to Washington to meet with Carter. There Carter remarked that the differences between the two sides were "absolutely insignificant," whereas Begin referred to them as "grave issues." On March 7 Carter flew to Cairo to meet again with Sadat and on March 10 he told the People's Assembly that he was "personally committed" to working out a solution to the "issues of concern to the Palestinians." Carter then flew to Israel and spoke before the Knesset, returning to Egypt with Begin's reaction to his proposals. On the West Bank, demonstrations broke out against the proposed treaty, but the next day the Carter draft was approved by the Egyptian cabinet.

Signed on March 26, 1979, the treaty embodied most of the points agreed on at Camp David but hedged these with side agreements. Most important was an annex between the United States and Israel in which the United States promised to provide Israel with oil for fifteen years, should it be unable to provide for itself (a previous agreement, made on September 1, 1975, had limited this supply to five years). A second protocol set forth various additional United States obligations, including the taking of "appropriate measures to promote full observance of the Treaty of Peace" and in the event of violation to "take such remedial measures as it may deem appropriate, which may include diplomatic, economic and military measures."

It had been a herculean effort by the President and his aides, and certainly the most sustained, high-level diplomatic effort of the United States government on the Middle East. Within the narrow confines of Egypt and Israel, it had succeeded. During the year Egypt and Israel were to implement the treaty, so that by the beginning of 1980 the two countries were very close to normal relations. Yet one is left with a nagging question: What, in the broader sense of American policy in the Middle East, had been accomplished?

Those who favored the treaty have felt that by taking one step at a time, by moving where movement was possible on the Egyptian-Israeli front, it would be possible to create a certain momentum that would inevitably bring about peace. The critics have argued that to start with Egypt precluded real progress on the central issue—namely, the fate of the Palestinians—and not only would not be conducive to the settlement of that issue but would drive the Palestinians to greater desperation and would force toward their position even such "moderates" as Saudi Arabia. (As one Saudi government official put it privately, "We can understand compromise, but you cannot force them to take absolutely nothing.") And so the violence has continued.

The desire to reduce the heavy yearly outlay on "security" was certainly one motive for President Sadat's visit to Jerusalem. Yet, ironically, armament expenditures not only decreased but actually increased, and in precisely those categories most expensive in terms of what Egypt most needs: hard currency. President Sadat, having isolated himself from all non-Egyptian Arab support, needed particularly to cater to the desires of his armed forces for billions of dollars' worth of the latest and most sophisticated American equipment.

The most pressing argument for the Egyptian-Israeli settlement, in terms of American self-interest, was that having broken the Arab front, it would enable each of the other Arab states to follow suit. Achieving peace would make the area safe for the United States and would close it to Russia. The effect has been precisely the reverse. The immediate result was that all but two Arab states— Oman and the Sudan, not the most useful of allies for Egypt— agreed to recall their diplomatic missions from Cairo and to sever all economic and political ties. Significantly, Saudi Arabia was among these. The Egyptians angrily charged Saudi Arabia with fostering the spread of Communism in the Middle East—not a charge that had often been laid at the Saudis' door.

On the Palestinian issue, the estrangement was even more complete. President Carter, who had spoken so warmly of the "homeland" upon entering the White House, was by August 1979 moved to say, "I am against any creation of a separate Palestinian state. I don't think it would be good for the Palestinians. I don't think it would be good for Israel. I don't think it would be good for the Arab neighbors of such a state." And so the "step-by-step" process led only to the first step and then stopped. It solved one problem at the grave risk of increasing the immediacy and danger of a host of other problems, precisely at the time that the Iranian revolution appeared to strike at the foundation of American policy throughout the area.

Although this is not the place to discuss the Iranian revolution,* it raised matters of great import to the United States in the Arab world. Could Islam be turned into a new revolutionary force, with possibly dangerous consequences for Saudi Arabia and thus for the supply of American oil? And with one of the two "pillars" supporting American policy in the Persian Gulf now removed, and the other angered by American policy over the American-sponsored Egyptian defection from the Arab camp, would there not be a major opportunity for Soviet intervention? Almost immediately, partial answers—or attempts at answers—appeared. A curious demonstration, armed and violent to be sure, but isolated and doomed from the beginning, took place in the holy precincts of Mecca on November 20, 1979. It was the first serious, public challenge to the Saudi regime in memory, and although it was quelled and its participants were executed, it was an unnerving experience. Rumors then circulated widely that the Mecca out-

---

* Significantly, the PLO found common cause with the Iranian revolutionaries, another group of "outsiders." Almost effortlessly, Yasir Arafat fell into a slot defined as anti-Shah, anti-American, and anti-Israel, and symbolically occupied the Israeli embassy in Tehran with his delegation just a month after the Shah was forced into exile.

break was only the tip of an iceberg of discontent. These seemed partially substantiated by the discovery that the participants in the riots were of humble, native background without extensive foreign contacts. On the day after the Mecca siege began, the U.S. embassy in Islamabad, Pakistan, was attacked by a mob. Three days later, the American government revealed that it had developed plans to evacuate its embassies in eleven Islamic countries. On December 2, the American embassy in Libya was besieged by a mob estimated at 2,000 people. Saudi Arabia deployed about half of its army to the Eastern Province after demonstrations were reported there against the royal family. And on December 26, in an unrelated but disturbingly juxtaposed action, the Soviet Union quadrupled the number of its troops in Afghanistan. The Soviet Union, faced with the likelihood that its friends in the Afghan government would fail to withstand an anti-Communist rebellion, intervened with large military forces and effectively conquered the country. In so doing, the Russians opened another frontier with Iran and created a neighborhood with Pakistan: after two hundred years, they appeared to have won "the Great Game." Obviously, these moves cannot be attributed to the separatist policies of Egypt, but there is little doubt that they helped create an atmosphere in which American interests could be probed. What they portend for the future among the Palestinians and their supporters is another matter, one far more grave and dangerous.

In the short term, there is no doubt that Saudi Arabia—despite having "proven" the American alliance when in 1978 it requested and was promised advanced jet fighters, the same promise the United States had made to Israel and Egypt—found itself increasingly estranged from the American government. Urged to hold the line on oil, it did so until the end of 1979. Its oil generally sold for $2 to $12 a barrel less than other OPEC oil, and it kept a reasonable relationship between its oil prices and the prices of the Western industrial goods and services it was purchasing. Early in 1980, however, for the first time it allowed its prices to leap-frog those of some of its neighbors. This move came after publication in the Middle East of the fact that the American government, having urged Saudi restraint, had sold one consignment of American-produced oil to Japan for $40 a barrel. It also followed a sharp exchange with President Carter over the question of Palestine.

In 1980, the United States needed to import 8.3 million barrels. Cost was thus a critical issue for the nation. In general, it was taken care of by market forces. Indeed, discounted for inflation, the price of oil fell by 56 percent between 1950 and 1970. Yet the rise in demand meant that whereas in 1970 the United States was spending $1.3 billion for imported oil, in 1980 the bill was about $73 billion (and note that *total* American exports in 1979 were valued at just $182 billion). Taken together with other aspects of American appetites, particularly for Japanese goods, this trend boded ill for the future. What to do about it had already become an issue in the Carter administration.

The most obvious way to accrue large amounts of money is to sell arms. They are expensive, are easy to transfer, and benefit the most organized and export-minded American industry. Moreover, demand for them is present—a country always wants an F15 jet even if it has too many F4 jets. In fiscal year 1978, the United States sold Saudi Arabia over $5 billion worth of military equipment, and Saudi Arabia spent approximately $2,000 per capita on "security." The dangers inherent in aggressive arms sales by the superpowers were made manifest in Iran, Ethiopia, and other countries. Nonetheless, the temptation became very great to handle payments in this manner. Soviet pressure was always a justification.

The only feasible long-term oil strategies, however, are restraint and the development of alternative sources of energy. Restraint is difficult, since there probably will be no dramatic event or crisis to enable a president to make a convincing case, as President Carter failed to do with his "moral equivalent of war" speech early in his administration. Even if the urgency is accepted, moreover, it will be harder yet for America to readjust its very geography, which is now built of concrete and asphalt to suit the automobile. Such a policy would require our cities to shrink and our priorities to change. And who will be brave enough, in seeking electoral support, to tell Americans these things? The development of alternative sources of energy is possible, but long-term and costly. Although the Carter administration began the process, it did not last long enough or, perhaps, have sufficient dedication to carry it through. Then, in the next decade, as the price of oil slipped and talk of an "oil glut" became common (if short-sighted), the various energy-saving and alternative-energy programs were dropped from the Reagan administration budgets. The fact was simply that the American public did not regard the matter with the seriousness it deserved and was to pay a price for this neglect by the end of the Carter administration, when the balance of payments, of which imported oil was a major factor, turned disastrously against America.

As the Carter administration drew to a close, it had become clear that, viewed from America, the power line-up in the Middle East had changed. Saudi Arabia, the main producer of oil, had moved from being a little-known, unimportant desert kingdom to the most important of America's trading partners; for at least the foreseeable future, its stability and friendship seemed nearly vital to American interests. Measured in these scales, the Camp David Accords and the Egyptian-Israeli peace treaty, great achievements though they were, still do not constitute a comprehensive policy. Such a policy was not devised in the Carter administration. In the past, it could have been an "area" policy, dealing with already complex and difficult problems, but for the 1980's to be successful, a policy had to guide the American nation in its broader problems with the Soviet Union; treat in acceptable ways the Palestine conflict, on which large numbers of American Jews felt religious and moral commitments and upon which the Arabs felt similar and opposite imperatives; and handle the great issues of America in the world economy.

27

American Policies of the 1980's

THE Reagan administration inherited what appeared to be a new situation in the Middle East: by ratifying the Camp David Accords, the Egyptians had broken up the Arab coalition against Israel; by releasing the U.S. embassy staff in Tehran, the Iranian government had taken the pressure off the hostage crisis; and with oil in abundant supply and prices falling, the administration was quietly scaling down the Carter administration's programs designed to promote fuel savings and to find alternative sources of energy. But within two years it found that most of the old problems remained. America remained heavily dependent on oil imported from the Middle East; the Arab-Israeli conflict took on a new dimension with the Israeli invasion of Lebanon; and in the chaos of the Lebanese civil war, hostage taking again became a major issue. Nevertheless, for reasons that lay partly outside the Middle East, the decade of the 1980's marked a fundamental turning point in American relations with the Arab world.

In considering both the continuities and the changes in the 1980's, it is useful to begin with the view from Washington. The United States, like all major powers, had interests and objectives in various parts of the world. The Middle East was just one of its concerns. More important, at least some of its objectives were contradictory, while others required actions or inactions that either

were unpopular at home or were judged not worth the effort necessary to achieve them. Yet they often demanded attention. When
seen in this light, the art of managing foreign relations is that of
keeping a vision of the forest in mind while picking a way through
the trees and underbrush. This chapter will look at how, in what
ways, and at what cost a path was found—and to what extent it
was lost—in the 1980's.

During the Reagan and Bush years the central objectives of
American policy remained what they had been for a generation,
namely to prevent the "loss" of all or a significant part of the Middle East to the Soviet Union, to prevent the outbreak of a regional
war of such magnitude as to involve the United States and the
Soviet Union, and to continue to ensure the United States and its
allies access to petroleum on "acceptable" terms.

That these objectives would be attained was never in doubt in
the 1980's. There was never a realistic possibility that the Soviet
Union would gain ascendancy in the Middle East. Bogged down
in its long and costly war in Afghanistan, the USSR generally
downplayed its efforts in the area. It did take advantage of the
openings given by Syria's and Iraq's need for Soviet military equipment and technical help; and it may have flirted with the possibility
of a deal with Libya to acquire Mediterranean port facilities. But
these actions never posed serious dangers to American policy.
Then, around 1987, as pressures on its economy mounted and
General Secretary Gorbachev began to set forth his new policy, the
Soviet Union began to cooperate with American efforts in various
parts of the Middle East, and it ended the decade actively supporting U.S. policy in the Gulf. Yet, as we shall see, Reagan administration officials regarded Soviet penetration of the Middle East as an
issue of such transcendental importance as to allow it virtually to
eclipse other considerations.

American access to oil on satisfactory terms was likewise generally secure in the 1980's. Despite the Iraq-Iran war and until the
Iraqi invasion of Kuwait in August 1990, there was too much
rather than too little oil on the market. Consequently, the price of
oil was driven down, falling by nearly 50 percent in dollar terms
and by much more when discounted for inflation. Transport of oil
to markets became a temporary concern during the Iraq-Iran war,
when each side tried to interfere with the shipments of the other,
and Iran also threatened the Arab oil producers who were helping
Iraq financially. But resolute American action—including escort-
ing tankers, sweeping the Persian Gulf for mines, and reflagging

Kuwaiti tankers with the American flag in 1987—with help from the European powers and the Soviet Union, contained this danger.

The Soviet Union sought no confrontation with the United States in the Middle East, although for a brief time in 1982–1983 there was danger of an inadvertent engagement in Lebanon, when the United States and Syria exchanged fire over Syrian antiaircraft and artillery positions that were partly manned by Soviet personnel.

Judged in terms of these three central objectives, which had been the core of American policy for thirty years, the Reagan administration's conduct of American relations with the countries of the Middle East, and through them with other countries, was highly successful.

Of course, the United States had a variety of other objectives as well. Some were treated as little more than pious hopes, such as encouraging the growth of democratic institutions or opening state-dominated economies to Western-style capitalism.

Between those objectives designated as primary and those meriting mention but no serious expenditure of effort was a layer of "second-tier" objectives. None of these was "vital" but some were important; rarely, however, could they be consistently addressed. One that always hovered just at the edge of the operational concern of the State Department and the White House was the achievement of a durable peace between the Israelis and the Arabs. Although nothing comparable to the Camp David effort of the Carter years was mounted, this issue occupied much of the attention that secretaries of state and the presidents gave to the Middle East.

From time to time, one or more secondary issues would assume great importance. Two that in the 1980's occupied a great deal of public attention were the containment or eradication of terrorism and the release of American hostages. Acutely aware of the agony of the Carter administration over hostages in Iran, the Reagan administration was to be deeply concerned over the fate of American hostages in Lebanon.

Each new administration, of course, inherits programs from its predecessor. The Reagan administration, like those before it, began with hundreds of programs in operation. Many of these were continued, sometimes without critical review, because they were already in place and because stopping or curtailing them would have required painful, unpopular, or reputation-harming acts that no one wished to undertake. An example of these was the form of the American aid program to Egypt. Pressure to continue or even expand existing programs, or to begin new ones, was felt whenever they were regarded as important in helping to keep friendly governments in power and in dissuading them from turning for substitutes to enemies of the United States. Military assistance was, of course, the prime example of such programs. Particularly in the Reagan administration, with its emphasis on American armament buildup, arms supply to friends abroad may be said virtually to have shifted from being a "tool" of foreign affairs into being a significant policy in its own right.

Such issues show how difficult it was for an American secretary of state to concentrate on the important, overwhelmed as he often was by the urgent; but there were yet another two levels or categories to which he had to pay attention. One consisted of policies, programs, or general lines of action undertaken more in response to the desires or needs of important American constituencies than in pursuit of any national interest in foreign affairs. Another consisted of policies dictated by the actions of America's allies and adversaries. Arms sales may, at least in part, be regarded as an example of both categories.

The obverse of the coin of arms sales illustrates another problem in foreign policy formulation—namely, to anticipate and take steps to guard against future dangers inherent in actions that, when initiated, seemed convenient, beneficial, or even necessary. The United States and the Soviet Union, along with Britain, France, Germany, China, and other countries, found it attractive to sell or give arms, or to upgrade those given by others, to countries in the Middle East during the 1980's. One result of these policies was that a number of countries in the Middle East (including Iran, Iraq, Syria, Israel, Egypt, and Libya) acquired vast inventories of conventional as well as significant amounts of chemical and biological weapons, and Israel, at least, has also acquired an inventory of nuclear bombs. Now virtually every country in the Middle East has surface-to-surface missiles, some of which are capable of reaching far beyond the Middle East.

In the highly volatile political conditions of the area, some of these weapons have passed out of the hands for which they were intended. For example, during the Iraqi invasion of Kuwait, Iraq seized a significant number of American HAWK and TOW missiles that had been given to Kuwait when it appeared threatened by Iran. This is a blatant case; but even when they remained in the hands of governments for which they were intended, sophisticated weapons were not generally subject to the elaborate and expensive controls exercised by the Great Powers. Even when no accidents have occurred and weapons have not been used, unintended arms races have been stimulated, and categories of weapons (such as chemical and biological) and long-range delivery systems (particularly involving missiles) have become common.

Instead of pursuing arms control, which is unpopular both with suppliers and with recipients, each administration for thirty years had sought to balance, at each higher stage of escalation, the arms available to the various countries. By the advent of the Reagan administration, the whole Middle East was armed to the teeth. This trend has had a number of adverse and potentially dangerous effects. The most obvious was that it put a tremendous strain on already fragile economies and diverted to unproductive uses funds that were urgently needed for development and social welfare projects. A second was that Western and Soviet arms supply policies in the 1950's and 1960's certainly stimulated the militarization of Third World societies. The resulting growth of military bureaucracies made the achievement of democratic and responsible governments, surely a fundamental if long-term American objective, less likely. A third effect was that once large and lethal weapons inventories were in place, governments were more inclined to use them. A fourth was that as each country acquired more sophisticated weapons, it was less likely to feel bound by the dictates of international law or the consensus of the United Nations. Iraq offers the most urgent example of the third and fourth dangers.

Thus, as we shall see in the confrontation with Iraq in 1990, the Bush administration was faced with the results of decades of easy arms supply. It was forced to try three measures to cope with ensuing dangers. First, it stationed more than a quarter of a million American troops in the Arab world. This has been expensive, with a yearly cost, even without hostilities, that is considerably higher than the entire amount spent by the United States on the Arab world since World War II, and would have been impossible had the Soviet Union not cooperated. Second, it searched for ways to get Iraq to agree to scale down (or eliminate) its advanced weapons capabilities. This is obviously a very difficult policy to force upon Iraq or any other country once its army has the weapons. Had Iraq already acquired nuclear weapons (as have Israel, India, and perhaps Pakistan), it would be nearly impossible. Even short of nuclear weapons, it became possible only at the cost of hostilities and even then probably only temporarily. Under almost any leadership, as the examples of India and Pakistan show, countries will pay virtually any amount to attain parity with their neighbors.

In the early 1980's this issue came to a focus in the Iraq-Iran war. The United States gave Iraq credits for roughly half a billion dollars' worth of foodstuffs, as well as priceless intelligence on Iranian troop movements. Then, under the stress of the hostage issue (over which it thought Iran exercised crucial influence) and its covert action against the Sandinista government of Nicaragua (for which Congress refused further funding), the White House furnished weapons to Iran to use against Iraq. This was the essence of the so-called Iran-Contra affair. Allegedly, Admiral John Poindexter was about to go much further, by starting to arrange the release of Shia terrorists held in Kuwait and by providing Iran with satellite photos of Iraqi troop movements, when he was stopped by the secretary of state and the deputy director of the CIA.*

While beginning to explore the possibility of getting our current adversary, Iraq, to scale down, the United States initially took the traditional and relatively painless solution in seeking to balance what Iraq had by supplying Israel and the "friendly" Arab states with still more weapons. If the past is any guide, this policy will prove to be both dangerous and short-term. Yet, as R. Jeffrey Smith wrote in the *Washington Post* on October 29, 1990, "Although Secretary of State James A. Baker 3d has said that the United States favors establishment of a regional 'security arrangement' aimed at constraining Mr. [Saddam] Hussein's future acquisition or use of biological, chemical, and nuclear weapons, no administration official has endorsed the idea of limiting future weapons sales of conventional weaponry in the region." On December 12, 1990, after a meeting with Soviet Foreign Minister Eduard Shevardnadze, Secretary of State Baker announced that after the resolution of the Gulf crisis, some form of arms control program would be high on the American agenda of objectives.

Apart from weapons proliferation and overt hostilities, some of the shortfalls in U.S. foreign policy in the past have resulted from the U.S. government's failure either to balance the complexity of its own objectives or to comprehend the hopes, fears, and political realities of those with whom it had to deal. We shall see examples of both of these in dealings with Syria and Israel over the war in Lebanon from the beginning of the decade.

With some sense of the complex demands and murky atmo-

---

* Bob Woodward, *Veil: The Secret Wars of the CIA, 1981–1987* (New York, 1987), pp. 434–435, 503.

sphere in which American policies were to be implemented, let us now review what actually happened, what failed to happen, and how the United States fared in the 1980's.

Warfare and anarchy in Lebanon remained a persistent challenge to U.S. foreign policy throughout the entire decade, although reactions to that challenge varied from encouragement of the actions of Israel, to direct military intervention, to diplomacy, to benign neglect. As discussed in detail in Chapter 22, Lebanon's turmoil in the 1980's was preceded by a long and complex series of events.

During twelve years of strong rule under two Maronite presidents, beginning in 1958, Lebanon changed dramatically socially and economically but made no significant political adjustments to these changes. Some of its constituent communities, led by the Druze, demanded a reordering of political power to give them a larger voice. No compromise was reached. The dominant Maronites used the power of the state to enforce the status quo. Their adversaries, mainly the Druze and the Muslims, forced the issue of change. And needing allies, they involved the Palestinians, who had come to Lebanon in two waves following the 1948–1949 Arab-Israel war and the 1970 Jordanian civil war, and who by then constituted about 10 percent of the population. Public order broke down, and the national army melted away into the rival communities. In 1974 and 1975, hardly a day passed without a major gun battle. Since the Palestinians were also striking at Israeli targets from bases in Lebanon, the Israelis got involved, first in clandestine support of the Maronite government and then through large-scale commando raids on Palestinian targets in Lebanon. The Israelis also began creating a new Lebanese Christian army with American equipment. By January 1976, Lebanon had become embroiled in a full-blown civil war.

The Syrians watched these developments in fear that Israel would take over all of Lebanon and use it as a base against Syria. In June 1976, ironically (as it seemed in the early 1980's) at the request of the Lebanese government, some 20,000 Syrian troops poured into Lebanon. These troops enabled the Christian government to drive the Druze-led coalition south across what came to be known as the "Green Line" that divided Lebanon in half. Attempt after vain attempt was made to enforce cease-fires; some sixty were negotiated in a single year. The war disintegrated into chaos as old coalitions splintered and new gangs arose. Each neighborhood became a "nation" while the nation lived in anarchy. Even young children were armed with assault rifles, and every person was a potential target. The machine gun was law.

In March 1978, some 12,000 Israeli troops invaded and occupied the southern third of the country. The invasion only exacerbated the problem, however, as it created another quarter of a million refugees. Israeli forces were gradually replaced by a UN peacekeeping force, while the Syrians, reversing their position, tried to destroy the Maronite militias over which they had lost control and, in the process, turned Beirut into a wasteland.

On June 6, 1982, Israel again invaded Lebanon with the hope of imposing a strong Maronite government on the whole country, except for the southern "security zone," which was then and remains occupied by its own army and the Lebanese military force it had created. That policy, the "Sharon Plan," almost immediately proved expensive, unpopular, and unlikely to succeed. So Israel sought first to destroy the PLO and then to extricate itself from the Lebanese quagmire. But it sought to leave behind a pro-Israeli government that could impose its will on the country. This was the task in which it sought American assistance.

The Reagan administration was willing to take on this new responsibility, in part because it feared that continued chaos in Lebanon might invite Soviet intervention or bring about the domination of what President Reagan proclaimed to be almost as bad: the Soviet Union's "surrogate," Syria. A second reason was the administration's sensitivity to the fact that in the chaos of Lebanon, Americans were being kidnapped and murdered. Yet another reason was probably operative: the U.S. government was alarmed at the possibility that Israeli occupation of Beirut would trigger a general Middle Eastern war and perhaps drag in the Soviet Union.

The initial American response was thus not to support Israeli action but to attempt to stop it. In direct contacts with Tel Aviv, the United States demanded an Israeli withdrawal, but when the issue came before the UN Security Council, the United States vetoed the resolution. Administration officials thought that they had received a pledge from Israel on June 16, 1982 (denied by General Sharon on July 2), not to enter Beirut. Thus, when the UN General Assembly demanded an Israeli withdrawal, the United States sided with Israel in a 127-to-2 vote. And when the issue again came before the Security Council, the United States again used its veto; but as a gesture of private anger, it suspended delivery of advanced jet fighters to Israel.

Although nothing has been officially revealed, there is indirect evidence that the Reagan administration was involved in secret peace negotiations with the PLO immediately before the Israeli invasion and may have used pressure on Israel to delay its invasion.*

As a result of these conflicting concerns, the unpopularity of the Israeli invasion, the terrible effects on Lebanon, the danger of renewed Syrian action, and the possibility of negotiations with the PLO, the United States proposed the creation of a United Nations force to garrison Beirut. Israel refused and, in compromise, the United States agreed on July 6 to station a small contingent of Marines in Lebanon as part of a multinational force to monitor the Israeli-enforced withdrawal of the PLO from Beirut. America thus found itself physically involved in the struggle for Lebanon. Within days, however, the administration began to have second thoughts on the open-ended nature of its involvement and began to withdraw its force. Two events forced it to change its plan. On September 15, 1982, the president-designate of Lebanon, Bashir Gamayel, was assassinated, and on September 17 hundreds of civilians in two refugee camps on the outskirts of Beirut were massacred by the Maronite militia under Israeli control. Shocked, the United States reintroduced and considerably augmented its troops in Lebanon, on condition of Israeli withdrawal from Beirut.

Relations with Syria remained cool. For years they had not been friendly, but after the Americans announced a $300 million increase in military assistance for Israel, the Syrians entered into a military assistance pact with the Russians in December 1982. The United States government put Syria on its list of those countries sponsoring terrorism and criticized its brutal suppression of a religious rebellion in the city of Hama in February 1982. Senior administration officials deprecated the will and ability of the Syrians to play a useful role in solving the Lebanese problem and essentially excluded them from negotiations the United States undertook with the Israelis and Lebanese. Using highly publicized "shuttle diplomacy," President Reagan sent ambassador-at-large Philip Habib on visits to the capitals of the Middle East to try to find some point of entry for a peace initiative. The one substantive result of this venture was that on May 17, 1983, Secretary of State Shultz obtained Israel's partial and conditional agreement to withdraw from most of Lebanon. But the condition was a parallel Syr-

* See Arthur Hertzberg, "The Impasse over Israel," *New York Review of Books,* October 25, 1990.

ian withdrawal, and Syria, having been excluded from the negotiations despite the advice of senior American diplomats and experts and the counsel of the president of Lebanon, Amin Gamayel, refused to play the part assigned to it. So the agreement was stillborn.

In the aftermath of this misadventure, relations with Syria, which the United States regarded as the patron of terrorists and as a Soviet ally, deteriorated still further. The Syrians took the unusual step of declaring Ambassador Habib persona non grata. Then, as relations grew more strained, a number of incidents occurred, mostly involving the warring Lebanese factions. American positions were fired upon from areas controlled by the Druze and Muslims, who were regarded as being under Syrian control. On September 12, 1983, President Reagan authorized the Marines to use "aggressive self-defense"; on September 17, naval warships fired on Syrian-held areas and two days later on Druze-held areas.

Fighting intensified in the mountains above Beirut between the Druze and other community militias on the one hand and the Falange (Kataib-based Maronite forces) of President Amin Gamayel. The Soviet Union accused the United States and Israel of preparing "a new [round of] war" in Lebanon, and the Syrian government warned that the escalation in fighting might bring about a renewed Syrian involvement. On September 21 President Reagan reacted, in a speech in which he blamed Syria and the Soviet Union for the growing desperateness of the situation.

From its position as an outside critic of the Israeli invasion, the United States had moved inexorably, in the eyes of some of the Arab partisans, to the role of a participant in the civil war. Increasingly caught in the crossfire, American troops had come under attack from time to time by Israel, Syria, and the various militias. Then on October 23 in Beirut, 241 U.S. Marines were killed in a suicide attack on their barracks.

Faced with a situation it seemed unable to handle or, at times, even to comprehend, one in which violence was endemic and appeared often pointless, the administration decided to withdraw from active involvement on the ground. On February 7, 1984, President Reagan ordered the Marines out of Lebanon. They were quickly followed by the forces of France and Italy.

Four points arising in the Lebanese war should be underscored here because they affected America in the 1980's in a variety of fields.

The first is that the Israelis thought (correctly, most commentators believed) that they had received a "green light" for their 1982

455

invasion of Lebanon from the U.S. secretary of state, Alexander Haig.* If the American intention was, in fact, to use Israel to try to solve the Lebanese-Syrian-Palestinian predicament, which seems unlikely, it was a move of great danger to other American interests throughout the Middle East and, as it turned out, particularly in Lebanon. Perhaps the decision received more care in formulation than yet appears, but such documents and interviews as have since become available indicate that it did not. Planned or unplanned, it was to lead to America's assumption of a military role in Lebanon, the loss of nearly 300 American lives, and a considerable blow to American prestige.

The second point is that the two Israeli invasions of Lebanon, particularly the one in 1982, shattered what remained of Lebanon's political stability and unleashed forces that created a maelstrom. As Yitzhak Rabin, speaking as Israel's minister of defense, later admitted to the Knesset, the Palestinian *Intifada* (uprising) was a continuation of what Israel mistakenly had begun in Lebanon. And although the Israeli invasion certainly did not initiate terrorism or hostage taking, it contributed to their spread and frequency.

The third lesson pointed up by the Lebanese experience is that many, probably most, states in the world today are only superficially coherent "nation-states." This is particularly true in Africa, Asia, and the Middle East. Often, as in Lebanon, they are fragile coalitions of minorities in which the dominant group has come to represent the whole. Since its ascendancy commonly derives from or was augmented by the former European imperial power, this group may be regarded as unfairly using its power against the others. In Lebanon, the Maronite community had been favored by the French during their mandate and managed to solidify its control in the immediate postwar era. The other communities were assigned lesser roles and restricted in their access to state power. More recently, a Maronite faction, organized around the Kataib or Falange, managed to parlay its covert alliance with Israel into an American military assistance program designed to give it overwhelming power in the form of a "national army." This army, in fact only one among several militias, was to be the cudgel with which the Falange intended to beat the other minority communities into acceptance of its hegemony.

Despite warnings from the officers of the Department of State and the Central Intelligence Agency about this basic political real-

* See Ze'ev Schiff, "Green Light, Lebanon," *Foreign Policy* (1983): 73ff.

ity so evident from Lebanese history, the Reagan administration found itself dragged into intercommunal violence. Increasingly caught in the crossfire, it watched angrily as the "national army" was torn apart. When it tried to intervene to save the army, the United States became, in the eyes of the Lebanese, simply another contender in the violent grab for power. Having failed politically, it found the superior fire power of the U.S. Navy of no avail. Finally, lacking any useful or sustainable role, it sailed away from Lebanon in futile indignation.

As discussed in Chapter 22, the last act in this drama was not played out until October 1990, when a reconstituted government, established as a result of inter-Arab negotiations and led by a new Maronite president, Ilias al-Hrawi, managed to win the cooperation of most of the other communities and the backing of the United States. Hrawi invited the Syrians into Beirut to suppress the Falange splinter of the army. It was this force, then being led in rebellion against the Lebanese government by General Michel Aoun, which the Reagan administration had mistakenly thought could create national unity.

The fourth point illustrated by America's involvement in Lebanon is how easy it is for the strong to disregard or disdain the interests of less powerful states which are located in the neighborhood and which therefore have historical and strategic interests that cannot long be brushed aside. For Lebanon, this meant Syria. Syria is not only a neighbor of Lebanon but one that depends upon Lebanese facilities, particularly the ports, for outlets to the sea. Syrians tended to regard Lebanon as a part of "historic Syria" and also remembered how Lebanon was used by France in the 1920's and 1930's as a bastion of its Middle Eastern imperialism. This is not just an obstructionist ploy of the expansionist and dictatorial government of Hafez al-Assad; assertion of a "vital" national interest in Lebanon has been the policy centerpiece of a variety of Syrian governments for more than half a century. Thus, to cut Syria out of the negotiations that were intended to establish the political and military posture of Lebanon, as Ambassador Habib and Secretary of State Shultz did, was bound to be self-defeating. The policy had to change—and in fact did, when the United States signed in Damascus a new agreement, negotiated by the Saudis, on restoration of peace in Lebanon.

Throughout the 1980's the challenge of terrorism occupied a great deal of the attention that the Reagan administration devoted to the Middle East. As a result of intense public sentiment and extensive press coverage, it was an issue no American government could afford to seem to neglect or tolerate. Thus, while containing terrorism was not a central or core objective of American policy, it often seemed more urgent than any other.

In our understandable abhorrence of terrorism, Westerners who live in politically open societies with at least a consensus on law can lose sight of how it is regarded by those who do not. In the last half-century, terrorism has been used for political purposes by peoples all over the world in every culture and religion. Merely condemning it as illegal is evidently not effective, for it is usually adopted by those who regard themselves as living in an essentially illegal or extralegal situation. Nor, by and large, have police measures worked. Even where military force is used overwhelmingly and tens of thousands of suspects are detained, little progress has been made in stopping it when those who engage in it believe it is their only means of action. As one group is detained or killed, others step forward to take its place, unless the conditions that made them turn to terrorism change.

Political terrorism was a major concern of the Reagan administration in all its efforts to deal with the conflict in the Middle East. Spectacular and dreadful events such as the explosion of Pan American flight 103 on December 21, 1988, over Lockerbie, Scotland, brought the issue of terrorism home to Americans, most of whom had never understood the more subtle and complex issues of the Middle East. Kidnappings and murders of Americans and others in Lebanon were covered by the media in all their lurid and heartrending detail.

The terrorists, no doubt, fully intended that their acts would focus attention on their causes. The methods they used and the targets they chose show that this was a part of their goal. But the reaction of the U.S. Congress, the administration, and the public was generally quite different from the one they sought. Whereas the terrorists had presumably hoped to force concessions on their demands in the Middle East and to dispirit the U.S. government, most Americans concluded that terrorists were simply vicious criminals.

In the long history of terrorism, repugnance for terrorists' acts has been a consistent danger to their causes. Armenian terrorists in the Ottoman Empire at the end of the nineteenth century tried to bring down bloody repression upon themselves as a means to force the European powers to intervene. Likewise, Serbian terrorists sought to break up the fragile Austro-Hungarian Empire by forcing it to commit repressive acts against its minorities. When such left-wing opponents of Western governments as the Industrial Workers of the World sought to dramatize the plight of the very poor, the public saw them merely as "bomb-throwing anarchists."

In World War II, in contrast, Americans sympathized with terrorists who opposed the Nazis. Regarding the "freedom fighters" against imperialism at the end of the war, our reactions were mixed. We did not take kindly to the Vietnamese who fought the French, but we empathized with such Jewish terrorists as the Irgun and the Stern Gang in their fight against the British in Palestine, even when their actions were spectacularly violent. Our feelings have varied from time to time and group to group with regard to the Basque ETA, the Irish Republican Army, the PLO, the Peruvian "Shining Path," and other groups. For the most part, the public has reacted not to their political "statements" but to the peril and discomfort it experienced as a result of their deeds. This was the case during the 1980's, when the Reagan administration found in the acts of the primarily Arab and Persian terrorists yet another reason not to sympathize with their causes.

In the Arab world in the 1980's, America confronted three distinct kinds of political violence. The first type was supported by governments and involved various means of violent action. Throughout the decade, the United States clashed repeatedly with Libya over Libya's alleged support of terrorism and other issues. The second type was the terrorism of anarchy, of which Lebanon provided the best-known model in the 1980's. And the third was the organized terrorism of underground groups, which in the Middle East meant the more extreme factions of the Palestinians, most notably the Abu Nidal group.

For the Reagan administration, the issue of state-sponsored terrorism came into focus primarily on Libya. On April 29, 1981, at the conclusion of a visit to the Soviet Union by Colonel Muammar al-Qaddafi, the Russians and the Libyans issued a joint communiqué decrying "attempts by imperialist circles to equate international terrorism with the liberation struggle of peoples." This was precisely the linkage proposed by the Americans. Indeed, a few days later, on May 6, President Reagan closed down the Libyan embassy in Washington for supporting "international terrorism." In August, after *Newsweek* published a story saying that the CIA planned to assassinate Colonel Qaddafi, the Libyan Bureau for Foreign Liaison (Libya's foreign ministry) complained that America was preparing some sort of hostile act, and a few days later protested that America was holding naval exercises in an area claimed by Libya as its territorial waters. As Lisa Anderson wrote,

> The Reagan Administration came into office determined to take a new and apparently more consistent position toward Libya. Qadhdhafi was selected for special attention by the United States as the symbol of all the United States finds repugnant in international affairs—support for international terrorism, opposition to a peaceful solution of the Arab-Israel conflict, and support for a diminished US role in the world. The expulsion of the Libyan diplomats was accompanied by much fanfare and the longstanding tacit US agreement not to challenge Qadhdhafi's declaration of 200-mile territorial waters was abandoned. (*Middle East Journal*, vol. 36, 1982)

On August 19, 1981, in an air encounter 100 kilometers off the Libyan coast, U.S. fighter planes shot down two Libyan planes. While President Reagan denied that the American maneuvers had been provocative, most observers agreed that the fleet exercises were the first steps in a new policy that would lead to attempts to punish Qaddafi for his promotion of terrorism.

Qaddafi presumably thought he perceived a pattern of action designed to lead to his downfall. On June 7, 1982, Hissen Habré, who was widely believed to be a protégé of the CIA, seized power in neighboring Chad. To the east, American-supported Egypt was openly hostile. Leaders in the Sudan had proved themselves unfriendly. So Qaddafi had to look further afield for allies. With both Ethiopia and South Yemen, which were Marxist and avowedly anti-American states, he established close ties, furnishing them with over $1 billion in aid. What he heard from the Yemenis could not have dampened his worries: from them he learned of a CIA-sponsored sabotage team which the Yemenis had captured and forced to confess in March of that year.* To attempt to create other allies, he played host on August 31 to members of some 360 "liberation movements" and other organizations from 86 countries, including the United States. The theme of the conference was "the legitimate uprising of the disinherited against their oppressors." If the "disinherited" were to win freedom, ran the Lib-

---

* Bob Woodward, *Veil: The Secret Wars of the CIA, 1981–1987* (New York, 1987), p. 215.

yan theme, they had to use what the wealthy and strong called terrorism but which, after all, was their only weapon. The Libyans' propaganda effort was not wholly successful. Although many groups were willing to accept Libyan money, few evinced trust in Libya's would-be prophet of the new crusade, Muammar al-Qaddafi. In impotent rage, Qaddafi reportedly spoke of having President Reagan assassinated.

In November 1982, gossip circulated in Washington that Libya was planning an attempt on President Reagan's life. Stories of Libyan hit-squads operating in America were aired on television and at the President's news conference. Expressing outrage and innocence, Libya requested a UN investigation of the charge. Ironically, Libya then itself became the victim of terrorism when a Libyan airliner was hijacked by three Lebanese Shiis. (They demanded the release of a Lebanese Shii, Imam Musa Sadr, who, they believed, was being held captive in Libya.) On December 10, President Reagan called on all U.S. citizens in Libya to leave the country. Through "back-door" channels, the administration reportedly sent a message to Qaddafi warning him that the United States would forcibly react to any attack on its interests. But on the day before Christmas, administration officials announced that the "Libyan hit-team" had "suspended" operations. And then, early in 1983, reports were received in Europe that another coup had been attempted in Benghazi.

What is one to make of these events—which are but a small sample of those that took place in the 1980's? Were they the result of paranoia, of realistic fears, of attempts to "destabilize"? Or did something else lie behind them? There are seldom firm answers in the world of covert operations. But it is clear that, rightly or wrongly, Libya had perceived American policy as aiming to overthrow its government. For its part, America was certain that Libya was supporting acts of terrorism against Americans, possibly even aiming to murder the President, and it sought to force Libya to change its policy.

How did Libya and the United States get on this collision course? The answer to this question requires a brief review of the experience that shaped the lives of the young officers whom Muammar al-Qaddafi led to power. In 1911, during the lifetime of Qaddafi's father, Libya was invaded by Italy. That invasion and World War I severed Libya from the Ottoman Empire, but its status remained confused until 1922, when the new Italian Fascist government, looking for a glorious adventure, determined to conquer the country. The campaign lasted for more than a decade and was one of the most brutal of the twentieth century. By 1936, around the time Qaddafi was born, the Libyan population had been reduced by fighting, famines, emigrations, and executions to about half what it had been in 1922. In World War II, Libya was the scene of great battles between the German Afrika Korps and the British; cities were laid waste, and thousands of rural Libyans lost their lives to bullets or to the millions of mines that were sowed by the two armies. By the end of the war, Libya was so poor and devastated— it was then thought to have almost no economic resources, and its total educated cadre consisted of just seven university graduates— that only Italy and the Soviet Union offered to take on the task of administering it. In 1951, to sidestep both unwelcome suitors, the British arranged through the UN that Libya be made independent under a British-sponsored monarch.

That is probably all that would have been heard of Libya had it not been for the discovery and exploitation of two of Libya's resources: in 1959, large reserves of oil were found; and at about the same time, the United States realized that the clear skies over Libya and its vast empty tracts of land offered the perfect gunnery range for NATO's air command. Wheelus Field, near Tripoli, became a vast American military city. The increasingly corrupt cabal of courtiers around the king profited enormously. These two beacons, military modernity and wealthy corruption, caught the eyes of the younger army officers. Young Colonel Qaddafi was the man who organized and effected the coup d'état of September 1, 1969.

Qaddafi, who had been born in the last and bitter days of Italian rule just before World War II, grew up in poverty. Like many young men, including his hero Gamal Abdul Nasser of Egypt, he found the army his ladder to education and a better life. He studied at the new military school and received some advanced training in England. As a military man, he was attracted by the bright, shiny hardware then so evident at the American air base, but he had inherited a deep fear and even a hatred of the Westerners who had shot their way back and forth across Libya for half a century. So it was not surprising that one of his first acts after taking power was to ask the Americans and the British to vacate their military bases.

Qaddafi's new regime then focused its attention on domestic problems. Reallocation of oil revenues made possible a spectacular change in the people's well-being. Within a decade, literacy increased from less than 20 percent to over 75 percent, medical care became universally available, and great improvements were made in transportation and housing. Yet Qaddafi was not satisfied by, indeed was discouraged by, these developments. Reacting against what he perceived to be the Libyans' increased interest in creature comforts, he took upon himself the mission of leading them toward "higher aims."

Already in 1973, Qaddafi had launched a campaign to try to energize or politicize his countrymen. This goal became the obsession of his life. And, reacting against him and what he was attempting, opponents organized in 1975 the first of a sequence of attempted coups. Qaddafi, in turn, became ever more doctrinaire, developing his own retort to both communism and capitalism in what he called the "Third International Theory." He affected a quasi-mystical new role, as a guru of the "disinherited" or "philosopher of the revolution." Che Guevara and Frantz Fanon entered his pantheon. To establish both his new position and his doctrine, Qaddafi set about organizing "revolutionary committees." These ultimately became a sort of informal political inquisition within Libya. They also formed the basis for the network he sought to establish abroad to control the Libyan émigrés who fled from his regime to Europe and America. Those who opposed him began to question his sanity, to accuse him of paranoia, and to find evidence of increasing savagery in his suppression of opposition.

Up to about 1973, relations between America and Libya, while not cordial, were correct. The United States had vacated Wheelus Field when asked to do so, and it is widely believed that the CIA had even given Qaddafi some help in foiling one of the attempted coups. But in the 1973 Egyptian-Israeli war, Libya played a prominent role in organizing use of what was called the "oil weapon," raising prices and limiting access to oil. Qaddafi made no secret of his feeling that Israel was the American proxy in the Middle East and that therefore the United States was responsible for the plight of the Palestinians and the continued humiliations of the Arabs.

Qaddafi was particularly infuriated when Nasser's successor, President Anwar Sadat, appeared (in Qaddafi's estimation) to turn Egypt into an American puppet. From about 1975, relations with Washington soured, and the United States blocked delivery of aircraft purchased by Libya. Charges were traded between the two governments over terrorism—the U.S. maintaining that Qaddafi was funding Palestinian and other terrorist groups, and Qaddafi claiming that Israeli attacks on Arabs such as the 1978 invasion of Lebanon could not have been organized without American approval. In 1979, a mob sacked the American embassy in Tripoli. Yet throughout this troubled period, Libyan oil exports to the

United States remained a major tie: about 40 percent of Libyan oil, a particularly light and low-sulfur grade, went to American buyers.

During this period, and up to the early 1980's, whatever Qaddafi did was enhanced or cushioned by the flow of oil income. After 1982, however, oil revenues (which provided 99 percent of Libya's earnings) plummeted from $22 billion to $5 billion. Many development projects were stopped, social welfare projects were curtailed, and even the appetite of his army for fancy new equipment had to be curbed. The fall in oil revenues also forced Qaddafi to scale down Libya's support for foreign groups.

In the view of the American government, the lull in Libyan support for terrorism was brief and never complete. Beginning in July 1984, a series of mysterious explosions damaged ships in the Red Sea. Within two weeks, Lloyds of London reported that sixteen vessels had claimed they had hit what seemed to be mines. At first, Iran was suspected of being behind the attacks, but Ayatullah Khumaini denounced the action. Then, on October 2, the U.S. government announced that "persuasive circumstantial evidence" pointed to Libya as the author of the mining. Meanwhile, American, British, French, Italian, Dutch, and Soviet ships began sweeping the Red Sea for mines.

Libya remained heavily dependent on foreigners and foreign organizations. Qaddafi's speeches and interviews show that this dependence was becoming ever more galling to him. And it was not only a question of what happened in distant markets, where he could not control the price of Libya's oil; he could see the dependence all around him in Libya. It has been estimated that by 1980, about 60 percent of Libya's unskilled labor and more than half of its professional labor force consisted of foreigners. Worse, Libya grew less than 40 percent of its food, although 30 percent of the work force was employed in doing so. In the economy as in military affairs, Qaddafi found himself dependent upon a system that he disliked, feared, and envied, but could not master.

He chose to try to change the system by getting rid of the vestiges of the hated past. He had done so in Libya, but, Qaddafi evidently concluded, Libya could never be strong or truly independent so long as the Arab world was disunited and the other Arab rulers were willing to do the bidding of the West. Probably it is this belief that led him, as it had led Nasser before him, into covert activities designed to overthrow those Arab governments that opposed him and to disrupt the actions of their foreign allies. He openly proclaimed his support for suicide attacks on American targets in the Middle East. Further afield, he gave some financial support for the development in Pakistan of an "Islamic bomb." At his order, Libya began involvement with an abortive attempt to keep Idi Amin in power in Uganda, with a military adventure in Chad, and with support for the IRA and the revolutionary movement in Iran.

Qaddafi's actions were often dangerous, and always idiosyncratic. While he spoke passionately and irresponsibly on the Palestine problem, ever favoring the more radical and violent of the Palestinian factions, he consistently opposed the Palestine Liberation Organization. He would not allow the PLO to attend the Afro-Asian Solidarity Conference in Benghazi in March 1985, and for many years refused to let it have an office in Libya. His arbitrary actions created considerable distrust even among those who had benefited from his covert largess. Persian religious leaders, on whom he had pinned considerable hopes, were outspokenly hostile to him after they assumed power, and his chosen allies in Sudanese politics were anxious not to be publicly identified with him.

Yet he refused to give up his subversive activities, and all the coup attempts against him failed. In the face of opposition, he appeared to become even more aggressive. Relations with the United States deteriorated still further when America became convinced that the December 1984 terrorist attacks in airports in Rome and Vienna had been instigated by the Libyans. In January 1986, President Reagan cut all economic ties with Libya, froze Libyan assets, and ordered all Americans out of Libya. On February 4, 1986, Israeli fighter planes forced a Libyan airliner to land in Israel. On March 4, the General People's Congress, meeting in Benghazi, called for the formation of suicide teams to attack American and Israeli targets. At this point, the United States decided to stage "freedom-of-navigation exercises" (the ninth since 1973) in waters claimed by Libya in the Gulf of Sidra. In the predicted clash, the Libyans shot at American aircraft, which in turn attacked Libyan radar posts and other targets. The Libyan government (according to American intelligence sources) then ordered its offices overseas to organize attacks on American facilities in Europe.

Clearly, relations between the Americans and Libyans had reached a flash point. As *New York Times* correspondent Edward Schumacher commented in *Foreign Affairs* (in the winter of 1986–87 issue), "If the ouster of Qaddafi has not been the Administration's avowed goal, it clearly has become a virtual obsession."

The flash occurred on April 5, 1986, when a bomb exploded in a Berlin discothèque, killing one American and wounding about eighty others. U.S. officials charged that Libya was behind the bombing. President Reagan publicly described Qaddafi as "the mad dog of the Middle East." A few days later, the American ambassador to the United Nations, General Vernon Walters, flew to Europe to try to convince America's allies that Libya had become a legitimate target for U.S. military action. His mission was not a complete success, but on April 15 the American air force carried out a massive bombing raid on targets around Tripoli and Benghazi. No one doubted that the prime target was Qaddafi himself. He survived, but his infant adopted daughter was killed and two of his sons were gravely wounded.

Opinion polls showed that more than 70 percent of the American public approved of the President's decision to launch the raid. In Europe, governments varied in their reactions. Prime Minister Margaret Thatcher's government strongly supported the action—it had allowed the American aircraft to take off from bases in Britain. France had refused to allow American aircraft to overfly French territory. Italy and Germany were privately critical of the raid. And the public in both England and Germany was about two-to-one opposed. The press, in a poll covering seventy-one major European newspapers, found opposition to be about 95 percent. As Robert Oakley, who was U.S. ambassador-at-large for counterterrorism, wrote in *Foreign Affairs* in 1987, the American action was seen by "some Europeans as rash, Rambo-like use of force rather than diplomacy by the United States, provoking Qaddafi and strengthening his position instead of stopping terrorism." However, upon consideration of the evidence, the foreign ministers of the European Community met on April 21 to condemn Libyan terrorism and to call for a drastic reduction in the number of Libyans allowed to reside in Europe. Subsequently, in Tokyo, leaders of the seven major industrial powers issued a joint condemnation "of international terrorism in all of its forms, of its accomplices and of those, including governments, who sponsor or support it."

In the aftermath of the attack, Qaddafi retired from the public eye, and speculation was rife that he had given up the struggle with America. But the lull was brief. More important, it seemed to some that the American attack on Qaddafi had the effect of undermining domestic opposition to him (which opposition would then be accused of comprising American agents and being in the pay of the CIA) and of driving him closer to the Soviet Union; but the attack had less effect on his support of "international terror-ism" than did the fall in the price of oil or the expulsion of the hundreds of Libyans living or studying in Europe.

Possibly recognizing this, the United States turned to other de-vices to bring the campaign home to Qaddafi. For the rest of the year, it put its emphasis on a destabilization or "disinformation" campaign that spread rumors of impending coup attempts. No coup materialized. And gradually the confrontation faded away. Ironically, a lessening of tensions seemed to promote a more peaceful Libya. In April 1990, Qaddafi called on Muslims every-where to release hostages and prisoners of conscience in honor of the Muslim holy month of Ramadan. In August, he reportedly ordered some seventy "liberation movements" from around the world to close their offices in Libya, stopped funding the more extreme Palestinian groups, and began to support the mainline PLO under Yasir Arafat. In an interview with an Egyptian newspa-per in October, Qaddafi admitted that Libya had supported groups accused of terrorism but had halted aid when it became clear that the groups were doing the Arab cause more harm than good. He also indicated that he would welcome talks with the United States on improving relations.

The polar opposite of state-supported terrorism can be observed in Lebanon. There, it was precisely the *lack* of a state that promoted violence but favored relatively small-scale violence. About the size of Connecticut, Lebanon has long been a refuge for religious and ethnic minorities and is rich in well-remembered history; it is, therefore, a deeply divided but intensely social country. Whereas their ancestors had fled to Lebanon to escape other oppressors, the Lebanese could not avoid one another. Each group found it was hard to move without stepping on the toe of a neighbor. Feuds were deeply rooted and vengeance was culturally approved. Out-side powers (America, Israel, Syria) maintained the only large-scale, mobilized military forces in the country. So when local communities—the Druze, Shiis, Sunnis, Maronites, what remained of the Palestinians, and others—created organized armed forces, they had to cast them in a different form. As these factions en-gaged in skirmishes, vendettas, and battles with one another and with the outside powers, a new hybrid evolved. That hybrid was not precisely "guerrilla warfare," since the militias often used con-ventional military doctrine and heavy equipment. More often, faced with military formations they could not match, the Lebanese readily took up what I have termed the weapon of the weak, namely terrorism. Terrorism was particularly congenial to the Shiis and their Iranian allies, who were consistently on the margins of power (See Chapter 21). But in the anarchy that prevailed throughout the 1980's, every faction engaged in terrorism.

What particularly concerned the United States government, of course, was the series of attacks on its citizens. A number of American journalists, businessmen, and others were kidnapped; the local office of the CIA was virtually wiped out in a bomb attack; the president of the American University of Beirut was murdered; and a massive car bomb explosion killed 241 Marines. Citizens of England, France, and other countries were similarly attacked, seized, or killed. And among the Lebanese groups, kidnappers and murderers claimed thousands of victims.

In its attempts to deal with terror in Lebanon, the administration was frankly baffled. CIA director William Casey was an activist who wanted to strike preemptively at terrorists, and President Reagan occasionally threatened publicly to do so. But such evidence and interview materials as has come to light, partly in the hearings of the Senate and House committees on intelligence, suggests that the United States never had intelligence of the quality, certainty, and timeliness required. A special FBI team composed of experts in locating kidnap victims was sent to Lebanon and failed in its mission. And, finally, in the CIA's one major effort at counterterror action, namely the attempt on the life of a prominent Shia leader in Beirut on March 8, 1985, a car bomb killed 80 people and wounded 200 but failed to harm the target, Shaikh Fadallah. According to the *Washington Post* (May 12, 1985), Reagan and Casey then disbanded their counterterrorist venture, which they gave up, allegedly, when the CIA found that it could not control the groups it had already organized: the groups' commitment to old feuds and demands for vengeance overrode their willingness to take orders from their American sponsors. So in dealing with Lebanon, America and the European powers fell back on a policy of public condemnation, private negotiation through third parties (including the 1985 arms-for-hostages deal with Iran), cash payoffs, and occasional prisoner swaps that included even a group of Iraqi Shiis who were held in Kuwaiti jails for trying to blow up the United States embassy in Kuwait.*

---

* In September 1987, Bob Woodward, an editor of the *Washington Post*, published an account of his conversations with former CIA director William Casey about the plans to set up counterterror groups all over the Middle East. See Wood-

In the chaos of Lebanon, kidnapping had grown virtually into a wholesale enterprise by 1985. The various factions splintered into ever smaller subdivisions. No one group had significant real power, but to kidnap a person required little power. In addition to dozens of Westerners, whose names were noted by the press, hundreds of Lebanese were abducted and traded among the groups for temporary concessions or the return of yet other hostages. No one knew what to do about this lawlessness; indeed, many of the "groups" were merely shadows that acquired acronyms or names and then disappeared.

On April 2, 1985, the Israeli government transported to Israel 1,100 Lebanese it was holding prisoner. Israel regarded the move not as the "taking of hostages" but as the removal of potentially dangerous people from the Lebanese scene. The United States and other states denounced the move as a violation of Geneva Conventions which ban such deportations. Denunciations did not, however, cause the Israelis to return the prisoners. The Shia Amal organization, to which most of the prisoners belonged, did not have the military power to stop the Israelis, but on June 14 some of its members seized a TWA jet with 153 passengers aboard and forced it to land in Beirut (where they murdered a U.S. Navy passenger). The hijackers demanded the release of the Shia prisoners and offered to trade Greek citizens on the flight for Lebanese prisoners held in Greece.*

President Reagan threatened on June 17 to send an American commando team to Lebanon to liberate the hostages, but senior American officials privately admitted that they had no real military option. Israel guardedly offered to liberate some 700 Shia prisoners, but the United States apparently told Israel privately that it did not favor this course, since it would be a "concession to terrorism." Angered at Washington's stance, Yitzhak Rabin said that America "should not play games" with Israel over the issue. Unilaterally, Israel released 31 prisoners. Then, on June 24, in a surprising about-face, Vice-President George Bush commented that the Shia prisoners in Israel were being held in violation of international law

---

ward, *Veil: The Secret Wars of the CIA, 1981–1987* (New York, 1987), pp. 393–395. On the plan devised by National Security Council director Admiral John Poindexter, his assistant, Lt. Colonel Oliver North, and CIA director William Casey to secure the release of the Shiis, see p. 503. These reports, for the most part, cannot be separately confirmed, as the documents either have been destroyed or are being withheld.

* See Charles W. Maynes, "Lost Opportunities," *Foreign Affairs*, 64 (1985): 425.

and should be released. Egyptian president Husni Mubarak, who was assisting America as an honest broker, warned against any attempt to liberate the American hostages by force. Finally, on June 28, after behind-the-scenes negotiations in which President Assad of Syria played a role, U.S. officials announced that the 39 remaining hostages would be released and that Israel would "soon afterwards" release 735 prisoners, but they claimed that "no deal had been struck." Deal or no deal, the Lebanese Shiis showed that terrorism could be made to work. It also showed that nothing else would have worked. Legal precedents were ignored and public pronouncements were ineffectual.

Among those who learned this lesson were the Israelis. On July 28, 1989, an Israeli special force entered Lebanon and kidnapped a Shia imam by the name of Shaikh Abd al-Karim Ubaid. Ubaid was said to be associated with one of the Lebanese factions known as Hizbullah (Arabic: "the Party of God"), which was thought to be holding two captured Israeli soldiers. In the process of seizing the shaikh from his home, the Israelis also kidnapped two other villagers and killed a neighbor who witnessed their act. Privately, American officials were highly critical of the Israeli kidnappings. The *New York Times* reported on August 17 that for eight days the Israelis had refused an American request for information on the operation, even when asked by President Bush. Initially, the Israelis offered to trade Ubaid for the captured Israeli soldiers; then they offered to trade all Israeli-held Lebanese prisoners for all Israeli and Western hostages held in Lebanon.

Somewhere between the state-organized terrorism of Libya and the anarchy of Lebanon were various groups of Palestinians (discussed in Chapter 16) engaged in terrorist attacks on Israeli, American, and other targets. Many of the original groups had splintered into competing factions, among which the one led by Abu Nidal was considered to be particularly dangerous. In the 1980's, their actions were largely denounced by the mainline PLO, and the more violent groups regarded the PLO as traitors to the Palestinian cause. PLO representatives in Athens, Rome, Paris, and other cities were murdered by these extremists.

In the world of clandestine operations, groups that are outwardly bitter enemies occasionally cooperate actively and frequently move tacitly in a parallel fashion. For this reason, perhaps, Israeli security forces have rarely attacked the more violent and extreme of the Palestinian groups, which are themselves the bitter enemies of Israel's most serious political opponent, the PLO. Palestinian Arab terrorists of the Abu Nidal faction and terrorists of the Jewish Armed Resistance *both* claimed to have murdered the PLO's representative in Paris on July 23, 1982.

Of course, individual events can rarely be sliced out of a sequence and treated as separate units. They tend, like old-fashioned feuds, to become self-perpetuating. For example, on September 15, 1985, three Israelis were killed on Cyprus. Israel decided that the PLO was responsible and two weeks later carried out an air raid on the PLO offices outside of Tunis, killing more than seventy people; six days after that, a group of Palestinians took over the S.S. *Achille Lauro* and killed an American Jewish passenger in cold blood. A few days later the hijackers surrendered. As part of a complex deal, they were to be flown over the Mediterranean in an Egyptian airliner. Knowing this, the American government sent fighter planes to force down the airliner and capture the three men. And so it went, to the next round of attack and reprisal.

By the end of the decade, some students of terrorism had concluded that police and military action alone was unlikely to put an end to terrorist acts. The British, even using ruthless and massive measures in the last days of the Palestine Mandate, had failed to prevent Jewish terrorists from blowing up the King David Hotel right in the center of Jerusalem; in Northern Ireland, they have likewise failed to eradicate the IRA. France vainly employed extreme measures against the Algerians in a long and bitter war. Israel has been battling various groups of Palestinians for twenty years and holds thousands of alleged terrorists in prison camps, but no sooner is one group broken up, arrested, or killed than another comes to replace it. Air raids have certainly killed many Palestinian guerrillas (along with numerous innocent bystanders), and officially sanctioned Israeli hit-squads have killed many more in Tunis, Stockholm, Athens, and Beirut. But there is little evidence of success.

And it is possible that, bad as the problem of political terrorism was in the 1980's, it could be much worse in the future. Ironically, with the end of the Cold War between the United States and the Soviet Union, ethnic and religious minorities or "proto-nations" may become more rather than less desperate and may be willing to use ever more violent and spectacular means to publicize their causes and achieve their ends.

So long as conditions are conducive to terrorism, it will continue.

What are those conditions? The most important of them is probably frustrated nationalism. Despite the challenges of other ideologies and now even of a resurgence of religion, ours remains an age of nationalism. Put simply, to be unable to express one's nationality in statehood is to be put beyond the law—to be made, literally, an outlaw. So long as large numbers of people are convinced that they are thwarted in their aspirations to self-determination and that they have no legal means for redress of grievance, they will fight with whatever means they can muster. Generally, those means equate to terrorism. Thus, any serious attempt to eradicate terrorism, while obviously not neglecting all prudent security measures, must both open legal means of redress and offer some means of working toward self-determination.

This, of course, takes us to the root problem of the Middle East: what to do about the roughly three million Palestinians in the diaspora and the nearly two million living under Israeli occupation. Each American president has laid out an answer, some more indirect or nonpolitical than others. Earlier proposals dealt with redefinitions of frontiers (a Dulles plan), divisions of river water (the Johnston Plan), compensation of refugees (the Johnson Plan), and so on. The most serious in terms of implementation was the one outlined in the Camp David Accords, but the Accords, like previous plans, circumvented the core issue, Palestinian self-determination, and dealt with bilateral Egyptian-Israeli relations. Wherever more recent proposals have come to focus on political problems, the United States position has been that the parties themselves must work out the details and method of implementation, while the United States can offer only advice and help.

President Reagan announced his own proposal for the Middle East on American television on September 1, 1982. More piously than practically, in view of both the already declared and largely implemented Israeli government settlements policy and the already demonstrated lack of American capacity or will to alter it, he called for an exchange of "territory for peace." He urged a form of accommodation between the Palestinians and the Jordanians, to provide a new synthesis. In whatever form this new synthesis took shape, it would avoid clashing with the Israeli determination that the Palestinians never be allowed to become a state; they would be only a component of Jordan, which would negotiate on their behalf with the Israelis.

The key role fell to King Husain. Always eager to try to define a means of avoiding conflict, he had engaged in virtually nonstop covert negotiations with the Israelis ever since he had come to the throne. And he indicated that he would like to try again to find some means of positive action. But he also indicated that he was dubious about this approach. He pointed out that negotiations would be mere formalities if the occupied territories were to be treated as what the Israelis called accomplished "facts": then there would be nothing on which to negotiate. Husain was also aware that without the active support of the PLO, he would be putting himself and his government in an extremely dangerous and exposed position. Yet under the Reagan plan, the PLO were to be told that they could have no part in the negotiations over the future of their people and that, even if the negotiations were successful, they would be excluded from political power. For them, it was a "no-win game." And for Husain, even if these problems could somehow be pushed aside, was it much better? He was asked to expose his throne, lay his prestige on the line, and compromise himself vis-à-vis the Israelis on the word of the United States, a country he no longer really trusted.*

The President, however, felt sufficiently sanguine about his proposal that he instructed his ambassador in Tel Aviv to deliver a personal démarche to Israeli Prime Minister Begin to the effect that the United States would not support the existence of additional Israeli settlements in the occupied territories as a precondition for a peace settlement.

Israel not only rejected the Reagan plan the day after it was announced and the prime minister had received the President's démarche, but answered President Reagan's call for a halt in the construction of new Jewish settlements in the occupied territories by announcing an accelerated program for additional settlements. And in January 1983, the Israeli government set off a major advertising campaign to promote settlements. Arafat, after halfheartedly flirting with Reagan's proposal and discussing it at length with King Husain, was forced by his colleagues also to reject it.†

During the 1980's, the U.S. government was constantly faced with fundamental legal and political issues arising from two aspects of the continuing problem of the Palestinians. One was the harsh policy of the Israeli occupation forces, and the other was the deter-

* As Husain and others often pointed out, he had been promised by President Johnson sixteen years before, in 1973, that the Israelis would be out of the occupied territories in six months; so he was wary of any American promises.

† See Eric Rouleau, "The Future of the PLO," *Foreign Affairs,* 62 (1983): 147ff.

mination of the Israeli government to convert the occupied territories into Jewish-owned and -settled land. Already in August 1981, despite its own bilateral démarches to Israel pointing to the illegality of the Jewish settlements in the occupied territories, the Reagan administration vetoed a Security Council resolution which also rejected their legal basis.

As Larry Fabian wrote in *Foreign Affairs* in 1983,

> Israeli settlements are but the surface manifestations of a vast and often esoteric network of security, political, and socioeconomic policies that have tightened Israel's grip over the West Bank and the Gaza Strip since 1967, embracing all aspects of daily life for the million-plus resident Palestinians, as well as all-important dimensions of planning for the future of these occupied lands. Over the years Washington's ritual protests against the settlements have produced dreary testimony to American ineffectuality and Israeli tenacity. The State Department first protested against the settlements in the summer of 1967, soon after the first new dot or two began appearing on the West Bank map, and regular protests followed.

These matters were to become increasingly critical during the Palestinian *Intifada* which began in 1987 (see Chapter 22). After years of employing tactics of military confrontation, shootings, beatings, arrests without charges, destruction of houses belonging to relatives of the arrested, administrative detention, and expulsion, leaders of the Israel Defense Force publicly admitted having reached the conclusion that the uprising, which except for rocks and knives was always unarmed and often peaceful, could not be suppressed by military force, since it was an outpouring of nationalist aspirations.

Both the Reagan and the Bush administrations from time to time expressed sympathy with the plight of the approximately two million Palestinians living in territories occupied by Israel. But they were constrained from implementing a consistent policy for a number of reasons. First, the U.S. Congress would tolerate few criticisms of Israel, and frequently urged the administrations into ever more favorable action, even during periods of strained relations or condemnations of Israeli policy. Second, many of the criticisms were aired at the United Nations, and the American government feared that any move that gave the United Nations a major role in the Middle East would be exploited by the Soviet Union to acquire a larger role in the area for itself. Thus, America often found itself criticizing the Israeli government for actions documented by Amnesty International, the International Red Cross, or even the U.S. Department of State, but then vetoing Security Council resolutions embodying the same evidence and the same criticisms. A recent example occurred on February 7, 1989, when the State Department annual report on human rights commented on the "substantial increase in human rights violations" in the occupied territories, violations that had caused "many avoidable deaths and injuries."

Iraq's invasion of Kuwait on August 2, 1990, forced the United States to put aside its disdain for the United Nations as an actor in the Palestine problem. Since President Bush decided to invoke the United Nations as the patron of the primarily American move to force Iraq to disgorge Kuwait, he could not very well prevent the United Nations from becoming involved in the *Intifada*. Thus, the United States—reluctantly, to be sure, and negotiating to scale down the terms and conditions—voted on October 12 in favor of a British-drafted UN Security Council resolution that condemned Israeli use of excessive force in suppressing a Muslim demonstration at Temple Mount (or, as Muslims call it, the Haram ash-Sharif).

The United States vote represented a significant change of policy. That change was not only forced upon the Bush administration by its decision to use the United Nations to legitimize and rally support for its move to bring about Iraqi withdrawal from Kuwait; it was also made possible by the change in its relationship with the Soviet Union. The reason for preventing United Nations involvement in the Middle East, namely the fear that it would give the Soviet Union an opening there, was no longer compelling. Indeed, from about 1987, the United States had welcomed, warily at first, Soviet actions that paralleled its own in the Gulf, and by 1990 was actively seeking Soviet support. Thus, when Israel rejected the UN resolution and refused to receive the representative of the Secretary General in Israel, the United States also tacitly approved, on November 1, a call from Secretary General Pérez de Cuéllar for the convening of a conference of the 164 signatories to the Fourth Geneva Convention to discuss ways to protect the inhabitants of the occupied territories from Israel.

Relations with the PLO underwent significant though less certain changes in the late 1980's. For nearly twenty years, despite sympathy with the plight of the Palestinians and agreement with limited aspects of their aspirations, successive American administrations had felt themselves unable to enter into serious negotiations. Indeed, in the Nixon administration, secretary of state Henry Kissinger had promised the Israelis to avoid even talking with Palestinians, and in the Carter administration unauthorized contacts had cost the American ambassador to the United Nations, Andrew Young, his job. The issue on which the United States government drew the line was its insistence that the PLO give up what the latter termed "armed struggle" against Israel. Each American administration demanded that Yasir Arafat recognize Israel's right to exist as a state.

Arafat repeatedly said to diplomats and journalists that he would make the necessary declaration, but that he would or could do so only if the United States would openly affirm the right of the Palestinians to self-determination. This the U.S. government would never agree to do. It argued that to make such a statement would be tantamount to recognizing the Palestinians as a state; this was something, the United States government argued, that must come in the course of peace negotiations. The impasse lasted until 1988.

In February of that year, Secretary of State Shultz expressed a desire to talk with Palestinian intellectuals during a visit to Israel. The PLO leadership, while at first welcoming the move, decided that the American intent was to find an alternative to the PLO leadership which could be used to legitimize aspects of American and Israeli policy toward the Palestinians. It was not until after the commencement of the United States dialogue with the PLO in Tunis in December that Palestinians in the occupied territories agreed to meet with American officials.

The full story of the negotiations that led up to the Tunis meeting is still not public. One account,* based mainly on interviews with Arafat, assigns a critical role to Swedish foreign minister Sten Andersson, who managed to clarify exactly what the U.S. government demanded to begin talks with the PLO and also managed to get Arafat's approval of the terms. They included, it is said, "unconditional recognition of the existence of Israel, the acceptance of UN resolutions 242 and 338, and the renunciation of terrorism." Arafat affirmed his acceptance, on behalf of the PLO, of these terms on December 14, 1988, in a press conference in Geneva.

One of the final foreign policy acts of the Reagan administration

* Janet Wallach and John Wallach, *Arafat: In the Eyes of the Beholder* (New York, 1990).

was Secretary of State Shultz's finding that the PLO had renounced terrorism and agreed to recognize Israel and that, therefore, the United States could commence talks with it. Talks were immediately opened at the U.S. embassy in Tunis.

But, of course, it was a long way from the holding of bilateral United States–PLO talks to undertaking work on the peace process. It was not—and still is not—clear exactly how that could be accomplished. The Israeli government has adamantly refused to deal directly with the PLO and has consistently said that it would not consider a peace settlement that involved the creation of a Palestinian state. So, in a sense, the old impasse was simply moved to a new level.

Recognizing this, Secretary of State James Baker put forward on March 13, 1989, a proposal to approach peace talks in "two tiers." Separate but simultaneous moves, he suggested, would be made, on the one hand, toward lessening tensions or ending hostilities in the occupied territories, and, on the other hand, toward defining a final settlement. The next day, he told members of the U.S. Congress that "if meaningful negotiations were not possible between Israel and the Palestinians [in the occupied territories], then I suppose we . . . would then have to see negotiations between Israelis and representatives of the PLO." A week later, the *New York Times* published summaries of Israeli press accounts of an Israeli intelligence analysis which asserted that the *Intifada* could not be crushed and that it could be halted only with the cooperation of the PLO, since there was no serious leadership in the occupied territories separate from the PLO. Briefly, it seemed that the Israeli government might move toward acceptance of Baker's plan. The next day, however, Israeli Prime Minister Shamir dashed any hopes that his government would deal with the PLO.

Meanwhile, Yasir Arafat came under attack by leaders of the so-called hard-line groups for his apparent willingness to enter into talks with the United States; and in the occupied territories, hostilities between the Israelis and the Arabs reached new levels of intensity. On May 22, 1989, apparently reacting to events there, Secretary Baker addressed the issue of the takeover of the occupied territories, saying that Israel should "lay aside once and for all the unrealistic vision of a greater Israel [and] reach out to Palestinians as neighbors who deserve political rights." According to the *New York Times,* Baker's speech brought an angry retort from Prime Minister Shamir the next day. But on July 12, the assistant secretary of state, John Kelly, testified before the House Foreign

Affairs Committee that Israel itself had undertaken secret negotiations with the PLO.

In the months that followed, negotiations were begun over a plan put forward by Secretary Baker that aimed at getting talks started between the parties. The terms put forward by Israel and published in the *Washington Post* on December 7, 1989, stipulated that a meeting would take place in Cairo in which Palestinians who were "satisfactory" to Israel would take part and at which the subject would be an Israeli proposal for elections in the occupied territories. By the end of February 1990, no agreement had been reached either on the final agenda or on the Palestinian delegation, whose composition Israel continued to demand the right to determine. On February 22, President Bush reportedly warned Israel that if it did not make the compromises necessary to get the peace process under way, the United States would cease to pressure the Palestinians to accept its initiative. Little if any further progress was made before the Iraqi invasion of Kuwait.

During the 1980's, partly as a result of the Camp David Accords but also because Egypt seemed the best candidate to rally moderate Arab governments to contain the growth of Soviet influence in the Middle East, Egypt became America's most favored Arab country and received more American aid than any other Middle Eastern country except Israel. Great efforts were made to facilitate Egyptian development, with the aim of making Egypt the most powerful and modern of the Arab countries and a voice for an American-defined policy of accommodation with Israel and opposition to the Soviet Union. But the results have been disappointing. Although the population continued to grow at a rapid rate, the economy did not. Land reclamation netted only marginal lands of low productivity, despite great effort. People flocked to the cities because living in the countryside meant having to forgo modern medical attention, having to be content with education only at the primary level, and having to live without clean, running water. So agriculture declined. By 1982, Egypt was buying half of its food abroad.

The country did become energy self-sufficient by 1983 and, largely because of the savings on energy costs, the economy showed great statistical growth. Remittances from the workers who flocked in the tens of thousands to such countries as Iraq also contributed significantly to the growth during the early 1980's. Still, Egypt needed at least $2 billion yearly from abroad to balance its expenditures. By 1982, the United States was committing approximately that amount in civil aid plus a sizable amount in military aid. The purpose of the military aid was never fully spelled out. Military experts generally have concluded that the Egyptian army was less combat-ready in 1985 than it had been fifteen years before and that, therefore, the purpose of American aid was presumably not to create a powerful military machine. More likely, the primary purpose was to ensure the army's cooperation with the civilian government. The army was rightly seen as the most powerful element in the coalition that kept the Egyptian government in power. A secondary purpose was the army's foreign affairs role. An adequate even if not impressive army could at least deter Libyan ambitions in the Sudan and balance and augment the smaller, American-equipped army of America's other Arab ally, Saudi Arabia.

The military aid was easy to absorb, but the slack and inflexible Egyptian economy proved unable to absorb more than about two-thirds of the civil aid. As growth slowed, existing strains became more noticeable. Among the new middle classes, who suffered the most from a 30-percent rate of inflation, the malaise was particularly evident. Expectations for Sadat's "Opening" (Arabic: *Infitah*) to capitalism had faded; consequently, when Husni Mubarak took over the presidency, after Anwar Sadat was assassinated by a Muslim fundamentalist group on October 6, 1981, he signaled his retrenchment from unabashed capitalism by firing Sadat's chief economic planner.

From 1975 to 1990, Egypt received more than $15 billion from the United States and a similar amount from other donors. Despite that, Egypt's growth rate in the mid-1980's fell to less than 5 percent. The amount of foreign exchange needed to cover debt obligations rose from 35.1 percent of foreign exchange earnings in 1984 to 45.8 percent in 1986. Already by 1984 Egypt had debt service requirements of $536 million, which about equaled the yearly amount of dollars coming in from U.S. aid. Thus, the result of years of American effort has been not the creation of a vigorous ally but the establishment of a permanent Egyptian dependency on America. This is a problem that has yet to be addressed, but it is one that will become increasingly urgent as America's own foreign exchange problems worsen in the 1990's.

The first step taken to alleviate Egypt's burden of foreign debt was a result not of an assessment of the country's needs but of the crisis precipitated by Iraqi president Saddam Husain. America needed Egypt's support in the Gulf crisis, and signaled its gratitude for that support by forgiving Egypt's $7.1 billion military debt. It was a debt that probably was never collectible in any case, but it is one that surely will have to be followed by other write-offs.

There seems no end to the Egyptian economic and social problem. By the turn of this century, barring war or plague, the population will have soared virtually beyond control. Already there are signs that hope for the future—a crucial prerequisite to the accomplishment of modernization—is fading. Egyptians are turning in ever larger numbers away from the national development program President Nasser offered them and the consumer society President Sadat offered them, and are embracing religious fundamentalism. This is a trend that is essentially opposed to the spirit and direction of American policy and one that frightens those who lived through the Iranian revolution. Yet it is a tendency virtually impervious to outside influence. Though apparently only a remote possibility today, a fundamental change in Egyptian society may become a major issue for Americans in the generation ahead.

The tragic civil war in the Sudan received relatively little attention from the United States government during the 1980's, although nongovernmental aid agencies took a hand in trying to prevent the worst ravages of famine and disease. To appreciate the depth and extent of the problems of the Sudan, it is necessary to understand how the vast area, roughly one-fourth the size of the United States, became a single country.

The Sudan as it now exists was demarcated by the European powers according to *their* own relative power and access, rather than according to any indigenous social or political realities. The primarily Nubian northern area bordering on Egypt is relatively homogeneous, being both Muslim and Arabic-speaking. The center, focused on the capital, Khartoum, is also Arabic-speaking and Muslim and thinks of itself as Arab. The south is a vast, poorly interconnected area peopled by a number of more or less autonomous "Nilotic" tribes. During British rule, little attempt was made to bring about a fusion of the various groups. The British did not impose the Arabic language on the south, where English became the lingua franca. Nor was much effort put into easing relations among the tribes or into giving them a sense of supra-tribal loyalties or identity. The British did, however, permit or encourage the work of missionaries, who converted parts of several of the tribes from animism to Christianity. Thus, in addition to various geographical and social distinctions, the north and the south spoke different languages and adopted different religions.

Not long after independence, the Sudan began its first major civil war, a long and wasteful conflict that, in the end, resolved none of the problems that had caused it. When Jafaar Numairi took power in a military coup in 1969, he attempted to use the army to impose upon the Sudan a sense of national order. In this, his government resembled other Arab military regimes. And he began various programs of national development, including exploitation of the country's meager oil reserves and the creation of a new agricultural project in the south, based on the Jonglei canal and swamp-draining system on the White Nile south of Malakal. The southerners saw these projects, and the Numairi regime as a whole, as aspects of northern tyranny. Worse, they bridled at the attempt by the Khartoum government to impose Islamic law on all of the Sudan.

After an interval of peace, in which nothing was settled, civil war broke out again. Led by Colonel John Garang, a Sudanese army officer from the Dinka tribe, rebels demanded an end to the military cliques that had ruled the Sudan and an end to Islamic hegemony. Fighting a savage guerrilla or "bush" campaign, with some help from the Marxist government of Ethiopia, Garang's followers forced work to stop on the Jonglei canal after 1983. They also brought to a halt all work on new oil fields, after Numairi structured the pumping and refining facilities so that the south would get little benefit from them. Area by area, they began a series of attacks and sieges that paralyzed the south.

During this time, the Sudanese economy, never very strong, deteriorated. United States aid amounted to a critical $375 million in 1983 and 1984, and the Sudan was borrowing large amounts from Arab and international lending agencies. Then, in 1983 and 1984, the Sudan suffered a catastrophic drought. Various non- and quasi-governmental agencies from a number of Western countries, along with the United States government, provided food aid, but efforts to get food to stricken areas were often nullified by the civil war.*

Jafaar Numairi was overthrown in April 1985, after ruling for sixteen years, and was replaced by a joint military-civilian government. The new regime attempted to bring a halt to the civil war but misunderstood the aims of the southerners. It assumed that once Numairi was out of the picture, the rebels would accommodate to Khartoum. They were wrong. By that time, the rebels were demanding a total restructuring of the state with, possibly, moves

* See Ann Lesch, "A View from Khartoum," *Foreign Affairs*, 65 (1987): 807ff.

toward regional autonomy. So the war continued. After a year, the interim government was replaced by a grandson of the famed nineteenth-century national-religious leader, the Mahdi. Sadiq al-Mahdi, a bright, tolerant, Oxford-educated man, took his turn at trying to reach an accord with the southern rebels in the summer of 1986 and on several subsequent occasions. The two sides inevitably parted on the issue of what to do about Islamic law: the north would not give it up, and the south would not accept it.

During the war, what had been generally ignored in the past could no longer be hidden—the fact that, bad as the split between north and south was, it was only one of several fissures in Sudanese society. Tribes in the south—the Dinka, Nuer, Shilluk, and others—fought one another, while "Arabs" attacked Nubians in the north. The whole country was caught in a vortex of hostilities.

By October 1988, hundreds of southerners were starving to death every day as a result of the civil war. Early in 1989, the United States offered to act as honest broker between the rebels and the government, and on March 2, the United States announced that at its request, the Soviet Union had agreed to urge the Ethiopian government to pressure the rebels toward negotiations. By that time, the rebels controlled almost all of Equatoria province, centered on the town of Juba. On May 1, a cease-fire went into effect in most areas, so that food convoys began to get through to the worst-hit areas. Then, on June 30, the military again intervened to overthrow the government of Sadiq al-Mahdi. The United States had, meantime, virtually stopped its aid program, already reduced to very modest proportions, because the Sudan was unable to meet the crippling repayments schedule.

So the Sudan, a vast and imposing area astride the mighty Nile River, wretchedly poor and deeply in debt, is lacerating itself into a sort of African Lebanon.

The case of the Sudan points up two messages. On the one hand, particularly in Africa, the countries we see uniformly colored on the map are often not, in fact, nation-states. On the other hand, as the memory of centralized Western control vanished, the natives could replace imperialism only with military control, but that control was merely a veneer. Almost nothing was—or, given the resources, could be—done to homogenize the country. As in Lebanon, the dominant local group (in Lebanon the Maronites and in the Sudan the Muslim "Arabs") gained ascendancy and used the power of the state for its own benefit. Other groups were shortchanged, excluded, or beaten down. Otherwise laudable development efforts were skewed to benefit the dominant group wherever possible, while wasteful or inappropriate projects were undertaken because politicians and merchants made money from them. The army was the major beneficiary. The things it wanted were often the most expensive and always the least useful; they were also the easiest to absorb. So long as the Cold War remained the major criterion of the powers, countries such as the Sudan were tolerated, indeed encouraged, in their wasteful expenditures and in their failure to address their fundamental political and social problems, because policy makers were guided by the compelling argument that "if we don't do it, *they* will." One of the questions that American policy can and should—indeed may have to—address in the 1990's, is what can be done about the Sudan.

Saudi Arabia presents almost the mirror image of the Sudan. Whereas the Sudan must hold out its battered cup for charity, Saudi Arabia, with a gross national product ten times larger and a literacy rate two times higher, can buy talent and equipment from anywhere in the world.

For America, the essential interest in Saudi Arabia is, quite simply, oil. Not only does Saudi Arabia have the largest reserves of any single country in the world—almost as much as Iraq, Kuwait, the UAE, and Qatar combined—but its reserves, at the present level of exploitation, should last at least a generation longer than those of any other oil-producing country. Prior to the 1990 crisis, roughly one of every twelve barrels of oil consumed in the United States came from Saudi Arabia.

In addition to its importance as a producer of energy, Saudi Arabia has been a completely stable, conservative monarchy, relatively popular with its citizens, and one engaged in a commendable development program in an area where most of the other states have been erratic or consistently "radical" in their policies. It has also been a major trading partner of the United States, a large-scale purchaser of American goods, and, before the decline in the price of oil in the mid-1980's, a mainstay for the American monetary system. For a time, its central bank, SAMA, was the largest purchaser of U.S. government debt obligations. As has often been said, if Saudi Arabia did not exist, the United States would have tried to invent it.

Thus, when Iraq invaded Kuwait on August 2, 1990, and many feared that its tanks would roll on toward the Saudi Arabian oil fields, President Bush began a form of military intervention in the

Middle East that quite simply dwarfed anything the United States had ever even contemplated in the past. Not only did America rush in about a quarter of a million troops, but President Bush announced that the United States was prepared to sell Saudi Arabia approximately $20 billion worth of military equipment.

Already in 1987 the strategic importance of the Gulf states had been called into question by the war between Iran and Iraq (see Chapter 21). On January 19 of that year, the Soviet Union took the lead in what became a naval convoy system by sending a group of cargo ships, escorted by one of its frigates. A week later, the U.S. Navy began deploying ships in the Gulf and moved a carrier task force to a position just outside the Straits of Hormuz. In response, Iran began to station missiles at sites adjacent to the straits.
Kuwait then announced that it had considered the idea of putting its sizable tanker fleet under the American flag, to give it a sort of immunity from Iranian attack. Iran's ambassador to the UN replied that such an action would make no difference to Iran in its blockade of Iraq. On April 21, both the United States and the Soviet Union issued warning statements. The Soviet Union commented that it would reply "firmly" to any attack on its flag, while America indicated that it was negotiating with Kuwait over the modalities of reflagging Kuwaiti ships. By this time, the Gulf was swarming with naval vessels and aircraft. The first casualty—ironically, given that the identified enemy was then Iran—came not from Iran but from Iraq, when an Iraqi jet fired a missile at the U.S.S. *Stark* off Bahrain on May 17. Iraq apologized and offered to pay compensation, and the incident passed. Then, on July 6, the U.S. Navy began convoying American ships through the Gulf, and on July 22 began moving reflagged Kuwaiti tankers up the Gulf.
The first serious clash with the Iranian navy came on September 22, when navy helicopters set fire to a mine-laying ship. In October 1987, Iran struck an American-flagged Kuwaiti tanker with a "silkworm" missile, and in retaliation American naval ships shelled and set fire to Iranian oil-drilling installations, radar stations, and communications sites. Finally, on February 25, 1989, after the Iraq-Iran cease-fire, the Soviet foreign minister proposed that both the USSR and the United States remove their fleets from the Gulf. The crisis appeared to be winding down, but as it turned out, it was only approaching a new phase—the Iraqi phase.

In the bitter aftermath of the Iranian revolution, when America watched impotently as its former friends were exiled, imprisoned, or executed and its embassy staff was held hostage, when almost daily pronouncements proclaimed it to be "the Great Satan" and its embarrassing confidential records were published, the conflict between Iran and Iraq was not unwelcome (see Chapter 21). In that conflict, Iraq seemed the lesser of two evils. In 1984, after seventeen years, the United States and Iraq reopened diplomatic relations. During the next few years, the United States "tilted," as the current expression had it, toward Iraq in the conflict; the U.S. government chose to overlook aspects of the Iraqi regime that it found abhorrent, including widespread civil rights abuses and lack of democratic institutions. Even after Iraq was no longer in danger of being overwhelmed by Iran, the United States government maintained its "tilt" toward Iraq. Moreover, it failed to assess accurately President Husain's long-term aims and ambitions. This failure was to prove costly as the 1990's began.

About the time the UN Security Council had unanimously adopted Resolution 598, calling for a cease-fire, withdrawal of troops behind the old frontiers, exchange of prisoners, and an inquiry into responsibility for starting the Iran-Iraq war, Iraqi president Saddam Husain met Syrian president Hafez al-Assad in Jordan. On November 9, 1987, at that meeting, the two leaders achieved a partial rapprochement. Allegedly, in return for Assad's agreement to end this split in the Arab camp, Syria received a large contribution in aid from the member states of the Gulf Cooperation Council. The meeting appeared to be a major diplomatic success for Saddam Husain, as it opened the possibility of considerably increasing Iraq's oil exports and enhancing its security.

With the war winding down, and particularly after a cease-fire had been achieved on August 20, 1988, Iraq found itself with a series of unresolved problems. The Kurdish issue in the north remained troubling, and the Iraqi army took advantage of the hostility it shared with Iran and Turkey toward the Kurds (all three countries violently opposed Kurdish nationalism) to engage in savage "search and destroy" missions in Kurdish areas of Iraq. In some of these attacks, Iraq employed chemical weapons, killing hundreds of Kurds and causing tens of thousands of them to flee across the mountains into Iran and Turkey.

Iraq also found itself burdened with a huge debt as a result of the war. Vast amounts of money had been received, under various conditions, from Kuwait, Saudi Arabia, the UAE, and other Arab states. But of course the war soaked up every cent the Iraqi government could spare. It was probably not unduly worried about repayment but needed to acquire new funds. Development efforts had been virtually stopped for a decade. Capital needs were, consequently, enormous but unspecified.

In its current economic circumstances, Iraq would have found it difficult, even if it had wished, to disband its one-million-man army. It lacked any significant ongoing projects that could provide jobs for the demobilized soldiers. But the government had no desire to disband the army. It was the battle-hardened and well-equipped army that made Iraq the most powerful of the Arab countries. No other Arab leader, neither Hafez al-Assad nor Husni Mubarak, commanded a comparable force. To give it up would be to return to something like second-class status. Moreover, Iraq remained convinced that sooner or later, Israel would mount a major attack against it. The Israeli bombing of the Iraqi nuclear facility in June 1981 was rarely discussed in Baghdad, but constituted a reminder of what Iraqis regarded as Israel's implacable hostility.* The army thus constituted both an irreplaceable asset and a huge financial drain.

What to do with it? This is a question that Saddam Husain no doubt pondered. Now that the frontier with Iran was more or less secure, now that the Kurds had been at least temporarily beaten down and friendly relations continued with the Turks, and now that relations with Hafez al-Assad had improved as a result of a late-November meeting in Jordan, Saddam Husain moved to neutralize Saudi Arabia. Almost unnoticed by the outside world, he and King Fahd of Saudi Arabia signed a nonaggression pact in Baghdad on March 27, 1989. The one country missing from this tour of the Iraqi frontiers was, of course, Kuwait.

Iraq's relations with Kuwait have long been ambiguous, for several reasons. First of all, Iraqis have believed for generations that Kuwait was artificially split off from Iraq and that it remains an integral part of Iraq. In the nineteenth century, Kuwait was nominally part of the province of Basra, which was one of the three Ottoman Empire provinces that became Iraq. In fact, the little port was so poor that no one paid much attention to it. But in 1898, on hearing of a Russian plan to build a railway to the Gulf (an element in their recurrent nineteenth-century nightmare of a Russian as-

---

* Some Israelis apparently believed that Israel could have exploited the hostility between Syria and Iraq in order to reach some sort of understanding with Iraq. See Ze'ev Schiff, Shlomo Gazit, et al., quoted in Laurie A. Mylroie, "After the Guns Fell Silent: Iraq in the Middle East," *Middle East Journal*, 43 (1989): pp. 51ff. But the fact is that Israel and Iraq remained as hostile as Israel and Syria.

sault on India), the British determined to put a "stopper" in the neck of the Gulf. At first, their aim was simply to keep Kuwait autonomous. But within a few years the rather vague Russian threat was replaced by a more substantial German-Turkish threat. And so, on November 3, 1914, they decided to make Kuwait a British protectorate.

At the end of World War I, the British assumed the mandate for Iraq and installed a British-"advised" government under the nominal leadership of King Faisal, whom the French had chased out of Syria. No sooner had the new Iraqi government been organized than it began to claim Kuwait as an integral part of its domain. This claim remained in effect throughout the years of the monarchy. However, British power was sufficient to prevent any serious attempt to press this claim until after the 1958 Iraqi coup. In June 1961, the government of General Abdul Karim al-Qasim pressed the old claims for hegemony over Kuwait. At that time, Britain was still the major foreign power in the Gulf and derived great financial rewards from its position in Kuwait. Britain not only obtained oil from its holding in the Kuwait Oil Company, but used its influence to get the Kuwaitis to invest their profits in the English economy on a vast scale. At that time, the British government informed the United States that Kuwait was a nearly vital national interest.*

So Britain took the initial steps to preserve Kuwaiti independence. It encouraged Jordan, over which it exercised considerable influence, to take the lead in establishing a mixed Arab force in Kuwait to block the Iraqi threat. Kuwait then shrewdly moved to give as many Arab states as possible an economic stake in preserving the status quo.

Meanwhile, Kuwait became an enchanted land. Its oil resources, now estimated at nearly 100 billion barrels, are concentrated in an area somewhat smaller than New Jersey, of which only about 8 percent is even marginally usable. Consequently, a modest development program produced a dramatic impact. If the streets were not paved with gold, it was because Kuwait invested vast amounts of money abroad; the publicly admitted amount is in excess of $100 billion. Kuwaitis became the super-rich of the Arab world. They gave or lent large amounts of money through the Kuwait Fund for Arab Economic Development, which became a sort of

---

* In 1961–1962, as a member of the Policy Planning Council, I wrote the U.S. government policy paper on oil in the Gulf to which the British government reacted.

regional World Bank and which accomplished important works in many poorer countries. Yet perhaps inevitably, the Kuwaitis excited hostility and envy by flaunting their wealth before their poorer neighbors. Even in Saudi Arabia, they were not popular. Saudi Arabia charged that Kuwait was exceeding the oil-production quotas set by the members of OPEC and so was driving down Saudi revenues. In short, despite their attempt to give other Arab states a stake in keeping them independent, the Kuwaitis appeared isolated, disliked, but enormously rich, and hence the perfect target for attack. It was that target on which Saddam Husain set his sights.

American reaction to the August 2, 1990, Iraqi invasion was swift and spectacular. For once, the United States faced an issue in the Middle East in which it perceived no ambiguity. President Bush even likened the Iraqi aggression to Hitler's attack on Czechoslovakia. Nothing about the Iraqi regime excited public sympathy. Its civil rights record was appalling. Its brutal suppression of the Kurds was suddenly remembered. Iraq's use of chemical weapons was a damning indictment of its past actions, and its presumed attempt to develop nuclear arms was regarded with dread.*

On the day the invasion took place, the UN Security Council condemned the action; and four days later, it approved a trade embargo. On August 8, the first American forces arrived in Saudi Arabia. The same day, declaring that American "economic independence" was jeopardized, President Bush explained that he had put troops in Saudi Arabia to defend the nations of the Gulf. Meanwhile, Iraqi state television broadcast a statement proclaiming that Kuwait was an integral part of Iraq. On August 22, Bush announced the call-up of military reservists, and three days later the Security Council authorized the enforcement of the embargo.

Both Saudi Arabia and Kuwait offered to pay a part of the costs

---

* Despite reports to the contrary, Iraqi nuclear potential was not a clear and present danger. As Tom Wicker pointed out in the *New York Times* of December 5, 1990, "To get from Iraq's current stage of nuclear development to weapons production took Pakistan about 11 years—and Pakistan had a more advanced scientific and technological establishment, as well as the tacit willingness of the U.S. to let the effort proceed." Moreover, the amount of enriched uranium Iraq is known to have, some 12.5 kilograms, is less than the amount needed to make even a single primitive explosive device, and has been otherwise accounted for by the International Atomic Energy Agency; nor could Iraq manufacture a usable bomb without at least one test, which would be immediately known through satellite observation.

of the operation, but Saudi Arabia was at first reluctant to appear to ask for American help. Other Gulf states were even more reticent. After initially gloating over Iraq's problems, Iran used them to secure what it had failed to achieve in a decade of war, namely establishment of the Iranian-Iraqi frontier on the thalweg of the Shatt al-Arab. (A "thalweg" is the deep point of a river—the optimum navigational channel.) Having accomplished that objective, Iran reversed course and expressed solidarity with the Iraqi regime against the United States, although it agreed to uphold the UN blockade. Turkey closed down the Iraqi pipeline that ran through its territory. Even Libya and Syria supported the American-mobilized move. Although Syria remained on the United States' list of nations supporting terrorism, Secretary of State Baker welcomed its participation in the American-commanded troop deployment in Saudi Arabia.

In contrast to actions and pronouncements by the Syrians, Saudis, and Egyptians, the Palestinians charged the United States with hypocrisy in denying any "linkage" between the issue of Kuwait and the issue of the occupied territories. They pointed out that Israel had been in occupation of the West Bank and Gaza since 1967, and that despite repeated UN resolutions, similar to the ten directed at Iraq, Israel had refused to get out. No one, they pointed out, had moved to force Israel out as the United States then proposed to do with Iraq. The United States, in reply, denied any "linkage" between the two occupations. It pointed out that Israel had seized the occupied territories in a war, whereas Iraq had attacked Kuwait in peacetime. Iraq, naturally, sought not only to draw a parallel between the two issues but to claim that its action would force the United States to come to terms with the Israeli occupation; it therefore attempted to cast itself in the position of the protector of the Palestinians and the champion of the Arab world. While this ploy did not meet with approval from the Arab governments, it gained some credence among the Arab public. It is partly for this reason that the conservative governments of the Gulf were reluctant to associate themselves completely with the United States on this issue.

Jordan, with a large population of Palestinians, with friendly ties to Iraq, with some 70,000 of its citizens formerly employed in Kuwait, and with heavy dependence upon Saudi largess, found itself caught in an impossible position. Immediately after the Iraqi invasion, King Husain sought some means of accommodation by flying to America to meet with President Bush, but he was told that the United States insisted on an unconditional withdrawal before any kind of accommodation could be discussed.

Strong, indeed unprecedented, support for the United States' policy came from the European countries and from the Soviet Union. The latter privately warned Iraq of grave consequences of a failure to withdraw, provided America with details on the functioning of Iraqi military equipment, and sent a senior Soviet official, Dr. Yevgeni Primakov, to Iraq to meet with President Husain to search for a peaceful solution. In apparent thanks for Soviet support, Saudi Arabia reestablished diplomatic relations with the USSR, which had been interrupted more than half a century before. The Soviet Union declined to join the United States in military action, and urged that every possible avenue short of war be actively explored. It did, however, join the United States in setting a deadline for Iraqi compliance with the United Nations' demand for withdrawal.

What exactly was the American position? As initially stated, it was to get Iraq to withdraw unconditionally from Kuwait; that was the action demanded by the UN resolution. As Iraq's position remained fixed, President Bush, while still insisting only on Iraqi withdrawal from Kuwait, apparently came to believe that an acceptable settlement would have to involve the dismantling of a part of Iraq's armed forces, the destruction of its chemical-weapons stocks and production facilities, and an end to its nuclear development program. Privately, American government officials have said they assume that in light of such a humiliation, Saddam Husain would not survive as the Iraqi leader.

The UN Security Council established a deadline of January 15, 1991, for the Iraqi withdrawal from Kuwait and authorized the use of force after that date to compel withdrawal. During the last days of December, the United States offered to meet with the Iraqi leaders in Baghdad and to have the Iraqi foreign minister come to Washington. Iraq replied with a date for the Baghdad meeting which the United States found to be too close to the UN deadline. A compromise was reached for a meeting in Geneva between the U.S. secretary of state, James Baker, and the Iraqi foreign minister, Tariq Aziz. The meeting was inconclusive, each government charging the other with a lack of desire to reach a peaceful solution. Baghdad showed no willingness to discuss withdrawal from Kuwait even in a last-minute meeting with the UN secretary general, Pérez de Cuéllar. On January 15, time ran out. A day later, the United States and other members of the coalition launched the first of a series of massive air and missile attacks on Iraq. These were followed by a land invasion that speedily crushed the Iraqi army and unleashed long-pent-up separatist movements among the Kurds in the north and the Shiis in the south.

As 1991 began, it was clear that the political and diplomatic map of the Middle East would be dramatically altered. No longer was the problem of "security" an aspect of the Cold War: the United States and the USSR were actively cooperating on the Gulf crisis; and Syria, still on the U.S. government's list of countries supporting terrorism, was cooperating with the American-led coalition along with Saudi Arabia and Egypt. No longer would the United States remain offshore and seek to influence events with limited applications of air power and naval demonstrations. Rather, it put a large proportion of its total armed forces ashore and engaged in the most massive air, sea, and land operations since the Vietnamese war. Spectacular as these have been, dramatically portrayed on television in every American living room, they are merely the first step in what must eventually be a complex diplomatic, political, and economic process that will reconstitute a new Middle East.

Great anomalies remain to be worked out; some indeed may have been either created or exacerbated by the war in Iraq. It is possible that having joined the coalition against Saddam Husain, the governments of some Arab countries will be vulnerable to attempted coups or civil unrest. To some degree, their fate will depend upon forces already at work in the Arab world that have been pressing for a radical restructuring of the societies along Islamic lines. A defeated Iraq will pose almost as many problems as the prewar Iraq (though these will be less urgent). How can the country be restructured? What kind of relationship will it develop with its neighbors? Will they attempt to profit from its weakness in order to seize territory or impose influence on its restructured government? How can the defeated and presumably disillusioned returning troops be reintegrated into civil life? How will Iraqi oil be brought back onto the international market? These are just some of the major questions that will confront the Bush administration in the aftermath of the war with Iraq. Beyond these war-related issues still looms the Palestine problem.

Difficult as crises are, it is well to remember that they are not only times of danger but also times of flexibility, when resolute and well-informed statesmen can address issues that in normal times are often unaddressable. It is not beyond the wildest dream that a new and better Arab world could emerge from this crisis. The war has left terrible damage. Development projects that have taken decades to build in Iraq and Kuwait have been destroyed; damage to the oil facilities of Kuwait by Iraq is immense; the ecological losses in the Gulf through the spillage of oil by Iraq have been devastating. The cost of the war has been heavy and money for rebuilding will have to come from oil revenues. The shock of the war and reconstruction will be felt throughout the already weakened world economy, and secondary shock waves, political as well as economic, can be expected in a number of the Arab states.

And so, as 1991 begins, the Middle East is the knife edge on which the fate of much of the world is poised.

Suggested Reading
Index

Suggested Reading

T HE purpose of the following list is to suggest further reading on the various subjects treated in broad brush strokes in this book. Obviously it cannot be exhaustive in any section. Only reasonably accessible works in European languages are included.

GENERAL WORKS on the Arabs or on the whole Middle Eastern area abound; unfortunately, generality often masks ignorance of the specific.

Beginning students will profit by reading Jean Sauvaget, *Introduction à l'histoire de l'Orient Musulman*, Eléments de Bibliographie (Paris, 1946) which, although now out of date, remains a valuable guide. The second edition has been recast by Claude Cahen and appears as *Introduction to a History of the Muslim East: A Bibliographical Guide* (Berkeley, 1965). More detail is usually to be found in the *Encyclopedia of Islam,* now being issued in a new edition, in Leiden. James D. Pearson (compiler), *Index Islamicus* (Cambridge, 1958 and subsequent years) is the shelf list of articles in periodicals in the University of London School of Oriental and African Studies arranged by subjects. Leonard Binder (ed.), *The Study of the Middle East: Research and Scholarship in the Humanities and the Social Sciences* (New York, 1976), offers a new type of aid to the perplexed student, a sort of professional analysis of the problems of studying the Middle East by some of the foremost contemporary scholars.

Among the periodicals which deal with Middle Eastern affairs, the *Middle East Journal* is probably the most accessible and useful. Published in Washington, D.C., quarterly since 1947, it includes articles, book reviews, surveys of other periodicals, and a chronology, which make it particularly valuable to students of the modern period. *The International Journal of Middle Eastern Studies* (Cambridge, quarterly since 1970) is the major professional journal now edited in America. Magazines come and go, but these are useful for various periods and places: The Italian magazine *Oriente Moderno* is most valuable for the period of the 1920's and 1930's, as is the English *Journal of the Royal Central Asian Society.* The French journal *Orient*, published three times yearly since 1957, contains, among other useful features, frequent translations of significant treaties and pronouncements from the Arab countries. *Studia Islamica*, dealing less with the modern period, contains many significant articles on the history and culture of the Arabs; it is published in Paris, roughly every six months.

Most of the general studies contain bibliographies. None, obviously, can be kept up to date. Perhaps the best way to keep reasonably up to date is through the reviews in the *Middle East Journal, International Affairs,* and *Foreign Affairs* quarterly.

A number of newspapers and magazines provide good coverage of Middle Eastern events. In times of crisis they become prolix, but they wither away in times of calm. Seldom do they offer information on the more subtle shifts in the society, the economy, or intellectual life. Among the best are the *The New York Times, The Washington Post, The Wall Street Journal, The Christian Science Monitor, The Independent,* and *Le Monde.*

THE PEOPLE ON THE LAND is a topic covered in a wide assortment of works. On the bedouin, Alois Musil, *The Manners and Customs of the Rwala Bedouins* (New York, 1928); George W. Murray, *Sons of Ishmael* (London, 1935); Henri Charles, *La Sédentarisation entre Euphrate et Balik* (Beirut, 1942); Harold R. P. Dickson, *The Arab of the Desert* (London, 1949); Henri Charles, *Tribus moutonnières du Moyen-Euphrate* (Beirut, 1939); and John L. Burckhardt, *Notes on Bedouins and Wahabys* (London, 1831), are all classics of description. Important information is also to be found in John C. Glubb, "The Bedouin of North Arabia," in the *Journal of the Royal Central Asian Society,* 1935; and, in the same journal in 1938, E. Epstein, "The Bedouin of Transjordan." All considered, the most masterly survey of bedouin life is Robert Montagne, *La Civilisation du désert* (Paris, 1947).

Among the more recent accounts are Roy H. Behnke, Jr., *The Herders of Cyrenaica* (Urbana, 1980), which shows the impact on bedouin society of the discovery of oil; William Lancaster, *The Rwala Bedouin Today* (Cambridge, 1981); and Jörg Janzen, *Nomads in the Sultanate of Oman* (Boulder, 1986), which describes the people of Dhofar immediately after the end of the tribal war in 1975.

On the nonbedouin rural Arabs, perhaps the best overall studies are André Latron, *La Vie rurale en Syrie et au Liban* (Beirut, 1936); and Jacques Weulersse, *Paysans* (Paris, 1941). The Egyptian peasant is treated in Henry Ayrout, *The Eyptian Peasant* (new edition, Boston, 1963); Jacques Berque, *Histoire sociale d'un village Egyptien au vingtième siècle* (Paris, 1957); and Hamed Ammar, *Growing Up in an Egyptian Village* (New York, 1954). Emrys Peters, "Aspects of Rank and Status among Muslims in a Lebanese Village," in Julian A. Pitt-Rivers, *Mediterranean Countrymen* (Paris, 1936), is the product of one of the most detailed studies ever made of Arab village life. The "marsh Arabs" of Iraq are the subject of Shakir M. Salim, *Marsh Dwellers of the Euphrates Delta* (London, 1962); Fulanain (pseud.) *Haji Rikkan, Marsh Arab* (London, 1927); and Wilfred Thesiger, *The Marsh Arabs* (London, 1964). *Fellah and Townsman in the Middle East: Studies in Social History* (London, 1982) is a collection of the work of the outstanding Israeli historian of the modern Arabs, the late Gabriel Baer.

Studies of urban life and the relations of the city to the countryside include three excellent Arabic novels, now available in English: Tawfiq el-Hakim, *The Maze of Justice* (London, 1947); Taha Hussein, *An Egyptian Childhood* (London, 1932); and idem, *The Stream of Days* (London, 1948). C. Hurgronje, *Mekka* (London, 1931); and John L. Burckhardt, *Travels in Arabia* (London, 1829), give fascinating pictures of Arabia at the beginning and end of the nineteenth century. Edward W. Lane, *The Manners and Customs of the Modern Egyptians* (London, 1836 and many subsequent editions), is one of the great classics of description of all time. It was a by-product of the half a lifetime which Lane spent in Cairo translating a huge lexicon of Arabic. For another keen and sympathetic portrait, see Janet Abu-Lughod, *Cairo: 1001 Years of the City Victorious* (Princeton, 1971). Albert de Boucheman, *Une Petite cité caravanière: Suhné* (Damascus, n.d.), shows a typical desert outpost. Fredrik Barth, *Sohar: Culture and Society in an Omani Town* (Baltimore, 1983), is an anthropological study on a little-known area at the time of the beginning of modernization. Of wider scope and more filled with data are two other commendable collections of studies, J. Metral and G. Mutin (eds.), *Politiques urbaines dans le monde arabe* (Paris, 1984); and N. C. Grill, *Urbanisation in the Arabian Peninsula* (Durham, 1984). A more prospective or even prescriptive look is Ismail Serageldin and Samir al-Sadek (eds.), *The Arab City* (Riyadh, 1982). Earlier tradition is the subject of André Raymond, *The Great Arab Cities in the Sixteenth to Eighteenth Centuries* (New York, 1984). More specialized is a volume on medieval Cairo: J.-C. Garcin et al., *Palais et maisons du Caire* (Paris, 1982).

Aspects of geography of the Arab Middle East are dealt with in John I. Clarke and Howard Bowen-Jones, *Change and Development in the Middle East* (London, 1981), which is a collection of papers on the geography of the Middle East. The particular importance of water is brought out in Nazim Moussly, *Le Problème de l'eau en Syrie* (Lyon, 1951). Peter Beaumont, Gerald H. Blake, and J. Malcolm Wagstaff, *The Middle East: A Geographical Study* (New York, 1976), is perhaps the best and most modern general geographical survey of the Arab world. Now gradually becoming available are magnificent maps from the United States Geological Survey, along with composite satellite photographs of whole countries. For the first time, one can *see* Yemen, for example, in Map 1-1143-A, Miscellaneous Investigations Series (Reston, Va., 1978). Richard Bulliet, *The Camel and the Wheel* (Cambridge, 1975), gives an insightful reinterpretation of the "underpinning" of the Arab conquests and medieval commerce.

Demography is the subject of a growing literature, as population pressures continue to work against the best efforts of development planners. Gabriel Baer, *Population and Society in the Arab East* (New York, 1964); John I. Clarke and William B. Fisher, *Populations of the Middle East and North Africa* (New York, 1972); Arumugam Thavarjah et al., *Demographic Measures and Population Growth in the Arab Countries* (Cairo, 1970); and Charles A. Cooper and Sidney S. Alexander, *Economic Development and Population Growth in the Middle East* (New York, 1972), all deal with aspects of demography. Many studies by the World Bank likewise contain important information on demography.

TRAVELERS have been one of the most notable sources of literature on the Middle East. Perhaps the most famous but least read is Charles M. Doughty, *Arabia Deserta*, which was first published in 1888 and which has been through dozens of editions since. Doughty is the subject of an excellent study by David G. Hogarth (New York, 1929). Almost as curious a man as Doughty was William Gifford Palgrave, who wrote of his crossing of Arabia in 1862 in his *Narrative of a Year's Journey through Central and Eastern Arabia* (London, 1865). Lady Anne Blunt gives a charming account of her trip to northern Arabia in *Pilgrimage to Nejd* (London, 1881). David G. Hogarth, *The Penetration of Arabia* (New York, 1904), gives background on a number of the travelers. Harry St. J. B. Philby is the author of a number of books of Arabian travel. Perhaps the greatest of the English explorers is Wilfred Thesiger, whose *Arabian Sands* (London, 1959) is unsurpassed. A camel trip across Arabia is described by William R. Polk and William J. Mares in *Passing Brave* (New York, 1973). The same two authors have translated, illustrated, and annotated a great pre-Islamic poetic description of the desert: *The Golden Ode* (Chicago, 1974). Georg August Wallin, *Travels in Arabia: 1845 and 1848* (Naples and New York, 1979), is an account, newly reissued, of one of the great nineteenth-century journeys across Arabia.

THE ANCIENT ARABS are best shown in their own literature. Obviously, this is best understood in Arabic, but the non-Arabist will profit from Charles J. Lyall, *Ancient Arabian Poetry* (London, 1930), which contains not only a wide sample of translations but a superb introduction. Two other surveys which put the classical literature in perspective are Hamilton A. R. Gibb, *Arabic Literature* (London, 1925); and Reynold A. Nicholson, *Literary History of the Arabs* (Cambridge, 1953). The heart of pre-Islamic literature is translated in William R. Polk and William J. Mares, *The Golden Ode;* and in Lady Anne Blunt and Wilfrid Scawen Blunt, *The Seven Golden Odes of Pagan Arabia, Known Also as the Moallakat* (London, 1903). The scene in Arabia of that period is sketched in Henri Lammens, *Le Berceau de l'Islam* (Rome, 1914); idem, *La Mecque à la veille de l'Hégire* (Beirut, 1924); and idem, *La Cité arabe de Taif à la veille de l'Hégire* (Beirut, 1922).

The rise of Islam is the subject of a vast literature reflecting the authors' attitudes toward the religion. Some of the primary materials are translations of Arabic texts. To begin with the Koran (or Qur'an), however, is probably unwise. Even Arab Muslims read the Koran with the help of a teacher and a commentary. The best translation, however, is very good. It is Marmaduke Pickthall, *The Glorious Koran* (London, 1930). To begin, one should read one or more of the following: Richard Bell, *Introduction to the Qur'ān* (Edinburgh, 1953); Hamilton A. R. Gibb, *Mohammedanism* (New York, 1955), which is possibly the best general introduction to the whole religious system; Authur S. Tritton, *Muslim Theology* (London, 1947); idem, *Islam: Belief and Practices* (London, 1951); and

Robert Roberts, *The Social Laws of the Qorân* (London, 1925). A more detailed account of the Koran itself is given in Arthur Jeffery, *The Qur'an as Scripture* (New York, 1952). Jean-Paul Charnay, *Sociologie religieuse de l'Islam* (Paris, 1977), offers one of the few serious if still overly formalistic sociological studies of Islam.

The life and times of Muhammad are treated in a number of works. Among the standard texts are William M. Watt, *Muhammad at Mecca* (Oxford, 1953); and idem, *Muhammad at Medina* (Oxford, 1956). The older study by William Muir, *Life of Mahomet* (London, 1894), is still delightful and valuable; but perhaps the best all-round introduction is Tor Andrae, *Mohammed: The Man and His Faith* (London, 1936). Patricia Crone has recently set out a radically different interpretation of early Islam in a series of books and articles; see especially *Meccan Trade and the Rise of Islam* (Princeton, 1987).

Maurice Gaudefroy-Demombynes, *Muslim Institutions* (London, 1950), is the best introduction to the social elaboration of Islam. Gustav von Grunebaum, *Islam: Essays in the Nature and Growth of a Cultural Tradition* (London, 1955); and idem, *Medieval Islam* (Chicago, 2nd ed., 1953), are significant contributions to the subject. Ira Lapidus, *Muslim Cities in the Later Middle Ages* (Cambridge, 1967), is a masterly study of the Syrian cities in the Mamluk period; and A. H. Hourani and S. M. Stern (eds.), *The Islamic City* (Oxford, 1970), presents papers on a variety of subjects covering law, guilds, town planning, and social life in Baghdad, Damascus, and other Islamic cities. Noel J. Coulson, *A History of Islamic Law* (Edinburgh, 1964); and idem, *Conflict and Tensions in Islamic Jurisprudence* (Chicago, 1969), give an excellent account of the development of Islamic law. The "world view" of the great medieval Muslim scholars is given in Seyyed Hossein Nasr, *An Introduction to Islamic Cosmological Doctrines* (Cambridge, Mass., 1964).

Special topics in Islam are treated in Reynold A. Nicholson, *The Mystics of Islam* (London, 1914); Arthur J. Arberry, *Sufism* (London, 1950); and Dwight M. Donaldson, *The Shi'ite Religion* (London, 1933). Detailed coverage on virtually every conceivable aspect of Islam is given in the *Encyclopaedia of Islam;* those articles of particular interest on the religion have been separately published in Hamilton A. R. Gibb and Johannes H. Kramers, *Shorter Encyclopaedia of Islam* (Leiden, 1953). Finally, Gustav von Grunebaum, *Muhammadan Festivals* (New York, 1951), is a good companion to have if one is living in a Muslim country.

THE CONQUESTS AND EARLY CALIPHATE are introduced in G. R.

Hawting, *The First Dynasty of Islam: The Umayyad Caliphate*, A.D. *661–750* (Carbondale, 1987). The conquests are the subject of an excellent essay by Carl H. Becker in *The Cambridge Medieval History* (Cambridge, 1936); and of Michael J. de Goeje, *Mémoire sur la conquête de la Syrie* (Leiden, 1900). Stanley Lane-Poole, *A History of Egypt in the Middle Ages* (London, 1914), deals with the Arab invasion and subsequent history; Hamilton A. R. Gibb, *The Arab Conquests in Central Asia* (London, 1923), deals with the invasions in the East. Various articles by Gibb on other aspects of the caliphate are reprinted in Stanford J. Shaw and William R. Polk (eds.), *Studies on the Civilization of Islam by Hamilton A. R. Gibb* (Boston, 1962). The cultural aspects of medieval Arabic civilization as they affected medieval Europe are covered in Thomas W. Arnold and Alfred Guillaume, *The Legacy of Islam* (Oxford, 1931). Other general histories of note are Carl Brockelmann, *History of the Islamic Peoples* (New York, 1947); Bernard Lewis, *The Arabs in History* (London, 1950), which has a somewhat narrower scope; Philip K. Hitti, *History of the Arabs* (London, 1951), which is much more detailed but less critical; and a series of accounts by General Sir John B. Glubb (Pasha), beginning with *The Great Arab Conquests* (London, 1961), and including *The Empire of the Arabs* (London, 1963), which are primarily of interest in that they are written by a soldier-statesman who posed questions of a different order from that of the questions asked by the scholarly Orientalists of established repute. F. E. Peters, *Allah's Commonwealth: A History of Islam in the Near East, 600– 1000 A.D.* (New York, 1973), concentrates on issues often avoided in the general surveys: law, philosophy, and theology; the work is primarily an intellectual history. The caliphate is the subject of a virtually undiscriminating reading of the Arabic chronicles in William Muir, *The Caliphate: Its Rise, Decline and Fall* (Edinburgh, 1915). The Umayyad caliphate is the subject of a number of excellent works, including Henri Lammens, *Etudes sur le règne du Calife Omaiyade Mo'awia Ier* (Leipzig, 1907); idem, *Etudes sur le siècle des Omayyades* (Beirut, 1930); Julius Wellhausen, *The Arab Kingdom and Its Fall* (Calcutta, 1927); and Mohammed A. Shaban, *Islamic History, A.D. 600–750* (Cambridge, 1971).

The Abbasid caliphate of Baghdad is dealt with in a number of studies. Recent reinterpretations are Moshe Sharon, *Black Banners from the East* (Jerusalem, 1983); see also Jacob Lassner, *The Shaping of Abbasid Rule* (Princeton, 1980). Still valuable are the essays in Theodor Nöldeke, *Sketches from Eastern History* (Edinburgh, 1892). The bureaucratic breakdown of the empire is the subject of Harold

Bowen, *Life and Times of 'Ali ibn 'Isa* (Cambridge, 1928). The cultural recovery of Islam in an age of political decline is described in Adam Mez, *The Renaissance of Islam* (London, 1937).

One of the most valuable pieces of scholarship in recent times is S. D. Goitein, *A Mediterranean Society: The Jewish Communities of the Arab World as Portrayed in the Documents of the Cairo Geniza*, 5 vols. (Berkeley, 1967 and subsequent editions), which illuminates not only the Egyptian Jewish community but aspects of the Middle Ages throughout the Mediterranean.

THE PERIOD OF THE ALIEN EMPIRES is covered in some of the general studies noted above. Steven Runciman, *History of the Crusades* (Cambridge, 1952–1954), is a masterly and well-written account; other articles on the Crusades are contained in Marshall W. Baldwin (ed.), *The First Hundred Years*, vol. 1 of *A History of the Crusades* (Philadelphia, 1955). Hamilton A. R. Gibb (trans.), *The Damascus Chronicle of the Crusades* (London, 1932); and Philip K. Hitti (trans.), *Memoires of an Arab-Syrian Gentleman* (New York, 1929), present Arab views of the Crusades. Claude Cahen, *La Syrie Nord à l'époque des Croisades* (Paris, 1940), is one of the best studies available. George Vernadsky, *The Mongols and Russia* (New Haven, 1953), discusses the Mongols more insightfully, though with less detail on the Middle East, than other works. Henri Lammens, *La Syrie: Précis historique* (Beirut, 1921), deals with the whole sweep of Syrian history; the Mamluk period is covered in Maurice Gaudefroy-Demombynes, *La Syrie à l'époque des Mamelouks* (Paris, 1923); and Ira Lapidus, *Muslim Cities in the Later Middle Ages* (Cambridge, Mass., 1967), is an excellent study of life in Damascus and Aleppo under the Mamluks. Lebanon is being treated in a series of volumes by Adel Ismail, *Histoire du Liban du XVIIe siècle à nos jours,* of which vol,. 1, *Le Liban au temps de Fakhred-Din II,* was published in Paris in 1955.

A. L. Udovitch, *The Islamic Middle East, 700–1900* (Princeton, 1981), has given us a new appreciation of more than a millennium of history.

THE LATER MIDDLE AGES and the period just prior to the "impact of the West" have been the subject of many studies. Those that focus more narrowly on particular towns or districts are particularly valuable. One is Abraham Marcus, *The Middle East on the Eve of Modernity: Aleppo in the Eighteenth Century* (New York, 1989). Hamilton A. R. Gibb and Henry Bowen, *Islamic Society and the West* (Oxford, 1950, 1957), is a major study of the Arab areas under the Turks. See also George Stripling, *The Ottoman Turks and the*

Arabs (Urbana, Ill., 1942); Stephen H. Longrigg, *Four Centuries of Modern Iraq* (Oxford, 1925); Henri Dehérain, *L'Egypte turque* (Paris, n.d.); Abraham N. Poliak, *Feudalism in Egypt, Syria, Palestine and Lebanon, 1250–1900* (London, 1939). Life in Cairo is the subject of a separate study in Marcel Colombe, "La Vie au Caire au 18éme siècle," Conférences de l'Institut Français d'Archéologie Orientale (Cairo, 1951); more detailed is Stanford J. Shaw, *Ottoman Egypt in the Age of the French Revolution* (Cambridge, Mass., 1964).

THE IMPACT OF THE WEST is also the subject of a growing number of studies. Among the general studies, see Charles Issawi, *The Fertile Crescent, 1800–1914* (Oxford, 1988), a valuable collection of documents on economic history during a pivotal period. William R. Polk and Richard Chambers (eds.), *The Beginnings of Modernization in the Middle East* (Chicago, 1968), collects studies by some of the most distinguished students of the period; and Charles Issawi (ed.), *The Economic History of the Middle East, 1800–1914* (Chicago, 1966), collects the source materials, with comments by the editor.

On THE LEVANT, see Kamal S. Salibi, *The Modern History of Lebanon* (New York, 1965); Iliya F. Harik, *Politics and Change in a Traditional Society: Lebanon, 1711–1845* (Princeton, 1968); and William R. Polk, *The Opening of South Lebanon* (Cambridge, Mass., 1963), all of which deal with Arab affairs under Turkish rule. The Levant in the period of European economic expansion is the subject of the masterly study of Dominique Chevallier, *La Société du Mont Liban à l'époque de la Révolution Industrielle en Europe* (Paris, 1971). Moshe Ma'oz (ed.), *Studies on Palestine during the Ottoman Period* (Jerusalem, 1975), consists of forty papers given during a conference at the Hebrew University in 1970. It is a work of very high quality but, like all such collections, lacks coherence; it particularly needs a synthesizing introduction. The attempt of the Ottoman Empire to set its house in order is dealt with in Moshe Ma'oz, *Ottoman Reforms in Syria and Palestine, 1840–1861* (London, 1968). More general is M. A. Cook (ed.), *Studies in the Economic History of the Middle East* (London, 1970).

On EGYPT, a recent study is Afaf Lutfi al-Sayyid Marsot, *Egypt in the Reign of Muhammad Ali* (Cambridge, 1984), which deals with the formation of modern Egypt in the aftermath of Napoleon's invasion. A flawed but stimulating view of the course of change is Peter Gran, *Islamic Roots of Capitalism: Egypt, 1760–1840* (Austin, 1978).

Helen A. Rivlin, *The Agricultural Policy of Muhammad 'Alī in Egypt* (Cambridge, Mass., 1961); and Gabriel Baer, *History of Landowner-*

ship in Modern Egypt, 1800–1950 (London, 1963), deal with rural problems. Moustafa Fahmy, *La Révolution de l'industrie en Egypte et ses conséquences sociales au 19e siècle, 1800–1850* (Leiden, 1954), treats urban changes. James Heyworth-Dunne, *Introduction to the History of Education in Modern Egypt* (London, 1938), treats cultural affairs; and John Bowring, *Report on the Commercial Statistics of Egypt and Syria* (London, 1840), is a mine of information on economic affairs. Egypt under the impact of the West is wonderfully described in Edward W. Lane, *Manners and Customs of the Modern Egyptians* (London, 1836 and subsequent editions); and in Antoine B. Clot, *Aperçu général sur l'Egypte* (Paris, 1840). Gabriel Baer, *A Social and Economic History of Egypt* (Chicago, 1969), gives a new dimension of nineteenth-century history. An overall view is contained in Peter M. Holt, *Political and Social Change in Modern Egypt* (London, 1968). The best general treatment of Egypt is François Charles-Roux, *L'Egypte de 1801–1882* (Paris, n.d.) On the Persian Gulf, see Arnold T. Wilson, *The Persian Gulf* (London, 1928).

On the "coming of the west," see Robert L. Tignor, *Modernization and British Colonial Rule in Egypt, 1882–1914* (Princeton, 1966). David S. Landes, *Bankers and Pashas* (Cambridge, Mass., 1958), is fascinating and can be put in a wider Middle Eastern context with Herbert Feis, *Europe: The World's Banker* (New Haven, 1930). Matthew S. Anderson, *The Eastern Question, 1774–1923* (New York, 1966), is a very good synthesis of the European view, as is William L. Langer, *The Diplomacy of Imperialism* (New York, 1935). Zaki Saleh, *Mesopotamia, 1600–1914* (Baghdad, 1957), gives a good account of Iraq in tandem with the spirit of Wilfrid S. Blunt, *The Secret History of the English Occupation of Egypt* (New York, 1922). The Crimean War is dealt with, in its Near Eastern aspects, in Harold W. V. Temperley, *The Crimea* (London, 1934). John Marlow, *World Ditch: The Making of the Suez Canal* (New York, 1964), is a good account of that great engineering feat. The English view of imperialism is best set out in Lord Cromer, *Modern Egypt* (London, 1908); and idem, *Abbas II* (London, 1915). More scholarly and balanced is Afaf Lutfi al-Sayyid, *Egypt and Cromer* (London, 1968).

The political impact and Egyptian reaction are the subject of Nadav Safran, *Egypt in Search of Political Community* (Cambridge, Mass., 1961); Jacob Landau, *Parliaments and Parties in Egypt* (New York, 1954); Jamal Ahmad, *The Intellectual Origins of Egyptian Nationalism* (London, 1960); Charles C. Adams, *Islam and Modernism in Egypt* (London, 1933); Malcolm H. Kerr, *Islamic Reform* (Berkeley, 1966); and Albert H. Hourani, *Arabic Thought in the Liberal Age, 1798–1939* (London, 1962).

The nationalist religious and linguistic revival is still the subject of surprisingly heated controversy, but there remain many areas of ignorance. Jaroslav Stetkevych, *The Modern Arabic Literary Language* (Chicago, 1970), provides, for the first time, a means of sensing what people were trying to do when they clung to language as a means of preserving their sense of identity. Elie Kedourie, *Afghani and Abduh: An Essay on Religious Unbelief and Political Activism in Modern Islam* (London, 1966); and Nikki R. Keddie, *An Islamic Response to Imperialism* (Berkeley, 1968), tear into the religious façade of the political movement without seeming to understand the fears and hopes of Middle Easterners. Morroe Berger, *Islam in Egypt Today* (Cambridge, 1970), deals with broader social and political issues.

WORLD WAR I is dealt with in a number of studies and collections of memoirs, as well as in official dispatches. On Iraq, the most important works, written by the chief political officer of the British forces, are Arnold T. Wilson, *Loyalties: Mesopotamia, 1914–1917;* and idem, *A Clash of Loyalties, 1917–1920* (London, 1930, 1931). Edouard Brémond, *Le Hédjaz dans la guerre mondiale* (Paris, 1931), gives a French view of the "reality" behind the Lawrence of Arabia legend. Lawrence's own account, Thomas E. Lawrence, *Seven Pillars of Wisdom* (New York, 1926), should be read with critical works not far away. Philip Knightley and Collin Simpson have provided what will probably remain the definitive account in *The Secret Lives of Lawrence of Arabia* (London, 1969). Sir Ronald Storrs, *Orientations* (London, 1937), gives one of the most fascinating views of the period. Lady Bell (ed.), *The Letters of Gertrude Bell* (London, 1927), gives a view of happenings in Baghdad similar to that of Storrs on events in Cairo and Jerusalem.

Among the official documents, Ernest L. Woodward and Rohan Butler (eds.), *Documents on British Foreign Policy, 1919–1939,* first series, vol. 4 (London, 1952), is essential for the critical year 1919. The terms on which the Arabs entered the war are set out and discussed in Cmd 5957: *Correspondence between Sir Henry McMahon and the Sharif Hussein of Mecca, July 1915–March 1916* (London, 1939); Cmd 5964; *Statements Made on Behalf of His Majesty's Government during the Year 1918 in Regard to the Future Status of Certain Parts of the Ottoman Empire* (London, 1939); and Cmd 6974: *Report of a Committee Set Up to Consider Certain Correspondence between Sir Henry McMahon and the Sharif of Mecca in 1915 and 1916* (London, 1939). *The Balfour Declaration* is a masterly work by Leonard Stein (London, 1961). A fascinating insight into the critical work of Sir Mark Sykes both on the Balfour Declaration and on the Sykes-Picot

Agreement is given in Christopher Sykes, *Two Studies in Virtue* (New York, 1953).

Elie Kedourie, *England and the Middle East, The Destruction of the Ottoman Empire, 1914–1921* (London, 1956), is well written. Perhaps the best work on the English role during this period and later periods is Elizabeth Monroe, *Britain's Moment in the Middle East* (Baltimore, 1963), although Sir Reader Bullard, *Britain and the Middle East* (London, 1951), is a good introduction. American efforts are the subject of Harry N. Howard, *The King-Crane Commission* (Beirut, 1963); and the work at the Peace Conference is ably covered in Harold W. T. Temperley, *The Peace Conference of Paris*, vol. 6 (London, 1921). The Arabs' efforts are described best in Zeine N. Zeine, *The Struggle for Arab Independence* (Beirut, 1960). A fascinating comment on Arab-Zionist negotiations is Moshe Perlmann, "Chapters of Arab-Jewish Diplomacy, 1918–1922," in *Jewish Social Studies,* 6 (1944): 123ff. Misunderstandings between the British and the French are sketched in Henry H. Cumming, *Franco-British Rivalry in the Post-War Near East* (London, 1938). The immediate postwar period is summed up in Arnold J. Toynbee, *The Islamic World since the Peace Settlement: Survey of International Affairs, 1925,* vol. 1 (London, 1927). Three other works deserve careful attention. Doreen Ingrams, *Palestine Papers, 1917–1922* (London, 1972), lets the statesmen and agents speak for themselves, with short bridging sections. Isaiah Friedman, in *The Question of Palestine, 1914–1918* (New York, 1973), presents more a lawyer's brief than a history, arguing that there is no essential conflict among promises Great Britain made to Arabs, Jews, and others. Aaron S. Klieman, *Foundations of British Policy in the Arab World: The Cairo Conference of 1921* (Baltimore, 1970), is the best work on the meetings which set the main lines of British policy at the end of World War I.

THE MANDATES PERIOD is the subject of an ever-growing volume of literature. The yearly reports to the League of Nations on the mandates are a treasure house of information. J. C. Hurewitz (ed.), *The Middle East and North Africa in World Politics* (New Haven, 1979), is a collection of documents on the period of Anglo-French supremacy in the Middle East, 1914–1946.

On SYRIA AND LEBANON, Philip Khoury, *Syria and the French Mandate* (London, 1987), now replaces S. H. Longrigg's earlier work, *Syria and Lebanon under French Mandate* (London, 1958). Albert H. Hourani, *Syria and Lebanon* (London, 1946), and Nicola A. Ziadeh, *Syria and Lebanon* (London, 1957), are still useful. In addition to

Zeine N. Zeine, *The Struggle for Arab Independence* (Beirut, 1960), R. de Bontant-Biron, *Comment la France s'est installée en Syrie* (Paris, 1923), sets out the beginnings of French power. Edmond Rabbath, *L'Evolution politique de la Syrie sous mandat* (Paris, 1928), and Pierre Rondot, *Les Institutions politiques du Liban* (Paris, 1947), are very important for an understanding of domestic affairs. An independent view is given in Domenico Censoni, *Siria e Libano del Mandato all'indipendenza, 1919–1946* (Bologna, 1948); and the difficulty the French had with the Druze (and others) is described in Général Andréa, *La Révolte druze et l'insurrection de Damas, 1925–1926* (Paris, 1937). An overall view, but at something of a distance, is given in Quincy Wright, *Mandates under the League of Nations* (Chicago, 1930). The Republic of Lebanon is the subject of Michael C. Hudson, *The Precarious Republic* (New York, 1963).

Iraq is the subject of many studies by Englishmen. A basic book is Stephen H. Longrigg, *Iraq, 1900–1950: A Political, Social and Economic History* (London, 1953). A more modern view is given in Peter Sluggett, *Britain in Iraq, 1914–1932* (London, 1976). Still valuable on earlier periods is Philip W. Ireland, *'Iraq* (London, 1937).

EGYPT has been the subject of increasingly detailed studies, such as Afaf Lutfi al-Sayyid Marsot, *Egypt's Liberal Experiment, 1922–1936* (Berkeley, 1977), which shows how Egypt tried to establish some sort of democracy. A more narrow focus on economics is to be found in Eric Davis, *Challenging Colonialism: Bank Misr and Egyptian Industrialization, 1920–1941* (Princeton, 1983). Older and more general studies include Marcel Colombe, *L'Evolution de l'Egypte, 1924–1950* (Paris, 1951). Following the 1952 coup, however, much of the overt political history of that period seemed to many writers of less consequence than underlying social and economic changes, of which more below. Anglo-Egyptian relations are soberly described in the Royal Institute of International Affairs, *Great Britain and Egypt, 1914–1951* (London, 1952); and, somewhat more vigorously and impartially, in John Marlow, *Anglo-Egyptian Relations, 1800–1953* (London, 1954). The sort of biting satire of Egyptians in the 1930's referred to in the text is Claude S. Jarvis, *The Back-Garden of Allah* (London, 1939), which went through nine printings, although banned in Egypt; see also idem, *Oriental Spotlight* (London, 1937).

On (TRANS)JORDAN, there is little of lasting value. One work that is useful is Mary Wilson, *King Abdullah, Britain and the Making of Jordan* (Cambridge, 1987).

The topic of the PALESTINE MANDATE has used up several times more printer's ink than all the rest of the topics of this book combined. I myself have contributed to the deluge in William R. Polk, David Stamler, and Edmond Asfour, *Backdrop to Tragedy: The Struggle for Palestine* (Boston, 1957). For the beginner, the book contains a comprehensive bibliography, a complete set of maps, a concise history, and the assembled viewpoints of an American, an English Zionist, and a Palestine Arab. Perhaps the best study of the political aspects of the Palestine problem is Jacob C. Hurewitz, *The Struggle for Palestine* (New York, 1950). Robert Montagne, "Pour la paix en Palestine," *Politique Etrangère* (1938), is important for an understanding of the Arab mood of the 1930's; and Abraham Granott, *The Land System in Palestine* (London, 1949), is a valuable account of the basis of the problem in the Mandate. The many official studies must be read and are about the best, in terms of academic standard and readability, of any published. Cmd 5479: *Palestine Royal Commission Report* (London, 1937), and *A Survey of Palestine, Prepared in December 1945 and January 1946 for the Information of the Anglo-American Committee of Inquiry* (Jerusalem, 1946), are extremely valuable. Somewhat less useful is the *United Nations Special Committee on Palestine Report* (Lake Success, N.Y., 1947). George Kirk, *The Middle East in the War* (London, 1952), and idem, *The Middle East, 1945–1950* (London, 1954), are of great value.

Until relatively recently, THE SUDAN was treated primarily as a preserve for anthropologists. The best anthropological studies are those dealing with the Nilotic tribes of the south, particularly Edward E. Evans-Pritchard, *The Nuer* (Oxford, 1940), and idem, *Witchcraft among the Azande* (Oxford, 1937). Peter Holt, *The Mahdist State in the Sudan, 1881–1898* (Oxford, 1958), is the best work on the brief period of Sudanese independence under its religious revival movement. The story is taken up in Robert O. Collins, *Land beyond the Rivers: The Southern Sudan, 1898–1918* (New Haven, 1971) and in Peter Holt, *A Modern History of the Sudan* (New York, 1961). Muddathir Abd al-Rahim, *Imperialism and Nationalism in the Sudan* (London, 1969), deals with institutional growth under the British. The Sudan has generally been neglected in recent years, but this neglect is partly remedied by Peter K. Bechtold, *Politics in the Sudan: Parliamentary and Military Rule in an Emerging African Nation* (New York, 1976).

More recent books become more political. A collection of papers on many aspects of the Sudan is Martin Daly (ed.), *Modernization in the Sudan* (New York, 1986). A general history of the premodern period is John Voll and Sarah Voll, *The Sudan* (Boulder, Colo., 1985). Bona Malwal, *People and Power in the Sudan* (London, 1981), looks at the problem of national integration. Tim Niblock, *Class and Power in Sudan* (Albany, 1987), analyzes the period from 1898 to 1985. On the influence of Islam, see Carolyn Fluehr-Lobban, *Islamic Law and Society in the Sudan* (London, 1987).

LIBYA UNDER ITALIAN RULE has thus far received very little attention. Claudio G. Segre, *Fourth Shore: The Italian Colonization of Libya* (Chicago, 1975), deals with some aspects, neither the more brutal nor the broader, of Italy's invasion and its attempt to turn Libya into an Italian Egypt. It is a comment on Libya that, as Segre remarks, no Libyan has described the Libyan perspective on this long and violent episode in colonialism.

THE ARABIAN PENINSULA divides into those countries that maintained their independence, Saudi Arabia and Yemen, and those that became British protectorates. Until relatively recently, neither group received much attention. The best accounts of the premodern period are those by travelers and civil servants. In addition to those noted above under TRAVELERS, see Harry St. J. Philby, *The Empty Quarter* (London, 1933), Harold Ingrams, *Arabia and the Isles* (London, 1942); Doreen Ingrams, *A Survey of Social and Economic Conditions in the Aden Protectorate* (Eritrea, 1949); and Hugh Scott, *In the High Yemen* (London, 1942).

On the United Arab Emirates, see Rosemarie Said Zahlan, *The Origins of the United Arab Emirates* (New York, 1978), which describes events, and particularly the UAE's relations with Britain, between the two world wars. On Oman, see Patricia Risso, *Oman and Muscat* (New York, 1986), which deals with the eighteenth century; and John Peterson, *Oman in the Twentieth Century* (London, 1978). On Bahrain, Talal Farrah, *Protection and Politics in Bahrain, 1869–1915* (Beirut, 1985), illustrates with documents from the British archives how Britain took over Bahrain as a protectorate in the nineteenth century. See also Fuad Khuri, *Tribe and State in Bahrain* (Chicago, 1980), which shows how the oil industry virtually created modern Bahrain. Fred Lawson, *Bahrain: Modernization of Autocracy* (Boulder, Colo., 1989), is essentially a study of British control over Bahrain. On Qatar, see Rosemarie Said Zahlan, *The Creation of Qatar* (London, 1979). On Aden, Z. H. Kour, *The History of Aden* (London, 1981), covers the history of the mid-nineteenth century.

The whole peninsula is covered in a series of articles in Derek Hopwood (ed.), *The Arabian Peninsula* (London, 1972). See also

Ahmad Mustafa Abu Hakima, *History of Eastern Arabia, 1750–1800* (Beirut, 1965); R. Bayly Winder, *Saudi Arabia in the Nineteenth Century* (New York, 1965); and Robert G. Gandau, *Oman since 1856* (Princeton, 1967). Gary Troeller, *The Birth of Saudi Arabia: Britain and the Rise of the House of Saud* (London, 1976), concentrates on British relations with Abdul Aziz ibn Saud from 1910 to 1926, as reflected in the British archives.

Prior to World War I, Britain was interested in the Gulf primarily for its value as a route to India and because Britain feared that others, notably Germany and Russia, might seek to use the route to challenge its own position in South Asia. These were the major reasons for Britain's creation of protectorates in the several shaikhdoms. The British view of this process is set forth in John B. Kelly, *Britain and the Persian Gulf, 1795–1880* (New York, 1968); Abdul Amir Amin, *British Interest in the Persian Gulf* (Leiden, 1967); and Charles Belgrave, *The Pirate Coast* (London, 1966). Donald Hawley, *The Trucial States* (New York, 1971), deals with the modern period. Jacqueline S. Ismael and Tareq Y. Ismael, "The Politics of Social Change in the Arab States of the Gulf: The View from Within," *Middle East Journal,* 32, no. 3 (1978), discusses and summarizes six Arabic-language books on current society and politics of the Gulf states, and is particularly valuable for its insights into current thinking about the recent past among Arab intellectuals.

WORLD WAR II AND ITS AFTERMATH in the Middle East are dealt with in two large studies by George Kirk: *The Middle East in the War* (London, 1952), and *The Middle East, 1945–1950* (London, 1954). Also see William Roger Louis, *Imperialism at Bay* (New York, 1978); and idem, *The British Empire in the Middle East, 1945–1951* (Oxford, 1984). For a useful summary of the Middle East as viewed strategically by Britain during the war, see John Keegan, *The Second World War* (London, 1989). German policies in the Middle East are the subject of Lukaz Hirszowicz, *The Third Reich and the Arab East* (London, 1966).

The period of turbulence following World War II, marked by formal independence and coups, is covered in a number of works. George Kirk, *The Middle East in the War* (London, 1952), is a good beginning. John Kimche, *Seven Fallen Pillars* (New York, 1953), is a harsh but accurate description; and Musa Alami, "The Lesson of Palestine," *Middle East Journal,* 3 (1949), is an Arab critique of Arab affairs. Albert Hourani, "The Decline of the West in the Middle East," *International Affairs,* 3 (1953–1954), is a sensitive and deep study of Arab-European relations. Edgar O'Ballance, *The*

Arab-Israeli War (London, 1952), sets out the events of the Arab defeat in Palestine.

The Egyptian coup of 1952 and its aftermath are dealt with in a number of books. One of the best is Jean and Simon Lacouture, *Egypt in Transition* (New York, 1958). Egypt under Nasser is described in Keith Wheelock, *Nasser's New Egypt* (New York, 1960); Panayiotis J. Vatikiotis, *The Egyptian Army in Politics* (Bloomington, Ind., 1961); and idem, *Egypt since the Revolution* (New York, 1968). More recent and from a different perspective is Jacques Berque, *Egypt, Imperialism and Revolution* (New York, 1972).

The view from the inside is given in Gamal Abdul Nasser, *The Philosophy of the Revolution* (Washington, 1955); Mohammed Naguib, *Egypt's Destiny* (New York, 1955); and Anwar Sadat, *Revolt on the Nile* (London, 1957). Highly critical views of Nasser's Egypt are Hassan Riad, *L'Egypte Nassérienne* (Paris, 1964); and Anouar Abdel-Malek, *Egypt: Military Society* (New York, 1968). One of the best analyses of post-Nasser Egypt is an article by Roland Delcour in *Le Monde,* which is reprinted in English in the *Guardian* (September 22, 1973) as "Egypt's 'Corrected' Revolution."

On Nasser and his colleagues, see Wilton Wynn, *Nasser of Egypt: The Search for Dignity* (Cambridge, Mass., 1959). P. J. Vatikiotis, *Nasser and His Generation* (New York, 1978), attempts to place Nasser in the context of Egyptian life. Perhaps the best book on both Nasser and Sadat is John Waterbury, *The Egypt of Nasser and Sadat* (Princeton, 1983). More biographical are David Hirst and Irene Beeson, *Sadat* (London, 1982); and Ghali Shoukri, *Egypt: Portrait of a President—Sadat's Road to Jerusalem* (London, 1981). These give informed and generally unfavorable views of Sadat. A much more favorable view is given in Felipe Fernandez-Armesto, *Sadat and His Statecraft* (London, 1983).

The situation in Syria is well described in Gordon Torrey, *Syrian Politics and the Military, 1945–1958* (Columbus, Ohio., 1964); and Patrick Seale, *The Struggle for Syria, 1945–1958* (London, 1965). Iraq has yet to receive comparable treatment. Michael Ionides, *Divide and Lose* (London, 1960); and Caractacus (pseud.), *Revolution in Iraq* (London, 1959), give the best book-length accounts. Also see William R. Polk, "The Lesson of Iraq," *Atlantic Monthly* (December 1958), for the immediate aftermath of the July coup in Baghdad. King Hussein of Jordan, *Uneasy Lies the Head* (New York, 1962), describes this era of turbulence from another angle. The intra-Arab consequences are the subject of Malcolm Kerr, *The Arab Cold War* (New York, 1971). William R. Polk, *The Elusive Peace: The*

Middle East in the Twentieth Century (London, 1979), is an interpretative essay on Arabism, Zionism, and the great powers, with special emphasis on the Palestinian problem.

On Egypt after 1952, see John Waterbury, *Egypt: Burdens of the Past, Options for the Future* (Bloomington, 1978), which is a collection of essays on the problems Egypt faced in the 1970's (and still faces today); idem, *Hydropolitics of the Nile Valley* (Syracuse, 1979), looks at the Nile linkage of Egypt and the Sudan in all its dimensions. Khalid Ikram, *Egypt: Economic Management in a Period of Transition* (Baltimore, 1980), is essentially the report of World Bank missions to evaluate Egyptian prospects. And on Egypt after Sadat, see Robert Springborg, *Mubarak's Egypt* (Boulder, Colo., 1989).

THE SUEZ CRISIS, a major trauma in the Middle East, inspired a number of books. Recently, it has been reassessed on the basis of many declassified governmental documents. See William Roger Louis and Roger Owen, *Suez 1956: The Crisis and Its Consequences* (London, 1989). In fact, however, most of the information has long been public. The earlier accounts include Anthony Nutting, *No End of a Lesson* (London, 1967), which benefits from the author's inside knowledge of the British Cabinet; Anthony Moncrieff (ed.), *Suez: Ten Years After* (London, 1967), which synthesizes the memories and views of many of the key participants; and Erskine B. Childers, *The Road to Suez* (London, 1962), which is very good. Hugh Thomas, *Suez* (New York, 1967), draws heavily upon the BBC series by Moncrieff and upon Israeli sources. Guy Wint and Peter Calvocoressi, *Middle East Crisis* (London, 1957), gives a good account of the events leading up to the crisis, while Michael Adams, *Suez and After* (Boston, 1958), shows its effects. The U.S. Department of State publication *The Suez Canal Problem* (Washington, 1956) gives many of the documents. Selwyn Lloyd, *Suez 1956: A Personal Account* (London, 1978), is not only personal but also self-serving and shows that little wisdom has been gained since the event.

Both THE JUNE 1967 AND OCTOBER 1973 WARS produced a motley array of memoirs, eyewitness accounts, and instant histories. The best to date on the June war are Michael Howard and Robert Hunter, *Israel and the Arab World: The Crisis of 1967* (London, 1967); Nadav Safran, *From War to War* (New York, 1969); Kenneth Love, *Suez: The Twice-Fought War* (New York, 1969); Walter Laqueur, *The Road to Jerusalem* (New York, 1968); and Maxime Rodinson, *Israel and the Arabs* (London, 1968). Insight Team of the Sunday

Times, *Insight on the Middle East War* (London, 1974), and Walter Laqueur, *Confrontation: The Middle East and World Politics* (New York, 1974), can be recommended on the October 1973 war. See also William R. Polk, "Why the Arabs Went to War," *Washington Post* (October 14, 1973). Some of the disparity in sophistication between the Arab and Israeli armies is shown in Edgar O'Ballance, *The Electronic War in the Middle East, 1968–1970* (Hamden, Conn., 1974), which, although now outdated, is still very interesting for its sidelights on recent technological and military history. In *The Road to Ramadan* (New York, 1975) Mohammed Heikal, the outstanding journalist of the Arab world and a confidant of Gamal Abdul Nasser and, at first, of Anwar Sadat, offers his interpretation of and personal experiences in the decade before the October 1973 war. On the Egyptian background to the 1973 war, see Hassan El Badri et al., *The Ramadan War, 1973: An Egyptian Report* (Boulder, Colo.: Westview Press, 1977).

The literature on PALESTINE AND THE PALESTINIANS is enormous, and constantly growing. Following are a few works, covering different areas, that I have found useful. Elias H. Tuma and Haim Darin-Drabkin, *The Economic Case for Palestine* (New York, 1978), argues that a Palestinian state is feasible on the meager lands realistically held to be available. Shaul Mishal, *West Bank / East Bank: The Palestinians in Jordan, 1949–1967* (New Haven, 1978), and Ann Mosley Lesch, *Political Perceptions of the Palestinians on the West Bank and the Gaza Strip* (Washington, 1980), deal with the complex relations of the Palestinians and Jordan. John W. Amos II, *Palestinian Resistance: Organization of a Nationalist Movement* (New York, 1980), describes the resistance groups; Ian Lustick, *Arabs in the Jewish State* (Austin, 1980), analyzes the Israeli system of control of its Arab minority. The two extremes of Israeli policy are shown by Rabbi Meir Kahane, *They Must Go* (New York, 1981); and Mark A. Heller, *A Palestinian State* (Cambridge, 1983). Kahane advocates expelling the rest of the Palestinians, whereas Heller believes that the creation of a Palestinian state is the least bad of all Israeli alternatives. Yossi Melman and Ran Raviv, *Behind the Uprising* (Westport, Conn., 1989), uses Israeli sources to look at the secret attempts by Israel and King Husain of Jordan to find a modus operandi; more detailed is Avi Shlaim, *Collusion across the Jordan* (New York, 1988). Zachary Lockman and Joel Beinin (eds.), *Intifada: The Palestinian Uprising against Israeli Occupation* (Boston, 1989), is a collection of papers, some very good, on various aspects of the uprising; better is the work of Don Peretz, long-time student of the Palestine prob-

lem, *Intifada* (Boulder, Colo., 1990). The long-disputed history of
the Palestinian refugees is discussed authoritatively on the basis of
Israeli sources in Benny Morris, *The Birth of the Palestinian Refugee
Problem, 1947–1949* (Cambridge, 1987); on Gaza see Paul Cossali
and Clive Robson, *Stateless in Gaza* (London, 1986); and Sara Roy,
The Gaza Strip (Jerusalem, 1986). Edward Said, *After the Last Sky:
Palestinian Lives* (New York, 1986), is a very personal exploration
of the refugee experience.

Older studies, dealing with issues that are still alive, include Julian J. Landau, *Israel and the Arabs* (Jerusalem, 1971); Yehoshefat
Harkabi, *Arab Attitudes toward Israel* (New York, 1972); idem, *Fedayeen Action and Arab Strategy* (London, 1970); and Shlomo Avineri
(ed.), *Israel and the Palestinians: Reflections on the Clash of Two National Movements* (New York, 1971). A collection of articles on many
aspects of the Palestine problem was edited by Ibrahim Abu-
Lughod as *The Transformation of Palestine* (Evanston, Ill., 1971). The
Palestine Liberation Organization Research Center in Beirut has
published a number of books and pamphlets setting forth its views.
The Institute for Palestine Studies, also in Beirut, issues comprehensive documentary collections on contemporary Palestinian, Israeli, inter-Arab, and international developments relating to the
Palestine problem. Finally, the United Nations Works and Relief
Agency publishes accounts of the refugees under its care.

On what is TERRORISM to some and armed struggle or national
liberation to others, see William B. Quandt, Fuad Jabber, and Ann
Mosely Lesch, *The Politics of Palestinian Nationalism* (Berkeley,
1973); and Gerard Chaliand, *The Palestinian Resistance* (Harmondsworth, Engl., 1972). The Islamic aspects of the current situation
are brought out in Johannes J. G. Jansen (trans.), *The Neglected
Duty* (New York, 1986), which gives the view of Sadat's assassins
on the Islamic justification for their deed. Robin Wright, *Sacred
Rage: The Wrath of Militant Islam* (New York, 1986), gives a more
generalized portrait of terrorism throughout the area. As'ad Abu
Khalil, "Internal Contradictions in the PFLP," *Middle East Journal*,
41 (1987): 361ff., is one of the most complete studies of this wing
of the Palestinian resistance. A fuller account of the main Palestinian organization is Helena Cobban, *The Palestine Liberation Organization* (Cambridge, 1984). B. E. O'Neill, *Armed Struggle in Palestine*
(Boulder, Colo., 1978), focuses on the military or paramilitary aspects of the guerrilla movement. David Hurst, *The Gun and the
Olive Branch* (London, 1977), is still valuable on the problem of
violence. More police-like and less analytical are David C. Martin

and John Walcott, *Best Laid Plans: The Inside Story of America's War against Terrorism* (New York, 1988); Stephen Segaller, *Invisible Armies* (London, 1987); Charles Villeneuve and Jean-Pierre Péret, *Histoire secrète du terrorisme* (Paris, 1987); and James Adams, *The Financing of Terror* (London, 1986).

On ARMS TRADE, see Lewis Snider, *Arabesque: Untangling the Patterns of Supply of Conventional Arms to Israel and the Arab States* (Denver, 1973). The opposite position is given in Aaron S. Klieman, *Israel's Global Reach: Arms Sales as Diplomacy* (McLean, Va., 1985).

On HUMAN RIGHTS, see the review article by Linda Malone, "Human Rights in the Middle East," *Middle East Journal,* 38 (1984): 733ff.

On the activities of THE UNITED NATIONS, see Milton Viorst, *Reaching for the Olive Branch: UNRWA and Peace in the Middle East* (Bloomington, Ind., 1989); and John MacKinlay, *The Peacekeepers: An Assessment of Peacekeeping Operations at the Arab-Israel Interface* (London, 1989).

On THE INDEPENDENT COUNTRIES, readers can consult the following works.

On JORDAN, perhaps the best (of a very thin field) is Peter Gubser, *Jordan* (Boulder, Colo., 1983). Also see Panayiotis J. Vatikiotis, *Politics and the Military in Jordan* (New York, 1967). Frederick G. Peake, *A History of Jordan and Its Tribes* (Miami, 1958), and John B. Glubb, *The Story of the Arab Legion* (London, 1948), are the product of the two creators of the military force of Jordan. A more current book is Aqil Hyder Hasan Abidi, *Jordan: A Political Study, 1948–1957* (New York, 1965).

The long and tragic CIVIL WAR IN LEBANON has produced a flood of books. These are a few I have found particularly useful: Walid al-Khalidi, *Conflict and Violence in Lebanon* (Cambridge, 1979), is perhaps the best systematic treatment of the Lebanese conflict; Marius Deeb, *The Lebanese Civil War* (New York, 1980), is also very good; Adeed Dawisha, *Syria and the Lebanese Crisis* (New York, 1980), shows how and why Syria intervened in Lebanon in 1976. The struggle among the Shiis is discussed in Augustus Norton, *Amal and the Shi'a* (Austin, 1987); another aspect of Shia life is taken up in Fouad Ajami, *The Vanished Imam* (Ithaca, 1986), which is about the activities and subsequent presumed kidnapping and murder of Musa al-Sadr. A powerful and emotional Israeli critique of the Israeli invasion is Jacobo Timerman, *The Longest War: Israel in Lebanon* (New York, 1982). The massacre of Palestinians during the invasion was probed by the (Israeli) Kahan Commission. For its findings, see *The Beirut Massacre* (New York, 1983). A very good, accessible, and humane book is Thomas L. Friedman, *From Beirut to Jerusalem* (New York, 1989).

LIBYA IN QADDAFI'S TIME is discussed in Marius Deeb and Mary Jane Deeb, *Libya since the Revolution* (New York, 1982); Jonathan Bearman, *Qadhafi's Libya* (London, 1986); and John Wright, *Libya: A Modern History* (Baltimore, 1982). John Davis, *Libyan Politics: Tribe and Revolution* (Berkeley, 1988), is an anthropologist's insightful view of politics in postrevolutionary Libya. Omar El Fathaly and Monte Palmer, *Political Development and Social Change in Libya* (Lexington, Mass., 1980), is a description of the first decade after the 1969 coup d'état. Two collections of papers contain a variety of information: E. G. H. Joffe and K. S. McLachan, *Social and Economic Development of Libya* (Boulder, Colo., 1982), and J. A. Allen, *Libya since Independence* (New York, 1982). John P. Mason, *Island of the Blest: Islam in a Libyan Oasis Community* (Athens, Ohio, 1977), is a rather elementary study of a Libyan community. John K. Cooley, *Libyan Sandstorm* (New York, 1982), is a first-rate journalist's account of Qaddafi's revolution.

On SYRIA, see John Devlin, *The Ba'th Party* (Stanford, 1976), which tells the history of the party in Syria up to 1966. Patrick Seale, *Asad* (Berkeley, 1989), places the Syrian leader in his national context.

Most books on the PERSIAN GULF are concerned with great-power strategy and the oil issue. Among the best is Alvin J. Cottrell et al., *The Persian Gulf* (Baltimore, 1980), which is a general survey of the background of the societies and geography of the Gulf. The attempts by the Gulf states to form a protective league are discussed in R. K. Ramazani, *The Gulf Cooperation Council* (Charlottesville, Va., 1988); and Erik Peterson, *The Gulf Cooperation Council* (Boulder, Colo., 1988). R. K. Ramazani, *The Persian Gulf and the Strait of Hormuz* (Amsterdam, 1979), is a study of the strategic implications of the narrow opening of the Gulf for the surrounding powers.

On KUWAIT, see Jacqueline S. Ismael, *Kuwait: Social Change in Historical Perspective* (Syracuse, 1982), which gives an excellent introduction to modern Kuwait. Y. S. F. al-Sabah, *The Oil Economy of Kuwait* (London, 1980), and M. W. Khouja and P. G. Sadler, *The Economy of Kuwait* (London, 1979), analyze Kuwait's oil and financial policy and institutions.

On SAUDI ARABIA: Fouad al-Farsy, *Saudi Arabia* (London, 1978), offers a study of Saudi Arabia as it was preparing for its development efforts. William Quandt, *Saudi Arabia in the 1980s* (Washington, 1981), is one of the most comprehensive books on Arabia from an American policy perspective. Robert Lacey, *The Kingdom* (London, 1981), is an engaging collection of gossip. David Holden and Richard Johns, *The House of Saud* (New York, 1981), is a more sober and more balanced account. Nadav Safran offers a more distant view in *Saudi Arabia: The Ceaseless Quest for Security* (Cambridge, 1985).

On QATAR: Rosemarie Said Zahlan, *The Creation of Qatar* (London, 1979), and Ragaei El Mallakh, *Qatar: Development of an Oil Economy* (New York, 1979), are complementary; one provides historical background and the other describes current, essentially economic, reality.

On BAHRAIN: Fred Lawson, *Bahrain: Modernization of Autocracy* (Boulder, Colo., 1989), is essentially a study of British control over Bahrain.

On YEMEN: John E. Peterson, *Yemen: The Search for a Modern State* (Baltimore, 1982), is perhaps the best book to start with on Yemen; a more detailed study is Robert Burrowes, *The Yemen Arab Republic* (Boulder, Colo., 1987). Charles F. Swagman, *Development and Change in Highland Yemen* (Salt Lake City, 1988), analyzes the efforts to develop rural Yemen. Robert Stookey, *South Yemen: A Marxist Republic in Arabia* (Boulder, Colo., 1982), was the first and is still probably the best study on the now more or less merged south of Yemen. Robin Bidwell, *The Two Yemens* (Boulder, Colo., 1983), is an analysis of the two Yemens in the 1970's.

On IRAQ: Hanna Batatu, *The Old Social Classes and the Revolutionary Movements of Iraq* (Princeton, 1979), is a remarkable study (based on British and Iraqi security service materials) of the political movements leading to the Baath seizure of power. The Qasim period is the subject of M. Khadduri, *Republican Iraq* (New York, 1969); and of Uriel Dann, *Iraq under Qasim* (New York, 1969). Samir al-Khalil (pseud.), *Republic of Fear* (Berkeley, 1989), is a powerful indictment of Saddam Husain and the Baath regime. Tim Niblock (ed.), *Iraq: The Contemporary State* (New York, 1982), is a collection of papers; those dealing with social change after 1958 are particularly valuable. A generally favorable view of Saddam Husain is given in Fuad Matar, *Saddam Hussein: The Man, the Cause and the Future* (London, 1981).

On THE IRAQ-IRAN WAR: Shirin Tahir-Kheli and Shaheen Ayubi have edited a series of papers, *The Iraq-Iran War* (New York, 1983), which bring out some of the complexities of that war. Shahram

Chubin and Charles Tripp, *Iran and Iraq at War* (Boulder, Colo., 1988), argue that Iraq attacked Iran to prove its power.

On THE KURDISH PROBLEM and the aspirations of the Kurdish people in Iraq (as distinct from the Kurds in Iran and Turkey), see Chris Kutschera, *Le Mouvement national kurde* (Paris, 1979), which is perhaps the best book on the Kurdish attempt to create a state. Edmund Ghareeb, *The Kurdish Question in Iraq* (Syracuse, 1981), is complementary in that it discusses the way the Iraqi government handled the Kurdish issue from 1968 to 1975 and how Iran and Israel sought to use the Kurds to weaken the Iraqis. Saad Jawad, *Iraq and the Kurdish Question, 1958–1970* (London, 1981), details the complex relations between the Iraqi government and the Kurds.

SOCIAL CHANGE is a relatively new subject for books on the Arab world. A recent study by Paul Shaw, *Mobilising Human Resources in the Arab World* (London, 1983), looks at labor migration, the economic role of women, and other issues from the perspective of the International Labor Organization. An older but still valuable source is Manfred Halpern, *The Politics of Social Change* (Princeton, 1963). Gabriel S. Saab, *The Egyptian Agrarian Reform, 1952–1962* (New York, 1967), discusses the rural aspects of social change. One approach to analyzing social change is William R. Polk, "Analyzing Social Change: The Middle East," *Bulletin of the Atomic Scientists* (January 1967). Hassan el-Saaty, "The Middle Classes in Egypt" (Cairo, 1957), and Sydney N. Fisher (ed.), *The Military in the Middle East: Problems in Society and Government* (Columbus, Ohio, 1963), are also valuable. Eliezer Be'eri, *Army Officers in Arab Politics and Society* (New York, 1970), and Jacob C. Hurewitz, *Middle East Politics: The Military Dimension* (New York, 1969), discuss the role of the military in social change. Jean-Jacques Waardenburg, *Les Universités dans le monde arabe actuel* (The Hague, 1966), is one of the rare studies on education. Trends in Egypt are dealt with in Patrick O'Brian, *The Revolution in Egypt's Economic System, 1952–1965* (London, 1966); Gabriel S. Saab, *The Egyptian Agrarian Reform, 1952–1962* (New York, 1967); and Richard H. Dekmejian, *Egypt under Nasir* (Albany, 1971). A detailed chronology of the coups in the whole Arab world is given in George M. Haddad, *Revolutions and Military Rule in the Middle East* (New York, 1971, 1973). Charles Issawi, "Economic and Social Foundations of Democracy in the Middle East," *International Affairs* (1956), is a sobering account of the lack of a basis in the current scene for democratic institutions.

THE ECONOMY of the Arab countries is a relatively new subject. Though much useful work was done by the Middle East Supply

Centre during World War II, the first comprehensive study was the Clapp Commission Report, United Nations Conciliation Commission for Palestine, *U.N. Economic Survey Mission for the Middle East* (Lake Success, N.Y., 1949). The rural base of the economy is the subject of Doreen Warriner's shocking and powerful books, *Land and Poverty in the Middle East* (London, 1948), and *Land Reform and Development in the Middle East* (London, 1957). On industry, see Ali A. I. El-Gritly, *The Structure of Modern Industry in Egypt* (Cairo, 1948); Kathleen M. Langley, *The Industrialization of Iraq* (Cambridge, Mass., 1961); and Arthur D. Little, Inc., *A Plan for Industrial Development in Iraq* (Cambridge, Mass., 1956). The International Bank studies *Iraq* (Baltimore, 1952), *Syria* (Baltimore, 1955), and *Jordan* (Baltimore, 1957), are comprehensive. Edmond Asfour, *Long-Term Projections of Supply and Demand for Agricultural Products in Saudi Arabia* (Beirut and Washington, 1965), is a pioneering study of Arabia; idem, *Syria: Development and Monetary Policy* (Cambridge, Mass., 1959), is about the best on Syria. Charles Issawi, *Egypt in Revolution* (London, 1963), the third edition of a book first published in 1947, is in a class by itself. Large numbers of books have been published on the economy of the Arab world since the first edition of Issawi's work. Most are derived from doctoral dissertations or consultants' reports and deal with narrow issues. Several serious and important works may be singled out for particular mention. Dr. Yusif Sayigh, *The Economies of the Arab World: Development since 1945*, and idem, *The Determinants of Arab Economic Development*, both published in London in 1978, are good places to begin. Excellent studies are Donald Mead, *Growth and Structural Change in the Egyptian Economy* (Homewood, Ill., 1967); Bent Hansen and Girgis A. Marzouk, *Development and Economic Policy in the UAR (Egypt)* (Amsterdam, 1965); Charles Issawi and Mohammed Yaganeh, *The Economics of Middle Eastern Oil* (New York, 1962); and Ragaei el Mallakh, *Kuwait* (Chicago, 1968). Marion Clawson et al. *The Agricultural Potential of the Middle East* (New York, 1971), is very good.

The World Bank and affiliated organizations, various United Nations agencies, and the various countries now publish comprehensive economic reports and their plans. Surveys are available from the United Nations Department of Economic and Social Affairs, *Economic Development of the Middle East, 1945–54* (New York, 1955), with supplements in later years. Finally, the economic research center at the American University of Beirut publishes occasional papers on the economy of the Middle East.

On aid offered by the Arabs to other Arabs and to Africans and

Asians, see Michele Achilli and Mohamed Khalidi, *The Role of the Arab Development Funds in the World Economy* (London, 1984), which gives the statistics on the relatively large-scale aid doled out by the Arabs to Africans and Asians.

On OIL, see Ian Skeet, *OPEC: Twenty-five Years of Prices and Politics* (Cambridge, 1988), and Pierre Terzian, *OPEC: The Inside Story* (London, 1985), which are complementary studies. Oil is the subject of a number of historical works. A convenient one, from a British point of view, is S. H. Longrigg, *Oil in the Middle East* (London, 1968).

On ways to reduce American dependence on Middle Eastern oil, see Douglas Bohi and Milton Russell, *Limiting Oil Imports* (Baltimore, 1978), which, though outdated, is an important stimulus to current thought. On the main oil producer, see Aaron David Miller, *Search for Security: Saudi Arabian Oil and American Foreign Policy* (Chapel Hill, 1980), and Michael B. Stoff, *Oil, War and American Security* (New Haven, 1980), which deal with the American quest for oil during and immediately after World War II.

On ARAB SELF-CONCEPTIONS, see Fouad Ajami, *The Arab Predicament* (Cambridge, 1981), and Georges Corm, *Fragmentation in the Middle East: The Last Thirty Years* (London, 1988), which look at the inability of the Arabs to get their own thoughts in order.

On their thoughts about themselves, one would do best to consult the literature in Arabic. Increasingly, it is becoming available in English and French translation. Among the works of note, see Naguib Mahfouz, *Miramar* (London, 1978); idem, *Children of Gebelawi* (London, 1981); idem, *The Beggar* (New York, 1986); idem, *The Beginning and the End* (New York, 1985); Yusuf Idris, *The Cheapest Nights* (London, 1978); idem, *In the Eye of the Beholder* (Chicago, 1978); Denys Johnson-Davies (ed. and trans.), *Egyptian Short Stories* (London, 1978); Taha Husain, *The Call of the Curlew* (Leiden, 1980); and idem, *An Egyptian Childhood* (London, rpt. 1981). The American Council of Learned Societies in Washington began in 1953 to publish a series of translations of significant Arabic political studies, in its Near Eastern translation program; little noticed when they first appeared, many of them have acquired new relevance, particularly the works dealing with Islam.

The upsurge of Islam is not only producing new accounts but also causing the "resurrection" of older and often neglected books. See John L. Esposito, "Islam and Politics," *Middle East Journal*, 36 (1982): 415ff.; and idem, *Islam: The Straight Path* (Oxford, 1988). Wilfred Cantwell Smith, *On Understanding Islam* (The Hague, 1981), is a collection of essays on various aspects of Islam.

On SECULAR NATIONALISM AND ARABISM, Nicola Ziadeh, "Recent Arabic Literature on Arabism," *Middle East Journal* (1952), provides a now outdated but useful survey. Mohammed B. Alwan, "A Bibliography of Modern Arabic Fiction in English Translation," *Middle East Journal* (Spring 1972), is a good survey. Hazem Z. Nuseibeh, *The Ideas of Arab Nationalism* (Ithaca, N.Y., 1956), is disappointing. William R. Polk, *What the Arabs Think* (New York, 1952), is based on the thought of the "new men" of Iraq. Albert Hourani, *Arabic Thought in the Liberal Age* (London, 1962); George Antonius, *The Arab Awakening* (London, 1938); Charles C. Adams, *Islam and Modernism in Egypt* (London, 1933); Hamilton A. R. Gibb, *Modern Trends in Islam* (Chicago, 1947); and Sylvia G. Haim (ed.), *Arab Nationalism* (Los Angeles, 1962), all deal with aspects of the background to contemporary developments. Walter Z. Laqueur, *Communism and Nationalism in the Middle East* (London, 1956), and idem, (ed.), *The Middle East in Transition* (New York, 1958), bring the account more up to date. Leonard Binder, "Radical Reform Nationalism in Syria and Egypt," *Muslim World* (1959), pushes an analysis of ideology about as far as it can go. The best account of the foreign policy of the Arabs is Charles D. Cremeans, *The Arabs and the World* (New York, 1963). The topic of the intellectual life of the Arabs has not attracted many American scholars, in part, no doubt, because of the problem of language and because few Arabs have achieved a praiseworthy critical appreciation; an exception is Abdallah Laroui, whose *La Crise de intellectuels arabes: Traditionalisme ou historicisme?* (Paris, 1974) is provocative and enlightening. An earlier period is viewed in a very different way in Hisham Sharabi, *Arab Intellectuals and the West: The Formative Years, 1875–1914* (Baltimore, 1970). A. I. Dawisha, *Egypt in the Arab World* (New York, 1976), is almost unique in analyzing the Egyptian role in inter-Arab affairs from an Arab perspective (Dawisha is Iraqi). One of the most able Israeli scholars on the Arab lands is Menahem Milson, whose *Society and Political Structure in the Arab World* (New York, 1973) is a collection of papers by various authors on some issues of the recent past.

On AMERICAN POLICY, studies have kept up with the change of policies and administrations. Sourcebooks on American policy, incomplete though they certainly are and always years behind the times, are provided by the series of volumes known as *Foreign Relations of the United States*. Important years have single volumes devoted to the Near East, South Asia, and Africa. They are published by the Government Printing Office in Washington, D.C., for the historical office of the Department of State. Official publications on

United States policy include a series by Harry N. Howard, which includes *Development of U.S. Policy in the Near East, 1945–1951* (Washington, 1952); *U.S. Policy in the Near East, South Asia and Africa, 1951–1952* (Washington, 1953); *U.S. Policy in the Near East during 1953* (Washington, 1954); *U.S. Policy in the Near East during 1954* (Washington, 1955); and *U.S. Policy in the Near East during 1955* (Washington, 1956). An essay by Richard H. Nolte and William R. Polk, "Toward a Policy for the Middle East," *Foreign Affairs* (July 1958), may still have interest. John Badeau, *The American Approach to the Arab World* (New York, 1968), attempts to analyze the nature of American policy toward the Arabs in light of the experiences of the Kennedy administration. William B. Quandt, *Decade of Decisions: American Policy toward the Arab-Israeli Conflict, 1967–1976* (Berkeley and Los Angeles, 1977), was prepared just before the author became a member of the staff of the National Security Council and is thus important not only for itself but as an insight into thinking about American policy in the Carter administration.

Periodic collections of documents, as in *United States Policy in the Middle East, September 1956–June 1957* (Washington, 1957), hearings before congressional committees, and speeches printed in the State Department *Bulletin* provide source materials. *Foreign Relations of the United States* (Washington, U.S. Government Printing Office) has now been published, by year. Generally one volume covers the Near East, South Asia, and Africa and includes the basic documents on the area. It is a useful work but difficult to assess because often it is the informal papers and the corridor conversation, more than the final documents, which give insight into foreign relations.

Attempts to influence American policy in the Middle East are detailed in *Activities of Non-Diplomatic Representatives of Foreign Principals in the United States,* Hearings before the Committee on Foreign Relations, United States Senate, 88th Congress, 1st Session, (Washington, U.S. Government Printing Office, 1963).

Zionist influence in America is clearly no longer the taboo subject it used to be. Nowadays Arab, American, and above all Israeli authors write freely on it without fear of being attacked as anti-Semites: Edward Tivnan, *The Lobby: Jewish Political Power and American Foreign Policy* (New York, 1987), gives a rare glimpse of the efforts of Zionists to influence American policy. Abdo A. Elkholy, *The Arab Moslems in the United States* (New Haven, 1966), deals with attempts at assimilation of the scattered Arab, primarily Lebanese, groups in America. What this and other works make clear is that the Arabs do not, in any sense, constitute a "community." Recently, perhaps as a result of the changing relations between America and the Arab world, Arabic-speaking immigrants are increasingly conscious of and willing to exhibit their Arabic origins. Three Christian groups are discussed in Philip M. Kayal and Joseph M. Kayal, *The Syrian-Lebanese in America: A Study in Religion and Assimilation* (Boston, 1975).

AMERICAN MISSIONARY ACTIVITY in the Middle East is the subject of a number of works, including Abdul Latif Tibawi, *American Interests in Syria, 1800–1901* (London, 1966); David H. Finnie, *Pioneers East* (Cambridge, Mass., 1967); Robert L. Daniel, *American Philanthropy in the Near East* (Athens, Ohio, 1970); and Joseph Grabill, *Protestant Diplomacy and the Near East, 1870–1927* (Minneapolis, 1971).

On Egypt and American aid, see William J. Burns, *Economic Aid and American Policy toward Egypt* (Albany, 1985). On the Gulf, see the perceptive if now somewhat outdated study by Emile Nakhleh, *The Persian Gulf and American Policy* (New York, 1982). David E. Long discusses the complex American relationship with Saudi Arabia in *The United States and Saudi Arabia: Ambivalent Allies* (Boulder, Colo., 1985), which makes points worth considering today.

On PEACE SEEKING: A general background to efforts to find a way out of the Arab-Israel impasse is provided by Saadia Touval, *The Peace Brokers* (Princeton, 1982). William B. Quandt, *Peacemaking and Politics* (Washington, 1986) is an insider's view; its sequel is given in William B. Quandt (ed.), *The Middle East: Ten Years after Camp David* (Washington, 1988), which is a symposium on what happened to the accords and what might be done after them. An Egyptian viewpoint is given by former Egyptian foreign minister Mohammed Ibrahim Kamel, *The Camp David Accords* (London, 1986). Atif Kubursi, *The Economic Consequences of the Camp David Agreements* (Beirut, 1981), argues that the accords were not in the Arab interest.

For an Arab view of American policy toward the Palestinian problem, see Mohammed K. Shadid, *The United States and the Palestinians* (New York, 1981), which argues that American policy has shifted gradually from pity to confrontation to some degree of understanding of the politics of the problem.

THE SOVIET ROLE AND OBJECTIVES (and American attitudes toward them) have changed so recently and radically that there is only historical interest (and not much of that) in most of the "policy" books of recent years. Two that are still worth reading are Aryeh Yodfat, *The Soviet Union and the Arabian Peninsula* (New York, 1983); and Gallia Golan, *The Soviet Union and the Palestinian Liberation Organization* (New York, 1980). The latter is a sophisticated Israeli view of a complex relationship. An informed Russian view of American policy and regional discord is Y. M. Primakov, *Anatomy of the Middle East Conflict* (Moscow and Chicago, 1979).

Of mainly historical value are Ivar Spector, *The Soviet Union and the Muslim World, 1917–1958* (Seattle, 1959); and Walter Z. Laqueur, *The Soviet Union and the Middle East* (New York, 1959). Aaron Klieman, *Soviet Russia and the Middle East* (Baltimore, 1970), is a competent analysis. Inevitably, Soviet activities in the Middle East are the subject of much speculation. A good, if thin, introduction is provided in R. D. McLaurin, *The Middle East in Soviet Policy* (Lexington, Mass., 1975). Much more detail is devoted to a narrower subject in Jon D. Glassman, *Arms for the Arabs: The Soviet Union and War in the Middle East* (Baltimore, 1975). Alvin Z. Rubinstein, *Red Star on the Nile: The Soviet-Egyptian Relationship since the June War* (Princeton, 1977), is less lurid than the title suggests; indeed, the author concludes that the Egyptians got the better part of the deal and that the Soviets derived little benefit and exercised less influence. Russian writings on the Middle East are viewed in a review article by Oles M. Smolansky, *Middle East Journal*, 30 (1976).

Index